GOVERNING FORTUNE

Governing Fortune

· · · · · · · · · · · · · · · · · ·

CASINO GAMBLING IN AMERICA

Edward A. Morse and Ernest P. Goss

The University of Michigan Press   Ann Arbor

Copyright © by the University of Michigan 2007
All rights reserved
Published in the United States of America by
The University of Michigan Press
Manufactured in the United States of America
∞ Printed on acid-free paper

2010   2009   2008   2007   4   3   2   1

A CIP catalog record for this book is available from the British Library.

Library of Congress Cataloging-in-Publication Data

Morse, Edward A., 1962–
    Governing fortune : casino gambling in America / Edward A. Morse
and Ernest P. Goss.
      p. cm.
    ISBN-13: 978-0-472-09965-8 (cloth : alk. paper)
    ISBN-10: 0-472-09965-5 (cloth : alk. paper)
    ISBN-13: 978-0-472-06965-1 (pbk. : alk. paper)
    ISBN-10: 0-472-06965-9 (pbk. : alk. paper)
    1. Casinos—Economic aspects—United States.   2. Casinos—
Social aspects—United States.   3. Gambling—Economic aspects—
United States.   4. Gambling—Social aspects—United States.
    I. Goss, Ernest, 1950–   II. Title.

HV6711.M67   2007
338.4'77950973—dc22   2006028160

PREFACE

This book explores the legal and economic environment of casino gambling in the United States. The authors draw upon their respective backgrounds to offer important (and often interrelated) insights to those wrestling with the policy dilemmas presented by legalized gambling. Rather than providing a polemic against gambling or an apology for it, this book is designed to provide an analysis of the industry to allow policymakers and interested citizens to make informed and thoughtful choices. By evaluating what is known—as well as the limits of that knowledge—this book casts additional light on the costs and benefits of legalized casino gambling and the policy decisions affecting its regulation.

After a brief examination of the historical roots of casino gambling in chapter 1, chapter 2 explores the growth of casino gambling generally, including both commercial and tribal casinos. Casino ownership has become a corporate enterprise, and this chapter also explores the major players in this industry and marketplace perceptions of its future prospects.

Casino gambling is often touted for its ability to create jobs, to generate tax revenues, and to encourage economic growth. As in other contexts, visible effects from investment and legal changes are often accompanied by invisible ones, which can be difficult to measure and evaluate. These benefits and costs are the subject of chapters 3 through 5. Chapters 3 and 4 examine the benefits claimed from casinos, focusing particularly on taxes and economic development. The conclusions are surprising. For example, casinos appear to create jobs but not growth in personal income. While casinos provide new sources for tax collections, their impact on tax relief is dubious.

Chapter 5 explores problem gambling and surveys significant research into social costs associated with gambling. It is critical of the industry's approach toward social costs, which exploits the limits on social science research methods and the complex causes of human social problems. Although there is still much to be learned, available research suggests that these costs are significant counterweights to the putative benefits of the industry—a risk that policymakers have been willing to ignore for the purpose of political gain from expanded casino gambling.

Chapters 6 through 11 explore the regulatory environment in which casinos operate, including the respective roles of state, federal, and tribal governments in designing and enforcing gambling laws. Gambling regulation has generally been left to the states, though federal influence is also evident, particularly in matters involving Native American tribes and those touching upon constitutional issues. This regulatory structure is not without its problems: interstate competition affects both the economics of gambling as well as its impact on citizens. States have generally used their preeminent regulatory position to foster a partnership with the industry that enhances industry profits and government revenues, paying little attention to efforts to curtail the effects of problem gambling. Early efforts toward adopting limits or constraints in some states have largely been abandoned in favor of industry-friendly rules.

Challenges to state sovereignty come from technology and the market forces of international competition. Chapter 10 explores the challenges presented by the Internet, including an analysis of recent World Trade Organization proceedings affecting the impact of international trade agreements on the continued viability of federal and state laws governing gambling. Tribal gaming also presents a potential challenge to state sovereignty that the federal government has encouraged and protected, and these issues are explored in chapter 11.

Chapter 12 concludes with an examination of liability issues affecting the future of the gaming industry, including lawsuits from victims of problem gambling behaviors and their potential impact on government approaches to regulation. Earlier approaches to regulation, which helped to foster the growth of this industry, may now need to be changed to address the real problem of social costs. This chapter outlines an innovative proposal involving individual licensing as a means to balance the liberty interests of individuals against the social costs generated from problem gambling behavior.

CONTENTS

FIGURES

TABLES

I. A Brief History of Gambling in America

Gambling has a long and ambivalent track record. At various points in history, gambling has been despised and criminalized, tolerated, and embraced—often at the same time. An appreciation of the historical development of social attitudes and government policies toward gambling is a helpful beginning point in understanding the current state of affairs with regard to casino gambling. Despite government efforts to stamp it out, gambling remains a persistent part of the human experience. History shows us that what cannot be defeated is often assimilated. This is the case with gambling in America.

EARLY ENGLISH HISTORY

English common law, which was influential in the formation of laws pertaining to gambling in the United States, reflects the deep historical roots of gambling as a leisure activity. The common law, which reflects customary practices, did not proscribe gambling per se.[1] Early statutes affecting gambling practices were aimed at perceived collateral effects of gambling, some of which seem curious by current standards. For example, an English statute in 1388 directed men subject to military service to abandon their pursuit of games, including tennis, football, and dice, based on the concern that such activities detracted from their military preparedness.[2] Similar concerns that men were gambling instead of practicing their archery skills provided the basis in 1541 for additional statutes prohibiting games, including cards and dice.[3] Significantly, these statutes did not outlaw gaming altogether, as games played at home during Christmastime were expressly allowed. Public gaming, on the other hand, was often thought to result in a breach of the peace resulting in an assorted list of crimes.[4]

Despite attempts to constrain gambling behavior through legal proscriptions, commoners and nobility alike retained their affection for gambling.[5] The ascension of the Stuarts to the throne in 1603 signaled an era of expansive gambling practices in both private and public forums. Gambling had become "a national pastime" that respectable persons found difficult to avoid in ordinary social intercourse.[6] However, the proliferation of gambling among the aristocrats raised concerns about adverse effects on the social structure through the loss of family estates through high-stakes wagering.[7] These concerns prompted statutory reforms in 1664 and later in 1710 that were aimed at regulating gambling rather than absolutely prohibiting it.[8] For example, notes and other security agreements given in payment of gambling debts were declared void; losers of sums over ten pounds could sue to recover their losses within three months, and if they failed to do so a third party could sue for treble damages.[9] However, these statutes retained a royal privilege for gambling within the royal palaces during the residence of the Queen.[10]

The disparate treatment of the royals and their subjects exposed the absence of an articulated moral foundation for prohibition apart from instrumental goals in preserving public order. The propriety of that public order was also drawn into question. Some argued that gambling put the rights of Englishmen at risk by jeopardizing the estates of the aristocracy, who were thought to be a bulwark against the excesses of the Crown.[11] Others looked at the propensity for gambling to circulate property as having positive effects on the social order, as it allowed for the redistribution of wealth.[12] Risk-taking behavior in military officers was also thought to have a salutary effect on their ability to lead.[13]

As the industrial and mercantile economy continued to grow, economic considerations grew to have a significant role in setting the parameters for gambling behavior. Government policy that would emerge across the sea in the American colonies would be influenced primarily by these considerations, though the religious worldviews of the early founders also had some effects in shaping social and ultimately government views about gambling.

GAMBLING IN COLONIAL AMERICA

Economics played a pivotal role in early prohibitions against gaming in the New World. Just as their English counterparts needed militia with strong archery skills, the American colonists needed productive citizens to withstand the rigors and hardship of early colonization efforts. Assuming that gambling undermined the colonists' work ethic, some of the colonies sought to limit gambling through legal measures. During its first year of existence, the Massachusetts Bay Colony outlawed dice, cards, and other games thought to induce the colonists toward idle or unprofitable use of time.[14] In fact, early statutes in both Massachusetts and Connecticut even went so far as to proscribe idleness as a punishable offense.[15]

Though such provisions now seem quite odd in a society where leisure is an important value—perhaps even rising to the level of a human right—the struggles of the times arguably may have demanded it. Difficult winters, diseases, and other travails presented a battle for survival.[16] Those who failed to engage in productive activities drained the resources of the larger group, which had little margin to maintain a safety net for those who could work but chose not to work. Of course, this public position abated as economic prosperity was achieved. For example, a Massachusetts statute in 1737 officially recognized an appropriate role for moderate pursuit of social games (though not gambling) in a manner consistent with a pursuit of other gainful activity: "All lawful games and exercise should not be otherwise used than as innocent and moderate recreations, and not as trades or callings, to gain a living or make unlawful advantage thereby."[17]

It should be noted that not all of the American colonies had similar approaches toward idleness. In New York, which was initially settled by the Dutch, gambling was commonplace.[18] The arrival of English rule in 1660 apparently had only modest effects on gambling, as it was not until 1741 that the first antigambling statute was enacted. Like many other statutes of this kind, it was enacted in response to the negative consequences of frequent public gambling.[19] Similar laws arose in other states, which focused not only on disorderly conduct associated with gambling houses but also on the negative effects on family welfare from gambling losses and the perceived corruption of youth.[20]

The southern colonies were also more tolerant toward gambling, and some commentators attribute this to the influence of the landed aristocracy, who emphasized and valued the pursuit of pleasure, as compared to the New England farmers' emphasis upon the importance of hard work in economic prosperity.[21] Gambling among plantation owners was thought to be common, and it suited their pursuit of a carefree lifestyle detached from the rigors of daily farmwork.[22] Even in Virginia, which took a more restrictive approach toward gambling than other southern colonies, public gambling was outlawed but gambling in private homes was permitted. As one commentator suggested, this legislation "did not really strike a blow at the way of life of the tidewater aristocrats; if anything, prohibitions of public gambling struck at the pleasures of the poor, who, unlike the rich, did not have the space in their own houses for large-scale gaming."[23]

Lotteries were also common. Their utility as fund-raising devices in support of public works and charitable pursuits allowed lotteries to flourish during early colonial periods.[24] Lotteries helped to finance projects at universities, including Harvard, Yale, and Princeton, as well as public works projects such as roads, schools, and river transportation. Even churches were built through lottery financing.[25]

THE EARLY REPUBLIC

As the nation emerged from the Revolutionary War, legislators in the Northeast continued to be hostile to gambling as a commercial or professional activity.[26] Public gambling and professional gamblers were the primary targets of antigambling laws.[27] Private game playing that did not involve wagering was allowed, but these activities occurred in a social environment that championed honest labor as the means to success and looked with skepticism on attempts to provide a shortcut to riches.[28]

Despite the benign treatment of gambling in English common law, the developing law in the United States turned more strongly against it. For example, in *Irwin v. Williar,* the Supreme Court observed: "In England, it is held that the contracts, although wagers, were not void at common law, and that the statute has not made them illegal, but only non-enforceable, [citation omitted] while generally, in this country, all wagering contracts are held to be illegal and void as against public policy."[29] In a Massachusetts case, Justice Holmes characterized wagering contracts as void as against public policy because they are "vicious."[30]

The common law concept of public nuisance also grew to encompass the maintenance of a gambling house as an activity that interfered with public morals, a classification shared with houses of prostitution and other activities classified as "indecent" and "profane."[31] However, gambling houses were also associated with disturbances and quarrels, particularly if cheating was involved, which also affected the public peace.[32] In this sense, the gambling house shared some characteristics with another public nuisance, the "common scold"—"a troublesome and angry person who, by brawling and wrangling among his or her neighbors, breaks the public peace, increases discord, and [by so doing] becomes a public nuisance to the neighborhood."[33]

As populations migrated westward, the frontier presented many new opportunities for gambling practices to develop outside the constraining effects of the established social order of the early colonies. Nevertheless, public gambling, and in particular gambling of a professional nature, was specifically targeted as being a threat to the public good once a legal establishment began to emerge. For example, an 1823 act in Kentucky was specifically targeted toward professional gambling activities:

> The object of the legislature[ ] was not to suppress gaming generally; but to pr[o]scribe a particular species of gambling, by punishing, rigorously, a notorious class of professional gamblers. Former laws were deemed sufficient for discountenancing the ordinary games of chance. But a more public and severe sanction was ascertained to be necessary for the extirpation of a vice, which had taken deep root, and was seen and felt to be peculiarly pernicious and demoralizing.[34]

The Missouri Supreme Court provided a similarly harsh description of the business of running a gambling operation, along with a more tolerant view of the individual gambler:

> To set up, or keep, or carry on a faro-bank . . . is an offense a great deal more injurious to the public morals, than the act of betting upon the gambling device so set up or conducted. The former is followed as a profession, and its professors go about, seducing the unwary, and holding out temptations to dissipation and vice, and leading thousands to ruin. The latter offense is committed often in the thoughtlessness of the moment—to amuse an idle hour, and without a clear perception of the corrupting associations and vicious habits to which the practice so often tends.[35]

However, in other states, an individual gambler's conduct was considered equally reprehensible. An early Tennessee statute provided that one convicted of gambling lost his right to hold public office for a period of five years.[36] As a Tennessee court explained, dark assumptions about gambling underlay this decision:

> Governments legislate to suppress general evils, without reference to possible or probable exceptions. Gaming, as a general evil, leads to vicious inclinations, destruction of morals, abandonment of industry and honest employment, a loss of self-control and respect. Frauds, forgeries, thefts, make up the black catalogue of crime, the closing scene of which generally ends in highway robbery and murder. The American and European journals are full of cases of the most distressing nature; of bankers, merchants, clerks to banking institutions, men in almost every description of trust, public and private, becoming bankrupts and thieves, to the ruin of themselves and others. Look for the source of their misfortune; you find it in lotteries, loo, faro, thimble, dice and the like.[37]

In the frontier regions west of the Mississippi, gambling flourished before formal governmental control was established. The nature of that control ranged from prohibition to regulation, depending on the state. In plains states such as Kansas and Nebraska, which were dominated by local farming communities, absolute bans were enacted soon after territorial statutes were granted.[38] However, rather than attempt to curtail idleness or sloth, these laws focused on the disruption of social order and other excesses associated with public gambling.[39] There was no particular aversion to private forms of gambling, and light penalties tended to be applied toward those who were unfortunate enough to be caught.[40] Horse racing, which would have a tendency to reflect progress in animal husbandry that was useful to the plains farmers and ranchers, even enjoyed a preferential status when it came to enforcement of gambling debts.[41]

In the far West, where farming communities were not the dominant political structure, early governments embraced licensing and regulation as a means of limiting the disruptive effects of cheating and other violent consequences associated with gambling.[42] Montana, for example, imposed substantial fees on gambling operators for each establishment and each faro, poker, or roulette table.[43] Cheating (and violence) still existed under this scheme,[44] which apparently involved little more than an attempt by the government to raise money from gambling activity. Eventually, even these states gradually enacted antigambling legislation, though the public sentiment against gambling was comparatively weak. Penalties were modest, reflecting a more laissez-faire approach toward regulation than in states with orientations toward farming communities.[45]

TRANSITIONS TO MODERN LEGALIZED GAMBLING: THE NEVADA EXPERIENCE

Nevada merits special attention in this historical discussion due to its preeminence as a gambling destination and its long-standing acceptance of commercialized gambling. However, early Nevada settlers possessed conflicting value systems: Mormon pioneers held strong antigambling views, while prospectors seeking the mother lode were quite tolerant of the risk taking associated with gambling and apparently practiced it with alacrity.[46] Congress established the Nevada Territory in 1861, and its first territorial governor pushed through a statute banning all gambling and imposing stiff penalties, which included both fines and prison terms.[47] To the consternation of the territorial governor (and probably others, including the Mormon pioneers), gamblers flouted these laws. Soon after Nevada achieved statehood in 1864, the state legislature substantially reduced the penalties for gambling, and in 1869 it took the further step of legalizing gambling.[48]

The legalization position was accompanied by a system of licensing and regulation, which was ostensibly motivated by the desire to curtail, if not eliminate, gambling altogether. The license fees, which ranged from $250 to $500 every three months, were thought to be sufficiently high to make it impractical for most gambling establishments to carry on their businesses. As a committee report stated, "[V]ery few, if any[,] will be able or willing to pay the heavy license required, and the practicable result will be: to close once and forever hundreds of low dens and 'dead falls' which now disgrace our principal towns."[49] The legislators' predictions were wildly erroneous, however, and gambling (primarily of a small stakes variety) remained a common activity in Nevada towns.

In addition to imposing license fees, which generated revenue to support government services, regulations controlled other aspects of gambling as well. For example, Nevada prohibited minors from gambling and provided their parents with the right to pursue a civil action for damages against the owner of a gambling establishment who permitted a minor to gamble.[50] Nevada legislation also limited gambling activities to the back room or to upper floors, where available.[51] Thus, despite legalization of gambling, Nevada's public policy toward gambling reflected sufficient social concern to keep it out of the reach of children and out of public display.

One additional regulation added in 1877 is particularly noteworthy in its concern for the social consequences of gambling: it prohibited debtors and men with wives and dependent minor children from gambling.[52] Those who gambled with such persons were guilty of a misdemeanor.[53] The extent to which the state enforced this provision is unclear, but it furnishes an interesting approach toward addressing the consequences of excessive gambling losses—a topic that will be taken up later.

Oddly enough, the permissive attitude toward other forms of gambling in early Nevada history did not extend to lotteries, which were expressly prohibited by the Nevada Constitution.[54] The Nevada Supreme Court rebuffed early legislative efforts to authorize a lottery to raise funds for state government. In *Ex Parte Blanchard,* the court reasoned that English statutes declaring lotteries to be a public nuisance were part of the common law in Nevada and that Nevada's constitutional provisions proscribing lotteries withheld legislative power to authorize a lottery.[55] Thus, a statute enabling a lottery for the seemingly beneficent purpose of "providing means to erect an insane asylum" was held to be unconstitutional.

A similar enabling provision was also rebuffed in a later case on similar grounds, with some additional moralizing by the court:

> We are of opinion that the facts stated in the articles of incorporation, in the statute, and in the information, show that the scheme is one whereby the legislature of this state, in consideration of the sum of $250,000, to be placed in the state treasury, to the credit of the "insane and charitable fund," attempted to authorize the managers of the "Nevada Benevolent Association" to enrich their own pockets, at the expense of the people of this and other states, by holding out promises of the great and sudden gains that might be acquired by the ticket-holders; that golden prizes would be "the lure to incite the credulous and unsuspecting into this scheme."[56]

Thus, public law seemed to express the sentiment that private casino-style games offered a sporting chance, while lotteries represented a corrupt exercise of government power that took advantage of its weaker citizens. (Though some might criticize this position as anomalous, it is not completely devoid of a foundation given the low payouts associated with the typical state-run lottery.)

Nevada's era of regulated legalized gambling ended abruptly in 1909 when the legislature once again banned gambling and imposed severe penalties.[57] Over the next two decades, which included the implementation of Prohibition with the ratification of the Eighteenth Amendment in 1919, individuals frequently violated both antigambling and antialcohol laws without significant consequences, albeit in private clubs and other locations outside of public view.[58]

However, in 1931, the Nevada legislature once again passed a legalization bill that ushered in the modern era of regulated casino gambling in the state.[59] Instead of prospectors, these modern casinos drew in patrons from California and eventually from other states, as they enjoyed an effective monopoly on legalized casino gambling in the United States until New Jersey approved casino gambling in 1976 and opened its first casinos two years later.[60] During the ensuing period, regulatory efforts would be refined and strengthened to address concerns about corruption and other criminal activity. Moreover, gambling would become entrenched as a legitimate business and entertainment option in that state and, ultimately, in many others that sought to emulate the Nevada model.

THE MODERN ERA

Though states other than Nevada had generally retained the approach of imposing criminal sanctions on gambling activities, notable exceptions began to emerge. Horse racing was a popular exception, which was sometimes considered "sport" in order to circumvent otherwise applicable gambling restrictions.[61] Unlike casino-style games, horse racing also supported an industry that had other economic impacts extending beyond the track, including breeders, farms, and feed stores. These arguments may have helped to distinguish horse racing from other forms of gambling that remained legally prohibited.

Economic needs of state and local governments also affected the acceptance of pari-mutuel betting on horse races. Some attribute the Great Depression as a catalyst for legalization, as states sought new revenue sources to address fiscal shortfalls.[62] Charitable gambling, such as bingo, also grew to be widely accepted as a fund-raising method.[63] Here, stakes were generally limited, and profits went to what could be considered "good causes" rather than into private coffers. Nevertheless, constitutional amendments were sometimes required to permit even charitable gambling, thus reflecting very strong antigambling sentiments that had to be overcome.[64]

Fiscal interests have undoubtedly played a significant—if not the most significant—role in this metamorphosis from gambling as taboo to gambling as a tool of the state.[65] State lotteries taught the important lesson that significant revenues could be gained from willing participants, some of whom were already being served by illegal numbers rackets. State lotteries have enjoyed explosive growth in the latter part of the twentieth century and into the twenty-first, taking in more than $48.8 billion in 2004 in forty-one states and the District of Columbia, up from $45.18 billion in 2003.[66] Per capita spending on lotteries in these states averages $183, ranging from a low of $9.27 in sparsely populated North Dakota to $1,370.95 in Rhode Island, where video lottery terminals (close cousins of slot machines) are allowed.[67] Of this $48.8 billion in 2004 revenues, an estimated $13.9 billion was returned to the states, with the remainder paying for expenses for the promotion of the lottery and the prizes awarded to players.[68]

Casinos also offer significant potential for public revenues, though the model for earning those revenues is typically different. States have chosen to license private firms to run casinos and to impose taxes on gaming activities.[69] In 2004, commercial casinos posted gross gaming revenues (defined as the amount wagered minus payouts to winning players) of nearly $29 billion,[70] with an additional $16.2 billion estimated for tribal casinos.[71] As of 2005, commercial casino gambling is currently available in only eleven states, while twenty-eight states allow tribal casinos.[72]

Many other states have more limited gambling activities, such as keno, bingo, card rooms, pull-tabs, and horse or dog racing. Few states have resisted legalization of gambling in some form, with Utah and Hawaii being the most notable exceptions. When all is totaled, estimated spending on gambling in the United States ranges from $72 billion to as much as $100 billion, depending on how the base is measured.[73] By comparison, Americans spend each year approximately $9.5 billion at the movies, $10.3 billion at theme parks, $23.8 billion on DVD and video rentals, and $51 billion on cable television.[74] Though $100 billion is less than 1 percent of the gross domestic product in the United States (which in 2004 was about $12 trillion), it is nevertheless a large figure. Moreover, it does not include illegal gambling, which still exists as an illicit alternative.

The history of gambling in America discussed here is considerably abbreviated, but it does permit us to make some general observations. First, a desire to gamble seems deeply rooted in human experience. Despite some moral objections to gambling, belief in luck has had a powerful influence in American culture.[75] A demand for gambling is likely to continue to exist for the foreseeable future, as patrons continue to be attracted by the hope that they will be lucky.

Government has at various times attempted to prohibit gambling through criminal sanctions, which have focused primarily on professional or commercial operations. However, laws of this nature have not always enjoyed widespread public acceptance. Regulating gambling, rather than letting it freely propagate according to market demands, is emerging as the dominant governmental approach. What might have started on a small scale with bingo or charitable operations has eventually expanded to more lucrative gambling options.

Government has thus chosen to exploit the public's belief in luck rather than repress it. In the case of lotteries, government itself is the operator and promoter. When commercial gambling operations are involved, gambling no longer involves a sterile redistribution of resources among participants. Instead, it becomes a means for gambling providers to reap substantial profits. Government has effectively harnessed this profit motivation to turn casinos into tools for tax collection, and in the process traditional characterizations of gambling as a vice have been overturned in favor of more positive characterizations.

Despite the fact that social costs have had a significant role in the legal suppression of gambling throughout its history, policymakers have given only limited attention to the nature and extent of social costs in designing regulations for the industry. From a political perspective, a "see no evil" approach is understandable: costs associated with the gambling industry are diffused and difficult to measure, whereas benefits (such as jobs and tax revenues) are tangible and quantifiable.[76] Interstate competition magnifies pressures toward legalization, as gambling proponents cite significant gaming tax revenue losses to the state from patrons willing to cross state lines to gamble.

Resistance to these pressures is not always futile, as evidenced by the fact that many states are without casinos and have relatively limited options for legal gambling. However, continued resistance is also difficult. Political pressures from interstate competition, growing antitax sentiments, and libertarian values of personal freedom all potentially contribute to an expanding role for legalized gambling, despite uncertainties about social costs. Unfortunately for the industry, as well as for the states that have enjoyed its largesse, in some locations the market is maturing, and much of the easy money has already been made. For most Americans, a casino is now within an easy traveling distance—and the prospects of gambling on the Internet may bring it even closer to home.

In 1999, the National Gambling Impact Study Commission urged policymakers to slow the expansion of gambling so that researchers and government could learn more about the social impacts of gambling, stating in part:

> The members of the Commission agree that there is a need for a "pause" in the growth of gambling. The purpose of the pause is not to wait for definitive answers to the subjects of dispute, because those may never come. Instead the purpose of this recommended pause is to encourage governments to do what, to date, few, if any, have done: to survey the results of their decisions and to determine if they have chosen wisely; to ask if their decisions are in accord with the public good, if harmful effects could be remedied, if benefits are being unnecessarily passed up.[77]

That recommendation was essentially ignored, as gambling continued to expand. However, the social science community has continued to learn about the industry, and it has produced some disturbing results about some of the negative social impacts of the industry. The regulatory environment has also continued to change, as the industry and government begin to deal with these looming social issues.

The chapters that follow explore some of these social and economic impacts of the casino gambling industry, as well as the regulatory environment in which they occur. Policymakers face difficult choices in the years ahead, and the discussion that follows is designed to provide a basis for reflection and understanding of this industry and the dilemmas that it presents.

2. Casino Expansion in the United States

From 1931 until 1976, Nevada held an effective monopoly on legalized casino gambling in the United States. However, that monopoly soon began to fracture as other states changed their approaches toward the gambling industry. New Jersey became the first state outside of Nevada to add casinos by legalizing casino gambling in Atlantic City in 1976 and opening its first casino two years later. It was more than a decade before other states began what has become a landslide in the expansion of U.S. commercial casinos.[1] Indian tribes soon joined in, adding casino facilities in thirty-three states between 1987 and 2005. Gambling supporters in the eleven commercial casino states and the thirty-three tribal casino states viewed casinos as an efficient device for generating tourism and economic development, as well as tax revenues for state and local governments.

Perhaps more emphatically, Indian tribes embraced gambling as a means to achieve economic development and to provide jobs for unemployed tribal members. In many cases, the close proximity of gambling opportunities across state lines influenced decisions for legalization as governments sought to compete for the gambling dollars of citizens from neighboring states. This legislative design of cross-border competition is evidenced by the fact that the vast majority of commercial casinos outside of Nevada are within two miles of state borders. Thus, many government officials viewed casinos as a reaction to the lure of casinos directly across the state line.

Since its expansion outside of Nevada and New Jersey, casino gambling has proven to be a growth industry with its pattern of growth highly resilient to negative conditions in the general economy. Even the tragic events of September 11, 2001, brought only a temporary setback for the industry, as patrons soon returned to gaming. Although reductions in air travel affected

Nevada casinos negatively, other venues reachable by automobile posted gains, allowing the casino industry to post overall growth even during that economically troubled year.[2]

Over the past decade, Americans' gambling losses at casinos grew at a rate twice that of the growth in the overall economy. In 2004, revenues for commercial casinos reached nearly $29 billion, up more than 7 percent from $27 billion in 2003.[3] Racetrack casinos—"racinos"—reflected an even stronger growth in revenues, taking in $2.9 billion in 2004, up more than 30 percent from $2.2 billion in 2003. As of 2004, the American Gaming Association reported a total of 445 commercial casinos operating in eleven states and twenty-four racinos operating in seven states.[4]

Tribal casinos have also experienced phenomenal growth. In 2004, there were 228 tribes operating 405 gaming facilities in thirty states.[5] These tribal facilities collected approximately $19 billion in gaming revenues in 2004. This reflects a 14.3 percent compound annual growth rate since 1997—dramatically higher than commercial casinos' growth of 6.8 percent annually.[6] However, not all of the tribal facilities are full-service casinos, as some include card rooms, bingo, or more limited forms of gambling. Class III casinos, which offer gaming opportunities that are comparable to those of commercial casinos (i.e., those owned by private firms), are available in twenty-three states.[7]

The following discussion explores casino growth in greater detail, focusing first on commercial casinos, next on their counterparts run by the Indian tribes, and then on racetrack casinos or racinos. The final section of this chapter examines how the explosive growth in casino gambling has affected firms that own the commercial casinos and manage the tribal casinos.

COMMERCIAL CASINOS

Figure 2.1 shows states that currently have legalized commercial casino gaming along with the date that the first casino was constructed in the state. Years of legalization were Nevada in 1931; New Jersey in 1976; Iowa, Louisiana, and South Dakota in 1989; Colorado, Illinois, and Mississippi in 1990; Indiana and Missouri in 1993; and Michigan in 1996. Pennsylvania and Florida will soon join these states, as both states legalized slot machines in 2004. Pennsylvania will allow up to sixty-one thousand slot machines at locations across the state.[8]

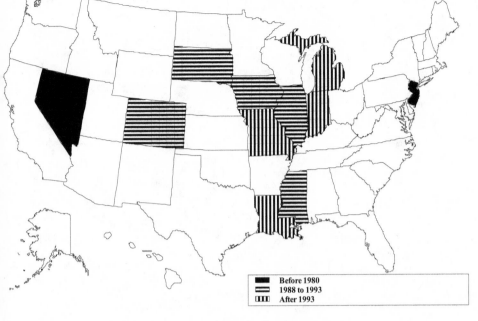

Fig. 2.1. First year of commercial casino operations

Figure 2.2 details the location of commercial casinos by county for 2003. Fifty-seven counties in the United States currently offer commercial casino gaming. Outside of Nevada, most commercial casino activity is located near either a river or a body of water, which often also forms a geographic border between states. In part, this is due to the fact that many states use public nostalgia for riverboat gambling to support the expansion of casino gambling. However, this also reflects the reality of cross-border competition for gambling patrons. For example, most of Iowa's thirteen casinos are located on the state's border with Nebraska (four casinos) and on the state's border with Illinois (seven casinos). Only two of Iowa's thirteen casinos are located more than three miles from the state border.[9]

Table 2.1 shows gross casino revenues by state between 1999 and 2004, along with the annual growth rate from 1999 to 2004. Iowa and Indiana experienced the most rapid growth during this period, with annual growth rates of 16.6 percent and 16.5 percent, respectively. New Jersey experienced the slowest annual growth rate during this period at 3.7 percent.

Fig. 2.2. Commercial casino counties, 2003

TABLE 2.1. Commercial casino AGR by state and growth rate, 1999–2004

	AGR (in millions of dollars)						Compound Annual Growth (%)
	1999	2000	2001	2002	2003	2004	1999–2004
Colorado	479.0	631.8	631.8	719.7	698.2	725.9	8.7
Illinois	1,100.0	1,700.0	1,800.0	1,800.0	1,709.0	1,718.0	9.3
Indiana	1,100.0	1,700.0	1,800.0	2,100.0	2,229.0	2,369.0	16.6
Iowa	496.0	887.0	922.9	972.3	1,024.0	1,064.0	16.5
Louisiana	1,300.0	1,800.0	1,800.0	2,000.0	2,017.0	2,163.0	10.7
Michigan	N.A.	743.6	1,000.0	1,100.0	1,130.0	1,189.0	12.5
Mississippi	2,200.0	2,649.0	2,701.0	2,700.0	2,700.0	2,781.0	4.8
Missouri	853.0	997.7	1,100.0	1,300.0	1,330.0	1,473.0	11.5
Nevada	8,100.0	9,600.0	9,500.0	9,400.0	9,625.0	10,562.0	5.5
New Jersey	4,000.0	4,300.0	4,300.0	4,360.0	4,490.0	4,807.0	3.7
South Dakota	44.0	51.8	58.6	66.3	70.4	78.0	12.1
U.S.	19,672.0	25,060.9	25,614.3	26,518.3	27,022.6	28,929.9	8.0
As % of U.S. GDP	2.12	2.55	2.54	2.53	2.46	2.47	

Source: American Gaming Association and U.S. Bureau of Economic Analysis.

This difference may be explained, in part, by the fact that Iowa and Indiana are newer casino markets, whereas Atlantic City, New Jersey, is a more mature market, having casinos that have operated since 1978. Michigan, the latest state to add casinos to its economic mix, experienced growth of 12.5 percent per year between 2000 (the first full year of operation) and 2004. Nationwide, commercial casino revenues, termed "adjusted gross receipts" (AGR),[10] grew from $8.3 billion in 1990 to $28.9 billion in 2004. This reflects a compounded yearly growth rate of almost 8 percent—more than three times the rate of inflation and more than twice the rate of U.S. economic growth as measured by the nation's gross domestic product.

Revenues per casino visitor also vary significantly among the commercial casino states. Table 2.2 lists attendance and average revenue per visitor by state for 2004. Spending per casino visitor ranged from $27 in Missouri to $209 in Nevada.[11] The average visitor across the United States spent $91 per casino visit in 2004. However, the 319 million visits or attendance came from 54.1 million individuals. Thus, on average, each individual who visited a casino in 2004 lost $535 for the full year.

Table 2.3 ranks casino locations across the United States based on 2004 AGR. While locations in Nevada and New Jersey, states with the older

TABLE 2.2.   Commercial casino attendance and AGR per visitor, 2004

	Attendance	Compound Annual Growth 2001–4 (%)	AGR per Casino Visitor ($)
Colorado	N.A.	N.A.	N.A.
Illinois	15,300,000	−6.6	112
Indiana	26,730,000	10.5	89
Iowa	19,540,000	0.2	54
Louisiana	40,890,000	−3.8	53
Michigan	N.A.	N.A.	N.A.
Mississippi	55,260,000	−0.9	50
Missouri	54,200,000	4.5	27
Nevada	50,500,000	0.6	209
New Jersey	33,230,000	0.8	145
South Dakota	N.A.	N.A.	N.A.
U.S.	319,000,000	−0.4	91

Source: American Gaming Association.
N.A. = not available

casinos, are ranked highly, new casino locations in Indiana, Michigan, and Mississippi have moved up rapidly in the rankings. Proximity to large population bases appears to be a significant factor in the AGR potential of commercial casino facilities. This also suggests the importance of local patronage to the successful casino.

TRIBAL CASINOS

The development of tribal casino gambling traces its roots to the Supreme Court's 1987 decision in *California v. Cabazon Band of Mission Indians*,[12] where the Court held that the state of California lacked authority to apply its regulatory statutes to gambling activities conducted on Indian reservations.[13] Tribal sovereignty in these matters was subordinate only to the federal government, and state power to regulate was thus dependent on congressional authorization. Congress quickly responded to this decision in 1988 by en-

TABLE 2.3.   **Ranking of casinos by location, 2001, 2003, 2004**

Rank				
2004	*2003*	*2001*	Location	2004 AGR ($)
1	1	1	Las Vegas—Strip	5.555 billion
2	2	2	Atlantic City, NJ	4.806 billion
3	3	3	Chicagoland (IL, IN)	2.346 billion
4	4	N.A.	Connecticut (Indian)	1.646 billion
5	6	5	Tunica, MS	1.199 billion
6	5	4	Detroit, MI	1.189 billion
7	8	6	Biloxi, MS	911.45 million
8	7	7	Reno/Sparks, NV	903.45 million
9	9	8	Southeast Indiana	885.90 million
10	11	10	St. Louis (MO, IL)	848.41 million
11	10	9	Shreveport, LA	835.51 million
12	12	12	Boulder Strip (NV)	791.69 million
13	14	13	Kansas City, MO	701.39 million
14	13	11	Las Vegas—Downtown	663.28 million
15	15	15	New Orleans	608.80 million
16	16	14	Laughlin, NV	595.32 million
17	17	16	Black Hawk, CO	524.04 million
18	18	19	Lake Charles, LA	462.07 million
19	19	18	Council Bluffs, IA	418.18 million
20	24	N.A.	Charlestown, WV (racino)	360.23 million

Source: Innovation Group, October 2001, 2003, 2004.

N.A. = not available

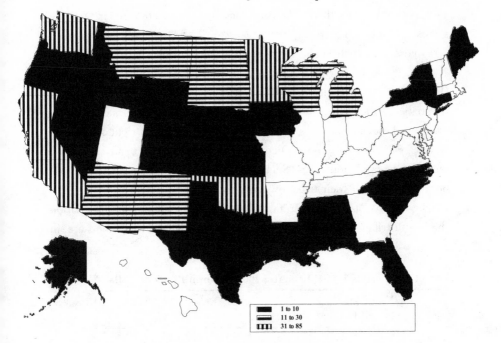

■■■	1 to 10
≡≡≡	11 to 30
‖‖‖	31 to 85

Fig. 2.3. Number of tribal casinos by state, 2004

acting the Indian Gaming Regulatory Act (IGRA),[14] which attempted to balance the interests of the states and of the tribes located within their geographical borders.

The IGRA was intended to accomplish several policy goals, which included (1) promoting tribal economic development and self-sufficiency; (2) providing a regulatory base to protect Indian gaming from organized crime, to ensure that the tribe is the beneficiary of the gaming operation, and to ensure the fairness and honesty of the gaming operation; and (3) establishing the National Indian Gaming Commission to assist in these purposes.[15] The IGRA essentially recognized tribal rights to operate gaming facilities on their reservations commensurate with the types of gaming that could otherwise be operated under state law.

Figure 2.3 shows the number of tribal casinos in each state as of 2004.[16] There were 405 tribal gaming facilities in the United States in 2004 compared to 385 in 2003. In 2004, Oklahoma had the largest number of tribal casinos at 85, followed by California at 56 and Minnesota and Washington each with 31. Class III tribal casino facilities are located in 192 counties across the United States.

Table 2.4 lists tribal casino AGR (i.e., wagers less winnings) by state from 2002 to 2004. California had the highest AGR at $5.3 billion, followed by Connecticut at $2.2 billion and Arizona at $1.5 billion. The data indicate that tribal casino AGR is quickly approaching that of commercial casinos. In some of these states, tribes have been granted exclusive rights to operate casinos, which have often included opportunities to exploit gaming markets with large population bases. Such operations can provide significant economic benefits for their tribal owners.

The top five states listed in table 2.4 all have exclusive gaming relationships with tribal governments, with no commercial casinos in the state. In-

TABLE 2.4.   Tribal AGR by state, 2002–4 (in millions of dollars)

State	2002	2003	2004	Growth 2002–4 (%)
Alaska	8.1	8.4	8.5	4.9
Arizona	1,094.2	1,218.3	1,533.7	40.2
California	3,678.1	4,699.9	5,324.3	44.8
Colorado	54.1	55.2	57.4	6.1
Connecticut	2,054.4	2,157.0	2,231.9	8.6
Florida	572.1	642.0	862.0	50.7
Idaho	94.2	103.9	140.0	48.6
Kansas	165.0	169.8	171.3	3.8
Louisiana	444.1	448.1	372.7	−16.1
Michigan	965.0	969.9	971.0	0.6
Minnesota	1,309.4	1,326.8	1,343.3	2.6
Montana	15.0	15.5	16.3	8.7
Nevada	45.0	44.0	51.6	14.7
New Mexico	576.9	613.6	707.4	22.6
New York	275.0	577.3	730.5	165.6
North Dakota	89.0	95.0	96.9	8.9
Oklahoma	461.1	641.8	939.3	103.7
Oregon	418.9	433.9	460.1	9.8
South Dakota	44.5	50.0	53.0	19.1
Washington	707.8	888.0	987.5	39.5
Wisconsin	980.7	991.5	1,004.1	2.4
Other states	850.0	872.1	974.3	14.6
All states	14,902.6	17,022.0	19,037.1	27.7

Source: Indian Gaming Industry Report, 2005–6.

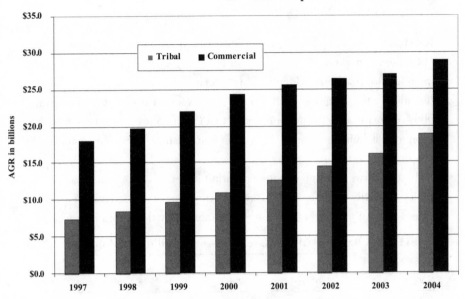

Fig. 2.4. Tribal versus commercial AGR, 1997–2004

terestingly, between 2002 and 2004, tribal AGR growth in states without commercial casinos was much higher than in states with commercial casinos. Collectively, tribal AGR in states with no commercial casinos grew by 44.5 percent, while tribal AGR in states with commercial casinos actually declined by 3.0 percent between 2002 and 2004. This indicates the importance of exclusive agreements between the tribes and the states in terms of producing higher growth rates in gambling revenue.

Tribal casino AGR has been growing at a rate that even surpasses the healthy growth rate of their commercial counterparts. Figure 2.4 attests to the rapid growth in casino gambling in terms of AGR. The aggregate AGR from tribal casinos increased from $8.2 billion in 1997 to more than $19.0 billion in 2004, an annual growth rate of nearly 14.2 percent. In contrast, the growth rate for commercial casinos slowed somewhat during this period to an average of 6.8 percent per year. Significantly, if these growth trends continue, the gap in AGR between commercial and tribal casinos will soon no longer exist. This growth trend is certainly not surprising given the favorable tax treatment afforded tribal casinos—a topic that is explored in greater detail in chapters 4 and 11.

RACINOS

Racetrack casinos (racinos) are an increasingly important segment of the U.S. casino market. A racino is defined as a horse-racing track that also includes slot machines, video gambling terminals, or other casino features. Included in the category are also dog-racing tracks that offer the same gambling opportunities. Proponents assert that racinos allow states to derive the economic benefits of gaming while containing gaming expansion to current racetrack facilities.

In 2004, twenty-four racinos operating in seven states generated $2.78 billion in AGR, which was up from $2.20 billion in 2003. However, more than $190 million of the increase was produced by the addition of four ra-

TABLE 2.5.   Racino AGR by state, 2002–4 (in millions of dollars)

State	2002	2003	2004	Growth 2002–4 (%)
Delaware	565.9	502.0	553.32	−2.2
Iowa	316.1	330.3	337.48	6.8
Louisiana	114.6	168.9	280.97	145.2
New Mexico	141.3	149.8	149.68	5.9
New York	N.A.	N.A.	192.45	N.A.
Rhode Island	281.0	333.5	383.8	36.6
West Virginia	596.0	717.1	882.4	48.1
Total	2,014.9	2,201.6	2,780.1	38.0

Source: American Gaming Association, yearly surveys.
N.A. = not available

TABLE 2.6.   Top racino markets, 2004 (in millions of dollars)

Rank	Top Markets	2004
1	Charlestown, WV	360.24
2	Providence, RI	304.77
3	Dover/Harrington, DE	297.70
4	Delaware Park/Wilmington, DE	261.60
5	Chester, WV	255.73
6	Wheeling, WV	192.12
7	Des Moines, IA	161.47
9	Council Bluffs, IA	133.94
9	Lake Charles/Vinton, LA	128.39
10	Shreveport, LA	84.24

Source: American Gaming Association, 2004 survey.

cinos in New York in 2004. Also 2004 marked the first full year of operation for two of Louisiana's three racinos.

Table 2.6 lists the top racino markets for 2004. As presented, Charlestown, West Virginia, was the largest racino market at $360.24 million in 2004 AGR. In fact, Charlestown's racino AGR was significant enough to place this market in twentieth place in terms of overall casino markets for 2004, up from twenty-fourth place in 2003.

Table 2.7 provides comparative data for commercial casinos, tribal casinos, and racinos for 2004. While there were more commercial casinos in 2003 than tribal casinos, the number of casinos added in the past few years clearly favors tribal casinos, with all 192 tribal casinos added in the past fifteen years. During this same period of time, only 175 commercial casinos were created. Table 2.7 also shows that a significant difference exists in the share of AGR going to government coffers, with 16.4 percent of commercial AGR paid to state and local governments but only 6.1 percent of tribal AGR being paid to state and local governments in lieu of taxes. (These tax differentials are the product of limits on the state taxing powers accorded to Indian tribes, a topic addressed in greater detail in chapter 11.)

Table 2.7 also shows the significantly higher tax rate paid by racinos, whose average tax rate is more than double that of commercial casinos. However, Iowa racinos sued the state of Iowa, claiming that the state's practice of taxing racetrack gambling at a higher rate than riverboat gambling violated

TABLE 2.7.   Comparison of commercial casinos, tribal casinos, and racinos

	Commercial	Tribal	Racinos
Number of casinos, 2004	445	405	24
Total 2004 AGR (in billions of dollars)	28.9	19.0	2.8
AGR per casino (in millions of dollars)	65.0	47.0	115.8
AGR growth, 2002–4 (%)	9.1	27.7	38.0
Taxes or revenue sharing, 2004 (in billions of dollars)	4.7	0.9	1.1
Effective tax or revenue sharing rate, 2003 (%)	16.4	4.7	38.6

Sources: Authors' calculation based on American Gaming Association surveys and *Indian Gaming Industry Report.*

Note: For Iowa and Louisiana, the AGA includes racino AGR with casino AGR. The total tribal casinos of 405 includes Class II (no slots or table games) and Class III (slots and/or table games).

the Fourteenth Amendment's Equal Protection Clause. The Iowa Supreme Court ultimately agreed with the industry on state constitutional grounds, despite a temporary victory for the state in the U.S. Supreme Court.[17]

INDUSTRY LEADERS

While casino gambling has expanded rapidly in the United States, the companies owning and/or managing the casinos have likewise grown at a brisk rate. Table 2.8 lists the largest casino firms in the United States according to market capitalization. Also listed in table 2.8 are the return on equity and current price-earnings ratios of each firm. For companies earning a positive income, the price-earnings ratio is calculated by dividing the current price

TABLE 2.8.   Casino leaders in market capitalization, 2005

Name of Company	Stock Exchange Symbol	Market Capitalization (in millions of dollars)[a]	Return on Equity (%)[b]	Price-Earnings Ratio[c]
Las Vegas Sands Corp.	LVS	12,700	42.8	26.8
MGM Mirage	MGM	10,200	13.4	29.0
International Game Tech	IGT	9,600	20.2	25.4
Harrah's Entertainment	HET	7,700	3.8	16.9*
Caesars Entertainment Inc.	CZR	6,400	2.9	68.5
Wynn Resorts LTD	WYNN	4,800	−17.1	39.6*
Boyd Gaming Corp.	BYD	4,800	20.5	30.1
Station Casinos	STN	4,300	31.4	32.1
Penn National Gaming	PENN	2,700	21.8	32.2
Scientific Games	SGMS	1,900	21.7	32.7
Ameristar Casinos	ASCA	1,410	21.4	22.0
Argosy Casino	AGY	1,360	22.4	17.5
Aztar Casino	AZR	1,130	6.2	18.4
Isle of Capri	ISLE	774.2	4.1	77.3
Century Casinos	CNTY	102	12.9	24.8
Diamonds	DIA	N.A.	N.A.	16.2
Spyders	SPY	N.A.	N.A.	16.0

Source: Reuters and Yahoo.com.

[a]Market capitalization is equal to the number of shares of stock outstanding multiplied by the stock price.

[b]Return on equity is equal to the profits divided by total net worth of the firm.

[c]The price-earnings ratio is calculated by dividing the price of the stock by the earnings over the past year.

*Indicates forward price-earnings ratio.

N.A. = not available

by last year's operating income. For companies with a negative income, the price-earnings ratio is calculated by dividing the current price by next year's income as estimated by analysts tracking the stock.[18]

Las Vegas Sands, with a market capitalization of $12.7 billion, is the largest publicly traded casino company listed on the New York Stock Exchange or the NASDAQ Exchange. Las Vegas Sands also had the highest return on equity at 42.8 percent, but not the highest price-earnings ratio. Despite having a return on equity of only 2.9 percent, Caesars had the highest price-earnings ratio of 68.5. Typically a high price-earnings ratio stems from high projected earnings growth rate or lower risk as assessed by investors. The median price-earnings ratio for the casino firms listed in table 2.8 is 30.0. This compares to 16.2 for the thirty Dow Jones industrial firms traded as Diamonds and 16.0 for the five hundred firms that make up the Standard and Poor's Index and traded as Spyders.[19] This data suggest that investors are estimating higher growth, or lower risks, for casinos than for other large firms in the United States.

Table 2.9 shows casino revenues by year for the casino companies listed in table 2.8.[20] As presented, Pennsylvania National Gaming experienced the highest rate of annual growth at 108.9 percent, and Station Casinos experienced the lowest rate of annual growth at 2.8 percent. Harrah's, with over $4 billion in casino revenues, was the top casino company. However, among the ten firms, only Station Casinos had a lower growth rate in revenues than Harrah's. Growth rates for firms listed in table 2.9 are considerably higher than casino AGR. In fact, the revenue growth of Pennsylvania National Gaming was roughly ten times that of casino AGR across the United States, while revenue growth of Las Vegas Sands was more than four times that of U.S. casino AGR. AGR is just one component of casino revenues, with other revenues coming from the sale of food and beverages and other items.

Table 2.10 lists casino revenues as a percentage of total revenues by year by company. Pennsylvania National Gaming casino revenue as a percentage of total revenue was the highest among the companies at 87.0 percent, while International Game Tech was the lowest at 46.8 percent. Table 2.10 shows clearly that casino revenues represent a significant and, in some cases, preponderant share of total company sales or revenues. However, five of the ten firms experienced a decline in casino revenues as a share of total revenues. In

TABLE 2.9. Casino revenues, 1997–2004 (in thousands of dollars)

	Las Vegas Sands	Harrah's	Caesars	International Game Tech	Boyd Gaming Corp.	Penn National Gaming	MGM Mirage	Station Casinos	Ameristar Casinos	Century Casinos
1997	N.A.	1,338,003	1,832	282,820	323,707	5,712	457,206	600,847	173,077	19,096,857
1998	N.A.	1,660,313	1,587	347,099	722,124	37,396	410,605	509,149	216,345	19,036,621
1999	N.A.	2,424,237	2,269	353,064	733,677	55,125	873,781	764,089	247,416	22,726,004
2000	N.A.	2,852,048	3,480	401,014	868,983	159,589	1,913,733	807,880	286,438	27,703,000
2001	227,240	3,235,761	3,271	374,942	912,427	366,166	2,163,808	659,276	551,648	30,096,000
2002	256,484	3,688,416	3,337	882,432	1,045,082	494,271	2,189,720	638,113	678,642	30,607,000
2003	272,804	3,853,150	3,212	1,059,539	1,073,736	976,411	2,075,569	648,664	760,376	31,869,000
2004	708,564	4,077,694	2,872	1,163,416	1,454,884	992,088	2,223,965	730,584	856,901	N.A.
Annual growth rates (%)	46.1	17.3	6.6	22.4	24.0	108.9	25.4	2.8	25.6	8.9

Source: Authors' calculations from Reuters and Yahoo! data.

N.A. = not available

addition to casino revenues, total revenues include food and drink sales, hotel rentals, and entertainment ticket sales.

Table 2.11 lists operating income as a percentage of revenues for all companies reporting results. This measure of profitability ranged from 14.6 percent to 49.1 percent. For 2004, Las Vegas Sands experienced the highest rate at 49.1 percent, and International Game Tech had the second highest rate at 32.8 percent. Interestingly, these two firms earned a high proportion of their revenues from noncasino sources. The firms that depended more heavily on casino revenues tended to experience lower earnings rates.

In order to accomplish the revenue growth listed in table 2.9, casinos spend heavily on advertising and promotion. According to Christiansen Capital Advisors, the casino industry currently spends 2.5 percent of casino

TABLE 2.10.   Casino revenues as a percentage of total revenues

	Las Vegas Sands	Harrah's	Caesars	International Game Tech	Boyd Gaming Corp.	Penn National Gaming	MGM Mirage	Station Casinos	Ameristar Casinos	Century Casinos
1997	N.A.	75.7	71.2	38.0	64.7	5.1	51.3	73.0	78.1	94.0
1998	N.A.	75.9	68.9	42.1	67.6	24.3	48.9	73.6	75.5	94.6
1999	N.A.	73.2	71.4	38.0	67.8	32.2	58.1	75.6	76.2	93.8
2000	N.A.	74.8	71.1	39.9	69.4	54.3	54.4	76.3	77.4	93.1
2001	36.1	75.7	71.4	31.3	74.6	70.5	49.0	72.3	83.2	89.8
2002	39.0	76.0	71.7	47.8	77.0	75.2	49.1	73.7	84.2	90.7
2003	37.0	75.5	72.1	49.8	77.0	84.0	48.0	70.1	83.5	88.4
2004	56.3	75.4	68.3	46.8	75.3	87.0	47.6	69.3	84.0	N.A.

Source: Authors' calculations from Reuters and Yahoo! data.
N.A. = not available

TABLE 2.11.   Net operating income as a percentage of revenue

	Las Vegas Sands	Harrah's	Caesars	International Game Tech	Boyd Gaming Corp.	Penn National Gaming	MGM Mirage	Station Casinos	Ameristar Casinos	Century Casinos
1997	N.A.	12.1	7.8	25.7	11.6	8.7	21.4	10.2	12.6	0.0
1998	N.A.	13.2	13.1	26.6	11.6	12.6	15.7	9.4	1.1	3.2
1999	N.A.	14.5	12.6	12.5	12.6	10.4	14.0	2.9	7.9	9.6
2000	N.A.	7.4	14.2	26.6	14.3	15.6	15.3	22.9	−6.1	13.5
2001	20.7	13.6	8.9	33.0	9.5	15.0	14.2	15.4	17.3	17.5
2002	24.3	16.1	12.3	28.8	12.1	15.5	17.2	16.8	14.3	18.4
2003	25.3	14.2	10.3	31.3	10.7	15.8	16.5	15.2	15.4	20.2
2004	49.1	14.6	14.8	32.8	15.3	18.7	20.4	24.4	15.6	N.A.

Source: Authors' calculations from Reuters and Yahoo! data.
N.A. = not available

revenues on advertising and promotion.[21] In an effort to lure increasing numbers of patrons, casinos continue to spend heavily on new promotions. The promotion competition between casinos tends to get pretty intense, especially in the major markets. For example, eight casinos compete for gambling patrons in the Chicago area. One of the large casino companies, Harrah's, recently initiated its $1,000,000 Treasure Hunt. Customers at Harrah's properties nationwide throughout the year earned an entry into the contest by the frequency of their gambling visits. The customers earned an opportunity to travel to Las Vegas on November 10, 2005, to search for a treasure chest containing $1 million in a remote desert location. This is an example of Harrah's efforts to increase repeat business.

At the Grand Victoria Casino in Elgin, Illinois, all dice players have to do is roll each of the six point numbers (4, 5, 6, 8, 9, and 10) during a single "hand" of their roll at a live craps game. Should the shooter roll all the numbers at least once before rolling a 7 the player wins a bonus payment of four thousand dollars in cash.

In 2002, Majestic Star in Detroit ran a promotion on table games entitled "Money for Nothing, Chips for Free." On Thursdays from January to October 2002, the staff members at Majestic Star randomly selected a table every ten minutes. Every player at that table who was using his or her Club Majestic card received free gaming chips, in amounts ranging from five to one hundred dollars.

Caesars in Tunica, Mississippi, offers what they term Grand One Players Club. By earning thirty thousand or more slot points or six hundred hours of rated play on table games with a twenty-five-dollar average bet or the equivalent, players can join the Grand One Players Club. Play must be accumulated in a twelve-month period. Patrons earn a 25 percent cash back bonus seven days a week. They also earn free spa services, including one free spa or salon service per month, VIP restaurant seating, VIP valet retrieval, VIP self-parking, VIP show seating, VIP hotel check-in, VIP reservation services, preferred tee times at Cottonwoods golf course, free room upgrade, invitation to private Grand One member events, and extra sweepstakes entry tickets. Final membership is determined by a combination of various play criteria and management approval.

Table 2.12 shows casino promotion spending by company from 1997 to 2004. Interestingly, Las Vegas Sands, the most profitable casino, grew their casino promotion budget at a rate much slower than all of its competitors, except for Station Casinos. Thus, the two low-growth casino firms, in terms of promotion spending, were the two casinos with the highest operating income as a percentage of revenues. It may be that low-earning casinos responded to their low earnings by increasing their promotion spending. Table 2.13 lists casino promotion spending as a percentage of revenues.

In order to investigate the relationship among promotion spending, operating income, and casino income, we calculate correlation coefficients between each relationship. A correlation coefficient measures the degree to which two variables are linearly related or associated. As the strength of the

TABLE 2.12.   Casino promotion spending

	Las Vegas Sands	Harrah's	Boyd Gaming Corp.	Penn National Gaming	MGM Mirage	Station Casinos	Ameristar Casinos	Century Casinos
1997		$147,432	$44,308		$63,733	$53,426	$15,530	
1998		$184,477	$93,772		$66,219	$49,176	$22,071	$753,063
1999		$286,539	$94,547		$112,560	$67,892	$24,618	$672,153
2000		$340,438	$98,268		$286,343	$67,659	$28,224	$653,120
2001	$42,594	$565,758	$120,656		$407,071	$72,816	$36,598	$755,000
2002	$34,208	$717,628	$128,547	$27,713	$428,318	$73,281	$108,406	$3,943,000
2003	$44,856	$782,050	$141,459	$74,324	$415,643	$67,365	$128,272	$4,424,000
2004	$61,514	$862,806	$198,033	$65,615	$434,384	$67,857	$165,461	$4,657,000
Growth (%)	13.0	28.7	23.9	54.0	31.6	3.5	40.2	35.5

Source: Authors' calculations based on data from Reuters.

TABLE 2.13.   Casino promotion spending as a percentage of casino revenues

	Las Vegas Sands	Harrah's	Boyd Gaming Corp.	Penn National Gaming	MGM Mirage	Station Casinos	Ameristar Casinos	Century Casinos
1997		11.0	13.7		13.9	8.9	9.0	
1998		11.1	13.0		16.1	9.7	10.2	4.0
1999		11.8	12.9		12.9	8.9	10.0	3.0
2000		11.9	11.3		15.0	8.4	9.9	2.4
2001		17.5	13.2		18.8	11.0	6.6	2.5
2002	17.3	19.5	12.3	5.6	19.6	11.5	16.0	12.9
2003	14.0	20.3	13.2	7.6	20.0	10.4	16.9	13.9
2004	10.8	21.2	13.6	6.6	19.5	9.3	19.3	

Source: Authors' calculations based on data from Reuters.

relationship between two variables increases, so does the correlation coefficient. A correlation coefficient can range between -1, perfectly and negatively related to $+1$, perfectly and positively related. A correlation coefficient of 0 means that there is no linear relationship between the variables. For example, the correlation coefficient between the temperature measured in Fahrenheit and centigrade is $+1$.

Table 2.14 lists correlation coefficients between each of the variables. According to the results, operating income and promotion spending are positively related with a small correlation coefficient of 0.163. On the other hand, operating income and casino revenues are negatively related with a larger correlation coefficient of -0.496, and operating income and casino revenues are also negatively associated with a correlation coefficient of -0.454. Perhaps low-earning casinos, in order to remedy the problem, are spending more aggressively on promotion. Moreover, casinos that make a large share of their revenues from noncasino activities appear to be earning higher operating incomes.

Almost 300 tribal casinos and 175 commercial casinos have been constructed during the past fifteen years, with more on the way. For many Americans, access to casino gambling is more convenient than ever. Though the growth of commercial casinos appears to have slowed somewhat, tribal casinos are continuing to expand. Tax and legal structures appear to be contributing to this disparate growth, as tribes have achieved competitive advantages over their commercial counterparts in building and opening new operations.

Although some states have benefited from tribal operations through the granting of exclusive rights (a topic explored further in chapter 11), those with both commercial and tribal facilities must draw the vast majority of state revenues from commercial operations. Thus, a shift toward tribal gam-

TABLE 2.14. Correlation coefficients, 1997–2004

	Promotion Spending	Operating Income	Casino Revenue
Promotion spending	1.000		
Operating income	0.163	1.000	
Casino revenues	−0.496	−0.454	1.000

Source: Authors' calculations.

ing potentially threatens an important source of tax revenues. Moreover, the potential for stagnation of casino collections as markets mature should awaken government officials to the danger of heavy reliance on growing revenue streams from casino operations. The nature and extent of those revenues, and their rising importance in each of the casino states, are considered in chapter 3.

Company financial statements indicate that casino company earnings and revenues have been growing robustly since 1997. Furthermore, investors are rewarding casino companies by bidding up the stock prices of the companies to the point where their price-earnings ratios are significantly above market averages. This indicates that investors expect casino profits to continue to grow at a pace exceeding that of the average publicly listed corporation.

3. Tax Revenues from Casinos

As presented in chapter 2, legalized casino gambling has emerged as a significant growth industry in the United States. State and local governments are willing participants in this expansion as they have increasingly looked to casino gambling as a new source of tax revenues, with citizens generally supporting the expansion of gambling. For many citizens, funding government activities with "voluntary" casino tax collections presents an attractive alternative to raising traditional or noncasino taxes. Additionally, with the promise of job and income growth, states have embraced gambling and casino wagering as tonics to remedy economic lethargy. However, it is unclear whether the addition of casino gambling actually reduces the tax burdens of citizens and is a net benefit to the community. Certainly the economic benefits or costs of casino expansion may depend on whether the added casinos are tribal or commercial.

TRIBAL CASINO PAYMENTS

Given significant differences between the taxes paid by commercial casinos and the payments in lieu of taxes paid by tribal casinos, the benefits to the community are likely to depend crucially on whether the casino is commercial or tribal. Indian tribes occupy an unusual legal status in our federal system. Tribes possess a limited sovereignty consistent with their status as "domestic dependent nations."[1] This sovereignty has limited state and local governments' ability to obtain funds via taxation from the operation of tribal casinos. The legal consequences of tribal status are discussed at length in chapter 11.

According to estimates by Meister in his 2005–6 *Indian Gaming Industry Report*, tribal casinos, despite any legal responsibility to pay state and local

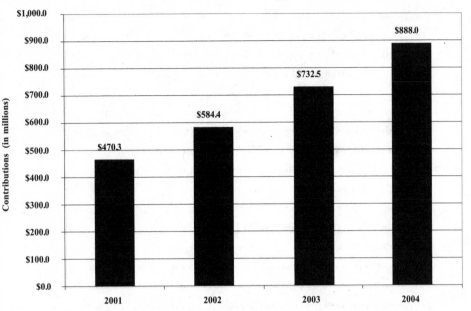

Fig. 3.1. Tribal casino contributions to state and local government, 2001–4 (in millions of dollars)

casino taxes, contributed $888.0 million to state and local governments on 2004 AGR of $19.0 billion.[2] This represents an average "tax" rate of 4.7 percent. Figure 3.1 shows that tribal contributions to state and local government tax coffers have risen from $470.3 million in 2001 to $888.0 million in 2004.

Despite the IGRA limits on state taxing powers, states have been allowed to negotiate gaming compacts that extract a payment for granting exclusive gaming rights to tribal interests. For example, this model is followed in Connecticut, which has no commercial casinos but two tribal casinos. By granting exclusive rights to the tribes, Connecticut reaped $411.4 million in payments in lieu of taxes from these two casinos in 2004, or approximately 46 percent of total tribal contributions to state and local governments in 2004. Thus, the two Connecticut casinos racked up an average of $205.7 million in tax receipts while the remaining 403 tribal casinos brought in an average of slightly less than $1.2 million in tax revenue.

Table 3.1 shows tribal casino contributions to state and local governments by state for 2003 and 2004. As listed, California and Connecticut accounted for almost 70 percent of total tribal contributions to state and local governments in 2004. Two of the states listed in table 3.1, Louisiana and Michigan, also had commercial casinos within their borders. Several other states had tribal casinos but did not report any tribal casino contributions. These include Colorado, Florida, Iowa, Kansas, Montana, Nevada, North Dakota, Oklahoma, and South Dakota.

As presented in table 3.1, Wisconsin tribes expanded their payments from casino gambling to state and local governments at the strongest pace in the nation between 2003 and 2004. Wisconsin Potawatomi tribal officials contend that the $40.5 million the tribe paid to the state in 2003 made it the largest business taxpayer in the state that year.[3]

Table 3.2 lists effective tax rates by state by year for tribal casinos. Even though the effective tax rates remain low, they have grown each year. As presented for 2004, Connecticut collected the highest rate from tribal casinos at 20.3 percent and Minnesota netted the lowest rate at 1.2 percent. This wide gap in effective tax collections is easily explained. As stated earlier, tribal casinos opened pursuant to the IGRA are not subject to state and local taxes on gaming revenues. State taxing powers are limited to recovering amounts necessary to cover regulatory costs, with amounts above this as

TABLE 3.1.   Tribal contributions to state and local governments, 2003, 2004

	2003 ($)	2004 ($)	Growth 2003–4 (%)
Connecticut	396,400,000	411,400,000	3.8
California	131,600,000	153,200,000	16.4
Arizona	26,100,000	70,100,000	168.6
Wisconsin	16,700,000	68,000,000	307.2
New York	39,000,000	57,100,000	46.4
New Mexico	36,900,000	39,500,000	7.0
Michigan	31,500,000	31,400,000	−0.3
Minnesota	16,100,000	16,100,000	0.0
Washington	8,900,000	9,900,000	11.2
Oregon	8,900,000	9,500,000	6.7
Louisiana	10,200,000	8,500,000	−16.7
Idaho	5,200,000	7,000,000	34.6
Alaska	300,000	300,000	0.0
*Other states	4,700,000	6,000,000	27.7
Total all states	732,500,000	888,000,000	21.2

Source: Indian Gaming Industry Report 2005–6.

purely voluntary contributions. Thus, tribal casinos not only fail to generate gaming taxes, but they may also erode the tax base through competition with commercial activities.

As listed in table 3.2, California's tribal casinos, with an average tax rate of 3.6 percent in 2004, represent an important contrast to Connecticut's. In March 2000, California governor Gray Davis signed unbreakable twenty-year compacts with sixty-one tribes, giving them a monopoly casino industry. However, in June 2005 Governor Davis's replacement, Governor Arnold Schwarzenegger, announced deals with five of California's casino-owning Indian tribes to provide the state with $150–200 million annually.[4] Schwarzenegger, like many other U.S. governors, is bumping up against increasing demands for state dollars while at the same time facing the barrier of tribal sovereignty. Politicians in states with commercial casinos are experiencing a much more positive environment, at least in terms of casino tax receipts.

COMMERCIAL CASINO TAX COLLECTIONS

As stated earlier, tax rates on commercial casinos are typically more than five times those of tribal casinos, depending on the state. Table 3.3 shows the

TABLE 3.2.   Tribal casino payments in lieu of taxes as a percentage of AGR, 2001–4

	2001	2002	2003	2004
Connecticut	20.7	19.7	19.6	20.3
New York	N.A.	N.A.	7.1	10.4
New Mexico	0.4	6.0	6.0	6.5
Wisconsin	2.7	2.4	1.5	6.3
Idaho	1.2	1.1	4.4	5.9
Arizona	N.A.	N.A.	2.1	5.8
California	0.8	2.0	3.1	3.6
Michigan	3.4	3.5	3.6	3.6
Alaska	3.9	3.7	3.6	3.6
Oregon	2.3	2.1	2.1	2.2
Louisiana	2.3	2.1	2.1	1.7
Washington	0.5	1.1	1.2	1.3
Minnesota	1.2	1.2	1.2	1.2
Other states	0.3	0.1	0.1	0.2
Total	3.7	3.9	4.3	5.2

Source: Author calculations based on Meister data.

N.A. = not available

legislated casino tax rates on commercial casinos in each state where they exist. Marginal tax rates range from 6.25 percent in Nevada to as much as 70 percent in Illinois. In addition to tax rates on AGR, many states also assess admission fees for each gambler, but these admission fees are paid by the casino from the proceeds of the casino and are not dependent on the gambling losses, or AGR, of the casino patron. However, the experience of each state has varied as widely as the characteristics of the populations of the states.

Based on the rates listed in table 3.3, the American Gaming Association (AGA) estimates that commercial casinos paid $4.7 billion in wagering taxes alone in 2004—a figure that does not include income, property, and sales taxes that casinos also contribute to public coffers. This represents an average tax rate on AGR of 16.4 percent. The 445 commercial casinos operating in eleven states have become an increasingly powerful tax-generating engine for specific locales of the United States, with tax collections from casinos

TABLE 3.3.   Legislated casino tax rates by state, 2005

Colorado	Graduated tax rate with a maximum tax of 20% on gross gaming revenue
Illinois	Graduated tax rate from 15% to 70% of gross gaming revenue, $3–5 per patron admissions tax
Indiana	Graduated tax rate from 15% to 35% of gross gaming revenue, $3 per patron admissions tax
Iowa	Graduated tax rate with a maximum tax of 22% on gross gaming revenue
Louisiana	Riverboat casinos: 21.5%; land-based casino: $60 million annual tax or 21.5% of gross gaming revenue, whichever is greater; racetrack casinos: 18.5% tax on gross gaming revenue,[3] 18% of net revenue paid to horsemen
Michigan	24% tax on gross gaming revenue (11.9% to city of Detroit, 12.1% to state of Michigan); effective tax rate of 23.02% (including taxes and fees)
Mississippi	Graduated tax rate with a maximum state tax of 8% on gaming revenue; up to 4% additional tax on gaming revenues may be imposed by local governments
Missouri	20% tax on gross gaming revenue, $2 per patron admission fee per excursion split between home dock community and the state
Nevada	Graduated tax rate with a maximum tax of 6.75% on gross gaming revenue; additional fees and levies may be imposed by counties, municipalities, and the state, adding approximately 1% to the tax burden
New Jersey	8% tax on gross gaming revenue plus a community investment alternative obligation of 1.25% of gross gaming revenue (or an investment alternative 2.5% on gross gaming revenue), 4.25% tax on casino ancillaries effective July 1, 2003*
South Dakota	8% tax on gross gaming revenue, gaming device tax of $2,000 per machine per year

Source: American Gaming Association, 2005 survey.

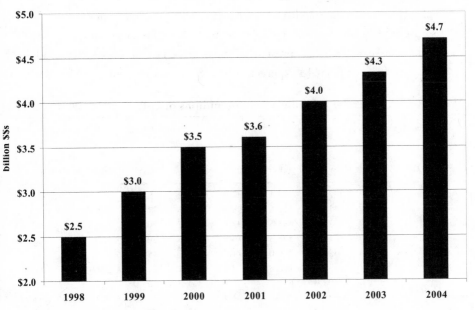

Fig. 3.2. Commercial casino wagering taxes paid, 1998–2004 (in billions of dollars)

growing much faster than overall tax collections. Figure 3.2 shows how casino tax collections have grown between 1998 and 2004.

As presented in figure 3.2, tax collections from casinos increased from $2.5 billion in 1998 to $4.7 billion in 2004, a growth of 88.0 percent or a compound yearly growth rate of 11.1 percent. According to the U.S. Census Bureau, from 1998 to 2004 the annual compound growth rate for federal tax collections was only 0.1 percent and was 3.8 percent for state taxes.

Table 3.4 shows tax collections from casino gambling by state. As listed for 2004, Nevada collected the largest sum at $887.0 million, while South Dakota collected the smallest sum at $11.9 million. Michigan, opening its commercial casinos in 1999, experienced the highest yearly growth rate at 70.0 percent, while Mississippi experienced the lowest annual growth rate at 4.4 percent.

Table 3.5 presents average tax rates by state from 1998 to 2004. The average tax rate is calculated as tax collections from casinos divided by the total net gambling revenues, or AGR, of casinos. As listed in table 3.5, Illinois levied the highest average tax rate at 46.7 percent, while Nevada assessed the lowest tax rate on casino revenues at 8.4 percent for 2004. Table

3.5 also indicates the stability of tax revenues as a percentage of AGR, with the average tax rate increasing by slightly more than three percentage points in the five-year period. As presented, the average tax rates on AGR for all casino states rose from 13.2 percent in 1998 to 16.4 percent in 2004. Ad-

TABLE 3.4.   Commercial tax collections (in millions of dollars), 1998–2004

	1998	1999	2000	2001	2002	2003	2004	Compound Yearly Growth 1998–2004 (%)
Colorado	63.0	728.0	82.1	92.0	98.2	95.6	99.6	8.7
Illinois	337.0	419.0	512.0	555.2	666.1	719.9	801.7	16.4
Indiana	370.0	425.0	453.5	492.6	544.7	702.7	760.5	13.7
Iowa	96.0	214.0	206.3	216.9	249.3	209.7	252.7	16.9
Louisiana	315.0	324.0	381.0	374.8	414.2	448.9	436.9	7.3
Michigan	N.A.	30.0	170.8	219.3	249.1	250.2	279.4	70.0
Mississippi	262.0	302.0	320.0	322.6	331.7	325.0	333.0	4.4
Missouri	251.0	275.0	304.0	322.7	357.6	369.0	403.1	8.1
Nevada	586.0	635.0	707.6	688.0	718.7	776.5	887.0	5.8
New Jersey	319.0	330.0	342.0	342.4	403.7	414.5	470.7	5.4
South Dakota	3.4	3.7	4.8	4.5	5.1	5.5	11.9	10.3
All casino states	2,602.4	3,685.7	3,484.1	3,631.0	4,038.4	4,317.5	4,736.5	10.7

Source: American Gaming Association, 1998–2004 surveys.
N.A. = not available

TABLE 3.5.   Average tax rate on AGR for commercial casinos by state, 1998–2004 (%)

	1998	1999	2000	2001	2002	2003	2004
Colorado	13.2	11.4	13.0	14.6	13.6	13.7	13.7
Illinois	30.6	29.9	30.1	30.8	37.0	42.1	46.7
Indiana	33.6	28.3	26.7	27.4	25.9	31.5	32.1
Iowa	19.4	25.0	23.3	23.5	25.6	20.5	23.7
Louisiana	24.2	23.1	21.2	20.8	20.7	22.3	20.2
Michigan	N.A.	18.1	23.0	21.9	22.6	22.1	23.5
Mississippi	11.9	12.1	11.9	11.9	12.3	12.0	12.0
Missouri	29.4	29.3	30.5	29.3	27.5	27.7	27.4
Nevada	7.2	7.1	7.4	7.2	7.6	8.1	8.4
New Jersey	8.0	7.9	8.0	8.0	9.3	9.2	9.8
South Dakota	7.7	7.7	9.3	7.7	7.7	7.7	15.3
U.S.	13.2	13.4	13.9	14.2	15.2	16.0	16.4

Source: Author calculations based on American Gaming Association data. Tax rate is equal to total gaming taxes paid divided by AGR.
N.A. = not available

ditionally, it must be noted that these percentages do not include admission fees, which are not considered part of AGR. The data in table 3.5 suggest that the national recession encouraged legislators to revisit this financial source to help solve the state and local fiscal crisis, with the average tax rate growing by a full percentage point between 2001 and 2002.

Table 3.6 shows the relative dependence of each commercial casino state on casino tax collections, with Nevada and Mississippi depending more heavily on casino tax generation to finance government activities than other casino states. In terms of the share of taxes collected from casinos, states ranged from 1.1 percent for South Dakota to 18.7 percent for Nevada. Data indicate that each state's casino tax collections grew more quickly than other tax receipts, thus showing an increasing reliance among the casino states on casino taxes. Iowa experienced the largest increase in casino taxes as a percentage of total tax collection, growing by 2.9 percentage points in six years.

Data in the preceding tables understate the increasing dependence of states on casino tax collections. For example, on June 23, 2005, Pennsylvania governor Edward G. Rendell issued the following statement after the Pennsylvania Supreme Court issued a ruling in *Pennsylvanians Against Gambling Expansion Fund, Inc. et al., v. Commonwealth of Pennsylvania, et al.,* upholding Act 71, which expanded gaming in Pennsylvania.

TABLE 3.6.   Casino taxes as a percentage of total tax collections, 1998–2004

	1998	1999	2000	2001	2002	2003	2004
Colorado	1.0	1.1	1.1	1.3	1.4	1.4	1.4
Illinois	1.7	2.0	2.1	2.4	3.0	3.2	3.1
Indiana	3.6	4.0	4.3	4.7	5.2	6.0	6.4
Iowa	2.0	4.3	4.0	4.2	5.0	4.1	4.9
Louisiana	5.3	5.4	5.7	5.1	5.9	6.2	5.4
Michigan	N.A.	0.1	0.7	1.0	1.1	1.0	1.2
Mississippi	5.9	7.4	7.2	6.6	6.6	6.4	6.5
Missouri	3.0	3.2	3.5	3.6	4.1	4.2	4.4
Nevada	18.3	20.6	21.2	19.7	21.9	18.4	18.7
New Jersey	1.9	1.9	1.8	1.8	2.1	2.0	2.2
South Dakota	0.5	0.5	0.6	0.5	0.5	0.5	1.1
All casino states	2.6	2.9	3.1	3.2	3.6	3.7	3.9

Source: Authors' calculations based on American Gaming Association and U.S. Census Bureau data.

N.A. = not available

The Administration is incredibly pleased that the Supreme Court upheld the majority of Act 71, which legalizes slot machine gaming in the commonwealth. It is a complete vindication of the Act, the process and the hard work and thoughtful drafting that many people put into creating this bill.[5]

And in 2004, the Michigan House of Representatives passed a bill doubling the tax rate on Detroit's three casinos, pushing it to 36 percent. The Michigan casinos warned that, if taxed at the higher rate, they would not build the new hotels they had promised for downtown Detroit and would have to reduce marginal operations, such as table games, with resulting job losses. Furthermore, casino officials made the case that such action could actually result in lower tax collections for the state, as it did in Illinois when the state raised taxes on its riverboat casinos and the state experienced a 6.6 percent drop in gaming revenues. In the end both sides compromised, and Michigan governor Jennifer Granholm signed a bill that increased tax rates on casinos from 18 percent to 24 percent.

But does increasing the casino tax rate produce higher casino tax collections? Just as expressed by Michigan casino leaders, Illinois presents an interesting case on the sensitivity of gambling tax collections to changes in gambling tax rates. In 2003, the Illinois legislature and the governor implemented a top-tax rate of 70 percent on AGR. Illinois's new wagering tax ranged from 15 percent of AGR up to $25 million, but it increased to 37.5 percent on AGR between $25 million and $50 million and escalated to 70 percent for AGR over $250 million. Prior to 1998, Illinois's wagering tax had held steady at a flat 20 percent when the state began to tap the industry for added revenues and implemented massive tax hikes, first a 50 percent rate in 2002 followed by the more recent increase to 70 percent in 2003.

Figure 3.3 profiles Illinois effective tax rates and Illinois AGR as a percentage of U.S. AGR from 1998 to 2004. As presented, from 1998 to 2001, when Illinois effective tax rates on casino AGR ranged from 25.9 percent in 1998 to 30.8 percent in 2001, Illinois expanded its relative position in the United States, growing from 5.6 percent of U.S. AGR in 1998 to 7.0 percent in 2001. However, beginning in 2002, the first year of the large tax hike, Illinois's growth in AGR moved below U.S. AGR, with its share dropping to 5.9 percent by 2004. These data, at least superficially, indicate the sensitivity of gambling revenues to tax rates on AGR.

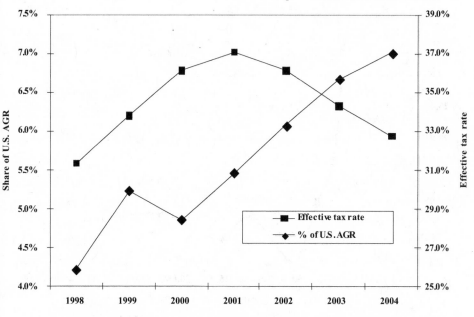

Fig. 3.3. Illinois casino tax rates and AGR as percentage of U.S. AGR, 1998–2004

Figure 3.4 shows average tax rates versus percentage of U.S. AGR for the eleven commercial casino states for 2004. There appears to be a negative relationship. That is, higher casino tax rates produce lower casino market shares.

HOW ARE CASINO TAXES SPENT?

Each commercial casino state has enacted legislation that specifies how casino tax collections will be spent. The spending targets vary widely and are often used to support popular causes, in addition to sharing revenues with state and local governments. For example, Colorado directs that regulatory costs must first be repaid from gaming revenues, after which 28 percent is distributed for the purpose of funding historical preservation grants. Such grants would be important for the purpose of developing tourism.[6] The remainder is divided between state and local governments. In contrast, Illinois allows local governments to share 5 percent of AGR and half the admission tax, but the remainder of its substantial tax collections goes to the state.[7]

Indiana's code contains a complex set of directions for revenue disposition, which vary by the type of casino involved. A substantial portion of these revenues—up to 37.5 percent—is required to be deposited in a special

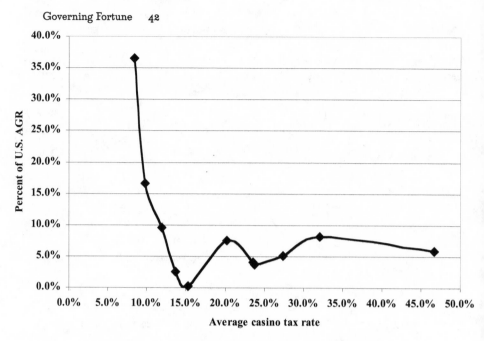

Fig. 3.4. Average casino tax rates versus percentage of U.S. AGR for 2004

property tax replacement fund.[8] Both state and local governments potentially benefit from gaming revenues according to complex formulas apparently designed to mollify different political constituencies.

Both Iowa[9] and Louisiana[10] share requirements that a portion of their casino revenues be deposited into a fund designated to address problem gambling. In Iowa, a special fund is also available to fund community improvements.[11] Targeted spending benefits in Louisiana include education and law enforcement. Michigan shares similar policy goals, as its laws specify that the distribution of casino tax revenue shall go to K–12 public education in Michigan and to capital improvements, youth programs, and tax relief in the city of Detroit.[12] Michigan's casino legislation also creates certain funds for the operation of the Michigan Gaming Control Board to license, regulate, and control casino gaming and funds for compulsive gambling prevention programs and other casino-related state programs.[13]

As these varying provisions illustrate, funding important public activities like historical preservation or education can involve providing additional tax revenues instead of tax relief. However, when the funds are primarily available to the state general fund, or when they are designated for the purpose of tax relief, the political promise inherent in casino gambling deserves closer scrutiny.

DO CASINOS GENERATE TAX RELIEF?

Each year the AGA surveys approximately one thousand adults from across the nation to gauge attitudes toward casino gambling in America. In the surveys between 1996 and 2005, the AGA asked respondents whether they thought legalized casino gambling was a good way to add to tax collections without raising noncasino patrons' taxes. Figure 3.5 shows the percentage of survey participants who agreed that this was an effective methodology of tax generation. As displayed, 67.0 percent of those surveyed in 2005 agreed with this taxing methodology.

While over the past decade between 60 and 70 percent of Americans judged casinos as a good method of raising tax collections, it is debatable whether casinos provide any tax relief for taxpayers in the state. To combat local opposition, politicians appear to have taken the position that it is good policy to attract casino spending from other states. The location of new casinos reflects the targeted goal of attracting cross-border patronage. Outside of Nevada, a high share of commercial casinos is within close proximity of the state border. Political leaders consider these cross-border patrons as a rich deposit of tax revenues from nonconstituents. Moreover, to the extent that gambling produces social costs, these costs are likely to return home along with the gambler, thus becoming a drain on another jurisdiction's social services. Iowa, for example, receives roughly 50 percent of its casino tax collections from four of its thirteen casinos that are located less than one mile from its border with Nebraska.[14]

Unfortunately, the quest for tourism-funded gambling has been hard to achieve, and it is not always possible to raise revenues from residents of other states. As casinos proliferate, interest in tourism for the purpose of gambling understandably wanes. As a result, casino revenues (and associated taxes) come increasingly from local patrons. Local patronage still generates gambling taxes from willing participants, which might be viewed as politically preferable to forced exactions from the general population. Governor Rendell of Pennsylvania announced that the tax revenue from the sixty-one thousand slot machines allowed by recent legislation would be used to provide property tax relief. Clearly, political leaders in Pennsylvania, much like

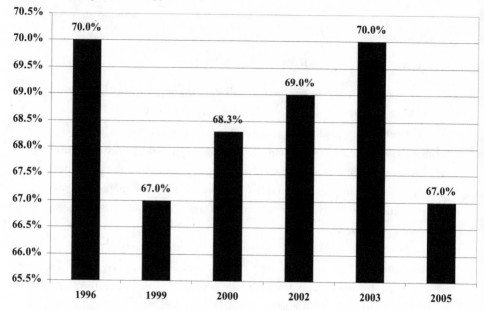

Fig. 3.5. Percentage of Americans who think legalized casinos are a good way of generating tax collections (*Source:* AGA Surveys, 1996–2005)

their counterparts in other states, view gambling as a ready and willing source of tax dollars. However, expanded gambling also presents a concern that local citizens (including those who do not participate in gambling at all) may also be bearing some hidden social costs. To this extent casinos would provide little tax relief.

Table 3.7 shows taxes as a percentage of personal income from 1998 to 2004. In 1998, noncasino taxes as a percentage of personal income were 6.6 percent in noncasino states and 6.1 percent in casino states. However, by 2004, the rate had dropped to 6.1 percent for noncasino states and 5.8 percent for casino states. Thus during the period of rapid growth in casino revenues and tax collections, the effective tax rate in noncasino states dropped more than in casino states. While this is certainly not definitive, it does suggest that casinos have not played an important role in reducing the tax burden for taxpayers in casino states.

Table 3.8 provides a measure of the extent to which casinos provide relief from local taxes. The table shows taxes per one thousand dollars of personal income for casino states and for noncasino states for 1991 and 2001. The year

1991 was chosen because, except for Nevada and New Jersey, no casinos had opened in any states at that time. The year 2001 was selected because it was the latest year for which both state and local tax data were available.

For property taxes, noncasino states clearly had a more positive experience than casino states. In terms of state property taxes, noncasino state taxes, per one thousand dollars in personal income, declined by 51.2 percent while casino state taxes actually rose by 75.0 percent. For local property taxes, much the same is calculated, with noncasino state taxes declining by 32.0 percent and casino state taxes declining by a much smaller 13.4 percent. Much the same trend is detected in other taxes. For example, sales taxes per one thousand dollars of personal income in noncasino taxes declined by 29.7 percent and 17.6 percent for state and local sales taxes, respectively. But for noncasino states, sales taxes per one thousand dollars of personal income declined by a much lower 2.4 percent and 3.5 percent for state and local taxes, respectively. This same pattern is observed in income taxes and overall taxes, as noncasino state taxes, per one thousand dollars of personal income, dropped by much higher rates than casino state taxes.

Table 3.9 contains data for the same two time periods, 1991 and 2001. Only categories for which the definition of spending did not change between the two years are listed. Data indicate that noncasino states reduced their

TABLE 3.7.   Noncasino taxes as a percentage of personal income, 1998–2004

	1998	1999	2000	2001	2002	2003	2004
Colorado	5.1	5.2	5.0	4.7	4.4	4.2	4.2
Illinois	5.4	5.5	5.9	5.5	5.3	5.3	5.6
Indiana	6.7	6.7	6.1	5.9	5.7	6.2	6.0
Iowa	6.7	6.5	6.4	6.2	5.8	5.8	5.3
Louisiana	5.8	5.8	6.1	6.4	5.8	5.8	6.2
Michigan	N.A.	7.4	7.8	7.5	7.3	7.6	7.3
Mississippi	7.6	6.7	6.9	7.2	7.4	7.0	6.8
Missouri	5.8	5.8	5.5	5.6	5.2	5.1	5.0
Nevada	5.0	4.3	4.3	4.3	3.9	4.9	4.9
New Jersey	5.7	5.7	5.7	5.6	5.5	5.8	5.7
South Dakota	4.2	4.1	4.4	4.6	4.8	4.7	4.5
Total casino states	6.1	6.0	6.1	5.9	5.7	5.8	5.8
All noncasino states	6.6	6.6	6.7	6.5	6.1	6.1	6.1

Source: Author calculations from U.S. Census Bureau data.

N.A. = not available

n spending per $1,000 of personal income at a much higher rate than
 states. Noncasino states reduced their education spending by 16.7
..cent for state expenditures and 0.6 percent for local expenditures. Casino
states actually increased their relative education spending at the state level by

TABLE 3.8.   Taxes per $1,000 of personal income, casino versus
noncasino states, 1991, 2001

	State Taxes		Local Taxes	
	Noncasino States	Casino States	Noncasino States	Casino States
Property, 1991	$1.78	$0.66	$34.90	$38.90
Property, 2001	$0.87	$1.15	$23.74	$33.67
Percent change	−51.2	75.0	−32.0	−13.4
General sales, 1991	$23.13	$20.95	$4.97	$4.26
General sales, 2001	$16.26	$20.46	$4.09	$4.11
Percent change	−29.7	−2.4	−17.6	−3.5
Income—individual & corp., 1991	$26.93	$24.57	$3.10	$0.92
Income—individual & corp., 2001	$19.37	$22.63	$2.15	$0.78
Percent change	−28.1	−7.9	−30.7	−15.1
All taxes, 1991	$70.76	$62.67	$47.40	$47.01
All taxes, 2001	$48.72	$59.60	$33.51	$41.86
Percent change	−31.1	−4.9	−29.3	−11.0

Source: Authors' calculations based on U.S. Census Bureau data.

TABLE 3.9.   Government spending per $1,000 of personal income,
casino versus noncasino states, 1991, 2001

	State Spending		Local Spending	
	Noncasino States	Casino States	Noncasino States	Casino States
Education, 1991	$5.81	$6.78	$2.05	$2.37
Education, 2001	$4.84	$7.02	$1.48	$2.36
Percent change	−16.7	3.5	−28.1	−0.6
Parks and recreation, 1991	$0.55	$0.60	$2.70	$2.78
Parks and recreation, 2001	$0.09	$0.22	$0.49	$0.85
Percent change	−83.4	−63.6	−82.0	−69.4
Housing and community development, 1991	$0.34	$0.32	$3.64	$1.74
Housing and community development, 2001	$0.05	$0.06	$0.37	$0.30
Percent change	−85.9	−80.8	−89.9	−82.9

Source: Authors' calculations based on U.S. Census Bureau data.

3.5 percent but reduced their relative education spending at the local level by 0.6 percent. Given that in many states, a high share of casino revenues goes to education, this is not surprising.

Much the same pattern is calculated for parks and recreation and housing and community development spending with expenditures per $1,000 of personal income declining at a faster pace for noncasino states than for casino states.

Another method of examining the impact of casinos on taxes is to analyze the change in the relative size of state and local government before and after the introduction of a casino. The location quotient (LQ) is one of the most frequently used tools in economic geography to examine how a particular change, in this case a new casino, changes the distribution of employment. This technique compares the county economy to the state economy, in the process attempting to identify specializations in the local economy. To calculate the LQ you simply divide the county's share of employment in an industry by the state's share of employment in the same industry. Equation (1) below indicates how the LQ is calculated.

$$LQ = \% \text{ of county employment in industry K} / \% \text{ of state}$$

$$\text{employment in industry K.} \tag{1}$$

According to equation (1), an LQ of 1.0 indicates that a county has its expected share of employment in industry K. On the other hand, suppose a county has 10 percent of its workforce in state and local government and the state has only 5 percent of its workforce in state and local government. In this case the LQ is 2.0, indicating that the county has twice its expected share of employment in state and local government. Casino opponents argue that casinos produce an increase in the size of the local police force, thus precipitating an increase in the county's LQ for government workers. However, irrespective of casinos, a county's LQ may be greater than 1.0. For example, a county with a state prison would likely have an LQ for government greater than 1.0.

But by comparing a county's LQ for state and local government employment before and after the addition of a casino, one can determine the extent to which the size of government expanded to accommodate the increased social services demands produced by the casino or contracted due to economies of scale for the delivery of social services. Alternatively, a decline in the LQ indicates that the county's nongovernment sectors grew more robustly than these same industries at the state level, pointing to potential benefits to the county's taxpayers from casino operations.

Table 3.10 compares casino counties by state for the year before casinos were added and for 2003. As presented, five of ten states[15] experienced little change in the relative size of government between the introduction of casinos and 2003. Iowa, Illinois, Indiana, Michigan, and Missouri had LQs in 2003 virtually the same as LQs prior to the introduction of casinos. On the other hand, four states experienced a reduction in the relative size of the government sector after the introduction of casinos. Colorado, Mississippi, New Jersey, and South Dakota all experienced a relative decline in the size of the government sector upon the introduction of casinos. Only Louisiana saw the relative size of its government sector expand significantly with the introduction of casinos.

Data in table 3.10 provide evidence that casino counties in Colorado, Mississippi, New Jersey, and South Dakota grew the relative size of their nongovernment workforce at a much faster pace than noncasino counties in the state, with significant declines in the LQ for government. On the other hand, casino counties in Louisiana, with a significant increase in the LQ for government, expanded the relative size of their government workforce at a much faster pace than noncasino counties in the state.

However, average LQs for casino counties in the state likely mask changes for a particular county. As listed in table 3.11, the impacts at the individual

TABLE 3.10.   Average government location quotients for casino counties before casino operations and in 2003

Casino Counties in	First Year of Casino Operations	LQ before Casinos	LQ in 2003
Colorado	1991	1.36	0.86
Iowa	1991	0.72	0.72
Illinois	1991	1.04	1.04
Indiana	1995	0.97	0.96
Louisiana	1993	0.87	0.95
Michigan	1998	0.98	0.99
Missouri	1994	0.77	0.77
Mississippi	1992	0.82	0.69
New Jersey	1978	1.30	0.94
South Dakota	1989	1.14	0.90

Source: Author calculations from U.S. Bureau of Economic Analysis.

TABLE 3.11. Impact of casino on goverment location quotient

State	County	FIPS	Year Casino Opened	LQ before Casino	LQ in 2003	Change
IL	Rock Island	17161	1992	0.79	0.88	0.09
LA	Orleans	22071	1994	0.93	1.02	0.09
IA	Lee	19111	1991	0.82	0.90	0.09
MO	Jackson	29095	1994	0.88	0.94	0.06
MO	Clay	29047	1994	0.91	0.97	0.06
IN	Lake	18089	1996	1.02	1.07	0.05
MO	St Charles	29183	1994	0.74	0.79	0.05
MO	Buchanan	29021	1994	1.06	1.12	0.05
LA	Caddo	22017	1994	0.90	0.94	0.05
MS	Greenville	28151	1994	0.98	1.01	0.03
IA	Woodbury	19193	1993	0.77	0.80	0.03
IA	Dubuque	19061	1991	0.48	0.51	0.03
IL	Tazewell	17179	1991	0.88	0.90	0.02
LA	Calcasieu	22019	1993	0.88	0.90	0.02
IL	Kane	17089	1991	0.97	0.98	0.01
MS	Adams	28001	1993	0.81	0.82	0.01
IA	Clinton	19045	1991	0.76	0.77	0.01
LA	East Baton Rouge	22033	1994	1.29	1.30	0.01
MO	Platte	29165	1994	0.60	0.61	0.01
IN	Vanderburgh	18163	1995	0.64	0.65	0.01
IA	Polk	19153	1995	0.74	0.73	−0.01
IA	Osceola	19143	2000	0.74	0.73	−0.01
IA	Scott	19163	1991	0.66	0.63	−0.03
MO	St Louis	29189	1994	0.65	0.61	−0.04
IL	Will	17197	1992	1.33	1.27	−0.05
LA	Jefferson	22051	1994	0.62	0.56	−0.06
MO	Lewis	29111	2001	1.29	1.22	−0.07
IA	Pottawattamie	19155	1996	0.95	0.88	−0.08
MS	Hancock	28045	1992	0.76	0.67	−0.09
MS	Harrison	28047	1992	0.74	0.64	−0.09
MS	Warren	28149	1993	0.69	0.60	−0.10
IN	LaPorte	18091	1997	1.30	1.19	−0.10
MO	Cooper	29053	1996	1.44	1.32	−0.12
IL	St Clair	17163	1993	1.10	0.96	−0.14
IN	Harrison	18061	1998	1.09	0.94	−0.15
LA	Bossier	22015	1994	0.91	0.76	−0.15
IA	Clayton	19043	1994	1.02	0.86	−0.15
IN	Dearborn	18029	1996	1.18	1.01	−0.17
MO	Pemiscot	29155	1995	2.18	1.99	−0.18
SD	Lawrence	46081	1989	1.14	0.90	−0.24
CO	Teller	8119	1991	1.30	1.02	−0.28
IL	Massac	17127	1993	1.53	1.25	−0.28
MS	Coahoma	28027	1994	1.36	1.06	−0.30
NJ	Atlantic	34001	1978	1.30	0.94	−0.35
IN	Switzerland	18155	2000	1.46	1.01	−0.45
MS	Tunica	28143	1992	0.92	0.32	−0.60
IN	Ohio	18115	1996	1.67	0.93	−0.74
CO	Gilpin	8047	1991	1.79	0.59	−1.20

Source: Author calculations based on U.S. Bureau of Economic Analysis data.

county level before and after the opening of a casino are more enlightening. According to the results, twenty-one counties experienced an increase in the relative size of government, with Rock Island County in Illinois seeing the largest rise in the size of government. On the other hand, twenty-seven counties saw a decline in the relative size of government before and after the introduction of casinos, with Gilpin County in Colorado experiencing the largest decline in the relative size of government.

How do casino counties that appeared to benefit from casinos in terms of the relative size of government differ from those that did not? Table 3.12 lists answers to that question by comparing counties in which the LQ for government increased (column 1) to counties in which the LQ for government decreased (column 2). As presented, counties that benefited tended to have a smaller population, lower density, and lower per capita income. Furthermore, counties in which the LQ for government declined experienced higher income, population, and employment growth over the course of the decade than counties in which the LQ for government increased.

Results in table 3.12 are not unexpected. They indicate that counties like Gilpin in Colorado, which was small in population, income, and employment before the casino opening, tended to benefit more than counties that were large in terms of population, income, and employment before the casino opening, such as Orleans in Louisiana, a county large in all three of these factors.

TABLE 3.12.   Profile of gainers and losers in casino counties

	Increased Relative Size of Government	Decreased Relative Size of Government
Population before casino	154,200	31,735
Population density before casino (persons per square mile)	281	64
Population growth, 1990–2003 (%)	3.5	7.4
Per capita income before casino ($)	17,657	15,461
Per capita income growth, 1990–2003 (%)	60.9	67.9
Employment before casino	84,056	13,224
Employment/population, 2003 (%)	58.8	53.6
Employment growth, 1990–2003 (%)	10.9	22.7

Source: U.S. Bureau of Labor Statistics, U.S. Census Bureau, U.S. Bureau of Economic Analysis.

State and local governments have become increasingly dependent on gambling taxes to support spending. From the data, it is clear that states derive significant tax advantages from commercial casinos in comparison to tribal casinos, with the tax rate almost four times as high for commercial casinos. Only Connecticut's 20.0 percent rate rivals that of commercial casino states.

While tax collections from casinos have grown dramatically over the years, data suggesting significant benefits to the taxpayer in the casino state are less compelling. Taxpayers in casino states did not experience benefits in terms of taxes as measured against personal income. Moreover, data indicate that casinos have no perceptible impact on property taxes. However, with only sixty-one commercial casino counties, impacts are difficult to detect.

Data indicate that the benefits to the taxpayer are likely dependent on the characteristics of the county before the opening of the casinos. Data suggest that counties with smaller and less dense populations and lower per capita income tend to benefit from casinos more than otherwise situated counties.

4. Casinos as Economic Development Tools

Local and state governments look at casinos as sources of taxes, gamblers see casinos as entertainment venues, and pathological gamblers gauge casinos as adversaries. Other entertainment providers view casinos as competitors but with inherent and insurmountable advantages. A wide swath of policymakers asserts that casinos create economic opportunities in the form of more jobs and higher pay for area residents. These casino advocates argue that casinos promote tourism, create jobs, spur economic development, and generate additional tax revenue for education and other needs. However, other policymakers and researchers contend that casinos simply rearrange employment in the area, offering no significant change in employment opportunities or in income gains. In the previous chapter, we examined the casino as a tool to reduce or alter relative tax burdens. In this chapter, we investigate casino contributions to economic development as defined by job growth, income growth, and changes in unemployment rates.

In a 2004 study published by the Federal Reserve of St. Louis, researchers examined the impact of casinos on economic development.[1] The lead researcher, Thomas Garrett, concluded that casinos create true economic development only when there is an increased "value" to society. He found that the addition of casinos into an area may produce business bankruptcy and higher levels of unemployment for the areas, thus reducing value. He found that the net change in local area jobs may be less than the additional casino jobs. At the same time, however, he noted that casino gaming may increase total employment when casinos indirectly generate noncasino jobs in the local area as a result of increased demand for noncasino goods and services. Furthermore, he concluded that casinos may have a positive impact on area income when previously unemployed workers become employed or when

52

individuals move into the area to take new casino jobs. A portion of the added income will then be spent on locally provided goods and services such as housing and entertainment.

In a 2005 research study, Garrett and Nichols, examining three destination casino areas, concluded that casinos do indeed export bankruptcy to the state in which the casino patron resides.[2] Using survey data, the authors calculated the number of visits from each state to casino resort destinations in Nevada, New Jersey, and Mississippi and found strong evidence that states having more residents who visit out-of-state casino resorts have higher bankruptcy filings. And in a 2005 study, Goss and Morse found that, after an initial increase in personal bankruptcy rates, counties that legalized casino gambling experienced lower personal bankruptcy rates during the first several years of casino operations.[3] However, the researchers concluded that those rates then increase, rising above those of noncasino counties after nine years of operations. By the thirteenth year of casino operations, the estimated bankruptcies per one thousand in population are 6.7 for counties that added casinos compared to 5.2 for noncasino counties. For the period of time covered by their analysis, this amounts to a compound annual growth rate in personal bankruptcies that is 2.3 percent higher for the county that added a casino than for an equivalent noncasino county.

Focusing on tribal casinos in a 1998 study, the Economics Research Group concluded that casinos make important job contributions to an area.[4] In examining 214 tribes, they found that the unemployment rate had fallen by 13 percent for tribes with casinos while there was no change for tribes without casinos. And in investigating four tribal casino locations, they measured significant declines in the unemployment rate before and after the casino opened. They calculated that for the Ho-Chunk tribe in Wisconsin, the rate declined from 19 percent to 6 percent; for the Oneida tribe, also in Wisconsin, the unemployment rate decreased from 19 percent to 4 percent; for the Chippewa tribe in Michigan, the rate dropped from 49 percent to 32 percent; and for the Sioux tribes in North Dakota and South Dakota, the unemployment rate plummeted from 62 percent to 29 percent.

In a 1998 study of one hundred communities, forty of which had casinos, the National Opinion Research Center (NORC) at the University of Chicago reported that communities with a casino within a fifty-mile radius experienced a 1 percent decline in their unemployment rate, a 17 percent decrease in unemployment insurance benefit payments, and a 13 percent drop in per capita welfare costs. In comparing reservations with casinos against reservations without casinos, Taylor and Kalt found that between 1990 and 2000 real per capita income grew by 36 percent, 21 percent, and 11 percent for tribes with casinos, tribes without casinos, and the United States, respectively.[5] During the same period the researchers calculated that unemployment rates declined by 4.8 percent, 1.8 percent, and 0.5 percent for tribes with casinos, tribes without casinos, and the United States, respectively. Clearly, their evidence implies significant positive economic development impact for tribal populations with casinos.

Goss concluded that yearly operation of an Omaha, Nebraska, casino would add $17.5 million in yearly wages and salaries, $58.4 million in yearly sales and support, and 1,008 jobs for the metropolitan area, with roughly $27.0 million in tax collections added each year.[6] However, for the rest of Nebraska outside of Omaha, he estimated that yearly operation of an Omaha, Nebraska, casino would reduce yearly wages and salaries by $6.3 million, yearly sales by $24.7 million, and jobs by 613.[7] He found that an Omaha, Nebraska, casino would likely increase the yearly crime rate by 1.5 percent to 7.9 percent but would have negligible impacts on the area's poverty rate. The primary reason for the low impact on crime and other social parameters is due to the fact that the Omaha Metropolitan Statistical Area (MSA) had three exisiting casinos on the Iowa side of the MSA.

The remainder of this chapter investigates casinos as business entities and as instruments of economic development. The next section investigates how this rapid growth in overall gambling revenues has affected the size of the casino.

THE TYPICAL U.S. CASINO

As presented in earlier chapters, the casino industry is a high-growth industry, with AGR expanding at a compound annual growth rate of 8.0 percent over the past five years. Typically, companies experiencing high growth, such as casinos, tend to pay less attention to cost cutting. However, when revenue growth slows, corporations, including casinos, begin to focus on costs and the bottom line. To date, casinos have yet to experience significant pullbacks in growth and have consequently paid less attention to costs and more consideration to revenues.

Just as casino AGR has expanded, the average size of U.S. casinos has increased steadily since 1998. Table 4.1 profiles casino size from 1998 to 2003 based on data from the U.S. Census Bureau's *County Business Patterns*. In 1998, the average stand-alone casino in the United States employed 201 workers. By 2003, the average stand-alone casino employed 265 workers. During this same period of time, casino hotels grew from an average workforce of 988 employees in 1988 to 1,208 employees in 2003. Furthermore, in 1998, 11.4 percent of stand-alone casinos employed more than 500 workers, while 30.6 percent employed fewer than 5 workers. By 2003, 15.9 percent of stand-alone casinos had employment levels greater than 500, but only 17.7 percent had workforces less than 5 workers. In 1998, 47.8 percent of casino hotels employed more than 500 workers and 10.2 percent employed fewer than 5 workers. By 2003, 59.2 percent of casino hotels employed more than 500 workers while only 6.3 percent employed fewer than 5 workers.

During this time span, U.S. casino employment rose by 11.0 percent per year, while the annual payroll increased by 16.4 percent per year. Consequently, average pay for stand-alone casino workers climbed from $21,792 in 1998 to $25,134 in 2003.[8] Table 4.2 shows casino employment and pay trends between 1998 and 2003. For casino hotels, average pay grew from $23,771 in 1998 to $26,121 in 2003. For both stand-alone and casino hotels, average pay was significantly higher than for the average firm in the amusement and recreation industry and in the accommodation industry. The inescapable fact from the data in tables 4.1 and 4.2 is that stand-alone casinos and casino hotels are

TABLE 4.1.   Average employment size for casinos, 1998–2003

	Average Number of Employees per Casino		Percentage with 1–4 Employees		Percentage with More than 500 Employees	
	Stand-alone Casinos	Casino Hotels	Stand-alone Casinos	Casino Hotels	Stand-alone Casinos	Casino Hotels
1998	201	988	30.6	10.2	11.4	47.8
1999	235	1,071	27.5	10.8	13.9	50.2
2000	280	1,082	23.6	10.4	15.5	48.6
2001	278	976	26.5	9.9	15.5	45.7
2002	292	907	23.3	15.9	15.5	44.4
2003	265	1,208	17.7	6.3	15.9	59.2

Source: Authors' calculations from U.S. Census Bureau, *County Business Patterns.*

growing in employment size and average pay, making them even more prized by the economic development community and politicians.

Table 4.3 lists the number of casinos, number of casino workers, and percentage of the workforce employed by commercial casinos in each state for the year 2004 as reported by the AGA. Supporters of casino expansion often point to the positive economic contributions of casinos, particularly in the area of employment. According to the AGA, 445 commercial casinos in eleven states employed 349,210 workers in 2004, for an average of 785 workers per casino. These workers earned an aggregate of $11.837 billion, or an average of just over $33,600 per worker.[9] AGA data differ from U.S. Census data due to different definitions of casinos and methodology used to count employment.

The average number of workers per casino ranged from 51 in South Dakota to 3,793 in New Jersey. The impact of casino employment is clearly more significant in Nevada than in any other state, as over 17 percent of its workforce is employed in casinos. Mississippi places a distant second, with approximately 3 percent of its workforce employed in casinos, with other states trailing far behind. However, it should be noted that table 4.3 overstates the number of casino workers since it includes hotel and lodging employees. There is a significant difference between the numbers reported by the AGA and by the U.S. Census Bureau. The AGA lists 445 commercial casinos while the U.S. Census Bureau reports 562 casinos. This difference may stem from the number of smaller casinos in some states, particularly South Dakota, that are not counted as casinos by the AGA. These smaller casinos are often simply a portion of a restaurant or convenience store that has been designated as a casino and separated from the rest of the establishment.

TABLE 4.2.   Employees and payroll for U.S. casinos, 1998–2003

	Number of employees		Annual pay per employee ($)			
	Stand-alone Casinos	Casino Hotels	Stand-alone Casinos	Casino Hotels	Amusement & Recreation	Accommodation
1998	119,820	291,489	21,792	23,771	15,449	17,586
1999	128,446	298,890	23,956	25,546	16,360	18,530
2001	150,218	311,576	23,913	26,135	16,858	19,453
2002	156,151	296,839	25,664	26,402	17,241	19,634
2003	163,956	301,909	25,134	26,121	17,591	20,113

Source: Authors' calculations from U.S. Census Bureau, *County Business Patterns.*

Data in the preceding tables show, to no one's surprise, that casinos create gambling jobs. However, the salient economic development question is, What impact do casinos have on the size of the noncasino workforce and on the value of income in the area where the casino is located?

Of course casinos have added casino jobs. However, opponents of casinos argue that they cannibalize other jobs in the leisure and hospitality industry. In order to investigate this issue, we once again calculate location quotients.[10] An LQ less than 1.0 indicates that the state has less than the nation in the leisure and hospitality industry exclusive of casino jobs. An LQ greater than 1.0 indicates that the state has a larger share of total employment in leisure and hospitality than the nation, again exclusive of casino jobs. Table 4.4 lists LQs for each casino state for the year before casinos were opened in the state and for 2005. Leisure and hospitality data were not available for Nevada and New Jersey for the year preceding casinos opening in those states. Additionally, reliable data were not available for racino states.

Data presented in table 4.4 indicate that in three states, Colorado, Iowa, and South Dakota, casinos appeared to draw jobs from noncasino firms. However, for the remaining six states, and for casino states in total, casinos appeared to not pull jobs from other firms in the leisure and hospitality industry and instead increased the state's share of employment in noncasino

TABLE 4.3.   Commercial casino employment by state, 2004

State	Number of Casinos	Number of Casino Workers	Casino Employment as % of Total Workforce
Colorado	46	7,703	0.3
Illinois	9	8,628	0.2
Indiana	10	17,377	0.6
Iowa	13	8,799	0.6
Louisiana	18	20,048	1.1
Michigan	3	7,572	0.2
Mississippi	29	28,932	2.7
Missouri	11	11,200	0.4
Nevada	258	191,620	17.7
New Jersey	12	45,501	1.2
South Dakota	36	1,830	0.5
Total	445	349,210	1.3

Source: American Gaming Association and U.S. Bureau of Labor Statistics.

TABLE 4.4.   Leisure and hospitality location quotients for casino states before casino opening and for 2005

	Year Casinos Opened	LQ before Casinos	LQ for 2005
Colorado	1991	1.21	1.14
Illinois	1991	0.87	0.93
Indiana	1995	0.89	0.94
Iowa	1991	0.91	0.90
Louisiana	1993	0.83	0.89
Michigan	1998	0.95	0.97
Mississippi	1992	0.33	0.80
Missouri	1994	0.99	1.00
South Dakota	1989	1.12	1.07
All casino states		0.93	0.96

Source: Authors' calculations based on U.S. Bureau of Labor Statistics data.

leisure and hospitality firms. Of course, this result could stem from increases in casino jobs reducing jobs outside of leisure and hospitality.

DO CASINOS CREATE NONCASINO JOBS AND HIGHER INCOME?

Critics of casinos argue that increases in employment tied to gambling are offset by losses in other nongambling entertainment firms. In addition, others argue that casinos tend to make a location less desirable for other nongambling establishments, thereby failing to increase overall employment or to actually reduce noncasino employment. Table 4.5 shows employment growth from 1995 to 2002 for noncasino counties compared to counties that added casinos in 1993 and 1994. Casino counties are further divided into tribal and commercial casinos.

As presented, counties that added a tribal casino in 1993 or 1994 experienced much stronger employment growth than either noncasino counties or commercial casino counties. The superior employment growing experience of tribal casinos may stem from the fact that tribal casinos are more likely to locate in rural or nonurban counties and will attract casino patrons and dollars from outside the county. This finding is consistent with findings in chapter 3. But, importantly, data in table 4.5 indicate that noncasino counties grew their employment at almost twice the rate of commercial casino counties.

Table 4.6 compares per capita income growth for noncasino counties, tribal casino counties, and commercial casino counties. Again commercial casino counties experienced the poorest growth, while tribal casinos saw the best growth. But the performance gap between the three groups is much smaller.

Data presented in tables 4.5 and 4.6 provide evidence that, in terms of job and income growth, tribal casino counties outperformed both non-casino and commercial casino counties and noncasino counties outperformed casino counties. One could certainly argue that factors other than casinos produced the differences listed in the tables. In order to disentangle

TABLE 4.5.   Change in county employment, 1995–2002 (%)

| | | Added Casino in 1993 or 1994 | |
	Noncasino	Tribal Casino	Commercial Casino
1995–96	2.0	4.8	1.8
1996–97	2.2	4.1	1.9
1997–98	2.5	4.0	1.5
1998–99	1.9	3.6	1.2
1999–2000	2.3	3.2	1.2
2000–2001	0.0	0.9	−0.4
2001–2	−0.1	1.1	−0.6
1995–2002	11.3	23.8	6.7

Source: Authors' calculations based on U.S. Bureau of Labor Statistics and Census Bureau data.

TABLE 4.6.   Change in county per capita income, 1995–2002 (%)

| | | Added Casino in 1993 or 1994 | |
	Noncasino	Tribal Casino	Commercial Casino
1995–96	6.0	5.3	4.4
1996–97	4.5	4.0	4.6
1997–98	4.9	5.1	5.1
1998–99	3.2	3.5	2.4
1999–2000	5.0	5.0	5.5
2000–2001	3.6	4.2	3.5
2001–2	1.6	2.3	2.6
1995–2002	32.8	33.3	31.7

Source: Authors' calculations based on U.S. Bureau of Labor Statistics and Census Bureau data.

the impact of casinos from other factors affecting per capita income and employment growth, we apply regression analysis to the data. Equations (4.1), (4.2), and (4.3) list the regression equation against factors hypothesized to affect economic development. Data concerning population, income, and employment for each county were obtained for each county from the U.S. Census Bureau. Such data permit our regression formula to evaluate different parameters and their potential impacts on economic development. We also combed various data sources to determine the first date in which a Class III or commercial casino opened in a particular county. In some cases when actual data were not available, we assumed that a tribal casino opened in the same year as the compact date associated with the operating tribe. Given the long time periods for operation of casinos in Nevada and Atlantic City, we excluded from our analysis all Nevada and New Jersey counties. This permitted a focus on relatively recent additions to the casino market, which would allow a more robust examination of the exogenous impact of the casino as opposed to other county-specific factors.

$$
\begin{aligned}
Emp = {} & \beta_0 + \beta_1 \, PopDen + \beta_2 \, PBlack + \beta_3 \, PO55 + \beta_4 \, P2054 \\
& + \beta_5 \, PU20 + \beta_6 \, NE + \beta_7 \, MA + \beta_8 \, ENC + \beta_9 \, WNC \\
& + \beta_{10} \, ESC + \beta_{11} \, WSC + \beta_{12} \, MT + \beta_{13} \, Year \\
& + \beta_{14} \, Casino + \beta_{15} \, Time + \beta_{16} \, Time^2 + \varepsilon. \qquad (4.1)
\end{aligned}
$$

$$
\begin{aligned}
PCapInc = {} & \beta_0 + \beta_1 \, PopDen + \beta_2 \, PBlack + \beta_3 \, PO55 + \beta_4 \, P2054 \\
& + \beta_5 \, PU20 + \beta_6 \, NE + \beta_7 \, MA + \beta_8 \, ENC + \beta_9 \, WNC \\
& + \beta_{10} \, ESC + \beta_{11} \, WSC + \beta_{12} \, MT + \beta_{13} \, Year \\
& + \beta_{14} \, Casino + \beta_{15} \, Time + \beta_{16} \, Time^2 + \varepsilon. \qquad (4.2)
\end{aligned}
$$

$$
\begin{aligned}
URate = {} & \beta_0 + \beta_1 \, PopDen + \beta_2 \, PBlack + \beta_3 \, PO55 + \beta_4 \, P2054 \\
& + \beta_5 \, PU20 + \beta_6 \, NE + \beta_7 \, MA + \beta_8 \, ENC + \beta_9 \, WNC \\
& + \beta_{10} \, ESC + \beta_{11} \, WSC + \beta_{12} \, MT + \beta_{13} \, Year \\
& + \beta_{14} \, Casino + \beta_{15} \, Time + \beta_{16} \, Time^2 + \varepsilon. \qquad (4.3)
\end{aligned}
$$

The dependent variables Emp, PCapInc, and URate represent the county's level of employment, per capita income, and unemployment rate, respectively. Table 4.7 contains a description of each variable used in the estimation of the three equations. This formula includes data on race and age, which other studies have shown to have a disproportionate impact on economic outcomes within a population.[11] Additionally, instead of using a continuous variable for Year, we use a binary variable for each year of the data except for 1990.

Table 4.8 lists the results from the estimation of equations (4.1), (4.2), and (4.3). As indicated, all casino variables are statistically significant in both estimations. As presented, commercial casinos have a positive impact on per capita income and employment and a negative impact on the county's unemployment rate. Tribal casinos have a positive effect on employment but a negative impact on per capita income and the county's unemployment rate. In all cases the influence of casinos is statistically significant.

However, the impact of a casino on the county differs according to how long the casino has been in operation. For per capita income, the influence rises, reaches a maximum, and then begins to decline. For the county's unemployment rate, the casino's impact also rises, reaches a maximum, and then begins to decline. In other words, the impact of time on each is humped-shaped. For employment, the effect of a casino on employment declines, reaches a minimum, and then begins to increase. That is, the shape of the relationship between employment and time is U-shaped.

Thus, for a county adding a commercial casino (1) per capita income rises with the opening of the casino, reaches a maximum impact in eight years, and then begins to decline; (2) employment increases with the opening of the casino, begins to decline for two years, reaching a minimum, and then begins to grow; and (3) the county's unemployment rate declines with the opening of the casino, grows for four years, and then begins to decline again. For a county adding a tribal casino, the impacts on employment and unemployment rates are the same as those for commercial casino counties. On the other hand, tribal casinos reduce per capita income upon opening. After two years of rising and positive impacts on per capita income, casino operations begin to negatively affect per capita income.

Figure 4.1 profiles per capita income differences between commercial

TABLE 4.7. Definition of variables used in estimation of equations (4.1, 4.2, 4.3)

Variable	Mnemonic	Description
Employment	Emp	County employment in thousands; Source: U.S. Bureau of Labor Statistics.
Per capita income	PCapInc	County per capita income in thousands; Source: U.S. Bureau of Economic Analysis.
Percent unemployment	Urate	County unemployment rates; Source: U.S. Bureau of Labor Statistics.
Population density	PopDen	County population per square mile; Source: U.S. Census Bureau.
Percent black	PBlack	Percentage of county population that is black; Source: U.S. Census Bureau.
Percent over 55	PO55	Percentage of population over the age of 55; Source: U.S. Census Bureau.
Percent 30–54	P3054	Percentage of population ages 30–54; Source: U.S. Census Bureau.
Percent under 20	PU20	Percentage of population under age 20; Source: U.S. Census Bureau.
New England	NE	A binary variable equal to 1 if county is located in the New England region; equal to 0 otherwise.
Mid-Atlantic	MA	A binary variable equal to 1 if county is located in the Mid-Atlantic region; equal to 0 otherwise.
East North Central	ENC	A binary variable equal to 1 if county is located in the East North Central region; equal to 0 otherwise.
West North Central	WNC	A binary variable equal to 1 if county is located in the West North Central region; equal to 0 otherwise.
East South Central	ESC	A binary variable equal to 1 if county is located in the East South Central region; equal to 0 otherwise.
West South Central	WSC	A binary variable equal to 1 if county is located in the West South Central region; equal to 0 otherwise.
Mountain	MT	A binary variable equal to 1 if county is located in the Mountain region; equal to 0 otherwise.
Year	Year	A binary variable equal to 1 for each year of the sample; equal to 0 otherwise.
Casino	Casino	A binary variable equal to 1 if the county adds a casino; equal to 0 otherwise.
Time	Time	Number of years that casino is in existence; 0 for noncasino counties.
Time^2	Time^2	Time × Time; added to recognize the nonlinear relationship between the length of time a casino is in business and its economic impact.

Note: The New England region includes Connecticut, Maine, Massachusetts, New Hampshire, Rhode Island, and Vermont. The Mid-Atlantic region includes New Jersey, New York, and Pennsylvania. The East North Central region includes Illinois, Indiana, Michigan, Ohio, and Wisconsin. The West North Central region includes Iowa, Kansas, Minnesota, Missouri, Nebraska, North Dakota, and South Dakota. The South Atlantic region includes Delaware, District of Columbia, Florida, Georgia, Maryland, North Carolina, South Carolina, Virginia, and West Virginia. The East South Central region includes Alabama, Kentucky, Mississippi, and Tennessee. The West South Central region includes Arkansas, Louisiana, Oklahoma, and Texas. The Mountain region includes Arizona, Colorado, Idaho, Montana, Nevada, New Mexico, Utah, and Wyoming. The Pacific region includes Alaska, California, Hawaii, Oregon, and Washington.

casino counties and counties without casinos and between tribal casino counties and counties without casinos. For commercial casinos, the difference is negative after fifteen years. For tribal casinos, it is negative throughout the operating life of the casino.

Figure 4.2 profiles employment differences between commercial casino

TABLE 4.8.   Impact of factors on county per capita income and employment

	Per Capita Income		Employment		Unemployment Rate	
	Coefficient	T-value	Coefficient	T-value	Coefficient	T-value
Population density	0.740*	24.166	19.321*	32.951	−0.016	−0.700
Percent black	−5.155*	−11.717	145.946*	17.650	1.241*	3.847
Percent 30–54	16.814*	10.142	33.466	1.777	−8.037*	−5.281
Percent over 55	34.626*	20.696	170.661*	8.999	−3.607*	−2.342
Percent under 20	43.365*	28.955	423.142*	25.620	10.434*	7.385
Mid-Atlantic	1.736*	5.267	64.809*	4.594	−0.080	−0.359
New England	4.116*	8.832	75.563*	3.767	−0.534	−1.697
East North Central	−0.318	−1.397	8.799	0.920	−0.321*	−2.073
West North Central	−1.880*	−8.734	−30.139*	−3.447	−2.566*	−17.173
East South Central	−2.749*	−12.544	−42.922*	−4.526	0.284	1.916
West South Central	−3.205*	−14.135	−22.312*	−2.323	−0.969*	−6.231
Mountain	−1.500*	−5.283	−22.172	−1.859	−0.805*	−4.156
Y91	0.471*	14.504	0.645*	1.962	1.097*	32.354
Y92	1.416*	42.787	1.096*	3.256	1.504*	43.716
Y93	1.883*	55.419	2.076*	5.965	0.976*	27.794
Y94	2.633*	75.039	3.280*	9.062	0.245*	6.794
Y95	3.094*	84.35	4.773*	12.493	−0.015	−0.407
Y96	4.207*	109.528	6.007*	14.885	0.101*	2.609
Y97	5.120*	132.656	7.397*	18.227	−0.311*	−7.999
Y98	6.211*	166.53	9.103*	23.372	−0.683*	−18.029
Y99	6.997*	189.631	10.803*	28.139	−0.955*	−25.418
Y00	8.108*	219.466	11.891*	30.914	−1.210*	−32.166
Y01	8.946*	241.715	11.742*	30.458	−0.594*	−15.764
Y02	9.354*	252.212	11.566*	29.927	−0.034	−0.913
Commercial casino	0.687*	5.148	3.693*	2.702	−0.490*	−3.584
Tribal casino	−0.379*	−4.130	3.426*	3.666	−0.357*	−3.758
Casino × time	0.096*	4.784	−0.909*	−4.500	0.031	1.502
Casino × time × time	−0.006*	−4.878	0.1790*	14.483	−0.004*	−3.369
Constant	−7.964*	−6.449	−126.209*	−8.477	7.591*	6.628
R^2 (%)	95.2		99.5		83.3	

* Indicates that coefficient is statistically significant at .05 level

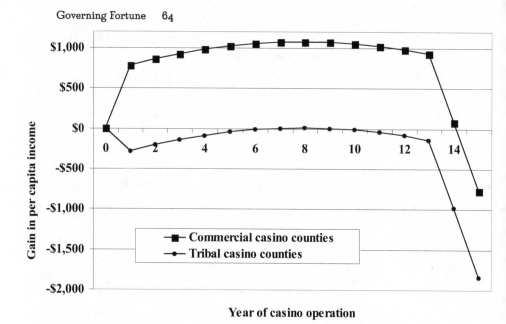

Fig. 4.1. Estimated per capita income gain for casino counties versus noncasino counties

counties and counties without casinos and between tribal casino counties and counties without casinos. For both commercial and tribal casinos, the difference is positive and grows over the life of the casino. The figure shows virtually no difference between the job creation impacts of tribal casinos and commercial casino.

Figure 4.3 tracks unemployment rates for commercial casino counties, tribal casino counties, and noncasino counties. Commercial and tribal casino counties are estimated to have unemployment rates less than counties without casinos for the first fifteen years of operations. Thus in terms of employment impacts, both tribal and commercial casinos create additional job opportunities in the county in which it is located.

Table 4.9 summarizes estimates based on regression results in table 4.8. Column 1 shows the compound annual growth in per capita income from the three groups of counties—commercial casino counties, tribal casino counties, and noncasino counties. Results indicate that noncasino counties grew at a rate exceeding that of the other two groups. Columns 2 and 3 show differences among the three groups for employment and unemployment. In both

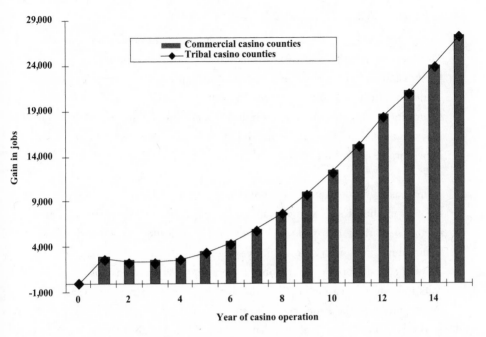

Fig. 4.2. Estimated employment gain for casino counties versus noncasino counties

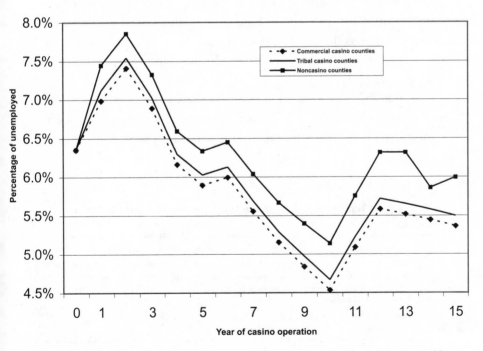

Fig. 4.3. Comparison of county unemployment rates—commercial casino, tribal casino, and noncasino

cases, casino counties performed at a higher level than noncasino counties. Thus results indicate that casinos tend to have a positive influence on job growth and unemployment rates but have a negative impact on per capita income growth. This result may stem from the high share of casino and other entertainment workers who are employed part-time but are included in the job numbers. These workers, because they work fewer hours, earn less. However, we do not test this hypothesis here.

Increasingly, local and state government policymakers are turning to casino gambling to fill budget gaps. In an effort to "sell" expanded casino gambling to their constituencies, these political leaders espouse the economic development creation abilities of the casinos. However, data in this chapter cast doubts on the income-generating powers of casinos. Our results indicate that casinos tend to dampen income growth but increase job opportunities in the counties where they are located.

Regression results indicate that casinos, both tribal and commercial, create substantial job opportunities in terms of new jobs and lower unemployment rates. Furthermore, the gains tend to grow as the casino remains in the county. Contrarily, casinos reduce per capita income, and the reduction gets larger as the casino remains in the county. The addition of part-time casino and entertainment workers due to casino operations may explain this phenomenon.

Additionally, data presented in this chapter and in chapter 3 indicate that casinos have not reduced the relative tax burdens of residents in states with commercial casinos. Data show that taxes, as a share of personal income, ei-

TABLE 4.9.   Change in economic factors after 15 years of casino operation (%)

	Compound Annual Change in Per Capita Income	Compound Annual Change in Employment	Change in Unemployment Rate
Commercial casino counties	3.0	4.2	−1.0
Tribal casino counties	2.7	4.1	−0.9
Noncasino counties	3.2	1.7	−0.4

Source: Estimation from regression models.

ther rose more dramatically or dropped less significantly in states with commercial casinos in comparison to states without commercial casinos. Instead, casinos appeared to produce increases in relative public spending on areas such as education and parks and recreation.

5. Social Costs

Economic development, employment opportunities, and new sources of tax revenues are not the only potential consequences of legalized casino gambling. Concerns about negative social impacts from gambling have long formed a part of the underpinning for criminal proscriptions against it. Policymakers considering whether to change those proscriptions are thus confronted with the question of whether these traditional concerns about social costs are well founded and, if so, whether these costs may exceed any promised benefits.

Evaluations of costs and benefits are part of the legislative process, and social science data form part of the grist for the legislative mill. However, legislators also enjoy political prerogatives, which allow them to make choices that may not always optimize costs and benefits. As one court has noted, "The power [of the legislature] to decide, to be wrong as well as to be right on contestable issues, is both [a] privilege and curse of democracy."[1] Casino gambling presents one of these contestable issues.

Although abundant evidence exists for the proposition that gambling—and more specifically gambling that reaches pathological levels—produces negative social consequences, much of the evidence that provides a direct link between gambling and associated negative consequences involves specific incidents with problem gamblers. Empirical research using sound social science methods has also offered proof on these issues, but that proof is not incontrovertible. Social problems often have multiple causes, and teasing out the extent of contribution by gambling alone has proven to be a daunting task. Given that benefits such as new sources of tax revenue are often more easily measurable than the costs (including hidden substitution effects),[2] industry supporters have seized on the comparative uncertainty surrounding costs as a basis for forging ahead with expanded gambling options.

Nevertheless, the available research supports the proposition that gamblers externalize costs to others. It also supports the likelihood that these costs are substantial. A policy response that neglects these likelihoods is becoming less sustainable as more is learned about gambling effects. The discussion that follows provides an overview of some of the significant research on pathological gambling conditions, as well as important considerations affecting the extension of that research to estimate social costs associated with the gambling industry.

PATHOLOGICAL AND PROBLEM GAMBLING

Social costs from gambling primarily flow from a relatively small segment of the population for whom gambling is not harmless recreation. Much is known about the nature of pathological gambling and its less severe manifestations, sometimes referred to as "problem gambling." The American Psychiatric Association defines pathological gambling in its *Diagnostic and Statistical Manual of Mental Disorders* (DSM-IV) as "persistent and recurrent maladaptive gambling behavior that disrupts personal, family, or vocational pursuits."[3]

According to the DSM-IV, pathological behavior is indicated by five or more of the following conditions: (1) a preoccupation with gambling; (2) a need to gamble increasing amounts in order to achieve desired excitement; (3) repeated unsuccessful efforts to control gambling; (4) restlessness and irritability when attempting to control gambling; (5) using gambling as a means to escape from problems; (6) "chasing" one's losses; (7) lying to conceal the extent of one's gambling; (8) committing illegal acts to finance gambling; (9) jeopardizing relationships (including employment or education) because of gambling; and (10) relying on others to relieve desperate financial situations caused by gambling.[4]

The decision to choose five manifestations as a cutoff for measuring pathology may be conservative, as some experts suggest that four manifestations may be a more appropriate figure.[5] Fewer than five of these behaviors could still produce substantial negative personal and social consequences, and this behavior is often considered under the rubric of "problem gambling."[6] NORC, whose survey on gambling-related social problems was utilized by the National Gambling Impact Study Commission, used the term "at-risk" gambler to define someone who has experienced losses of more than one hundred dollars in a single day and reports only one or two DSM-IV criteria, whereas a "problem gambler" has the same loss experience but reports three or four of these criteria.[7]

Differences in formulating screening tools to identify and diagnose gambling-related behavioral problems account for some variation in research results concerning the number of problem or pathological gamblers.[8] As one study explains: "There is no particular number of symptoms at which true pathological gambling suddenly manifests itself—the designation of pathological gambling is a matter of degree."[9]

The DSM-IV explains that the pathology rarely occurs with the first bet. A course of experience with gambling is required for most people: "There may be years of social gambling followed by an abrupt onset that may be precipitated by greater exposure to gambling or by a stressor."[10] Thus, as gambling opportunities proliferate, it stands to reason that more pathology is likely. The NORC survey indicates that past-year gambling in casinos increased from 10 percent of the population in 1975 to 29 percent by 1998.[11] In contrast, bingo declined from 19 to 6 percent, and horse racing declined from 14 to 7 percent during the same period, suggesting that the marketplace has substituted casino gambling for other games of chance.[12] For 2004, the AGA estimates that 54.1 million Americans visited a casino.[13] This represents about one-fourth of the estimated 2004 adult population, which numbers approximately 212 million.[14]

Pathological gambling is considered a chronic disorder, much like alcoholism. This means that once it develops there is a tendency for recurrence.[15] For this reason, diagnosis of pathological gambling focuses on ascertaining a subject's lifetime experiences, as well as more recent ones. However, lifetime orientations can create problems in estimating the magnitude of the impact of negative gambling-related behaviors in a particular year. For this reason, some studies have included questions about past-year behavior in addition to lifetime time frames.

The causes of pathological gambling are still under investigation. As one study has observed, "Research into the causes of [pathological] gambling is in its infancy compared to research into the causes of other addictive behaviors."[16] Like alcohol dependence, pathological gambling may have an inherited component, as it is more common among people whose parents experience similar pathology.[17] Recent studies have also indicated that brain chemistry affects pathological gambling behavior, including a study in the

Archives of Neurology suggesting that stimulation of dopamine receptors might be responsible for pathological gambling as a complication related to the treatment of Parkinson's disease.[18]

Differences between machine gambling (e.g., slot machines and video lottery terminals) and other forms of gambling may also be reflected in the development of pathological gambling. An empirical study by Breen and Zimmerman indicates that machine gamblers develop problem gambling conditions sooner (1.08 years versus 3.58 years) than their counterparts who gamble in more traditional forms.[19] These researchers note that the differing latency period may be attributable to other factors, such as the convenience and availability of machines. However, the difference also may be due to the stimulus variables provided by gambling machines, including the reinforcement of "small wins," "near misses," and continuous action, which is not prevalent in more traditional gambling forms.[20]

Some research suggests that men tend to experience pathological gambling more than women. The DSM-IV indicates that male problem and pathological gamblers outnumber females by a ratio of 2 to 1.[21] The NORC study shows a similar disparity in 1998, with male pathological and problem gambling at a lifetime rate of 3.7 percent, while only 1.9 percent of females are similarly affected.[22] A nationwide survey conducted from August 1999 to October 2000 by Welte et al. indicated that current-year indications of pathological or problem gambling were in a somewhat closer relationship for males and females, approximately 1.3 to 1.[23] A comparison of the results for the Welte survey and the NORC study for the combined group of problem and pathological gamblers based on current experience is presented in table 5.1.

The DSM-IV also reports that the onset of pathology in males is generally earlier, potentially beginning in adolescence.[24] For this reason, public health authorities have warned against efforts to provide "casino nights" for young people.[25] Although such activities may be well-intentioned efforts to substitute what might be viewed as harmless fun for potential incidents of alcohol abuse, they may ultimately lead to substituting another pathology. Antigambling activists have also seized on this concern in connection with the sale of games and toys with gambling themes.[26]

Racial differences in gambling pathology may also exist. The Welte survey shows that blacks and Hispanics have higher combined rates for problem and pathological gambling than whites.[27] However, the NORC survey produced similar directional results for blacks but lower incidents for Hispanic gamblers. See table 5.1 for comparative results reflecting the past-year experiences of these demographic groups.

White gamblers significantly outnumber those of other races, such that the higher percentage of minority problem gamblers does not necessarily translate into a larger absolute number of problem gamblers from minority communities.

The extent of problem gambling in the United States remains an issue about which experts disagree, in part because of the differing approaches for determining what constitutes a problem gambler. The NORC study concluded that, in 1998, problem and pathological gamblers totaled 1.5 percent of the adult population, or approximately 5.5 million people. An additional 15 million were considered at risk. If those figures are updated to reflect the estimated adult population for 2004 based on U.S. Census Bureau data, the results are approximately 5.7 million problem and pathological gamblers, with an additional 16.3 million at risk. These figures are displayed in table 5.2.

It should be noted that the figures in table 5.2 simply extrapolate the results from a 1998 survey to an updated population. They do not take into account the possibility that additional casino facilities may have increased the manifestation of problem gambling behaviors.

Alternatively, if survey results focusing on casino patrons[28] are applied

TABLE 5.1.   Selected demographic characteristics of problem and pathological gamblers (based on past year experiences)

	Welte, et. al. (%)	NORC (%)
Sex:		
Male	4.10	1.70
Female	2.90	.90
Race:		
White	1.80	1.10
Black	7.70	3.20
Hispanic	7.90	0.80
Asian	6.50	N.A.
Native American	10.50	N.A.

N.A. = not available

against the base of estimated casino visitors in 2004, the estimated total for problem and pathological gamblers increases slightly. This methodology also generates a higher proportion of pathological gamblers, who are likely to generate higher social costs. These figures are displayed in table 5.3.

The differing pathology rates between types of casino facilities reflected in the NORC survey data present interesting possibilities for further research to ascertain the basis for the differences. One possibility is that riverboats may involve a greater percentage of local patrons, who visit frequently based on convenient access from their work or home, with relatively fewer tourists traveling to visit them as destination facilities, such as Nevada or Atlantic City casinos.

Using the more recent findings of the Welte study, the total for pathological gamblers grows still larger. The Welte study used two different screens

TABLE 5.2.   Estimated population of problem and pathological gamblers

	NORC Percentage	Estimated 2004 Adult Population	Estimated 2004 Affected Population
Non-gambler	14.40	212,103,606	30,542,919
Low-risk	75.10	212,103,606	159,289,808
At-Risk	7.70	212,103,606	16,331,978
Problem	1.50	212,103,606	3,181,554
Pathological	1.20	212,103,606	2,545,243
Total problem and pathological gamblers:	5,726,797		

Source: National Opinion Research Center data, lifetime survey.

TABLE 5.3.   Estimated problem and pathological gamblers based on NORC surveys of casino patrons applied to 2004 casino visitors

	Riverboats (%)	Tribal (%)	Nevada & Atlantic City Casinos (%)	Average (%)	Casino Visitors 2004 (AGA)	Estimated Population
Non-gambler	0.00	0.00	0.70	0.23	54,100,000	126,233
Low-risk	67.20	73.10	68.10	69.47	54,100,000	37,581,467
At-Risk	15.60	16.40	22.10	18.03	54,100,000	9,756,033
Problem	6.30	6.00	3.40	5.23	54,100,000	2,831,233
Pathological	10.90	4.50	5.40	6.93	54,100,000	3,750,933
Total Problem and Pathological Gamblers			6,582,167			

TABLE 5.4.   **Estimated problem and pathological gamblers (Welty)**

Methodology	Overall %: (lifetime basis)	Estimated 2004 Adult Population	Estimated Problem & Pathological Gamblers
SOGS (20 factors)	11.50	212,103,606	24,391,915
DIS (10 factors)	4.80	212,103,606	10,180,973

for problem gambling, one of which was based on the ten DSM-IV criteria and the other of which was based on the twenty criteria under the South Oaks Gambling Screen (SOGS) developed by Lesieur and Blume.[29] The results in both cases were higher than the NORC survey, as shown in table 5.4.

As the study explains, "The reason that the SOGS produces higher rates of pathological gambling than the DIS [Diagnostic Interview Schedule from DSM-IV] is that it is easier to obtain five positives from 20 variables than from 10 variables."[30] Nevertheless, even the more conservative definitional approach generates a substantially larger population of problem and pathological gamblers than the previous methodologies, suggesting that one in twenty adults in the United States—or perhaps as many as one in nine—may have a gambling problem. Problem and pathological gamblers may account for up to 15 percent of gambling losses, making them a significant contributor to the industry's profitability.[31]

Despite technical disagreements about measuring the number of problem gamblers, there is general agreement that this pathology generates personal hardship and pain for the individual and also for others. As the National Gambling Impact Study Commission recognized, "All [researchers] seem to agree that pathological gamblers 'engaged in destructive behaviors, they run up large debts, they damage relationships with family and friends, and they kill themselves.'"[32] However, the extent of these costs and related issues involving the causal link between pathology and particular negative outcomes is contested. Herein lies the battleground between industry advocates and detractors.

SOCIAL COST RESEARCH

Research into the social cost impact of introducing a casino encounters several challenges that are often interrelated. First, researchers face the formidable problem of distinguishing between causation and correlation. When one looks at the problems often associated with gambling, such as crime, divorce, bankruptcy, or suicide, it is quite clear that multiple causes may contribute to these problems. It is true that problem gamblers sometimes resort to theft or embezzlement, and significant thefts could cause a business bankruptcy. Debt incurred from excessive gambling could cause marital stress, resulting in personal bankruptcy and possibly divorce or other family-related problems. Complications from divorce spill over into other social problems, which have links to the financial well-being of the former spouses, including unpaid child support, which was estimated at a staggering $95 billion in 2003.[33]

What is not clear in each of these examples is the extent to which some other dysfunctional behavior might also be a contributing, if not intervening, cause of the event. Problem gamblers often share other pathologies, such as alcoholism, that provide additional basis for causation. A significant correlation appears between alcohol abuse and gambling pathology. The Welte study shows that drinkers averaging more than four drinks a day are more than five times as likely to become problem or pathological gamblers than their teetotaling counterparts.[34] This statistic is consistent with previous studies summarized in the National Gambling Impact Study Commission Report.[35]

Nevertheless, free drinks are allowed in several states with commercial casinos. As one court has noted, "[T]he absence of a regulation barring gambling by a drunk patron cannot be considered an oversight or mistake. At the very least the State condones casino patrons drinking while they place bets, and the policy of providing free drinks on request could arguably be said to actively encourage this conduct."[36] The AGA justifies this practice based on customer demands, while adding that "Avid casino players like to be at the top of their game and therefore avoid the consumption of alcohol."[37]

Other disorders, such as emotional or mental health concerns, are also more prevalent in the population of pathological and problem gamblers. The NORC study indicates that problem and pathological gamblers are more than twice as likely to seek mental health treatment than their nongambling or low-risk gambling counterparts.[38] This correlation does not show whether the mental health problem is caused by gambling or whether persons with mental health problems in the first place (or at least a predisposition toward them) are more likely to experience gambling problems. Nevertheless, if either of these conclusions were true, it would present a significant problem for policymakers interested in the public health ramifications of gambling.

Similarly, the NORC study indicates that gamblers generally have higher divorce rates than nongamblers. Approximately 53.5 percent of pathological gamblers, 39.5 percent of problem gamblers, and 36.3 percent of at-risk gamblers had been divorced, as compared with only 18.5 percent of nongamblers and 29.8 percent of those classified as low-risk gamblers.[39] As noted previously with regard to mental health, this data alone is insufficient to show conclusively that divorce occurs on account of gambling as opposed to other problems. However, these significant differences in divorce rates do raise concerns; they do not suggest that expanded gambling is helping to improve these social conditions.

Research also shows that gambling pathologies may vary according to age. Welte et al. showed that problem and pathological gambling prevalence declined significantly in populations over the age of sixty-one.[40] The NORC study similarly showed diminished levels of problem or pathological gambling for those over the age of sixty-five.[41] More recently, researchers examined whether recreational gambling (with problem or pathological gambling specifically included) had a relationship to the health of older adults. Although their research indeed found a positive correlation between the subjective reports of health in the recreational gambling population, correlation also did not necessarily point to causation in this case. As the researchers recognized, there are limits to the conclusions that can be drawn from these results.

> Recreational gambling in older adults may allow for increased socialization, community activity, and travel, which may in turn be reflected in more positive ratings of health. Such an effect may not be evident in younger adults, perhaps because other social or occupational activities take priority. It is also possible that a greater proportion of older, as compared with younger, adults are too sick to gamble and are categorized in the nongambling group, making the older gamblers appear healthier. These sicker older adults might have more limited access to transportation or lack the energy or motivation necessary for specific types of gambling.[42]

The complex sources of causation of many social problems present formidable obstacles in knowing with precision the extent of causation that can be attributed to adding a casino to the environment. Problem gambling conditions may also already exist on account of other gambling sources, including illegal gambling, available prior to the introduction of a casino. Agnostic positions as to causation have academic appeal, and they are often adopted by the industry when it seeks to promote its business.

For example, research has shown that proximity to a casino increases the likelihood for manifestations of problem gambling. Most problem and pathological gamblers live within 50 miles of a casino. Using lifetime experience figures from the NORC study,[43] approximately 4.4 percent of the population within 50 miles of a casino represents problem or pathological gamblers. In contrast, less than half of this proportion lives farther away: approximately 2.1 percent of the population living within 51 to 250 miles of a casino falls into the problem or pathological category, and 2.5 percent of the population living more than 250 miles from a casino is similarly affected. Looking instead at the annual experience figures, the proportion is even more dramatic: approximately 2.4 percent of the population within 50 miles represents problem or pathological gamblers, whereas only 0.9 percent of the population living within 51 to 250 miles and only 0.7 percent living more than 250 miles from a casino are similarly affected.[44] Stated differently, one is about two times as likely to find a problem gambler within 50 miles of a casino.

These findings make sense intuitively, as more convenient access to gambling presents the possibility for more frequent gambling experiences, which in turn could result in the kind of losses associated with problem gambling behavior. Nevertheless, these results were questioned in one recent study, which pointed out that

it is not possible to determine if (a) the availability of gambling caused this inflated prevalence rate, (b) more people with gambling problems settled in areas closer to major opportunities to gambling, (c) casinos locate in areas that already have a high rate of disordered gambling, or (d) casinos locate in areas with a disproportionately vulnerable population. To understand fully the overall repercussions of gambling on society, a significant research effort is necessary to document the complex interaction among these health and socioeconomic variables, as well as their short- and long-term costs.[45]

Although additional research probably would be helpful, the level of skepticism expressed here borders on the absurd. Policymakers don't have the option of waiting for these questions to be solved with certainty. They must ultimately reach conclusions based on likelihoods rather than scientific precision. To suggest that the industry locates casinos where disordered gambling or particularly vulnerable populations already exist presupposes secret industry knowledge about illegal gambling and/or problem gamblers that is apparently not available to the research community. Alternatively, it presupposes that the industry is very "lucky" in choosing those locations. Neither of these presuppositions is a plausible explanation of the correlation shown here.

The gambling industry often uses this skeptical approach to challenge the findings of research that generates results that are inconvenient for its business goals. It has also been known to engage in dubious uses of statistics to advocate industry-friendly positions. Consider, for example, the AGA's position on bankruptcy, as articulated on its Web site. In support of its position that there is no linkage between casinos and bankruptcy, the AGA cites the following example:

> According to data maintained by the Administrative Office of the U.S. Courts and population statistics from the most recent census (2001), Utah and Tennessee were ranked first and second respectively in 2002 in terms of the number of bankruptcy filings per household. Utah is the only state in the country with absolutely no form of legalized gaming whatsoever, and Tennessee's only gaming is a state-run lottery that is still in the process of coming on-line.[46]

We have also observed industry advocates using this argument in local debates on the issue of expanded gambling.

The fact that high bankruptcy rates exist in Utah and Tennessee, where no legalized casino gambling exists, is entirely consistent with the proposition that bankruptcy is caused by other factors besides excessive gambling losses. But that proposition is hardly contestable. Significantly, this example does not speak at all to the question of whether the introduction of a casino to a jurisdiction has a differential impact over time, which is at the heart of what the industry is questioning here.

Similarly, on the issue of crime, the AGA points to examples where crime rates have dropped in cities with casinos and, in some cases, in cities where casinos have been added.[47] Conversely, it points to increases in crime in locations such as Orlando, where noncasino entertainment is offered.[48] In the case of Atlantic City, which the General Accounting Office (GAO) discussed in some detail as an example of a location where crime rates had increased after casinos opened,[49] the AGA dismissed these results and focused instead on experiences of the past five years, where crime rates have dropped.[50]

The problem for researchers is to ascertain the effects of crime based on the change in conditions attributed to adding casinos instead of to other sources. Crime trends nationally have generally declined. According to the Bureau of Justice Statistics, property crimes have declined substantially during the past three decades.[51] Violent crimes have similarly declined, particularly so in the last decade.[52] However, particular jurisdictions can experience different results based on a number of factors, including employment, economic conditions, and the impact of particular features of the legal system. To the extent that criminals take into account penalties and enforcement efforts, changes in the legal system can also impact crime rates, thus reflecting interjurisdictional competition in setting legal penalties.[53]

The powerful tool of regression analysis is available to evaluate the differential impacts of casinos on a macro level. By looking at casino and noncasino jurisdictions over longer periods of time, and adjusting for other significant differences that appear among these jurisdictions, the impact of casinos on such matters as crime and bankruptcy can be ascertained with reasonable confidence. These results are not free from uncertainty, but they do present powerful evidence that deserves consideration in the policy analysis of casino gaming. Recent research using this methodology has produced strong evidence of a correlation between casinos and crime and between casinos and bankruptcy. Some significant research in these areas is briefly discussed next.

Casinos and Crime

Although several previous studies failed to show a correlation between casinos and crime, a more recent study by the economists Grinols and Mustard took on the task of measuring the externalized costs associated with crime attributed to casino gambling.[54] Grinols and Mustard examined county-level data for the period 1977–96, focusing on data for reported crimes in counties with casinos and in counties without casinos. Their model also accounted for fifty-eight other variables, including demographic factors such as race, sex, and age; unemployment; and personal income.

When one charts the aggregate crime rates for counties with casinos, a decline appears between 1990 and 1996, a time of rapid expansion of casinos. As Grinols and Mustard point out, some researchers claimed that this data suggested that casinos reduced crime. However, a more appropriate measure would focus on the differential experiences between casino and noncasino counties over this period, not a simple evaluation of a trend line. When a more complex analysis is completed, the result is that crime dropped 12 percentage points more in counties without casinos than in the casino counties.

Grinols and Mustard also broke new ground in showing another feature of casinos: the fact that their impacts on crime vary over time after opening. Although crime may drop in the year of opening or in the year or two thereafter, they found statistically significant increases for all crimes except murder. In most cases, these increases occurred after the first two years of operation, reflecting a time lag between opening and the eventual impact on increasing criminal activity.

These results are theoretically consistent with plausible impacts of the casino industry on criminal behavior. As Grinols and Mustard point out, casinos could potentially reduce crime by providing increased wages and positive economic development growth. However, crime would likely increase to the extent that those development opportunities would not be realized or employment growth in other sectors of the economy would be harmed as a result of locating a casino in the jurisdiction. (As discussed in chapter 4, it appears questionable whether these putative benefits from casinos are in fact realized in many jurisdictions.)

In addition to these indirect effects on crime from economic development impacts, Grinols and Mustard also point to the crime experiences of problem and pathological gamblers as a significant factor explaining crime trends in casino counties. The proliferation of casinos decreases the cost of "buying" gambling services, thus increasing consumption by problem gamblers. Some of those gamblers will resort to crimes to pay for this increased consumption. Grinols and Mustard cite studies by the Maryland Department of Health and Mental Hygiene (1990), showing that 62 percent of a Gamblers Anonymous group had committed illegal acts as a result of gambling, and by the noted gambling researcher Dr. Henry Lesieur (1998), showing that 56 percent of those in gambling treatment had engaged in stealing to finance gambling.[55]

A more recent study by the U.S. Department of Justice also appears to confirm a linkage between problem and pathological gambling and crime. The study sampled arrestees in Las Vegas, Nevada, and Des Moines, Iowa. The percentage of problem or pathological gamblers among these arrestees was three to five times higher than that of the general population.[56] Moreover, nearly one-third of the arrestees identified as pathological gamblers admitted to committing robbery in the previous year, and approximately 13 percent had assaulted someone for money.[57]

However, the study also indicated that "pathological gamblers were no more likely to be arrested for property or other white collar crimes (larceny, theft, embezzlement, and fraud) than nongamblers and low-risk and at-risk gamblers. . . . Rather, they were most likely to be arrested for such offenses and probation or parole violations, liquor law violations, trespassing, and other public order offenses."[58] Despite the absence of the property crime link in arrests, it is significant that more than 30 percent admitted to committing robberies in the past year—more than double the percentage for nongambler arrestees.[59] Thus, arrests based on other categories of offenses may mask other criminal behavior—including property-related crimes—for which no arrest was made.

The time lag for crime manifestation in Grinols and Mustard's study may be partially explained by the time period needed for problem gambling behavior to fully manifest itself. However, Grinols and Mustard also suggest another possibility for growing crime rates: perhaps casinos attract visitors who are more prone to commit crime or to be victims of crime.

The AGA points to the theory that higher crime rates around casinos may be linked to higher levels of visitors coming into the area.[60] The theory goes that more visitors create more opportunities for criminals, which ultimately translate into more criminal incidents. Thus, visitors should be counted in computing crime rates, so that per capita figures based on residents are effectively diluted by the increased population of visitors. Grinols and Mustard raise an intriguing counterargument: if more visitors induce more crime, then one should witness higher crime rates whenever there are a lot of visitors to a jurisdiction and not just in cases of casinos. However, cities with large tourist magnets—such as the Mall of America in Bloomington, Minnesota; Disney World in Orlando, Florida; and the country music mecca of Branson, Missouri—are cited as counterexamples where large numbers of visitors did not produce similar crime experiences to their casino-laden counterparts. For example, the Mall of America had 7.7 more visitors than Las Vegas, but its crime rate (as adjusted to take into account visitors per local resident) is less than one-fifteenth of that in Las Vegas.[61]

Examples such as these do not necessarily prove an assertion that the population of casino visitors either causes or attracts more crime. More research is needed to explain these differing crime rates. For example, differences in legal penalties and enforcement priorities can have significant effects on changing crime rates, and these changes are not reflected in bare statistics of criminal convictions in a given period. Displacement of crimes as a result of changing the probability of detection and the applicable sanction is well documented in economic and criminology research.[62] Future research models affecting gambling impacts on crime will also need to take these possibilities into account. However, one additional point also should be noted: to the extent that communities with casinos actually invested more resources into law enforcement after the casino opened, then it is entirely possible that casino impacts on crime are understated rather than overstated.

These correlations between casinos and crime should present significant concerns for policymakers considering the introduction of a casino or for those with casinos operating for a short period within their jurisdictions. The impacts of crime do not only affect the victim and the taxpayers through costs of enforcement and incarceration. Crime may also negatively affect property values and personal income.[63] Investments of significant additional resources may thus be required to address the potential impact of crime on the local community.

After adjustments for other factors, Grinols and Mustard estimate that approximately 8.6 percent of property crimes and 12.6 percent of violent crimes in counties with casinos were due to adding the casino. They translate this into casino-related costs of seventy-five dollars per adult (in 1996 dollars). This means that a casino potentially imposes significant aggregate costs, though as discussed later, the effects of those costs may be diffused among different groups and governmental jurisdiction, thus complicating political decisions in these areas.

Casinos and Bankruptcy

Bankruptcy is another area where casinos may have negative impacts on the surrounding community. As noted previously, the AGA rejects the proposition that casinos can be linked to increased bankruptcy rates. The AGA states in part that "A series of independent government studies conducted during the late 1990s failed to establish a link between casinos and bankruptcy, and statistics support that finding."[64] These include the NORC study, the GAO review of the National Gambling Impact Study Commission Report, and a U.S. Treasury Department study completed in 1999.[65] A closer look at these materials reveals that they indeed fall short of providing conclusive proof of a significant impact of casinos on bankruptcy, but they nevertheless present results that are not favorable to the industry on this question. If the question were framed differently, and the industry were forced to prove conclusively the absence of a link between casinos and bankruptcy, the industry could not meet this standard based on the contents of these studies.

The NORC study examined bankruptcy experiences based on extensive telephone surveys. It found that both problem and pathological gamblers experienced elevated bankruptcy rates as compared with the general population. Pathological gamblers had a bankruptcy rate of 19.2 percent, as compared with 5.5 percent and 4.2 percent for low-risk gamblers and nongamblers, respectively.[66] Although the rate for problem gamblers of 10.7 percent was only "marginally statistically significant,"[67] it was nevertheless used as the basis for estimating the costs that these gamblers imposed on others.

The elevated bankruptcy rates for these populations, which are likely to grow as a result of more convenient access to casinos, suggest a significant impact. To illustrate, assuming 19.2 percent of the 3.75 million estimated pathological gamblers computed in table 5.3 filed for personal bankruptcy, this group alone would produce nearly 720,000 bankruptcy petitions. By comparison, in 2003 there were 1.6 million annual personal bankruptcy filings.[68] Although these petitions would probably not appear in the same year, they still represent a significant pool from which future bankruptcy petitions may come.

The GAO study was also less favorable to the industry than the AGA suggests. First, it reported the NORC study results on bankruptcy experiences from problem and pathological gamblers without questioning them. Although it noted that NORC had also found no significant change in per capita bank-ruptcy rates in communities where casinos were introduced,[69] those rates were not the source of the social cost estimate that NORC provided to the National Gambling Impact Study Commission.

The GAO study also included a case study of Atlantic City, New Jersey. Here, the GAO observed that Atlantic County (in which Atlantic City is lo-cated) showed higher bankruptcy rates than New Jersey or the nation in general for the period 1990–98. In fact, during 1994–98, the Atlantic County rate was double the rate for New Jersey, which approximated the nationwide rate. However, the GAO reported that it was unable to ascertain the basis for that change. The GAO was also unable to ascertain the effects of opening casinos, which occurred in 1978, because county-level data were "not readily obtainable" from the Administrative Office of the United States Courts for that period. The GAO also surveyed officials in government agencies and private industry to ask them about the heightened rate, and their answers were inconclusive.

Rather than provide a ringing endorsement of the proposition that casi-nos don't cause bankruptcies, the results of the GAO study tip the scale on the side of being concerned about negative consequences more than they allay those concerns. They highlight the need for more research to cover longer time periods associated with our experience with casino gambling.

The Treasury Department study cited by the AGA surveyed the available literature on the relationship between bankruptcy and casinos and engaged in a limited empirical analysis of bankruptcy data in certain jurisdictions.[70] In re-viewing the available literature, the Treasury Department concluded in part:

> While most available studies have pointed toward a connection between gambling and bankruptcy and have found various linkages, none has "proven" that gambling causes bankruptcy. Even among the population of people who went bankrupt because of gambling, there is a question of whether they might, due to a generalized lack of risk aversion, have lost their assets anyway, through other high-risk behaviors.[71]

The Treasury Department thus apparently agrees that some people went bankrupt because of gambling but that gambling was not the only "high-risk behavior" engaged in by these patrons. This is hardly comforting. It is also worth noting that the Treasury Department study agreed that the highest risk group of gamblers have bankruptcy rates that are roughly two percentage points higher than the rate for occasional gamblers. However, it ultimately dismisses any significance from this difference based on the small population for this group.[72]

The Treasury Department also undertook some of its own empirical research in the form of regression analysis, and it found that gambling effects were inconclusive at the statewide level. However, the study cautions that this analysis was based on a small sample and highly aggregated data.[73] Thus, this failure to find a measurable impact is hardly the last word on the subject.

It is important to put each of these studies into a proper context. First, they were done during a period when there were fewer new casinos opened than we have today. These empirical studies did not take into account the dramatic growth in the number of casinos that has occurred in the past several years since the latest study was completed. Moreover, the time period when new casinos were opened—and thus the opportunities for observation of social costs—was comparatively brief. Interpreting these findings to say "not yet" or "not now" is quite different from interpreting them to mean "not ever." For this reason, more recent studies with a longer time frame of reference deserve greater attention.

Barron, Staten, and Wilshusen recently examined county-level bankruptcy data for the period 1993–97 in counties with commercial casinos, as well as contiguous counties within fifty miles of a casino.[74] They concluded that casinos had a positive and statistically significant impact on increased personal bankruptcy rates. Casinos did not account for the entire increase in bankruptcy filings that occurred nationwide during the 1990s, but their regression analysis showed the likelihood that casinos had some impact on this increase.

We have constructed our own investigation, which operates on an expanded data set covering more years and more observations than the Barron study.[75] We include data from the period 1990–2002 covering both commercial casinos and Class III tribal casinos, which were excluded from the Barron assessment. We focused on time lags between the introduction of the casino and the emergence of bankruptcy experiences. As Grinols and Mustard have demonstrated with casinos and crime, it is conceivable that casino operations may also affect bankruptcy rates differently according to the duration of their operations.

Our data set also focuses on bankruptcy experiences in the county in which the casino is located, and it thus ignores the effects on contiguous counties as identified in the Barron study. This more limited focus probably provides a more conservative measure of bankruptcy impacts, to the extent that it may potentially exclude many gambling patrons of cross-border casinos from the analysis of the casino county and in fact would include them instead in a noncasino county where they reside. Given that a large number of casinos are located along state borders in order to take advantage of trade from noncasino states, this assumption probably understates the differential impact on bankruptcy rates from casinos.

Using a regression analysis that takes into account endogenous factors including population, race, age, personal income, and employment, we examined county-level bankruptcy trends over the period 1990–2002. Focusing on the cohort of counties in which a casino first opened during the relevant period (thus eliminating Nevada and Atlantic County in New Jersey from the mix due to the extended presence of casinos during this period), we then sought to examine the impact of those casinos on bankruptcy rates.

Significantly, we found that the bankruptcy impacts varied according to the duration of operation of casinos within the county. The addition of casinos had a positive and statistically significant impact on individual bankruptcy rates in the first year of operations. Thereafter, casino counties tended to experience bankruptcy rates that were slightly lower than the rate for an equivalent noncasino county. After about the third year, the bankruptcy rate then steadily grew, outpacing the noncasino county in the ninth year of operations, with an increasingly widening gap between them in subsequent years.

Figure 5.1 profiles the estimated bankruptcy rates for casino counties and noncasino counties based on this regression model. Over the twelve-year period, bankruptcy rates in casino counties grew by 180 percent, while bankruptcy rates in noncasino counties grew by only 117 percent. Beginning from a rate of 2.4 bankruptcies per 1,000, the casino county is estimated to grow to 6.7 per 1,000, while a noncasino county would grow to 5.2 per 1,000. For the period of time covered by this analysis, this reflects an increase of more than 2 percent in the annual growth rate for bankruptcy over this period for counties with casinos over their noncasino counterparts.

Although the last word on bankruptcy and casinos has yet to be written,

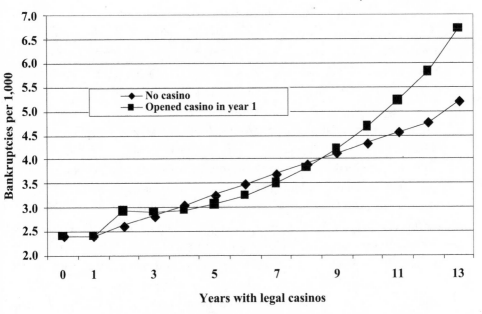

Fig. 5.1. Estimated individual bankruptcy rates—casino versus noncasino county

the available data do suggest that casinos can be linked to bankruptcies. The evidence from surveys of problem gamblers is itself a strong indication that a significant population may be affected by bankruptcy. Even if other behaviors may have contributed to bankruptcy, gambling also appears to be a contributing factor. The empirical evidence of county-level bankruptcy filings provides similarly strong indications that adding a casino has the potential for longer-term manifestations of bankruptcy experiences. As positive economic impacts from employment or tourist patronage fade (as illustrated in chapter 4), the possible negative impact on local populations may then be realized.

ESTIMATING THE INCIDENCE AND MAGNITUDE OF SOCIAL COSTS

Identifying the social problems associated with casino gambling is only part of the process of evaluating the cost side of the ledger for casino gambling. Negative social consequences associated with casino gambling must also be analyzed to determine the incidence of the cost, focusing particularly on those costs that are externalized by the gambler or the industry to others. In addition, estimates of the magnitude of these costs need to be developed.

This process can be dauntingly complex. Consider, for example, the case of a personal bankruptcy triggered by problem gambling. One potential cost involves the debt that is discharged as a consequence of bankruptcy proceedings. Here a creditor has incurred a cost because the debtor's reciprocal promise to repay is effectively nullified by a discharge granted under federal bankruptcy laws.[76] From an economist's perspective, this loss does not necessarily reflect a social cost, as it involves a transfer in which one party (the debtor) is arguably better off by the amount that the other (the creditor) is worse off.[77] Nevertheless, to the extent that the unpaid debt is attributable to losses at the casino, the debtor apparently gambled at the expense of another.

The immediate incidence of this loss appears to fall on the unpaid creditor, but ultimately others may bear this cost. The creditor may address the expected loss in advance by charging its customers more for credit or for the underlying goods or services sold on credit. In this case, some portion of the externalized cost may get passed along to the creditor's customers, which could include both gamblers and nongamblers.

Whether this impact affects local or distant markets might also be considered. For example, a financial institution issuing a credit card with a nationwide customer base could potentially spread this loss over a broader geographical market than the traditional corner store, which generations ago sold goods on personal credit to neighborhood patrons. Changes in bankruptcy laws enacted in April 2005 will potentially enhance protections for these creditors, particularly credit card issuers, from the discharge of indebtedness by problem gamblers. This legislation specifically carves out as nondischargeable any debt to a single creditor over $500 incurred within ninety days of a petition for so-called luxury goods or services.[78] Although this category is not specifically defined, gambling would arguably be included. Further, certain cash advances aggregating over $750 within seventy days of a bankruptcy petition are presumed to be nondischargeable.[79] These provisions could ultimately work against problem gamblers, leaving them with fewer options to discharge their debts. The impact of these provisions on future behavior, and whether that reflects an appropriate policy balance by requiring costs to be internalized by those with pathological conditions, remains to be worked out after this legislation becomes effective.

Bankruptcy also involves other costs, including the transaction costs associated with bankruptcy proceedings. Unlike the costs associated with the debt, these are typically incurred in the jurisdiction where the debtor lives or owns a business. Venue will generally be appropriate in the federal district court where the domicile, residence, principal place of business, or principal assets of the debtor are located.[80] Thus, to the extent that gambling patrons live or own a business in a jurisdiction other than the one in which they regularly gamble, these costs are effectively exported from the casino jurisdiction. A recent study indeed suggests that casinos export bankruptcy costs to the jurisdictions from which they draw visiting patrons.[81]

Some of these transaction costs are jointly paid by the gambler and the creditors, including filing fees, court costs, and the fees paid to legal counsel. Others are borne by taxpayers, who provide funds to support the bankruptcy courts and related judicial machinery administering this area of law. Concepts of variable and fixed costs are potentially relevant here, as the real impact of problem gambling–related bankruptcy is arguably at the margin: Given that bankruptcy has many causes other than gambling, bankruptcy courts and their associated staffs would be needed at some level whether there were casinos or not.

The incidence of costs imposed on taxpayers also raises issues involving jurisdiction. To the extent that federal courts are involved, federal taxes support these activities, thus affecting a diffusion of costs beyond the local region. Other examples of social costs, such as crime-related costs imposed on local law enforcement, may have more direct impacts on local taxpayers. Thus, the type of cost may thus reflect more or less scrutiny from a local taxpayer or politician who is sensitive to the question of who bears the costs and who obtains the benefits.

These issues of incidence are often not addressed in the literature discussing the impact of social costs, which focuses on the bigger picture of the aggregate costs and benefits. However, these issues are potentially relevant to policymakers and legislators, who must consider political interests of their particular constituencies. The impact on one's own constituents, as opposed to the impact on others, creates a powerful incentive for decision making that ignores the impact of costs that may be exported to others. In this sense, the politics of gambling at state and local levels may often violate the Golden Rule, as exports of social costs to another jurisdiction (or to taxpayers accountable to another level of government) are omitted from the total calculus of costs that might otherwise affect decisions about the benefits of gambling.

Estimating the magnitude of these costs presents other significant challenges. First, the statistical base for estimating the contribution of gambling to the social problem must be determined. One approach to this issue focuses on the costs attributed to behaviors associated with problem and/or pathological gamblers. This approach seeks to estimate the marginal contribution of these behaviors to the expected incidence of social costs in populations without problem or pathological gambling experiences. The other approach looks broadly at the results of regression analysis associated with conditions before and after a casino has been added, seeking to ascertain the marginal contribution from all aspects of the casino rather than only from those affected by problem gambling.

Both approaches are subject to the challenges of multiple causation. In other words, some members of these populations could have contributed to these costs regardless of whether legalized casino gambling was present in their community. Estimates that do not separate the impact of other causal factors from that of gambling pathology are subject to challenge. Regression analysis that controls for multiple contributing factors provides a basis to limit the effects from other causes, but the analysis is only as good as the available data.

Data concerning the marginal contribution of problem and/or pathological gamblers have the advantage of being more available and easier to work with than more complex regression models. For example, the NORC study estimated the costs associated with the various social conditions—including lost employment, bankruptcy, criminal justice, divorce, and health issues—from an extensive survey population.[82] By differentiating the experience rates for problem and pathological gamblers over other groups, an estimate of the associated cost can be developed.

However, this estimation method often focuses on incidents per problem or pathological gambler. If a problem or pathological gambler is diagnosed based on lifetime experiences, derivation of an annual estimate of costs is highly uncertain.[83] The NORC survey also queried the population about prior year incidents, which provided a basis for estimating annual impacts on some problems but not on others. More research into the longitudinal patterns of pathological and problem gamblers may yield a more accurate picture of annual costs than this simple methodology.

Grinols has explored this issue thoughtfully and extensively in a recent book, in which he summarizes the results from studies that sought to measure social costs associated with problem and/or pathological gambling.[84] These costs spanned a range of nine different categories, including crime (which included subcategories of costs associated with apprehension and police, adjudication, and incarceration), business and employment costs (including lost productivity, lost time, and unemployment), bankruptcy, suicide, illness, social service costs (including therapy and treatment costs), family costs (associated with divorce and separation), and so-called abused dollars, which refers to money acquired from relatives and friends under false pretenses for use in gambling.[85]

Grinols examined nine studies that computed estimated costs for pathological gamblers. An average of data for studies, adjusted to 2003 dollars, generates an estimated cost per pathological gambler of $10,330.[86] The cost per problem gambler, which was based on three studies examining only a partial listing of costs, was estimated at $2,945.[87] If these costs are applied to estimates of total pathological and problem gamblers developed previously in this chapter, the totals range from $47 billion to $161 billion (see table 5.5). The lower end of this range compares favorably with the lifetime estimates of the NORC study, which was also adopted by the National Gambling Impact Study Commission.

TABLE 5.5.   Estimated aggregate social costs

	Grinols Cost Estimate ($)	NORC Patron Survey (table 5.3) ($)	Aggregate Cost ($)
Pathological	10,330	3,750,933	38,747,141,333
Problem	2,945	2,831,233	8,337,982,167
Total			47,085,123,500
	Average Grinols Cost[a]	Welte Study (table 5.4)	
SOGS	6,638	24,391,915	161,901,333,755
DIS	6,638	10,180,973	67,576,208,872

[a]This figure is a simple average of the Grinols cost estimates for problem and pathological gamblers. As referenced in tables 5.2, 5.3, and 5.4 above, the ratio of problem gamblers to pathological gamblers varies in each estimate, with more problem gamblers in one example and more pathological gamblers in two examples. A simple average approximates equal occurrences of each category.

In addition to these aggregate effects on social costs, other costs not listed here may also be relevant. Some of them are inherently personal and difficult to value in monetary terms, such as the pain inflicted on families affected by the problem gambler. Though these kinds of costs are beyond the scope of an economic analysis, they are very real from a human perspective. Problem and pathological gamblers are likely to contribute significantly to casino profits—and government coffers. The NORC study indicated that 15 percent of AGR comes from problem and pathological gamblers.[88] A 1996 study by Grinols and Omorov indicated that a much higher figure was justifiable—perhaps as much as 52 percent.[89] A report prepared by two researchers from the University of Lethbridge on the sources of revenues in Canadian casinos indicated that the proportion of revenue coming from problem gamblers may vary according to the type of game involved. This study, which was based on diary entries for a sample of Canadian gamblers in Ontario, indicated these approximate proportions for different types of gambling. In rank order, the rough proportions are "60% gaming machines; 53% horse racing; 22% casino table games; 22% bingo and raffles; and 19% lotteries."[90]

Given the prevalence of electronic gaming machines in casinos in the United States,[91] the 60 percent estimate for gaming machines suggests that casinos and racinos depend heavily on problem gambling behavior. Even if more conservative measures are used, the revenues from problem gambling are likely to be significant, presenting a dilemma for the industry. It might seem socially responsible to be concerned about problem gamblers. However, getting too concerned might be very bad for business.

As discussed in the chapters that follow, governments have paid comparatively little attention to social costs, and in particular the plight of problem and pathological gamblers, in determining the parameters of the regulatory environment for casino gambling. Instead, they have focused on keeping the industry profitable and using it as a tool for tax collection. The available data on social costs suggest that this is a serious error and that a head-in-the-sand approach of academic agnosticism is no longer a sustainable position for making gambling policies.

6. Regulating Gambling—An Introduction

> [T]he power of the State to establish all regulations that are reasonably necessary to secure the health, safety, good order, comfort, or general welfare of the community . . . can neither be abdicated nor bargained away, and is inalienable even by express grant.
>
> *Atlantic Coast Line R. Co. v. Goldsboro*, 232 U.S. 548, 558 (1914)

> [H]e who stirs the devil's broth must needs use a long spoon.
>
> *Marshall v. Sawyer*, 301 F.2d 639, 648 (9th Cir. 1962)
>
> (Pope, J., concurring)

In our federal system, regulatory functions are diffused among federal, state, and local governments. In theory, the Founding Fathers designed the federal government with limited powers, thus constraining its ability to encroach upon the governing role of the states. The Tenth Amendment reinforces this design: "The powers not delegated to the United States by the Constitution, nor prohibited by it to the States, are reserved to the States respectively, or to the people."

In practice, however, the federal government's delegated powers have often been exercised rather expansively. In particular, Article I, Section 8, Clause 3 of the United States Constitution grants to Congress the power "[t]o regulate Commerce with foreign Nations, and among the several States, and with the Indian Tribes." Since most activities have some connection with or effect upon commerce, the permissible scope of federal regulation has indeed broadened. Though the Supreme Court has recently expressed some limitations on the scope of the commerce powers,[1] it is difficult to raise a successful constitutional objection to federal legislation regulating (or perhaps even prohibiting) gambling activities under those powers. Alternatively, Congress could also exercise its taxing powers under Article I, Section 8, Clause 1 to regulate or even prohibit gambling.[2] For example, Congress could enact a large federal excise tax on gambling transactions to effectively eliminate legalized gambling by making it uneconomical.

Despite these extensive powers, the federal government has exercised a restrained approach in its oversight of gambling. The states provide most laws involving the regulation of gambling. As political subdivisions of the state, local governments function much like agencies in exercising governmental power, which is effectively derived from the state.[3] Federal policy has generally supported state autonomy over gambling matters, intervening only in limited circumstances to address such matters as interstate aspects of gambling, criminal activities, and gambling conducted by Native American tribes. Federal tax laws specifically applicable to gambling focus primarily on information reporting, and they have only limited effects on the industry's gambling operations.

Significant state regulatory structures affecting commercial casino gambling are discussed in this chapter, followed by more extensive state-specific expositions in chapters 7 and 8. Federal laws regulating gambling, including the peculiar regulatory posture of Native American gaming and the special problems of the Internet, are discussed in chapters 9 through 11.

STATE REGULATION: WIELDING THE POLICE POWER

A state's authority to regulate (or prohibit) gambling is traditionally associated with so-called police power, which was the subject of some early Supreme Court litigation. In *Stone v. Mississippi*,[4] a corporation challenged the validity of state legislation abrogating its power to conduct a lottery, which the state had previously granted through a corporate charter. The corporation claimed that this legislation impaired contractual rights in violation of the Contracts Clause in Article I, Section 10, Clause 1 of the United States Constitution.[5]

The Court rejected this challenge and confirmed the state's power to regulate gambling, stating in part:

> [Lotteries] are not, in the legal acceptation of the term, *mala in se,* but, as we have just seen, may properly be made *mala prohibita.* They are a species of gambling, and wrong in their influences. They disturb the checks and balances of a well-ordered community. Society built on such a foundation

would almost of necessity bring forth a population of speculators and gamblers, living on the expectation of what, "by the casting of lots, or by lot, chance, or otherwise," might be "awarded" to them from the accumulations of others. Certainly the right to suppress them is governmental, to be exercised at all times by those in power, at their discretion. Any one, therefore, who accepts a lottery charter does so with the implied understanding that the people, in their sovereign capacity, and through their properly constituted agencies, may resume it at any time when the public good shall require, whether it be paid for or not. All that one can get by such a charter is a suspension of certain governmental rights in his favor, subject to withdrawal at will. He has in legal effect nothing more than a license to enjoy the privilege on the terms named for the specified time, unless it be sooner abrogated by the sovereign power of the State. It is a permit, good as against existing laws, but subject to future legislative and constitutional control or withdrawal.[6]

The Court's views reflect the sentiments of the times about gambling; that is, it was not wrong in itself (*mala in se*), though it tended to have negative effects that states could constrain through regulation or prohibition.[7] It is also interesting to note that the Court advanced the belief that lotteries were even more damaging to the social fabric than other forms of gambling and that some government regulation was preferable to none in this area.

[T]his court said, more than thirty years ago, speaking through Mr. Justice Grier, in *Phalen* v. *Virginia* (8 How. 163, 168), that "experience has shown that the common forms of gambling are comparatively innocuous when placed in contrast with the wide-spread pestilence of lotteries. The former are confined to a few persons and places, but the latter infests the whole community; it enters every dwelling; it reaches every class; it preys upon the hard earnings of the poor; and it plunders the ignorant and simple." Happily, under the influence of restrictive legislation, the evils are not so apparent now; but we very much fear that with the same opportunities of indulgence the same results would be manifested. If lotteries are to be tolerated at all, it is no doubt better that they should be regulated by law, so that the people may be protected as far as possible against the inherent vices of the system; but that they are demoralizing in their effects, no matter how carefully regulated, cannot admit of a doubt.[8]

The police power reflects the ideal of government protecting citizens from one another and, perhaps in some cases, from themselves. For many years, governments have chosen criminal sanctions as the method of exercising the police power to stamp out gambling (particularly in its professional or commercial forms) or at least to constrain its impact on society through deterrent effects. Fraud, cheating, and the economic hardship associated with losing more than a patron could afford, as well as other collateral effects associated with gambling losses, including crime, violence, and strained family relationships, were among the concerns to be addressed. Governments attempted, in general, to reduce these problems by limiting the available opportunities to gamble. Attaching a criminal penalty also reinforced other social values, such as accumulating wealth by earning, saving, and investing for the future rather than by quick gains from beliefs in luck or chance.

However, criminal sanctions provide an imperfect solution to the regulation of gambling. Defects in the statutory scheme, such as incomplete definitions of proscribed forms of gambling, sometimes leave gaps to be exploited.[9] As in other industries, technological changes, including the development of electronic communication media, change the way that business is done; laws must also change to encompass these new technologies.[10] Lawmakers must also take care to adjust the system of criminal penalties to take into account current social conditions and beliefs. A penalty that is judged too harsh will impede prospects for conviction and make enforcement less likely, while a penalty that is seen as too lenient will not deter the proscribed behavior.[11]

Even if lawmakers produce perfectly written statutes, enforcing them is another matter. The fact that gambling is not viewed as *malum in se* may lead to lax enforcement efforts, as officials direct scarce resources toward activities that they believe present more serious social problems. Corrupting influences may also be at work as illicit gambling profits may also find their way to affect the decisions of law enforcement officials.[12] This in turn may create the need for still more laws, and probably federal oversight, to address the problem of state and local corruption.[13]

Even with the most efficient criminal sanctions, some individuals will continue to demand gambling services and will seek out this demand through an underground economy that is beyond the effective reach of governmental authority. Negative collateral effects from gambling still exist in this environment, though they presumably affect fewer patrons.

Of even greater significance to policymakers may be the fact that substantial profits generated in this underground economy are beyond the reach of the government's taxing power. Though governments may tax illicit gains,[14] the collection of such taxes presents a real problem. The prospect of capturing tax and other economic benefits from this underground economy presents a tempting target for those seeking a solution for fiscal needs without the negative political consequences of raising taxes.

Legalization may make illicit alternatives less desirable for both patrons and providers who would prefer to avoid the sanctions and stigma associated with illegal activity. However, it is unlikely to eliminate the underground economy. Regulations impose costs, which increase individual incentives to circumvent the regulatory system. For example, even when options for legalized gambling exist, patrons may continue to choose illegal gaming based on a desire to attain better odds or to avoid tax consequences on winnings.[15]

Thus, criminal sanctions continue to play an important role even in those states that choose the path of legalization. However, such sanctions serve a different function in the legal and social order, in that they tend to protect the state's fiscal interests by channeling behavior away from illegal alternatives and into taxable gambling activities. Their role as a transmitter of social values is compromised by the existence of government-sanctioned outlets for similar behavior.

Legalizing an activity, coupled with the promotion of that activity through advertising, will generally increase the level of that activity that was once prohibited.[16] Some commentators have suggested that legalization may even increase illegal forms of gambling by reducing the stigma associated with gambling.[17] Even if this is not the case, policymakers must recognize that increasing the opportunities for legal gambling activities is likely to exacerbate social problems associated with gambling. As discussed in chapter 5, bankruptcies, crimes, and other negative consequences mean that some of the costs associated with gambling activities may be externalized to others. In an ideal world, a regulatory approach should address these costs and limit their imposition upon others.

STATE REGULATORY STRUCTURES

States with legalized casino gambling have pursued different approaches to licensing and regulating gaming operations, but those approaches share some common features. For the most part, regulatory behavior tends to focus upon the goal of developing public confidence in gaming as a legitimate form of entertainment. Such efforts must overcome years of history and cultural bias: recall that "maintaining a gambling house" was generally considered as a public nuisance to be abated.[18]

To achieve this end, regulations need to address consumer concerns about fraudulent, unfair, or otherwise dangerous practices that potentially affect gaming patrons. Regulators must disassociate criminal elements from state-sanctioned gambling establishments. They must also protect patrons from unscrupulous gaming operators and threats or violence due to gaming losses. Enhancing the legitimacy of the industry will also tend to channel patrons and service providers away from illegal alternatives, which is important for governmental success in capturing the economic benefits that otherwise lurk in the underground economy.

Regulations also must ensure that government-imposed taxes and fees are accurately assessed and collected. Much like owners, governments are concerned about getting their share of the financial rewards generated from a gambling enterprise. Without adequate internal controls and reporting, a cash-based business such as a casino provides a fertile environment for siphoning money back into the underground economy. (The federal government shares this interest with the states. As discussed in chapter 9, it also imposes regulations to prevent money laundering and to protect other fiscal and security interests.)

In many jurisdictions, the regulatory structure also seeks to ensure the economic viability of gaming as an enterprise in the state. States often accomplish this by limiting the supply of gaming licenses, thus preserving what amounts to an oligopolistic status for licensed casinos. This structure tends to ensure that the state will have a reliable flow of tax dollars from an operation with an adequate market share to support a profitable operation, thereby attracting private capital to invest in the casino infrastructure.

Having fewer but larger facilities may also provide other efficiency gains from a regulatory perspective. For example, it is undoubtedly easier to monitor the compliance of fewer larger establishments than many small ones. Moreover, to the extent that the providers are largely made up of publicly traded corporations, additional resources (including government agencies, such as the Securities and Exchange Commission) are available to monitor and regulate the financial responsibility of the industry.

Nevertheless, a structure favoring a limited number of providers also has potential downside risks. The award of a discretionary gambling license increases the possibility that private companies[19] will receive public largess based on their political influences. Though it may be possible to structure licensing decisions in a competitive way to ensure that the public captures a larger portion of the benefits associated with gaming, this is not the dominant approach in jurisdictions with a limited number of licenses.[20]

Finally, government may also seek to address some of the negative consequences of legalized gambling on patrons and their families stemming from excessive gambling losses. Regulations have generally overlooked these consequences on individuals, which are often indirect and hidden, in favor of market competition for the gaming dollar. In part, this regulatory gap may be due to the exigencies of developing an effective business model that will produce the expected revenues promised to constituents. Governments that depend upon tax revenues from gaming operations understandably find it easier to choose a path that maximizes the industry's gains, which may come at the expense of the citizens they are supposed to protect.

Protections for those vulnerable to compulsive gambling behaviors are especially weak, often involving counseling and treatment options that are effective, if at all, after considerable financial and other damage has occurred. The compulsive gambler is thus exposed to ever-expanding opportunities for legal gaming, leaving families and others (including nongamblers) exposed to the attendant social and economic losses from this behavior.

Though a comprehensive state-by-state review of efforts to regulate gambling is beyond the scope of this book, a review of the particular regulatory structures and practices in a few states provides a flavor of different approaches taken and the relative balance achieved between promotion of the industry and protection from its excesses. Nevada's system is well developed and oriented heavily toward the promotion of gambling as a significant part of the state's economy, reflecting its position as an early adopter of legalized gambling as part of the entertainment and tourism industry. As such, it provides a baseline for comparison with approaches taken in other states that have followed Nevada's lead in legalizing casino gambling.

7. Casino Regulation in Nevada

As the leading destination for casino gambling in the United States, Nevada has a long-standing commitment to the gaming industry as an important part of its economy.[1] Nevada has designed a regulatory scheme that links the growth and success of the industry to public trust and confidence in the integrity of the industry and all those who deal with it. As stated in the Gaming Control Act:

> All establishments where gaming is conducted and where gaming devices are operated, and manufacturers, sellers and distributors of certain gaming devices and equipment . . . must therefore be licensed, controlled and assisted to protect the public health, safety, morals, good order and general welfare of the inhabitants of the state, to foster the stability and success of gaming and to preserve the competitive economy and policies of free competition of the State of Nevada.[2]

Because of Nevada's position as the state with the largest casino industry and the longest history of legalized gambling, its regulatory model merits serious attention from those concerned with gaming regulation.

BASIC MECHANISMS OF CONTROL

Nevada pursues its regulatory purposes through two agencies: the Gaming Control Board and the Gaming Commission. The Gaming Commission consists of five members, who are appointed by the governor.[3] In an effort to maintain political neutrality, no more than three members may come from the same political party[4] and no member may currently hold elective office or an official capacity in a political party.[5] In an effort to maintain neutrality from the industry, no member may hold a pecuniary interest in a gaming establishment.[6] The commission has authority to issue gaming licenses and to promulgate regulations affecting the industry.[7]

The Gaming Control Board consists of three members, also appointed by the governor.[8] Like commission members, board members are precluded from holding an elected office or serving as an official in a political party.[9] One member must be a certified public accountant or otherwise qualified to practice public accounting and must also possess expertise in corporate finance, auditing, economics, or gaming.[10] Another member must be selected "with special reference to his training and experience in the fields of investigation, law enforcement, law or gaming."[11]

The board's mission is stated as follows:

> The State Gaming Control Board governs Nevada's gaming industry through strict regulation of all persons, locations, practices, association, and related activities. Through investigations, licensure, and enforcement of laws and regulations we protect the integrity and the stability of the industry and ensure the collection of gaming taxes and fees that are an essential source of State revenue.[12]

An extensive staff, which is organized in six functional divisions, assists the board in carrying out its duties.

The Audit Division, which has a professional staff of more than one hundred employees, audits casinos with more than $3 million in revenue to ensure compliance with applicable gaming laws and proper reporting of gaming revenue.[13] It utilizes traditional audit techniques as part of regular, systematic reviews of casino operations, and it also performs covert operations or other special investigations as needed to detect money laundering, "skimming," or other illegal activities.[14]

Investigative functions are also carried out by two other divisions: the Investigation Division and the Enforcement Division. The Investigation Division carries out background investigations on prospective licensees.[15] The Enforcement Division's responsibilities include investigating suspected criminal activity, monitoring for involvement of organized crime, and checking the backgrounds of prospective employees.[16] The Enforcement Division also recommends to the board persons to be added to the "List of Excluded Persons."[17] As discussed later in the chapter, this list has proved controversial, as it provides a state-sanctioned means for private firms to

deny access to specific individuals in an effort to protect the industry's reputation and to further law enforcement efforts.

The Tax and License Division is responsible for collecting all taxes imposed on gambling. It also issues gaming licenses pursuant to the direction of
the Gaming Commission, performs compliance reviews for licensees with
less than $3 million in gaming revenues, and monitors Indian gaming in Ne-
vada.[18] Gaming taxes and related fees and licenses totaled $819,380,000 in
fiscal 2004, representing 19.6 percent of total revenues.[19]

Other divisions are designed to deal with specialized problems. The Corporate Securities Division monitors publicly traded companies and their
subsidiaries operating gaming businesses in Nevada.[20] Since the Nevada legislature changed state law to lift restrictions affecting the ability of publicly
traded companies to hold gaming licenses, these companies now control approximately three-fourths of gaming revenues in the state.[21] Finally, the
Technology Division provides laboratory and field testing for electronic devices and software to ensure their integrity for gaming patrons.[22]

Licensing for casino owners and employees is a central feature of Nevada's
regulatory system. It is unlawful for an "owner, lessee, or employee" to carry
on any gaming activity without a license.[23] "Restricted" licenses are available
to those who choose to operate fewer than fifteen slot machines in an environment that is ancillary to another business, such as in a restaurant or convenience store.[24] Operators and employees of casinos with more than fifteen
devices or with table games require an "unrestricted" license.[25]

A prospective licensee bears the burden of proving his or her qualifica-
tion.[26] The following criteria apply in making licensing decisions:

An application to receive a license or be found suitable must not be
granted unless the commission is satisfied that the applicant is:
  (a) A person of good character, honesty and integrity;
  (b) A person whose prior activities, criminal record, if any, reputa-
       tion, habits and associations do not pose a threat to the public in-
       terest of this state or to the effective regulation and control of
       gaming or charitable lotteries, or create or enhance the dangers
       of unsuitable, unfair or illegal practices, methods and activities in
       the conduct of gaming or charitable lotteries or in the carrying on
       of the business and financial arrangements incidental thereto; and

(c)   In all other respects qualified to be licensed or found suitable consistently with the declared policy of the state.[27]

Operators who apply for a casino license must further establish business competence and experience and prove that adequate financing for the casino operation comes from a "suitable source."[28] Even lenders to casino operations must meet character requirements,[29] and others doing business with the casino may also be subjected to licensing requirements.[30]

Licensing standards serve a public purpose in protecting patrons and others doing business with the casino industry. For example, ensuring the financial wherewithal to meet operational demands tends to ensure that casinos are able to carry out their financial obligations to winning patrons. However, licensing standards also serve another important purpose, which was instrumental in gaining public acceptance for the industry: freedom from association with criminal elements. The Nevada Supreme Court explained this purpose in an early case.

> Throughout this country, then, gambling has necessarily surrounded itself with an aura of crime and corruption. Those in management of this pursuit who have succeeded, have done so not only through a disregard of law, but, in a competitive world, through a superior talent for such disregard and for the corruption of those in public authority.
>
> For gambling to take its place as a lawful enterprise in Nevada it is not enough that this state has named it lawful. We have but offered it the opportunity for lawful existence. The offer is a risky one, not only for the people of this state, but for the entire nation. Organized crime must not be given refuge here through the legitimatizing of one of its principal sources of income. Nevada gambling, if it is to succeed as a lawful enterprise, must be free from the criminal and corruptive taint acquired by gambling beyond our borders. If this is to be accomplished not only must the operation of gambling be carefully controlled, but the character and background of those who would engage in gambling in this state must be carefully scrutinized.[31]

This 1957 opinion was written shortly after an extensive study of organized crime was commissioned by the United States Senate. In 1950, Senator Estes Kefauver, who chaired the Senate Committee to Investigate Organized Crime, delegated to the American Bar Association the responsibility for investigating and evaluating local law enforcement mechanisms and their effectiveness against organized crime.[32] This study, which was issued in 1952, raised important issues concerning the tension between the structurally desirable feature of local law enforcement and control, which is inherent in our federal system, and the deleterious effects of corruption on its effectiveness. If Nevada was to avoid encroachment by federal law enforcement,[33] it was effectively required to demonstrate that its regulatory agencies and its gambling industry were free from the taint of criminal elements.

AGENCY DISCRETION: LICENSING

The Casino Control Act grants extensive discretion to the commission in granting or denying licenses to casino operators and key employees, and that discretion is critical to maintaining the integrity of the industry. The act provides in part: "The commission has full and absolute power and authority to deny any application for any cause it deems reasonable."[34] The act also makes it clear that a license is not a property right but is instead a revocable privilege.[35] Nevada law provides no recourse to judicial review for a prospective licensee whose application is denied.[36] This feature has survived constitutional challenges, leaving the commission with nearly plenary powers over those to whom licenses are granted.

For example, in State v. Rosenthal,[37] the Nevada Supreme Court upheld the commission's denial of a license to Frank Rosenthal, who functioned as a key employee of a Las Vegas casino. In support of its decision, the commission had made the following findings about Rosenthal:

> The applicant is a person whose licensing by the State would reflect or tend to reflect discredit upon the State of Nevada by reason of: A) A North Carolina court finding of guilt for conspiracy to bribe an amateur athlete; B) Testimony of Mickey Bruce in Senate subcommittee hearings that applicant attempted to bribe him to throw outcome of 1960 Oregon-Michigan football game; C) Statements by police officers Dardis and Clode to Senate subcommittee and to Florida Racing Commission that applicant admitted he was corrupting public officials in return for protection; D) The applicant's being barred from race tracks and pari-mutual operations in the State of Florida.[38]

In reversing a lower court's finding that the board's decision violated Rosenthal's due process rights, the Nevada Supreme Court treated gambling as a special case suited for the state's exercise of "police powers" outside the scope of federal constitutional protections.

> Gaming as a calling or business is in the same class as the selling of intoxicating liquors in respect to deleterious tendency. The state may regulate or suppress it without interfering with any of those inherent rights of citizenship which it is the object of government to protect and secure.[39]

A legislative decision to leave licensing matters to the discretion of the commission and to provide no resort to judicial review did not offend due process. As a *prospective* licensee, Rosenthal was not deprived of any current property right. Moreover, deference to agency discretion was consistent with the legislature's purpose in regulating legalized gambling. Specialized knowledge was required to effectively regulate the gambling industry,[40] and the qualifications and experience of the commission made it especially well qualified to exercise this discretion.[41]

The commission also serves as the primary decision maker in cases involving revocation or other disciplinary matters affecting licensees. However, judicial review is provided in this context.[42] Unlike the prospective licensee, a holder of an existing license does possess rights that are entitled to due process protections.

AGENCY DISCRETION: BLACKLISTING

The List of Excluded Persons or "Black Book" provides another tool for the state to reinforce its efforts to legitimize the gaming industry. The commission is authorized by statute to create a list of persons "whose presence in the establishment is determined by the board and the commission to pose a threat to the interests of this state or to licensed gaming, or both."[43] The criteria for exclusion include a broad range of activities:

(a) Prior conviction of a crime which is a felony in this state or under the laws of the United States, a crime involving moral turpitude or a violation of the gaming laws of any state;

(b) Violation or conspiracy to violate the provisions of this chapter relating to:

     (1) The failure to disclose an interest in a gaming establishment for
        which the person must obtain a license; or

     (2) Willful evasion of fees or taxes;

  (c) Notorious or unsavory reputation which would adversely affect pub-
      lic confidence and trust that the gaming industry is free from crimi-
      nal or corruptive elements; or

  (d) Written order of a governmental agency which authorizes the ex-
      clusion or ejection of the person from an establishment at which
      gaming . . . is conducted.[44]

Exclusion may not be based on invidious categories, including race, color, creed, national origin or ancestry, or sex.[45] However, the commission need only find one of the permissible enumerated criteria for exclusion in order to support a decision to exclude.[46] The stated criteria allow for exclusion based on information that would be insufficient for a criminal conviction. For example, regulations provide that hearsay evidence—as reflected in reports by federal or state legislative or executive agencies—may be used to establish a "notorious or unsavory reputation" as a basis for exclusion.[47] Associating with illegal sports betting or influencing the outcome of collegiate sporting events is also grounds for exclusion.[48]

The commission's decision is subject to judicial review, but a reviewing court's ability to reverse such a decision is constrained by statute, which limits relief to such circumstances involving a decision that is "unsupported by *any* evidence" or "arbitrary or capricious or otherwise not in accordance with law."[49] The commission is permitted to take punitive measures against any establishment or related individual who "knowingly fails to exclude" a listed person.[50] Listed persons who attempt to enter a casino or otherwise have contact with the industry may be charged with a gross misdemeanor.[51]

The Black Book was initially used to target known members and associates of organized crime, and it was apparently used sparingly during its early years. For example, after existing for more than twenty years, only nine persons were listed in 1987.[52] As of May 2005, thirty-nine persons were listed.[53] Several added to the list in recent years have been included for crimes involving efforts to improperly manipulate electronic gambling devices.[54] Thus, although the origins of the list may have been rooted in protecting the public reputation of the industry, it also protects the casinos from economic losses by providing a centralized means of notice from those with a propensity for electronic theft.[55]

Those selected for inclusion in the Black Book enjoy limited due process rights, which are grounded in the significant reputational interests affected by inclusion.[56] In *Spilotro v. State,*[57] Anthony Spilotro, an organized crime figure who had been placed in the Black Book, unsuccessfully challenged the constitutionality of the Nevada statutes. Among other things, Spilotro alleged that the Nevada scheme violated substantive due process by punishing him for his status or associations. The court rejected this argument, stating in part: "the purpose of the statutes is regulatory, not penal. The exclusionary list is designed not to punish those listed for past bad behavior, but to protect the interests of the State and the licensed gaming industry, by avoiding any potentially significant criminal or corruptive taint and thus maintaining public confidence and trust in the gaming industry."[58] These regulatory purposes also formed the basis for rejecting his argument that inclusion on the list was an unconstitutional bill of attainder, which required a criminal penalty for that status to attach.[59]

The court also rejected challenges based on Spilotro's right to travel, association, and access to public places, which would be affected by inclusion on the list. In particular, it found that no such rights exist for access to casinos.[60] The court found that the rules governing the Black Book were a "reasonable method of achieving a legitimate end of protecting the state's vital gaming industry and thus comply with substantive due process and procedural due process."[61]

Commentators have been critical of the list as a means of regulation, particularly because of the potential impact on economic and associational rights from inclusion, which may be based on evidence that falls short of constitutional sufficiency for a criminal conviction.[62] However, the peculiar nature of casino gambling apparently forms the basis for granting some latitude to the state in choosing the means to accomplish its regulatory purposes.

That latitude is also evident in Nevada's treatment of so-called card counters, who may be excluded from casinos for conduct that does not involve cheating or criminal activity but that instead might threaten the industry's economic well-being. The exclusion of card counters is not expressly sanctioned by state statute; it is the product of a common law rule giving owners of private establishments the right to refuse service to those whom they choose. Although the Gaming Control Act requires that gambling be available to the public, it also specifically allows this "common law right" to continue. The act states that it does not

(a) Abrogate or abridge any common law right of a gaming establishment to exclude any person from gaming activities or eject any person from the premises of the establishment for any reason; or

(b) Prohibit a licensee from establishing minimum wagers for any gambling game or slot machine.[63]

In *Uston v. Hilton Hotels Corporation,*[64] a card counter challenged the legality of a casino's practice of excluding him from the casino, even though his name was not found in the Black Book. Uston had neither cheated nor committed an illegal act; he claimed that his only offense was that he was a "better than average blackjack ('21') player." As the court explained, a "card counter" is "a person that attempts to know every card both in and out of the deck, thereby enhancing his chances of placing a favorable wager."[65] Card counting does not guarantee success, but by evaluating the cards that have been played and by making larger bets as more cards are played (and thus more cards are known), a card counter is able to gain some advantage in assessing the odds affecting a particular hand.[66]

Uston based his claim, in part, on a civil rights statute, 42 U.S.C. § 1983, which requires state action as a predicate. Here, even though his exclusion was not caused by any positive action of a government official or agency, such as the Gaming Control Board or Gaming Commission, Uston alleged "that the actions of the defendants in preventing him from playing the game of '21' were tantamount to state action (1) because of the extent to which the State of Nevada regulates the gaming industry, and (2) because the State of Nevada, charged with the enforcement of the gaming laws, has refused to prohibit the discrimination against card counters."[67]

The court found these arguments to be without merit, stating in part: "Mere state regulation of a private industry in and of itself does not constitute state action. Something more, more in the nature of a substantial and direct state involvement in promoting the challenged activity, must be demonstrated in order to establish state action."[68] In this case, Uston could not show that the state had "to any significant degree promoted or participated in the exclusion of persons suspected by gaming establishments to be

card counters or in Uston's words, 'better than average black jack players.' "[69] The state's inaction—that is, its failure to compel casinos to admit
him because he was not on the List of Excluded Persons—would not give
rise to a cause of action in these circumstances.[70] Having failed to show any
basis for invidious discrimination, Uston was thus left without any legal
recourse under federal law in these circumstances. Moreover, given the specific reservation of the common law right to exclude, it appears that no recourse exists under Nevada state law either.

The *Uston* court is probably correct that no federal civil rights violation
arises from being excluded from a casino because you are perceived to be a
better than average player. Other courts have reached a similar conclusion.[71]
However, the distinction between government action and inaction—that is,
turning a blind eye toward a conspicuous practice—in a pervasively regulated industry is difficult to draw. It is also potentially troublesome from a
political perspective. The fact that state law permits casinos to exclude players considered to be an economic threat reveals the state's interest as a de
facto participant in the gambling business. It also reinforces the state's vital
economic interest in ensuring that casinos are on the winning side of the
gaming equation, even to the detriment of particular citizens.[72]

It strains logic to assert that permitting casinos to adopt exclusionary
practices reinforces consumer confidence in the fairness of the gaming industry. A New Jersey court considering a similar claim by Uston raised these
points.

> The exclusion of persons who can play the licensed games to their advan-
> tage may diminish public confidence in the fairness of casino gaming. To
> the extent persons not counting cards would be mistakenly excluded,
> public confidence might be further diminished. However, the right of the
> casinos to have the rules drawn so as to allow some reasonable profit
> must also be recognized in any realistic assessment. The Commission
> should consider the potentially broad ramifications of excluding card
> counters before it seeks to promulgate such a rule. Fairness and the in-
> tegrity of casino gaming are the touchstones.[73]

Regulators in New Jersey have taken a different approach than Nevada.
Rather than allowing casinos to exclude card counters, New Jersey allows
casinos to take special measures to address the economic threat of card

counters, including reshuffling cards, increasing the number of decks being played, limiting the number of hands that may be played at one time, and lowering betting limits for suspected card counters.[74] However, under either approach, card counters are still not treated the same as other gamblers who lack their skills; the economic interests of the casinos triumph over a skilled player's potential advantage.

CREDIT RULES

Credit is ubiquitous in commerce, and it is commonly understood that granting credit facilitates consumer spending. However, easy access to credit in the emotion-laden environment of a casino also presents the potential for patrons to exacerbate their losses, perhaps to the point of excess. Gaming experts have indicated that credit may account for more than half of the revenues generated in Nevada's larger casinos and that it is an especially critical business practice for casinos that compete for the patronage of foreign gamblers.[75]

Oddly enough, prior to 1983 Nevada followed the common law rule that gambling debts were legally unenforceable.[76] Nevertheless, the industry was apparently quite successful in collecting debts outside the judicial process. Experts in this area estimated a historical collection rate of 95 percent.[77] However, more permissive credit rules in New Jersey, which permitted the enforcement of gambling debts, caused the Nevada gaming industry to seek changes in its laws to ensure that Nevada gamblers would continue to view their debts as valid.[78] The current provision states in part: "A credit instrument accepted on or after June 1, 1983, and the debt that the credit instrument represents are valid and may be enforced by legal process."[79] In order to cut off potential defenses to gambling debts based on compulsive gambling, the statute also provides in part that

A patron's claim of having a mental or behavioral disorder involving gambling:

(a) Is not a defense in any action by a licensee or a person acting on behalf of a licensee to enforce a credit instrument or the debt that the credit instrument represents.

(b) Is not a valid counterclaim to such an action.[80]

Nevada's statutory abrogation of its common law doctrine undoubtedly favors the commercial viability of casinos. The board still regulates a casino's credit practices, including requirements for information gathering to ensure a patron's creditworthiness and to prevent the use of credit as a money-laundering device.[81] It also regulates collection practices to prevent collection abuse.[82] Otherwise, the responsibility for using credit within one's means lies solely with the patron.

While casinos may use the courts to collect debts from their patrons, patrons with claims against casinos for unpaid jackpots or other winnings are required instead to participate in an administrative proceeding before the board or, in cases under five hundred dollars, before a hearing examiner appointed by the board.[83] The statute here essentially provides that, outside of the statutorily prescribed procedures for administrative review, "gaming debts that are not evidenced by a credit instrument are void and unenforceable and do not give rise to any administrative or civil cause of action."[84] After participation in this administrative process, patrons or licensees who are aggrieved by a final decision of the board may petition for judicial review.[85]

Market forces reinforce a casino's interest in paying off jackpots or other winnings, as contrary practices would tend to dry up the market for patrons rather quickly.[86] A casino that fails to pay off a valid jackpot also places its license at risk, which creates an additional disincentive for refusing payment.[87] However, in a rare litigated case where a casino refused to pay, the letter of the law was applied in favor of the casino. This case involved a nineteen-year-old who was lucky enough to win a slot machine jackpot in excess of $1 million. His luck ended, however, when the casino discovered that he was a minor ineligible to gamble under Nevada law.[88] The casino asserted his minority as a contractual defense to payment, claiming that a minor could not form a valid contract under Nevada law. The board agreed with the casino, as did both the Nevada Supreme Court and the Ninth Circuit.[89]

On one hand, this result tends to reinforce government efforts to prevent minors from gambling. By removing the incentive of a large jackpot, a minor might well be deterred from trying to play at all. On the other hand, if undetected minors can win smaller jackpots that do not generate attention from the casino, they might still seek to play despite this ruling. A casino benefits from losses incurred by minors, just as it benefits from the losses of other players.

However, allowing minors to gamble potentially subjects casino operators to disciplinary actions, including fines and the possibility of losing a gaming license.[90] The threat of discipline encourages casino efforts to monitor and exclude minor patrons. That incentive would be strengthened if casinos were also obligated to pay off winnings and to restore losses incurred by minor patrons. This less restrictive approach reflected in current law appears to favor the casino's economic interests.

PROBLEM GAMBLING

Direct efforts to address concerns about the excesses of gambling patrons—including the effects of compulsive gambling—are virtually nonexistent in Nevada. In 1998, the Gaming Control Commission adopted regulations that required its licensees to take some minimal steps toward concerns about problem gambling. First, the regulations require licensees to post information for its patrons.

> Each licensee shall post or provide in conspicuous places in or near gaming and cage areas and cash dispensing machines located in gaming areas written materials concerning the nature and symptoms of problem gambling and the toll-free telephone number of the National Council on Problem Gambling or a similar entity approved by the chairman of the board that provides information and referral services for problem gamblers.[91]

Second, licensees are also required to conduct training programs for their employees about the nature of problem gambling. The purpose of such training appears limited, however, as the regulation specifically provides that "[t]his subsection shall not be construed to require employees of licensees to identify problem gamblers."[92]

Third, certain licensees are required to develop procedures for self-regulation by patrons: "Each licensee that engages in the issuance of credit, check cashing, or the direct mail marketing of gaming opportunities, shall implement a program . . . that allows patrons to self-limit their access to the issuance of credit, check cashing, or direct mail marketing by that licensee."[93]

Public appropriations to treat problem gambling have been nonexistent in Nevada, as this problem has been left in private hands. However, in 2005, Governor Kenny Guinn proposed an appropriation of two hundred thousand dollars over two years to help create a problem gambling program.[94] Although the industry privately funds programs to help problem gamblers, public funding has not previously addressed this issue.[95] Critics point out that the amount of this appropriation pales in relation to the taxes generated from gambling (which, as noted previously, exceed $800 million annually). However, only seventeen states provide some funding for problem gambling.[96] Thus, Nevada's prior funding practices (or lack thereof) do not seem that unusual by this standard.

Although regulations recognize the existence of problem gambling, they do very little to interfere with the business practices of the casinos and the putative freedom of patrons to make their own decisions about how much to lose. Nevada's regulatory approach requires a high level of personal responsibility among gamblers for their own choices. Such an approach is consistent with the business goals of casino operators, particularly when high rollers (so-called whales), who are often from foreign countries, constitute a specific and highly profitable segment among gambling patrons. (As one commentator has quipped, "In Las Vegas, compulsive gambling is defined as 'devoted casino customer.'")[97]

Nevada law provides separate licensing provisions applicable to so-called international gaming salons, which require a minimum of five hundred thousand dollars as a cash deposit or line of credit as a prerequisite to admission[98] and a minimum wager of five hundred dollars.[99] Salon operators must limit admission to those who meet approved financial criteria,[100] which tends to ensure that patrons who participate in this high-stakes environment can afford potentially big losses. Limitations on losses certainly seem incongruous within such an environment. However, patrons with more modest means can undoubtedly still lose more than they can afford without entering an international gaming salon.

The Gaming Commission has taken some steps toward constraining the methods of payment accepted in electronic devices used in gaming, which tend to limit excessive losses by those of more modest means. In 1995, the state legislature adopted a statute that proscribed electronic transfers from a financial institution directly to a gaming device through a credit card.[101] However, the statute was silent as to transfers using debit cards. In May 2003, the Gaming Commission rejected a plan to allow ATM cards in slot machines.[102] The Gaming Control Board recommended further study of the impact of using ATM cards on compulsive gambling, and the commission acquiesced in this recommendation.[103] The commission has also enacted a rule prohibiting the location of an ATM within a designated gaming area of a restricted licensee.[104] Such a restriction might also tend to limit impulse gambling at these locations.

Nevada's casino-friendly rules appear to have been quite effective at developing a successful model for generating economic benefits from the gaming industry. Gaming taxes, which make up nearly 20 percent of state revenues, provide an important source for public funds. Nevada imposes no income taxes on individuals or corporations, but it does have a sales tax, which generates a share of state revenues that is comparable to gaming taxes.[105] Given the substantial dependence on tourism in this economy, it is likely that tourists pay a substantial share of these taxes.

Local taxes in Nevada also appear quite modest. According to one study, a family of four living in Las Vegas and earning $100,000 per year paid an average of $4,217 in state and local taxes, which is well below the national median figure of $8,896.[106] By comparison, that same family in Omaha, Nebraska—a city without legalized casino gambling—paid $8,635.[107] Nevertheless, the tourist-oriented model achieved in Nevada, and particularly in the destination resorts of Las Vegas, has proved difficult to replicate in other venues. Other states have chosen to take slightly different approaches to regulating casinos, which are discussed in the following chapter.

8. Casino Regulation in Other States

Prospects for tourism, economic renewal, and tax relief have provided the impetus for other states beyond Nevada to legalize and regulate casino gambling. New Jersey was the first to pursue this course, approving a constitutional amendment in 1976 to permit casinos in Atlantic City.[1] New Jersey casinos were operational two years later, providing legal competition to the casinos that had long enjoyed an effective monopoly in the United States.

More than a decade later, casino gambling began to expand in the Midwest. Nostalgia for the halcyon days of riverboats and the untamed West provided the model for distinguishing casinos in this region from those in Nevada and New Jersey. In 1989, Iowa became the first midwestern state to legalize riverboat casinos, which policymakers hoped would draw tourists and alleviate economic stagnation in the agricultural and manufacturing sectors of its economy.[2] Other states in the Mississippi River valley, including Illinois, Missouri, Louisiana, and Mississippi, soon followed with riverboat gambling of their own, creating energetic interstate competition for casino patrons.

Land-based operations sprang up in South Dakota, which added limited-stakes casinos in 1989 in the tourist town of Deadwood.[3] Colorado followed suit by enacting laws in 1991 to permit limited gaming in the tourist communities of Cripple Creek, Blackhawk, and Central City.[4] All of these destinations focused on tourist nostalgia for the Old West and further distinguished their brand of gambling by maintaining a limited stakes variety.

Other eastern states decided to cash in on the consumer demand for gambling. Rhode Island, Delaware, and West Virginia added casino-style gambling to their racetracks in an effort to shore up an ailing horse-racing industry. New Mexico added racinos in 1999, and New York followed this trend in 2004.

Pennsylvania also enacted legislation in 2004 that would allow slot machines across the state, with openings expected in 2006.[5] Florida voters likewise paved the way in 2004 by approving a constitutional amendment that would allow slot machines at racetracks in Miami-Dade and Broward Counties.[6] Table 8.1 lists all states with commercial casinos or racinos (i.e., racetrack-based facilities with slot machines or similar games) in 2004, along with associated operations and AGR.

In these states regulatory approaches toward casino gaming share many common features, which borrow heavily from the earlier experiences in Nevada. Licensing is a common central feature of control, and background investigations are a prerequisite to the granting of a casino license. In this sense, licensing provides the important assurance for the public that the casino industry is not tainted by an association with criminal elements.[7] Regulations also affect the fairness of games, the exclusion of minors, and the collection of applicable taxes.[8]

States have also adopted variations from Nevada's regulatory model, as

TABLE 8.1.   Commercial casino/racino operations by state (2004)

	Legalized Year	Opening Year	Number of Operations	2004 AGR Rank	2004 AGR (in millions of dollars)
Colorado	1990	1991	46	11	726
Delaware*	1994	1995	3	12	553
Illinois	1990	1991	9	6	1,718
Indiana	1993	1995	10	5	2,229
Iowa	1989	1991	13	8	1,401
Louisiana	1991	1993	18	4	2,442
Michigan	1996	1999	3	9	1,189
Mississippi	1990	1992	29	3	2,781
Missouri	1993	1994	11	7	1,473
Nevada**	1931	1931	258	1	10,562
New Jersey	1976	1978	12	2	4,807
New Mexico*	1997	1999	5	15	150
New York*	2001	2004	4	14	192
Rhode Island*	1992	1992	2	13	384
South Dakota	1989	1989	36	16	78
West Virginia*	1994	1994	4	10	882

Source: American Gaming Association.

*Racinos Only

**Excludes operations with less than $1 million AGR.

they have sought to adapt gambling to their particular social and economic needs. Variations have commonly involved restricting the location of gambling operations, imposing betting or loss limits, and requiring programs to address concerns about problem gamblers. Channels for distributing government revenues from gaming also differ among the states. Though these revenue features do not directly affect gaming itself, they potentially affect the structure of political support for casino gaming. Given deeply rooted antagonism toward casinos in many communities, these changes have proved highly significant in engendering local support for expanded gaming.

Although a comprehensive review of regulation in all commercial casino states is beyond the scope of this chapter, a brief look at regulatory variation among them provides valuable insight into the nature of this industry and the manner in which states have adapted their legal and economic structures for gambling in their communities. It also provides an interesting backdrop for examining the political forces at work in this environment, including dynamic forces of interstate competition. Regulatory trends seem to be moving in favor of practices that enhance the profitability of the industry, with only modest efforts toward addressing effects of problem gambling.

We begin with New Jersey, the largest of Nevada's land-based casino competitors. We then turn to an extended discussion of Iowa, which provides an interesting case study of how a kinder, gentler form of gambling gave way to more industry-friendly practices in the face of interstate competition for gambling dollars. Two other states with geographical constraints on their casino facilities, Missouri and Mississippi, merit brief discussion for their variations in casino regulation. Finally, we conclude with a look at the tourist model adopted in South Dakota, the smallest of these commercial casino states.

NEW JERSEY

New Jersey's state constitution was amended in 1976 to allow the legislature to authorize "gambling houses or casinos."[9] Among other things, this constitutional amendment limited the scope of legalized gambling to the confines of Atlantic City, a long-standing tourist destination that had fallen into disrepair.[10] New Jersey voters apparently found this constraint acceptable, as they had defeated a previous referendum in 1974 that would have allowed state-owned casinos anywhere in the state with consent from local voters.[11]

This amendment was not based solely on economic development but also on more lofty goals of assisting elderly and disabled citizens with the tax revenues from these enterprises. The amendment specifically required any enabling legislation to restrict the use of revenues from gaming as follows:

> State revenues derived therefrom to be applied solely for the purpose of providing funding for reductions in property taxes, rental, telephone, gas, electric, and municipal utilities charges of eligible senior citizens and disabled residents of the State, and for additional or expanded health services or benefits or transportation services or benefits to eligible senior citizens and disabled residents, in accordance with such formulae as the Legislature shall by law provide.[12]

Targeting casino revenues toward a visible and popular end, rather than merely adding a source of funds for general revenues, might have been helpful in generating popular support for a constitutional change.

In response to this constitutional amendment, the New Jersey legislature adopted the Casino Control Act, which forms the basis for casino regulation. The stated policies and purposes attending the act emphasize the potential for casinos to bring economic development and support to the tourist, resort, and convention industry of the state. However, these policies and purposes also attempted to carve out for New Jersey a different atmosphere for gaming from that in "other jurisdictions" (i.e., Nevada).

> Restricting the issuance of casino licenses to major hotel and convention facilities is designed to assure that the existing nature and tone of the hospitality industry in New Jersey and in Atlantic City is preserved, and that the casino rooms licensed pursuant to the provisions of this act are always offered and maintained as an integral element of such hospitality facilities, rather than as the industry unto themselves that they have become in other jurisdictions.[13]

This goal of linking casino gambling to the hospitality industry in Atlantic City suggests that gambling was originally intended as an ancillary form of entertainment for venturing tourists. However, it is doubtful whether this goal has been realized, as illustrated by a comparison with a sister gaming city—Las Vegas. As of 2000, Atlantic City and Las Vegas both generated approximately $4.3 billion in gaming revenues. However, Las Vegas generated another $4.3 billion in other nongaming revenues, while the comparable amount in Atlantic City was only $0.4 billion—a mere $12 per patron.[14]

The geographical proximity of Atlantic City to other major metropolitan areas, including New York, Philadelphia, and Washington, D.C., has made it a popular destination for commuters. Census data for 2000 indicate that approximately 25 million adults live within 150 miles of the city.[15] Despite comparable figures for Atlantic City and Las Vegas gaming revenues, Atlantic City has fewer than 12,000 hotel rooms, as compared with over 120,000 hotel rooms in Las Vegas.[16] Over 98 percent of visitors to Atlantic City casinos arrive by car or bus.[17]

Restricting casinos to Atlantic City, rather than allowing them throughout the state, potentially served another legislative purpose besides redevelopment: it made access to casino gambling less convenient for New Jersey residents. Restricting casinos to the environs of a coastal city known as a tourist destination would not create easy and ubiquitous access to casino gambling commonly linked to problem gambling behavior.[18] Targeting visitors rather than local patrons creates a more attractive model for gambling, as new dollars are brought into the jurisdiction and consequences from problem gambling are likely to return home with the visitors.

Despite this focus, policymakers eventually realized the New Jersey residents could also be affected by casinos, as well as other forms of gambling available in the state. According to the 2000 census, Atlantic County, in which Atlantic City is located, had about 252,000 residents, and about one-fourth of them were under the age of eighteen.[19] When counties that border Atlantic County are included, the total population balloons to nearly 2.2 million.[20] These New Jersey residents living in close proximity to the casinos in Atlantic City meant local patronage and the potential for problem gambling.

The legislature passed a bill in 2001 to create a mechanism for problem gamblers to exclude themselves voluntarily from a casino.[21] In 2002, this self-exclusion program was expanded to include other gambling venues, including racetracks and off-track betting facilities.[22] The program entails fairly rigorous requirements for participation. An individual seeking exclusion is required to personally appear in state offices located in Atlantic City or Trenton in order to submit a form with pertinent information requesting exclusion for either one year, five years, or a lifetime.[23] The person submitting the request is also required to acknowledge the following statement:

I am voluntarily requesting exclusion from all gaming activities at all New Jersey licensed casinos and simulcasting facilities because I am a problem gambler. I certify that the information that I have provided above is true and accurate, and that I have read and understand and agree to the waiver and release included with this request for self-exclusion. I am aware that my signature below authorizes the Casino Control Commission to direct all New Jersey casino licensees to restrict my gaming activities in accordance with this request and, unless I have requested to be excluded for life, until such time as the Commission removes my name from the self-exclusion list in response to my written request to terminate my voluntary self-exclusion. I am aware and agree that during any period of self-exclusion, I shall not collect any winnings or recover any losses resulting from any gaming activity at all licensed casinos and simulcasting facilities, and that any money or thing of value obtained by me from, or owed to me by, a casino licensee as a result of wagers made by me while on the self-exclusion list shall be subject to forfeiture.[24]

The self-exclusion list is maintained by the Casino Control Commission and distributed to every casino licensee.[25] A photograph of each self-excluded person, as well as a description of that person, is also provided to each licensee for the apparent purpose of aiding in the identification of self-excluded persons who nevertheless attempt to gamble.[26] The identity of those on the list is treated as confidential information, except that it may be disclosed to appropriate casino employees, including those of other licensees in Atlantic City, to assist in enforcement efforts.[27] Licensees bear no liability for disclosure or publication of the identity of members on the list that is not willfully unlawful.[28]

Licensees are required to develop procedures that will ensure that gaming privileges are not extended to self-excluded persons.[29] They must also ensure that credit is not extended to them; that no complimentary goods and services are provided; and that no solicitations, mailings, promotions, or other promotional materials are sent to them.[30] In the event that self-excluded persons do gamble, they are not allowed to collect their winnings or recover their losses.[31] In the event that such persons do collect winnings, they are subject to forfeiture to the commission.[32]

Licensees are statutorily exempt from any liability associated with failing to withhold gaming privileges from a self-excluded person who is allowed to gamble.[33] Although the losses incurred by an excluded person who succeeds in gambling are potentially subject to forfeiture, that possibility occurs only if there was "willful violation" of the self-exclusion regulations.[34] Thus, the economic incentives for vigorous enforcement of the self-exclusion provisions are limited indeed.

These provisions have questionable significance in addressing the concerns of problem gambling. As of January 2003, after more than one year of this program, only 139 people had signed up for self-exclusion, and 10 of these had dropped out, apparently due to the elapse of the one-year period in their exclusion request.[35] Some critics cite a lack of publicity as responsible for the weak response.[36]

This plan also appears vulnerable to other criticism. First, in order to be placed on the self-exclusion list, the patron must admit that he or she is a "problem gambler."[37] Patrons may associate problem gambling with "pathological gambling," which is listed in the DSM-IV.[38] Some people may be deterred from participating in the program because they associate it with admitting to a mental illness or disorder. Moreover, such an admission may be inaccurate for some people, who wish to be excluded before problem gambling behavior has manifested itself. For example, a patron may suffer from depression or manic episodes that lead to gambling behavior that is not considered pathological gambling but might lead to unwanted losses.[39]

Other disorders, such as alcoholism or compulsive shopping, could potentially be assisted from a self-exclusion program. A recovering alcoholic might wish to be excluded from the local pub, and a compulsive shopper might wish to be excluded from the mall.[40] However, popular support for government programs in these areas would appear dubious. Enlisting private business firms to assist adults in monitoring their own behavior is likely to prove unpopular, especially when such assistance is contrary to the firm's economic interests. The ubiquity of opportunities to engage in common activities like shopping or drinking—for example, shopping centers, bars, and liquor stores—also makes it impractical to disseminate information about the affected person so that a business could comply. Moreover, private businesses not accustomed to extensive regulation might resent any requirement that they expend their resources in such a manner.

The comparatively controlled and limited environment of casino gaming establishments makes enforcement of a self-exclusion list plausible in this context. However, as a practical matter, monitoring and excluding patrons may still present a challenge for those who don't utilize players' clubs or electronic payment mechanisms, which provide reliable identification without significant surveillance efforts.

For a protection short of self-exclusion, a patron may also request suspension of credit privileges at a casino.[41] The effect of such a suspension is less significant than exclusion, as it does not affect one's ability to gamble. Such requests may be submitted by mail as well as in person, and they are effective for a minimum of thirty days and thereafter until a request for reinstatement is accepted by the commission.[42] However, the ubiquity of modern credit means that credit can be accessed through other providers, thus allowing a determined patron to gamble excessively if he or she chooses to circumvent the ban on casino credit. Nevertheless, suspending casino credit may erect a barrier to impulsive behavior that could, in some cases, prevent excessive losses.

IOWA

Iowa legalized casino gaming in 1989 by permitting low-stakes riverboat gambling on the Mississippi River and on certain inland waters.[43] One commentator described the regulatory structure that emerged from this legislation as focusing on these six attributes:

> First, that wagering be for low stakes and that no member of the public suffers substantial losses. Second, that proceeds from gaming benefit the public good. Third, that Iowa regulate gaming. Fourth, that gaming be associated with activities that promote tourism. Fifth, that gaming operators contribute to the state economy by hiring Iowa residents and using and promoting Iowa goods. Sixth, that gaming raise tax revenue.[44]

Although most of these attributes may still be found in the current gaming industry in Iowa, competitive pressures have eliminated the "low stakes" requirement and substantially diluted any regulatory orientation toward protecting the public from substantial losses. In this sense, Iowa provides an interesting case study about how well-intentioned regulations eventually fell by the wayside in the pursuit of greater profits for the industry and tax revenues for state and local governments.

The gaming laws enacted in 1989 ensured that any casino gaming operation would be quite different from that which would be found in either Las Vegas or Atlantic City. First, real vessels were required: prospective licensees were required to "develop, and as nearly as practicable, recreate boats that resemble Iowa's riverboat history."[45] Those boats—known as "excursion gambling boats"—had to live up to their name by actually embarking on gambling excursions for a minimum number of days each year.[46] Gambling activities were restricted to no more than 30 percent of the available square footage of an excursion boat.[47] Licensees were also required to ensure that Iowa goods and services were used in operations, and a portion of the boat was required to be reserved "for the promotion and sale of arts, crafts, and gifts native to and made in Iowa."[48]

As in other jurisdictions, minors were prohibited from gambling. However, minority was initially defined at eighteen years old rather than twenty-one.[49] The legislature vacillated on this definition over the next few years, as the age of minority was increased to twenty-one in a bill passed a few days later in 1989.[50] The minimum gambling age was reduced once again to eighteen in 1991[51] and then increased to twenty-one in 1994,[52] where it remains today.[53]

In addition to these regulations affecting the business operations of riverboat casinos, the legislation also provided strict wagering and loss limitations. Casino patrons were allowed to wager a maximum of five dollars per play, with a maximum loss limit of two hundred dollars per excursion.[54] A requirement that all gambling be conducted with tokens or chips, rather than money, made it feasible to enforce these limits.[55] Moreover, during the "excursion season" (April through October)[56] gambling was restricted to such times when the boat actually went on an excursion; in the off-season, the gaming commission established rules for entry and exit that would support the loss limitations.[57] Licensees were also prohibited from lending money to patrons for gambling purposes, thus eliminating a source of credit that could lead to losses beyond what the patron could afford.[58]

This approach geared toward protecting gamblers from excessive losses did not last for long. Building a gaming industry on the excursion boat model presented considerable risks in an environment of mobile facilities and interstate competition. By 1993, three of the five riverboats that had been licensed for the Mississippi River had pulled up anchor and left the state.[59] News reports indicate that one of these boats, the *Dubuque Casino Belle,* was profitable for its first year of operation, but patronage declined as gamblers chose to visit facilities in other states with more liberal betting limits and regulations.[60] Patrons were apparently voting with their feet, and they apparently didn't like the state making decisions about how much or when they could bet.

In 1994, riverboats returned when the Iowa legislature dropped the loss and betting limits and Iowa counties with riverboats approved gaming rules that were friendlier to the business interests of casinos.[61] The legislature responded to pressure from both gambling interests and local government officials by taking several measures that would enhance the competitive position of Iowa boats against competitors in other states, including Illinois. Local governments lobbied for the removal of loss limitations because they wanted additional local revenues from a projected increase in their share of casino profits to address needs imposed by catastrophic flood damage along the Mississippi River valley.[62]

In addition to eliminating the wagering and loss limitation, the 1994 legislation also eased other restrictions. Though riverboat excursions were still required, requirements for a specific duration and limited access by patrons during other times when the boats were docked were eliminated, as they were no longer needed to support the loss limits. Thus, patrons were free to come and go from the boats as they pleased whenever the boats were docked.[63] The availability of slot machines was also expanded from the boats to dog and horse racetracks, which had previously been limited to pari-mutuel wagering on races.[64] As a protective measure, however, casinos were also prohibited from accepting credit cards for gambling purposes.[65] Later rules would also prohibit any form of electronic dispensing of cash or credit on the gambling floor.[66]

This 1994 legislation did not reflect a situation where the state government imposed its will on local citizens who had previously approved a kinder, gentler form of gambling. The law required local citizens to weigh in on these changes through a referendum process.[67] Thus, the removal of the loss and wagering limitations, as well as the expansion of slot machines into dog- and horse-racing tracks, required the approval of local voters, and such approval was readily given.

Local voting is an important feature of Iowa's regulatory system. The state racing and gaming commission possesses extensive powers to license and regulate casino gambling on excursion boats.[68] These powers even extend to setting payout levels for authorized games and slot machines.[69] However, the commission's power to award a license is predicated upon local voter authorization for casino gambling.[70] In the event that a local referendum fails, a license may not be issued and existing licenses may be revoked. Another referendum may not be held again for at least eight years.[71] After approval, periodic referenda to continue legalized gambling must also occur.[72] Iowa's history indicates that counties have sometimes rejected legalized gaming under similar provisions.[73] However, once gaming has become operational, voters have given overwhelming approval to subsequent referenda.[74]

Another feature of the 1994 legislation was the expansion of slot machines at racetracks. This created two types of casinos in Iowa: racetrack casinos ("racinos"), which could offer slot machines along with horse or dog racing but not other games, and excursion gambling boats, which could offer slot machines and other approved games but no wagering on races.[75] While the repeal of loss limitations alleviated the financial stress on the riverboats, the prospect of slot machines at racetracks was designed to improve the financial picture of racing establishments.

The plight of Prairie Meadows, a horse-racing facility financed substantially by bonds issued by Polk County, was apparently an important influence on the decision to expand gambling via slot machines. The original construction of this facility in 1987 was financed by bonds guaranteed by Polk County, and that guarantee was soon called upon as the track fell short of its financial projections.[76] Losses mounted in this facility, and the county eventually became the owner of the track in 1993, issuing general obligation bonds to finance this acquisition.[77]

By the time slot machines had been approved at racetracks in 1994, debt at Prairie Meadows totaled $89.3 million.[78] Within two years after opening, this entire debt was repaid.[79] Profits from expanded slot machines thus extracted Polk County taxpayers from a difficult financial situation without raising local taxes. However, it made slot machine gambling more accessible to patrons in the central part of the state, which was not otherwise served by excursion boats. Moreover, it involved county government as an owner of a gambling facility (albeit as a landlord)—which was quite different from the typical role of local governments in other facilities.

Iowa law provides an ownership and tax structure that ensures that local communities obtain some direct benefits from casino revenues. Gaming licenses must be held by a "qualified sponsoring organization,"[80] which is essentially a nonprofit corporation that is eligible for tax-exempt status.[81] The sponsoring organization may contract with another firm to manage the operation, and this firm is also subject to licensure and approval of the gaming commission.[82] Sponsoring organizations are liable for taxes on admissions for each person entering an excursion boat, which are payable to the gaming commission.[83] Cities and counties in which an excursion boat is docked may also impose an admission fee of not more than fifty cents, which is payable to their respective general fund.[84] Licensees must also pay additional assessments to cover licensing costs and other costs of criminal investigations, which are payable to the state's general fund.[85]

The main tax burden on the licensees, however, is the wagering tax. This tax applies on a sliding scale to AGR,[86] ranging from 5 percent on the first $1 million to 10 percent on the next $2 million to 22 percent on amounts over $3 million.[87] Prior to amendment in 2004, a separate, higher tax rate was imposed on AGR at racetrack enclosures, which increased by 2 percent each year, from 22 percent in 1997 to as much as 36 percent in 2004.[88] Racetrack interests successfully challenged this differential tax system in the Iowa Supreme Court, but that ruling was subsequently reversed by the U.S. Supreme Court, which upheld the differential tax rates as a proper legislative classification under the U.S. Constitution.[89] However, the Iowa Supreme Court subsequently persisted in its position that the scheme was unconstitutional, resting its decision on state constitutional grounds.[90] The legislature subsequently changed the differential to make it smaller, limiting the upper level to 24 percent for racetrack enclosures without competing riverboat casinos in the same jurisdiction.[91]

Of this wagering tax, 1 percent is designated to be shared by the city and county government in which the facility is located.[92] One-half of 1 percent (raised from three-tenths of 1 percent in 2004) is designated for a state "gambling treatment fund."[93] The remainder is allocated to the general fund.[94] Thus, most of the gaming tax revenue from casinos finds its way into the central coffers of the state rather than into local government hands.

Of the amounts allocated to the general fund, totals in excess of $60 million are supposed to be dedicated to other state programs designed for the development of recreation, tourism, infrastructure, and schools.[95] For the fiscal year ending June 30, 2003, the state's share of these wagering taxes from riverboats was $120,872,266 and the corresponding amount from racetracks was $57,835,883.[96] Cities and counties reaped a total just short of $10 million, and the gambling treatment program received just under $3 million.[97] Of course, local governments also received additional property taxes and other tax receipts associated with the operation of the gaming business in their locale.[98]

This management structure, which leaves qualified sponsoring organizations in control of gaming, makes it possible for the legislature to impose this additional requirement upon such organizations:

> A qualified sponsoring organization licensed to operate gambling games under this chapter shall distribute the receipts of all gambling games, less reasonable expenses, charges, taxes, fees, and deductions allowed under this chapter, as winnings to players or participants or shall distribute the receipts for educational, civic, public, charitable, patriotic, or religious uses.[99]

A special rule for racetrack operations with debt requires such operations to pay off debt first before engaging in charitable distributions.[100] Racetrack operations may also use receipts from their slot machines to supplement purses paid to dog or horse owners, thus supporting that segment of the racing industry.[101]

Qualified sponsoring organizations are expressly prohibited from making political contributions or other kindred payments.[102] However, this is not to say that they lack the power to affect public opinion about gaming through the distribution of their charitable grants. For example, as of 2002, the Iowa West Foundation, holder of licenses for three casinos in the Council Bluffs area in the far western part of the state, had paid out over $106 million in grants.[103] Through the first half of 2003 alone, it paid out over $7.9 million in grants to cities, counties, and charitable organizations in western Iowa.[104] Such grants are powerful public relations tools, as the libraries, swimming pools, community centers, fire stations, and other highly visible public projects are funded with gaming dollars.

The state also utilizes gaming revenues through other conspicuous programs, which include the Vision Iowa and the Community Attraction and

Tourism (CAT) funds. These funds were established by the legislature in 2000 for the purpose of providing funding for construction projects that support recreation, entertainment, and cultural activities.[105] Both of these funds are administered by a thirteen-member board, who are appointed by the governor.[106] An additional fund for school infrastructure is administered by the Iowa Department of Education.[107]

The Vision Iowa fund receives $15 million annually from wagering tax revenues, while the CAT fund receives $12.5 million.[108] These funds are structured to share the resources generated from wagering taxes throughout the state, including counties and cities without gambling facilities. One-third of the CAT fund revenues are specifically reserved for cities with populations below ten thousand and for the bottom one-third of counties by population.[109] Through these funds, Iowa achieves a redistribution of economic benefits from gambling to counties without gambling facilities—or the population base to support one. Residents of these counties can thus point to a visible community infrastructure improvement—such as a swimming pool, theater, or community center—that would perhaps have been unaffordable without gambling dollars. Such practices would appear to kindle additional political support for gaming in the state.

As for the less visible effects of gambling—namely, the social problems associated with it—the state's primary commitment appears to be the resources committed to the gambling treatment fund. Historically, the legislature had diverted a substantial portion of this fund to other uses, including substance abuse, wellness programs, children's programs, and the Iowa Veterans home.[110] In 2004, the legislature expanded this fund by raising the total cap from commercial casino taxes to $6 million, with an additional $500,000 from the Iowa lottery.[111] This expansion addressed concerns about redirected funds and the level of commitment to gambling treatment, which studies have shown to be quite effective for gamblers who seek it.[112] Redirected funds required cuts in advertising, making it difficult to reach the intended audience of problem gamblers.[113] The head of the state gambling treatment program estimates that twenty thousand Iowans have severe gambling problems, with an additional forty to sixty thousand experiencing problems that could escalate without treatment.[114]

In 2004, Iowa expanded its approach to problem gambling by enacting a self-exclusion provision similar to that used in New Jersey.[115] Prior to this law, the Iowa Gaming Association supported a voluntary self-exclusion provision applicable to people in treatment for problem gambling, but this approach was without the force of law.[116] This law does not specify the process but only requires licensees to come up with such a process. Through its trade organization, the industry came up with an exclusion program that involves an irrevocable, lifetime exclusion from all properties in Iowa.[117] The exclusion form also points out that when signing up for this program "the ultimate responsibility to limit access to any Iowa casino remains mine alone." It also contains an extensive release from any liability associated with a failure to comply with the ban. An excluded gambler must attest to the following statement:

> I will not seek to hold the Casino or any other Iowa casino liable in any way should I continue gambling at any casino despite this exclusion request. I agree to indemnify this Casino and any other casino for any liability the casino may incur relating to this request. Specifically, I, for myself, my family members, heirs, and legal representatives hereby release and forever discharge the Casino and all other Iowa casinos, all of their direct and indirect subsidiaries, their partners, agents, employees, officers, affiliates, directors, successors, and assigns, and those with whom the Casino may lawfully share information regarding this exclusion, including the Iowa Racing and Gaming Commission and any contractor or Internet Services Provider that offers services on the behalf of these entities (collectively, the "Released Parties"), from any and all claims in law or equity that I now have or may have in the future against any or all of

TABLE 8.2.   Iowa gambling treatment fund expenditures (2001–5 (est.))[a]

Fiscal Year	Fund Revenue ($)	Program Expenditures ($)	Redirected Funds ($)
FY 2005 (est.)	6,000,000	4,310,000	1,690,000
FY 2004	3,875,436	1,970,428	1,690,000
FY 2003	3,579,350	1,714,479	1,690,000
FY 2002	3,503,005	1,714,443	2,057,298
FY 2001	3,261,636	1,898,762	1,874,750

[a]See Iowa Gambling Treatment Fund: Revenues, Expenses, Redirects at http://www.1800betsoff.org/pdf/revenue_redirect.pdf (accessed May 16, 2005)

the Released Parties arising out of, or by reason of, the performance or non-performance of this Self-Exclusion Request, or any other matter relating to it, including the release of information contained in this form. I further agree, in consideration for the Released Parties' efforts to implement my exclusion, to indemnify and hold harmless the Released Parties to the fullest extent permitted by law for any and all liabilities, judgments, damages, and expenses of any kind, including reasonable attorneys' fees, resulting from or in connection with the performance or non-performance of this self exclusion request.[118]

The enabling statute provided that "[t]he state and any licensee . . . shall not be liable to any person for any claim which may arise from this process." However, this broad release language arguably goes beyond the statute in providing for indemnification for legal fees, including those which may test the limits of this liability exclusion.

The Iowa statute focuses on incentives for the gambler rather than on incentives for the casino to enforce the self-exclusion ban. It imposes a sensible requirement that casinos must pay out any winnings by an excluded person to the gambling treatment fund instead of to the winning patron.[119] This creates a disincentive for the excluded patron to stray back to the casino for more betting. However, given the likelihood that players lose over time, the casino nevertheless benefits from such play to the extent that they may keep the excluded patron's losses.

Iowa regulations also require disclosure of the average payout percentage of slot machines.[120] Such disclosure reflects some movement toward regulatory models adopted in other areas, such as tobacco and alcohol, where information and/or warnings of risks are presented as an attempt to ameliorate harms to citizens from such activities. However, no empirical studies indicate whether this disclosure is effective at reducing any incidence of problem gambling behavior. Considerable variation may nevertheless exist among machines grouped together for averaging purposes. Moreover, a casino manager might advertise low payouts for slot machines with small wagers and high payout percentages on high-wager machines. In this way, patrons may be coaxed into betting at higher-value machines, which, over time, might offer a better return. In doing so, these patrons may be wagering more (and perhaps more than they can afford to lose), thus increasing house profits.

Finally, Iowa's approach to interstate competition also merits discussion. Iowa's casinos in Council Bluffs are within a metropolitan statistical area that spans eight counties, including four counties in the neighboring state of Nebraska with no legalized casino gaming opportunities. Although Nebraska permits noncasino gambling, including a lottery, pari-mutuel betting on horse racing, and keno, casino gambling is prohibited. It is well known that Nebraska residents patronize Council Bluffs casinos, and this fact was highly touted in efforts to legalize casinos in Nebraska funded by an organization known as Keep the Money in Nebraska.[121]

In November 2004, Nebraska voters considered ballot initiatives to provide a legal framework for casino gambling. These legalization initiatives were ultimately defeated, thus allowing Iowa to continue tapping the Nebraska market without in-state competition.[122] However, in anticipation of this vote, the Iowa legislature crafted changes in its gambling laws to strengthen the industry's position in the event of cross-border competition from a Nebraska-based casino. Among other things, this legislation eliminated any requirement that excursion boats must cruise.[123] This would eliminate a competitive disadvantage to land-based facilities, such as those proposed in Nebraska.

In addition, the 2004 legislation included a rather unusual provision allowing expansion through gambling via moored barges in Council Bluffs on "the earlier of July 1, 2007, or the date any form of gambling games, as defined in this chapter, is operational in any state that is contiguous to the county where the licensee is located."[124] Since Nebraska failed to legalize casino gambling, this right to accelerate expansion did not arise. Nevertheless, this legislation signaled the government's resolve to support stiff competition in the face of future legalization efforts across the border.

The Iowa Racing and Gaming Commission approved a significant expansion to a racetrack casino in Council Bluffs early in 2005, as well as other expanded gambling venues in interior Iowa communities in May 2005.[125] Although one of these venues is near Albert Lea, Minnesota, and it may be designed to attract patronage from non-Iowans, others are located in interior counties far from state borders, which would be expected to draw patronage from Iowans. Thus, the cross-border patronage that has been fueling facilities on the eastern and western borders of the state is likely to be displaced by Iowa residents with more convenient access to gambling in nearby communities.

Not only does Iowa compete for patrons from across its borders, but its regulatory structure also attempts to source goods and services for gambling from Iowans as opposed to workers and companies outside the state.

> The [Racing and Gaming] commission shall require that an applicant utilize Iowa resources, goods, and services in the operation of an excursion gambling boat. The commission shall develop standards to assure that a substantial amount of all resources and goods used in the operation of an excursion gambling boat emanate from and are made in Iowa and that a substantial amount of all services and entertainment are provided by Iowans.[126]

Though this patent attempt to discriminate in favor of local goods is of questionable legal validity, it has nevertheless resulted in businesses establishing Iowa offices to service casino customers. This practice keeps more revenue in Iowa communities, but it compounds the political pressures for cross-border competition in Nebraska. Not only are Nebraska patrons losing money in Iowa casinos, but their businesses are also handicapped when it comes to tapping into the economic benefits from the goods and services consumed by that industry. It remains to be seen how long this political tension will continue before Nebraska, too, joins the ranks of commercial casino states.

MISSOURI

Like its neighbor Iowa, Missouri also chose a riverboat model for its casino gaming industry. Missouri voters approved a referendum allowing excursion boat gambling on the Mississippi and Missouri Rivers, subject to loss limitations of five hundred dollars per excursion, in November 1992.[127] During the following year, the legislature enacted a revised version of riverboat gambling, which changed the terms of the referendum in several respects but retained the essential features of riverboat gaming with a loss limitation of five hundred dollars per excursion.[128] The validity of this legislation was quickly challenged; under then applicable provisions of the Missouri Constitution, games of skill were permissible but games of chance were constitutionally prohibited as unlawful lotteries.[129] Since some games conducted aboard excursion boats (including slot machines) could appropriately be classified as games of chance, a portion of the enabling legislation was declared unconstitutional.[130]

This judicial development gave rise to a subsequent referendum in 1994, which allowed such games on excursion boats subject to local voter approval.[131] However, another legal challenge soon emerged, this time based on the definition of where gambling could lawfully occur. The referendum had approved games of chance "only upon the Missouri and Mississippi Rivers," and the plaintiffs claimed that this language affected the validity of gaming licenses issued for gaming facilities located on "artificial spaces" filled with river water but not contiguous to the river. The Missouri Supreme Court agreed that such facilities were not contemplated by the constitutional amendment, thus limiting riverboat gambling in the state to those facilities that are truly on the river or on water contiguous thereto.[132] Given its unique geography, this means that Missouri's casinos will be located near borders with Kansas and Nebraska on the west and Illinois on the east, with a few distributed along the Missouri River, which crosses the northern half of the state.

Despite the competitive pressures of the no-limit gambling adopted in Iowa, Missouri has continued to impose a loss limit of five hundred dollars per person per two-hour excursion period.[133] The Missouri Gaming Commission's annual report points out that Missouri is the only jurisdiction in the world that imposes a loss limitation on its patrons.[134] The commission asserts that this system puts Missouri casinos at a competitive disadvantage to their neighbors in Iowa, Kansas, and Illinois. As the commission explains:

> The reason the loss limit renders Missouri casinos less competitive is that customers do not like it. Those who use Missouri casinos find the loss limit a patronizing intrusion by government into a private business transaction. Perhaps more important to the issue of competitiveness are those who dislike the loss limit so much that they refuse to patronize Missouri casinos, choosing instead to visit casinos in neighboring jurisdictions or to gamble illegally at truck stops and private clubs.[135]

Missouri facilitates this loss limitation system through a requirement for cashless wagering—patrons are required to use tokens or chips, whether in electronic or physical form, for all gambling transactions.[136] Unlike Iowa, Missouri does not require any formal disclosure of payout ratios, but it does impose a limit that no device may pay out at less than an 80 percent rate.[137] Missouri also prohibits casinos from lending to patrons, though credit card or debit card transactions on-site, as well as check cashing, may be permitted.[138]

The Missouri Gaming Commission has also asserted that no evidence exists that the five-hundred-dollar loss limit has effectively curbed problem gambling behavior.[139] A survey of problem gamblers indicates that 90 percent agree with the commission, while about 8 percent believe the loss limit helped them.[140] Although a loss of even five hundred dollars per excursion could easily add up to significant amounts with repeated visits, such a limit may protect against large and significant wagers that could bankrupt either an individual or, if significant enough, perhaps even a casino.

The commission has also reported that fewer than 1 percent of its patrons ever buy in for the full five-hundred-dollar amount, which suggests that most patrons are unaffected by this limit.[141] Nevertheless, the fiscal impact of higher-stakes gamblers is apparently significant. The comparative win per patron (which reflects the average AGR from all patrons) visiting a Missouri casino is substantially lower than its counterpart in Illinois. For example, figures for 2000 indicate that the Missouri patron lost thirty-six dollars versus nearly sixty-seven dollars for riverboat gamblers in Illinois.[142] It thus appears that a small number of patrons may be responsible for a significant portion of casino revenues, and this loss limitation prevents Missouri casinos from capturing revenues from these patrons.

Analysts have predicted that the loss limitation alone results in more than $282 million in lost industry revenues. Moreover, the inability to compete for higher-stakes gamblers means other lost revenues, such as those attributed to facility expansions.[143] Significant political capital is apparently attached to this five-hundred-dollar limit, despite what appears to be a modest effect on the typical gambling patron.

Although the legislature appears steadfast in retaining the five-hundred-dollar limitation, it has taken other steps to enhance industry profitability by keeping it competitive with its cross-border competitors. Legislation passed in 1999 removed an artificial limitation on boarding, which required patrons to queue up for entry at specified times.[144] Patrons complained about this practice, and the legislature overturned this limitation in part to allow Missouri casinos to compete more effectively with Illinois, which had also abandoned this requirement. Though this was probably good for the casino business, it was also good for the state and local tax coffers, as it meant that higher taxes for admission fees could be imposed. Missouri imposes a two-dollar admission tax for each "cruise" period of two hours. With no barriers on entry, a patron who entered the casino a few minutes before the new cruise period and stayed three hours would thus generate three admissions taxes, whereas the previous barrier to entry would have only generated two.[145]

Legislation passed in August 2000 also enhanced industry profitability by allowing so-called vend-to-meter transactions.[146] Prior to this legislation, slot machine players were required to insert tokens for each spin. This caused considerable delay, thus reducing the volume of player wagering and ultimately industry profits. The legislation allowed players to obtain paper credits, which could then be used in slot machines instead of tokens. The commission reported this change as patron friendly: "The benefit to the patron is that they no longer have to expend the physical effort of inserting the token into the slot machine. This benefit is real when you consider it can save the patron from inserting as many as two thousand tokens [i.e., one hundred dollars played in a nickel slot machine] on one transaction."[147]

However, the commission also notes that this significantly increases player wagering and thus state tax revenues: "The average slot play per patron for the six months prior to vend-to-meter was $573 while the average slot play per patron for the last six months of the fiscal year was $679, an increase of 19%. Therefore, the annualized statewide increase in gaming revenue, assuming 22.7 million patrons and a slot hold percentage of 6.4%, is $154 million."[148] Though faster play would also mean faster problems for problem gamblers, this consideration was apparently outweighed by the goal of enhanced revenues.

Missouri has adopted a legal mechanism for voluntary self-exclusion by problem gamblers, similar to that adopted in New Jersey.[149] Individuals who seek self-exclusion are required to state that they are "problem gamblers" as a prerequisite to inclusion on the list of "disassociated persons."[150] Casinos are absolved from any liability associated with their actions in enforcing, or failing to enforce, the terms of membership on the list.[151] However, unlike New Jersey's system, which allows exclusion for periodic terms, Missouri's system requires exclusion for life.[152] The justification for this difference is presumably based on the lifelong nature of pathological gambling conditions. Moreover, listed persons are subjected to a criminal penalty for trespassing if they attempt to enter a casino facility.[153]

Like Iowa, Missouri also maintains a compulsive gamblers fund for gambling treatment, which is funded in part from gaming revenues.[154] The Port Authority of Kansas City also maintains a fund for problem gamblers, which they reportedly plan to use to fund studies of problem gambling and the effectiveness of treatment programs.[155]

The number of gambling facilities licensed in Missouri is a matter of discretion for the Missouri Gaming Commission.[156] It exercises this discretion to ensure that existing markets have the capacity to absorb new facilities without substantially impacting other operations.[157] Thus, industry profitability is a significant consideration in granting new licenses, thus reflecting the state's support for the financial well-being of an industry that contributes substantially to state coffers, albeit at the expense of some of its residents.

Recent commission decisions that have focused on expanding the St. Louis gambling market indicate an increasing focus on gaining revenues from Missouri residents. Jefferson County, which borders the St. Louis metropolitan area on the south along the Mississippi River, was characterized as an "underserved" market. Casinos in the northern part of the city, including suburban St. Charles and Maryland Heights, were drawing patrons from their local communities at two to three times the rate of those who gambled in Jefferson County. Patronage from these local residents would thus presumably increase with another facility, increasing the tax revenues contributed to state coffers.[158]

Licensing is also conditioned upon local approval in the area where the riverboat would be docked or otherwise located.[159] Local government may also submit recommendations to the commission concerning the number and identity of licensees in their area, along with the terms of any local revenue-sharing agreement with a licensee.[160] Although the bulk of gaming taxes is payable to the state,[161] local governments are entitled to 10 percent of gaming taxes plus whatever other amounts they may agree to obtain from licensees.[162] Local governments thus may exercise considerable economic muscle over the benefits they ultimately extract from licensees.

MISSISSIPPI

Mississippi has also pursued legalized casino gaming with a riverboat motif, approving enabling legislation on June 29, 1990.[163] Lotteries are constitutionally proscribed in Mississippi, but the legislature asserted its authority to legislate upon gaming matters notwithstanding this proscription.

> The legislature is prohibited from legislating upon lotteries and permitted by virtue of its inherent powers to legislate upon gaming as the occa-

sion arises. The Legislature derives its power to legislate upon gaming or gambling devices from its inherent authority over the morals and policy of the people and such power shall not be considered to conflict with the constitutional prohibition of lotteries.[164]

The Mississippi Gaming Control Act was patterned after the Nevada Gaming Control Act.[165] However, Mississippi's approach differs somewhat from other states in several respects.

First, there is the matter of location. Like its upstream competitors, Mississippi based its gaming industry on a riverboat model—though in its case the riverboat terminology is apparently used rather loosely. Mississippi law limits the sites for legal casino gaming to "vessels" located in the "Mississippi River or navigable waters within any county bordering on the Mississippi River" or in "waters within the State of Mississippi, which lie adjacent to the State of Mississippi south of the three (3) most southern counties in the State of Mississippi."[166] These geographic limits ensure that Mississippi casinos can draw from border states as well as from Gulf Coast counties known to be frequented by tourists. However, any real connection to navigable waters or any significant form of water transportation is quite tenuous.

Although the Mississippi Supreme Court has rejected the Mississippi Gaming Commission's attempt to grant a permit to construct a casino on a manmade waterway, many facilities have nevertheless been approved in manmade waterways.[167] In fact, long canals made it possible to locate facilities very close to Memphis, Tennessee, which permits these facilities to draw customers across state lines.[168] Inland casinos are frequently constructed far from the river by dredging a channel, filling it with floodwater or water pumped in from the river, and floating in a barge.[169]

Moreover, a "vessel" for purposes of this statute need only float on water and be at least 150 feet long.[170] As one commentator has explained, "Although dockside casinos are floating structures, they are not designed or intended to be used in navigation as a means of transportation. This intent is evidenced by the fact that a majority of dockside casinos are permanently moored to land-based structures and lack any means of self-propulsion."[171] As another commentator has noted, "Interestingly, only the gambling equipment needs to float, other parts of the casino can be on dry land. The 'floating' casinos often have more square footage on land than on water. In fact, most of the casinos in Tunica [County] 'look about as seaworthy as Sears Tower.' "[172]

Locating casinos on the river or in coastal areas may tend to constrain the availability of gambling to local citizens by imposing a geographic barrier.[173] At the same time, this approach tends to enhance access by customers from bordering states. However, despite a stated policy against land-based casinos,[174] the industry nevertheless appears to have largely discarded this constraint, insofar as dockside casinos may already resemble their counterparts that are otherwise located on land. The devastating effects of Hurricane Katrina on the coastal areas of Mississippi ultimately produced a change in this policy against land-based casinos in the Biloxi area. Legislation was approved in October 2005 allowing land-based casinos to be constructed within eight hundred feet of the shore in the three most southern counties of Mississippi, thus potentially improving the safety of these casinos in future storms.[175]

Mississippi's approach to local control over granting casino licenses also represents a departure from that of most other states.[176] Mississippi effectively allows gambling in the specified counties bordering the Mississippi River and the Gulf Coast unless local citizens mobilize and petition against legalization. State law requires that a prospective licensee must give notice of intent to apply for a license to the Mississippi Gaming Commission.[177] The prospective licensee is also required to publish this notice for three weeks in a local newspaper in the county where the prospective licensee seeks to do business.[178] Local citizens then have thirty days from the date of the last publication of notice to mobilize a petition drive. If at least fifteen hundred registered voters or twenty percent of the registered voters of the county, whichever is less, sign the petition, then the matter of licensure is put to a local vote.[179] Otherwise, if the petition effort fails, the board of supervisors of that county is required to adopt a resolution effectively authorizing legal gaming in that county.[180] Thus, the default rule favors legalization, and local citizens must undertake a significant effort to prevent that default rule from being implemented.

Of course, the prospective licensee must obtain approval from the Mississippi Gaming Commission for a license, and such approval requires the typical character and fitness requirements.[181] In addition, the site must be approved and environmental permits must be obtained for that particular location.[182] However, the number of licenses is not otherwise limited; the commission may issue a license to any qualified person, without any constraint on the number of licenses based on the need for additional gaming facilities.[183] In contrast, the Iowa Racing and Gaming Commission is specifically authorized to limit the number of gaming licenses.[184] The Missouri Gaming Commission is similarly empowered to determine the number of excursion boat licenses in a given county, although local governments may submit recommendations on this question.[185]

The brisk competition inherent in Mississippi's comparatively laissez-faire attitude toward casino licensing necessarily entails the possibility of winners and losers among casinos, as well as among their patrons. At least two casinos in the state have gone bankrupt and others have consolidated or reorganized.[186] Given that casinos in Atlantic City and Nevada have also filed for bankruptcy from time to time, this unrestricted licensing approach does not appear to have caused significant casino failures. However, the expansion in Mississippi has apparently slowed: in 2005 there were twenty-nine commercial casinos in the state, which is one less than it had in 1997.[187] With statewide gaming revenues of $2.7 billion in 2004, Mississippi only trails behind Nevada and New Jersey in terms of its overall market share for casino gambling.

SOUTH DAKOTA

South Dakota's gambling industry is relatively small, with gross revenues of only $78 million in 2004.[188] Its approach to regulating gambling is also somewhat unique. South Dakota was the first state after New Jersey to legalize casino gambling, with casinos opening in the town of Deadwood on November 1, 1989.[189] Voters in Deadwood approved a measure to allow "limited card games and slot machines" by a vote of 690 to 230, thus bringing casinos to this small town in the Black Hills of western South Dakota.[190]

Deadwood's reputation as a Wild West town that started in the Black Hills gold rush in 1876 provides the base for nostalgic tourism in the area. Modern interest in this town has also been rekindled through the HBO series *Deadwood,* which is set in this historic community.[191] Colorful characters such as Wild Bill Hickok once frequented Deadwood saloons, and tourists are reminded that they can play in the same casino where he was reportedly killed while playing cards.[192] As a historical matter, Deadwood also had a reputation for other vices: in its early days an estimated 90 percent of the female population were prostitutes.[193] However, in keeping with the family tourism tradition common to the Black Hills region, casinos in this area are remarkably family oriented. South Dakota casinos are unique in that minors are allowed on the gaming floor with their parents,[194] though persons under the age of twenty-one are proscribed from playing gambling games.[195]

South Dakota's policies toward gaming reflect the standard reiteration of licensing and regulation as the bedrock of public trust in the integrity of the games and in their freedom from criminal elements.[196] The South Dakota Commission on Gaming is the agency responsible for such regulation, and its actions are similar to those in other jurisdictions, including licensing and inspection of casino facilities and their operators.[197] However, casinos in Deadwood were ushered in based on a very strict limited-stakes model, in which no more than five dollars could be bet at any time.[198] Efforts to raise this amount by referendum in 1993 failed, but in 2000 efforts to raise the limit to one hundred dollars were successful, and this limitation remains in force today.[199] Maximum bets of one hundred dollars may nevertheless generate significant losses for patrons, but such limits also serve to protect the house. Without the possibility of large individual bets, the house removes any threat that a lucky patron might "break the bank" with a winning high-stakes gamble.

South Dakota has also attempted to limit the size of its casinos with a law restricting each licensee to no more than thirty table games and slot machines.[200] However, cooperative efforts by multiple licensees are permitted, which effectively allows several licensees to operate under one roof in what looks like a single casino.[201]

Casino gambling in this town has not become an engine for development as measured by population growth. According to U.S. Census Bureau figures, Deadwood's population has declined by more than 24 percent, from 1,830 in 1990 to only 1,380 in 2000.[202] Main street shops and stores once frequented by tourists have been displaced by casino operations, which have located in historic structures downtown or in newer structures designed to fit the historic Wild West motif.[203] Deadwood's remote location from major population areas coupled with family-oriented tourism make it a difficult choice for a casino market. In an era where major casino operators are building bigger and flashier facilities to attract patrons, the limited size and stakes variety of casino found here is unlikely to generate significant patronage by those seeking a destination for gambling.

Although South Dakota voters were willing to approve the increased betting limits for Deadwood casinos in 2000, it is interesting to note that these same voters narrowly defeated an attempt to remove another form of gambling—video lottery terminals—which is much more widespread. Video lottery terminals resemble slot machines, but they restrict bets to a maximum of two dollars and their payout is restricted to one thousand dollars.[204] These machines can be found throughout South Dakota in bars and taverns, with a maximum of ten machines per establishment.[205]

State law charges the lottery commission with maximizing revenue from these machines, and the state is entitled to half the revenues generated from these machines, all but 0.5 percent of which is to be used for property tax reduction.[206] In fiscal 2004, the property tax reduction fund received over $110 million, which is over one-tenth of the total state revenues of $938 billion.[207] In contrast, the Deadwood casinos generate a total of $78 million in annual gaming revenues, of which less than $12 million is in the form of taxes, which are spent on tourism, county government, and a separate gaming commission fund.[208]

Despite this significant contribution to state coffers, a constitutional amendment to repeal the video lottery failed by a reasonably narrow margin on November 7, 2000.[209] Such narrow approval of a practice that generates such significant state revenues for a popular purpose—property tax reduction—reflects deep public skepticism about gambling in that state. Given the demographics of a state like South Dakota—a small population spread over a large land area, with concentrated populations in cities in the far east (Sioux Falls) and far west (Rapid City)—the practice of restricting casino-style gambling to a limited tourist venue keeps these games beyond the reach of most residents. However, tribal gaming operations are also accessible in nine other venues in the state. As will be discussed in chapter 11, those tribal casinos are, in part, a trade-off that South Dakotans must accept for their limited experiment with casinos in Deadwood. Nevertheless, easy access to the close cousins of slot machines—video lottery terminals—has expanded gambling in the state in a manner that obfuscates somewhat the significance of gambling in that state's economy.

COMMON THEMES

Once gambling expanded into New Jersey, it was only a matter of time before others joined the bandwagon. In fact, it is surprising that it took over a decade for Iowa and the other riverboat states to adopt plans for expanded gambling. States like Iowa and Missouri reflect the well-intentioned beginnings of an expanded gaming industry that was supposed to be different from the commercial norm. Cultural distinctives, including riverboat or Wild West motifs, as well as gambler-friendly limits on betting and losses were initially designed to keep gambling as lighthearted fun. This was undoubtedly part of the early political "selling" of the idea of expanded gambling.

Those distinctives soon gave way to more commercially friendly forms of regulation. The desire to generate more gaming revenues, with resulting profits for business and taxes for government, gave way to regulations that promoted more efficient means to extract revenues from patrons. Mississippi's rules regarding vessels show the lengths to which legal definitions can be stretched in order to facilitate expanded play, particularly if that means the ability to attract valuable cross-border patronage. Interstate competition plays a significant role as these states also court more lucrative forms of play to attract cross-border patronage. In doing so, however, their own citizens appear to be an increasingly large source of patronage.

South Dakota, in contrast, continues to have only a tiny casino industry, as continuing restrictions tend to stunt further investment and growth. South Dakota's lottery—particularly through the prevalence of video lottery terminals—suggests competition from another state-supported form of gambling, which further limits the potential for casino growth in that jurisdiction. Lottery competition is also being felt in other states, including Iowa, which has issued a moratorium on new touch-screen lottery terminals, a close cousin to slot machines, in convenience stores and other businesses.[210] This moratorium is based in part on concerns about problem gambling (including access by minors) and in part on the competitive impact with Iowa's casino industry.

As will be discussed in later chapters, electronic gambling has proved to be an instrument for growth in the gaming industry, and this appetite for electronic forms of competition may present additional pressures on the states. The federal government's role in assisting the states with gambling enforcement is discussed in chapter 9. The particular threats presented by the Internet are explored in chapter 10.

9. Regulating Gambling: The Federal Government's Role

The federal government has traditionally considered gambling to be a matter of public morality or social welfare that should be left to the purview of the states. Though federal laws and regulations addressing national concerns about money laundering, tax evasion, and organized crime may affect casino operations, the extent of federal interference in the business of legalized gambling within the United States has historically been quite limited. For the most part, federal laws can be viewed as supporting and reinforcing the framework for regulation developed by each state rather than imposing a consistent and coherent national policy. The federal government has sometimes intervened to address cross-border conflicts, which arise on account of the limited jurisdictional reach of the enforcement powers of the states; otherwise, it has been remarkably restrained in this area.

Deference to state sovereignty presents both social and political advantages. It allows social policies to be developed by government officials who are presumably attuned to local values and politically accountable to the citizens most affected by their decisions. It also allows for policy experimentation, which has been touted as one of the strengths of our political system. As U.S. Supreme Court justice Louis Brandeis once said, "It is one of the happy incidents of the Federal system that a single courageous state may, if its citizens choose, serve as a laboratory; and try novel social and economic experiments without risk to the rest of the country."[1]

However, technological developments have made it increasingly difficult to constrain the effects of any "gambling experiment" within a state's geographical borders. Effective transportation systems, coupled with the proliferation of gambling establishments, have put gambling opportunities within easy reach of a substantial portion of the population in the United States. These features heighten prospects for interstate competition for gambling patrons, which creates special pressures on state and local governments in close proximity to jurisdictions with legalized gambling.

Potentially even more significant are developments in communications technologies that have made it possible to expand gambling operations without regard to geographical borders. Telephone, wireless, and Internet technologies make it possible for gambling operations to be located remotely from their patrons. The prospects of revenue flows to unregulated (and untaxed) providers outside the state raise both fiscal and public welfare concerns for state governments, which are difficult to address given limitations on their enforcement jurisdiction.

The Internet has elevated the locus for these concerns to the international arena. By allowing patron relationships to develop in a virtual environment, without the need for local agents or facilities, the Internet presents the possibility for casinos and their patrons to bypass traditional law enforcement methods. The enforcement of federal criminal proscriptions to constrain the growth of gambling, to control its effects, and to preserve revenue sources for the states emerges as a potentially significant federal function in this changing environment.

The discussion in this chapter provides an overview of significant federal laws that currently constrain or affect gambling activities. Constitutional questions also lurk here, as the Commerce Clause and the First Amendment may constrain the states from doing what they wish to do. Even international trade agreements may constrain government authority in this area. The particular problems of Internet gambling are addressed in some detail in chapter 10. Tribal gaming, which presents a different policy approach involving federal intrusion on state sovereignty in favor of tribal sovereignty, is discussed in chapter 11.

A CASE STUDY IN FEDERAL POLICY: COMPETITION IN STATE LOTTERIES

In understanding the current posture of federal-state relations with regard to gambling activities, it is important to recognize that cross-border impacts from gambling are not only a recent phenomenon. Federal government efforts to address interstate and international aspects of gambling—and to exercise restraint in doing so—have a long pedigree in our nation's history. However, government intervention in this context is rooted primarily in concerns about state welfare and revenue rather than in any national interests in uniform treatment of the subject of gambling. Moreover, that intervention occurs in the shadow of important constitutional structures, including the Commerce Clause, that are designed to shape the contours of government authority over commercial activities.

The cross-border effects of state lotteries provided one of the earliest demands for federal regulation of gambling issues. Current federal laws in this area are rooted in an 1895 statute[2] that the Supreme Court upheld against a constitutional challenge in *Champion v. Ames*.[3] Champion had been indicted for conspiracy to transport lottery tickets across state lines. The tickets in question were issued by the Pan-American Lottery Company, which held a monthly drawing in Asuncion, Paraguay.[4] Champion argued that the statute criminalizing his conduct exceeded Congress's powers under the Commerce Clause. The Court disagreed, explaining in part:

> Congress . . . does not assume to interfere with traffic or commerce in lottery tickets carried on exclusively within the limits of any state, but has in view only commerce of that kind among the several states. It has not assumed to interfere with the completely internal affairs of any state, and has only legislated in respect of a matter which concerns the people of the United States. . . . In legislating upon the subject of the traffic in lottery tickets, as carried on through interstate commerce, Congress only supplemented the action of those states—perhaps all of them—which, for the protection of the public morals, prohibit the drawing of lotteries, as well as the sale or circulation of lottery tickets, within their respective limits. It said, in effect, that it would not permit the declared policy of the states, which sought to protect their people against the mischiefs of the lottery business, to be overthrown or disregarded by the agency of interstate commerce. We should hesitate long before adjudging that an evil of such appalling character, carried on through interstate commerce, cannot be met and crushed by the only power competent to that end.[5]

Congress thus chose to limit the scope of its regulation to purely interstate or, in the case of importation, international activities. It did not impose restrictions on the states, even though it may well have thought that such restrictions were advisable based on the Court's moral characterization of lotteries.[6]

This restrained approach proved inadequate to the task of suppressing interstate activities in carrying out a lottery business. In *Francis v. United States*,[7] decided the same day as *Champion v. Ames*, the Court set aside a conviction under this same statute in the case of agents who transported slips of paper representing chances in a game known as "policy."[8] In this case, the lottery drawing was held in Ohio, but the lottery company had agents in other states, including Kentucky, where the defendants resided. After selling tickets, the agents made duplicate slips of paper indicating the numbers the customer had chosen, which were then transported to Ohio to assist the company in determining the identity of the winner.

Though this practice seemingly circumvented the intent of the federal statute upheld in *Champion v. Ames*, the Supreme Court gave a strict interpretation to that statute, holding that the agents' conduct was outside the confined scope of its criminal prohibition. The agents were not transporting lottery tickets themselves, only slips of paper representing the numbers chosen on the tickets. The tickets sold to customers did not leave the state, and the slips were not equivalent to the tickets because the lottery prize would ultimately not be awarded without the original ticket.[9] Such an interpretation made it possible for schemes like this one to operate so long as local law did not prohibit them.

The statutory gap exposed in *Francis* would soon reemerge in the late twentieth century when private firms sought to use electronic means to transport lottery information across state lines. Sensing that profits could be made through trafficking in lottery tickets from different states, entrepreneurs sought to use computer technology to communicate lottery information between out-of-state patrons who wanted lottery tickets and purchasing agents located within the state sponsoring the lottery. Conveniently for these firms, the Court's decision in *Francis* remained good law and the applicable federal statute was essentially unchanged: no tickets were being transported across state lines, only intangible signals from one computer to another.[10]

In response to this practice affecting state lotteries, Pennsylvania adopted a criminal proscription against selling lottery tickets from another state.[11] In *Pic-A-State v. Pennsylvania*,[12] a Pennsylvania firm carrying on a business in facilitating the sale of out-of-state lottery tickets challenged the validity of this state law under the dormant Commerce Clause. The firm's argument was simple and elegant: (1) lottery tickets were objects of commerce, and their sale in interstate commerce was a proper matter for federal regulation; (2) Congress had not prohibited this method of commercial exchange; (3) Pennsylvania citizens can legally purchase Pennsylvania lottery tickets, thereby reflecting state policy that lotteries are not unlawful; and (4) the Pennsylvania statute proscribing the sale of tickets from another state facially discriminates against interstate commerce and is presumptively invalid.[13]

The federal district court substantially agreed with this argument, finding in part that Congress had not given the states a free pass from Commerce Clause constraints.

> [W]hile [Congress] has legislated to facilitate the operation of legal state lotteries, it has never characterized as worthy of protection a state's right to choose to allow its citizens to play only its own state-sponsored lottery. Its emphasis has been on protecting the states that choose to prohibit lotteries. Thus, whatever the authority of an individual state to authorize a state lottery or to allow no lotteries at all, that state's authority remains bound by the dormant Commerce Clause just as it is in other subject areas.[14]

Applying a heightened level of scrutiny, the court proceeded to examine whether the state's purposes behind this facially discriminatory act "could be as well served by nondiscriminatory means."[15] Here, the state's concerns, which included risk of fraud from these agencies and (probably more important) the loss of revenues to the Pennsylvania lottery and its preferred programs of caring for elderly citizens, were insufficient to support the statute. According to the court, Pennsylvania could regulate the ticket agencies much like it regulated its own lottery sellers; it could also impose taxes on sales of such tickets to make up for lost revenues.[16] Thus, it struck down the Pennsylvania statute as unconstitutional.

The state appealed to the U.S. Court of Appeals for the Third Circuit, and during the pending appeal, Congress passed the Violent Crime Control and Law Enforcement Act of 1994.[17] Despite the seemingly inapplicable title of this law, it included a provision that effectively made the conduct of a business like that of Pic-A-State a federal crime, unless participating lottery states enacted a compact for interstate sales.[18] According to the Third Circuit, Congress's intervention here impacted the Commerce Clause analysis applicable to the Pennsylvania statute: "Where Congress has proscribed certain interstate commerce, Congress has determined that that commerce is not in the national interest. Where such a determination has been made by Congress, it does not offend the purpose of the Commerce Clause for states to discriminate or burden that commerce."[19]

Here, Congress had not preempted the field of lottery ticket sales. Instead, it had carefully crafted this provision to support state regulatory efforts, including the allowance of interstate sales with the support of an interstate compact.[20] In these circumstances, the Pennsylvania statute complements, rather than conflicts with, the federal criminal statute.[21] As a result, the state statute remained valid and was not preempted by the federal provision.[22]

Pic-A-State raised one final constitutional challenge, which the Third Circuit also rejected. In *Pic-A-State PA, Inc. v. Reno,*[23] Pic-A-State argued (much like Champion had done years before) that Congress's enactment of the federal criminal ban against selling interstate lottery tickets exceeded its power under the Commerce Clause. Adding a modern twist to the Champion case, however, Pic-A-State argued that Congress's regulation in this area presupposed that lotteries were "evils" to be constrained and that this was no longer true in light of the legalization of lotteries in over thirty states.[24] It also argued that Congress's choice constituted an irrational restraint of trade.[25]

The Third Circuit wasted little time in disposing of these arguments and by doing so reaffirmed the propriety of the protective role undertaken by Congress in these circumstances. Here, the putative status of lotteries as "evils" was irrelevant to the court, as long as there was some rational basis for the legislation. Loss of state revenue to out-of-state competition, coupled with the need to protect state sovereignty over such matters, was a sufficient basis for upholding the act under a rational basis standard.[26] The court noted: "Although many states have legalized lotteries, some have not. Congress could rationally decide to legislate in support of the policies of nonlottery states by placing the regulation of lotteries within the discretion of each state and prohibiting out-of-state interference."[27]

In further support of the rational basis for congressional action, the court also stated:

In the context of the one-hundred year history of [18 U.S.C.] § 1301 and the Federal regulation of lotteries, Congress could rationally conclude the need for an amendment to close a loophole created by advances in technology unforeseeable at the time the statute was originally drafted. Congress believed that since the sale of lottery tickets across state lines was illegal, the sale of interests in tickets across state lines by computer should be illegal as well. We believe the Commerce Clause requires no more indication of rationality for us to uphold the statutory scheme adopted by Congress.[28]

This brief saga affecting the cross-border conflicts in connection with the sale of lottery tickets provides some important lessons for understanding the unusual regulatory environment being cultivated here. In response to consumer demand, commercial interests spawned innovation that pushed the limits of existing state laws. Instead of adopting a singular national policy, Congress continued to leave the status of gambling through lotteries in the hands of the states. Rather than resolving the issue itself, Congress provided a default rule that protected state interests but also allowed a different result to be achieved through state cooperation.

What is particularly unusual here is that instead of encouraging robust competition among the states offering lotteries, Congress chose to protect state fiscal interests by effectively restraining trade. To the extent that gambling is viewed as merely another form of commerce, such a protectionist approach would probably not be tolerated. For example, the states would surely not be allowed to preclude their merchants from selling apples grown elsewhere if domestic apples were available. Thus, despite modern attempts to characterize gambling as merely another form of entertainment, Congress clearly viewed it differently than other commercial ventures.[29]

In part, this special treatment may reflect the close relationship between commercial gambling establishments and the taxes that they pay to state governments. State governments obtain considerable revenues from gaming taxes; competition threatens this revenue stream. Whether this relationship is a sufficient justification for different treatment is debatable. Other industries might also provide important contributions to the tax rolls if they are protected from competition. Nevertheless, the difference remains.

FEDERAL CRIMINAL SANCTIONS AFFECTING GAMBLING ENTERPRISES

Federal criminal statutes applicable to gambling other than lotteries reflect a similarly restrained approach that is sensitive to state interests. Instead of imposing a uniform federal standard, these laws generally define proscribed activities in relation to the legal status of the activity within the affected states. Moreover, their application is generally limited to activities with interstate and international effects, where the independent enforcement actions of the states are likely to be ineffective.

By erecting barriers to cross-border gaming operations, these laws serve multiple purposes. They protect the viability of state revenue streams obtained from legalized operations by making the detection and prosecution of illegal activities more likely. They support the policies of states that have chosen to follow the path of prohibiting gambling within their borders. They also assist the federal government in its efforts to stamp out organized crime, a problem that often involves interjurisdictional dimensions.

Significant federal statutes that potentially affect cross-border gambling operations include the Wire Act,[30] the Interstate Transportation of Paraphernalia Act,[31] and the Travel Act.[32] These three laws were originally enacted in 1961 as part of anticrime legislation; only limited amendments have occurred since that time. A provision of more recent vintage, the Professional and Amateur Sports Protection Act,[33] was enacted in 1992. Highlights from each of these laws are explored in the next sections.

The Wire Act (18 U.S.C. § 1084) and Related Legislation

The Wire Act was enacted in 1961 as part of a package of legislation proposed by Attorney General Robert F. Kennedy to address concerns connected with gambling and organized crime.[34] The Wire Act provides in part:

> Whoever being engaged in the business of betting or wagering knowingly uses a wire communication facility for the transmission in interstate or foreign commerce of bets or wagers or information assisting in the placing of bets or wagers on any sporting event or contest, or for the transmission of a wire communication which entitled the recipient to receive money or credit as a result of bets or wagers, or for information assisting

in the placing of bets or wagers, shall be fined . . . or imprisoned not more than two years, or both.[35]

According to the legislative history, this new law was designed "to assist the various States . . . in the enforcement of their laws pertaining to gambling, bookmaking, and like offenses and to aid in the suppression of organized gambling activities."[36] Government officials were particularly concerned that modern gambling operations were using telephone and other electronic means to facilitate illegal gambling activities that primarily benefited organized crime.[37]

Conduct proscribed by this statute is limited to that of persons "engaged in the business of betting or wagering." The scope of activity that rises to the level of being in the business of betting or wagering has proved controversial. For example, in *Pic-A-State,* the federal district court agreed that the Wire Act did not apply to the lottery ticket vendor, as it was not engaged in the business of wagering or betting because "they set no odds, accept no wagers and distribute no risks."[38] Both the Eighth and Ninth Circuits have held that placing bets on behalf of others is not a requirement for conviction; a person wagering for his own account could potentially be included.[39] On the other hand, the act has been interpreted as not reaching a bettor who regularly placed bets with a friend in the business of gambling.[40] In one case, even betting between eight hundred and one thousand dollars per day, three or four times per week, was held insufficient to be engaged in the business of betting or wagering.[41]

Despite this uncertainty, it is plain that the Wire Act was not designed to reach the casual gambler; such activities would be punished, if at all, under state law. Unlike other regulatory efforts, there is no intent here to preempt state law and occupy the field. The act specifically provides that "[n]othing in this section shall create immunity for criminal prosecution under any laws of any State."[42] On the other hand, federal prosecution could also occur without the necessity for state cooperation, a desirable feature when local law enforcement was corrupted or otherwise unable (such as through a lack of resources or through jurisdictional conflicts) to step in and enforce local gambling laws.

The act is also careful to preserve the rights of states to allow legalized gambling. Subsection (b) provides in part: "Nothing in this section shall be construed to prevent . . . the transmission of information assisting in the placing of bets or wagers on a sporting event or contest from a State or foreign country where betting on that sporting event or contest is legal into a State or foreign country in which such betting is legal."[43] At the time this legislation was enacted, Nevada was the only state where remote betting was legal. As explained in the legislative history,

> [T]he transmission of gambling information on a horserace from a State where betting on that horserace is legal to a State where betting on the same horserace is legal is not within the prohibitions of the bill. Since Nevada is the only State which has legalized offtrack betting, this exemption will only be applicable to it. For example, in New York State pari-mutuel betting at a racetrack is authorized by State law. Only in Nevada is it lawful to make and accept bets on the race held in the State of New York where pari-mutuel betting at a racetrack is authorized by law. Therefore, the exemption will permit the transmission of information assisting in the placing of bets and wagers from New York to Nevada. On the other hand, it is unlawful to make and accept bets in New York State on a race being run in Nevada. Therefore, the transmission of information assisting in the placing of bets and wagers from Nevada to New York would be contrary to the provisions of the bill.[44]

Legality in both states is a prerequisite for protection under this exception, and courts have held that proof of violation of a state statute is not a predicate to prosecution under the Wire Act.[45] States thus maintain a prerogative to legalize the use of interstate communications in connections with gambling, but they have not taken this route. Typical provisions limit legal gambling to situations of in-person contacts, thus keeping the effects (and profits) of such activities within the state where the bet is placed.[46]

Two other statutes originally enacted in 1961 addressed the related problems of interstate travel to facilitate unlawful gambling and the transportation of gambling paraphernalia. The Travel Act[47] provides a federal criminal penalty (including fines and imprisonment for up to five years) on the following persons:

> whoever travels in interstate or foreign commerce or uses the mail or any facility in interstate or foreign commerce, with intent to—

(1) distribute the proceeds of any unlawful activity; or . . .

(2) otherwise promote, manage, establish, carry on, or facilitate the promotion, management, establishment, or carrying on, of any unlawful activity.[48]

For this purpose, "unlawful activity" includes "gambling . . . offenses in violation of the laws of the State in which they are committed or of the United States."[49] The scope of the Travel Act extends to interstate activities, though the mere fact that people cross state lines to participate in gambling that might violate local law has been held to be outside the scope of this provision.[50]

The Interstate Transportation of Paraphernalia Act[51] addresses a related problem of transporting items used in illegal gambling activities. The act provides in part:

Whoever, except a common carrier in the usual course of its business, knowingly carries or sends in interstate or foreign commerce any record, paraphernalia, ticket, certificate, bills, slip, token, paper, writing, or other device used, or to be used, or adapted, devised, or designed for use in (a) bookmaking; or (b) wagering pools with respect to a sporting event; or (c) in a numbers, policy, bolita, or similar game shall be fined under this title or imprisoned for not more than five years or both.[52]

Like the Travel Act, this act also contains exceptions for items involved in a state where gambling is legal.[53] Manufacturers of gaming devices are also subject to additional rules that require them to register with the attorney general prior to manufacturing gaming devices and that provide criminal sanctions on the interstate transportation of such devices without proper registration and record keeping.[54] In this way, federal law supports state efforts to prevent illegal gambling, while also providing a means for federal intervention to combat organized crime.

The Professional and Amateur Sports Protection Act

Though the Wire Act specifically includes "bets or wagers on any sporting event or contest" within its scope, it also contains a specific exemption for state-sponsored gambling. In 1991, some members of Congress became intensely interested in issues surrounding gambling on sporting events. However, unlike previous legislation that was motivated by a desire to bolster law enforcement efforts in the battle against illegal gambling operations run by organized crime, the legislation that would emerge would instead be motivated primarily by concerns about the proliferation of state-sponsored forms of legalized gambling. In breaking with its tradition of legislating to support state discretion on legalized gambling, Congress enacted legislation that partially banned state-sponsored sports betting, effective January 1, 1993.

Sports have enjoyed a special role in American culture. As the legislative history to the Professional and Amateur Sports Protection Act[55] points out, "Sports are national institutions, and Congress has recognized a distinct federal interest in protecting sports from corruption."[56] As early as 1964, Congress had expressed this interest by making it a federal crime to attempt to influence a sporting contest by bribery.[57] The reported cases under this antibribery law primarily involve offenses relating to horse racing,[58] which was a more common form of legalized gambling at the time the law was enacted. Illegal betting on other sports also existed long before this provision was enacted, though state law provided the basis for criminal proscription.[59]

Concerns about the corrupting effects of gambling on important American values tied to sports formed a part of the basis for further legislation in this area. The legislative history to the Sports Protection Act quotes Paul Tagliabue, commissioner of the National Football League, in part:

> Sports gambling threatens the character of team sports. Our games embody our very finest traditions and values. They stand for clean, healthy competition. They stand for teamwork. And they stand for success through preparation and honest effort. With legalized sports gambling, our games instead will come to represent the fast buck, the quick fix, the desire to get something for nothing. The spread of legalized sports gambling would change forever—and for the worse—what our games stand for and the way they are perceived.[60]

In particular, concerns were expressed about the effects of gambling on young people, in terms of both the erosion of core values and the contribution to problem gambling behaviors. The legislative history continues:

> The committee is especially concerned about the potential effect of legalized sports gambling on America's youth. Beyond impairing the values sports represent to our young people, new technologies are being con-

sidered that, while designed to make gambling more convenient for adults, also would make gambling more convenient for children. . . . Youngsters would inevitably find sports gambling schemes that utilize these new technologies to be highly seductive.

Teenage gambling-related problems are increasing. Of the approximately 8 million compulsive sports gamblers in America, 1 million of them are under 20. Teenagers gamble on sports, lotteries and card games. *Governments should not be in the business of encouraging people, especially young people, to gamble.*[61]

It is significant to note that in this situation congressional concern was focused on the impact of legalized gambling rather than illegal forms. In fact, the interstate competition for gambling provided the basis for intervention.

Sports gambling is a national problem. The harms it inflicts are felt beyond the borders of those states that sanction it. The moral erosion it produces cannot be limited geographically. Once a state legalizes sports gambling, it will be extremely difficult for other states to resist the lure. The current pressures in such places as New Jersey and Florida to institute casino-style sports gambling illustrate the point. Without Federal legislation, sports gambling is likely to spread on a piecemeal basis and ultimately develop an irreversible momentum.[62]

Although federal interference in this context would undoubtedly affect the states' ability to raise revenues by expanding legalized gambling options, the majority did not find that to be a persuasive basis for rejecting the bill: "The answer to state budgetary problems should not be to increase the number of lottery players or sports bettors, regardless of the worthiness of the cause. The committee believes the risk to the reputation of our Nation's most popular pastimes, professional and amateur sporting events, is not worth it."[63]

Moreover, the Senate Judiciary Committee believed that the legalization of sports gambling would, in many cases, potentially lead to more social costs. The committee report quoted the commissioner of baseball, Francis T. Vincent Jr., in part: "once the moral status of sports betting has been redefined by legalization . . . many new gamblers will be created, some of whom inevitably will seek to move beyond lotteries to wagers with higher stakes and more serious consequences."[64] Thus, sports gambling was effectively analogized to a "gateway drug," with potentially deleterious moral and social consequences.

Despite these articulated concerns about the moral fabric, the Sports Protection Act did not go as far to repair it as logic might have dictated. In recognition of the political realities, the act contained a "grandfather provision" that prevented retroactive application to Oregon, Delaware, and Nevada, which had already instituted sports-related lotteries. The legislative history is particularly solicitous of Nevada's interests, stating in part that the committee had no "desire to threaten the economy of Nevada, which over many decades has come to depend on legalized private gambling, including sports gambling, as an essential industry."[65] Thus, it would appear, the youth in these jurisdictions would have to gain the values taught by fair competition in sport through some other means.

Republican senator Charles Grassley submitted a minority report that took the majority to task for this legislation. First, he found that it substantially intruded into states' rights by constraining them from raising revenues through expanded gambling options. The Reagan Justice Department agreed with Grassley on this point in opposing the bill.[66] Second, and perhaps more trenchant in effect, Senator Grassley pointed out that the bill would effectively grant a federal monopoly to the three states affected by the grandfather provision. He also pointed out the perverse effects that such grandfathering would have on the purported moral values advanced by the majority. Leveling a charge specifically at the professional sports leagues, who helped support the bill, he stated in part: "If the professional sports leagues were truly concerned about the risk of 'fixed' games, the integrity of professional sports, and the protections of their alleged trademarks, they would be seeking to prohibit this $1.8 billion head-to-head sports wagering industry in Nevada."[67] He further pointed out that the sports leagues benefited from this interest in sports wagering, as evidenced by the fact that Jimmy "The Greek" Snyder offered wagering advice in National Football League pregame shows and that virtually every major newspaper printed "point spreads" and similar wagering advice.[68]

Senator Grassley also took issue with another fundamental belief of the majority: that making sports betting illegal would prevent the growth of gambling. To the contrary, Senator Grassley suggested that "the principal beneficiar[ies] will be organized crime and the local bookie."[69] In the majority's view, legalization leads to greater demand for both legalized and illegal gambling. On the illegal side, the majority cited testimony from an FBI agent to the effect that "illegal entrepreneurs can always 'outmarket' their legitimate counterparts, offering credit, better odds, higher payout, and, most important, tax-free winnings."[70]

It remains to be proved empirically whether Senator Grassley or the majority was correct on this point. However, the economic rationale expressed by the majority seems hard to contradict. Anecdotal evidence of betting in the United Kingdom suggests that gambling has indeed proliferated there once it was legalized. On most any block in London, betting shops can be found. Betting lingo has found its way into the language of the popular culture, reflecting a ubiquity of gambling that is in stark contrast to the United States today,[71] though this may not always be so.

Sports betting is also common on college campuses today. The National Collegiate Athletic Association (NCAA) announced that FBI agents would be meeting with all thirty-two teams in the collegiate basketball championships in 2006 (compared to only the final four teams in 2005) due to results from a study showing widespread gambling among college athletes.[72] According to this study, which the NCAA completed in 2003 through a survey of twenty-one thousand student athletes, gambling among college athletes was common, despite NCAA rules to the contrary. Approximately 35 percent of male athletes and 20 percent of female athletes reported wagering on a sporting event in the past year, which is in direct violation of NCAA rules.[73] Though such wagering might include comparatively innocuous behavior, such as participation in a sports pool for an unrelated sport, the study indicated that about 2 percent of men's football and basketball athletes had been asked to affect the outcome of a game.[74] One percent of football players and 0.5 percent of men's basketball players admitted to accepting money to play poorly.[75] Less than 5 percent of male athletes and less than 0.5 percent of female athletes were categorized as problem or pathological gamblers.[76] Nevertheless, these results suggest that gambling is a growing problem on campuses and that sports gambling may already be affecting the integrity of athletic competitions.

OTHER FEDERAL REGULATIONS: TAX AND MONEY LAUNDERING RULES

In addition to federal criminal proscriptions that affect the scope and extent of legalized gambling operations, other federal laws can also affect casino operations. Though a complete review of every form of federal regulation is beyond the scope of this text, two areas merit particular attention: tax and money laundering rules.

Taxing Gambling Businesses

It has been said that "the power to tax is the power to destroy."[77] Tax policy undoubtedly has a regulatory dimension, as the Supreme Court has explained:

> The lawmaker may, in light of the "public policy or interest served," make the assessment heavy if the lawmaker wants to discourage the activity; or it may make the levy slight if a bounty is to be bestowed; or the lawmaker may make a substantial levy to keep entrepreneurs from exploiting a semipublic cause for their own personal aggrandizement.[78]

Although Congress has the power to impose taxes that would effectively destroy the economic viability of gambling businesses, it has chosen not to do so.[79] Apart from a limited exception for certain federal excise taxes, Congress has chosen not to burden gambling businesses with significant tax assessments that differ from those applicable to other trades or businesses. Instead, this power has been left to the states, which have exercised this power with alacrity.

Section 4401 of the Internal Revenue Code imposes a federal excise tax on persons in the business of accepting wagers, but this tax has little economic significance for state-authorized gambling businesses. First, the code defines wagers in a very restrictive manner:

> The term "wager" means—
>   (A) any wager with respect to a sports event or a contest placed with a person engaged in the business of accepting such wagers,
>   (B) any wager placed in a wagering pool with respect to a sports event or a contest, if such pool is conducted for profit, and
>   (C) any wager placed in a lottery conducted for profit.[80]

The term *lottery* is further restricted to exclude any game in which wagers are placed and prizes are determined and paid out in the presence of those playing the game.[81] Specific exemptions also exist for wagers placed in pari-mutuel enterprises licensed under state law, any coin-operated devices, and state-conducted lotteries.[82] Thus, the typical table games and slot machines played at a casino would be outside the scope of this tax.

Second, even if a wager would fall within the applicable definition, as in the case of sports betting, the tax rate on legal wagers is only 0.25 percent of the wager.[83] An annual tax of fifty dollars is also imposed on persons accepting wagers under these provisions that are not otherwise exempt.[84] Thus, the tax burden, if any, on legal operations from this federal excise tax would be quite modest.[85]

Illegal operations are subject to a higher tax rate of 2 percent and an annual tax of five hundred dollars.[86] Prior to amendment in 1974, the rate of this federal excise tax was 10 percent.[87] The 1974 amendments also responded to the Supreme Court's ruling in *Marchetti v. United States*,[88] which held that registration requirements associated with this excise tax as applied to taxpayers involved in illegal gambling activity violated their Fifth Amendment right against self-incrimination. Under current law, strict limitations on disclosure to law enforcement agencies apply to cure these Fifth Amendment infirmities.[89]

A significant tax on wagers, as opposed to taxes on winnings, would undoubtedly cut into the house's margin on gambling and potentially make the business of gambling uneconomical. For example, in some table games such as blackjack, a skilled player may allow a house advantage of less than 1 percent.[90] If even a 2 percent wagering tax was imposed on the casino, the game would produce virtually certain losses for the house in the long run if payouts remained the same. The only way to change such a result would be to change the rules so as to increase the house advantage or reduce payouts, which would effectively shift the incidence of that tax to the players. This may channel demand for legal gambling activities to illegal ones, or it may simply depress the demand altogether given the increase in costs.

Taxing Gamblers

Income tax rules affecting the treatment of a gambler's winnings and losses can also affect the economics of gambling transactions and thus indirectly affect the demand for legalized gambling. For federal income tax purposes, winning bets generate gross income, which may in turn generate income tax liability. As a technical matter, the amount of gross income is the excess of the winning payout over the amount of the wager; the portion of that payout that represents the initial wager should be treated as a nontaxable return of capital.[91] However, few gamblers have only winning bets during a taxable year. Losing bets may be deductible against gambling winnings, thus reducing taxable income, but, as explained later, such deductions are subject to restrictions that potentially limit their effectiveness. As a result, the government can be viewed as a partner of the winning gambler, but the losing gambler is an orphan.

Since 1934, the Internal Revenue Code has imposed a special limitation on the deductibility of gambling losses: "Losses from wagering transactions shall be allowed only to the extent of the gains from such transactions."[92] In contrast, taxpayers engaged in other business or profit-seeking activities are potentially allowed to deduct losses from one business activity against gross income from other business activities; moreover, excess losses may be carried to other tax years.[93]

This limitation on the deductibility of gambling losses reflects the policy judgment that gambling activities are different from other business or profit-seeking ventures. As the Supreme Court observed in a 1987 tax case,

> Federal and state legislation and court decisions, perhaps understandably, until recently have not been noticeably favorable to gambling endeavors and even have been reluctant to treat gambling on a parity with more "legitimate" means of making a living.[94]

The differential treatment accorded to gambling transactions may reflect vestiges of moral disapproval, and commentators have criticized aspects of the current tax structure on this basis.[95]

However, the differential treatment of gambling is not without some rational basis. Though gambling may entail profit-seeking motivations, gambling is primarily a pleasure-seeking activity in which patrons tolerate losses as the price of entertainment. Though some people may gamble with sufficient continuity and regularity to establish that their primary motivation in gambling is to seek income or profit, this is the exceptional case. In reality, the odds of most games are stacked against the gambler, leaving few opportunities to exploit specialized knowledge or skill to overcome the house advantage. (Poker may represent one of the few games in which the skilled competitor maintains an advantage over other players.) Further, the legislative history suggests that Congress was also concerned about the practices of gamblers who would report their losses but fail to report their winnings; such a practice is negated by the rule limiting the deduction of losses.[96]

The gambler who earns (or attempts to earn) his or her livelihood through gambling is allowed to deduct gambling losses (including related expenses) directly against his or her winnings, but only to the extent thereof.[97] Unlike the professional trader of stocks or securities, the professional gambler is not allowed tax benefits for losses in excess of gambling winnings.[98] This is perhaps a concession to congressional doubt about the validity of a profit motivation in this context but also perhaps a judgment about the comparative value of the gambler's contribution to the social good. A speculative day trader in stocks, whom some would consider to be engaged in a similar activity to the gambler, at least provides liquidity in the capital markets; the gambler can make no similar claim.

For those who engage in gambling primarily for pleasure (albeit also motivated by the hope for profit), losses are subject to the same special restriction as professional gamblers; that is, they cannot be used to offset income from sources other than gambling. However, they are also subject to a further restriction on their deductibility: unlike professionals, who can deduct losses directly against their winnings and are taxed (if at all) only on the net result, a casual gambler is required to treat gambling losses as an itemized deduction.[99] Among other things, this rule can cause hardships for taxpayers seeking tax benefits based on limitations imposed on adjusted gross income. For example, the tax court recently ruled that a low-income taxpayer appropriately lost a portion of her earned income credit due to gambling winnings, even though such winnings were offset entirely by losses that were allowed as an itemized deduction.[100] A middle-class taxpayer with significant gambling activity may also find that he or she is ineligible to obtain such benefits as the child tax credit, deductions for certain retirement contributions, and tuition payments to pursue higher education.[101] These effects tend to undermine the purposes that are otherwise intended by these social welfare provisions that are built into the tax code, and that denial occurs regardless of whether the taxpayer experiences true economic gains commensurate with reportable winnings.

Moreover, all gambling taxpayers must meet a burden of proof in substantiating their loss deductions. In Revenue Procedure 77-29,[102] the Internal Revenue Service set forth guidelines for the proof required to document gambling losses. These guidelines state in part:

> An accurate diary or similar record regularly maintained by the taxpayer, supplemented by verifiable documentation will usually be acceptable evidence for substantiation of wagering winnings and losses. In general, the diary should contain at least the following information:
> 1) Date and type of specific wager or wagering activity;
> 2) Name of gambling establishment;
> 3) Address or location of gambling establishment;
> 4) Name(s) of other person(s) (if any) present with taxpayer at gambling establishment; and
> 5) Amount(s) won or lost.[103]

In addition, the procedure suggests:

> Where possible, the diary and available documentation generated with the placement and settlement of a wager should be further supported by other documentation of the taxpayer's wagering activity or visit to a gambling establishment. Such documentation includes, but is not limited to, hotel bills, airline tickets, gasoline credit cards, canceled checks, credit records, bank deposits, and bank withdrawals.[104]

These substantiation requirements have been characterized as being more stringent than those imposed on taxpayers in other contexts.[105] To the extent that the gambler is unable to meet the burden of proof, any tax benefits from losses are effectively denied. Few gamblers keep sufficient records to satisfy this burden, thus exposing them to potential liability on audit.

It is a familiar rule of tax law that deductions are matters of legislative grace and that taxpayers have the burden of establishing the right to a deduction before they are allowed to reduce their tax liability.[106] It would be possible for Congress to design a tax system that would tax winning bets but treat losing bets as nondeductible personal consumption expenditures. Although the current system may indeed work this harsh result on gamblers who do not itemize deductions or who cannot meet the burden of proof, better treatment is possible for those who can comply.

In fact, the deductions available to gamblers may actually work out better than the result obtained for taxpayers engaged in so-called hobby activities, which lack the requisite profit motivation to be considered a trade or business. Section 183 of the code disallows deductions incurred in connection with such to the extent that those deductions exceed the gross income generated from that activity. Moreover, these deductions are allowable only as itemized deductions, which in this case are subject to a "floor" or limitation based on 2 percent of adjusted gross income.[107] Gambling losses are not subject to this 2 percent "floor," and casual gamblers are thus in a better situation than the hobbyist involved in other pursuits where pleasure, rather than profit, is the dominant motivation.

Tax rules affecting gambling winnings and losses potentially affect the odds associated with positive economic outcomes from gambling. As the effective tax rates increase, the expected value of any positive economic outcome decreases. To illustrate, consider the recent case of the gambler who decided to sell all his worldly goods and bet the proceeds on a single spin of a roulette wheel in Las Vegas.[108] The typical roulette wheel in the United States consists of thirty-eight numbered slots, containing the numbers 1–36, 0, and 00.[109] Only numbers 1–36 are colored red or black, and a bet on either red or black produces a payout of "even money" or double the amount bet. In these circumstances, a bet on either red or black produces a winning probability of 47.37 percent and a losing probability of 52.63 percent, reflecting a house advantage of 5.26 percent.[110]

Assuming a stake of $100,000 was wagered on red, the gambler could potentially double his money if he won. However, the expected value of the bet would be $94,740, reflecting a deduction for the house advantage:

$$\frac{\text{Probability}}{.4737} \times \frac{\text{Payout (pretax)}}{\$200,000} = \frac{\text{Expected Value}}{\$94,740}.$$

Thus, pure logic would not support this wager; the gambler is already starting out with a disadvantage to the house. He must believe he will be "lucky" in order to proceed with this bet.

Just how lucky he must be depends on the probability assigned to winning bets. It is interesting to note that this gambler staked all his wealth on a bet with a relatively high probability, nearly even odds. Had he chosen instead to bet on a single number, the odds against him would be much higher (37 to 1, or about 2.63 percent), but that bet would have produced a much higher payout (35 to 1 instead of 2 to 1) if it was successful. Nevertheless, the house advantage on this bet is still 5.26 percent, despite the fact that there is a greater potential for gain.[111] Thus, the expected value of the wager is similar in each case. Presumably, this gambler chose a less risky alternative because of the comparatively high probability of walking away with nothing.

This analysis ignores the effect of taxes imposed on winnings, which could significantly lower the true value of the expected payout. If this gambler is successful in betting red, his $200,000 payout will consist of $100,000 of return of capital and $100,000 of taxable income. Assuming for illustration purposes an average income tax rate of 20 percent, the after-tax value of the payout is $180,000, not $200,000. As a result, the expected value of the bet is really $85,266, not $94,740:

$$\underset{.4737}{\underbrace{\text{Probability}}} \times \underset{\$180,000}{\underbrace{\text{Payout (after tax)}}} = \underset{\$85,266}{\underbrace{\text{Expected Value}}}.$$

Thus, the outcome is even less attractive from the gambler's perspective when the government's share of the winning bet ("government's advantage") is also added to the house advantage.

Whether tax considerations actually change behavior in a particular case would, of course, depend on the gambler. It is doubtful that the gambler who risks all on one spin is acting on pure reason. Few recreational gamblers probably understand or consider the tax consequences of their behavior. For example, the lower-income taxpayer with gambling losses probably does not consider the loss of her eligibility for the earned income credit as she considers the consequences of gambling winnings and losses.[112] Nevertheless, whether the gambler is engaged in a single wager or repeated transactions, these tax rules can have a real effect on the expected value of winning. The gambler has to be much luckier than the odds might otherwise indicate in order to come out ahead when tax effects are considered. Few gamblers probably understand this phenomenon, or they learn about it when it is too late and a tax deficiency is proposed.

Of course, taxpayer compliance with these rules is another consideration; tax avoidance undoubtedly occurs in the context of many gambling transactions. The house advantage in casino games means that the predicted results for casino gamblers who bet regularly will, as a general matter, experience net losses from gambling activities, giving little tax significance to the population when viewed as a whole. However, relatively large jackpots from progressive slot machines, bingo, or lotteries present the possibility that some gamblers may indeed have significant tax liability in a given tax year because their winnings exceed their losses—or more particularly the losses that they are able to prove. These taxpayers face the greatest risk of discovery in the event they improperly report their tax liability, as the code imposes financial reporting requirements on gambling businesses that are designed to identify such taxpayers to the government.

Section 6041 of the code generally imposes an information-reporting requirement on taxpayers engaged in a trade or business who make payments totaling six hundred dollars or more in "rent, salaries, wages, premiums, annuities, compensations, remunerations, emoluments, or other fixed or determinable gains, profits, and income."[113] This general rule applies to table game winnings.[114] However, some gambling activities are subject to more specific regulations, which require a casino to collect information and report payments of twelve hundred dollars or more from a bingo game or slot machine play, without regard to the amount wagered.[115] These regulations also require reporting for winnings of fifteen hundred dollars or more from a keno game, but this amount is reduced by the amount wagered in that game.[116]

Information reports provide an audit trail for the Internal Revenue Service to track down gamblers with potential tax liability. In some cases, an audit also produces evidence that the taxpayer failed to report not only winnings reported on the Form W-2G but also other winnings that were not subject to these reporting requirements. Losses, on the other hand, are not subject to similar reporting requirements. As a result, in a system in which the proof of winnings is assisted by the casino and the proof of losses is left to the taxpayer's own devices, a taxpayer may be unable to overcome the assessment of a deficiency, along with possible penalties.[117]

In addition to the reporting requirements, casinos may also be subject to income tax withholding requirements on certain winnings.[118] These withholding requirements impose additional administrative burdens on casinos and other gambling businesses when more significant payouts are involved. Like the information reporting requirements, these rules ensure that winners have an additional incentive for filing a return: they may ultimately get their withheld taxes back if they can prove sufficient losses were incurred to offset those large winnings. These rules also help to constrain the illegal practice known as "ten percenting"—paying another patron a percentage of winnings (often 10 percent) in order to provide false identity information to avoid tax compliance.[119] However, these withholding rules are not foolproof, as withholding is not required in all cases.[120] Only a system of purely electronic wagering, with a record of wins and losses, would ensure that all these transactions are properly reported.

MONEY LAUNDERING

The tax reporting and withholding rules previously described impose an administrative burden on casinos and other gambling businesses. In effect, casinos are legally required to assist in the enforcement of the income tax laws affecting their patrons. Rules governing the disclosure of large cash transactions also assist the government in the enforcement of tax laws, but their primary purposes involve detection and prevention of money laundering activities.

The term *money laundering* refers to the process by which criminal enterprises seek to mask the origins of cash generated through unlawful activities by associating it with legitimate sources.[121] Though money laundering enforcement efforts previously focused on domestic criminal enterprises (including drug trafficking), efforts to detect and suppress international terrorist organizations have gained attention in recent years.

Congressional findings in connection with anti–money laundering legislation passed in 2002 reflect an increasing concern about the impact of money laundering on the world economy and the particular threats raised by international actors. The following findings were revealed:

(1) money laundering, estimated by the International Monetary Fund to amount to between 2 and 5 percent of global gross domestic product, which is at least $600,000,000,000 annually, provides the financial fuel that permits transnational criminal enterprises to conduct and expand their operations to the detriment of the safety and security of American citizens;

(2) money laundering, and the defects in financial transparency on

which money launderers rely, are critical to the financing of global terrorism and the provision of funds for terrorist attacks;

(3) money launderers subvert legitimate financial mechanisms and banking relationships by using them as protective covering for the movement of criminal proceeds and the financing of crime and terrorism, and, by so doing, can threaten the safety of United States citizens and undermine the integrity of United States financial institutions and of the global financial and trading systems upon which prosperity and growth depend.[122]

Current law imposes reporting requirements on businesses that receive large cash deposits, in order to address these international and domestic threats from money laundering activity. These reporting requirements emanate from two different sources: the Bank Secrecy Act[123] and the Internal Revenue Code.[124]

Section 6050I of the Internal Revenue Code generally requires a person engaged in a trade or business who receives cash of more than ten thousand dollars in a single transaction, or two or more related transactions, to file a Form 8300 with the Internal Revenue Service.[125] Attempts to "structure" transactions by dividing them into smaller components that fall below the ten-thousand-dollar limit are prohibited.[126] Moreover, "cash" is defined to potentially include cashier's checks, money orders, traveler's checks, and similar instruments if the recipient "knows that such instrument is being used in an attempt to avoid the reporting of the transaction."[127]

Certain businesses may be exempt from reporting under section 6050I, including financial institutions that are subject to similar reporting requirements under the Bank Secrecy Act.[128] Casinos with gross annual gaming revenues over $1 million are within the scope of the Bank Secrecy Act and thus potentially fit this exemption.[129] However, exemption is discretionary and is granted on a case-by-case basis.[130] The Internal Revenue Service has specifically ruled that Class III Indian Casinos are within the scope of this exemption.[131] Small casinos—that is, those with annual gaming revenue of less than $1 million—are required to report under section 6050I.[132] Moreover, all casinos are required to report cash receipts in excess of ten thousand dollars in connection with nongaming businesses, including entertainment, shops, and hotels.[133]

Under the Bank Secrecy Act, casinos are obligated to report cash trans-actions over ten thousand dollars in connection with a broad range of trans-actions involving cash in or cash out. Cash-in transactions include

(A) Purchases of chips, tokens, and plaques;

(B) Front money deposits;

(C) Safekeeping deposits;

(D) Payments on any form of credit, including markers and counter checks;

(E) Bets of currency;

(F) Currency received by a casino for transmittal of funds through wire transfer for a customer;

(G) Purchases of a casino's check; and

(H) Exchanges of currency for currency, including foreign currency.[134]

Cash-out transactions include

(A) Redemptions of chips, tokens, and plaques;

(B) Front money withdrawals;

(C) Safekeeping withdrawals;

(D) Advances on any form of credit, including markers and counter checks;

(E) Payments on bets, including slot jackpots;

(F) Payments by a casino to a customer based on receipt of funds through wire transfer for credit to a customer;

(G) Cashing of checks or other negotiable instruments;

(H) Exchanges of currency for currency, including foreign currency; and

(I) Reimbursements for customers' travel and entertainment expenses by the casino.[135]

Verification of the identity of the person for whom the reportable cash is re-ceived is required,[136] thus providing a paper trail for law enforcement offi-cials to follow.

A specialized agency within the Treasury Department, the Financial Crimes Enforcement Network (known as FinCEN), issued regulations in 2002 to prescribe additional requirements for casinos in connection with the reporting of so-called suspicious transactions. It explained the enhanced focus on casino enterprises as follows:

[T]hese actions to expand the obligations of casinos reflect the continuing determination not only that casinos are vulnerable to manipulation by money launderers and tax evaders but, more generally, that gaming establishments provide their customers with a financial product—gaming—and as a corollary offer a broad array of financial services, such as customer deposit or credit accounts, facilities for transmitting and receiving funds transfers directly from other institutions, and check cashing and currency exchange services, that are similar to those offered by depository institutions and other financial firms.[137]

Perhaps even more significant is the fact that money launderers are believed to be efficient actors: "Money launderers will move their operations to institutions in which their chances of successful evasion of enforcement and regulatory efforts are the highest."[138]

The regulations prescribe the following standards that trigger a reporting obligation for a suspicious transaction:

A transaction requires reporting under the terms of this section if it is conducted or attempted by, at, or through a casino, and involves or aggregates at least $5,000 in funds or other assets, and the casino knows, suspects, or has reason to suspect that the transaction (or a pattern of transactions of which the transaction is a part):

(i)   Involves funds derived from illegal activity or is intended or conducted in order to hide or disguise funds or assets derived from illegal activity (including, without limitation, the ownership, nature, source, location, or control of such funds or assets) as part of a plan to violate or evade any federal law or regulation or to avoid any transaction reporting requirement under federal law or regulation;

(ii)   Is designed, whether through structuring or other means, to evade any requirements of this part or of any other regulations promulgated under the Bank Secrecy Act. . . .;

(iii) Has no business or apparent lawful purpose or is not the sort in which the particular customer would normally be expected to engage, and the casino knows of no reasonable explanation for the transaction after examining the available facts, including the background and possible purpose of the transaction; or

(iv)   Involves use of the casino to facilitate criminal activity.[139]

These standards are subject to criticism for their imprecision. Commentators expressed concerns about the difficulties of determining when a transaction is suspicious.[140] However, FinCEN retained this generalized approach, which is rooted in a fundamental belief in the advantages of experienced industry participants over government officials:

> [T]he employees and officers of those institutions are often more likely than government officials to have a sense as to which transactions appear to lack commercial justification (or in the case of gaming establishments, transactions that appear to lack a reasonable relationship to legitimate wagering activities) or that otherwise cannot be explained as constituting a legitimate use of the casino's financial services.[141]

In addition to the financial reporting rules, casinos are also subject to a complementary requirement to develop a monitoring program that evaluates customer activities for risks associated with money laundering.[142] As further explained in the preamble to the regulations:

> FinCEN wishes to emphasize that the rule is not intended to require casinos mechanically to review every transaction that exceeds the reporting threshold. Rather, it is intended that casinos, like every type of financial institution to which the suspicious transaction reporting rules of 31 CFR part 103 apply, will evaluate customer activity and relationships for money laundering risks, and design a suspicious transaction monitoring program that is appropriate for the particular casino in light of such risks. In other words, it is expected that casinos will follow a risk-based approach in monitoring for suspicious transactions, and will report all detected suspicious transactions that involve $5,000 or more in funds or other assets. A well-implemented anti-money laundering compliance program should reinforce a casino's efforts in detecting suspicious activity. In addition, casinos are encouraged to report on a voluntary basis detected suspicious transactions that fall below the $5,000 reporting threshold, such as the submission by a customer of an identification document that the casino suspects is false or altered, in the course of a transaction that triggers an identification requirement under the Bank Secrecy Act or other law.[143]

Compliance with the Bank Secrecy Act regulations is potentially costly to casinos. Estimated burdens published in the *Federal Register* in 2002 indicate that the currency transaction reporting requirement alone would affect 550 casinos, requiring 237,000 responses annually and a total of 94,800 human hours.[144] The suspicious transaction reporting requirements were thought to have a more limited impact, in that existing casino business practices already involve monitoring customers' information and thus may be amenable to being adapted to meet the requirements of those rules.[145]

These regulations may well contribute to enhanced enforcement efforts, but it is important to recognize that they have inherent limitations. Short of requiring all casino transactions to be conducted through electronic means, coupled with rigorous identity verification requirements for casino players, gaps will remain in this system designed for detection. Such a comprehensive, electronic-based system would be considered threatening to many gamblers, who would prefer that their activities remain private and out of the range of government supervision.

The suspicious transaction rules are particularly vulnerable to skepticism about their effectiveness. Although they do provide a legal means for cooperative activity by casinos, such cooperation is hardly in their economic interests, as it potentially involves the loss of a valuable customer. Casinos benefit from gathering information about their customers and their betting preferences, but learning "too much" might trigger a reporting obligation. It would be interesting to learn whether these regulations will ultimately have any impact on the information that casinos gather for their own business purposes, as well as whether they will make a positive contribution toward law enforcement efforts. Such information is likely to be kept as a trade secret by casinos, however, which will make sure it does not reach the light of day.

FIRST AMENDMENT CONSTRAINTS ON REGULATION OF CASINO ADVERTISING

One other topic merits attention in this chapter: the impact of the First Amendment on the regulation of commercial speech involving gambling businesses. State and local governments have occasionally sought to impose restrictions on advertising for gambling businesses, such as banning local advertising of casinos in an attempt to curb gambling by local citizens, while at the same time choosing to permit advertising in venues targeted toward tourists.[146] Although such restrictions might arguably serve a valid public interest in constraining social costs arising from local patrons, they constrain the commercial interests of the casino as well as the interests of those who might wish to hear that speech.

Interstate commerce issues also lurk here. Some forms of advertising, such as billboards and signs, may have a distinctly local impact, but others are less easily tied to particular geographic regions. Broadcast media are perhaps the most difficult to constrain, as their signals may reach well beyond the borders of a particular state. Congress weighed in on these conflicting interests by imposing a ban on radio and television broadcast advertising of information for any "lottery, gift enterprise, or similar scheme,"[147] terminology that has been interpreted to include casinos.[148] However, that ban has been weakened through statutory exceptions, including those allowing advertising for state-run lotteries and charitable gaming.[149] What was left of the ban was weakened even further by the Supreme Court's efforts to strengthen the protections available to commercial speech.[150]

This complex area has been the subject of extensive academic commentary, which will not be exhaustively explored in this context.[151] However, a brief discussion of several gambling-related cases that reached the Supreme Court is helpful in understanding the changing parameters of regulation of commercial speech and its effects on the regulation of casino advertising.

In *Posadas de Puerto Rico Associates v. Tourism Company of Puerto Rico*,[152] the operator of a Puerto Rican casino challenged government regulations that constrained the casino's ability to advertise. Puerto Rico had legalized casino-style gambling in 1948 for the purpose of generating tourism and enhancing the tax revenues available to the government.[153] The enabling legislation also imposed restrictions on casino advertising. In particular, section 8 provided that "[n]o gambling room shall be permitted to advertise or otherwise offer their facilities to the public of Puerto Rico."[154] Section 7 granted regulatory powers to a public corporation, which would implement these advertising restrictions.[155]

Regulations promulgated under section 7 essentially allowed casinos to advertise in venues that would be available primarily to tourists but prohibited advertising in venues that would target local Puerto Rican residents. For example, an advertisement in the *New York Times*, which might reach a local subscriber, would be permitted. However, advertising in local media would be restricted as to the content of casino gaming that could be included.[156] Although the effectiveness of these restrictions is disputable, their articulated purpose was to protect local residents from media exposure to the "experiment" of casino gambling, while at the same time allowing the casinos to fulfill their goals of promoting tourism.[157]

The Supreme Court noted that purely commercial speech was involved, and thus it invoked the so-called *Central Hudson* test:

> Under *Central Hudson,* commercial speech receives a limited form of First Amendment protection so long as it concerns a lawful activity and is not misleading or fraudulent. Once it is determined that the First Amendment applies to the particular kind of commercial speech at issue, then the speech may be restricted only if the government's interest in doing so is substantial, the restrictions directly advance the government's asserted interest, and the restrictions are no more extensive than necessary to serve that interest.[158]

Here, both residents and tourists could gamble legally, and affected advertising was neither misleading nor fraudulent. Thus, the analysis turned on the latter three elements of this test, which require the Court to consider the weight of the governmental interest and the fit between that interest and the means chosen to advance it.

First, the Court found that substantial government interests were present. The government's brief alleged legislative concerns that "[e]xcessive casino gambling among local residents . . . would produce serious harmful effects on the health, safety and welfare of the Puerto Rican citizens, such as the disruption of moral and cultural patterns, the increase in local crime, the fostering of prostitution, the development of corruption, and the infiltration of organized crime."[159] As the Court noted, "These are some of the very same concerns . . . that have motivated the vast majority of the 50 States to prohibit casino gambling. We have no difficulty in concluding that the Puerto Rico legislature's interest in the health, safety, and welfare of its citizens constitutes a 'substantial' governmental interest."[160]

The Court also found that the regulations directly advanced the government's interest in reducing the risks to the public associated with casino gambling. Even though other forms of gambling (such as cockfighting, horse racing, and lotteries) could be advertised locally, the Court deferred to the legislative judgment that particular harms associated with casino gambling could be singled out for protection.[161]

Finally, the Court found that the measure was not more extensive than necessary to serve the government's interest. The Court rejected an approach that would respond to social problems through allowing more speech rather than through constraining commercial speech. According to the Court, this was a matter to be reserved for the legislature.[162] The greater power to ban gambling included a lesser power of regulating commercial speech associated with gambling. As the Court explained,

> [I]t is precisely *because* the government could have enacted a wholesale pro-hibition of the underlying conduct that it is permissible for the government to take the less intrusive step of allowing the conduct, but reducing the demand through restrictions on advertising. It would surely be a Pyrrhic victory for casino owners such as appellant to gain recognition of a First Amendment right to advertise their casinos to the residents of Puerto Rico, only to thereby force the legislature into banning casino gambling by residents altogether. It would just as surely be a strange constitutional doctrine which would concede to the legislature the authority to totally ban a product or activity, but deny to the legislature the authority to forbid the stimulation of demand for the product or activity through advertising on behalf of those who would profit from such increased demand. Legislative regulation of products or activities deemed harmful, such as cigarettes, alcoholic beverages, and prostitution, has varied from outright prohibition on the one hand, see, *e.g.,* Cal. Penal Code Ann. § 647(b) (West Supp. 1986) (prohibiting soliciting or engaging in act of prostitution), to legalization of the product or activity with restrictions on stimulation of its demand on the other hand, see, *e.g.,* Nev.Rev.Stat. §§ 244.345(1), (8) (1986) (authorizing licensing of houses of prostitution except in counties with more than 250,000 population), §§ 201.430, 201.440 (prohibiting advertising of houses of prostitution "[i]n any public theater, on the public streets of any city or town, or on any public highway," or "in [a] place of business"). To rule out the latter, intermediate kind of response would require more than we find in the First Amendment.[163]

This dimension of the Court's analysis granted significant government power over commercial speech involving "vices" that nevertheless had legal status. In *United States v. Edge Broadcasting Company,*[164] the Court considered whether a Federal Communications Commission ban on lottery advertising in broadcast media satisfied the First Amendment. A radio station that was located in North Carolina (where the lottery was illegal) but that nevertheless reached customers in Virginia (where the lottery was legal) challenged this ban as violating its rights to commercial speech.

Although the government argued that the principle stated in *Posadas* that "the greater power to prohibit gambling necessarily includes the lesser power to ban its advertisement" should control the outcome here, the Court nevertheless required a full *Central Hudson* analysis.[165] However, the Court also recognized that "the activity underlying the relevant advertising—gambling—implicates no constitutionally protected right; rather, it falls into a category of 'vice' activity that could be and frequently has been, banned altogether."[166] The Court ultimately found that the requirements of *Central Hudson* were met and that the ban was appropriate to meet the substantial governmental interest in balancing the policies of states that prohibit lotteries against those that do not. As in *Posadas,* the Court in *Edge Broadcasting* was willing to defer to the legislative judgment about the validity of its policies rather than relying on the approach of answering commercial speech that hinders a government policy with counter-speech.[167]

This deferential approach to the legislature in matters involving "vice" would soon be abandoned, however, as the Court took a different tack toward commercial speech that refused to countenance a judgment that any legal activity could be characterized as "vice." In *44 Liquormart, Inc. v. Rhode Island,*[168] which involved a state ban on price advertising for liquor by state-licensed retailers, the Court explained that the deferential approach articulated in *Posadas* was an aberration that would no longer be followed. According to the Court, First Amendment jurisprudence was designed to embrace a skeptical view of outright bans of truthful commercial speech.

> Precisely because bans against truthful, nonmisleading commercial speech rarely seek to protect consumers from either deception or overreaching, they usually rest solely on the offensive assumption that the public will respond "irrationally" to the truth. The First Amendment directs us to be especially skeptical of regulations that seek to keep people in the dark for what the government perceives to be their own good.[169]

Based on this view, deference to the legislature on matters of suppressing commercial speech was inappropriate.

Because the 5-to-4 decision in *Posadas* marked such a sharp break from our prior precedent, and because it concerned a constitutional question about which this Court is the final arbiter, we decline to give force to its highly deferential approach. Instead, in keeping with our prior holdings, we conclude that a state legislature does not have the broad discretion to suppress truthful, nonmisleading information for paternalistic purposes that the *Posadas* majority was willing to tolerate.[170]

Moreover, the Court also rejected reliance on the "greater includes the lesser" principle as a basis for supporting government regulation of commercial speech.

Although we do not dispute the proposition that greater powers include lesser ones, we fail to see how that syllogism requires the conclusion that the State's power to regulate commercial *activity* is "greater" than its power to ban truthful, nonmisleading commercial *speech*. Contrary to the assumption made in *Posadas,* we think it quite clear that banning speech may sometimes prove far more intrusive than banning conduct. As a venerable proverb teaches, it may prove more injurious to prevent people from teaching others how to fish than to prevent fish from being sold. Similarly, a local ordinance banning bicycle lessons may curtail freedom far more than one that prohibits bicycle riding within city limits. In short, we reject the assumption that words are necessarily less vital to freedom than actions, or that logic somehow proves that the power to prohibit an activity is necessarily "greater" than the power to suppress speech about it.[171]

In a further retreat from its prior precedent in *Edge Broadcasting,* the Court also rejected the concept of a special class of commercial speech accompanying "vice" activities.

[T]he scope of any "vice" exception to the protection afforded by the First Amendment would be difficult, if not impossible, to define. Almost any product that poses some threat to public health or public morals might reasonably be characterized by a state legislature as relating to "vice activity." Such characterization, however, is anomalous when applied to products such as alcoholic beverages, lottery tickets, or playing cards, that may be lawfully purchased on the open market. The recognition of such an exception would also have the unfortunate consequence of either allowing state legislatures to justify censorship by the simple expedient of placing the "vice" label on selected lawful activities, or requiring the federal courts to establish a federal common law of vice. For these reasons, a "vice" label that is unaccompanied by a corresponding prohibition against the commercial behavior at issue fails to provide a principled justification for the regulation of commercial speech about that activity.[172]

Thus, the Court apparently takes an increasingly agnostic view about the moral dangers associated with activities that the legislature chooses to make legal and removes legislative prerogatives with regard to banning speech in these areas.

The significance of this change in approach for commercial speech involving gambling was further evidenced in the Court's 1999 decision in *Greater New Orleans Broadcasting Association, Inc. v. United States,*[173] which involved the application of regulations under 18 U.S.C.A. § 1304 to prohibit certain types of advertising for private legal casino operations via television media. Unlike the radio advertising in *Edge Broadcasting,* which occurred through a radio station located in a state in which the advertised gambling was illegal, the television stations involved in this case were located in Louisiana, where private casino gambling was legal. However, their signals potentially reached into states such as Texas and Arkansas, where private casino gambling was not legal.[174]

The government alleged that substantial interests were at stake, including familiar assertions about the social costs of commercial casino gambling.

> Underlying Congress' statutory scheme, the Solicitor General contends, is the judgment that gambling contributes to corruption and organized crime; underwrites bribery, narcotics trafficking, and other illegal conduct; imposes a regressive tax on the poor; and "offers a false but sometimes irresistible hope of financial advancement." With respect to casino gambling, the Solicitor General states that many of the associated social costs stem from "pathological" or "compulsive" gambling by approximately 3 million Americans, whose behavior is primarily associated with "continuous play" games, such as slot machines. He also observes that compulsive gambling has grown along with the expansion of legalized gambling nationwide, leading to billions of dollars in economic costs; injury and loss to these gamblers as well as their families, communities, and government; and street, white-collar, and organized crime.[175]

Although the Court grudgingly recognized that these interests could indeed be substantial, it also noted that federal policies in this area had changed substantially since the enactment of 18 U.S.C. § 1304 in 1975. Numerous exceptions had been appended to the broadcast ban, and the federal policy expressed in the Indian Gaming Regulatory Act had also effectively promoted casino gambling.[176] These inconsistencies proved to create a fatal flaw in the government's case. As the Court explained,

> The operation of § 1304 and its attendant regulatory regime is so pierced by exemptions and inconsistencies that the Government cannot hope to exonerate it. Under current law, a broadcaster may not carry advertising about privately operated commercial casino gambling, regardless of the location of the station or the casino. On the other hand, advertisements for tribal casino gambling authorized by state compacts—whether operated by the tribe or by a private party pursuant to a management contract—are subject to no such broadcast ban, even if the broadcaster is located in, or broadcasts to, a jurisdiction with the strictest of antigambling policies. Government-operated, nonprofit, and "occasional and ancillary" commercial casinos are likewise exempt.[177]

Since these exempt forms of casino gambling would presumably present the same kinds of social costs as private casino gambling, the government could not meet its burden. Moreover, the Court also suggested that other means could be used to address these social concerns that would not burden commercial speech.

> Ironically, the most significant difference identified by the Government between tribal and other classes of casino gambling is that the former is "heavily regulated." If such direct regulation provides a basis for believing that the social costs of gambling in tribal casinos are sufficiently mitigated to make their advertising tolerable, one would have thought that Congress might have at least experimented with comparable regulation before abridging the speech rights of federally unregulated casinos. While Congress' failure to institute such direct regulation of private casino gambling does not necessarily compromise the constitutionality of § 1304, it does undermine the asserted justifications for the restriction before us. There surely are practical and nonspeech-related forms of reg-

ulation—including a prohibition or supervision of gambling on credit; limitations on the use of cash machines on casino premises; controls on admissions; pot or betting limits; location restrictions; and licensing requirements—that could more directly and effectively alleviate some of the social costs of casino gambling.[178]

Congress's failure to require more restrictive forms of federal regulation thus proved inconsistent with the overall goals articulated in the restriction on casino advertising. The concern raised in *Posadas* as a reason for granting legislative deference, that is, that government might otherwise have to restrict the people's freedom to *do* the activity, was now embraced as a preferable one to restricting commercial speech about the activity.

As a result of the Supreme Court's change in views about the scope of First Amendment protections for commercial speech, it appears that policymakers will be unable to impose substantial restrictions on casino advertising in connection with decisions to regulate the gaming industry. Appropriate time, place, and manner restrictions (such as keeping casino ads from public schools or other environs targeted to minors) may well continue to be upheld under the *Central Hudson* analysis. Challenges to false or misleading speech may also be sustained, though misleading speech can be difficult to define. For example, would an advertisement inviting debtors to win their way out of financial worries by coming to the casino be acceptable commercial speech? As casino markets become more saturated and thus more competitive, more of these issues are likely to be presented.[179]

Whether the Court's change in approach is desirable from a policy perspective is a matter for debate. On one hand, the idea that consumers should have access to information that is neither false nor misleading appeals to our belief in reason and rational discernment. However, cultural matters of sensibility are also at stake, which are not easily dismissed. For example, would the Court be willing to apply its rationale to allow constant media bombardment to the type of services and prices available in connection with the legal prostitution services (which are allowed in some Nevada counties)? The real extent to which the courts are willing to reject the concept of "vice" for all activities that are legally permitted remains to be seen. A more culturally sensitive alternative of toleration without permitting commercial enterprises to flout cultural norms appears outside the realm of possibility under this approach.

To the extent that advertising for casino gaming has a negative impact on other cultural values, such as work, saving, and temperance, those values will apparently have to be addressed through counter-speech. Alternatively, to the extent that empirical research demonstrates a connection between advertising and problem gambling behavior, counter-speech might be needed. Whether the legislature will require the casino industry to fund such speech and whether they have the power to do so are issues that may be presented in the future; the tobacco industry currently faces similar issues that may provide some indication of future trends. (Those issues are discussed further in chapter 12.)

In the meantime, however, it is quite clear that protections for commercial speech do not extend to advertising unlawful activities.[180] The current illegality of Internet gambling in the United States means that targeting advertisers becomes a legitimate tool for enforcing antigambling laws, a topic discussed in the following chapter.

10. The Internet: Gambling's New Frontier

The technologies that have made the Internet so attractive to other commercial ventures have also attracted the gaming industry. Although the diffused and geographically ambiguous nature of the Internet makes it difficult to assess its economic impact, analysts at the General Accounting Office have estimated that more than $4 billion was wagered on the Internet in 2003.[1] The recent phenomenal growth of online poker, which is estimated to have grown from less than $100 million in 2002 to more than $1 billion in 2004, suggests continued expansion in online markets.[2] Some sources estimate online patron losses at $12 billion for 2005.[3]

The economic potential for Internet gambling may also be revealed through an indirect measure—the amount that online casinos have paid to promote their sites to potential patrons. Prior to federal government efforts to restrict Internet advertising, paid listings in commonly used search engines reflected competitive bids by commercial gaming interests, thus providing an indication of the commercial value placed on certain terms. As of April 2004, the top bid for the word *casino* as a paid placement on sites such as Yahoo! and Google was $14.97 per "click-through."[4] This appears to be a significant investment for the privilege of accessing a potential customer, who ultimately may not choose to wager on the site. However, one online gambling firm headquartered in Gibraltar, PartyGaming PLC, disclosed profits of $350 million on $600 million in revenues in 2004, suggesting that this kind of online advertising spending is not irrational.[5] As of August 2005, PartyGaming PLC had a market capitalization of 6.55 billion British pounds—more than that of British Airways.[6]

Growth in this industry has been substantial. In 1997, as few as thirty Web sites apparently offered online gambling.[7] Seven years later, several thousand sites offered some form of gaming services.[8] As many as seventy-six different jurisdictions may be offering some form of government license for Internet gambling.[9] The ubiquity of the Internet coupled with jurisdictional constraints on the efficacy of federal and state laws make the Internet a particularly challenging environment to regulate. The nature of that challenge and some potential means for dealing with it are discussed in the sections that follow.

THE BUSINESS MODEL FOR INTERNET GAMBLING

Internet gambling creates the possibility of reaping economic benefits without a significant investment in a physical plant or employee base. Unlike their traditional counterparts, Internet casino operations do not require extensive investments in lavish, customer-friendly facilities. Their secure servers can be located in inconspicuous buildings in remote locales; physical access and the creature comforts are not a consideration in the world of virtual gaming. Construction and maintenance of facilities require significant up-front investments for traditional casino operations, which create barriers to entry and significant ongoing cost, particularly in competitive tourist markets. For example, it has been reported that the failure of Trump-owned casinos in Atlantic City to make renovations and improvements put them at a competitive disadvantage to other newer casinos.[10]

Internet operations also do not require extensive employee staffing to serve the needs of their customers. Employees who run the games, such as dealers and croupiers, are instead replaced by computerized versions for online patrons. The pit boss and the supervisory personnel who are otherwise employed to watch over these employees are also unnecessary, as computer algorithms are designed to ensure against human foibles that might otherwise cheat the house of its advantage. Computer technologists and programmers thus substitute for other forms of human employment, providing a productivity advantage and likely reduction of overhead costs.

Both virtual and traditional casino operations share the common need for advertising to attract customers. First Amendment protections for commercial speech permit a broad range of advertising targeted at potential patrons for legal operations. Print and broadcast media frequently tout opportunities to gamble at legal casino operations, and thus media companies benefit indirectly from this enhanced demand for advertising. Even though advertisements may cross state lines into jurisdictions that do not permit casino gambling, state regulation or censorship of such advertising is likely to be unsuccessful as long as the casino's operation is legal and the advertising is not false or misleading.[11]

Though Internet gambling operations have also used traditional media,[12] most use the Internet as their primary medium to reach customers. Internet providers and users face a practical problem in finding one another, and search engines have been developed to address this problem. Search engines potentially provide access to available content without special costs or charges to the indexed sites, but the crowded marketplace has made this process somewhat cumbersome. The search term *casino* provides millions of "hits" on a typical search engine. The industry has therefore had to resort to more costly methods of targeting potential customers.

As previously noted, pay-for-listing services in major search engines provide one approach to distinguish an Internet casino from its competition. In a typical pay-for-listing arrangement, competitors submit bids to search engine providers for the privilege of a preeminent listing in search results associated with specified key words. These bids commit the site to pay the host a stated amount per click-through to the bidder's site. Unlike ads in broadcast or print media, where an approximation of the number of potential readers or listeners may be available but actual contact with the ad is unknown, click-through measurements provide a reasonably accurate indication of actual consumer interest.

However, a click-through does not necessarily consummate a customer relationship. Thus, the online casino continues to bear some risk. Assuming a rate of $14.97 per click-through, the casino would pay $14,970 to the advertiser for each thousand click-throughs. In order for that casino to be profitable, click-throughs would have to generate player relationships that would generate gaming losses to cover this customer acquisition cost plus other operational costs. Thus, for example, average losses of one hundred dollars per account would require a response rate of at least 150 customers per thousand click-throughs or 15 percent, in order to cover the advertising cost. As losses or response rates increase above these levels, profitability may be possible.

Predicting profitability based on the willingness to pay customer acquisition costs in an online business is hazardous, as many online firms that fit this profile failed during early phases of e-commerce applications on the Internet. However, regardless of whether these ads are profitable for the online casinos, they provide revenue to the online advertiser. In 2004, Yahoo! Inc. experienced record profits, which it attributed in part to online advertising.[13] While it is uncertain how much revenue it generated from casinos, the trend toward online advertising generally presents a picture of unrelenting growth. Reported earnings for 2005 indicate that online advertising generated $1.32 billion for Yahoo!—a 39 percent increase over 2004.[14]

In addition to paid placements, online casinos have a variety of other means to reach their Internet customers. Links to casinos through other Web sites provide another option for reaching casino customers. In these relationships, the online casino may offer the owner of a referring Web site a portion of the revenues or net winnings generated through their patrons.[15] In this manner, the online casino may acquire customers without a significant up-front payment, as in the case of a paid placement in a search engine. Of course, such an arrangement may pose other risks, including the monitoring and enforcement of the payment terms, which would be left to the site owners.

"Pop-up" advertising has also become a popular means for online casinos to advertise on the Internet. Despite annoying many Internet users to the point of developing blocking software as a means of self-help, they are apparently effective in attracting customers by matching and cross-selling similar content-based interests. For example, online gaming sites sometimes utilize adult entertainment themes to build upon the affinity of patrons for sex and gambling—not unlike their counterparts in Las Vegas who match sexually charged entertainment productions with their gambling operations. Pop-up ads for online casinos have even been reported to be found on a Web site designed to help compulsive gamblers.[16] Though this pop-up ad would undoubtedly reach the type of customer an online casino longs for (at least from an economic perspective), the placement certainly raises questions about social responsibility and the obligations that government may impose on gambling operators for the good of the public.

Licensing issues affect online casinos much like they affect their traditional counterparts. However, differences in the potential customer base of an online casino, as well as differences in the business model, affect the scope and impact of licensing decisions. The online gambling industry is currently located outside of the United States, and the economic interests of foreign governments hosting these operations are often at odds with the interests of the country from which patrons are likely to come. As one analyst has pointed out,

> The Internet gambling industry can be an attractive source of export earnings, with minimal infrastructure requirements. Additionally, the social cost of gambling is exported as the consequences of gambling addiction and problem gambling are bourne by the community in which the gambler lives. This can be an attractive proposition for those countries providing the access to online gambling and a troubling one for those supplying the gamblers.[17]

Licensing officials in jurisdictions with traditional casinos have some incentives to examine the operational impacts on local populations when determining the conditions for licensing. These concerns about community effects also provide incentives for casino operators to behave responsibly, to the extent that they depend on government cooperation for the purpose of renewing those licenses. Internet operations designed to attract foreign patrons have diminished interests in these areas. For example, it is doubtful that Internet operations will make any significant contributions toward social costs or community betterment affecting their patrons. Even cooperative advertising efforts to warn about problem gambling behaviors among online patrons would not be expected. In the current online environment, such efforts are simply not good for business.[18]

A NEED FOR REGULATION?

Gambling patrons also have economic interests that are integral to their participation in the online marketplace. The extent to which government regulation plays a role in ensuring patron security is an interesting, yet undeveloped, question. With traditional casinos, regulation provides an indication that games are being played fairly and that the casino is financially capable of paying off a winning bet. Other physical cues of reliability may also be available, such as the ability to watch dealers perform their tasks and to witness other patrons winning jackpots. In a traditional casino, not only do these cues indicate that the patron is getting his or her money's worth, but they also contribute to an atmosphere of excitement that may loosen a patron's purse strings.

Similar physical cues are generally unavailable online, as players are relegated to a private, computer-based experience. However, sophisticated online players may also access other sources of information. Here, the Internet's capacity for efficient information sharing may provide additional indications about the reliability of an online casino, which might even be used as a substitute for government regulation. Online patrons can share information in user groups, which provide an informal basis for comparing anecdotal Internet gambling experiences. For example, message boards at sites such as Winneronline.com provide a means for disgruntled players to share their concerns about nonpayment for a winning account.[19] Public relations representatives from online casinos have also been known to frequent such boards to address the problems raised by patrons.

Online patrons may also be able to access sites that are specifically devoted to sharing information about online casino payouts. Independent accounting firms such as PricewaterhouseCoopers provide audit services to casinos. This public attestation function is designed to bolster marketplace reliance on a secure and fair online gaming experience.[20] Web sites may also rank online casinos based on their payout rates.[21] However, it is up to the patron to determine whether these rates are accurate. Assuming disclosures are accurate, then the online player may even have an advantage over players in traditional casinos, which often do not advertise these rates.

Sports-betting sites avoid some concerns about fairness because the standards for winning and losing are readily available and accessible to patrons from reliable third-party sources. Thus, the online sports bettor need only concern himself or herself with the viability of the enterprise with whom the bet is placed; concerns about whether the electronic deck is stacked or the roulette wheel is rigged are not relevant, thus providing another level of security to the player. This added security, coupled with pervasive popular interest in sports and the belief that superior sports knowledge may provide an advantage, perhaps helps to account for the popularity of online sports betting.

Online patrons who rely on information-based monitoring are placing trust in private sources rather than in government-backed regulators. Given the information transparency that is possible in the online marketplace and the availability of private attestation functions, it is a fair question to ask whether government regulation would truly add to the reliability of online games. However, in the event of the financial failure of an online gambling firm, the player relying on private ordering principles would be well advised to be diversified. The prospects of pursuing claims in foreign courts may well prove daunting to most players, who would likely choose to cut their losses and move on.

The psychological profile of the online gambler is likely to involve a significant risk-taking component, which may limit the practical impact of inquiries into the nature and extent of government protections. Despite the potential risks, some gamblers seem intent on using online casinos without regard to their local legal status or to whether an effective means of government regulation and oversight exists among the many nations that permit some form of online gaming.

FEDERAL GOVERNMENT EFFORTS TO CONTROL ONLINE GAMBLING

Congress's tepid efforts to control sports betting in the Professional and Amateur Sports Protection Act, discussed in chapter 9, suggest the possibility that the federal government may possess a similarly limited commitment to preventing online gambling. Though critics have raised concerns about the protection of minors in the online forum, the increased social costs from online gambling, and even psychological harms from the potentially addictive character of video-based gambling activities, a comprehensive legislative solution has not been forthcoming.

This legislative failure may be attributed, in part, to the difficulty of enforcing what laws we currently have against online gambling. Even assuming that legislative goals can be identified, implementing legislation in an environment with jurisdictional as well as technological complexity presents formidable challenges.

THE FEDERAL GOVERNMENT STRIKES: PROSECUTION OF JAY COHEN

One of the most visible prosecution efforts affecting an international Internet gaming enterprise involves the case of *United States v. Cohen*.[22] This case has garnered significant international attention because of the application of U.S. laws to an individual conducting a business that is legally operating in a foreign country. In 1996, Jay Cohen left his position as a market maker at a San Francisco firm that traded in options and derivatives for an alternative risk-driven career as an international bookmaker. He became the president of the World Sports Exchange (WSE), a firm that began a sports-betting operation in the tiny Caribbean nation of Antigua and Barbuda.

Antigua and Barbuda are two small Caribbean islands with a combined population of about seventy thousand residents. According to the CIA's *World Factbook,* only about five thousand residents had Internet access as of 2001,[23] but that figure doubled to ten thousand in 2002, the latest year for which estimates are available.[24] Despite apparently limited Internet usage among Antigua natives, the island has nevertheless become a haven for Internet gaming firms. In 2001, the Antiguan government established a Free Trade and Processing Zone, which created a regulatory and tax structure that proved attractive for other firms interested in offering Internet gaming services. However, the WSE was ahead of the curve in choosing to begin its operations in Antigua before these incentives were enacted. The fact that gambling was legal in Antigua and that Antigua was also connected to the United States by an undersea fiber-optic cable (thus assuring Internet connectivity even during a hurricane) probably influenced its locational decision.[25]

WSE targeted customers in the United States by advertising in various media, including radio, newspaper, television, and the Internet. Customers who responded could set up accounts to bet with WSE via telephone or Internet. After depositing at least three hundred dollars via wire transfer into an account located in Antigua, the customer was allowed to instruct WSE to make bets on sporting events using those funds. Average accounts ran from one thousand to three thousand dollars, though some deposited as much as thirty thousand dollars.[26] WSE profited from a 10 percent commission on each wager.[27]

The prospects of Internet-based sports wagering proved attractive in the marketplace, as WSE had over sixteen hundred customers after its first year of operation. A *Wall Street Journal* story in April 1997 examined Cohen's new business venture, providing readers with an explanation of the business and a Web site address for potential customers and curiosity seekers to find out more.[28] Customers responded with gusto, including many from the United States. By November 1998, WSE had received over sixty thousand telephone calls from the United States.[29]

Unfortunately for Cohen, the media attention that proved so good for business also attracted the attention of law enforcement authorities. FBI agents in New York opened accounts and placed bets with WSE both by phone and by Internet.[30] On the basis of these contacts, Cohen was arrested and indicted for offenses in violation of the Wire Act, 18 U.S.C. § 1084(a). In particular, Cohen was charged with "(1) transmission in interstate or foreign commerce of bets or wagers; (2) transmission of a wire communication which entitles the recipient to receive money or credit as a result of bets or wagers, and (3) information assisting in the placement of bets or wagers."[31] He was ultimately convicted and sentenced to twenty-one months in prison.

Enforcement of laws against Internet gaming involves more than discovering and proving the elements of a crime. The government must establish personal jurisdiction over the defendant in order to exact a criminal punishment, and Jay Cohen squarely presented this problem. Although he was a U.S. citizen, the government could not reach him as long as he resided in Antigua. Instead of remaining in Antigua and evading the risk of prosecution, Cohen chose to surrender himself to authorities and to challenge the underlying basis for a violation of the Wire Act.

Unfortunately for Cohen, his challenge to the application of the Wire Act proved unsuccessful. Among other things, Cohen argued that he was entitled to protection under a safe harbor provision in the Wire Act, which provided in part that

> [n]othing in this section shall be construed to prevent the transmission in interstate or foreign commerce of information for use in news reporting of sporting events or contests, or for the transmission of information assisting in the placing of bets or wagers on a sporting event or contest from a State or foreign country where betting on that sporting event or contest is legal into a State or foreign country in which such betting is legal.[32]

Cohen argued that customers were only transmitting information and that the bet or wager was actually placed in Antigua.[33] However, the court found that the customers were indeed placing bets from the United States.[34] The trial judge's instruction to the jury explicitly referenced either telephone or Internet transmissions as being within the scope of the Wire Act.[35] Moreover, it was quite clear that such betting was illegal under New York law, and that provided a sufficient basis to find that he was not within the scope of the safe harbor.

Cohen's case also clarified that using telephone or Internet connections to transmit betting information could result in a violation of the Wire Act. Though Cohen had argued that he did not transmit information but merely received it, the court was unpersuaded.

> Cohen established two forms of wire facilities, internet and telephone, which he marketed to the public for the express purpose of transmitting bets and betting information. Cohen subsequently received such transmissions from customers, and, in turn, sent such transmissions back to those customers in various forms, including in the form of acceptances and confirmation. No matter what spin he puts on "transmission," his conduct violated the statute.[36]

Cohen was one of fourteen people indicted by federal prosecutors for offshore online gambling operations.[37] However, his case became a celebrated cause for the offshore betting community. Cohen petitioned the U.S. Supreme Court for review, and that petition was supported by the Antiguan government, which filed an amicus brief in support of Cohen's petition. Moreover, as discussed subsequently, the Antiguan government also chose to use the U.S. government's position in this case as a basis for challenging U.S. compliance with its treaty obligations involving international trade, which remains an ongoing dispute.

Though Cohen's case is significant, the language of the Wire Act may nevertheless impose limits on the federal law enforcement efforts directed toward Internet gambling. The operative provision of the Wire Act, 18 U.S.C. § 1084(a), states in relevant part:

> Whoever being engaged in the business of betting or wagering knowingly uses a wire communication facility for the transmission in interstate or foreign commerce of bets or wagers or information assisting in the placing of bets or wagers on any sporting event or contest, or for the transmission of a wire communication which entitles the recipient to receive money or credit as a result of bets or wagers, or for information assisting in the placing of bets or wagers, shall be fined under this title or imprisoned not more than two years, or both.[38]

First, the language of the Wire Act suggests that only those engaged in the business of placing bets are affected. It does not address the casual gambler, who might utilize the Internet to engage in online casino gambling.[39] Targeting casual gambling behavior on a large scale may be an unwise use of limited federal prosecution resources. However, the potential for federal enforcement of laws against Internet gambling may well deter some patrons from the activity. Any deterrent effect is nullified if the public knows that no basis for prosecution exists.[40]

Second, the scope of the Wire Act may be further limited by its reference to wagers "on any sporting event or contest." The Fifth Circuit has recently concluded that the Wire Act does not apply to casino gaming on the Internet because such wagering does not involve a "sporting event or contest."[41] The Fifth Circuit agreed with the rationale of the federal district court, which found that a "plain reading of the statutory language" supported by the legislative history required this result.[42]

However, this reading is contestable. The language "on any sporting event or contest" modifies the first appearance of "bets or wagers" in section 1084(a), but "bets or wagers" appears two more times in that statute without the limiting language. While it is true that the legislative history, which extends back to 1961, focused on sports betting, this predates the advent of the Internet and its potential to bring other kinds of gambling to remote bettors. A New York state court has agreed that the Wire Act does apply to online casino gaming, based in part on the broader purpose of preventing unlawful gambling.[43]

Members of Congress have recognized this potential deficiency in the language of the Wire Act, but proposed legislation to amend it has failed.[44] A failure to adopt an amendment does not necessarily mean that Congress approves of Internet casinos. The scope and extent of the current version of the Wire Act may yet be tested in other jurisdictions. As discussed subsequently, the Justice Department has used the threat of prosecution under "aiding and abetting" theories to address ancillary business participation in Internet casino gambling. Nevertheless, it is true that the current language does present some uncertainty and that Congress has yet to pass a comprehensive legal solution.

The international gaming community remains very concerned about the prospects of prosecution for Internet wagering activities such as those in *Cohen*. An amicus curiae brief in support of Cohen's petition for certiorari in the U.S. Supreme Court filed by the Antiguan government stated in part:

The Second Circuit's decision would criminalize not only the activities of American citizens in Antigua, but also activities of non-American citizens engaged in the betting or wagering business from Antigua, suppliers for that business, and even Antiguan governmental officials not protected by the doctrine of Sovereign Immunity.

Should the petition for certiorari not be granted and the present decision be allowed to stand, it would have a very negative impact on the Antiguan economy and hamper the country's efforts to create strong regulatory controls over all interactive wagering.[45]

Since the Supreme Court denied certiorari in this case, it remains to be seen whether the ultimate impact on Antigua will be as negative as predicted. As discussed subsequently, the World Trade Organization (WTO) proceedings involving Antigua provided one way for this nation to strike back against U.S. policy using trade laws. First, however, we look at what tools lie in the law enforcement arsenals of the states.

THE STATES STRIKE: INTERNET ENFORCEMENT EFFORTS

State laws may also affect the legality of Internet betting operations. Like their federal counterpart, state governments also face jurisdictional constraints. Finding an appropriate nexus between the criminal activity and the state is typically not the problem, but enforcing a judgment over the operator of an offending Web site may present an insurmountable practical barrier to effective legal governance. As a result, there are few reported cases in which state governments seek to prosecute Internet gaming operations.

People v. World Interactive Gaming Corporation[46] is a notable case in this area because of the state's ability to overcome those jurisdictional limitations. The World Interactive Gaming Corporation (WIGC) was incorporated in Delaware but maintained an office in New York. Through a wholly owned Antiguan subsidiary, Golden Chips Casino, Inc. (GCC), WIGC operated an Internet casino pursuant to a license from the Antiguan government. GCC promoted this casino on the Internet and through advertising in a national gambling magazine, and New York residents viewed these ads. Like its sports-betting counterpart, the WSE, the GCC required its Internet casino users to wire funds to an Antiguan bank account, from which bets would ultimately be made.

In June 1998, the attorney general's office downloaded gambling software from GCC's Antiguan Web site, and the following month they began placing bets. The GCC software asked users to enter their permanent address. If the user reported an address in a state that permitted land-based gambling, such as Nevada, the software granted permission for the user to gamble in virtual games, which included slot machines, roulette, and blackjack. If the user reported an address in New York, where land-based casino gambling was illegal, permission was not granted. However, New York users who were denied access could easily circumvent this restriction by changing the registration to Nevada, since the software did not monitor actual locations.

On the basis of this activity, the attorney general sought an injunction against WIGC to prevent it from "running any aspect of their Internet gambling business within the State of New York." WIGC challenged this action on jurisdictional grounds, but this challenge failed. WIGC managed this business from its offices in New York. It made administrative decisions and did computer research for the business in New York. It also worked with a New York–based design firm, Imajix Studios, to design graphics for the Web site. Even if its offices had not been in New York, these systematic and purposeful contacts with the state would have been sufficient to satisfy jurisdictional requirements.[47]

As for its subsidiary, GCC, personal jurisdiction would ordinarily be more difficult to establish. If GCC were treated as a separate legal entity, the state would be required to show that it had sufficient contacts with New York to support jurisdiction. However, in this case, such a showing was obviated by the court's determination that GCC's corporate form would not be respected on the ground that it was a "mere agent, department, or alter ego" of WIGC.[48] Here, WIGC "completely dominated" its subsidiary. The GCC Web site had been "purchased" by WIGC, which also provided administration services. GCC's top employees were hired by, and reported to, WIGC. Work on the servers that hosted the Web site was also done pursuant to contracts with service providers that were maintained by WIGC.

Thus, WIGC not only ignored corporate formalities but also provided support for the gaming operations of its subsidiary to an extent that it could be categorized as an agent of that subsidiary. It was relatively easy to find that WIGC was guilty of promoting gambling in violation of New York law. In fact, the court noted that violation of New York law had even occurred before any New York resident wagered on the GCC Web site, to the extent that their conduct in creating and soliciting patronage for unlawful games "materially aids [unlawful] gambling activity."[49] The fact that Internet gaming was legal in Antigua was not a defense, as these activities occurred in New York.

A similar case was also presented in Minnesota during the early years of Internet casinos. In *State v. Granite Gate Resorts, Inc.*,[50] the attorney general filed a complaint against a Nevada corporation and its principal officer, alleging that these defendants engaged in deceptive trade practices, false advertising, and consumer fraud based on designing and hosting an advertisement for an online wagering service based in Belize. Although the corporation and officer were both domiciled in Nevada, the state of Minnesota asserted jurisdiction based on the nature and extent of Internet contacts with Minnesota residents. The company's Web site advertised an online wagering service that was soon to become operational as "a legal way to bet on sporting events from anywhere in the world."[51] In addition, it explained how to subscribe to the service and provided a form to enroll on a mailing list and a toll-free number for Internet users to contact them. At least one Minnesota resident became part of the mailing list, and computers in Minnesota contacted the Web site several hundred times.

The Minnesota Court of Appeals concluded that the state had jurisdiction in these circumstances. Based on the quantity and quality of the contacts with the state through the Web site and the strong interests of the state in enforcing its consumer protection laws and regulating gambling, the court found that the jurisdictional threshold had been met. This meant that the state could proceed, imposing injunctive relief as well as civil penalties against the foreign corporation and its officer.

Other courts have similarly found personal jurisdiction over an online gambling operation based on contacts with state residents on interactive Web sites.[52] Though a purely passive Web site might not pass muster under current case law dealing with Internet jurisdiction, the typical casino gaming site would indeed have engaged in contracts with state residents over the Internet and in doing so would repeatedly transmit computer information to that jurisdiction. These activities would generally be sufficient to support a finding of personal jurisdiction, thus potentially subjecting the Internet casino to legally enforceable judgments.

The potential extent of jurisdictional reach is also illustrated in *Alitalia-*

Linee Aeree Italiane v. Casinoalitalia.com,[53] a case involving a trademark in-fringement claim against an Internet casino. Alitalia Airlines, an Italian cor-poration, brought suit in a federal district court in Virginia against an Inter-net casino operator based in the Dominican Republic. Alitalia alleged that the Internet casino had infringed its trademark as a result of the use of its corporate name in its Web site. Alitalia claimed that such usage created a false impression that the airline was supporting online gambling. It also claimed that such usage further tarnished its mark because the word *casino* meant *brothel* in Italian, thus suggesting to Italian-speaking users that Alitalia may be in another tawdry business.

At the heart of the case was the basis for personal jurisdiction in a Virginia court. Other than operating the Web site, which did indeed reach five Vir-ginia customers, the defendant corporation had no other contacts with Vir-ginia, as its operations were based entirely in the Dominican Republic. Nev-ertheless, the court found that these limited contacts were sufficient to provide personal jurisdiction over the site: "Defendant's contacts with these residents are sufficient to put the defendant on notice that it is purposefully directing its activities at Virginia, and that it should therefore foresee being haled into court in this forum."[54]

Though states may well have a legal foundation for pursuing online casi-nos that violate state gambling laws, such efforts are nevertheless likely to be fruitless in many cases. In the *Granite Gate Resorts* and *World Interactive Gaming* cases, the defendants were both incorporated in the United States. Thus, a valid judgment could potentially be enforced against assets and per-sons located in the United States through other courts with jurisdiction over those assets and persons. However, a well-advised Internet casino operator could easily avoid the mistakes that were made in those cases by incorporat-ing in a foreign jurisdiction and maintaining operational control outside of the United States. The fact that there are no more recent reported cases in-volving state attorneys general seeking relief from domestic Internet casino operations suggests that the Internet gaming marketplace has indeed learned these simple lessons and has avoided similar mistakes.

In a case like *Alitalia,* the defendant was located in the Dominican Repub-lic and apparently limited its base of operations accordingly. Enforcement of any judgment that affected operations in a foreign country would ordinarily require cooperation from a foreign government, which would have the power to compel the defendant to comply. Absent a treaty provision to aid in that enforcement, the chances of success would be doubtful. Thus, the domestic judgment would effectively have no impact on a foreign corporation operating an Internet casino site, as long as that corporation and its operators stayed outside of the jurisdiction of the United States.

ANTICYBERSQUATTING CONSUMER PROTECTION ACT: IN REM THEORY

Alitalia involved a somewhat unusual situation because the applicable federal statute forming the basis for relief, the Anticybersquatting Consumer Protection Act (ACPA), provides that if the plaintiff cannot get personal jurisdiction over the owner of that domain name, it could bring suit under a theory of in rem jurisdiction (i.e., jurisdiction based on the location of the property—the domain name) in a federal district court where the domain name is registered.[55] Although this kind of suit would not be effective for monetary damages, it could provide relief in the form of either cancellation or transfer of ownership of the infringing domain name.[56] Since the entity that controlled the registration of that Web site, Network Solutions, was a corporation domiciled in Virginia,[57] this relief would be effective without any concerns about enforcing a judgment in the Dominican Republic.

Although the ACPA is narrowly tailored to address the problems of trademark infringement, its approach of dealing with trademark infringement could potentially provide a framework for addressing Internet casino gaming enforcement. If Congress wished to impose a significant barrier to Internet gambling, it could enact a similar provision that would allow an in rem action against the offending Web site operating the online casino. Alternatively, to the extent that personal jurisdiction is proper based on contacts with domestic gamblers, a court might award a remedy of canceling or transferring the ownership of an offending domain name. Thus, state or federal government officials could effectively wrestle away control of Web sites that violate federal or state gambling laws through doing business with U.S. customers.

Current technology does permit Web sites to block access to patrons with Internet addresses in a particular country. Such technology is becoming increasingly important in addressing problems of content that may violate local laws, as was recently litigated in connection with challenges by the French government to Internet content offered by Yahoo! involving Nazi materials.[58] Such an approach might also provide an effective means to address a gaming operation that unlawfully does business with patrons within the United States, failing to implement good-faith efforts to block access to patrons in countries where Internet gaming is illegal.

Of course, there are significant political barriers to this approach. The Internet community would probably become apoplectic over a single nation's attempt to wrestle away control over Web sites based on the location of domain name registrars within their own jurisdiction. Such an approach has some intuitive appeal as a means of restoring domestic sovereignty over the scope of legal conduct in the gaming area, but this means of enforcement may also have unintended consequences. Internet domain name registrars might simply choose to locate in other countries that do not share a concern about the violation of domestic gambling laws in the United States. For example, a registrar could locate in a jurisdiction friendly to Internet gambling and register domain names for Internet casinos under its own geographical domain name system, thus foiling any attempts to affect their ownership via court judgments from the United States. An international treaty may be required in order to deal effectively with the enforcement issues presented by Internet casino operations.

TARGETING ADVERTISING AND FINANCE

Although government actors may directly challenge Internet gambling operations, the viability of Internet gambling operations may also be affected by indirect efforts. Legal challenges to the mechanisms for Internet payments and to advertising and support structures have made it more difficult to manage and operate a viable Internet gambling operation. In the long run, these efforts may prove most effective in reducing, though not eliminating, Internet gambling.

As discussed previously, advertising is a critical part of the business model for Internet gambling. Firms that provide advertising, whether in the form of paid placements on search engines, banner ads, or other more traditional forms, thus participate indirectly in the lucre of the Internet gambling industry, even though such gambling may not be legal in a particular jurisdiction. Although First Amendment protections extend to commercial speech, such protections do not extend to speech that facilitates the violation of federal or state laws.[59]

Federal prosecutors reportedly convened a grand jury investigation of Internet gambling that resulted in the issuance of subpoenas to broadcasters, publishers, and Web sites that advertise for offshore operations.[60] Prosecutors alleged that advertisers were "aiding and abetting" the violation of antigambling laws. Using a similar theory, federal marshals seized $3.2 million from Discovery Communications, a television and media company that owns the Travel Channel. These funds were payment for thirty-second commercials to be run in a six-month period during broadcasts of the World Poker Tour for ParadisePoker.com, an online poker site.[61]

Although the legal foundation for these tactics is far from certain, the potential for adverse legal ramifications has apparently affected major advertisers. Internet search engines Yahoo!, Google, and Lycos have agreed to stop running advertising for online casinos,[62] although Yahoo! indicated that it would continue to run these ads in markets outside of the United States. Major broadcasters such as Clear Channel Communications and Infinity Broadcasting have also stopped taking online gambling ads. Electronic Arts, an online video game provider, has followed suit, citing the potential for future "policy and legal" problems for the company.[63] Such actions are likely to make it more difficult for Internet gambling enterprises to reach their customers. However, determined patrons will probably be undeterred and will find other ways to access these sites through foreign sites providing links and advertising.

Legal challenges affecting the financing of Internet gambling activities may also threaten the growth of Internet gambling firms. Understanding the nature of a credit card transaction is an important prerequisite to understanding how payments are made and the allocation of payment risks under various payment mechanisms.

A credit card transaction typically involves several intermediaries between the merchant (casino) and the cardholder (patron).[64] Card associations, such as Visa and Mastercard, make a branded product available for issuance by financial institutions and provide rules for members of the association that affect the terms of card use as well as the payment rights and obligations of participating members.

Financial institutions such as banks issue credit cards to their customers, thus initiating a credit relationship with the cardholder. They may set credit limits based on credit information that the customer provides, and they may perform the billing and collection services for the cardholder, though often this role is outsourced to a third-party processor. The issuing institution thus makes money by extending credit and earning interest on any unpaid balances. It also makes money through sharing in the fees generated from merchants who receive payments through the customer's cards. Its primary risk derives from cardholders who default—a risk that can be managed by using credit filters and raising interest rates on unpaid balances.

Financial institutions may also be involved in the capacity of enrolling merchants to participate in the card payment service. These institutions, known as "acquiring banks," are effectively extending credit to the merchants. Merchants agree to receive payment from customers through means of the credit card and to process payment information through an established protocol. Merchants submit customer requests for credit through an extensive computer network to a processor, which in turn contacts the issuing bank for a determination of whether to approve credit for the customer. The merchant then sends records of its approved transactions to the acquirer, which in turn credits the merchant's account for the total amount of billings less an allowance based on a negotiated discount.

This discount from the merchant is intended to cover the expenses associated with payment and collection from the issuing bank, as well as other processing costs. Those expenses may be significant, particularly if the merchant is involved in a business where customers ultimately express dissatisfaction and dispute the charges. Gambling and pornography are notorious businesses for dissatisfied customers, particularly when an unsuspecting spouse has found out about secret online exploits. To the extent that a merchant engages in fraud or otherwise fails to deliver a product or service purchased with a credit card, a charge-back process occurs, which ultimately may reach the merchant. Herein lies an important dimension of risk for the acquiring financial institution: some merchants close their shops and flee the jurisdiction, leaving the acquirer to ultimately bear the loss.

This system generally works very well for consumers, who can effectively purchase with greater confidence by using the delay in time between purchase and payment on their account to their advantage. This time delay allows the customer to determine whether a merchant has held up his or her end of the bargain, to withhold payment, and to dispute the transaction under the card association rules. Merchants also benefit from this system, to the extent that it facilitates payment and increases sales opportunities.

Though other forms of payment may exist for a remote seller, such as wire transfers, checks, or money orders, each alternative form has its drawbacks. Wire transfers can result in fairly quick transfers of cash, but once that cash is gone, the advantage is clearly on the side of the transferee. Thus, a customer with doubts about the integrity of the merchant would probably be hesitant to use this method. Moreover, wire transfers are typically relatively expensive, making them unsuitable for frequent small consumer transactions.

Checks and money orders may be less expensive to process, but they may also involve considerable delay. There are also payment risks to consider. From the customer's perspective, a money order involves an immediate monetary outlay. A check may allow time for a stop payment order, though such an effort is certainly not as consumer friendly as under the dispute provisions of the credit card. Merchants also face payment risks, which are rooted in the creditworthiness of the customer. Though the merchant may compensate by waiting to deliver until a check has cleared, this entails further delay and hinders sales growth. A credit card, on the other hand, gives the customer the luxury of delayed evaluation of the transaction to ensure that the merchant is delivering what was promised, coupled with the speed and assurances of creditworthiness that the merchant desires.

The credit card industry is well acquainted with the risks associated with illicit operations, particularly those involving pornography or gambling. Acquiring financial institutions in the United States that seek Internet-based merchants typically include provisions that shun operations dealing in pornography or online gambling.[65] Offshore gambling operations that use credit cards often must establish relationships with foreign acquiring banks, which thus assume the credit risks associated with charge-backs and other defaults by merchants in the online gambling business.[66] The online payment service PayPal, which is sometimes used in lieu of credit card payments, includes provisions in its online user agreement that specifically preclude its use in connection with gambling and adult-oriented businesses.[67]

In addition to the risk of charge-backs, the possibility of legal liability on account of aiding and abetting an illegal operation is also presented. This concern is illustrated by recent litigation in which cardholders with Internet gambling losses brought a class action lawsuit against Mastercard, Visa, and the banks that issued their credit cards.[68] These plaintiffs alleged that the credit card companies and banks were part of a "worldwide gambling enterprise" with unnamed Internet casinos. By extending credit for gamblers and collecting on those debts, credit card companies had allegedly facilitated a criminal enterprise that violated federal and state criminal gambling laws. In particular, the plaintiffs alleged that such conduct constituted racketeering and unlawful collection of debt, which entitled them to civil remedies under the Racketeer Influenced and Corrupt Organizations Act (RICO).[69]

A claim of racketeering under RICO requires a showing of at least two predicate criminal acts based on either state or federal law.[70] Here, the plaintiffs alleged violations of the Wire Act, as well as violations of other federal provisions addressing mail and wire fraud. However, the court rejected these claims based on federal law. With regard to the Wire Act, the court limited its application to sports betting—conduct that was not pleaded in this case.[71] As for the fraud violations, it found that the plaintiffs failed to plead any fraudulent representations by the defendants in connection with any gambling activity.[72]

The plaintiffs also claimed that the defendants' conduct violated a Kansas criminal statute proscribing commercial gambling. The court ultimately considered two elements of that statute, which involved, "[f]or gain, becoming a custodian of anything of value bet or offered to be bet" and "[s]etting up for use or collecting the proceeds of any gambling device."[73] In this context, the particulars of Internet gambling worked in favor of the defendants, as the court found that the credit card companies did not violate these provisions.

In a typical transaction, the plaintiffs used their credit cards to purchase credits from the Internet casino prior to gambling. The credits are maintained in an account with the Internet casino, and the patron can access these credits for the purpose of placing bets. Losses are deducted from the account, but winnings are credited to the account. However, any net winnings are not credited to the patron's credit card but instead are paid by alternate mechanisms.[74]

Under these facts, the district court found that the extension of credit to the cardholder, in the form of purchasing credits, had occurred before any illegal gambling had occurred: "It is a temporal impossibility for the defendants to have completed their transaction with the plaintiff before he gambled and to then be prosecuted for collecting the proceeds of a gambling device, which can only take place after some form of gambling is completed."[75] Although an opinion of the Kansas attorney general found that placing bets from a computer in Kansas to an online casino would violate Kansas law, the court limited the scope of the legal violation to the activities of the plaintiffs and the online casinos, not to the activity of extending credit to the cardholder.[76] The Fifth Circuit agreed, noting that it was also impossible to "take custody" of a bet if the transaction with the credit card companies occurred before any bet was placed.[77]

Oddly, the facts in this case indicated that the ultimate charge on the cardholder's account did depend on the losses accrued. For example, one of the named plaintiffs, Thompson, had purchased $1,510 in credits using his Mastercard; he lost everything.[78] Bradley, the other named plaintiff, had purchased $16,445 in gambling credits, but his credit card billing statements showed only $7,048 in purchases at the casino.[79] This difference between purchases and billings suggests the possibility that the net result after winnings and losses was ultimately charged to his credit card. Otherwise, one would expect to see the charge of only $16,445 on his monthly statement. This also suggests that the amount ultimately paid by the cardholder to the issuing bank was determined after his gaming transactions had been completed. Though there were no net winnings, it strains credibility to believe that every transaction under the account was a losing transaction and that he lost only half the value of the account with no wins to offset those losses. No explanation of this factual discrepancy appears in the case.

The court's restrictive approach toward finding any violation of the Wire Act and applicable Kansas law helped to ensure that the credit card industry avoided significant financial liability as a result of Internet gambling losses in this case. Though the entire amount at stake is not stated in this litigation, two of the plaintiffs named in the litigation had lost several thousand dollars. Those similarly situated might number in the thousands, presenting substantial claims had this litigation been successful.

Even though the plaintiffs in this matter did not achieve a legal victory, the case nevertheless sent a strong cautionary message to the credit card industry. If the gamblers had been located in a state with more comprehensive antigambling laws, or if violations of the Wire Act could be clearly proven through involvement with Internet-based sports betting, it is plausible that a credit card company and the issuing bank could indeed face liability under RICO. Moreover, the concept of "aiding and abetting" violation of state laws through extending credit might lend itself to other plaintiffs seeking to establish liability, particularly when the identity of the Internet casino and the involvement in illegal gambling are known to those involved in processing these payments.[80] The Web site maintained by the Kansas attorney general stated in part in 2004:

> [P]ersons or organizations who knowingly assist Internet gambling organizations in any unlawful activity may themselves be held liable for that unlawful activity. Thus, for example, Internet access providers and credit card companies that continue to provide services to gambling organizations after notice that the activities of the organizations are illegal would be subject to accomplice liability.[81]

Legislation to cut off the mechanisms for funding Internet gambling has been before Congress but has not yet been brought to a final vote. The Internet Gambling Funding Prohibition Act was reported out of the Senate Committee on Banking, Housing, and Urban Affairs on October 27, 2003, which unanimously recommended passage. As explained in the committee report:

> The bill would prohibit gambling businesses from accepting credit cards, checks, or other bank instruments from gamblers who bet over the Internet. To accomplish this purpose, the bill would require designated payment systems to establish policies and procedures designed to identify and prevent transactions in connection with Internet gambling. Most financial institutions have some capacity to identify and block restricted transactions for the purposes of compliance with other laws, such as those relating to U.S. economic sanctions programs and money laundering prevention. Some participants in these payment networks have already voluntarily established policies to prohibit these types of transactions. Thus, it is anticipated that the costs of compliance imposed by this bill would be small. In addition, to the extent that individual gamblers will be precluded from using bank instruments, financial entities may experience some cost savings as they will be less likely to have gamblers defaulting on debts incurred.[82]

Although this bill was never enacted into law, the industry is apparently taking the concerns raised by the bill into account.

THE INTERNATIONAL GAMING INDUSTRY STRIKES BACK: WTO CHALLENGE

Further complexity in the international dimensions of Internet gambling arose in 2003, when the government of the Caribbean nation of Antigua and Barbuda brought a complaint against the United States before the WTO, arguing that the United States had unfairly discriminated against the online gambling services offered by Antiguan firms. Antigua claimed that the United States was in violation of the General Agreement on Trade in Services (GATS). In particular, Antigua claimed:

> The central, regional or local authorities of the United States allow numerous operators of United States origin to offer all types of gambling and betting services in the United States (sometimes via exclusive rights or monopolistic structures). There appears to be no possibility for foreign operators, however, to obtain an authorization to supply gambling and betting services from outside the United States.[83]

Antigua submitted an extensive list of federal and state statutes, as well as other legal sources, including attorney general opinions and cases such as *United States v. Cohen* and *World Interactive Gaming*, discussed previously.[84] It claimed that these sources together operated as "measures" that completely prohibited the remote provision of gambling services by a foreign operator. They further alleged that this prohibition violated obligations under GATS, to which the United States was a signatory nation.

The United States' initial response to these claims involved rather interesting legal posturing. Among other things, the United States' request for a preliminary ruling from the WTO panel contended that, as a technical matter, some of the authorities cited by the Antiguans were technically not measures at all, since they did not constitute legal instruments with functional lives of their own.[85] Thus, for example, a state attorney general opinion or an opinion of courts inferior to the U.S. Supreme Court was arguably not sufficient to serve as a measure under this standard.

More significant, however, was the United States' position that Antigua's bare citation of state and federal laws applicable in the United States, even if they were "measures," failed to meet its burden of proof in showing that these laws and regulations effected a "total prohibition" in violation of the

GATS obligations. Here, the United States used the complexity of its laws involving Internet gambling to its advantage; Antigua would be forced to explain how those laws created such a total ban. The United States asserted that "Antigua must not be permitted to hide behind the excuse that U.S. law is supposedly too complex and opaque; Antigua and its two outside law firms are certainly capable of identifying and attempting to establish a prima facie case as to specific measures if they choose to do so."[86]

This was an obligation that Antigua did not readily embrace. As it pointed out, the state of law in the United States was a matter of "significant debate within the United States legal community."[87] Moreover, Antigua recognized that it was caught on the horns of a dilemma.

> If [Antigua] were to have listed the Wire Act only there is little doubt that, at the stage when the United States needed to implement any recommendations and rulings resulting from this dispute, the United States would have taken the position that it needed only to disapply or adapt the Wire Act and could continue to apply other laws because these would have been outside the terms of reference of the Panel. This concern has been vindicated by the fact that the United States now adopts a very similar formalistic and obstructive approach in the Request.[88]

Thus, Antigua sought a more comprehensive solution based on the totality of effect of U.S. laws.

The Antiguan challenge also addressed the heart of the GATS treaty obligation: should gambling services be included within the scope of free trade commitments regarding "entertainment services (including theater, live bands and circus services)" and "other recreational services (except sporting)"?[89] The United States argued that remote gambling services were outside the scope of the ordinary meaning of these two terms. In fact, the exception of "sporting" could be viewed as an express elimination of gambling from the scope of this term, to the extent that the *Merriam-Webster's Collegiate Dictionary* defines *sporting* in part in relation to gambling.[90]

This position offered by the United States was arguably inconsistent with the dominant marketing practices of casino gaming operations in the United States. The gaming industry promotes its operations as involving entertainment and/or recreation. For example, the AGA's annual reports describe gambling in the same category as other entertainment options.[91]

Other countries, including eight European members of the WTO, specifically excluded gambling from this listing of services; the United States did not. Whether in hindsight the United States should have been expected to invoke a specific exclusion raises a provocative question: Was the cultural transformation of gambling from vice to entertainment sufficiently complete to hold the United States to a broader dimension for these terms? The United States devoted much of its submission to the historical, moral, religious, and practical justifications for treating gambling as a different matter than other services. On the other hand, Antigua argued about the nature and extent of gambling practices in the United States, which are indeed substantial.

Even if Antigua were to be sustained on this argument, however, the United States raised still other challenges for Antigua's position. Article XVII of GATS provides a basic rule according the same national treatment to domestic and foreign suppliers of scheduled services:

> In the sectors described in its Schedule, and subject to any conditions and qualifications set out therein, each Member shall accord to services and service suppliers of any other Member, in respect of all measures affecting the supply of services, treatment no less favourable than that it accords to its own like services and service suppliers.

Thus, to the extent that Antigua could show that the United States had adopted measures affecting the supply of "remote" gambling (i.e., accessible via the Internet or via telephone), were those measures effectively treating a foreign supplier differently from a domestic one? This question hinged on the extent to which Internet gambling was indeed the same as other forms of land-based gambling. If it was indeed a different product and both domestic and foreign providers are subject to the same restrictions on such remotely provided services, then Antigua would not have a viable claim.

The differences between remote gambling services and other gambling activities were briefly discussed in the first written submission of the United States, but still more extensive attention was directed to this issue in a second submission.[92] This submission went into considerable detail about operational and consumer characteristics, as well as the regulatory characteristics, which merit a distinction between remote and in-person gambling activities.

As for operational and consumer characteristics, the United States cited reports by consultants (including Bear Stearns) to the effect that Internet operations have different customers than land-based operations. In part, Internet customers choose this form of gambling because they want "the ability to indulge in gambling in seclusion without the stigma or effort required to go to a public gambling facility."[93] They also differ in psychological perceptions, including the motivation to gamble, physiological experiences, and socialization.[94] Thus, consumers perceive Internet gaming differently from in-person gambling experiences.

From a regulatory perspective, the United States also took the position that remotely provided gambling presents more significant threats than land-based operations in terms of organized crime, money laundering, and fraud.[95] Antigua attempted to address these issues through its own regulatory framework. However, such matters touching on national security would undoubtedly concern policymakers in the United States, who would not be content to entrust them to a foreign government, even a friendly one.

The public health dimension of online gambling also received attention from both sides. Though Antigua attempted to show that online gambling is no more addictive than other forms of gambling, the United States pointed to uncertainties about health effects posed by online play. For example, it cited the American Psychiatric Association's concerns about the dangers posed by the solitary nature of Internet gambling and the prospects of lengthy, uninterrupted play. However, even if Internet gambling was less addictive, the sheer potential magnitude of gambling in every location with an Internet connection raises the prospect of "an enormous growth in the opportunity for gambling and, consequently, for gambling addiction."[96]

Public health effects on minors posed a related threat. Whereas in-person contacts with casino gambling present many opportunities to detect and eliminate underage gambling, the online environment provides the possibility for minors to play online. The United States cited examples of child-oriented games licensed by the Antiguan government, which included "cartoon-like design, and childish iconography."[97] It also presented evidence that requiring identification through a credit card or debit card was not an effective means of preventing access by minors. Based on 1999 data, approximately 28 percent of minors between the ages of sixteen and twenty-two had at least one major credit card, and these figures were likely to understate current cardholders on account of extensive marketing efforts directed toward college students under the age of twenty-one.[98]

Finally, the United States also raised other arguments based on another provision of GATS, Article XIV, which provides several general exceptions.

> Subject to the requirement that such measures are not applied in a manner which would constitute a means of arbitrary or unjustifiable discrimination between countries where like conditions prevail, or a disguised restriction on trade in services, nothing in this Agreement shall be construed to prevent the adoption or enforcement by any Member of measures:
>
> (a) necessary to protect public morals or to maintain public order;
>
> (b) necessary to protect human, animal or plant life or health;
>
> (c) necessary to secure compliance with laws or regulations which are not inconsistent with the provisions of this Agreement including those relating to:
>
> i. the prevention of deceptive or fraudulent practices or to deal with the effects of a default on services contracts; . . .
>
> ii. safety.

Given the extensive history of U.S. laws directed toward protecting the public morals and public order and the concerns about public health and safety raised by online gambling, the United States also alleged that, if it was found to have generally prohibited remote gambling, it should be allowed to do so within the scope of these exceptions. The fact that remote access allowed gambling into uncontrolled settings that are particularly accessible to children raised a significant concern about public order and public morals.[99] Moreover, the uncertain controls over offshore funds also "could pose a risk to national security from terror and/or criminal organizations."[100]

The WTO dispute resolution panel released its 273-page report on November 10, 2004,[101] but a confidential draft released to the parties reached major news media as early as March 2004.[102] The decision was generally unfavorable to the United States, though it failed to address some of the more interesting policy dimensions outlined previously. Instead, it focused on more narrow legal grounds and arcane matters of treaty interpretation. The panel found that the United States had indeed made commitments under Article XIV of GATS with regard to gambling, though it may well have done so inadvertently.[103] It also found that U.S. laws (including both federal and state provisions) failed to accord services of Antigua a position no less favorable than that allowed to domestic providers.[104] Oddly, the panel acknowl-

edged that these laws "are designed so as to protect public morals or maintain public order," but it enigmatically concluded that the United States had
failed to meet its burden to show that its laws "are necessary to protect public morals and/or public order."[105] Moreover, the United States had failed to
show that its enforcement efforts were consistent with the requirements of
its treaty obligations.[106] In particular, the panel pointed to off-track betting
operations allowed for horse racing as allowing remote gambling via telephone or Internet.[107] The panel thus recommended that the United States
make conforming changes in its laws.[108]

This result sent immediate tremors throughout the gaming industry,
which wondered whether international competition through the Internet
would soon become available in the United States.[109] The ruling also raised
questions about unintended consequences of trade agreements, including
state sovereignty over gambling within their borders. It is doubtful that most
Americans would consider their state and local laws to be superseded by an
international treaty obligation, over which their state legislators and gover-
nors would have no say whatsoever. Despite the considerable merits of
global trade, the attempt to treat gambling as any other entertainment service arguably pushed beyond the current cultural sensibilities of most Americans, as well as threatened to undermine traditional regulatory structures
for gambling.

Antigua's jubilation over the ruling proved short-lived, as the United
States filed notice of appeal on January 7, 2005.[110] Antigua also appealed
certain elements of the decision, and third-party submissions were also filed
by other nations, including the European Community and Japan, which both
supported the proposition that the United States had indeed made a commitment for free trade in gambling services.[111] The Appellate Body issued its
decision on April 7, 2005, and this decision substantially pared back any impact of the panel decision.

First, the Appellate Body focused only on federal laws, ruling that Antigua had failed to make the prima facie case showing that state laws were
inconsistent with GATS treaty obligations.[112] The Appellate Body found,
however, that Antigua had made a prima facie case for inconsistency with regard to the federal Wire Act, the Travel Act, and the Illegal Gambling Business Act.[113] It also agreed with the panel that the United States had made a
commitment with regard to trade in gambling under GATS.[114]

As for the applicable federal laws, the Appellate Body agreed with the panel that these laws implicated public morals and public order, but it reversed its decision that these laws were not "necessary to protect public morals or to maintain public order." The Appellate Body explained that the "necessary" requirement involves a balance between the effectiveness of the measures in accomplishing domestic ends and the restrictive impact of the measure on international trade.[115] As a general matter, the United States had the burden to put forth evidence of these public purposes, and Antigua as respondent had the burden to show a reasonably available means to these ends that does not restrain trade.[116]

In this context, the Appellate Body found that the United States had indeed shown a prima facie case that these measures were necessary, noting that the panel had also recognized the close connection between these laws and important societal interests. Antigua's alternative, on the other hand, consisted solely in proposed consultations with the United States, which the Appellate Body found to be insufficient as an alternative means of addressing these interests.[117]

Despite these rulings favoring the United States, the Appellate Body also found that the United States had potentially discriminated against foreign gaming service suppliers in one respect: it appeared to allow off-track betting on horse racing in certain situations, pursuant to the Interstate Horseracing Act.[118] Thus, despite a failure to show enforcement discrimination favoring domestic suppliers over foreign suppliers with regard to the Wire Act, Travel Act, and Interstate Gambling Business Act, the Interstate Horseracing Act presented a potential problem.

The manner of bringing U.S. law into conformity with GATS in this situation continues to be the subject of negotiations between the United States and Antigua. An arbitrator was appointed to help resolve the dispute.[119] It appears that the United States will not take the position of opening up the Internet freely to gambling interests. However, the manner of enforcing domestic laws against Internet gambling remains an important issue.

The WTO dispute highlights the need for careful attention to international agreements in the quest for solutions to conflicts arising from the use of the Internet. Cultural differences about the role of gambling in society undoubtedly deserve greater attention in specific treaty negotiations; the current approach of Antigua and the WTO apparently disregards these significant concerns in seeking to enter markets in the United States by a side door left open by trade negotiators. It also remains to be seen whether the concerns raised about public health, public morals (particularly of youth), public safety, and national security will provide a sufficient impetus for federal legislation that will clearly and comprehensively address the legal status of online wagering activity. So far, these concerns have resulted in much bluster but no concrete actions from lawmakers.

Threats of enforcement of existing laws against Internet gambling, even though not completely successful in all venues, have undoubtedly curtailed the industry's growth online, as well as the behavior of industry actors. For example, a recent convention of online casino operators chose to meet in Toronto rather than in the United States, based on fears about arrest if they entered the United States.[120] The controversial efforts to seize cash from otherwise legitimate enterprises engaged in advertising will also get the attention of liability-conscious executives, making it more difficult for the industry to promote itself via traditional advertising media. However, patrons have still managed to find Internet businesses and to gamble. Reports of the recent public stock offering by PartyGaming PLC, a Gibraltar-based firm that has studiously avoided legal contacts with the United States, indicate that 90 percent of its $600 million in annual revenues come from American gamblers.[121]

Though law enforcement may send symbolic messages to this industry, the Internet is clearly not within its complete control. Internet gambling will remain an alternative outlet to those who choose to evade regulatory efforts in land-based casinos. This frontier will be hard to tame.

II. Tribal Gaming

Indian tribes occupy an unusual legal status in our federal system. On one hand, tribes possess a limited sovereignty consistent with their status as "domestic dependent nations."[1] This limited sovereignty means that tribal governments have some inherent powers, including powers of self-government, which are akin to those of a separate government entity.[2] This status serves as a barrier to state and local governmental interference with many aspects of tribal government. For example, states may not tax Indian lands, and the jurisdictional reach of their criminal and regulatory laws is constrained by principles of tribal sovereignty and self-governance.

On the other hand, their dependent status makes Indian tribes subject to the federal government's power, without particular representation in that government as allowed to the states. Congress's power over Indian affairs has been characterized as "plenary and exclusive," and this power is rooted primarily in the Indian Commerce Clause of the U.S. Constitution.[3] The Treaty Clause technically grants authority to the executive branch, but it has also been viewed as a source of legislative power in this area.[4] Congress in 1871 authorized no further treaties with Indian tribes, but already extant treaties were not affected by this rule. Thus some matters of tribal governance fall under the authority of treaty obligations rather than other federal statutes.[5]

The policies of the federal government toward the Indian tribes have vacillated over time. As the Supreme Court recently explained,

> Congress has in fact authorized at different times very different Indian policies (some with beneficial results but many with tragic consequences). Congressional policy, for example, initially favored "Indian re-

moval," then "assimilation" and the break-up of tribal lands, then protection of the tribal land base (interrupted by a movement toward greater state involvement and "termination" of recognized tribes); and it now seeks greater tribal autonomy within the framework of a "government-to-government relationship" with federal agencies.[6]

Tribes have not always benefited from their treatment at the hands of the federal government. Many of them have effectively disbanded, as their ability to pass on their cultural traditions and to maintain a sustainable economic way of life has been jeopardized by the encroachment of modern cultural and economic practices. However, some of the tribes that have survived have seized upon the popular interest in gambling as a means to provide economic development. Some tribes have been able to parlay their unique legal status into a preferred position in the gaming marketplace, where they have successfully attracted non-Indian patrons and their financial resources.

This path toward gambling put tribal governments on a collision course with the states in which tribal lands are located. Despite the fact that states had traditionally exercised authority over the legal status of gambling within their borders, tribes contended that gambling activities fell within the realm preserved for tribal sovereignty. Efforts of the Department of the Interior to bolster tribal self-determination and government through gaming fueled this conflict with the states, and the Supreme Court took up this issue in the seminal case of *California v. Cabazon Band of Mission Indians*.[7]

In *Cabazon Band*, Indian tribes with reservations in Riverside County, California, sought a declaratory judgment to the effect that neither state nor county government had any authority to enforce its gambling laws on reservation lands. The tribes had been offering card games and high-stakes bingo primarily to non-Indian patrons from surrounding communities who came to the reservation to gamble. The tribes had conducted these games pursuant to an ordinance approved by the secretary of the interior, which granted authority to operate the games and to use the revenues generated from them to improve the health, education, and welfare of tribal members. The games provided the sole source of income for the tribes, and they provided the major source of tribal employment.

The state of California and Riverside County intervened for the purpose of asserting that the tribes' practices violated state and local laws. Bingo was allowed in California, but it was limited to the context of charitable gaming. Among other things, California law required that operators of charitable bingo games must limit the stakes to $250 and that those operating the games must be unpaid workers. The tribes failed to comply with either of these requirements, and they challenged the state's power to impose them on games conducted on their reservations.

California's authority over criminal acts committed on the reservation was rooted in a specific grant from Congress, which extended criminal jurisdiction to offenses committed by or against Indians within all Indian country within the state.[8] However, Congress had not granted general civil regulatory authority over matters on Indian lands.[9] The character of the applicable state laws affecting gambling was thus at the heart of this litigation: Was the state seeking to enforce a criminal proscription (appropriate), or was it seeking to enforce civil regulatory provisions (not appropriate)? Drawing a bright line between these two categories is difficult, as enforcement of civil regulations might well involve a threat of criminal prosecution.

The Court's analysis ultimately focused on whether the rules are prohibitory or regulatory in nature—a balancing determination with somewhat mystical dimensions. On one hand, California limited bingo games to charitable operations; it had banned commercial gambling operations, in part because of concerns about attracting organized crime.[10] It also imposed limits on the prizes, which the tribes did not do.

On the other hand, California had also allowed gambling in other forms, including horse racing and card games, and it promoted gambling through its own state lottery. Bingo games were open to the public. California law imposed no express limit on the number of games that could be played or the amount that a participant could spend.[11] This general policy toward allowing and even promoting gambling apparently influenced the Court's decision that the law at issue was regulatory and thus not applicable in the tribal context.[12] Though high-stakes bingo may well attract organized crime, such matters were left to the province of federal prosecution under the Organized Crime Control Act.[13] However, the Court suggested that this concern was more theoretical than actual, as it noted the absence of a single federal prosecution connected with more than one hundred Indian bingo operations at that time.[14]

Rather than prosecuting gaming operations, the federal government had been encouraging them. President Reagan stated in 1983, "It is important to the concept of self-government that tribes reduce their dependence on federal funds by providing a greater percentage to the cost of their self-government."[15] The Department of the Interior had chosen gambling as a means of fostering employment and economic development within the tribes, and allowing state regulation would effectively hinder this important federal policy.[16]

The result in *Cabazon Band* caused considerable consternation in states with Indian lands. The Court's analysis greatly expanded the likelihood that tribal gambling operations could be developed without regard to competing economic and regulatory considerations of the states. On the economic side, the expansion of tribal gambling undoubtedly competes with state-sponsored gaming activities, which generate revenues for the public fisc. Under generally applicable principles of state taxation, Indian gaming would not generate those tax revenues.[17] Further, absent a framework for federal regulation of Indian gaming, legitimate concerns may also be raised about the involvement of criminal elements in this cash-oriented business.[18]

Protective interests of the state may also be presented: though gaming may well help to achieve federal goals in fostering economic development for tribes without other significant natural resources, this policy choice would also affect non-Indians, who are likely to be the primary patrons of those gambling establishments. As the dissent in *Cabazon Band* pointed out:

> [The tribes] and the Secretary of the Interior may well be correct, in the abstract, that gambling facilities are a sensible way to generate revenues that are badly needed by reservation Indians. But the decision to adopt, to reject, or to define the precise contours of such a course of action, and thereby to set aside the substantial public policy concerns of a sovereign State, should be made by the Congress of the United States. It should not be made by this Court, by the temporary occupant of the Office of the Secretary of the Interior, or by non-Indian entrepreneurs who are experts in gambling management but not necessarily dedicated to serving the future well-being of Indian tribes.[19]

Congress soon weighed in on these issues by enacting the Indian Gaming Regulatory Act (IGRA) of 1988. The IGRA addresses the extent to which the goals of tribal self-determination and self-sufficiency through Indian gaming should be balanced against state interests affecting the availability of gambling within their borders. Its stable legal foundation for tribal gambling has been responsible for considerable growth in tribal casino operations, including the applications of numerous groups to reestablish their tribal status in order to profit from offering casino gambling services.

OVERVIEW OF THE IGRA

The stated purposes of the IGRA, as set forth in the act itself, are as follows:

(1) to provide a statutory basis for the operation of gaming by Indian tribes as a means of promoting tribal economic development, self-sufficiency, and strong tribal government;

(2) to provide a statutory basis for the regulation of gaming by an Indian tribe adequate to shield it from organized crime and other corrupting influences, to ensure that the Indian tribe is the primary beneficiary of the gaming operation, and to assure that gaming is conducted fairly and honestly by the operator and the players; and

(3) to declare that the establishment of independent regulatory authority for gaming on Indian lands, the establishment of Federal standards for gaming on Indian lands, and the establishment of a National Indian Gaming Commission are necessary to meet congressional concerns regarding gaming and to protect such gaming as a means of generating tribal revenue.[20]

Toward these ends, the IGRA establishes a regulatory structure that is based on three different categories of gaming activity. Class I gaming is exclusively within the jurisdiction of the Indian tribe.[21] This category includes "social games solely for prizes of minimal value or traditional forms of Indian gaming engaged in by individuals as a part of, or in connection with, tribal ceremonies or celebrations."[22] These games have no real potential for commercial profit, and they would be unlikely to affect any competing state interests.

Class II gaming is subject to oversight by the National Indian Gaming Commission. This category includes games such as bingo and certain card games that are otherwise allowed by the state.[23] Slot machines are specifically excluded from Class II games.[24] Class II games can be economically significant, and they may only be carried on within states that permit such gaming "for any purpose by any person, organization or entity."[25] Thus, a state that adopts a public policy prohibiting gambling altogether may effectively enforce that policy on Indian lands within the state. However, a state that offers gaming privileges to others may not deny that privilege to tribes within its borders. This provision thus reflects an attempt to accommodate legitimate state concerns about the effects of gambling on its citizens while preventing discrimination against Indian operations.

Class II gaming operations require the approval of the chairman of the National Indian Gaming Commission, which is subject to several important conditions.[26] One of these conditions requires that the construction, maintenance, and operation of the gaming facility must adequately protect the environment and public health and safety. Although the tribe must comply with federal environmental laws, compliance with state or local building and safety codes is not necessarily required.

This application of local zoning or building codes was recently litigated in *Cayuga Indian Nation of New York v. Village of Union Springs.*[27] In 2004, a federal district court held that a tribe's construction of a gambling facility on reservation lands it had recently acquired from non-Indians was not subject to state or local zoning or building codes. The fact that non-Indians would be the primary patrons of the facility did not change this result. Thus, based on this decision, the particular parameters for satisfying the standard of public health and safety appear to be within the discretion of the tribe, subject to oversight by federal officials. However, late in 2005 this result was overturned on the basis of the U.S. Supreme Court's decision in *City of Sherrill v. Oneida Nation,*[28] which rejected the proposition that acquisition of land by a tribe restored aboriginal title and thus tribal sovereignty as a protection from local regulation. On the authority of *City of Sherrill,* the district court removed an injunction barring enforcement of zoning and building codes on the affected property.[29] Nevertheless, the application of zoning rules or building codes on historical reservation property would continue to present issues not resolved by this decision.

The rest of these conditions imposed on Class II gaming operations are designed to ensure the financial integrity of the operation and to safeguard benefits to tribal members. The Indian tribe must have the sole proprietary interest in the activity, or it must contract with a service provider that will meet similarly stringent operational standards. The net revenues from tribal gaming must be used for specified purposes, which include funding tribal government operations or programs, supporting the general welfare of the tribe and its members, promoting economic development, donating to charities, and supporting operations of local government agencies.[30]

The tribal operation is also subject to annual audits, which must extend to all contracts for supplies, services (other than legal or accounting), or concessions involving contract amounts in excess of twenty-five thousand dollars. These audits must be provided to the commission. In addition, the commission is empowered to engage in continuous monitoring, inspection, and oversight of the tribal operation.[31] Such financial oversight presumably addresses concerns about corruption and other criminal activities being funded with gaming revenues.

Along these same lines, the tribe must provide a monitoring system that ensures that background investigations are conducted on management and key employees of the gaming operation. These employees must meet licensing standards that ensure that "any person whose prior activities, criminal record, if any, or reputation, habits and associations pose a threat to the public interest or to the effective regulation of gaming, or create or enhance the dangers of unsuitable, unfair, or illegal practices and methods and activities in the conduct of gaming shall not be eligible for employment."[32]

The act recognizes the potential for these operations to generate sufficient income to the tribe that may even allow for per capita distributions of profits to tribal members.[33] However, such distributions may only be made if the commission is satisfied that the tribe has an adequate plan to support tribal government and economic development and that such plan has been adequately funded.[34] Moreover, the act expressly states that such distributions are subject to federal income taxation in the hands of the recipients.[35]

Though Class II gaming is subject to active monitoring and inspection by the National Indian Gaming Commission, the act also provides a means for tribes to minimize the commission's involvement and to engage in self-regulation. Tribes that have engaged in continuous operations of a Class II facility for at least one year may petition for the right of self-regulation. Such a petition requires showing that the tribe essentially has a clean record of operating fairly and honestly, that it has adequate systems for financial and operational integrity, and that it is fiscally sound.[36]

If the petition is granted, the tribal operation is still subject to the annual auditing requirement and must submit the results of such an audit to the commission. However, the tribe is otherwise exempt from the active intervention by the commission. In this way, the act provides a means for greater independence and self-government of the tribe with regard to gaming operations, while at the same time providing a limited means for the commission to identify and address problems through the annual audit.

The third category of gaming under the IGRA—Class III—encompasses all other forms of gambling not included in Classes I or II.[37] Thus, the traditional casino table games and slot machines—which are among the most lucrative forms of gambling available—are within this class. Not only are these activities economically significant, but they also present some of the greatest regulatory challenges.[38]

Much like Class II gaming, Class III gaming requires a tribal ordinance within a state that "permits such gaming for any purpose by any person, organization, or entity."[39] However, it also requires a tribal-state compact, which must be negotiated with the state and approved by the secretary of the interior.[40] The compact provisions may include the following subjects:

(i)   the application of the criminal and civil laws and regulations of the Indian tribe or the State that are directly related to, and necessary for, the licensing and regulation of such activity;

(ii)   the allocation of criminal and civil jurisdiction between the State and the Indian tribe necessary for the enforcement of such laws and regulations;

(iii) the assessment by the State of such activities in such amounts as are necessary to defray the costs of regulating such activity;

(iv)   taxation by the Indian tribe of such activity in amounts comparable to amounts assessed by the State for comparable activities;

(v)   remedies for breach of contract;

(vi)   standards for the operation of such activity and maintenance of the gaming facility, including licensing; and

(vii) any other subjects that are directly related to the operation of gaming activities.[41]

Thus, the IGRA gives considerable latitude to state governments in the negotiation of regulatory limits on gambling. For example, Arizona's model compact contains limits on the financial services available in gaming facilities, including restricting the location of ATM machines near gaming devices, prohibiting acceptance of electronic benefit transfer cards from welfare programs, and prohibiting the extension of credit by the casino.[42] Guidance about such matters as notices for persons with problem gambling, prohibitions on advertising aimed at minors, and self-exclusion programs for problem gamblers is also part of the compact process in Arizona.[43] States that prohibit certain types of Class III games may also extend those prohibitions to the tribal casino and may thus refuse to negotiate on such matters.[44] However, the fact that the state restricts Class III games to charitable purposes, even though embedded as a constitutional restriction, has been ruled an insufficient basis for restricting tribal gaming pursuant to a compact with the state.[45]

Though the states may negotiate over regulation of Class III gaming, it is significant to note that the IGRA provisions delineating the content of tribal-state compacts impose limits on taxes and fees that may be imposed on the sponsoring tribes. States may lawfully negotiate for financial assessments against the tribes, but paragraph (iii) permits this only "in such amounts as are necessary to defray the costs of regulating such activity." Paragraph (iv) allows taxation "by" the Indian tribe, but it does not permit taxation "of" the Indian tribe. This taxing issue is significant and merits further discussion.

TAXES AND TRIBAL CASINOS

State taxing power over tribes has long been subject to significant restraints, which protect the tribes from incursions by competing state and local government powers. Tribal members have been held to be exempt from state taxation on their income or property so long as it is sufficiently connected to reservation lands.[46] Limited incursions of this exemption from state taxation have been permitted at the pleasure of Congress. As the Supreme Court has stated:

> In keeping with its plenary authority over Indian affairs, Congress can authorize the imposition of state taxes on Indian tribes and individual Indians. It has not done so often, and the Court consistently has held that it will find the Indians' exemption from state taxes lifted only when Congress has made its intention to do so unmistakably clear.[47]

However, the Court has also recently imposed a limit on the property tax exemption associated with tribal lands when those lands were brought into the reservation through purchase.[48] This decision struck a balance in favor of the state and local tax base, as well as regulatory requirements applicable to activities on such lands, when such lands had been subject to state and local government sovereignty prior to acquisition. However, it does not speak to the issue of gaming taxes, which are highly significant for casino operations.

The IGRA is quite clear on the point that compacts are not to be used as a means of expanding the taxing powers of state and local government:

> Except for any assessments that may be agreed to under paragraph (3)(C)(iii) of this subsection, nothing in this section shall be interpreted as conferring upon a State or any of its political subdivisions authority to impose any tax, fee, charge, or other assessment upon an Indian tribe or upon any other person or entity authorized by an Indian tribe to engage in a class III activity. No State may refuse to enter into the [compact] negotiations . . . based upon the lack of authority in such State, or its political subdivisions, to impose such a tax, fee, charge, or other assessment.[49]

Elsewhere, the IGRA also provides that an attempt to impose any direct taxes on the tribe would be considered evidence of bad faith on the part of the state.[50]

Nevertheless, several states have obtained payments from tribes that appear to circumvent these provisions. Instead of characterizing these payments as taxes, they are treated as fees in exchange for the state's grant of exclusive rights to offer Class III gaming activities. Thus, to the extent that a state has sufficient tribal interests in operating casino facilities, it can effectively reap economic benefits for the state treasury by granting exclusive rights. This same opportunity is not available to states with both commercial and tribal facilities, as the state tax limitations will ordinarily apply in that situation.

California is one state in which an exclusive right is granted for tribal gambling. The preamble to the model compact adopted in California states in part:

> The exclusive rights that Indian tribes in California, including the Tribe, will enjoy under this Compact create a unique opportunity for the Tribe to operate its Gaming Facility in an economic environment free of competition from the Class III gaming referred to in Section 4.0 of this Compact on non-Indian lands in California. The parties are mindful that this

unique environment is of great economic value to the Tribe and the fact that income from Gaming Devices represents a substantial portion of the tribes' gaming revenues. In consideration for the exclusive rights enjoyed by the tribes, and in further consideration for the State's willingness to enter into this Compact, the tribes have agreed to provide to the State, on a sovereign-to-sovereign basis, a portion of its revenue from Gaming Devices.[51]

Under the California system, payments from tribal operations include both license fees and an assessment based on a stated percentage of net gaming revenues. License fees from gaming devices, which begin at $900 per device for 351 licensed devices per operation and increase to as much as $4,350 per device for operations with 1,251–2,000 licensed devices, are paid into a Revenue Sharing Trust Fund.[52] This fund is used to distribute revenues from gaming tribes to other tribes without gaming operations. Its progressive structure ensures that those tribes that are the most successful at gaming operations bear more of the burden for supporting other tribes that may lack a suitable geographic location to profit from a gaming operation.[53]

In addition, a percentage of the "net win" from establishments with more than 200 gaming devices is also paid over to a Special Distribution Fund. This percentage also reflects a progressive rate structure:

Terminals	Percentage
First 200	0%
Next 300	7%
Next 500	10%
Over 1,000	13%[54]

This Special Distribution Fund is subject to appropriations by the legislature for various purposes, including gambling addiction programs, grants to state and local government agencies affected by tribal gambling, regulatory costs, and "any other purposes specified by the Legislature."[55]

Arizona's model compact for tribal gaming similarly extracts a tribal contribution to the state in exchange for exclusivity rights. Its model compact provides as follows:

In consideration for the substantial exclusivity covenants by the State . . . the Tribe shall contribute for the benefit of the public a percentage of the

Tribe's Class III Net Win for each fiscal year of the Gaming Facility Operator as follows:

(1) One percent (1%) of the first twenty-five million dollars ($25,000,000.00);

(2) Three percent (3%) of the next fifty million dollars ($50,000,000.00);

(3) Six percent (6%) of the next twenty-five million dollars ($25,000,000.00); and

(4) Eight percent (8%) of Class III Net Win in excess of one hundred million dollars ($100,000,000.00).[56]

In the event that those exclusive rights are abrogated, the tribal contribution is substantially reduced, presumably to comply with the IGRA provisions limiting the state's taxing powers.[57] Of these total funds, 88 percent are allocated to the Arizona Benefits Fund, which is used to cover regulatory costs, problem gambling programs, education, trauma and emergency services, wildlife conservation, and tourism.[58] The other 12 percent of the funds are allocated to a separate fund that is used to help cities, towns, and counties fund "government services that benefit the general public, including public safety, mitigation of impacts of gaming, and promotion of commerce and economic development."[59]

Connecticut, home to the world's largest casino, has also granted exclusive rights to tribal operations, for which it extracts a payment of 25 percent of gross slot machine revenues from casinos operated on Indian lands by two tribes, the Mashantucket Pequot and the Mohegan.[60] This amount increases to 30 percent of gross revenues in the event that the total contribution from each of the two tribes falls below $80 million.[61] The tribes' "memorandum of understanding" with the state ensures that the obligation to make these payments to the state ends if the exclusive right is terminated by state law.[62] Revenues from tribal gaming are part of the state's general fund and are thus not subject to targeted spending requirements.[63]

Michigan had initially assessed additional fees against tribal operations, but it was forced to stop collecting those fees when commercial casinos obtained the right to offer gaming services in Detroit.[64] Pursuant to a compact with the state, the tribes were obligated to pay over 8 percent of their net win from electronic casino games as long as they held the "exclusive right to operate" those kinds of games in the state. Subsequent to that compact, the people of Michigan passed an initiative known as the Michigan Gaming Control and Revenue Act, which authorized up to three casino licenses in Detroit. The Sixth Circuit concluded that the exclusivity condition would end when a license was issued to a nontribal holder by the Michigan Gaming Control Board.[65]

Some commentators have argued that the payments to states in exchange for exclusive gambling rights are inconsistent with the IGRA.[66] However, the Ninth Circuit has recently upheld the California provisions in a tribal challenge that they were inconsistent with the IGRA. In a case entitled *In re Indian Gaming Cases,*[67] the tribe alleged that the financial assessments in the California compact violated the terms of the IGRA and showed a lack of good faith on the part of the state.

The tribe alleged that the Revenue Sharing Trust Fund, which was used to share revenues with nongaming tribes, constituted an unlawful tax that went beyond the scope of "assessments" allowed to defray the cost of regulating tribal gaming.[68] However, the Ninth Circuit rejected this claim, finding instead that the Revenue Sharing Trust Fund advances the congressional goals in the IGRA by "creating a mechanism whereby *all* of California's tribes—not just those fortunate enough to have land located in populous or accessible areas—can benefit from Class III gaming activities in the State."[69] Even if the fund contributions were "demanded" (as opposed to negotiated), and even if it was considered a "direct tax" on the tribes, the court was not concerned about this type of tax. According to the court, the IGRA does not convert any attempt to tax into conclusive proof of a lack of good faith: "the good faith inquiry is nuanced and fact-specific, and is not amenable to bright-line rules."[70] The fact that the fund actually originated in a tribal proposal and that it was adopted by all other tribes was also helpful in supporting its validity.

As for the Special Distribution Fund, the court had no trouble in finding that "all of the purposes to which money can be put are directly related to tribal gaming."[71] Even the fact that distributions could be made "for any other purposes specified by the legislature" was thought to be limited by the interpretational principle of *ejusdem generis,* meaning that it is limited to similar gambling-related purposes as set forth in the other examples of appropriate spending targets.[72] The fact that the state gave the tribe exclusivity rights bolstered the court's view that these kinds of payments were not contrary to the IGRA: "We do not find it inimical to the purpose or design of the IGRA for the State, under these circumstances, to ask for a reasonable share of tribal gaming revenues for the specific purposes identified in the SDF provision."[73] Unlike a situation where the state was using tax assessments to protect other gaming enterprises from competition by tribal casinos, here the state was granting a valuable exclusive right to operate free from other market forces.[74] Apparently, the court viewed some compensation for this right to be an appropriate action by the state, which was distinguishable from a more generalized exaction in the form of a tax assessment.

This case indicates that compacts may effectively impose payment obligations that look like taxes on the tribal operations, despite the strong language against taxation in the IGRA. However, the peculiar context of this case merits some caution before extending its result to all exclusivity arrangements. First, this case involved a single tribe's complaint about a compact system that approximately sixty other tribes had accepted. The potential to upset the entire regulatory structure affecting such a diverse group of tribal, state, and local government actors undoubtedly weighed heavily on the side of sustaining these practices, particularly when the vast majority of tribes had no objection to the practice.

Second, the California funds had limited purposes that closely related to ensuring tribal welfare and ameliorating ancillary negative effects of casino operations. As the court pointed out, the California compact

> differs in this respect from the revenue sharing provisions found in Tribal State compacts entered into by the States of Connecticut, New Mexico, and New York, for example. In those states, revenue derived from tribal gaming goes into the States' general funds. The legality of such compacts is not before us, and we intimate no view on the question.[75]

The fact that a state does not specifically earmark funds obtained from tribal gaming sources should not be dispositive of the validity of such assessments, but this case leaves open the possibility of a different result.

The constraint of state taxing powers raises some interesting political issues, which will need to be resolved in the near future. Non-Indian citizens have often been supportive of Indian gaming, in part because they want the option to participate in gaming activities that might otherwise be unavailable to them. For example, in both Arizona and California, Indian tribes have used public initiatives to legalize Indian gaming, which might otherwise not have occurred if the matter was left in the hands of their government officials. Local opposition based on concerns about spillover effects of casino operations on a local neighborhood is typically insufficient to impact gambling policy at the state level, where the enabling compacts are made. Tribal gaming operations have also grown in their political influence, as they have considerable resources to distribute in favor of candidates who will support their businesses.[76]

However, opposition to Indian gaming may be growing. The tax-favored status of tribal gaming operations played an important role in the 2003 California gubernatorial recall election. One journalist recounted the following ad sponsored by Arnold Schwarzenegger's campaign:

> "Their casinos make billions, yet they pay no taxes and virtually nothing to the state," pronounced Arnold Schwarzenegger in one of his campaign ads. "It's time the Indians pay their fair share. All the other major candidates take their money and pander to them." He stares into the camera. He shakes his head slowly back and forth. He squints hard. "I don't play that game."[77]

Despite tribal gifts of $8.2 million to his Democratic opponent, Lieutenant Governor Cruz Bustamonte, and $2.5 million to his competing Republican candidate, Tom McClintock, Schwarzenegger ultimately triumphed. It remains to be seen whether he will be successful in renegotiating the financial terms in which tribes are allowed to carry on Class III gaming to make them more favorable to the State.

Although California's fiscal crisis may be easing, there are other reasons to support a modification of the tax burdens imposed on Indian casinos. State and local governments are likely to incur ancillary social costs associated with casino operations that will exceed the direct costs of regulation allowed to be recovered under the IGRA. It is arguably appropriate to require casino operations to internalize those costs through payments to state and local governments. States with exclusivity agreements can address these issues indirectly through requiring revenue-sharing provisions in their compacts. However, states without exclusivity arrangements lack this option, as they are subject to the more stringent tax prohibitions of the IGRA.

States that legalize casino gambling for commercial enterprises are thus disadvantaged in their dealings with tribal operations. To the extent that patrons substitute play in a tribal operation instead of a commercial casino, revenues from direct taxes imposed on commercial casinos are lost. Moreover, enhancements to the state and local tax base from adding commercial casinos are largely unavailable for tribal casinos.[78] Their effective exemption from direct taxes on net gaming receipts, property taxes on facilities, and sales taxes on food and beverage operations clearly limits any tax contribution to the local community.

Tribal gaming operations may nevertheless generate some benefits for the local economy. For example, casinos may provide employment opportunities for non-Indians. They may also purchase goods and services from local businesses. However, these benefits may be offset by displacements in spending on local establishments, as local patrons spend their money in the casino instead of in other local businesses. Although it is difficult to gauge the magnitude of these competing economic flows, the disadvantage for local governments on the tax side of the ledger as compared with a similar commercial casino operation is quite clear.[79]

The tribal advantage inherent in this arrangement was an intentional feature of the IGRA. It was originally designed as an indirect means of delivering economic benefits to a group that has historically suffered from poverty and unemployment. However, generalizations about Indian tribes, as well as other ethnic or racial groups, can be hazardous.

Tribal membership is not limited to the poor and unemployed, and that remains true after a tribe is granted the valuable right to open a casino. For example, the Cabazon band in California, which initiated the Supreme Court case that is credited with generating the IGRA, has only fifty members,[80] yet it operates a casino facility that attracts 1.5 million visitors annually and contains nearly two thousand slot machines.[81] Similarly, the Chippewa tribe of Michigan is reported to hold a portfolio of $1.2 billion, giving each tribal member a net worth of more than $400,000. Adult tribal members receive $52,000 per year and children receive $13,000 per year from casino profits, without a requirement for meaningful work or participation in the enterprise.[82] Although these tribes may once have needed support in addressing poverty and unemployment, it is difficult to argue that a continuing economic advantage in a regulated industry is still needed in this case.

Aggregate tribal benefits from gaming are not necessarily transmitted to individual members of a tribe. Only about one-fourth of tribes engage in some form of per capita payments to tribal members.[83] The rest of the tribes purport to devote their revenues to services for tribal members, economic and community development, and charitable purposes. Questions have been raised about the effectiveness of tribal governance and disclosure concerning how gaming revenues are spent. A series of articles in the *Detroit News* in 2001 covered disputes that arose in the Sault Ste. Marie Chippewa tribe over the management of tribal wealth generated from its casino operations.[84] Tribal sovereignty means that tribal remedies may not meet the expectations of those who are accustomed to the political structures, due process, and legal remedies accessible outside the tribal context.

Efforts to share the benefits reaped from casino gaming with nongaming tribes, such as the California system discussed previously, have been quite limited in scope. Poverty and unemployment continue to be a problem in Indian communities, and many of them continue to be left out of the bonanza granted through Indian gaming. Most have no real opportunities to benefit from gambling because their geographic location gives them no access to a sufficient market of non-Indian patrons. Creating the prospects of extraordinary wealth for a few well-placed tribes through government-imposed advantages makes for dubious policy, which is likely to be reexamined if gambling continues to proliferate.

ENFORCING THE COMPACT PROCESS: PROBLEMS OF STATE SOVEREIGN IMMUNITY

The compact requirement in the IGRA provides a somewhat unusual approach toward resolving some of the practical and political problems involved in offering Class III gaming. Courts have described the compact approach as being rooted in the need for an appropriate regulatory system for Class III gambling; the absence of federal or tribal regulatory systems requires reliance on state models.[85] Since Class III games may only be held on tribal lands within states that have legalized those games, and then only to the extent that particular games are legal, the state would be expected to have regulatory systems in place for such games. However, it should be noted that the IGRA does not rule out the prospect of concurrent regulation by the tribes, provided that it is not inconsistent with or less stringent than the state regulatory requirements.[86]

The compact approach potentially has desirable political effects, to the extent that it requires a dialogue between the state and the tribe. Some have referred to this as an example of "cooperative federalism," to the extent that competing interests of federal, state, and tribal governments can be addressed through the compact.[87] In theory, this might produce amicable and effective solutions to problems presented by locating a tribal casino within the state. However, such solutions depend on good faith cooperation; human beings do not always behave that way, particularly when something as complex and controversial as gambling is involved.

The IGRA anticipates that tribal and state authorities may not reach agreement, and it provides for federal court jurisdiction over disputes initiated by the Indian tribes arising from a failure to enter into compact negotiations or to conduct negotiations in good faith.[88] However, these provisions have only limited effectiveness because the Supreme Court has held that Congress was not empowered to abrogate the sovereign immunity that the states enjoy in this context under the Eleventh Amendment.[89] Thus, a state may raise sovereign immunity as a defense against an action initiated by a tribe, thus bypassing the federal court's authority as a mechanism for enforcement.

In light of this legal development, the secretary of the interior promulgated regulations that deal with the possibility that a state may elect not to negotiate a compact and assert sovereign immunity in federal court.[90] The regulations state the following process:

> An Indian tribe may ask the Secretary to issue Class III gaming procedures when the following steps have taken place:
>
> (a) The Indian tribe submitted a written request to the State to enter into negotiations to establish a Tribal-State compact governing the conduct of Class III gaming activities;
>
> (b) The State and the Indian tribe failed to negotiate a compact 180 days after the State received the Indian tribe's request;
>
> (c) The Indian tribe initiated a cause of action in Federal district court against the State alleging that the State did not respond, or did not respond in good faith, to the request of the Indian tribe to negotiate such a compact;
>
> (d) The State raised an Eleventh Amendment defense to the tribal action; and
>
> (e) The Federal district court dismissed the action due to the State's sovereign immunity under the Eleventh Amendment.[91]

If a state raises sovereign immunity as a bar to litigation, these regulations provide a means for tribes to go directly to the secretary to seek permission regarding Class III gambling. The secretary must request a proposal from the state and may order mediation if the parties cannot reach agreement on which proposal to accept.[92] The secretary may ultimately either adopt the mediator's proposal or provide his or her own procedures consistent with the IGRA for Class III gaming to go forward.[93] This process has recently been invoked by the Kickapoo Traditional Tribe of Texas, but the state of Texas initiated litigation to block it, which was ultimately unsuccessful.[94]

It should be noted that tribes have sometimes chosen to act without a compact in place. For example, in California, a number of tribes had decided to engage in Class III gaming without a compact; then-Governor Wilson refused to negotiate for a compact until the tribes ceased these operations. As one court noted, "Because IGRA grants the federal government exclusive jurisdiction to prosecute any violations of State gambling laws in Indian country, the State's refusal to engage in negotiations was one of the few forms of leverage it possessed to force tribes to comply with IGRA's compacting requirement."[95] In Nebraska, which had not authorized Class III gaming, federal officials also had to intervene to enjoin tribal operations that violated state law and occurred outside of the IGRA provisions.[96] States and the tribes thus share a dependency on federal officials in this area.

THE SCOPE OF "INDIAN LANDS"

Indian gaming governed by the IGRA is restricted to that conducted on "Indian lands,"[97] a term that includes

(A) all lands within the limits of any Indian reservation; and

(B) any lands title to which is either held in trust by the United States for the benefit of any Indian tribe or individual or held by any Indian tribe or individual subject to restriction by the United States against alienation and over which an Indian tribe exercises governmental power.[98]

The parameters of these Indian lands are somewhat malleable to the extent that a tribe may acquire new lands that are held in trust for its benefit. The IGRA contemplates this possibility, and it imposes significant limits on the extension of gaming to trust lands acquired after October 17, 1988.

The legislative history speaks to the scope of tribal lands as follows:

> Gaming on newly acquired tribal lands outside of reservations is not gen-
> erally permitted unless the Secretary determines that gaming would be in
> the tribe's best interest and would not be detrimental to the local commu-
> nity and the Governor of the affected State concurs in that determination.[99]

Although these limits are designed to protect the interests of local communities that could be affected by the construction of a casino facility, those
protections have sometimes proved illusory.

New trust lands eligible for gaming are generally limited to parcels meeting certain requirements. For tribes with existing reservations, the IGRA
provides that gaming could be conducted on newly acquired trust lands
within or contiguous to the boundaries of that reservation.[100] This permits
a limited geographical expansion of the country in which gaming is permitted, but such expansion is anchored to the locus of the reservation. Thus,
this provision would generally prevent a tribe occupying a remote, rural
reservation from reaching an urban population center conducive to supporting a gaming operation.

For tribes with no reservation lands as of October 17, 1988, a different
rule was provided, depending on the location of the trust lands acquired for
their benefit. If the land was acquired in Oklahoma, gaming would be permitted if that land was within the tribe's former reservation or contiguous
to other land held in trust for the tribe.[101] If the land was outside of Oklahoma, gaming would be allowed on lands within the boundaries of the
tribe's "last recognized reservation within the State or States within which
such Indian tribe is presently located."[102] These rules similarly constrict the
possibility of expanding gaming by tribes that do not have a reservation but
wish to participate in a casino operation.

The IGRA nevertheless contains some exceptions to these restrictive
rules to accommodate the potential for Indian gaming on other trust lands.
The secretary of the interior is given discretion to allow Indian gaming if
these conditions are met:

> the Secretary, after consultation with the Indian tribe and appropriate
> State and local officials, including officials of other nearby Indian tribes,
> determines that a gaming establishment on newly acquired lands would

be in the best interest of the Indian tribe and its members, and would not be detrimental to the surrounding community, but only if the Governor of the State in which the gaming activity is to be conducted concurs in the Secretary's determination.[103]

This provision is designed to provide political protection for local communities potentially affected by casinos on newly acquired trust lands. The secretary is required to find that a casino "would not be detrimental" to the local community before he or she can permit gaming to occur. Local officials are entitled to consult with the secretary, thus providing input about any concerns that might make a casino undesirable for their community. The governor also has veto power, thus providing additional assurance that federal officials who are largely immune from local political accountability do not inappropriately dismiss local concerns in favor of the tribe.

Other exceptions to the general prohibitions on expanding tribal gaming include

> Lands . . . taken into trust as part of—
> (i)   a settlement of a land claim,
> (ii) the initial reservation of an Indian tribe acknowledged by the Secretary under the Federal acknowledgment process, or
> (iii) the restoration of lands for an Indian tribe that is restored to Federal recognition.[104]

The secretary may create new reservations, as well as restore lands to tribes that had previously lost their status through termination procedures adopted in the mid-1950s. However, that process occurs without the benefit of the political protections for local communities that may be affected. The process of restoration has generated bitter disputes between tribes, the federal government, and state and local governments, which have resulted in litigation.

A recent case that illustrates this conflict is *City of Roseville v. Norton*,[105] in which two cities in California and a local nonprofit organization known as Cities for Safer Communities (together referred to as "Cities") challenged the scope of the restoration exception outlined previously. In 1994, Congress passed legislation restoring tribal status to the Auburn Indian band, which had had no federally recognized existence since 1967, when Congress terminated its forty-acre reservation, distributed the lands in fee title to individuals, and terminated federal trust responsibilities over the tribe.[106] The 1994 legislation restored the tribe's status and authorized the secretary of the interior to take land back into trust to serve as a reservation for the approximately 247 members of the tribe. The Auburns did not seek to reacquire their original reservation, which was held in fee title by individuals (including non-Indians). Instead, they sought to acquire a 49.21-acre parcel of land for the purpose of constructing a casino.[107]

This location was apparently valuable for several reasons. It was close to the large population base of the Sacramento area. It was also located on the route to Reno, Nevada, a popular commercial casino destination approximately one hundred miles away. Experts had predicted that this location would be highly profitable, as it had the potential to capture a significant portion of the patronage that might otherwise go across the border to the casinos in Reno.

From the Cities' perspective, this location was objectionable. They claimed that the casino would create adverse impacts on their communities from crime, interference with planned residential developments, and interference with the family-oriented nature of the area.[108] They also argued that the Bureau of Indian Affairs was not legally authorized to proceed with the acquisition without a determination that the proposed gaming activity "would not be detrimental to the surrounding communities" and the consent of the governor.

In response, the Bureau of Indian Affairs took the position that the land was exempt from the finding of no community detriment, since this was within the exception for "restoration of lands" under the IGRA. It was also thus exempt from any requirement of consent from the governor. The bureau nevertheless treated this acquisition as a "discretionary" acquisition, which did require the balancing of the interests of the tribe against potential land use conflicts associated with the acquisition. However, this balancing of interests fell on the side of the tribe, thus allowing the approval of the acquisition.[109]

The district court dismissed the Cities' claims, and the District of Columbia Circuit Court of Appeals was ultimately called upon to decide the question of whether this land would be considered to be a part of a "restoration of lands," even though it was never a part of the Auburns' original reservation. In a lengthy analysis, the court of appeals agreed that the word *restoration* could encompass either of the interpretations sought by the parties. Thus, "neither side can prevail by quoting the dictionary."[110] However, when considering the purposes of the IGRA and the act restoring the Auburn tribe, the balance moved against the Cities' claims. Here, treating this acquisition as a "restoration of lands compensates the Tribe not only for what it lost by the act of termination, but also for opportunities lost in the interim."[111] A broader approach toward restoration was also deemed to be more consistent with the purposes of the IGRA to promote tribal economic development and self-sufficiency.[112] Moreover, it was also consistent with the purpose of the legislation restoring the Auburn tribes, which did not limit the selection of a reservation to particular lands but gave discretion to the secretary.[113]

This case suggests the possibility that tribal casino operations could be placed in many locations that have not traditionally been considered to be Indian lands and in fact were never characterized in this way. The Bureau of Indian Affairs is thus given extensive powers that effectively bypass the statutory protections granted to local governments in other contexts. In this case, the planned casino did turn out to be among the most successful in the country, with more than 3 million visitors and estimated profits of more than $300 million during its first calendar year of operations.[114]

However, traffic problems associated with that facility have been considerable. News reports indicated that cars were backed up for miles when the casino opened.[115] Those disruptions may have subsided somewhat as "opening day" has passed. Placer County, which was not a party to the litigation against the tribe, entered into a memorandum of understanding with the tribe in which the tribe agreed to pay traffic mitigation fees of $4.8 million and to make certain road improvements.[116] However, the Cities have obtained nothing. The extent of other concerns raised by the Cities remains to be seen, but they remain closed out of any governing process associated with an enterprise that could have a significant effect on their communities.

Even without a formal restoration act, as was the case in *City of Roseville,* the IGRA provisions on Indian lands may present other disputes over the expansion of Indian gaming. A particularly interesting case involves the Wyandotte tribe of Oklahoma, which sought to expand some two hundred miles into Kansas for the purpose of opening a casino. Faced with "meager financial resources and the dim prospects for gaming on its Oklahoma reservation,"[117] the Wyandottes acquired property adjoining an Indian cemetery in Kansas City, Kansas, and submitted an application to the secretary of the interior to take this land into trust for the purpose of developing and operating a casino on the land.[118]

The cemetery had once been part of lands acquired by the Wyandottes from the Delaware Nation of Indians in 1843.[119] Pursuant to an 1855 treaty, the Wyandottes agreed to dissolve the tribe, accept U.S. citizenship, and cede their lands to the United States. However, the cemetery was specifically singled out to be "permanently reserved and appropriated" as a burial ground.[120] Approximately two hundred Wyandottes chose not to accept citizenship, and Congress reconstituted this group as the Wyandotte tribe in 1867. This reconstituted tribe settled in Oklahoma. The Wyandottes were again terminated in 1956, but their status was restored in 1978. In 1984, Congress appropriated money to satisfy judgments obtained by the tribe for lands they had ceded to the United States; these funds were to be used to purchase lands that would be held in trust for their benefit.[121] These lands surrounding the cemetery were purported to be such lands.

The status of the cemetery as a reservation was very important to the Wyandotte's plan. If the cemetery was considered to be a Wyandotte reservation, the tribe could conduct gaming without the need for consultation with local government or approval from the governor of Kansas. The land would be considered "contiguous" to reservation land and thus outside the scope of these provisions involving the approval of state and local government. If these trust lands were not deemed contiguous, they would fall within the category of lands acquired after 1988, which would be subject to these provisions. Given the opposition of the governor, who was joined by other tribes operating competing casino facilities in pursing this litigation, such approval would not be forthcoming and the Wyandottes' plan would be thwarted.

Although the Tenth Circuit Court of Appeals held that the cemetery was not to be considered a "reservation," Congress enacted legislation that cast doubt on this result. Section 134 of Public Law 107-63 clarifies that the secretary of the interior has discretionary authority to determine whether land qualifies as a reservation.[122] For a brief period, the Wyandottes did indeed open a casino with Class II games on their acquired land. However, the National Indian Gaming Commission intervened and shut down the casino in early 2004, citing its view that the casino site did not meet the definition of "tribal land" under the IGRA.

The tribe's distant connection to the state of Kansas, where other local tribes do enjoy gambling privileges, undoubtedly put it in a more difficult political position than it might otherwise have occupied as a local tribe with roots in the community. The governor and the attorney general focused significant attention on the Wyandottes' operation, and they publicly announced their efforts to work with the National Indian Gaming Commission to stop it.[123]

It should be noted that a similar claim for Indian lands has been made based on a cemetery adjoining the campus of the University of California at Chico.[124] The state of California refused to negotiate a compact with the tribe, since the tribe had no land other than the cemetery. The tribe sued to compel negotiations, but the federal district court rejected that claim, stating in part:

> It is hard to believe that the Tribe really wants to negotiate to build a gambling casino on their burial ground, but that is what they argue. At oral argument, the Tribe's counsel admitted that the Tribe hopes to use lands outside the former Chico Rancheria, the subject of a pending fee-to-trust application, for a gaming facility. Thus, use of the cemetery parcel seems to be merely a pretense to force the State into negotiations in an attempt to forestall any delay in installing a future gaming facility on the land outside the former Chico Rancheria.[125]

More of these issues are likely to emerge as more tribes are recognized and Indian lands are restored. It is understandable that tribes will want to locate casino facilities near urban population centers, where they have the greatest prospects for success. The extraordinary potential for wealth generation in the right location certainly creates an incentive to pursue these opportunities through any legal means. However, the injection of gaming facilities into urban areas without the support of state and local governments and appropriate political mechanisms to address the externalities accompanying such facilities is problematic. Taken to the extreme, such efforts could prove to become catalysts for significant rethinking of the scope and extent of Indian gaming: the goose that lays the golden eggs may well be unintentionally devoured as a result of controversial extensions of gaming without substantial local political support.

THE LIMITS OF CLASS II GAMING:
WHAT IS A SLOT MACHINE?

A final issue with a potentially significant consequence to Indian casino operations involves the borderline between Class II and Class III gaming. The
IGRA specifically restricts slot machines to Class III gaming jurisdictions.
Though slot machines have long been a part of successful Las Vegas–style casinos, their popularity with consumers and casino operators has increased over
time. Technological improvements, including not only more lights and "bells
and whistles" but also appearances by famous personalities through audio and
video features, have increased the extent of their play.[126] Horse-racing facilities have scrambled to add slot machines, thus transforming into so-called racinos on account of the revenue-enhancing potential of slot machine play.

Despite their apparent popularity, slot machines have also been described
as the "crack cocaine of gambling" by antigambling activists.[127] Sophisticated
electronic features are designed to create conditions that are conducive to
continuous, repetitive play—conditions that also have a potential to manifest problem gambling behaviors.[128] Lured by the possibility of very high
(though very rare) payouts, coupled with intermittent smaller rewards,
players have been known to continue for hours. With a slot machine designed around a standard of six seconds between plays, the typical player
betting two dollars per play is wagering up to twelve hundred dollars per
hour.[129] Even with a relatively high average payout of 90 percent, this translates to gross profits of more than one hundred dollars per hour. The wealth-
generating potential from these machines for the casino operator, particularly with thousands of them on the floors of large casinos, is enormous.

The electronic features that make slot machine play so attractive to patrons have not escaped the notice of tribes operating Class II facilities, which
rely on more traditional games such as bingo and pull-tabs. The IGRA
specifically contemplates the possibility that "electronic aids" might be used
to assist players in these kinds of games.[130] However, recent decisions by the
Eighth Circuit and the Tenth Circuit Court of Appeals illustrate the technological blurring of the differences between electronic aids and slot machines. This blurring has potentially significant legal consequences for the
nature and extent of Indian gaming.

In *Seneca-Cayuga Tribe of Oklahoma v. National Indian Gaming Commission,*[131] the Tenth Circuit addressed the issue of whether "The Magical Irish Instant Bingo Dispenser System (the Machine)" constituted a slot machine, which would thus fall under the Class III gaming regulation system. The Machine dispenses paper pull-tabs from a roll containing up to seventy-five hundred individual tabs. When a player inserts money into the Machine and presses a button marked "DISPENSE," the Machine cuts a pull-tab card and dispenses it into a tray for the player to receive. The Machine is also capable of scanning a bar code on the tab, which displays the contents of the paper tab on a video screen viewed by the player. If the tab is a winner, the player takes the tab to a clerk, who confirms the win and pays out the appropriate prize.

As the court noted, "The game played with the Machine can be a high-stakes, high-speed affair. A winning ticket pays up to $1,199.00 per one-dollar play. When working properly, the Machine completes one play every seven seconds."[132] Thus, the Machine presumably helped to make a comparatively mundane game of pull-tabs more visually exciting. It would also make play more frequent and regimented, potentially enhancing the profitability for the operator.

The Tenth Circuit faced the issue of whether the Machine was essentially an electronic aid to playing pull-tabs, which were allowed as Class II devices, or whether, as argued by the government, the game was essentially an "electromechanical facsimile version of slots," which would thus constitute a Class III device.[133] The Machine was functionally similar to another device known as the "Lucky Tab II," which the District of Columbia Circuit had previously held to be an authorized Class II technologic aid. The Tenth Circuit essentially agreed. In evaluating the Machine, the court observed that the player was still essentially playing a pull-tab game.

> Although a pull-tabs player may opt to view the video display regarding the contents of the paper pull-tabs, players of the Machine must still manually peel back the top layer of the pull-tab to confirm victory, and it is that tab presented for visual inspection to a gaming hall clerk that entitles players to winnings. We thus reject the argument that the game played with the Machine is slots: although we acknowledge some superficial similarities between the two, pull-tabs, even when sped up, placed under lights, and depicted with a spinning machine on the side, is still pull-tabs.[134]

The Lucky Tab II machine was also the subject of litigation in *United States v. Santee Sioux Tribe of Nebraska*,[135] in which the federal government sought to enjoin a tribe from using the machines in its Class II facility. Here, too, Eighth Circuit followed the District of Columbia Circuit in finding that the machine merely facilitates the playing of paper pull-tabs.

> While this case presents a close call, we think the better view is that operation of the Lucky Tab II machines does not change the fundamental fact that the player receives a traditional paper pull-tab from a machine, and whether he or she decides to pull the tab or not, must present that card to the cashier to redeem winnings.[136]

As for the argument that the machines were facsimiles of slot machines, the court noted: "These machines may look and sound like slot machines, but they cannot make change, accumulate credits, or pay out winnings. Thus, they are not exact copies (the commonly understood definition of a facsimile) of a slot machine."[137]

The U.S. government filed a petition of certiorari for review of both of these cases, but the Supreme Court denied these petitions.[138] The states of California, Alabama, Connecticut, Texas, Minnesota, Nebraska, Nevada, South Dakota, and Texas—which all have within their borders Indian tribes that currently operate gaming facilities or may seek to do so in the future—submitted an amicus brief in support of the petition. These states claimed that ruling that the devices were technologic aids rather than slot machines "threatens substantially to undermine the only means available for States to ensure adequate regulation of slot-machine gambling conducted on Indian lands, vis., the negotiated tribal-state compact."[139]

The states argued that when slot machines are subject to the compact requirement as a Class III game, the states may exercise considerable control or oversight over the regulation of gambling. Moreover, in states like California, the compact not only limits the number of slot machines but also subjects those machines to license fees. Moreover, the Class III facilities must also comply with revenue-sharing requirements, which are not applicable to Class II operations. To the extent that these restrictions can be circumvented, the protections of the IGRA are made ineffective. As the states point out:

By virtue of the Tenth Circuit's decision, the Tribes' ability entirely to circumvent IGRA's negotiation obligations with respect to slot machines is merely a function of human creative ability to design slot machines that—in the case of pull-tab devices, for example—permit push-button "play" of a coded strip-roll of paper "pull-tabs," providing a visual and auditory display of the outcome represented by bells and the aligning of reels of a virtual "one-armed bandit." From the player's point of view—and, therefore, from the perspective of a need for negotiated compact treatment—these so-called "technologic aids" are indistinguishable in any meaningful sense from any other slot machine along the casino wall.[140]

Although the Supreme Court was apparently not persuaded of the need for its intervention, the significance of this controversy has not been lost on the National Indian Gaming Commission. On January 21, 2004, the commission announced the formation of a Class II Game Classification Standards Advisory Committee to provide more definitive technical standards and regulations for the parameters of Class II games. Representatives were named on March 8, 2004, approximately one week after the Supreme Court's denial of certiorari in the Eighth and Tenth Circuit cases. It remains to be seen whether the committee will indeed promulgate more restrictive rules on electronic aids. If they fail to do so, this may present another case in which aggressive and technically correct legal positions expose fundamental political flaws in the regulatory system, which in turn will generate more restrictive rules. Detailed draft regulations were released in March 2005, though final regulations have not been promulgated.[141]

TRIBAL POLITICAL INFLUENCE

As shown previously, tribes enjoy a privileged status under current law. It is not surprising that tribal governments have been active in political efforts designed to maintain their privileged status. The recent controversies surrounding the indictment and guilty plea of the lobbyist Jack Abramoff, whose clients included several Indian tribes with gaming operations, have brought these efforts to light.

The total amount spent by tribes to influence legislation at both state and federal levels is difficult to ascertain. This difficulty is partly attributable to the fact that funds may be channeled to grass roots organizations that do not engage in lobbying government representatives but instead provide other services. These kinds of expenditures are outside the scope of election law reporting. Expenditures at the state and local levels are also difficult to track, as they are also outside the scope of federal election laws. However, federal expenditures provide a window of insight on the political influence of tribes, which merits some attention.

The Center for Responsive Politics, which operates opensecrets.org, a Web site examining the political expenditures on behalf of various industries, provides some insight into the magnitude and direction for political contributions of the Indian gaming industry. Data compiled from reports to the Federal Election Commission show that the Indian gaming industry contributed an estimated $7.3 million in the 2004 election cycle.[142] Most of the industry contributions (approximately 68 percent, or $4.8 million) went to Democratic candidates.

Although $7.3 million may seem significant, this total is dwarfed by other industries. For example, defense contractors, which are highly connected to and dependent upon actions in the political world, spent over $15 million.[143] Pharmaceutical firms spent about $18 million.[144] The commercial gambling industry spent about $11 million.[145] All totaled, House and Senate candidates received over $1 billion in 2004.[146] Thus, the contributions of any particular industry look small indeed in relation to this massive total. Nevertheless, it is interesting to note some of the particular matters that invoked tribal lobbying and political efforts. For examples we need to look no further than some of Abramoff's clients.

One issue that focused tribal concerns on federal legislation involved the federal tax treatment of tribal governments. The Mississippi band of Choctaw Indians was one of Abramoff's clients with interests in this area. The Choctaws have extensive business holdings in Mississippi and other parts of the Southeast, extending into Mexico. Their Web site lists Choctaw enterprises in manufacturing, retail, service, and tourism as providing more than eight thousand jobs, making them one of the top ten employers in Mississippi.[147] Although the tribe touts manufacturing as the basis for its economic success, it cites the Silver Star Casino as "the largest and most profitable Choctaw Enterprise to date."[148]

The growing influence and profitability of tribal casinos were drawing attention from commercial casino competitors, which did not enjoy the tax-exempt status of Indian tribes on similar enterprises. As a result, the tax-exempt status of tribal governments was at risk of being legislatively overturned. Tribal governments mobilized in opposition to this legislation. Jack Abramoff's close connections to antitax groups, which were particularly influential in Congress during this period, proved useful in helping to defeat this legislation, which Abramoff characterized as another attempt to raise taxes.[149]

In the process of representing the Choctaws, however, Abramoff apparently exacted funds from the Choctaws through related enterprises engaged in grass roots lobbying, which made payments to Abramoff that were not disclosed to the Choctaws.[150] The tribe asserts that they have cooperated with the Justice Department's investigation and that they have reached a settlement with Abramoff's former law firm that resolves their claims for past misdoings while he was associated with the firm.[151]

Abramoff's political influence was also deployed by tribal governments to protect their casino enterprises from incursion by other tribes. The Tigua tribe's Speaking Rock Casino located near El Paso, Texas, which borders neighboring Louisiana, was the target of a lawsuit filed in 1999 by Texas attorney general John Cornyn (now a U.S. senator).[152] This suit sought to enjoin the tribe from continuing casino-style gambling on its reservation, which the state contended was in violation of Texas and federal law. The federal district court ruled in favor of the state, and the facility was enjoined from operating casino games otherwise prohibited to Texas citizens in 2002.[153]

The political intrigue surrounding this case is rooted in the tenuous status of tribal gaming in the hands of federal and state authorities. The tribe had its status restored pursuant to federal legislation, and the ability to pursue gambling on the reservation was a matter that was specifically addressed in the restoration bill. State and federal officials were consulted in this process, and the federal restoration act for the tribe ultimately tied the fate of gambling to Texas law.[154] The broader IGRA was held not to abrogate this provision, which was effectively considered a compact with the state of Texas.[155]

Since the fate of the tribe's gambling operations, as well as the employment of casino workers, was at stake in this litigation, it was theoretically possible to resolve the matter through changing Texas law. The tribe was reported to employ 785 people at the casino, with a payroll of $14 million.[156] Thus, intense local interests were affected.

Of course, not everyone would line up with the interests of the Tiguas and their employees on this matter. Neighboring casinos in Louisiana, also run by Native Americans, would stand to gain from the elimination of a cross-border competitor. In particular, the Coushatta tribe of Louisiana, which operated the Coushatta Casino Resort in nearby Kinder, Louisiana, reportedly utilized Abramoff's services on this matter.[157]

Grass roots political interests against expanding gambling would become a valuable tool in ensuring against a political solution favoring another Texas casino. Ralph Reed, former executive director of the Christian Coalition, was hired by Michael Scanlon, an Abramoff associate, and his firm was reportedly paid more than $4 million to engage in opposition to Texas casino expansion.[158] Though Reed, who was staunchly antigambling in his beliefs, refused to take money from casino-owning tribes, the use of an intermediary here apparently hid the source of this spending. In response to an extensive public relations campaign by the Tiguas against the efforts of Attorney General Cornyn, Reed promised to send fifty pastors as "moral support" for Cornyn.[159] Reed, who is a candidate for lieutenant governor in Georgia, has subsequently claimed not to have known about any connection between tribal contributions and his political work against expanded casinos.[160]

The Tiguas were apparently also unaware of Abramoff's efforts against them in the Texas legislature. Those efforts did not stop Abramoff from subsequently being retained by the Tiguas for the purpose of lobbying Congress in order to change the undesirable judicial outcome. However, the Tiguas reportedly had trouble paying their retainer. According to a report in the *Weekly Standard,* Abramoff proposed an "elder legacy plan," which involved taking out life insurance policies on older tribal members, with the proceeds being paid to Abramoff on their demise. The tribe rejected this plan.[161]

Political contributions by the Tiguas to individual representatives, including Ohio congressman Bob Ney, have been the subject of continuing interest as this saga continues to unfold.[162] Representative Ney resigned his post as chairman of the House Administration Committee in early 2006, for the apparent purpose of avoiding "distraction" from his committee work as a result of Abramoff-related investigations.[163]

The Coushatta tribe and the Choctaws of Mississippi also apparently involved Abramoff in lobbying against casino competition in Louisiana from a neighboring tribe, the Jena Choctaw. An e-mail by Abramoff to Italia Federici, head of a Republican environmental advocacy group called the Council of Republicans for Environmental Advocacy (CREA), stated in part:

> There is a tribe in Mississippi and Louisiana called the Jena Choctaw. They are a federally recognized tribe and trying to get a gambling compact in Mississippi and/or Louisiana. The Jens are also trying to get land put into trust (ostensibly for "economic development", but really for gambling). This is totally horrible for both the Choctaw in Mississippi and the Coushatta. The Interior Department BIA has sent a letter out (I will fax this to you right now at the [blank] number) soliciting local input, as if they are going to do this !! [W]e have to squash this very, very hard and fast.[164]

It should be noted that the CREA hosted social events at which Interior Secretary Gale Norton and other Department of the Interior officials were invited guests.[165] The tribes were solicited to participate in this organization as "trustees" through contributions of fifty thousand dollars.[166] This apparently provided at least the perception of acquiring greater access to these officials.

In each of these examples, tribal political influence was brought to bear on issues that were important to them. Their involvement appears no different from that of other business enterprises seeking to defend business turf or to extend favorable tax preferences. The criminal information against Abramoff suggests that tribes were indeed victims of Abramoff to the extent that their funds may have been channeled to organizations that benefited Abramoff without their knowledge. However, their intentions to obtain benefits from those expenditures—just as other enterprises benefit from lobbying expenditures—were also clear.

In addition to these specific payments to lobbyists, tribes also made significant political contributions to individual candidates through Abramoff and his associates. According to a recent investigation compiled by the *Washington Post*, Abramoff, members of his lobbying team, and tribal associates contributed over $4 million to individual politicians during the period 1999–2004.[167] The possibility that these contributions may have caused specific legislative actions is a matter worthy of investigation.

It is important to recognize that the special status enjoyed by the tribes provides particularly enticing circumstances for lobbying activity. Whenever a business activity or economic benefit is held at the pleasure of government to the exclusion of others, competing interests will have incentives to remove those benefits. Political activists thus enjoy a position that lends itself to the extraction of tribute to preserve the status quo. As illustrated in the previous discussion, purveyors of government influence may play both sides of the political fence, leaving the tribes caught in the middle. When fueled by the considerable cash profits of a successful tribal gaming operation, the influence of tribes on politics is a force to be reckoned with. Citizens also need to be watchful about such expenditures at the state and local level, particularly in jurisdictions affected by tribal casino operations.

12. Governing Fortune in a Changing World

As legal and geographic barriers have crumbled, casino patrons have experienced unprecedented opportunities to pursue the whims of fortune. Traditional legal proscriptions against professional gaming houses have been transformed into components of a regulatory structure that supports a large commercial industry. Instead of struggling to suppress the demand for gambling, governments have chosen to exploit it by channeling patrons toward state-approved providers that can capture tax revenues and provide legitimate employment opportunities.

Expanded gambling has also exposed dimensions of human weakness that otherwise might have remained latent. There is still much to learn about the nature and extent of problem gambling, but the extant data suggest that its dimensions are significant. The National Council on Problem Gambling estimates that 3 million adults in the United States meet criteria for pathological gambling each year, with another 2–3 percent (6–9 million) experiencing serious problems due to gambling.[1] As discussed in chapter 5, these figures may be conservative. Problem and pathological gamblers are a significant source of revenues for casino operations.

Problem gambling behavior affects nongamblers as well as gamblers. Our own research has found that opening a casino produces a significant increase in personal bankruptcy rates over time.[2] Each bankruptcy translates into losses for creditors, and the associated costs they incur are likely to be passed along to others. Other researchers have identified a correlation between casino gambling and crime. Some have estimated that criminal activity associated with casinos exacts aggregate costs that outweigh any countervailing aggregate economic benefits.[3]

Children and families are also apt to suffer from problem gambling be-

246

havior. Gambling spouses may incur debt secretly and impose legal responsibility for those gambling-related debts on a nongambling spouse. In some cases, gambling losses may mean that child support goes unpaid, potentially impacting dependent children and adding further strain to the social safety net. As of 2003, nationwide arrearages in child support totaled over $95 billion—a stunningly large number that has been growing over time.[4]

News accounts commonly report these negative consequences, including embezzlement from employers or clients, family discord and divorce, and even suicide as a result of excessive gambling losses.[5] More stories probably lie below the surface, as family-related problems involving human weakness tend to be hidden in order to avoid embarrassment. Industry advocates may continue to challenge the certainty of scientific proof about a connection between gambling and social costs, but as time goes on that position becomes harder to maintain. It is evident that the costs are not zero and that they are likely to be significant.

In this environment, government officials may experience tension between their desire to raise revenue from this industry and their traditional responsibilities to protect the public welfare. Personal freedom is a powerful political ideal, and some people connect the pursuit of gambling with the pursuit of happiness. However, even libertarian principles recognize the need to internalize costs from such pursuits. In this final chapter, we look further at the political and legal environment with an eye toward the future of industry regulation.

If legalized gambling persists in some jurisdictions (as it is likely to do), the paradigm for regulation needs to change to address the reality of externalized social costs. The current system may seem highly resistant to change, but that resistance may be softening. We suggest one possibility for change that may provide a suitable compromise between freedom and responsibility. It involves wrapping new technology around an old idea with deep historical roots: licensing gamblers.

THE CURRENT POLITICAL MILIEU

Policymakers have given surprisingly little attention to social costs in formulating casino gambling policies. In fact, the successful expansion of the industry has been achieved in significant part by ignoring them. Industry proponents have achieved political success by exploiting the fact that costs associated with the gambling industry are diffused and difficult to measure, whereas benefits (such as tax revenues) are tangible and quantifiable.[6] Casino promoters have adopted the strategy of shifting the burden of proof on social costs to their opposition, while at the same time touting the casino as a tonic for economic vitality, a politically attractive source for tax revenues from a voluntary and popular activity, and a vanguard of individual liberty.

Although casino promoters have achieved success with this approach, it has played best in times of economic difficulty. In those situations, social risk taking may seem to be a viable step on the path to prosperity. Government officials thus view the easy money offered by the casinos as a preferable alternative to offer to their constituents, particularly when other alternatives may be based on less popular options involving sweat, tears, and toil. In modern times, such alternatives are hardly the stuff of which political success is made.

Signs of change may nevertheless be on the horizon. Citizens have continued to scrutinize the collateral effects of casinos on economic and social structures. Grass roots political efforts have proven remarkably effective against coordinated and well-funded efforts from commercial casino forces. Even the industry itself appears to be willing to take greater steps to address problem gambling.

An apt example occurred in November 2004, when a majority of Nebraska voters rejected statewide initiatives to legalize casinos. Two separate initiatives were on the ballot—one sponsored by the legislature and the other sponsored by a coalition of pro-gaming interests (including prospective casino investors) known as Keep the Money in Nebraska.[7] Both initiatives sought to establish legal casinos in Nebraska to compete with facilities in neighboring states, particularly those in Council Bluffs, Iowa, which shares a border with Nebraska on the Missouri River across from Omaha, Nebraska's most populous city. Although competition between these two plans may have contributed to electoral division within pro-gambling forces, thus weakening their prospects for success, grass roots political opposition from a group known as Gambling with the Good Life[8] was also instrumental in this outcome.

Though reportedly outspent by twenty to one,[9] Gambling with the Good Life successfully mobilized voters, particularly those interested in the social costs associated with gambling. They used connections with local churches and civic groups to spread their message, which emphasized the deleterious effects of problem gambling as a counterweight to the putative economic benefits associated with expanded gambling. The leader of this group, Pat Loontjer, a housewife, volunteered her time and mobilized many other volunteers to do the same. She was also supported by visible public figures, including congressman and former University of Nebraska football coach Tom Osborne and "Oracle of Omaha" Warren Buffet, who helped spread a message favoring work and saving over the ephemeral riches associated with gambling. Some businesses, including restauranteurs concerned about displacement effects of casino spending, also joined in such efforts. With little spending in the mass media, Loontjer spearheaded a grass roots campaign based on people-to-people contact, town meetings, and yard signs spreading word of individual support.

In contrast, Keep the Money in Nebraska focused heavily on mass media advertising that emphasized the economic drain from Nebraska residents' gambling across the river in Iowa. Images of millions of dollars floating across the bridge linking Omaha to Council Bluffs casinos flooded the airwaves. When questioned about social costs, the pro-casino spokespersons took an aggressive position that such costs had not been proven. They chose instead to emphasize the economic benefits, including jobs and taxes, that legalized gambling could deliver if Nebraskans gambled at home.

After the election, Keep the Money in Nebraska continued to advocate for legal change in state casino policy. However, their position seems to recognize social costs as part of the gambling equation. Their Web site states in part:

> Nebraska continues to have the vast majority of its citizens frequent bordering casinos, extensive participation in sports book, an eruption of illegal machines in private clubs and out state bars, and rapid expansion of Internet gaming. *Between 3% and 5% of our population already has a gaming related behavior disorder.* That figure is very comparable to states with full fledged casino gaming. We have most all of the downsides of expanded gaming and simply none of the upsides. There is a silver lining in all this. We have the opportunity to focus on the best possible way to minimize the downside and deal with it in a socially responsible manner in the new petition language.[10]

To recognize that a significant percentage of the population has a gambling-related disorder seems a significant concession. It remains to be seen how any new initiative they intend to sponsor will address problem gambling issues. Discussion of new initiatives to legalize casino gambling for the ballot in November 2006 suggests that the issue will not go away quietly.[11]

Local citizens also rejected initiatives for slot machines in Miami-Dade County, Florida, in 2005, after a statewide initiative was approved. The approval process for this initiative illustrates the difficulty of including social costs into the economic calculus associated with new gambling legislation. Florida law requires that constitutional amendments proposed through citizen initiatives must include "an analysis and financial impact statement to be placed on the ballot of the estimated increase or decrease in any revenues or costs to state or local governments resulting from the proposed initiative."[12] An initial attempt to include a reference to costs associated with "problem gambling" in this statement was opposed by the attorney general.[13] The Florida Supreme Court resolved this issue in the government's favor. The following language ultimately appeared on the ballot:

> This amendment alone has no fiscal impact on government. If slot machines are authorized in Miami-Dade or Broward counties, governmental costs associated with additional gambling will increase by an unknown amount and local sales tax-related revenues will be reduced by $5 million to $8 million annually. If the Legislature also chooses to tax slot machine revenues, state tax revenues from Miami-Dade and Broward counties combined would range from $200 million to $500 million annually.[14]

Thus, although the initiative recognized the potential for governmental costs to increase, the only quantifiable costs involved foregone sales tax revenues to local government, which are quite modest in relation to the direct taxes that the state would gain from expanded gambling.

After gaining narrow approval for this initiative in a statewide election in November 2004, local voters were then required to give further approval to expanded gambling. Broward County voters approved the measure, but Miami-Dade voters apparently changed their minds and voted against it in March 2005, despite giving 57 percent approval the previous November. Broward County has experienced further delays in the installation of slot machines. Enabling legislation was delayed, as the legislature was unable to agree on regulatory details. Further litigation may ultimately be required to resolve these issues.[15]

In July 2004, Pennsylvania approved a measure to allow up to sixty-one thousand slot machines across the state.[16] Neighboring Maryland, despite threats that these machines could draw patrons across state lines, is holding fast against expanded gambling. Pro-gambling interests in Maryland spent more than $2.3 million on lobbying efforts during the 2004 legislative session, which is not insubstantial in relation to the total estimated spending on all issues of $30 million the prior year.[17] One commentator analogized the interstate competition to an "arms race" between states competing for gambling patrons.[18] If so, a "peace movement" may well be at work, as resistance to slot machines in Maryland has been going on for three years. Though lobbyist spending there remains large, it has declined, reflecting the possible concession to the political will against expanding the industry.[19]

These recent examples show that public resistance to gambling remains a force to be reckoned with. Citizens continue to be skeptical about the economic and social dimensions of gambling. Sometimes regional interest groups like Gambling with the Good Life help in the dissemination of academic research that is problematic for the industry, which otherwise might be relegated to the ivory tower. Other organizations, including the National Coalition Against Legalized Gambling and the National Coalition Against Expanded Gambling, have also disseminated this research, reaching community activists and thus supporting grass roots resistance efforts. Religious convictions may also be playing an important role in the actions of many gambling opponents, and this force continues to be influential in American politics.

Skepticism about the benefits of gambling may also be rooted in personal experiences. The proliferation of gambling has produced shared experiences with problem gambling, which may be spread interpersonally. Claims of tax relief may also ring hollow, as neighbors in gambling states are still likely to complain about their high taxes. Personal stories should not be underestimated as an animating force behind a resistance to expanded gambling. This kind of information has the potential to overcome the influence of corporately funded mass media efforts to communicate a more positive message. Moreover, in states with populist traditions (like Nebraska), voters may already have a skeptical predisposition toward positions advanced by well-heeled corporate sources.

In some areas of the country, gambling markets are also maturing. Although early casino adopters found it easy to tap into consumer demand, particularly from patrons living in bordering states that restricted legal casinos, later adopters have found a more competitive marketplace. The proverbial "low-hanging fruit" has been picked, and competition for gaming dollars is intensifying. One effect of this competition is that the industry must spend more and more to create an attractive gambling environment. The recent experience of Trump Hotels and Casino Resorts in Atlantic City provides anecdotal evidence of this trend: after restructuring under federal bankruptcy protection, it will invest heavily to refurbish the facility to compete with other newer properties in Atlantic City.[20] In Las Vegas, the new Wynn Las Vegas hotel has reportedly cost $2.7 billion to construct—topping a previous billion-dollar expenditure on the Bellagio as the most expensive new property in the city.[21] As previously discussed, the capital markets have also expressed skepticism about the future profitability trends for this competitive industry.[22]

The political nirvana of tourist-based gambling, in which a casino does attract new dollars to the local economy, has proved exceedingly difficult to achieve. Las Vegas is unusual in this respect, as it remains an important tourist destination even for those with local gambling options. A recent Zogby survey has even reportedly shown that a majority of New Jersey residents would prefer to gamble in Las Vegas over Atlantic City.[23] However, without significant market differentiation (such as through special amenities or other tourist attractions, which Las Vegas can readily offer), it seems unlikely that patrons interested in gambling will travel elsewhere for that purpose. As a result, casino revenues (and associated taxes) in many locations are likely to come increasingly from local patrons at their "hometown" casino.

Local patronage still generates gambling taxes from willing participants, which might be viewed as politically preferable to increasing forced exactions from the general population. However, local citizens (including those who do not participate in gambling at all) may also bear some hidden costs. Increased reliance on local patronage also spells trouble for any prospects of turning the casino into a positive force working for economic development. In contrast to losses from their nonresident counterparts, wagering losses from local patrons may displace other local consumption instead of bringing in new dollars to the local economy. Moreover, the typical taxing structures that redistribute public gambling revenues ensure that a portion of gambling losses will be transferred outside of the local economy. Prospects for significant local benefits from gambling become more remote as nonresident patrons are removed from the mix.[24] The associated social costs of these problem gamblers also remain localized instead of being exported to other jurisdictions where nonresidents return.

Although the political and economic forces discussed previously may provide a basis for constraining the expansion of gambling (or at least slowing that growth), jurisdictions with existing casino facilities face other difficulties. To the extent that government officials take steps to address the costs of problem gambling, they face the prospects of a corresponding decline in government revenues from gambling taxes—at least in the short run. Moreover, in an environment of interstate competition (which potentially extends internationally through the Internet), designing and implementing a more restrictive regulatory system proves daunting. Creating a competitive disadvantage with facilities in neighboring jurisdictions may not seem like a prudent business choice in an environment where interstate competition—a casino "arms race"—is under way.

Once casinos become established, inertial forces tend to ensure their continuity. Significant past investments in infrastructure and jobs, as well as government reliance on revenues from the industry, encourage preservation of the status quo. Moreover, the practical reality of reliable campaign contributions cannot be ignored. An industry with cash to spend whose existence is at the pleasure of the state or local government has a powerful incentive to continue giving to support that status.[25] Growing economic and political clout provides a basis for skepticism and suspicion about the degree of scrutiny that elected officials are willing to turn upon the industry and its effects on the larger society, even if social costs are being imposed.

Recent events in Iowa illustrate this basis for skepticism. In 2004, the Iowa legislature required a study of socioeconomic effects from gambling, which was to be completed prior to a vote on expanding casino gambling in that state.[26] However, it appropriated only ninety thousand dollars to complete this research[27]—quite a modest expenditure in relation to the more than $200 million in gambling taxes contributed annually to state coffers. The legislature also expected this work to be done in a compressed time frame of approximately five months. Such constraints on time and resources raise the question of how much the legislators really wanted to learn about the impact of casinos in their state.

Further intrigue also surrounds this study. A legislative committee initially selected Per-Mar Security, a firm from Davenport, Iowa, to perform this research. In doing so, it passed over proposals from academics, including those from two state universities. Per-Mar Security later withdrew from the engagement after local media reported that it had economic ties to the industry, as it had sold security equipment and provided services to an Iowa casino.[28] Legislators, some of whom also received campaign contributions from this firm, claimed not to know of this apparent conflict of interest.[29]

An academic group from the University of Northern Iowa was ultimately chosen to complete the study, but only after a considerable delay. Moreover, the state persisted in approving an $85 million expansion of a casino in Council Bluffs without the benefit of any results from the study.[30] Such expansion in the face of uncertainty about the nature and extent of social costs provides an additional source of skepticism about the extent to which the public good is being considered by those who regulate the industry.

The current regulatory system has worked effectively during a phase where growing the industry and enhancing its profitability have served both government and industry interests. However, it falls short of an ideal system, which would sort out those with problem gambling behaviors who impose costs on others while allowing other patrons to exercise freedom in pursuing their own conception of the good.

Self-selection has not proven effective as a means for exclusion, as those with gambling problems often don't respond until after they have experienced significant losses—and likely imposed costs on others. Moreover, self-exclusion mechanisms ultimately depend on the gambler's own initiatives, which have been known to be faulty. One patron reported gambling over eighty times after she enrolled in an exclusion program; prior to enrollment she had lost over four hundred thousand dollars in personal savings and incurred thousands more in debt.[31]

Technology may now provide an unprecedented means to identify problem gamblers and to help them control their tendencies. To civil libertarians, technology may pose a threat that conjures up the image of "Big Brother" intruding directly on their personal pleasure seeking. However, one Internet firm has adopted a software-based solution to monitor gambling patterns and to warn those who may be venturing into problem areas, including reckless betting behavior. These patrons are contacted by an employee described as a "recovering gambling addict" and counseled to seek help.[32] This practice seems contrary to the short-term economic interests of the casino, which would presumably benefit from high levels of consumption at all times.

However, such behavior is not uncommon in other business environments. For example, drinking establishments have been known to cut off customers who have overindulged. In part, they may do so for altruistic and noble reasons, such as genuine personal concern for their customer. But the threat of liability may also encourage this behavior as a self-interested means to reduce the risk of exposure to penalties or civil claims through the legal system. In the casino industry, where the fate of the industry may lie in the hands of government officials moved by political winds, it may also be prudent to consider these longer-term interests.

LITIGATION THREATS TO THE GAMBLING INDUSTRY: SOME RECENT CASES

As more information becomes known about the nature and extent of problem gambling, evidence of indifference to these problems, or of the knowing design of casino environs to take advantage of human weaknesses, could well shift legal and political winds against the industry. When government officials are unwilling to impose changes through regulatory channels, litigation can serve as a catalyst for change. The possibility that casino patrons or those harmed by problem gambling behavior may pursue claims against casinos or their affiliated suppliers lurks in the background as a potential future threat to the industry.

Those who find such a threat implausible should consider recent legal actions against the tobacco industry. Following complaints brought by individuals, state attorneys general and eventually the federal government sought redress for harms and costs associated with adverse public health effects associated with the industry. The fact that the industry was specially taxed and that the government carefully regulated the sale of its products was apparently an insufficient basis to stop these actions from going forward and producing large cash settlements. Government can be a fickle business partner when it becomes advantageous to do so.[33]

As for private claims, class action lawsuits can present a formidable threat for any industry. Given the extensive costs to litigate and the prevalence of the so-called American Rule in requiring each party to bear his or her own attorney's fees, an individual plaintiff with a small or even modest-sized claim for damages would not choose to incur the transaction costs necessary to obtain redress. Attorneys working on a contingent fee basis could become interested, however, in the event that multiple claims could be joined together, thus allowing the potential for aggregate recoveries to justify the substantial litigation costs.

In *Poulos v. Caesars World, Inc.,*[34] the Ninth Circuit considered whether casino patrons could maintain a class action lawsuit seeking damages from the casino industry. The plaintiffs had lost money playing video poker and electronic slot machines. They brought a civil RICO claim alleging that the casinos had "engaged in a course of fraudulent and misleading acts and omissions intended to induce people to play their video poker and electronic slot machines based on a false belief concerning how those machines actually operate, as well as the extent to which there is actually an opportunity to win on any given play."[35]

With regard to video poker, the plaintiffs claimed that the electronic version of the game did not replicate a random deal from a conventional deck of cards. The computerized version was, instead, more predictable for the house, thus giving the house a greater advantage than in a conventional game.[36] They similarly claimed that the electronic slot machines were designed to appear similar to their mechanical counterparts, but their results were also based on computer programming that did not match the odds from mechanical devices. In addition, they claimed that casinos could also program the electronic versions to generate "near misses" for patrons, thus manipulating players by inducing them to believe they had just missed a jackpot and otherwise inflating the perceived chances of winning.[37]

Unfortunately for the plaintiffs, the court found that their claims were not suitable for class certification because of problems with individual proof of causation. In a civil RICO claim, the plaintiffs must show that a defendant's conduct proximately caused the injury.[38] For example, a slot machine player might meet this burden by showing

> that the Casinos' failure to inform players that the electronic slot machines operate differently than their mechanical counterparts affected

her decision to play, or that she was influenced by the fact that electronic slot machines look like traditional slot machines. In turn, this would require her to establish that she was aware of how the mechanical slot machines operated, was unaware that the electronic slot machines operated differently than those machines, and was motivated to play the electronic slot machine based on her knowledge of these factors.[39]

Alternatively, a video poker player might show the causal link between the casino's conduct and her losses by establishing

> that she was an ace player in the traditional table poker game and played the video poker game, at least in part, because she was misled into believing that the video poker and table poker games functioned similarly and offered the same odds. It is not enough to say "I played the games and I lost money" or "I didn't make any money."[40]

People gamble for many different reasons, and not every potential member of the class would be expected to be able to prove causation in this manner. As the court observed:

> [T]here may be no single, logical explanation for gambling—it may be an addiction, a form of escape, a casual endeavor, a hobby, a risk-taking money venture, or scores of other things. The vast array of knowledge and expectations that players bring to the machines ensures that the "value" of gambling differs greatly from player to player, with some people playing for entertainment value or for any number of other reasons as much as to win. [41]

Although the court recognized that some securities cases had been allowed to proceed as class actions without a similar showing of reliance and causation, it distinguished those cases as involving claims based entirely on omissions. In this case, the plaintiffs alleged affirmative mislabeling and specific acts on the part of the casino defendants.[42] Thus, their class certification was denied.

The law firm of Lionel, Sawyer, and Collins, which represented casino industry defendants in this case, issued a statement that this case caused "a collective sigh of relief around the globe as the casinos and manufacturers locally, nationally, and internationally were able to rid themselves of what would have been a time-consuming, multibillion dollar lawsuit."[43] The plaintiffs' attorneys in this case vowed to fight on with individual cases, though the damages threat to the industry posed by these cases is undoubtedly less significant than if a class had been certified.

Other class action efforts on a state level have also proven unsuccessful. In *Kraft v. Detroit Entertainment, LLC,*[44] the Michigan Court of Appeals dismissed a class action lawsuit based on the Michigan Consumer Protection Act and common law claims of fraud and unjust enrichment. In this case, class members asserted that the slot machines they played were deceptive in that they misrepresented the chances of winning a large payoff by failing to disclose that the machines were programmed to stop more frequently on spaces with lower valued payoffs. The expansive regulatory system applicable to gambling was held to preempt all state law claims against the casino, thus providing extensive protection for the industry from legal liability. In essence, redress for the failure to disclose was limited to that which might be provided by the casino regulators, and the courts would not intervene.

Problem gamblers have also sought to recover on an individual basis for substantial losses flowing from their gambling behavior. In *Merrill v. Trump Indiana, Inc.,*[45] a compulsive gambler brought suit in federal court seeking $6 million in damages from a riverboat casino. The gambler, Mark Merrill, was at the time of the litigation serving time in a federal prison in Florida for robbing banks, an activity he traced to the need to cover substantial gambling losses at the defendant casino. As the court wryly noted, "Mr. Merrill, by his own admission, is a compulsive gambler. Like East and West, this is a twain that should never meet. But it did."[46]

Merrill alleged that he had requested that the casino evict him if he should ever show up to gamble. The casino's failure to do so formed the basis for his complaint. Merrill asserted both contract and tort theories under Indiana law, but the district court dismissed all of them. On appeal, Merrill focused solely on his tort claims—that is, that the casino had violated a duty of care or engaged in willful and wanton misconduct by allowing Merrill to gamble.

For the source of this duty of care, Merrill first focused on regulations promulgated by the Indiana Gaming Commission that required casinos to maintain an eviction list. However, these regulations were not enacted until 2000—after Merrill had incurred his losses. Even if the law had applied to

Merrill, the court refused to create a private cause of action from the regulation. A violation of the regulation might get the casino in trouble with the commission, but that did not necessarily form a basis for recovery by an individual.[47]

Merrill also sought to develop a common law basis for a duty, but the court similarly rebuffed this theory. Though a duty of care exists where the safety of a casino patron was at issue, those problems were not presented here. The court found that the closest analogy under common law was the duty of care that a tavern owner had to protect its patrons. Although Indiana law might allow a third party to recover for injuries caused by an intoxicated patron, that patron could not recover from his own injuries.[48] Here, the court assumed that the same rule would apply to a compulsive gambler. As for Merrill's claim of willful and wanton conduct, the court rejected it on the basis that no facts were presented that could lead a jury to find such misconduct by the casino. Thus, Merrill was out of luck; his case was dismissed.

Though the court's approach in *Merrill* appears to limit gambler claims based on their own losses, the analogy between casinos and tavern owners presents the potential for future claims by third parties injured by compulsive gamblers. For example, in Merrill's case, a bank from whom Merrill had stolen could have brought a claim against the casino on this theory. Suits like these face practical barriers, including the difficulty of proving a linkage between their losses and the casino's breach of a putative duty. Behavior such as bank robbery is subject to explanation by other intervening causes, including psychological and moral defects unrelated to gambling. Negligence on the part of claimants may also bar recovery, to the extent that they failed to prudently guard their own property to protect it from loss.

Nevertheless, common law theories such as this one present the potential for third parties to recover externalized costs from the industry. As with the tobacco industry, some commentators have suggested that the gaming industry may be subject to lawsuits to recover social costs imposed by pathological gambling behaviors on state and local governments.[49] Though such lawsuits have not yet materialized in the United States, growing evidence of the existence of connections between gambling and social costs may well be cause for concern.

The industry may find that government support is built on financial rewards; loyalty can change to the extent that financial rewards can be obtained through other means. The tobacco industry certainly discovered this truth. After years of paying extraordinary taxes on tobacco products and adapting to government requirements to warn potential customers, it has faced lawsuits by both the federal government and state attorneys general for billions more on account of perceived harms associated with the legal use of their product. Given the long-term manifestation period of public health effects from smoking, proactive changes by the tobacco industry proved too little too late. The gaming industry may find itself in a more favorable position, with the hope that changes in its practices could have more immediate positive effects.

CHANGING THE REGULATORY PARADIGM: A LICENSE TO GAMBLE?

Allowing people to make their own choices—and to suffer the consequences for them—is a politically attractive option. If gambling is just another form of entertainment, then perhaps society ought to be indifferent as to whether people want to spend their money playing coin-operated slot machines or video games. However, a closer inspection suggests that these activities may actually be quite different.

Unlike other forms of entertainment, gambling lacks well-defined boundaries for consumption. Although it is possible to overindulge in any activity, gambling involves spending as a form of recreation that can result in losing a fortune in a few moments. Gambling losses also appear to have an inverse relationship to normal consumption patterns: one is unlikely to believe that enjoyment increases as you lose more money. Moreover, the potential for addictive behavior that the bells and whistles of electronic slot machines and similar devices can induce may raise still other concerns, which are not present in most other forms of entertainment.

Our legal and moral traditions recognize that it is entirely appropriate to constrain behavior that imposes costs on others without their consent. The well-being of children also weighs heavily on the side of government reinforcement of individual responsibility versus the more abstract pursuit of the good. In particular, the potential for government intervention to regulate the demand side of gambling, rather than the supply side, merits some attention.

Licensing is an important component of the current regulatory structure. However, licensing focuses primarily on providers of gambling services rather than patrons. Licenses are required to operate a casino, and licensing requirements also extend to casino employees, who must undergo background checks and maintain a safe distance from those suspected of criminal enterprises. Licensing is intended to eliminate connections between casinos and criminal enterprises and to ensure that the state gets its share of the lucre generated from patrons. In many states, licenses also limit the supply of gambling services available to the public, which is likely to have positive effects on casino profits for existing licensees. In contrast, the demand side remains remarkably free, with the notable exception of proscriptions against gambling by minors.

A licensing requirement for gambling patrons would not be inconsistent with restrictions on other activities that potentially impact the community. Driving a car, owning a handgun (in many jurisdictions), and operating a restaurant all involve licensing functions that balance competing demands of personal liberty and public welfare. Moreover, such a concept is not entirely novel. Patron-based regulations extend all the way back to the Nevada frontier. An 1877 Nevada law prohibited gambling by debtors and persons with wives and dependent children.[50] Family members were given the power to inform gambling proprietors of ineligibility, and a misdemeanor criminal sanction was imposed on those who won money from ineligible gamblers.[51]

This law reflects the policy judgment that a bachelor miner could wager his silver with little impact on the economic health of others but that the person with debt or other support obligations could not. It is unclear whether this Nevada law significantly affected the incidence of gambling losses. However, in this era of rugged individualism, the apparent consciousness about the impact of gambling on the social order is remarkable. Instead of shifting social costs to others through government programs or legal structures (such as liberal bankruptcy laws), this approach seeks to reinforce individual responsibility to curtail those costs in the first place. At the same time, it preserves freedom for those with the capacity to bear these costs themselves.

Categorical restrictions on access to privileges such as gambling may be politically controversial, but the constitutional prerogative to impose restrictions on access to gambling is beyond serious question. Gambling is not a fundamental right.[52] As a result, the state can choose to regulate it by imposing conditions on access that are rationally related to legitimate state interests.[53] This should allow rather broad discretion in segmenting the patron market if the government wished to do so, provided that these categories were tailored toward achieving viable policy objectives.

Some categories would be more easily defensible than others. Relatively noncontroversial candidates for exclusion might include those receiving public assistance or those behind on child support payments. Each of these categories would appear able to withstand the applicable rational relationship analysis. When viewed in economic terms, a wager virtually always has a negative expected value equal to the house advantage. In the long run, gambling losses are likely, and those losses potentially displace dollars that might otherwise be used for beneficial purposes, such as support or maintenance of oneself or a minor child. When the state is advancing funds to assist individuals with those needs, restricting the ability to gamble seems appropriately connected to the desired end.

Another possible category might include those who have recently demonstrated financial irresponsibility through filing a bankruptcy petition. A discharge in bankruptcy allows the debtor to impose costs involuntarily upon unpaid creditors.[54] However, it is unclear whether this classification could be sustained under current law, which prohibits state discrimination against a debtor in matters of licensing based solely on the status of filing a petition in bankruptcy.[55] Section 525 of Title II of the U.S. Code is designed to reinforce the "fresh start" purposes of the Bankruptcy Code. The legislative history explains in part:

> The prohibition does not extend so far as to prohibit examination of the factors surrounding the bankruptcy, the imposition of financial responsibility rules if they are not imposed only on former bankrupts, or the examination of prospective financial condition or managerial ability. The purpose of the section is to prevent an automatic reaction against an individual for availing himself of the protection of the bankruptcy laws. Most bankruptcies are caused by circumstances beyond the debtor's control. To penalize a debtor by discriminatory treatment as a result is unfair and undoes the beneficial effects of the bankruptcy laws. However, in those cases where the causes of a bankruptcy are intimately connected with the license, grant, or employment in question, an examination into

the circumstances surrounding the bankruptcy will permit governmental units to pursue appropriate regulatory policies and take appropriate action without running afoul of bankruptcy policy.[56]

A federal bankruptcy court interpreted this provision in a case involving a debtor licensed as a horse trainer under Maryland racing law who challenged the loss of his horse training license after filing a bankruptcy petition. In these circumstances, the bankruptcy court found that it was appropriate for the state to impose a financial responsibility requirement and that such requirement was imposed on all trainers whether bankrupt or not. The court made it clear that enforcement was not a penalty for past irresponsibility but instead was focused prospectively on subsequent behavior.

> [The financial responsibility requirement] does not *per se* preclude one from obtaining a horse trainer's license because of impoverishment. There is no requirement in the rule that one must enjoy a certain position of wealth in order to qualify. Second, there is a subtle but important distinction between requiring a debtor to make good on outstanding debts (which are dischargeable in bankruptcy) as opposed to requiring licensees to demonstrate their *prospective* financial responsibility as a condition for the granting or renewal of licenses. This rule does not *per se* require the debtor to satisfy his outstanding judgments. Third, the prohibition against financial irresponsibility, in conjunction with the others enumerated above, is reasonably related to the protection and promotion of the horse racing industry in Maryland.[57]

The debtor in question had substantial gambling debts, as well as unpaid debts for feed and horses incurred while engaged in the business of being a trainer. Thus there was ample evidence apart from the bankruptcy petition itself to question his prospective financial responsibility.

If events unrelated to gambling, such as illness or lost employment, are the cause of bankruptcy, then excluding all bankrupt debtors from the privilege of gambling is potentially overbroad. If no future obligation exists to creditors, excluding the debtor from gambling arguably appears more like a penalty for past misbehavior than one protecting future social interests.

However, it should be noted that recent revisions to the bankruptcy laws have modified the extent to which a "fresh start" is available to debtors. Section

707 of the Bankruptcy Code imposes a new requirement on debtors with certain minimum levels of income to make payments to creditors out of a portion of their current disposable income.[58] Query whether restricting gambling privileges for these debtors would satisfy legitimate state interests by supporting the future obligation of repayment.

More dubious classifications might involve income testing, in an attempt to limit gambling to those who could "afford" to lose. Casino gambling in Great Britain was once limited to social clubs, which could define their own parameters for membership.[59] Limiting access to the comparatively wealthy presumably had some limiting effect on personal hardship from problem gambling behaviors. A recent proposal for casino gambling in Singapore imposes barriers to play by low-income residents in an effort to reduce social costs but to attract revenues from tourists. This proposal is meeting political opposition. After all, the rich may also have creditors, and even the poor have dreams to get "lucky."

An income cutoff as suggested in Singapore is both over- and underinclusive. If a person with modest income chooses to spend money on gambling and if that spending does not breach obligations to others, there is no rational basis to exclude him or her from pursuing an activity that the government otherwise defines as recreation. Whether one can gamble without externalizing the costs is hardly dependent solely on income, as wealthy gamblers may also have considerable debt, which is perhaps even larger in magnitude. As one commentator has written about the Singapore proposal:

> The casino doorman will ask: "Tell me your background first. . . . You are a well-known, but shady, businessman with three companies on the verge of bankruptcy? . . . In you go sir. The blackjack tables are to your left." "And you sir? . . . You've been a hard-working, taxi driver for 15 years? . . . Piss off, you peasant."[60]

Those with histories of problem gambling present a similar dilemma in crafting the limits for state action to protect citizens from their own bad choices. If harm to others becomes the touchstone for intervention, then a license might be used for the limited purpose of assisting those who wish help. For example, those seeking treatment could voluntarily surrender their licenses, thus providing a more robust approach to self-exclusion than the lists used in some states, which provide no real penalties for a casino's failure to exclude a listed member. Alternatively, the fact that a license provides a more robust means of tracking patronage could itself provide a means for intervention before losses mounted. This approach is used in the Netherlands, where casino staff members will approach patrons when their visits go up suddenly or when their visits exceed fifteen times per month.[61]

Licensing also offers the potential to internalize other costs within the gambling community. For example, whether one holds a license to gamble could be included on a credit report, allowing creditors to segment their customers and to make sophisticated pricing decisions based on differences in perceived risks. Losses associated with the gaming segment (such as in the form of a credit card default) could thus be shared among other gamblers rather than indirectly imposed on nongamblers. The insurance industry's treatment of smokers provides an apt example of this kind of segmented structuring to permit individual freedom while requiring participants to internalize the costs of the activity.

Of course, there are enormous practical barriers to a licensing program. In order to be effective, licensing would require greater dependence on electronic identification and gaming practices. The industry is already moving in this direction, as player's club programs become ubiquitous. Missouri casinos require that patrons register to enter a casino, a practice that is used to limit gaming purchases (and thus, indirectly, losses) during each gambling session. Electronic slot machines and even video lottery terminals could be programmed to comply with the goal of licensing. Tax reporting and money laundering concerns could also be addressed in this approach, if the political will can be mustered to address these concerns.

However, some other barriers must also be overcome. The interstate dimensions of modern casino gaming erect one such barrier, as licensing requirements in one state could be circumvented by patrons who choose to travel to a bordering state without such requirements. The experiences of Iowa and Illinois in the early 1990s showed the difficulty of imposing gambling restrictions in the form of loss limits, as riverboats floated elsewhere to pursue more lucrative markets without limitations on profit.[62] Patrons also followed, as they chose the kind of experience they wanted—which was free from limits on betting and losses. Tribal casinos would also create a knotty problem for a state-based scheme, as a tribal facility could provide a readily accessible alternative to the state-licensed casino imposing a licensing requirement.

Federal law could also be used to overcome these problems of interstate competition, but a federal role does not come without difficulty. Privacy advocates may well become apoplectic over the idea of a government licensing program of this magnitude, which would require databases to be maintained at state or federal levels to include those with licensing privileges and those who are barred from obtaining licenses. However, privacy is but one of the many competing values that are impacted in this arena. As recent terrorism threats have indicated, many citizens are willing to trade privacy for security. Such trade-offs may also be politically acceptable here, when doing so means reinforcing freedom for gamblers and nongamblers alike.

A federal scheme would also have to address a formidable future threat—that of circumventing government regulation through the Internet. Absent a comprehensive treaty dealing with Internet gambling providers, a regulatory scheme based on licensing could potentially be circumvented. However, this threat must be kept in perspective. Like drug addicts, gambling addicts may well pursue their addictions in realms that are not safe. But relegating their pursuits to unregulated markets undoubtedly deters some people from this behavior.

Although licensing would not avoid all of the social costs associated with legalized gambling, this concept has the potential to reduce those costs while at the same time safeguarding liberty for those who wish to gamble and can do so responsibly. From a political perspective, it is hard to argue for personal freedom when doing so involves the use of public funds devoted to the welfare of families and children or when personal obligations for child support go unpaid. If those kinds of gamblers are contributing substantially to industry coffers such that removing them threatens the industry's viability, then perhaps this industry should not be operating.

This book has shown that there are no easy solutions to the problems presented by casino gambling. The costs and benefits of legalized gambling each present elements that cannot easily be quantified. The dilemma can be illustrated by an encounter that one of us had recently with two gamblers. Both worked as nurses and had families to support. One of them had been to a casino before work that morning, where she reported losing four hundred dollars. She was visibly depressed, and she commented that she always seemed to lose when she needed the money the most. The other went occasionally with friends and wagered a total of fifty dollars "until it was gone," and she reported having a fabulous time.

Policymakers considering the expansion of legalized gambling should recognize that the responsible gambler probably represents the majority of the gambling population. They engage in an activity that apparently gives them pleasure and seems harmless enough. However, for the minority who lose more than they can afford, creating convenient access to gambling creates a significant potential for harm, not only to themselves but also to others. Although definitive answers to important questions, such as how much industry revenue comes from problem gamblers, have not been resolved, the available data suggest that this minority of the gambling population is providing a significant portion of the revenue. This presents a dilemma for jurisdictions where local gamblers are the primary source of patronage.

As Nelson Rose, a prominent academic commentator, observed more than a decade ago, "Throughout history, every society that has allowed casinos to cater to local customers has eventually outlawed gambling."[63] Professor Rose predicted a future crackdown on gambling to the extent that local populations become the source for gambling dollars.[64] This prediction has not yet come true in many jurisdictions. However, it may explain the reticence to expand gambling in other jurisdictions, where policymakers are not content to look solely at the positive side of the ledger.

In jurisdictions with significant gambling investments, the prospects of returning to a regime of criminal proscription are remote. As in the ancient myth, the contents of Pandora's box could not be returned once they had been released into the world. However, it should be remembered that this box also contained hope. If casino gambling is to persist, then regulators must address the serious problems it creates, even if that means that casino profits and state tax revenues suffer as a result. Informed citizens will be indispensable in ensuring that government officials are held accountable in this area. Continued attention from the academic community in addressing the critical questions presented by legalized casino gambling will play a vital role in sorting out the truth and bringing it to light. Governing fortune is hard work.

NOTES

CHAPTER 1

1. *See* THE DEVELOPMENT OF THE LAW OF GAMBLING: 1776–1976 at 3–4 (1977) [hereinafter DEVELOPMENT OF THE LAW OF GAMBLING]. This study was commissioned by the National Institute of Law Enforcement and Criminal Justice, Law Enforcement Assistance Administration of the United States Department of Justice, under the Omnibus Crime Control and Safe Streets Act of 1968. Much of the historical material in this chapter is drawn from this extensive and thorough work.

2. *Id.* at 4–5.

3. *See id.* at 5–7.

4. *See id.* at 6–7.

5. *See id.* at 7–13.

6. *See id.* at 12.

7. *Id.* at 12.

8. *Id.* at 13–16. The titles are instructive. The Statute of Charles II (1664) was entitled "An Act against deceitful, disorderly, and excessive gaming," *id.* at 13, while the Statue of Anne (1710) was entitled "An Act for the better preventing of excessive and deceitful gaming," *id.* at 15.

9. *Id.* at 16–17. Half the damage award would go to the plaintiff, the rest to the poor. Id. at 17. It is uncertain how the poor's share was actually administered. At this time, ten pounds was not an insubstantial sum, as it represented more than two hundred times the daily wages of common laborer (i.e., one shilling). *See id.* at 17 n.41.

10. *Id.* at 18.

11. *See id.* at 33.

12. *See id.* at 30.

13. *See id.*

14. *See id.* at 41.

15. *See id.* at 41–42.

16. *See id.* at 43.

17. *Id.* at 48.

18. *See id.* at 127–33.

19. *See id.* at 132.

20. *See id.* at 46–47.

21. *See id.* at 242–44.

22. *See id.* at 243.

23. *Id.*

24. *See* Ronald L. Rychlak, *The Introduction of Casino Gambling: Policy and Law,* 64 Miss. L.J. 291, 299–301 (1995).

25. *See id.* It should be noted that Harvard, Yale, and Princeton were also religiously affiliated institutions.

26. *See* Development of the Law of Gambling, *supra* note 1, at 72.

27. *See id.* at 65–72.

28. *See id.* at 64–65.

29. Irwin v. Williar, 110 U.S. 499, 510 (1885).

30. Harvey v. Merrill, 150 Mass. 1, 11, 22 N.E. 49, 52 (1889) ("It is now settled here that contracts which are void at common law, because they are against public policy, like contracts which are prohibited by statute, are illegal as well as void. They are prohibited by law, because they are considered vicious, and it is not necessary that a penalty be imposed in order to render them illegal.").

31. *See* W. Page Keeton et al., Prosser and Keeton on the Law of Torts 683–84 (5th ed. 1984).

32. *See, e.g.,* Developments in the Law of Gambling, *supra* note 1, at 68 ("General social disruption was thought to be another byproduct of the tavern scene.").

33. Black's Law Dictionary 1208 (5th ed. 1979).

34. Commonwealth v. Burns, 27 Ky. 177, 1830 WL 1856 (1830).

35. O'Blennis v. State, 12 Mo. 311, 1848 WL 4097 (1848). Faro was a fast-paced card game with a low house advantage and was frequently played on the frontier. For a description of this game, see <http://www.greedyhog-gambling.com/docs/faro-the-frontier-favorite.shtml> (visited May 23, 2006). The author of this Web site speculates that the demise of faro was attributable to such factors as a low house edge (less than 2 percent) and widespread cheating. *See id.*

36. State v. Smith, 10 Tenn. 272, 1829 WL 501 (1829).

37. *Id.*

38. *See* Development of the Law of Gambling, *supra* note 1, at 377–79. Concepts of Jacksonian democracy were thought to play an important foundational role in enacting these prohibitions.

39. *See id.* at 382.

40. *See id* at 380, 384, 389.

41. *See id.* at 381–82.

42. *See id.* at 387–89.

43. *See id.* at 388.

44. *See id.*

45. *See id.*

46. *Id.* at 403–6.

47. *Id.* at 407.

48. *Id.* at 410–12.

49. *Id.* at 411 n.93 (quoting a portion of a legislative committee report on the 1869 legalization act).

50. *Id.* at 416 n.6.

51. *Id* at 416 n.7. This regulation would be repealed in 1905. *See id.* at 426 n.41.

52. *Id.* at 416 n.8.

53. *See id.*

54. *Id.* at 417.

55. 1874 WL 3931, at 3 (Nev.).

56. State v. Overton, 1881 WL 4088, at 6–7 (Nev.).

57. DEVELOPMENT OF THE LAW OF GAMBLING, *supra* note 1, at 427.

58. *See id.* at 428–32.

59. *See id* at 432–41.

60. This is not to say that gambling was unavailable elsewhere. New Orleans was also well-known as a city that tolerated gambling, despite *de jure* criminalization. *See generally id.* at 286.

61. *See id.* at 362, 263–69.

62. *See id.* at 362.

63. *See id.* at 346, 364, 402.

64. *See id.* at 364.

65. *See, e.g.,* LaTour v. Louisiana, 778 So. 2d 557, 562–64 (La. 2004) (tracing the history of the transformation of gambling from vice to economic development tool in Louisiana).

66. *See* North American Association of State and Provincial Lotteries, *Fiscal Years 2002, 2003, and 2004 Lottery Sales and Profits,* available at <http://www.naspl.org/sales&profits.html>.

67. *See id.* The impact of video lottery terminals appears significant. In contrast to North Dakota, neighboring South Dakota had per capita lottery spending of $874.24. South Dakota has video lottery terminals; North Dakota does not.

68. *See id.*

69. Tax issues are addressed in greater detail in chapter 3.

70. *See* AMERICAN GAMING ASSOCIATION, STATE OF THE STATES 2 (2005), available at <http://www.americangaming.org/assets/files/uploads/2005_State_of_the_States.pdf>.

71. *See* ALAN MEISTER, INDIAN GAMING INDUSTRY REPORT 1 (2004) (estimating 2003 data); American Gaming Association, *Gaming Revenue: Current-Year Data* (August 2004), available at <http://www.americangaming.org/Industry/factsheets/statistics_detail.cfv?id=7>.

72. *See* American Gaming Association, *States with Gaming* (May 2005), available at <http://www.americangaming.org/Industry/factsheets/general_info_detail.cfv?id=15>.

73. *See* American Gaming Association, *Gaming Revenues: Current-Year Data* (August 2004), available at <http://www.americangaming.org/Industry/factsheets/statistics_detail.cfv?id=7>, which estimates the total at $72.87 billion. However, this includes lottery winnings of only $19.93 billion instead of the broader total of approximately $48 billion in lottery spending. If all lottery spending is included, the total would be approximately $30 billion higher.

74. *See* AMERICAN GAMING ASSOCIATION, STATE OF THE STATES 4 (2004) available at <http://www.americangaming.org/assets/files/uploads/2004_Survey_for_web.pdf>. The AGA shows only commercial casino spending in its comparison.

75. For an excellent historical and cultural analysis of the concept of luck in America, see JACKSON LEARS, SOMETHING FOR NOTHING (2003).

76. *See generally* GAO, IMPACT OF GAMBLING: ECONOMIC EFFECTS MORE MEASURABLE THAN SOCIAL EFFECTS (GGD-00-78, April 27, 2000), available at <http://www.gao.gov/new.items/gg00078.pdf>. The putative benefits and costs associated with gambling are discussed at greater length in chapters 3–5.

77. NATIONAL GAMBLING IMPACT STUDY COMMISSION REPORT at 47 (1999).

CHAPTER 2

1. These developments are chronicled in greater detail in chapter 8.

2. *See* AMERICAN GAMING ASSOCIATION, STATE OF THE STATES 5 (2002), available at <http://www.americangaming.org/assets/files/AGA_survey_2002.pdf>.

3. *See* AMERICAN GAMING ASSOCIATION, STATE OF THE STATES 2 (2005), available at <http://www.americangaming.org/assets/files/uploads/2005_State_of_the_States.pdf>.

4. *See id.*

5. *See* ALAN MEISTER, INDIAN GAMING INDUSTRY REPORT (2005–6).

6. *See id.*

7. *See id.*

8. See chapter 8 for more details on this legislation.

9. See chapter 8 for discussion of recent developments in Iowa that may expand casinos in interior locations.

10. AGR represents the gross gambling revenues minus winnings paid to the gambler.

11. Revenue per visitor in Missouri may be understated, however, due to the

fact that the Missouri system for regulation involves a five-hundred-dollar loss limit per "excursion." *See generally* Missouri Gaming Commission, Annual Report 2003, at <http://www.mgc.dps.mo.gov/annual%20reports/2003/annual2003.html>. If multiple excursions per visitor are taken into account, the AGR per patron is comparable to that in Iowa and Louisiana. Missouri's regulatory system is discussed in greater detail in chapter 8.

    12. 480 U.S. 202 (1987).

    13. A detailed discussion of the development of tribal gaming and its regulatory environment is provided in chapter 11.

    14. 25 U.S.C. §§ 2701–2721.

    15. *See* 25 U.S.C. § 2702.

    16. All tribal casino data in this chapter come from Meister, Indian Gaming Industry Report (2005–6).

    17. *See* Fitzgerald v. Racing Ass'n of Central Iowa, 675 N.W.2d 1, cert. denied 541 U.S. 1086 (2004). *See also id.,* 539 U.S. 103 (2003) (holding that the Iowa scheme satisfied federal constitutional constraints).

    18. This estimate comes from Yahoo.com or <http://finance.yahoo.com>.

    19. Diamonds (DIA) and Spyders (SPY) are shares of stock that are composed of a portion of the Dow 30 industrial companies and the S&P 500 companies, respectively.

    20. Only firms from table 2.8 with available financial statements are listed.

    21. Christiansen Capital Advisors promotion spending <http://news.mainetoday.com/indepth/gambling/030502blom.shtml> (accessed May 27, 2006). Harrah's promotion <http://brokopp.casinocitytimes.com/articles/678.html> (accessed May 27, 2006). Grand Victoria Casino <http://www.grandvictoria elgin.com/property/press1.php?UID=53> (accessed May 27, 2006). Majestic Star promotion spending <http://info.detnews.com/casino/newdetails.cfm?column= grochowski&myrec=109> (accessed May 27, 2006). Caesars in Tunica promotion spending <http://www.tunica-ms.com/events.htm> (accessed May 27, 2006).

CHAPTER 3

    1. *See* Cherokee Nation v. Georgia, 30 U.S. (Pet.) 1, 20 (1831).

    2. *See* Alan Meister, Casino City's Indian Gaming Industry Report, 28 (2005–2006).

    3. Wisconsin state officials confirmed that this statement was indeed correct. *See Milwaukee Journal-Sentinel,* June 23, 2005, at <http://www.jsonline.com/news/state/jun05/335634.asp>.

    4. <http://www.schwarzenegger.com/news.asp>.

    5. <http://news.findlaw.com/scripts/printer_friendly.pl?page=/prnewswire/20050622/22jun20051730.html>.

    6. <http://www.coloradogaming.com>.

7. <http://www.illinoiscasinogaming.org/industry_resources.htm>.

8. <http://www.in.gov/gaming>.

9. <http://www.state.ia.us/irgc>.

10. <http://www.dps.state.la.us/lgcb>.

11. See chapter 8 for further details.

12. "The day-to-day operating expenses of the MGCB are paid for by the Annual State Services Fee (this fee is not related to the casinos' gaming revenues). Each year, $2 million of this $25 million Fee goes toward compulsive gambling programs, administered by Michigan Department of Community Health. No single casino's share shall exceed 1/3 of the total Annual State Services Fee Adjusted annually by Detroit Consumer Price Index." See Michigan Gaming Control Board, at <http://www.michigan.gov/mgcb/0,1607_120_1395_1469_7138_11436_,00.html> (accessed May 26, 2006).

13. "The entire State Wagering Tax (8.1% of the casinos' Net Win) is deposited into the School Aid Fund for statewide K–12 classroom education. The City Wagering Tax (9.9% of the casinos' Net Win) may be used by the City of Detroit for hiring, training, and deployment of street patrol officers; neighborhood and downtown economic development programs designed to create local jobs; public safety programs such as emergency medical services, fire department programs, and street lighting; anti-gang and youth development programs; other programs that are designed to contribute to the improvement of the quality of life in the City; relief to the taxpayers of the City from one or more taxes or fees imposed by the City; capital improvements costs; and road repairs and improvements." See Michigan Gaming Control Board, at <http://www.michigan.gov/mgcb/0,1607,7-120-7863_15534_F,00.html> (accessed May 30, 2006).

14. See Iowa Racing and Gaming Commission, yearly reports, at <http://www.state.ia.us/irgc>.

15. Nevada is not considered, since ten of the sixteen counties in the state have casinos and the casinos had been in existence for many more decades than casinos in other states.

CHAPTER 4

1. Thomas A. Garrett, *Casino Gaming and Local Employment Trends,* 86 FED. RESERVE BANK OF ST. LOUIS REV. LEN. 9–22 (2004).

2. THOMAS GARRETT & MARK NICHOLS, DO CASINOS EXPORT BANKRUPTCY? (Federal Reserve Bank of St. Louis Working Paper No. 2005-19A, 2005), available at <http://research.stlouisfed.org/wp/2005/2005-019.pdf>.

3. ERNEST GOSS & EDWARD A. MORSE, THE IMPACT OF CASINO GAMBLING ON PERSONAL BANKRUPTCY RATES (1990–2002) (August 25, 2005, Social Science Research Network Working Paper), <http://ssrn.com/abstract=801185>.

4. S. Cornell, J. Kalt, M. Krepps, and J. Taylor, *American Indian Gaming Policy*

and Its Socio-Economic Effects. A Report to the National Gambling Impact Study Commission (Economic Resource Group, Inc. July 31, 1998).

5. Jonathon Taylor & Joseph Kalt, *American Indians on Reservations: A Databook of Socioeconomic Change Between the 1990 and 2000 Census* (Harvard Project on American Indian Economic Development, January 2005).

6. Ernie Goss, *The Economic Impact of an Omaha, Nebraska Casino.* Research report prepared for the Greater Omaha Chamber of Commerce, 2002, available at <http://www.outlook-economic.com/ResearchAndNews/Research/gambling.pdf>.

7. These losses result from the expectation that 13.7 percent of Omaha casino patrons will come from Nebraska outside of metropolitan Omaha. This results in reduced spending for the non-Omaha portion of Nebraska.

8. Data on tribal casino employment are not available on a consistent and timely basis. Consequently only commercial casino employment data are presented.

9. American Gaming Association, 2004 Report, at <http://www.americangaming.org/assets/files/2004_survey_for_web.pdf>.

10. In this case, state employment is compared to national employment. Thus LQ equals the percent of state employment in leisure and hospitality divided by the percent of national employment in leisure and hospitality. See chapter 3 for a discussion of LQs.

11. *See* Teresa A. Sullivan, Elizabeth Warren, & Jay Lawrence Westbrook, The Fragile Middle Class (Yale 2000). Data from studies in 1991 and 1997, which are both within the period analyzed here, suggest that bankruptcy filings are higher in demographic groups with people between the ages of twenty-five and fifty-four. *See id.* at 38–41. A 1991 study also indicated that African American racial groups had a higher proportion of bankrupt debtors in relation to population as compared with other ethnic groups. *See id.* at 41–50.

CHAPTER 5

1. *See* National Paint & Coatings Ass'n v. City of Chicago, 45 F.3d 1124, 1127 (7th Cir. 1995).

2. *See generally* GAO, Impact of Gambling: Economic Effects More Measurable Than Social Effects (GAO/GGD-00-78, April 27, 2000), available at <http://www.gao.gov/new.items/gg00078.pdf> [Hereinafter GAO Study].

3. American Psychiatric Association, Diagnostic and Statistical Manual of Mental Disorders 615 (4th ed. 1994) [hereinafter DSM].

4. *See id.* at 618.

5. *See* National Opinion Research Center, Gambling Impact and Behavior Study at 16, 20 (1999) (Report to the National Gambling Impact Study Commission) [hereinafter NORC Study].

6. *See, e.g.,* National Gambling Impact Study Commission Report at 4-1

(1999); Howard J. Shaffer & David A. Korn, *Gambling and Related Mental Disorders: A Public Health Analysis,* 23 ANN. REV. OF PUB. HEALTH 171, 174 (2002) ("subclinical or problem gambling is a milder form of pathological gambling") [hereinafter Shaffer & Korn (2002)].

7. *See* NORC Study, *supra* note 5, at 21.

8. *See id; see also* John Welte et al., *Alcohol and Gambling Pathology among U.S. Adults: Prevalence, Demographic Patterns and Comorbidity,* J. STUD. ALCOHOL 706–7 (September 2001) [hereinafter Welte Study].

9. Welte Study, *supra* note 8, at 708.

10. *See* DSM, *supra* note 3, at 617.

11. *See* NORC Study, *supra* note 5, at 7.

12. *See id.*

13. AMERICAN GAMING ASSOCIATION, STATE OF THE STATES 3 (2005), at <http://www.americangaming.org/assets/files/uploads/2005_state_of_the_states.pdf>.

14. *See* Population Division, U.S. Census Bureau, Table 1: Annual Estimates of the Population by Sex and Five-year Age Groups for the United States: April 1, 2000 to July 1, 2004 (NC-EST2004-01, Release Date June 9, 2005). This total includes all population ages twenty and over. This may overstate the population slightly to the extent that adults under age twenty-one are not permitted to gamble legally in casinos.

15. *See* NORC Study, *supra* note 5, at 21.

16. *See* Carlo C. DeClemente, Marilyn Story, & Kenneth Murray, *On a Roll:The Process of Initiation and Cessation of Problem Gambling Among Adolescents,* 16 J. GAMBLING STUD. 289, 294 (2000).

17. *See* DSM, *supra* note 3, at 617.

18. *See* M. Leann Dodd, Kevin J. Klos, et al., *Pathological Gambling Caused By Drugs Used to Treat Parkinson Disease,* 62 ARCHIVES OF NEUROLOGY (2005), available at <http://archneur.ama-assn.org/cgi/content/full/62.9.noc50009v1> (accessed July 13, 2005).

19. *See* Robert B. Breen & Mark Zimmerman, *Rapid Onset of Pathological Gambling in Machine Gamblers,* 18 J. GAMBLING STUD. 31 (2002).

20. *See id.* at 40–41.

21. *See* DSM, *supra* note 3, at 616–17.

22. *See* NORC Study, *supra* note 5, at 26, table 7.

23. *See* Welte Study, *supra* note 8, at 709.

24. *See* DSM, *supra* note 3, at 616.

25. *See* Iowa Department of Public Health, *Healthy Iowans 2010,* chap. 20, p. 10 (January 2000), available at <http://www.idph.state.ia.us>.

26. *See* National Coalition Against Legalized Gambling, *Addicts R' Us' Games Invade Children's Shelves,* 3 BET'S OFF BULLETIN (January 2005).

27. *See* Welte Study, *supra* note 8, at 706, 707.

28. *See* NORC Study, *supra* note 5, at 26, table a.

29. *See* H. R. Lesieur and S. B. Blume, *The South Oaks Gambling Screen (SOGS): A New Instrument for the Identification of Pathological Gamblers,* 144 AMER. J. OF PSY-CHOL. 1184 (1987).

30. *See* Welte Study, *supra* note 8, at 708.

31. *See* NORC Study, *supra* note 5, at 33–34.

32. *See* NATIONAL GAMBLING IMPACT STUDY COMMISSION REPORT at 4-1 (1999) (quoting National Research Council, *Pathological Gambling: A Critical Review* [April 1, 1999], Exec-2).

33. *See* United States Department of Health and Human Services, Office of Child Support Enforcement, Table 11: Total Amount of Arrearages Due FY 2003, available at <http://www.acf.hhs.gov/programs/cse/pubs/2004/reports/preliminary_data/table_11.html> (accessed June 3, 2005).

34. Welte Study, *supra* note 8, at 710.

35. *See* NATIONAL GAMBLING IMPACT STUDY COMMISSION REPORT at 4-7, table 4-3 (1999).

36. *See* Tose v. Greate Bay Hotel and Casino, Inc., 819 F.Supp. 1312, 1320 (D. N.J. 1993) (discussing New Jersey alcohol regulation in casinos).

37. *See* American Gaming Association, *Casino Alcohol Policies,* at <http://www.americangaming.org/Industry/factsheets/issues_detail.cfv?id=31> (last visited July 23, 2005).

38. *See* NORC Study, *supra* note 5, at 29–30.

39. *See id.* at 49.

40. *See* Welte Study, *supra* note 8, at 709.

41. *See* NORC Study, *supra* note 5, at 27.

42. Rani A. Desai et al., *Health Correlates of Recreational Gambling in Older Adults,* 161 AM. J. PSYCHIATRY 1672–79 (September 2004).

43. *See* NORC Study, *supra* note 5, at 27.

44. *See id.*

45. *See* Shaffer & Korn (2002), *supra* note 6, at 177.

46. *See* American Gaming Association, *Bankruptcy Fact Sheet,* available at <http://www.americangaming.org/Industry/factsheets/issues_detail.cfv?id=2> (last visited July 23, 2005).

47. *See* American Gaming Association, *Crime Fact Sheet,* available at <http://www.americangaming.org/industry/factsheets/issues_detail.cfv?id=23> (last visited July 25, 2005).

48. *See id.*

49. *See* GAO Study, *supra* note 2, at 35–42 (discussing the example of Atlantic City).

50. *See* American Gaming Association, *Industry Information,* available at

<http:// www.americangaming.org/industry/faq_detail.cfv?id=63> (last visited July 25, 2005).

51. *See* United States Department of Justice, Office of Justice Programs, *Bureau of Justice Statistics* (showing property crime rates from 1973 to 2003), available at <http:// www.ojp.usdoj.gov/bjs/glance/house2.htm> (last visited July 25, 2005).

52. *See id.* at <http://www.ojp.usdoj.gov/bjs/glance/cv2.htm>.

53. *See generally* Doran Teichman, *The Market for Criminal Justice: Federalism, Crime Control, and Jurisdictional Competition,* 103 MICH. L. REV. 1831 (2005).

54. Earl L. Grinols & David B. Mustard, *Casinos, Crime, and Community Costs,* 88 REV. ECON. & STAT. 28 (2006).

55. *See id.* These studies are also referenced in the NORC Study, *supra* note 5, at page 47.

56. *See* United States Department of Justice, Office of Justice Programs, *National Institute of Justice, Gambling and Crime Among Arrestees: Exploring the Link* (July 2004), at <http://www.nijrs.gov/pdffiles1/nij/203197.pdf> (last visited May 15, 2006).

57. *See id.*

58. *See id.*

59. *See id.*

60. *See* American Gaming Association, *supra* note 50.

61. *See* GRINOLS, *supra* note 53, at 32.

62. *See generally* Teichman, *supra* note 53, at 1831, 1839–49.

63. *See id.* at 1838.

64. *See* American Gaming Association, *Industry Information,* at <http://www .americangaming.org/industry/faq_detail.cfv?id=62> (last accessed July 25, 2005).

65. *See id.*

66. *See* NORC Study, *supra* note 5, at 46. It should be noted that other studies have also claimed that pathological or compulsive gamblers had a bankruptcy rate of approximately 20 percent. *See* Department of the Treasury, *A Study of the Interaction of Gambling and Bankruptcy* at 43 (July 1999). SMR Research claims 20 percent of compulsive gamblers were forced to file bankruptcy; interviews with bankruptcy lawyers indicated that 10–20 percent were bankrupt due to gambling debts; *id.* at 45 (University of Minnesota Medical School study of pathological gambling treatment patients showed 21 percent had declared bankruptcy); *id.* at 45–56 (Abt Associates, Inc., study indicated 20 percent rate for comparable population of pathological gamblers).

67. *See* NORC Study, *supra* note 5, at 46.

68. *See* Administrative Office of the United States Courts, Table 5A (U.S. Bankruptcy Courts Business And Nonbusiness Bankruptcy County Cases Commenced, By Chapter Of The Bankruptcy Code, During The Twelve Month Period Ended Dec. 31, 2003).

69. *See* GAO Study, *supra* note 2, at 21.

70. *See* Department of the Treasury, *supra* note 64.

71. *See id.* at 47.

72. *See id.* at 64.

73. *See id.* at 54.

74. John M. Barron, Michael E. Staten, & Stephanie M. Wilshusen, *The Impact of Casino Gambling on Personal Bankruptcy Filing Rates,* 20 CONTEMP. ECON. POL'Y 440–55 (2002).

75. ERNEST GOSS & EDWARD A. MORSE, THE IMPACT OF CASINO GAMBLING ON PERSONAL BANKRUPTCY RATES (1990–2002) (August 25, 2005, Social Science Research Network Working Paper), <http://ssrn.com/abstract=801185>.

76. *See* 11 U.S.C. § 727(a) (providing conditions for discharge in bankruptcy).

77. *See* NORC Study, *supra* note 5, at 45; *see also* EARL L. GRINOLS, GAMBLING IN AMERICA 134 (2004) (explaining this principle in connection with the analogous issue of theft losses).

78. *See* Pub. L. 109-9 at § 310 (amending 11 U.S.C. § 523).

79. *See id.*

80. 28 U.S.C. § 1408(a).

81. *See* THOMAS GARRETT & MARK NICHOLS, DO CASINOS EXPORT BANKRUPTCY? (Federal Reserve Bank of St. Louis Working Paper No. 2005-19A, 2005), available at <http://research.stlouisfed.org/wp/2005/2005-019.pdf>.

82. *See generally* NORC Study, *supra* note 5, at 38–60.

83. *See id.* at 52–53.

84. *See generally* GRINOLS, *supra* note 77, at 167–73.

85. *See id.* at 172–73 (table 7.1). Grinols also included a category for government regulatory costs, but none of the other studies included data on this issue.

86. *See id.*

87. *See id.* at 174 (table 7.2).

88. NORC Study, *supra* note 5, at 40.

89. E. L. Grinols & J. D. Omorov, *Development or Dreamfield Delusions? Assessing Casino Gambling's Costs and Benefits,* 16 J.L. & COMM. 58–60 (1996).

90. *See* Robert Williams & Robert Wood, *The Demographic Sources of Ontario Gaming Revenue* at 42 (Ontario Problem Gambling Research Center, June 23, 2004).

91. In Missouri casinos, where slot machine revenues are tracked separately from table games, slot machines typically generate the vast majority of AGR. The largest of these casinos, Harrah's in Maryland Heights, showed slot machine AGR of $263.573 million, more than 87 percent of total AGR of $300.775 million in 2004–5. These results are not atypical for other casinos in this jurisdiction. See MISSOURI GAMING COMMISSION, ANNUAL REPORT 2005, at the appendix, available at <http://www.mgc.dps.mo.gov/annual%20reports/2005/apx.pdf>.

CHAPTER 6

1. *See, e.g.*, United States v. Morrison, 529 U.S. 598 (2000) (finding the federal Violence Against Women Act was beyond Congress's Commerce Clause authority); United States v. Lopez, 514 U.S. 549 (1995) (finding that the Gun-Free School Zones Act of 1990 exceeded Congress's Commerce Clause authority). In *Lopez*, the Court identified three broad categories of activities that are within the scope of modern Commerce Clause authority: regulating use of the channels of interstate commerce; regulating and protecting instrumentalities of interstate commerce or persons or things in interstate commerce (including threats from intrastate activities); and regulating activities that have a "substantial relation" to interstate commerce. *See id.* at 558–59.

2. *See, e.g.*, United States v. Hallmark, 911 F.2d 399, 401 (10th Cir. 1990) ("Congress may, in any case, regulate or prohibit wagering activities pursuant to its enumerated powers; to do so by means of a tax would not violate the Constitution.") A Tenth Amendment argument against allowing federal taxation of wagering was considered "meritless."

3. *See* Hunter v. City of Pittsburgh, 207 U.S. 161 (1907).

4. 101 U.S. 814 (1879).

5. This provision states in part: "No State shall . . . pass any . . . Law impairing the Obligation of Contracts."

6. *Id.* at 821.

7. This conclusion follows from the fact that state governments and others had long utilized lotteries to fund worthy projects. As the Court explained, "We are aware that formerly, when the sources of public revenue were fewer than now, they were used in some or all of the States, and even in the District of Columbia, to raise money for the erection of public buildings, making public improvements, and not [i]nfrequently for educational and religious purposes." *Id.* at 818.

8. *Id.*

9. Such problems were confronted by the American Bar Association's Commission on Organized Crime as it evaluated the scope of state laws in the early 1950s. *See* Paul Bauman & Rufus King, *A Critical Analysis of the Gambling Laws, in* II ORGANIZED CRIME AND LAW ENFORCEMENT 74–76 (Morris Ploscowe, ed., 1952). This commission ultimately developed the Model Anti-Gambling Act to address these concerns.

10. For example, coverage of the Wire Act and its extension to Internet gaming, as discussed in chapter 10, provides an interesting modern example of this phenomenon.

11. *See* Bauman & King, *supra* note 9, at 75.

12. *See, e.g.*, United States v. Allen, 10 F.3d 405 (7th Cir. 1993) (prosecution of sheriff's department investigator for bribery arising from FBI sting operation involving illegal gambling operation in Indiana). A similar problem exists in other

criminal enterprises, such as the distribution of illicit drugs. *See, e.g.,* Eric Luna, *Drug Exceptionalism,* 47 VILL. L. Rev. 753, 796 (2002).

13. *See generally* Steven C. Yarborough, *The Hobbs Act in the Nineties: Confusion or Clarification of the Quid Pro Quo Standard in Extortion Cases Involving Public Officials,* 31 TULSA L.J. 781 (1996) (discussing the Hobbs Act as a means to prosecute corruption); Adam A. Kurland, *The Guarantee Clause as a Basis for Federal Prosecutions of State and Local Officials,* 64 S. CAL. L. REV. 367, 373 n.21 (1989) (citing federal legislation applicable to state and local corruption from gambling).

14. *See, e.g.,* United States v. Sullivan, 274 U.S. 259 (1927) (bootlegger's income was subject to tax despite being derived from illegal activity); James v. United States, 366 U.S. 213 (1961) (embezzled funds are held taxable).

15. *See, e.g.,* Alan Feuer, *7 Accused of Operating a Lucrative Citywide Betting Ring,* N.Y. TIMES, July 29, 2004, at <http://www.nytimes.com/2004/07/29/nyregion/29numbers.html> (accessed July 29, 2004) (referring to policy rackets in New York as "shadow Lotto" for those who want better odds and tax-free winnings); Suk Tom, *Illegal Gambling? Iowans Find Ways to Bet on It,* DES MOINES REGISTER, April 5, 2003, at 1B (2003 WL 6703144) (discussing similar attractions of illegal gambling to Iowans, despite legal outlets).

16. *See, e.g.,* Ronald L. Rychlak, *The Introduction of Casino Gambling: Public Policy and the Law,* 64 MISS. L.J. 291, 335–36 (1995) (noting that legalization encourages new gamblers to play, which in turn creates new potential problem gamblers).

17. *See, e.g.,* Theresa A. Gabaldon & John Law, *With a Tulip, in the South Seas: Gambling and the Regulation of Euphoric Market Transactions,* 26 J. CORP. L. 225, 260 (2001); Rychlak, *supra* note 16, at 349.

18. *See* W. Page Keeton et al., PROSSER AND KEETON ON THE LAW OF TORTS 683–84 (5th ed. 1984) (discussed in chapter 1).

19. Indian tribes may also benefit from government treatment. See chapter 11.

20. *See generally* Stephanie A. Martz, *Note, Legalized Gambling and Public Corruption: Removing the Incentive to Act Corruptly, or, Teaching an Old Dog New Tricks,* 13 J.L. & POL. 453 (1997).

CHAPTER 7

1. Nevada's Gaming Control Act states this commitment in part: "The gaming industry is vitally important to the economy of the state and the general welfare of the inhabitants." Nev. Rev. Stat. Ann. § 463.0129(a).

2. *Id.* § 463.0129(d).

3. *Id.* §§ 463.022, .024.

4. *Id.* § 463.023 (4).

5. *See id.* § 463.023(2).

6. *See id.* § 463.023(3).

7. *See, e.g., id.* § 463.150.

8. *Id.* §§ 463.030, .050.

9. *Id.* § 463.040(2).

10. *See id.* at § 463.040(5).

11. *Id.* at § 464.040(6).

12. <http://gaming.state.nv.us/about_board.htm>.

13. <http://gaming.state.nv.us/documents/pdf/audit_div_overview.pdf>.

14. *See id.*

15. *See* <http://gaming.state.nv.us/about_board.htm>.

16. *See id.*

17. *See id.*

18. *See id.*

19. *See* State of Nevada, *Citizen's Assets* (2004), available at <http://controller.nv.gov/CAFR_pdf_files/PopularReport01.pdf> (accessed May 3, 2005). Monthly fees imposed on holders of nonrestricted revenues, which are tied to the level of gross gaming revenues, are a substantial source of these taxes. Fees range from 3 percent for amounts under $50,000 per month to 6.25 percent for amounts in excess of $134,000 per month. *See* Nev. Rev. Stat. § 463.370(1). As discussed in chapter 5, these tax rates are modest in comparison to other gaming states. This potentially allows operators to invest more heavily in entertainment or other accoutrements designed to attract patrons.

20. *See id.*

21. *See* LIONEL, SAWYER & COLLINS, NEVADA GAMING LAW 27 (3d ed. 2000).

22. *See* <http://gaming.state.nv.gov/about_board.htm#tech> (visited May 22, 2006).

23. *See* Nev. Rev. Stat. Ann. § 463.0152.

24. *See id.* § 463.161.

25. *See id.*

26. *See id.* § 463.170(1).

27. *See id.* § 463.170(2).

28. *See id.* § 463.170(3).

29. *See id.*

30. *See id.* § 463.167.

31. Nevada Tax Commission v. Hicks, 310 P.2d 852, 854 (Nev. 1957). *See also* Kraft v. Jacka, 669 F.Supp. 333, 337 (D. Nev. 1987) ("The members of the State Gaming Control Board and the Nevada Gaming Commission are charged with the awesome responsibility of regulating the gaming industry in Nevada and keeping undesirable elements out of the gaming industry.").

32. *See* 1 ORGANIZED CRIME AND LAW ENFORCEMENT xvii–xxvi (Morris Poscowe, ed. 1952) (introduction by Senator Estes Kefauver).

33. The nature and extent of federal regulation of gambling are discussed in chapter 9.

34. Nev. Rev. Stat. § 463.220(7).

35. *Id.* § 463.129(2).

36. *Id.* at § 463.318(2) ("Judicial review is not available for actions, decisions and orders of the commission relating to the denial of a license or to limited or conditional licenses."). However, exceptions may exist for *ultra vires* acts of the commission or for decisions influenced by corruption, as suggested in Cohen v. State, 930 P.2d 125 (Nev. 1997). *See also* LIONEL, SAWYER & COLLINS, *supra* note 21, at 96. A remedy in federal court might be available in the event that a board's decision was based on racial animus or other criteria violating federal civil rights. Cf. Kaft v. Jacka, 669 F.Supp. 333 (D. Nev. 1987) (rejecting claim based on 42 U.S.C. § 1985 due to failure to show racial or other class-based "invidious discriminatory animus"), aff'd, 872 F.2d 862 (9th Cir. 1989), overruled on other grounds, Dennis v. Higgins, 498 U.S. 439 (1991).

37. 559 P.2d 830 (Nev. 1977).

38. *Id.* at 833 (quoting the commission report).

39. *Id.* (quoting State ex. rel. Grimes v. Board, 1 P.2d 570, 572 (Nev. 1931)).

40. *See id.* at 833.

41. *See id.* at 834.

42. *See, e.g.,* Nev. Rev. Stat. Ann. § 463.310(8).

43. *Id.* § 463.151.

44. *Id.* § 463.151(3).

45. *Id.* § 463.151(4).

46. *See* State v. Rosenthal, 819 P.2d 1296, 1299 (Nev. 1991).

47. NGR § 28.010(3).

48. Id. § 28.010(4).

49. Nev. Rev. Stat. Ann. § 463.317(3); *see also* Rosenthal, *supra* note 46, 819 P.2d at 1299.

50. Nev. Rev. Stat. Ann. § 463.154.

51. *Id.* § 463.156.

52. *See* Michael W. Bowers & A. Costandina Titus, *Nevada's Black Book: The Constitutionality of Exclusion Lists in Casino Gaming Regulation,* 9 WHITTIER L. REV. 313, 318 (1987).

53. <http://gaming.state.nv.us/loep_main.htm> (visited May 3, 2005). As of January 2006, only thirteen were listed.

54. *See, e.g.,* Brendan Riley, *Convicted Slot Cheat Added to Nevada's "Black Book,"* at <http://www.lasvegassun.com/sunbin/stories/nevada/2003/feb/20/022010167 .html> (discussing addition of Tommy Glenn Carmichael despite his attempts to use his cheating skills to improve slot machine security by inventing an "anti-cheating" device).

55. The Gaming Control Board also publishes a "most wanted list" on its Web site, which consists of those wanted in connection with casino-related crimes. *See*

<http://gaming.nv.gov/wanted_main.htm> (visited January 14, 2006). A list of those denied or found unsuitable for gaming licenses is also published, presumably for the benefit of those considering hiring these individuals or otherwise involving them in casino-related enterprises. *See* <http://gaming.nv.gov/unsuitable.htm> (visited January 14, 2006).

56. *See* Thomas v. Bible, 694 F.Supp. 750, 760–61 (D. Nev. 1988). *See also* Nev. Rev. Stat. Ann. §§ 463.152 (notice requirements) and .153 (hearing requirements). The statutorily prescribed right to notice and a hearing does not attach until after a name is placed on the list. *See* Thomas v. Bible, 694 F.Supp. at 759. However, in Spilotro v. State, 661 P.2d 467 (1983), the facts suggest that a hearing was granted before inclusion. *See id.* at 468–69.

57. 661 P.2d 467 (1983).

58. *Id.* at 470.

59. *See id.*

60. *See id.* at 471.

61. *Id.* at 472. Spilotro is followed in Rosenthal, *supra* note 46, 819 P.2d at 1300.

62. *See, e.g.,* Bowers & Titus, *supra* note 52, 313.

63. Nev. Rev. Stat. Ann. 463.0129(3).

64. 448 F.Supp. 116 (D. Nev. 1978).

65. *Id.* at 118 n.1.

66. *See also* Doug Grant, Inc. v. Greate Bay Casino Corp., 273 F.3d 173 (3d Cir. 2000) (discussing card-counting strategies).

67. Uston, *supra* note 64, 448 F.Supp. at 118.

68. *Id.* (citation omitted).

69. *Id.*

70. *See id.*

71. *See, e.g.,* Brooks v. Chicago Downs Ass'n, Inc., 791 F.2d 512 (7th Cir. 1986) (applying common law rule of exclusion in favor of Illinois racetrack in efforts to exclude "expert handicappers" from betting on horse races).

72. *Cf.* Marshall v. Sawyer, 301 F.2d 639, 648 (9th Cir. 1962) (Pope, J., concurring) ("True the gambling casinos are operated by individuals or corporations under state license, but in a very real sense, and in essence, the State of Nevada itself is in the gambling business, and its continued maintenance of that institution is vital to the State's life and its economy.").

73. Uston v. Resorts International Hotels, Inc., 445 A.2d 370, 376 (N.J. 1982).

74. *See* Campione v. Adamar of New Jersey, Inc., 714 A.2d. 299, 306–8 (N.J. 1998), for an overview of the history of the countermeasure regulations issued after *Uston.*

75. *See* Lionel, Sawyer & Collins, *supra* note 21, 256.

76. *See, e.g.,* State Gaming Control Board v. Breen, 661 P.2d 1309, 1311 (Nev. 1983); Sea Air Support, Inc. v. Herrmann, 613 P.2d 413 (Nev. 1980).

77. *See* Lionel, Sawyer & Collins, *supra* note 21, at 260.

78. *See id.*

79. Nev. Rev. Stat. § 463.368(1).

80. *Id.* § 463.368(6).

81. *See* Lionel, Sawyer & Collins, *supra* note 21, at 265–70. Money laundering is a federal offense. See chapter 9.

82. *See id.* at 270.

83. *See* Nev. Rev. Stat. § 463.361–.366.

84. *See id.* at 463.361(1).

85. *See id.* at 463.366.

86. Anecdotal evidence indicates that concerns about the reliability of games and the payoff of jackpots may deter some players from gambling via the Internet. See chapter 10.

87. *See* Nev. Rev. Stat. § 463.1405(3) (allowing revocation or suspension of "any cause deemed reasonable by the commission").

88. *See id.* § 463.350.

89. For a history of this action, *see* Erickson v. Desert Palace, Inc., 962 F.2d 694, 694–96 (9th Cir. 1991); Lionel, Sawyer & Collins, *supra* note 21, at 321–23.

90. *See* Nev. Rev. Stat. § 468.350.

91. NGC Regulation 5.170(2).

92. *Id. at* 5.170(3).

93. *Id.* at 5.170(4).

94. Elizabeth White, *Nevada Proposes Helping Problem Gamblers for the First Time,* Las Vegas Sun, February 19, 2005.

95. *See id.*

96. *See id.*

97. *See* John L. Smith, *Bennett's Bottom Line on Gambling out of Line in More Than One Way,* Las Vegas Rev.-J., May 7, 2003, available at <http://www.reviewjournal.com/lvrj_home/2003/May-07-Wed-2003/news/21266047.html> (last visited May 3, 2005).

98. *See* NGR 5.200(2)(f).

99. *Id.* at 5.200(3)(f).

100. *See id.* at 5.200(3)(i).

101. *See* Nev. Rev. Stat. § 463.3557. This provision was amended in 2002 to allow a transfer to an "interactive gaming system" if the commission promulgated regulations that authorized interactive gaming. *See id.* However, no such regulations have been forthcoming.

102. *See* Liz Benston, *Gaming Panel Shelves ATM Slots,* Las Vegas Sun, May 23, 2001 (2003 WL 7821332).

103. *See id.*

104. N.G.Reg. 3.015(8).

105. *See* State of Nevada, *supra* note 19.

106. *See* U.S. CENSUS BUREAU, STATISTICAL ABSTRACT OF THE UNITED STATES: 2002 (122d ed.), Table 433, Estimated State and Local Taxes Paid by a Family of Four in Selected Cities: 2000.

107. *See id.*

CHAPTER 8

1. *See* N.J. CONST. ART. 4, § 7, 2.D.

2. *See, e.g.,* CABOT ET AL., EDS., INTERNATIONAL CASINO LAW 59 (1991).

3. S.D. Stat. 42-7B-1 (1989).

4. Colo. Legis. S.B. 91-149 (June 4, 1991).

5. 2004 Pa. Legis. Serv. Act. 2004-91 (H.B. 2330) (July 6, 2004). This legislation was fueled by promises of property tax relief coupled with benefits for tourism and an ailing horse-racing industry. *See* Pennsylvania Governor's Message, July 31, 2004 (statement of Governor Edward G. Rendell). As of January 2006, the Pennsylvania Gaming Control Board had not yet awarded any operator licenses. The first application deadline was December 28, 2005. See Pennsylvania Gaming Control Board Receives 25 Application Submissions for Operator Licenses, January 9, 2006, at http://www.pgcb.state.pa.us/press/pr_010906.htm (visited May 18, 2006).

6. Florida's Broward County approved slot machines in a racino in March 2005, but voters in Miami-Dade County rejected them. *See* Theresa Walsh Giarrusso, *Go Guide 2005: Seven States Add Slot Machines,* ATLANTA JOURNAL AND CONSTITUTION, March 13, 2005, at K6 (2005 WLNR 3931048).

7. For example, the New Jersey Division of Gaming Enforcement provides the following explanation of its function:

> Licensure is the cornerstone of the regulatory system. Licenses are required of casino owners and operators, casino employees, and companies that do business with casinos in order to assure that those involved with this industry meet the statutory requirements of good character, honesty and integrity and to keep the New Jersey casino industry free from organized crime. The DGE conducts all licensing investigations and provides a recommendation to the Casino Control Commission, which has the power to grant or deny a licensing application

<http://www.state.nj.us/lps/ge/mission&duties.htm>. In Iowa, the Department of Criminal Investigation, Gaming Enforcement Bureau, is "responsible for regulatory enforcement and criminal investigation at all licensed gambling operations in Iowa. The bureau is required to conduct complete and thorough background investigations of business entities and individuals involved in gaming. The bureau maintains an investigatory staff at each of the licensed riverboat casinos and pari-mutuel facilities in Iowa." <http://www.state.ia.us/government/dps/dci/gaming.htm>.

8. *See, e.g.,* <http://www.state.ia.us/government/dps/dci/gaming.htm>

(discussing regulatory functions of Iowa's Department of Criminal Investigation, Gaming Enforcement Bureau).

9. N.J. Const. Art. 4, § 7, 2.D.

10. For a particularly bleak description of Atlantic City prior to casino gaming, *see* Rutgers School of Business, *The Future Impact of Gaming on Atlantic City 2003–2008* (2003), available at <http://camden-sbc.rutgers.edu/Alumni/Rutgers%20Gaming%20Study>. This study states in part:

> Atlantic City, once revered as America's Favorite Playground, now stood stark and gray against the barren seascape. Decades had passed since its heyday. The former gem of the East Coast had fallen into neglect and disrepair and had become a city long forgotten by tourists and travelers. But the turning point in its revival was drawing near.

Id. at 3. For further history on the constitutional amendment legalizing casino gambling and the enactment of the Casino Control Act, *see* New Jersey v. Trump Hotels & Casino Resorts, Inc., 734 A.2d 1160, 1165–73 (N.J. 1999).

11. Cabot et al., *supra* note 2, at 25.

12. N.J. Const. Art. 4, § 7, 2.D.

13. NJ ST 5:12–1

14. *See* Rutgers School of Business, *supra* note 10, at 5.

15. *Id.* at 4.

16. *Id.* at 5.

17. *See id.* at 4.

18. The National Gambling Impact Study Commission distinguishes between convenience gambling and destination resorts in terms of the efficacy for economic development and propensity for problem gambling behavior. *See* National Gambling Impact Study Commission Report at 7-4 (1999).

19. *See* <http://quickfacts.census.gov/qfd/states/34/34001.html>. It should be noted that the legal age for casino gambling is tewnty-one, so this estimate only approximates the adult population eligible for gaming.

20. *See* <http://quickfacts.census.gov/qfd/maps/new_jersey_map.html> (totaling populations in 2000 for Atlantic, Burlington, Camden, Cape May, Cumberland, Gloucester, and Ocean Counties). Assuming about one-fourth of the population is below the legal gambling age of twenty-one, this would mean that over 1.5 million adults eligible to gamble live in these counties alone.

21. *See* N.J.S.A. § 5:12-71.2.

22. *See* N.J.S.A. § 5:5-65.1.

23. *See* N.J. Admin. Code tit. 19, § 48-2.2.

24. *Id.* § 48-2.2(4).

25. *See id.* at §48-2.3(a).

26. *Id.* at § 48-2.3(b).

27. *See id.* at §§ 48.2-3(c) and (d); 48.2-4.

28. *See* N.J. Stat. Ann. § 5:12-71.2(e).

29. *See* N.J. Admin Code tit. 19, § 48-2.4.

30. *See id.*

31. *See* N.J.S.A. § 5:12-71.3(b).

32. *See id.* at § 5:12-71.3(c).

33. *See id.* at § 5:12-71.2(c).

34. *See id.* at § 5:12-71.3(d).

35. *See* Judy DeHaven, *Few Gamblers Opt for Self-Ban Plan,* NEWARK STAR-LEDGER, January 26, 2003 (2003 WL 10818365).

36. *See id.*

37. See chapter 5 for a discussion of the meaning of the terms *problem gambling* and *pathological gambling.*

38. *See* AMERICAN PSYCHIATRIC ASSOCIATION, DIAGNOSTIC AND STATISTICAL MANUAL OF MENTAL DISORDERS 615 (4th ed. 1994).

39. *See id.* at 617.

40. It should be noted, however, that compulsive shopping is not listed in the American Psychiatric Association's *Diagnostic and Statistical Manual of Mental Disorders.*

41. *See* N.J. Admin. Code tit 19, § 45-1.27A.

42. *See id.*

43. *See* 1989 Iowa Leg. Serv. 73 G.A., S.F. 124, Ch. 67 (West).

44. CABOT ET AL., *supra* note 2, at 59.

45. Iowa Code § 99F.7(2) (1989).

46. *Id.* § 99F.7(1) (1989).

47. *Id.* § 99F.7(5) (1989).

48. *See id.*

49. *See* 1989 Iowa Legis. Serv. 67, S.F. 124, Ch. 67 § 9(6) (April 27, 1989) (enacting Iowa Code § 99F.9(6)).

50. *See* 1989 Iowa Legis. Serv., 75, S.F. 525, § 6 (May 8, 1989) (amending Iowa Code § 99F.9(6)).

51. *See* 1991 Iowa Legis. Serv., ch. 144, S.F. 110, § 1 (May 9, 1991).

52. *See* 1994 Iowa Legis. Serv., ch. 1021, H.F. 2179, § 23 (Marcy 31, 1994).

53. *See* Iowa Code § 99F.9(5).

54. *See id.* § 99F.9(2).

55. *Id.* § 99F.9(4),(5).

56. *See* Iowa Code § 99F.1(8) (1993). This term was deleted from the code in 1994.

57. *See id.* § 99F.4(17) (1989).

58. *See* id. § 99F.7(9).

59. *See Third Gambling Boat Leaves Limited Bets Iowa,* CHI. TRIB., April 1, 1993 (1993 WL 11055799).

60. *See id.*

61. *See, e.g.,* Jeff Lehr, *Gambling Boat Nearly Ready,* Hawkeye (Burlington, Iowa), November 16, 1994 (1994 WL 3046389); Eva Lego, *Bettendorf Strikes Deal with Lady Luck,* Quad-City Times, August 3, 1994 (1994 WL 3071256) (casino boat agrees to return after two-year absence). *See also Iowa Lifts the Restrictions on Riverboat Casino Bets,* Chic. Sun-Times, May 29, 1994 (1994 WL 5556159) (noting that legislation put Iowa's vessels on "same footing" as Illinois vessels).

62. *See* Kathie Obradovich, *Governor Wants More Detail: Davenport Needs to Show More Proof That It Needs Betting Limits Lifted,* Quad-City Times, August 10, 1993 (1993 WL 3159488).

63. *See* 1994 Iowa Legis. Serv. 1021 (H.F. 2179), § 11 (March 31, 1994) (amending Iowa Code § 99F.4(17)).

64. *Id.* § 10 (amending Iowa Code § 99F.4(4)).

65. *See* Iowa Code § 99F.9(6) (added by 1994 Iowa Legis. Serv., ch. 1021, H.F. 2179, § 23 (March 31, 1994)).

66. *See* Iowa Code 99F.7(9)(b) (as amended by Acts 2004 80 G.A. ch. 1136, § 45 (effective May 6, 2004)).

67. *See* 1994 Iowa Legis. Serv., ch. 1021, H.F. 2179, § 17 (amending Iowa Code § 99F.7(10)(c)).

68. *See* Iowa Code § 99F.4 to .6.

69. *See id.* § 99F.4 (16), (17).

70. *Id.* § 99F.7(11).

71. *Id.* § 99F.7(11)(e). Legislation in 2004 amended this provision, increasing the previous term limit from two to eight years.

72. *See* Iowa Code § 99F.7(10)(d).

73. *See* <http://www3.state.ia.us/irgc/Referendum.htm> (last visited May 3, 2005) (showing results from 2003–4).

74. *See id.*

75. *See* Racing Ass'n of Central Iowa v. Fitzgerald, 648 N.W. 2d 555, 556–57 (Iowa 2002), *rev'd,* 123 S.Ct. 2156 (2003).

76. *See* Dan Johnson, *It's Been a Bumpy Ride for Prairie Meadows,* Des Moines Reg., August 25, 2002 (2002 WL 23124615).

77. *See id.*

78. *See id.*

79. *See id.*

80. Iowa Code § 99F.5(1).

81. *Id.* § 99F.1(14).

82. *See id.* § 99F.7(2).

83. *See id.* § 99F.10(2).

84. *See id.* § 99F.10.

85. *See id.* §§ 99F.10(4); 99F.10A.

86. *See id.* § 99F.1(1).

87. *Id.* § 99F.11.

88. *See id.*

89. *See* Fitzgerald v. Racing Ass'n of Central Iowa, 123 S.Ct. 2156 (2003), reversing, 648 N.W.2d 555 (Iowa 2002).

90. *See* Racing Ass'n of Central Iowa v. Fitzgerald, 675 N.W.2d 1 (Iowa), cert. denied 581 U.S. 1086 (2004).

91. *See* Iowa Code § 99F.11(2)(b),(c).

92. *Id.* § 99F.11(3).

93. *See id.*

94. *See id.*

95. *See* Iowa Code §§ 99F.11(4); 8.57(5)(e) (diverting amounts in excess of $60 million to other funds). The Vision Iowa fund is discussed later.

96. Iowa Racing and Gaming Commission, Report for Fiscal 2003, at <http://www3.state.ia.us/irgc/FYTD03.pdf>.

97. *See id.*

98. *Cf.* Iowa Code § 99F.7(12) (prohibiting delinquent status in payment of property taxes); (11) (allowing local docking fees to be charged).

99. *Id.* § 99F.6.

100. *See id.*

101. *See id.*

102. *See id.* ("A qualified sponsoring organization shall not make a contribution to a candidate, political committee, candidate's committee, state statutory political committee, county statutory political committee, national political party, or fundraising event as these terms are defined in section 56.2.").

103. <http://www.iowawestfoundation.org/2002annual/pg5.htm> (visited May 3, 2005).

104. *See* <http://www.iowagaming.org/WhatIsTheIGA/nonprofitlicense holders/iowawest.html> ("2003 Grant Recipients").

105. *See* Iowa Legislature Senate File 2447.

106. *See* Iowa Code §§ 15F.102 (defining board composition); 15F.103 (defining board duties).

107. *See id.* § 12.82.

108. *See* <http://www.visioniowa.org/vision.html> (Vision Iowa); <http://www.visioniowa.org/cat.html> (CAT).

109. *See* Iowa Admin Code § 211.4 (2).

110. *See Iowa Gambling Treatment Fund—Revenues, Expenditures, and Redirects,* at <http://www.1800betsoff.org/revenue_redirect.htm> (showing data for 1986–2005 (estimated)).

111. *See* Iowa Gaming Association at <http://www.buyiowafirst.org/Responsible Gaming/responsi.html> (visited May 3, 2005).

112. *See* Chris Clayton, *Gambling Treatment Touted,* OMAHA WORLD-HERALD, November 28, 2002, available at <http://www.responsiblegambling.org/articles/Gambling_treatment_touted.pdf>.

113. *See* William Petroski, *Gambling Treatment Sum to Jump,* DES MOINES REG., August 1, 2004, at 1 (2004 WLNR 16262408).

114. *See id.*

115. *See* Acts 2004 (80 G.A). ch. 1136, § 35 (adding Iowa Code § 99F.4(23)).

116. *See* Iowa Gaming Association Web site, www.iowagaming.org.

117. *See* Uniform Self-Exclusion Form (November 1, 2004), at <http://www.iowagaming.org/ResponsibleGaming/responsi.html>.

118. *See id.*

119. *See* Iowa Code § 99F.4(23) (2004).

120. *See* Iowa Code § 99F.7(16).

121. *See* <http://www.keepthemoneyinnebraska.com/>.

122. Portions of one of these initiatives, which had several parts, were approved, including a provision allowing the state to tax gaming revenues. Whether this reflected voter confusion or a simple desire to impose taxes is open to interpretation.

123. Iowa Acts 2004 (80 G.A). ch. 1136, § 62.

124. *Id.* § 41.

125. *See* William Petroski, *The Lucky Number Is 4,* DES MOINES REG., May 12, 2005, at 1 (2005 WLNR 7575901).

126. Iowa Code § 99F.7(4).

127. For a history of the initial process of legalized casino gaming on riverboats in Missouri, *see* Harris v. Missouri Gaming Comm'n, 869 S.W. 2d 58 (Mo. 1994).

128. *See id.*

129. *See id.*

130. *See id.*

131. *See* Akin v. Missouri Gaming Comm'n, 956 S.W. 2d 251 (Mo. 1997).

132. *See id.*

133. *See* Missouri Stat. Ann. § 313.805(3).

134. MISSOURI GAMING COMMISSION, ANNUAL REPORT TO THE GENERAL ASSEMBLY 8 (2004), available at <http://www.mgc.state.mo.us/annual%20reports/2004/annual2004.pdf> [hereinafter 2004 Annual Report].

135. *Id.* (footnotes omitted).

136. *See* Missouri Stat. Ann. §§ 313.805(13); 313.817(3).

137. *See id.* § 313.805(12).

138. *See id.* § 313.812(9).

139. 2004 Annual Report, *supra* note 134, at 8.

140. *See id.* at 11.

141. *See* MISSOURI GAMING COMMISSION, ANNUAL REPORT TO THE GENERAL

ASSEMBLY (2000) at 19 [hereinafter 2000 Annual Report], at <http://www.mgc.dps.mo.gov> (visited May 16, 2006).

142. *See id.* at 16.

143. *See Free Money,* ST. LOUIS POST-DISPATCH, March 5, 2005 (editorial) (2005 WLNR 3450184) (reporting that the Maryland Heights facility would initiate a $400 million expansion if loss limits were removed).

144. *See* 2000 Annual Report, *supra* note 141, at 9–10.

145. *See id.* at 18–19.

146. *See* MISSOURI GAMING COMMISSION, ANNUAL REPORT TO THE GENERAL ASSEMBLY (2001) at 27, at <http://www.mgc.dps.mo.gov/> (visited May 16, 2006).

147. *See id.*

148. *See id.*

149. *See* Missouri. Stat. Ann. § 313.813.

150. 11 MO ADC 45-17.020.

151. *See id.*

152. *See id.*

153. *See id.*

154. *See* Missouri Stat. Ann. §§ 313.842; 313.835(1).

155. *See* Rick Alm, *Gambling and Tourism: House Rules against Disgruntled Gamblers,* KANSAS CITY STAR, May 13, 2003 (2003 WL 19781395).

156. *See* Missouri Stat. Ann. § 313.812 (1).

157. *See* 2004 Annual Report, *supra* note 134, at 11 ("The Commission's practice of waiting to introduce new gaming capacity into a market until there is adequate demand allows Missouri licensees to remain profitable and encourages them to reinvest in Missouri.").

158. *See* 2000 Annual Report, *supra* note 141, at 30–34 (discussing the "St. Louis Expansion Process").

159. *See* Missouri Stat. Ann § 313.812(10).

160. *See id.* § 313.812(1).

161. *See id.* § 313.822 (imposing a 20 percent tax on AGR of gaming establishments).

162. *See id.*

163. *See* 1990 Miss. Laws Ch. 45, § 1 ff (enacting Mississippi Gaming Control Act), codified at Miss Code Ann. § 75-76-1 to -313.

164. *See* Miss. Code Ann. § 75-76-3(2). *See also id.* § 75-76-3(6).

165. *See* Ben H. Stone et al., *Site Approval of Casinos in Mississippi—A Matter of Statutory Construction, Or a Roll of the Dice?* 64 Miss. L.J. 363, 365 n.5 (1995).

166. Miss. Stat. Ann. § 97-33-1.

167. *Cf.* Miss. Gaming Comm'n v. Board of Education, 691 So.2d 452, 455 (Miss. 1997) *with* Miss. Casino Operator's Ass'n v. Miss. Gaming Comm'n, 654 So.2d 892 (Miss. 1995) (overruling gaming commission order allowing site loca-

tion in manmade canal, though recognizing other similar facilities had been approved).

168. Lynne Willbanks Jeter, *Tunica Ranked Third-Largest behind Las Vegas, Atlantic City,* MISS. BUS. J., December 14, 1998 (1998 WL 10300366).

169. *See* Ronald J. Rychlak, *The Introduction of Casino Gambling: Public Policy and the Law,* 64 MISS. L.J. 291, 310 (1995).

170. *See* Miss. Stat. Ann. § 27-109-1.

171. Henry N. Dick III, *Comment, Dockside Gambling and the Federal Maritime Lien Act:Why Dockside Casinos Should Not Be Considered Vessels for Purposes of the Federal Maritime Lien Act,* 64 MISS. L.J. 659, 669 (1995).

172. Rychlak, *supra* note 169, 64 Miss. L.J. at 310 (footnotes omitted).

173. *See id.* at 309.

174. *See, e.g.,* Miss. Gaming Comm'n v. Board of Education, 691 So.2d 452, 455 (Miss. 1997) ("The site, if approved, could and would open the State of Mississippi to inland land-based casino gaming.").

175. *See* 2005 Miss. Laws 5th Ex. Sess. Ch. 16 (H.B. 45) (approved October 17, 2005); *Mississippi to Let Casinos Move onto Dry Land: Governor to Sign Bill to Allow Gambling a Short Distance from Shore,* ASSOCIATED PRESS, October 4, 2005.

176. *See* Rychlak, *supra* note 169, 64 MISS L.J. at 308 (noting this approach is unlike every other state except Louisiana). However, in 1996, Louisiana's state constitution was amended to require local parish approval prior to the introduction of gambling in that state. *See* La. Const. Art 12, § 6(c) (1996).

177. *See* Miss. Stat. Ann. § 19-3-79(1).

178. *See id.*

179. *See id.* § 19-3-79 (3).

180. Miss. Stat. Ann. § 19-3-79(2).

181. *See, e.g.,* Miss Stat. Ann. §§ 75-76-67 (suitability determination by board); 75-76-73 (form and contents of license application). Special rules apply to corporate licensees, *see id.* §§ 75-76-201 to -215 (generally); 249-265 (public corporations), and to limited partnerships, *id.* §§ 75-76-219 to -231.

182. *See* Stone et al., *supra* note 165, at 363.

183. *See* Miss. Stat. Ann. 75-76-67.

184. *See* Iowa Code Ann. § 99F.7(1) ("The commission shall decide the number, location, and type of excursion gambling boats licensed under this chapter for operation on the rivers, lakes, and reservoirs of this state.").

185. *See* Missouri Stat. Ann. § 313.812(1).

186. *See* John M. Czarnetsky, *When the Dealer Goes Bust: Issues in Casino Bankruptcies,* 18 MISS. C. L. REV. 459, 460 (1997).

187. *See id.* at n.7 (citing thirty casinos in Mississippi in 1997); American Gaming Association at www.americangaming.org/Industry/state/statistics.cfm (listing twenty-nine casinos for Mississippi) (visited May 17, 2005).

188. *See id.*

189. *See* U.S. Casino Directory: South Dakota, at www.americancasinoguide .com/southdakota.shtml (visited May 17, 2005).

190. *See* S.D.C.L. 42-7B-1, Commission Note (2005).

191. *See* <http://www.hbo.com/deadwood/about/> (visited May 18, 2005).

192. *See* <http://www.americancasinoguide.com/southdakota.shtml> (visited May 18, 2005).

193. *See* <http://www.legendsofamerica.com/SD-Deadwood2.html> (visited May 18, 2005).

194. *See* <http://www.americancasinoguide.com/southdakota.shtml> (visited May 18, 2005).

195. *See* S.D.C.L. § 42-7B-35.

196. *See id.* § 42-7B-2.1.

197. *See id.* § 42-7B-11 (commission's powers).

198. *See* South Dakota Laws Chapter 374, § 12 (1989).

199. *See* S.D.C.L. § 42-7B-14.

200. *See id.* § 42-7B-16.

201. *See* <http://www.americancasinoguide.com/southdakota.shtml> (visited May 18, 2005).

202. <http://www.state.sd.us/bit/statistics/main_topics/sdcities_a_f.htm>.

203. *See* Barry M. Horstman, *Some Communities Win with Casinos, Some Lose,* CINCINNATI POST, September 18, 1997, available at <http://www.cincypost.com/ news/1997/gamble091897.html>.

204. *See* S.D.C.L. § 42-7A-38. The statute expresses the maximum credit as no more than $125 per credit value of $0.25 played. This amounts to $1,000 (8 × $0.25 = $2 maximum bet; 8 × $125 = $1,000).

205. *See* S.D.C.L. § 42-7A-37.1 (limited to bars and lounges); § 42-7A-44 (no more than ten per establishment).

206. S.D.C.L. § 42-7A-63.

207. *See* State of South Dakota, *General Fund Condition Statement,* at <http:// www.state.sd.us/bfm/budget/rec05/gfcdbud.pdf> (visited May 18, 2005).

208. *See* American Gaming Association, *Industry Information State Statistics,* at <www.americangaming.org/Industry/state/statistics.cfm> (visited May 11, 2005).

209. The vote was 146,428 (46.3 percent) for and 169,642 (53.7 percent) against. *See* S.D. Const. Art. 3, § 25 (reporters note).

210. *See* William Petroski, *Iowa Issues Moratorium on Video Gambling Machines,* DES MOINES REG., January 10, 2006, available at <http://www.desmoinesregister.com>.

CHAPTER 9

1. New State Ice Co. v. Liebman, 285 U.S. 282, 311 (1932) (Brandeis, J., dissenting).

2. *See* Pic-A-State Pa, Inc. v. Reno, 76 F.3d 1294, 1297 (3d Cir. 1996). Other

congressional acts to assist the states in controlling lotteries predate this 1895 statute. For a more complete history of these legislative attempts, *see* United States v. Edge Broadcasting, 509 U.S. 419, 421–22 (1993).

3. 188 U.S. 321 (1903). The text of this act reads as follows:

"§1. That any person who shall cause to be brought within the United States from abroad, for the purpose of disposing of the same, or deposited in or carried by the mails of the United States, or carried from one state to another in the United States, any paper, certificate, or instrument purporting to be or represent a ticket, chance, share, or interest in or dependent upon the event of a lottery, so-called gift concert, or similar enterprise, offering prizes dependent upon lot or chance, or shall cause any advertisement of such lottery, so-called gift concert, or similar enterprise, offering prizes dependent upon lot or chance, to be brought into the United States, or deposited in or carried by the mails of the United States, or transferred from one state to another in the same, shall be punishable in [for] the first offense by imprisonment for not more than two years, or by a fine of not more than $1,000, or both, and in the second and after offenses by such imprisonment only." 28 Stat. at L. 963. U. S. Comp. Stat. 1901, p. 3178.

Id. at 322. Current federal statutes applicable to lotteries include 18 U.S.C.A. §1301 (2003) (transporting lottery ticket); *id.* §1302 (mailing lottery ticket); *id.* §1303 (prohibiting postal employee from acting as agent of lottery).

4. 188 U.S. at 323.

5. *Id.* at 357–58.

6. However, it would later use its regulatory powers to prohibit federally insured banks from participating in lotteries—which arguably reflects an antilottery policy. *See, e.g.,* 12 U.S.C.A. § 25(a) (national banks); 12 U.S.C.A. §339 (state federal reserve member banks); 12 U.S.C.A. § 1829a (state nonmember banks); 12 U.S.C.A. § 1463 (state savings associations).

7. 188 U.S. 375 (1903).

8. *Id.* at 376.

9. *See id.* at 377–78.

10. *See* Pic-A-State, PA v. Pennsylvania, 1993 WL 325539 (M.D. Pa. 1993).

11. *See id.* The challenged statute is currently found at 72 Pa. St. Ann. tit. 72, § 3761-307(c).

12. *Id.*

13. *See generally id.*

14. *Id.* (footnotes 13 and 14 omitted).

15. *Id.*

16. *See id. See also* Pic-A-State PA, Inc. v. Pennsylvania, 43 F.3d 175, 177 (3d Cir. 1994) (summarizing the effect of the district court's memorandum decision). If those taxes proved discriminatory, however, the tax scheme could itself

be challenged. *See, e.g.,* Complete Auto Transit (prescribing tests for validity of discriminatory taxing schemes under Commerce Clause).

17. Pub.L. No. 103-322, 108 Stat. 1796 ("1994 Crime Control Act").

18. *See* Pic-A-State PA, Inc, *supra* note 16, at 176. As the court explained: "One portion of the 1994 Crime Control Act makes it a federal crime to knowingly transmit in interstate commerce information for the purpose of procuring interests in an out-of-state lottery if one is engaged in the business of procuring for a person in one State such a ticket, chance, share, or interest in a lottery . . . conducted by another State (unless that business is permitted under an agreement between the States in question or appropriate authorities of those States)." *Id.* at 177–78 (internal quotation omitted).

19. *See id.* at 179.

20. *See id.*

21. *See id.* at 180.

22. *See also* L.E. Services, Inc. v. State Lottery Commission of Indiana, 646 N.E.2d 334, 344–47 (Ind. App. 1995) (following a similar rationale in upholding an Indiana law proscribing the sale of out-of-state lottery tickets in Indiana).

23. 76 F.3d 1294 (3d Cir. 1996).

24. *See id.* at 1301.

25. *See id.*

26. In support of this conclusion, the court looked to the floor debates and quoted as follows from Senator Specter: "the right of a State to regulate lottery [*sic*] and gambling within its borders must be preserved. Federal gambling laws have traditionally enabled the States to regulate in-State gambling. Federal laws should continue to limit the proliferation of interstate gambling to preserve the sovereignty of States that do not permit certain forms of gambling." *Id.* at 1302 (citation omitted).

27. *Id.* at 1303.

28. *Id.*

29. As discussed in chapter 10, this differentiation between gambling and other forms of entertainment has recently been raised in challenges before the World Trade Organization.

30. 18 U.S.C.A. § 1084.

31. 18 U.S.C.A. § 1953.

32. 18 U.S.C.A. § 1952.

33. 28 U.S.C.A. § 3702.

34. *See* United States v. Borgese, 235 F.Supp. 286, 295–96 (1964); H.R. 967, 1961-2 USCCAN 2631.

35. 18 U.S.C. § 1084(a) (2003).

36. Letter from Robert F. Kennedy to The Speaker of the House of Representatives, April 6, 1961, *reprinted in* 1961-2 USCCAN at 2633.

37. *See id.*

38. Pic-A-State Pa., Inc. v. Pennsylvania, 1993 WL 325539 (E.D. Pa. 1993), *rev'd on other grounds,* 42 F.3d 175 (3d Cir. 1994).

39. *See* United States v. Scavo, 593 F2d 837 (8th Cir. 1979); United States v. Cohen, 378 F.2d 751 (9th Cir.), cert denied, 389 U.S. 897 (1967).

40. *See* United States v. Anderson, 542 F.2d 428 (7th Cir. 1976).

41. *See* United States v. Baborian, 528 F.Supp. 324 (D.R.I. 1981).

42. 18 U.S.C. § 1084(c).

43. 18 U.S.C.A. § 1084(b).

44. H.R. No. 967, 1961-2 U.S.C.C.A.N. 2631, 2632-33.

45. *See, e.g.,* States v. McDonough, 835 F.2d 1103 (5th Cir. 1988).

46. For example, Missouri law contains the following provision:

No licensee shall permit participation by a person in a game conducted in the licensed gaming establishment if such person is not physically present in the licensed gaming establishment during the period of time when such game is being conducted, and all games and the participation of patrons therein shall be entirely located and conducted on the licensed premises. (MS ST § 75-76-101)

47. 18 U.S.C.A. § 1952.

48. *Id.* § 1952(a).

49. *Id.* § 1952(b).

50. *See* Rewis v. United States, 401 U.S. 808 (1971).

51. 18 U.S.C.A. § 1953.

52. 18 U.S.C. § 1953(a).

53. *See id.* § 1953(b).

54. *See* 15 U.S.C.A. § 1171-78, which is also known as the Gambling Devices Transportation Act. *See* United States v. Bally Mfg. Corp., 345 F.Supp. 410 (D. La. 1972).

55. *See* P.L. 102-559, 106 Stat. 4227, *codified at* 28 U.S.C.A. §§ 3701-3704 [hereinafter Sports Protection Act].

56. S. Rep. No. 102-248, at 6 (1992), *reprinted at* 1992 U.S.C.C.A.N. 3553, 3557.

57. *See* 18 U.S.C.A. § 224.

58. *See, e.g.,* United States v. Pinto, 503 F.2d 718, 723 (2d Cir. 1974) (harness racing); United States v. Walsh, 544 F.2d 156 (4th Cir. 1976) (horse racing).

59. For an example of sports bribery prosecution under a state statute, *see* State v. De Paglia, 71 N.W.2d 601 (Iowa 1955) (involving attempted bribery of a basketball player to "shave points" in a Drake versus Iowa State game). The legislative history to 18 U.S.C. § 224 suggests that, although "[s]tate law enforcement agencies have done much to uncover and prosecute these [state] statutes . . . [i]t is felt that more must be done. Bribery of players or officials to influence the results of sporting contests is a challenge to an important aspect of American life—

honestly competitive sports." H.R. Rep. No. 1053 (1964), *reprinted in* 1964 U.S.C.C.A.N. 2250, 2251.

60. S. Rep. No. 102-248 at 5, 1992 U.S.C.C.A.N. at 3555.

61. *Id.*, 1992 U.S.C.C.A.N. at 3556 (emphasis added).

62. *Id.*

63. *Id.* at 7, 1992 U.S.C.C.A.N. at 3558.

64. *Id.*

65. *Id.* at 8, 1992 U.S.C.C.A.N. at 3559.

66. *See id.* at 12–13, 1992 U.S.C.C.A.N. at 3562–63.

67. *Id.* at 14, 1992 U.S.C.C.A.N. at 3564.

68. *Id.*, 1992 U.S.C.C.A.N. at 3565. Senator Grassley's commentary predated the widespread use of the Internet. As discussed in chapter 10, sports betting via the Internet is widely accessible despite the federal ban.

69. *Id.* at 16, 1992 U.S.C.C.A.N. at 3566.

70. *Id.* at 7, 1992 U.S.C.C.A.N. at 3558.

71. *See, e.g.,* Marc Carinci, *London: A Gambler's Paradise,* March 6, 2004, at <http://www.covers.com/covers/mall/articles/london_a_gamblers_paradise.asp>.

72. *See NCAA Steps Up Anti-Gambling Efforts,* ASSOCIATED PRESS, January 7, 2006.

73. *See 2003 NCAA National Study on Collegiate Sports Wagering and Related Behaviors,* available at <http://www.ncaa.org/library/research/sports_wagering/2003/2003_sports_wagering_study.pdf>.

74. *See id.*

75. *See id.*

76. *See id.*

77. *See* National Cable Television Ass'n v. United States, 415 U.S. 336, 341 n.4 (1974) (crediting Chief Justice Marshall with this statement).

78. *See id.* at 341 (footnote omitted).

79. *See* United States v. Hallmark, 911 F.2d 399, 401 (10th Cir. 1990).

80. I.R.C. § 4421(1).

81. *See id.* § 4421(2).

82. *Id.* § 4402.

83. *See id.* § 4401(a)(1).

84. *Id.* § 4411(b).

85. Nevertheless, its potential applicability to tribal gaming in the form of pull-tabs was apparently sufficiently significant to warrant litigation in the Supreme Court. *See* Chickasaw Nation v. United States, 534 U.S. 84 (2001) (upholding application of excise tax provisions to tribal gambling).

86. *See* I.R.C. §§ 4401(a)(2); 4411(a).

87. *See* H.R. Conf. Rep. No. 93-1401, *reprinted in* 1974 U.S.C.C.A.N 6232, 6232–33.

88. 390 U.S. 39 (1968).

89. *See* I.R.C. § 4424.

90. *See* <http://www.onlineblackjackreview.com/Online-Blackjack-Basic -Strategy-Odds.htm> (visited July 7, 2004).

91. *See* Hochman v. Commissioner, 51 T.C.M. (CCH) 311 (1986); GCM 37312 (November 7, 1977).

92. I.R.C. § 165(d); Commissioner v. Groetzinger, 480 U.S. 23, 32 (1987).

93. *See* I.R.C. 165(c)(1).

94. Commissioner v. Groetzinger, 480 U.S. 23, 32 (1987).

95. *See generally* Stephen A. Zorn, *The Federal Income Tax Treatment of Gambling: Fairness or Obsolete Moralism?* 49 TAX LAWYER 1 (1995), for an excellent discussion of these issues.

96. *See* Praytor v. Commissioner, T.C. Memo 2000-282 at n. 2.

97. *See id; see also* Rev. Rul. 54-339, 1954-2 C.B. 89.

98. *See* Commissioner v. Groetzinger, 480 U.S. 23, 32 (1987).

99. *See, e.g.,* Balot v. Commissioner, 81 T.C.M. (CCH) 1409 (2001).

100. *See* Petty v. Commissioner, T.C. Memo 2004-144.

101. *See, e.g.,* I.R.C. §§ 24(b) (child tax credit); 219(g) (retirement contributions for active participants in pension plans); 222(b) (deductions for qualified tuition and related expenses).

102. 1977-2 C.B. 538.

103. *Id.* at § 3.

104. *Id.*

105. *See* Zorn, *supra* note 95, at 7 ("While no one concerned with the effective administration of the tax laws would argue for eliminating the requirement that gamblers substantiate their winnings and losses in some way, the current rules are so out of touch with a realistic expectation of individual behavior as to invite creativity on the part of taxpayers."); 46–50 (discussing cases in this area that appear to relax the standards imposed by the service).

106. *See* Indopco v. Commissioner, 503 U.S. 79, 84 (1992); Norgard v. Commissioner, 939 F.2d 874, 878–79 (9th Cir. 1991).

107. *See* I.R.C. §§ 183; 63(d); 67(b).

108. *See Betting It All on Vegas Roulette Spin,* REUTERS, April 8, 2004.

109. *See* <http://wizardofodds.com/games/roulette.html> (visited July 2, 2004).

110. *See id. See also* <http://www.roulette-guru.com/roulette_odds.html> (visited July 2, 2004).

111. *See id.*

112. *See* Petty v. Commissioner, T.C. Memo 2004-144, discussed later.

113. I.R.C. § 6041(a).

114. *See* Lutz v. Commissioner, 83 T.C.M. (CCH) 1446, n. 4 (2002).

115. *See* Treas. Reg. § 7.6041-1.

116. *See id.*

117. *See, e.g.,* Lutz v. Commissioner, 83 T.C.M. (CCH) 1446, n. 4 (2002).

118. *See* I.R.C. §§ 6441; 3402(q).

119. *See, e.g.,* Lyszkowski v. Commissioner, T.C. Memo 1995-235 (discussing legislative history).

120. *See* United States v. Monteiro, 8761 F.2d 204, 211 (1st Cir. 1989).

121. *See* 31 U.S.C. § 1956(a)(1); United States v. Vanhorn, 296 F.3d 713, 717-18 (8th Cir. 2002); U.S. v. Peterson 244 F.3d 385, 390 (5th Cir. 2001).

122. Pub. L. 107-56. Title III, § 302, 115 Stat. 296.

123. Pub. L. 91-508, codified as amended at 12 U.S.C. § 1829b, 12 U.S.C. §§ 1951–1959, and 31 U.S.C. §§ 5311-5332. The applicable provisions governing reporting and disclosure requirements are found at 31 U.S.C. §§ 5311–5332.

124. *See* I.R.C. § 6051I.

125. *See* I.R.C. § 6050I(a).

126. *See id.* § 6050I(d).

127. *See id.* § 6050I(c)(1).

128. *See id.* § 6051I(c).

129. *See* 31 U.S.C. § 5312(a)(2)(X) and 31 C.F.R. § 113.11(n)(7)(i).

130. *See* Treas. Reg. § 1.6050I-1(d)(2).

131. Notice 96-57, 1996-2 C.B. 225. However, reporting requirements remain in effect for nongaming businesses, including shops, restaurants, entertainment, or hotels.

132. *See* Treas. Reg. § 1.6050I-1(d)(2).

133. *See id.*

134. *See* 31 C.F.R. § 103.22(b)(2).

135. *See id.*

136. *See id.; see also* 26 C.F.R. 1.6050I-1(e)(3) (verification requirements under tax provision).

137. *See* Financial Crimes Enforcement Network; Amendment to the Bank Secrecy Act Regulations—Requirement That Casinos and Card Clubs Report Suspicious Transactions, 67 Fed. Reg. 60722-01, 60723, n. 8 (September 26, 2002).

138. *See id.* at 60724.

139. 31 C.F.R. § 103.21(a)(2).

140. *See generally* 67 Fed. Reg. at 60725.

141. *See id.* at 60723.

142. *See id.* at 60725; 31 C.F.R. § 103.64.

143. *See id.* Additional practical guidance for casino compliance was later made available to casino operators. *See* Financial Crimes Enforcement Network, Suspicious Activity Reporting Guide for Casinos (2003), available at <http://www.fincen.gov/casinosarguidancefinal1203.pdf>.

144. 67 Fed. Reg. 67893-03, 2002 WL 31476627 (F.R.).

145. *See* 67 Fed. Reg. at 60728.

146. *See, e.g.,* Posadas de Puerto Rico Assoc. v. Tourism Co., 478 U.S. 328 (1986).

147. 18 U.S.C. § 1304.

148. *See* Greater New Orleans Broadcasting v. United States, 527 U.S. 195 (1999).

149. *See* 18 U.S.C. § 1307.

150. *See* Greater New Orleans Broadcasting v. United States, 527 U.S. 195 (1999).

151. *See, e.g.,* William H. Van Alstyne, *To What Extent Does the Power of Government to Determine the Boundaries and Conditions of Lawful Commerce Permit Government to Declare Who May Advertise and Who May Not?* 51 EMORY L. J. 1513 (2002); Mitchell N. Berman, *Commercial Speech and the Unconstitutional Conditions Doctrine: A Second Look at "The Greater Includes the Lesser,"* 55 VANDERBILT L. REV. 693 (2002); Martin H. Redish, *Tobacco Advertising and the First Amendment,* 81 IOWA L. REV. 589 (1996).

152. 478 U.S. 328 (1986). As a commonwealth of the United States, Puerto Rico is subject to First Amendment protections. *See id.*

153. *Id.* at 332 (citing 1948 Act).

154. *Id.*

155. *See id.*

156. *See id.* at 335–36.

157. *See id.* at 334.

158. *Id.* at 340.

159. *Id.* at 341 (quoting Brief for Appellees at 37).

160. *Id.*

161. *See id.* at 342–43.

162. *See id.* at 344.

163. *Id.* at 346–47 (footnote omitted).

164. 509 U.S. 418 (1993).

165. *See id.* at 425.

166. *Id.* at 426.

167. *See id.* at 434–35.

168. 517 U.S. 484 (1996).

169. *Id.* at 503 (citation omitted).

170. *Id.* at 509–10 (citations omitted).

171. *Id.* at 511 (footnote omitted).

172. *Id.* at 514 (citation omitted).

173. 527 U.S. 173 (1999).

174. *See id.* at 180–81.

175. *Id.* at 185–86 (citations omitted).

176. *See id.* at 187.

177. *Id.* at 190 (citations omitted).

178. *Id.* at 192 (citations omitted).

179. It should be noted that concerns about misleading speech in advertising led the National Gambling Impact Study Commission to recommend a pause in advertising and cooperative efforts at the development and adoption of "best practices" for advertising. *See* NATIONAL GAMBLING IMPACT STUDY COMMISSION REPORT 3-17–3-18 (1999).

180. *See* 44 Liquormart, Inc. v. Rhode Island, 517 U.S. 484, 497 (1996) ("[T]he First Amendment does not protect commercial speech about unlawful activities. *See Pittsburgh Press Co. v. Pittsburgh Comm'n on Human Relations,* 413 U.S. 376 (1973)").

CHAPTER 10

1. GAO, INTERNET GAMBLING: AN OVERVIEW OF THE ISSUES (December 2, 2002) (GAO-03-89).

2. *See* Kurt Eichenwald, *At PartyGaming, Everything's Wild,* N.Y TIMES, June 26, 2005. Bloomberg reports that Christiansen Capital Advisors estimate 2005 online gaming at $8.2 billion. *See Online Gambling Raises the Ante,* BLOOMBERG MARKETS, October 2005.

3. *See* Matt Richtel, *Wall Street Bets on Gambling on the Web,* N.Y. TIMES, Dec. 25, 2005 (reporting estimate from Christiansen Capital Advisors).

4. *See* Carl Blalik, *Lawyers Bid Up Value of Web-Search Ads,* WALL ST. J., April 7, 2004, at B1, c. 2. The term *casino* was sixth on the list of paid placements at $14.97, trailing "mesothelioma attorney" ($70.24), "car accident lawyer" ($50.00), "investment fraud" ($30.00), "Wisconsin mortgage" (19.00), and "conference calling" ($18.22). Though as a technical matter, *casino* might include traditional casino operations, each of the listed ads was for an online operation. As discussed subsequently, government efforts to block online casino ads on sites based in the United States call into question any subsequent estimates based on advertising rates.

5. *See* Eichenwald, *supra* note 2.

6. *See Online Gambling Raises the Ante, supra* note 2.

7. *See* Robin Kelley et al., *GAMBLING@HOME: Internet Gambling in Canada* at 2 (October 2001), available at www.cwf.ca.

8. *See id.* (estimating 1,200–1,400 sites in 2001). A Google search on April 8, 2004, using the term *online casino gambling* returned over 1.1 million Web sites, although many of those sites do not actually contain an online casino. *See also* Michael Totty, *Taming the Frontier,* WALL ST. J. (European ed.), January 31, 2003 (2002 WL-WSJE 3870150) (citing a Bear, Stearns estimate of 1,800 Internet gambling sites).

9. *See* <http://www.gamblinglicenses.com/licensesDatabase.cfm> (accessed January 17, 2006).

10. *See, e.g.,* Jodie T. Allen, *Trump's Latest Chumps,* U.S. NEWS & WORLD REP.,

April 12, 2004, at 35 ("[Trump Hotels & Casino Resorts] the profitless company struggled even to pay interest on its $1.8 billion debt, let alone make the invest-ments needed to keep up with flashy new competitors like the Borgata."); Amy Yee, *Trump Towers Above Casino Debt Issues*, FIN. TIMES, April 8, 2004, at 27 (2004 WL 75248936) ("The worn-out Taj Mahal, Trump Plaza and Trump Marina in Atlantic City, New Jersey are in urgent need of renovation. The casinos are struggling to compete with sleeker casinos like the Borgata, a [$1.1 billion] joint-venture be-tween MGM Mirage and Boyd Gaming that opened last summer.").

11. This issue is addressed in greater detail in chapter 9.

12. The World Sports Exchange, discussed later, is one example.

13. *See, e.g.,* Bambi Francisco, *Yahoo Hits Fresh 52-Week High after Q1,* April 8, 2004, at <http://www.marketwatch.com> (accessed April 14, 2004) (attributing success in part to strength in advertising, including its acquisition of Overture).

14. *See* Mylene Magdalinden, *Yahoo's Revenue Surges 39%, but Earnings Miss Expec-tations,* WALL ST. J., January 17, 2006, available at www.online.wsj.com.

15. *See, e.g.,* <http://adv.casinoblasters.com/index.php?bamse> (accessed April 12, 2004).

16. *See Casinos Bet on Gambling Addiction Web Site,* at <http://story.news.yahoo .com/news?tmpl=story&cid=573&ncid=573&e=4&u=/nm/20040412/od_nm/ casino_dc> (last visited April 12, 2004).

17. *See* Kelley et al., *supra* note 7, at 3.

18. We are aware of only one exception: Trinidad-based Casino Fortune em-ploys a software-based tool to identify problem gambling patterns to shut down ac-counts of gamblers manifesting problem behaviors. *See* Amy Eagle, *Taking Chances,* CHI. TRIB., December 15, 2004.

19. *See* <http://mb.winneronline.com/>.

20. *See* Max Drayman, *How PricewaterhouseCoopers Reviews Casino Payouts,* May 24, 2001, at <http://www.winneronline.com/articles/december2000/pwc.htm> (viewed April 12, 2004).

21. *See, e.g., Best Payout Percentages* at <http://www.winneronline.com/ bestpayouts/> (viewed April 12, 2004), showing a ranking of online casinos. It is interesting to note, however, that some of these casinos are also sponsors of the sites, which questions the independence of such listings.

22. 260 F.3d 68 (2d Cir. 2001), *cert. denied.* 536 U.S. 922 (2002).

23. Central Intelligence Agency, THE WORLD FACTBOOK, at <http://www.odci .gov/cia/publications/factbook/fields/2153.html> (accessed April 16, 2004).

24. *See id.* (accessed January 17, 2006).

25. *See* Rebecca Quick, *Entrepreneurs Roll the Dice on a New Site,* WALL ST. J., April 10, 1997, at B18 (1997 WL-WSJ 2416377).

26. *See id.*

27. *See id.*

28. *See id.*

29. *See* United States v. Cohen, 298 F.3d at 70–71.

30. *See id.* at 71.

31. United States v. Cohen, 260 F.3d at 71.

32. 18 U.S.C. § 1084(b)

33. *See* United States v. Cohen, 260 F.3d at 74–75.

34. *See id.* at 75.

35. *See id.* at 74–75.

36. *Id.* at 76. *See also* United States v. Tomeo, 459 F.2d 445, 447 (10th Cir. 1976) (finding it unlikely that Congress contemplated one-way communication in using the term *transmission*).

37. *See* Dean Starkman, *U.S. Charges 14 in Crackdown Bid on On-Line Betting,* WALL ST. J., March 5, 1998, at A8 (1998 WL-WSJ 3485072).

38. 18 U.S.C.A. § 1084(a).

39. Other aspects of the Wire Act are discussed in chapter 9.

40. Recently publicized efforts to address the problem of child pornography via the Internet, which has resulted in prosecutions of individuals based on seized credit card records from a domestic processor engaged in handling payments from offshore sites devoted to this material, suggest that prosecution efforts may be feasible where the commitment exists. *See* Cassel Bryan-Low, *Internet Transforms Child Porn into Lucrative Trade,* WALL ST. J., January 17, 2006, at A1.

41. *See, e.g.,* In re Mastercard International Inc., 313 F.3d 257, 261–62 (5th Cir. 2002).

42. *See* In re MasterCard, 132 F.Supp. 2d 468, 480 (E.D. La. 2001). *See also* Michael P. Kailus, *Do Not Bet on Unilateral Prohibition of Internet Gambling to Eliminate Cyber-Casinos,* 1999 UNIV. OF ILL. L. REV. 1045, 1060–61 (suggesting that "a plain language interpretation of [§ 1084] would seem to indicate that [it] applies only to wagering on sporting events"). However, this author also states that "a common sense interpretation" would include Internet casinos within the reach of the Wire Act. *Id.* at 1061.

43. *See* People v. World Interactive Gaming Corp., 714 N.Y.S.2d 844 (1999).

44. *See* In Re MasterCard, 132 F.Supp. 2d at 480–81; see also H. R. 4411, The Unlawful Internet Gambling Enforcement Act of 2005, which was introduced in the House on November 18, 2005 but was later referred to the Judiciary Committee where it remains as of May 19, 2006.

45. Brief of the International Financial Sector Regulatory Authority, 2002 WL 32136044 (April 12, 2002).

46. 714 N.Y.S.2d 844 (N.Y. Sup. 1999).

47. *Id.,* 714 N.Y.S.2d at 849.

48. *See id.* at 849–50.

49. *See id.* at 851.

50. 568 N.W.2d 715 (Minn. Ct. App. 1997).

51. *See id.* at 717.

52. *See, e.g.,* Thompson v. Handa-Lopez, Inc., 998 F.Supp. 738 (W.D. Tex. 1998) (finding personal jurisdiction over online casino domiciled in California in breach of contract claim brought by Texas gambler).

53. 128 F.Supp.2d 340, 347–51 (E.D. Va. 2001).

54. *See id.* at 350.

55. *See* 15 U.S.C.A. § 1125(d)(2)(A), (C).

56. *See* 15 U.S.C.A. § 1125(d)(1)(C) ("In any civil action involving the registration, trafficking, or use of a domain name under this paragraph, a court may order the forfeiture or cancellation of the domain name or the transfer of the domain name to the owner of the mark.")

57. *See* Alitalia-Linee Aeree Italiane v. Casinolitalia.com, 128 F.Supp.2d 340 (E.D. Va. 2001) 128 F.Supp.2d at 346, n. 14.

58. *See* Yahoo! Inc. v. La Ligue Contre Le Racisme Et L'Antisemitisme,— F.3d—, 2006 WL 60670 (9th Cir. 2006).

59. *See* 44 Liquormart, Inc. v. Rhode Island, 517 U.S. 484, 497 (1996), discussed in chapter 9.

60. *See* Matt Richtel, *Web Engines Plan to End Online Ads for Gambling,* N.Y. TIMES, April 5, 2004, at C1, col. 5, at <http://www.nytimes.com/2004/04/05/technology/05yahoo.html>.

61. *See* Matt Richtel, *U.S. Steps Up Push Against Online Casinos by Seizing Cash,* N.Y. TIMES, May 31, 2004, at <http://www.nytimes.com/2004/05/31/technology/31gambling.html>.

62. *See* Richtel, *supra* note 60.

63. *See* Matt Richtel, *Electronic Arts to Stop Advertising for Online Casinos on Its Website,* N.Y. TIMES, June 12, 2004, at <http://www.nytimes.com/2004/06/12/business/media/12gamble.html> (visited June 17, 2004).

64. *See generally* THOMAS P. VARTANIAN ET AL., 21ST CENTURY MONEY, BANKING & COMMERCE 57–59 (1998).

65. *See, e.g.,* <http://www.paymentonline.com/termsandconditions/> (paragraph G) (visited May 3, 2004).

66. For a more extensive account of credit-card industry practices, *see* Cura Financial Services v. Electronic Payment Exchange, Inc., 2001 WL 1334188 (Del. Ch.).

67. *See Paypal Acceptable Use Policy* (Amended November 5, 2005), available online at <http://www.paypal.com/cgi-bin/webscr?cmd=p/gen/ua/use/index_frame-outside>.

68. *See* In re Mastercard International, Inc., 313 F.3d 257 (5th Cir. 2002).

69. *See id.* at 260–61. The civil remedies provision is found at 18 U.S.C. § 1964.

70. *See id.* at 262.

71. *See id.*

72. *See id.*

73. *See id.* at 262, n.14 (citing Kan Stat. Ann. § 21-4304).

74. *See id.* at 260.

75. *See* In re Mastercard International, Inc., 132 F.Supp. 2d 468, 479 (E.D. La. 2001).

76. *See id.*

77. *See* In re Mastercard International, Inc., 313 F.3d 257, 262 (5th Cir. 2002).

78. *See id.* at 260.

79. *See id.*

80. *See, e.g.,* United States v. Kaczowski, 114 F.Supp.2d 143 (W.D.N.Y. 1999) (applying "aiding and abetting" and conspiracy theories to defendants involved in offshore gambling operations).

81. *Internet Gambling Warning,* at <http://www.ksag.org/contents/consumer/internetwarning.htm> (visited May 4, 2004).

82. *See* S. Rep. No. 108–173, 108th Cong., 1st. Sess. 2003, 2003 WL 22437220 (Leg.Hist.) at 15.

83. WTO, *United States—Measures Affecting the Cross-Border Supply of Gambling and Betting Services, Request for the Establishment of a Panel by Antigua and Barbuda,* WT/DS285/ (June 13, 2003).

84. *See* WTO, *supra* note 82, at WT/DS285/1/Add.1 (April 10, 2003) (updating request for consultations dated March 13, 2003, and entered into the record dated March 27, 2003, with a corrected annex of references to U.S. legislation).

85. *See* WTO, *United States—Measures Affecting the Cross-Border Supply of Gambling and Betting Services, Request for Preliminary Rulings by the United States of America,* WT/DS285 (October 17, 2003), at ¶¶ 3–10.

86. *Id.* at ¶ 21.

87. Comments on the United States' Request for Preliminary Rulings by Antigua and Barbuda (October 22, 2003), at ¶ 13. *See also* ¶ 12 ("It is doubtful that anyone could compose a definitive list of all United States laws and regulations that could be applied against cross-border gambling.").

88. *Id.* at ¶ 14.

89. *See* First Written Submission of the United States, November 7, 2003, at ¶ 69.

90. *See id.* at ¶¶ 69–72.

91. *See, e.g.,* AMERICAN GAMING ASSOCIATION, 2003 STATE OF THE STATES: THE AGA SURVEY OF CASINO ENTERTAINMENT 2 (2003) (comparing casino spending and attendance to other entertainment, such as zoos or major league baseball).

92. *See* Second Written Submission of the United States, January 9, 2004.

93. *Id.* at ¶ 34.

94. *See generally id.* at ¶¶ 34, 37–42.

95. *See generally id.* at ¶¶ 43–51.

96. *Id.* at ¶ 53.

97. *Id.* at ¶ 54.

98. *See id.* at ¶ 55.

99. *See id.* at ¶ 114.

100. *See id.* at ¶ 113.

101. *See* WTO, United States—Measures Affecting the Cross-Border Supply of Gambling and Betting Services (WT/DS285/R), (November 10, 2004).

102. *See, e.g.,* Scott Miller & Christina Binkley, *U.S. Ban on Web Gambling Breaks Global Trade Pacts, Says WTO,* WALL St. J., March 25, 2004, at A2. *See also* Kay Georgi & Phippe Vlaemminck, *WTO Panel Rules Against United States in Internet Gambling Case—What Does It Mean?* COUDERT BROTHERS LLP CLIENT ALERT, March 26, 2004.

103. *See id.* at ¶ 7.2–7.3.

104. *See id.* at § 6.607.

105. *See id.* at ¶ 6.535.

106. *See id.* ¶ 6.589.

107. *See id.* ¶ 6.595–6.600.

108. *See id.* ¶ 7.2–7.4.

109. *See, e.g.,* Miller and Binkley, *supra* note 102; Daniel Pruzin, *WTO Publishes Final Decision on Internet Gambling; U.S. to Appeal,* 9 BNA ELEC. COM. & L. REP. 940 (November 17, 2004).

110. *See* WTO, *United States—Measures Affecting the Cross-Border Supply of Gambling and Betting Services,* AB-2005-1 at ¶ 7 (April 7, 2005).

111. *See id.*

112. *Id.* ¶ 153.

113. *See id.*

114. *See id.* ¶ 213.

115. *See id.* ¶ 303.

116. *See id.* ¶ 310.

117. *See id.* ¶¶ 323–26.

118. *See id.* ¶¶ 360–69.

119. *See* Daniel Pruzin, *WTO Chief Appoints Arbitrator to Determine U.S. Compliance Deadline in Gambling Case,* BNA DAILY REP. FOR EXECUTIVES, July 6, 2005, at A-7.

120. *See* Matt Richtel, *An Industry That Dares Not Meet in the Country of Its Best Customers,* N.Y. TIMES, May 17, 2004, at <http://www.nytimes.com/2004/05/17/business/worldbusiness/17wager.html>.

121. *See* Eichenwald, *supra* note 2.

CHAPTER 11

1. *See* Cherokee Nation v. Georgia, 30 U.S. (Pet.) 1, 20 (1831).

2. *See* United States v. Lara, 541 U.S. 193, (2004).

3. *See id.*

4. *See id.* As the Court also pointed out, some of the federal government's powers over Indian tribes might also be rooted in preconstitutional practices, to the extent that the federal government has inherent powers rooted in its own sovereign status.

5. *See id.*

6. *Id.* (citations omitted).

7. 480 U.S. 202 (1987).

8. *See* 480 U.S. at 207 (citing 18 U.S.C. s 1162(a)).

9. *See id.* at 208.

10. *See id.* at 211.

11. *See id.* at 211.

12. *See id.* at 211. The county ordinance prohibiting card games was similarly defective, as it allowed municipalities to adopt rules that allowed card games, and two cities within the county had, in fact, done so. *See id.* at 212, n.11.

13. *See id.* at 212–14.

14. *See id.* at 214.

15. *See id.* at 217, n.20.

16. *See id.* at 217–22.

17. This concern was raised in the dissenting opinion in *Cabazon Band. See id.* at 224, 226 (Stevens, O'Connor, and Scalia, dissenting).

18. *See id.* at 222.

19. *Id.* at 227.

20. 25 U.S.C.A. § 2702.

21. *Id.* § 2710(a)(1).

22. *Id.* § 2703(6).

23. *See Id.* § 2703(7). Banked card games, in which players bet against the house, are specifically excepted from this definition. *See id.* The statute also grandfathers in certain card games in designated states that may not conform to these requirements. *See id.* at § 2703(7)(C).

24. *See id.* § 2703(7)(B)(ii). However, what constitutes a "slot machine" is a matter for litigation. *See infra.*

25. *Id.* § 2710(b)(1)(A).

26. *See id.* § 2710(b)(2).

27. 317 F.Supp.2d 128 (N.D. N.Y. 2004).

28. 125 S.Ct. 1478 (May 29, 2005).

29. Cayuga Indian Nation of New York v. Village of Union Springs, 390 F.Supp.2d 203 (N.D.N.Y. Oct 05, 2005).

30. *See id.*

31. *See* 25 U.S.C.A. § 2706.

32. 25 U.S.C.A. § 2710(b)(2)(F).

33. *See* 25 U.S.C.A. § 2710(b)(3).

34. *See id.*

35. 25 U.S.C.A. § 2710(b)(3)(D).

36. *See id.* § 2710(c). Regarding financial controls, the commission promulgated regulations in 1999 to provide minimum internal control standards for the industry. *See* 64 Fed. Reg. 590-01 (January 5, 1999).

37. *See* 25 U.S.C.A. § 2703(8).

38. *See, e.g.,* Seminole Tribe v. Florida, 517 U.S. 44, 48 (1996) (Class III is "the most heavily regulated of the three classes").

39. *See* 25 U.S.C.A. § 2710(d)(1)(B).

40. *See id.* § 2710(d)(1)(C). In some states, such as California, the constitution provides for Indian gaming pursuant to a model compact.

41. 25 U.S.C.A. § 2510(d)(3)(C).

42. Arizona Model Compact, ¶ 3(k).

43. *See* American Greyhound Racing v. Hull, 305 F.3d 1015, 1019 n. 3 (9th Cir. 2003) (citing year 2000 amendments to required provisions in compacts).

44. *See, e.g.,* Cheyenne River Sioux Tribe v. South Dakota, 3 F.3d 273, 279 (8th Cir. 1993) ("The 'such gaming' language of 25 U.S.C. § 2710(d)(1)(B) does not require the state to negotiate with respect to forms of gaming it does not presently permit."); Rumsey Indian Rancheria of Wintun Indians v. Wilson, 41 F.3d 421, 427 (9th Cir. 1994) (following 8th Circuit in *Cheyenne River Sioux*); Citizen Band Potawatomi Indian Tribe of Oklahoma v. Green, 995 F.3d 179 (10th Cir. 1993) (video lottery terminals prohibited under Oklahoma law could not be imported for use in a tribal casino).

45. *See* Dalton v. Pataki, 5 N.Y.3d 243 (2005) (holding that state constitutional constraint was preempted by IGRA, thus allowing tribal casino gambling pursuant to compact), cert. denied, 126 S.Ct. 742 (Nov. 28, 2005). The IGRA's language allowing tribal gambling where the state law permits it for "any purpose by any person, organization or entity" was a critical part of this decision. *See id.*, 5 N.Y.3d at 259.

46. *See, e.g.,* McClanahan v. State Tax Commission of Arizona, 411 U.S. 164 (1973) (Arizona could not impose state income tax on tribal member's income earned entirely from reservation sources); Moe v. Confederated Salish and Kootenai Tribes of Flathead Reservation, 425 U.S. 463 (1976) (nixing Montana state taxes on cigarette sales by tribal members on reservations and personal property taxes on motor vehicles).

47. Montana v. Blackfeet Tribe of Indians, 471 U.S. 759, 765 (1985).

48. *See* City of Sherrill v. Oneida Indian Nation, 544 U.S. 197 (2005).

49. 25 U.S.C.A. § 2510(d)(3)(D).

50. 25 U.S.C.A. § 2510(d)(7)(B)(iii)(II).

51. Model Tribal-State Gaming Compact, ¶ E, at <http://www.cgcc.ca.gov/enabling/tsc.pdf> (dated July 14, 2003) (last accessed May 21, 2004).

52. *See* In Re Indian Gaming Related Cases, 331 F.3d 1094, 1105 (9th Cir. 2003).

53. *See id.* at 1105, 1111.

54. *See id.* at 1105–6.

55. *See id.* at 1113.

56. Generic Arizona Compact ¶ 12(b), at <http://www.gm.state.az.us/compact.final.pdf> (last accessed May 21, 2004).

57. *Id.* at ¶ 3(h)(1).

58. *Id.* at ¶ 12(c); A.R.S. § 5-601.02(3).

59. *See* Model Arizona Compact ¶ 12(c); A.R.S. § 5-601.02(4).

60. *See* Veronica Rose, *Compact and Slot Agreement Amendments* (2002-R-0999), at <http://www.cga.state.ct.us/2002/olrdata/ps/rpt/2002-R-0999.htm> (visited May 24, 2004).

61. *See id.*

62. *See id.*

63. *See* In re Indian Gaming Related Cases, 331 F.3d 1094, 1114 n. 17 (9th Cir. 2003).

64. *See* Sault Ste. Marie Tribe of Chippewa Indians v. Engler, 146 F.3d 367 (6th Cir. 1998); *see also id.*, 271 F.3d 235 (6th Cir. 2001).

65. *See id.*, 146 F.3d at 373.

66. *See, e.g.*, Eric S. Lent, *Note, Are States Beating the House? The Validity of Tribal-State Revenue Sharing Under the Indian Gaming Regulatory Act*, 91 Geo. L. J. 451 (2003); Gatsby Contreras, *Exclusivity Agreements in Tribal-State Compacts: Mutual Benefit Revenue Sharing or Illegal State Taxation?* 5 J. Gender Race & Just. 487 (2002).

67. 331 F.3d 1094 (9th Cir. 2003).

68. *See id.* at 1110.

69. *Id.* at 1111.

70. *Id.* at 1113.

71. *See id.* at 1114.

72. *See id.* at 1113.

73. *Id.* at 1115.

74. *See id.* at 1115.

75. *Id.* at 1114, n.17.

76. *See* the subsequent discussion re: tribal lobbying. *See also* Melvin Claxton & Mark Puls, *Tribes Buy Clout with Casino Cash*, Det. News, December 30, 2001, at <http://www.detnews.com/specialreports/2001/chippewa/1230lead/1230lead.htm>.

77. Jan Golab, *Arnold Girds for Indian War*, American Enterprise Online (Jan./Feb. 2004), at <http://www.taemag.com/issues/articleid.17819/article_detail.asp>. As for the legal basis for these contributions, Golab further observes: "The Indian Gaming Regulatory Act of 1987 sets forth a list of specific purposes for

which tribal gaming revenues may be used. One of those is 'to promote the economic development of the tribe.' The Indians claim that campaign contributions qualify as 'promoting their economic development.' Critics cry foul." *Id.*

78. *But see* City of Sherrill v. Oneida Indian Nation, 544 U.S. 197 (2005), indicating that purchased lands formerly under state and local government control may still be subject to state and local taxing powers.

79. For an economic analysis of tax impacts, see chapter 4.

80. *See* <http://www.cabazonindians-nsn.gov/cgi-bin/ducs/display/o_content _cms/i_25> (last visited May 21, 2004).

81. *See* <http://www.fantasyspringsresort.com/> (last visited May 21, 2004).

82. *See* Mark Puls & Melvin Claxton, *Power Grab, Money Spur Tribal Expulsions,* DET. NEWS, Aug. 5, 2001, at <http://www.detnews.com/specialreports/2001/ chippewa/sunlead/sunlead.htm> (last visited May 25, 2004).

83. *See* National Indian Gaming Association, Library and Resource Center, Indian Gaming Facts, at <http://indiangaming.org/library/index.html> (last visited May 28, 2003).

84. *See* <http://www.detnews.com/specialreports/2001/chippewa/index .htm> (November 11, 2001).

85. *See, e.g.,* Pueblo of Santa Ana v. Kelly, 114 F.3d 1546, 1549 (10th Cir. 1997) (quoting from IGRA legislative history).

86. *See* 25 U.S.C. A. 2710(d)(5).

87. *See* Artichoke Joe's California Grand Casino v. Norton, 353 F.3d 712, 715 (9th Cir. 2003) (quoting district court decision).

88. *See* 25 U.S.C.A. § 2710(d)(7).

89. *See* Seminole Tribe v. Florida, 517 U.S. 44 (1996).

90. *See* 64 Fed. Reg. 17535-02 (April 12, 1999) (promulgating 25 C.F.R. § 291.1–.15).

91. 25 C.F.R. § 291.3.

92. *See id.* §§ 291.9–11.

93. *See id.* § 291.11.

94. *See* Texas v. United States, 362 F.Supp. 2d 765 (W.D. Tex. 2004).

95. *See* In re Indian Gaming Related Cases, 331 F.3d 1094, 1099 (9th Cir. 2003).

96. *See, e.g.,* United States v. Santee Sioux Tribe of Nebraska, 324 F.3d 607 (8th Cir. 2003).

97. *See generally* 25 U.S.C.A. § 2710.

98. *Id.* § 2704(4).

99. S. Rep. No. 100-446, at 8 (1988), reprinted in 1988 U.S.C.C.A.N. 3071, 3078.

100. *See* 25 U.S.C.A. § 2719(a)(1). It is possible for reservation lands to surround non-Indian lands, thus allowing expansion "within" the reservation as well as outside of it.

101. *See id.* § 2719(a)(2)(A).

102. *See id.* § 2719(a)(2)(B).

103. *Id.* § 2719(b)(1)(A).

104. 25 U.S.C.A. § 2719(b)(1)(B). Other special exceptions for tribes in Wisconsin and Florida are also included in the IGRA. *See generally* 25 U.S.C.A. §§ 2719(b)(2),(3).

105. 348 F.3d 1020 (D.C. 2003), *cert. denied,* 541 U.S. 974 (2004).

106. *See id.* at 1022.

107. *See id.* at 1022–23.

108. *Id.* at 1023.

109. *See id.* at 1024.

110. *Id.* at 1027.

111. *Id.* at 1029.

112. *See id.* at 1030.

113. *See id.* at 1031.

114. *See Appeals Court Sides with Tribe in Casino Challenge,* SAN DIEGO UNION-TRIBUNE, November 16, 2003, at <http://www.casinoman.net/Content/casino_gambling_news/gambling_news_article.asp?artid=2288> (indicating projected profits of $260 million); *Thunder Valley Deals Mostly Winning Hand,* SACRAMENTO BEE, May 30, 2004, at <http://www.casinoman.net/Content/casino_gambling_news/gambling_news_article.asp?artid=3073> (estimating between 3 and 3.7 million visitors and profits of approximately $300 million).

115. *See* Thomas J. Walsh, *Thunder Valley Casino Opens to Huge Crowds: Bumper-to-Bumper Traffic Greets Formerly Quiet Community of Lincoln,* RENO GAZETTE-JOURNAL, June 9, 2003, at <http://www.rgj.com/news/stories/html/2003/06/09/44205.php> (last visited June 6, 2004).

116. *See Thunder Valley Casino Update—Placer County, California,* at <http://www.placer.ca.gov/news/2003/6-4-03-casino-update.htm> (last visited June 6, 2004).

117. Sac and Fox Nation of Missouri v. Norton, 240 F.3d 1250, 1255 (10th Cir. 2001), *cert. denied,* 534 U.S. 1078 (2002).

118. *See id.* at 1256.

119. *See id.* at 1254.

120. *See id.*

121. *See id.* at 1255.

122. *See* City of Roseville, supra, 348 F.3d at 1029.

123. *See* Press Release, *Governor Sebelius and Attorney General Kline Take Action Against Wyandotte Casino,* September 9, 2003, at <http://www.accesskansas.org/ksag/contents/news-releases/sep09casino.html>.

124. *See* Mechoopda Indian Tribe of Chico Rancheria, California v. Schwarzenegger, 2004 WL 1103021 (unreported E.D. Cal. 2004).

125. *Id.* at n. 10 (citation omitted).

126. *See generally* Gary Rivlin, *Bet on It: The Tug of the Newfangled Slot Machines,* N.Y. TIMES MAGAZINE, May 9, 2004, at 42ff.

127. *See id.* at 74.

128. *See id.*

129. *See id.*

130. *See* 25 U.S.C.A. § 2703(7)(A)(i).

131. 327 F.3d 1019 (10th Cir. 2003), cert. denied, 540 U.S. 1218 (2004).

132. *See id.,* 327 F.3d at 1025.

133. *See id.* at 1040.

134. *Id.* at 1040–41.

135. 324 F.3d 607 (8th Cir. 2003).

136. *Id.* at 615.

137. *Id.* at 615, n.3 (citation omitted).

138. *See* Ashcroft v. Seneca-Cayuga Tribe of Oklahoma, 124 S.Ct. 1505 (March 1, 2004); United States v. Santee Sioux Tribe of Nebraska, 124 S.Ct. 1506 (March 1, 2004).

139. Brief of Amici Curiae at 1, 2004 WL 161450 (January 21, 2004).

140. *Id.* at 4.

141. *See* <http://www.nigc.gov/nigc/documents/announcements/devclass2505 .jsp> (visited January 16, 2006).

142. <http://www.opensecrets.org/industries/indus.asp?Ind=G6550> (visited January 16, 2006).

143. <http://www.opensecrets.org/industries/indus.asp?ind=D&cycle =2006> (visited January 16, 2006).

144. <http://www.opensecrets.org/industries/indus.asp?Ind=H04> (visited January 16, 2006).

145. <http://www.opensecrets.org/industries/indus.asp?Ind=N07> (visited January 16, 2006). For 2006 election-cycle contributions, the gaming industry ranks thirty-eighth among all contributing industries. *See* <http://www.opensecrets .org/industries/mems.asp>.

146. *See 2004 Election Overview: Stats at a Glance,* <http://www.opensecrets .org/overview/stats.asp?Cycle=2004> (visited January 16, 2006).

147. *See* <http://www.choctaw.org/economics/tribal_business_overview .htm> (visited January 17, 2006)

148. *See id.*

149. *See* Thomas B. Edsall, *Abramoff Allies Keeping Distance,* WASH. POST, November 8, 2004, at A23; Andrew Ferguson, *A Lobbyist's Progress,* WKLY. STAND., December 20, 2004, available at <http://www.weeklystandard.com/Content/Public/ Articles/000/000/005/022nwtca.asp?pg=2>.

150. The criminal information filed against Abramoff cites "Deprivation of

Abramoff's Clients' Right to Abramoff's Honest Services" regarding "a Native American tribal client based in Mississippi"—which could reasonably be assumed to be the Choctaws. The text of the information is available at www.citizensforethics.org/filelibrary/abramoff-info.pdf (visited January 16, 2006).

151. Press Release, *Mississippi Choctaws Respond to Abramoff Plea*, January 4, 2006, available at <http://www.choctaw.org/press_room/pr_2006_01_04.htm> (visited January 16, 2006).

152. *See* Texas v. Ysleta Del Sur Pueblo, 220 F.Supp. 2d 668 (W.D. Tex. 2001), aff'd 68 Fed. Appx. 659 (5th Cir. 2002), cert. denied, 540 U.S. 985 (2003). Ysleta Del Sur Pueblo is the formal name for the Tigua tribe.

153. *See id.*, 220 F. Supp.2d at 709–14 (order denying motion for reconsideration of modifying opinion, June 24, 2002).

154. *See id.* at 676–84 (discussing the legislative history of the restoration act).

155. *See id.* at 684–85.

156. *See* Letter from U.S. Representative Sylvestre Reyes (D-TX) to Senator Ben Nighthorse Campbell, Chairman, Indian Affairs Committee, dated September 24, 2004, available at <http://wwwc.house.gov/reyes/news_detail.asp?id=670>.

157. *See* Ferguson, *supra* note 149. The Senate Committee on Indian Affairs has released documents showing the involvement of various Texas and Louisiana tribal interests in the matter of Texas casinos. *See* <http://www.indian.senate.gov/exhibits2.pdf>. These include an e-mail dated November 12, 2001, from Abramoff associate Michael Scanlon to general counsel of the Couchattas, J. VanHorne, providing an article from the *Houston Chronicle* on November 11, 2001, as background on the litigation.

158. *See* Ferguson, *supra* note 149.

159. *Id.* (e-mail from Ralph Reed to Abramoff, November 14, 2001).

160. *See* Paul West, *Christian Rightist Seeks Georgia Office*, SAN FRAN. CHRON., March 27, 2005, available at www.sfgate.com.

161. *See* Ferguson, *supra* note 149. One open question about such a plan would be whether the tribe would have an insurable interest in older tribal members. It is easy to envision public policy objections, not to mention moral objections, to such a scheme.

162. *See Operation Open Doors*, WASH. POST, December 3, 2004, at A26, available at <http://www.washingtonpost.com/wp-dyn/articles/A30123-2004Dec2.html>.

163. *See GOP Congressman Latest Casualty in Abramoff Scandal*, at <http://indianz.com/News/2006/012026.asp>.

164. *See* United States Senate Committee on Indian Affairs, Oversight Hearing on Lobbying Practices, Exhibits Released to the Public November 17, 2004, available at <http://www.indian.senate.gov/2005hrgs/111705hrg/111705exhibits.pdf> (e-mail dated January 22, 2002).

165. *See id.* ("Contact Information for guests of September 24, 2001 dinner party" hosted by CREA).

166. *See id.* (various e-mails).

167. *How Abramoff Spread the Wealth,* WASH. POST, December 12, 2005, available at <http://www.washingtonpost.com/wp-dyn/content/graphic/2005/12/12/GR2005121200286.html>.

CHAPTER 12

1. *See* National Council on Problem Gambling, *Problem Gambling Resource and Fact Sheet* at <http://www.ncpgambling.org/media/pdf/eapa_flyer.pdf> (visited June 3, 2005).

2. See chapter 5.

3. *See* Earl L. Grinols & David B. Mustard, CASINOS, CRIME, AND COMMUNITY COSTS 88 REVIEW OF ECONOMICS AND STATISTICS 28 (February 2006), discussed in chapter 5.

4. *See* United States Department of Health and Human Services, Office of Child Support Enforcement, Table 11: Total Amount of Arrearages Due FY 2003, available at <http://www.acf.hhs.gov/programs/cse/pubs/2004/reports/preliminary_data/table_11.html> (accessed June 3, 2005).

5. Professor Grinols chronicles many of these reports in his recent book, GAMBLING IN AMERICA 146–66 (2004).

6. *See generally* GAO, IMPACT OF GAMBLING: ECONOMIC EFFECTS MORE MEASURABLE THAN SOCIAL EFFECTS (GGD-00-78, April 27, 2000), available at <http://www.gao.gov/new.items/gg00078.pdf>.

7. *See* <http://www.keepthemoneyinnebraska.com/> (visited June 4, 2005).

8. *See* <http://www.gamblingwiththegoodlife.com/> (visited June 4, 2005).

9. *See id.*

10. *See* www.keepthemoneyinnebraska.com (visited June 4, 2005) (emphasis added).

11. *See* Robynn Tysver, *Another Try at Casinos Eyed,* OMAHA WORLD-HERALD, January 17, 2006, at 1.

12. Florida Stat. Ann. § 100.371(a)(6).

13. Advisory Opinion to the Attorney General re Authorizes [*sic*] Miami-Dade & Broward County Voters to Approve Slot Machines in Parimutuel Facilities, 880 So.2d 689 (Fla. 2004).

14. *See* Official General Election Ballot, Miami-Dade County, November 2, 2004, at <http://elections.metro-dade.com/mdgen-eng.html> (accessed November 24, 2004).

15. *See* Amy Sherman, *Courts Now Get a Spin at the Slots,* MIAMI HERALD, May 25, 2005, at A1 (2005 WLNR 8244850).

16. 2004 Pa. Legis. Serv. Act 2004-71 (H.B. 2330) (PURDON'S) (approved July 4, 2004).

17. *See* David Nitkin, *Gambling Industry Puts Their Money on State Lobbyists,* BALT. SUN, June 1, 2005, at 2B (2005 WLNR 8671813).

18. *See id.*

19. *See Safe Bet,* BALT. SUN, June 9, 2005, at 14A (2005 WLNR 9156122).

20. *See* Donald Wittkowski, *Trump Hotels Postpones Emergence from Bankruptcy,* PRESS ATL. CITY, May 13, 2005, at <http://pressofatlanticcity.com> (accessed May 31, 2005).

21. *See* David Littlejohn, *Steve Wynn's $2.7 Billion Gamble,* WALL ST. J., May 17, 2005, at D10.

22. See chapter 2.

23. *See* John Curran , *New Jersey Gamblers Prefer LV, Study Says,* LAS VEGAS REV.-J., May 26, 2005, at <http//www.reviewjournal.com/lvrj_home/2005/May-26-Thu -2005/business/1885362.html>.

24. See chapter 4.

25. As discussed in chapter 11, tribal and commercial casino interests are both involved in political spending. *See also* Campbell Lynn, *$9.6 Million Contributed in Illinois in 10 Years,* DES MOINES REG., May 30, 2004 (2004 WL 74844624).

26. Iowa Acts, House File 2302, section 61.

27. *See Request for Proposals for a Study of the Socioeconomic Impact of Gambling on Iowans,* at <http://www.legis.state.ia.us/Contracts>.

28. *See* William Petroski, *Per Mar Withdraws from Iowa Gambling Study,* DES MOINES REG., October 22, 2004, at B1 (2004 WL 90800014); *see also* William Petroski, *Gambling Study Firm Has Ties to Casinos,* DES MOINES REG., October 19, 2004, at A1 (2004 WL 90799696); *State Should Walk Away,* DES MOINES REG., October 20, 2004, at A16 (2004 WL 90799026); William Petroski, *Gaming Critic Fears Study Will Be Biased,* DES MOINES REG., October 11, 2004, at B1 (2004 WL 90799242).

29. *See* Petroski, *Gambling Study Firm, id.*

30. *See* William Petroski, *State Approves Expansion of Casino in Council Bluffs,* DES MOINES REG., November 19, 2004, at B8 (2004 WL 100489586).

31. *See* Joel J. Smith, *Compulsive Gamblers Triple at Detroit Casinos,* DET. NEWS, October 14, 2004.

32. *See* Amy Eagle, *Taking Chances,* CHI. TRIB., December 15, 2004.

33. The Justice Department's recent decision to reduce the claim for punitive damages against the tobacco industry from more than $130 million to only $10 million further reinforces the view that political decisions can change the fortunes of an industry. *See* Eric Lichtblau, *Political Leanings Were Always Factor in Tobacco Suit,* N.Y. TIMES, June 19, 2005, at 1.

34. 379 F.3d 654 (9th Cir. 2004).

35. *Id.* at 663.

36. *See id.* at 660.

37. *See id.* at 661.

38. *See id.* at 664.

39. *Id.* at 665.

40. *Id.*

41. *See id.* at 665–66.

42. *See id.* at 666–67.

43. Liz Benston & Cy Ryan, *Gaming Industry Wins Key Ruling in Lawsuit*, LAS VEGAS SUN, August 11, 2004, at <http://www.lasvegassun.com/sunbin/stories/gaming/2994/aug/11/517321932.html>.

44. 261 Mich. App. 534, 683 N.W.2d 200 (2004).

45. 320 F.3d 729 (7th Cir. 2003).

46. *Id.* at 730.

47. *Id.* at 732. The court also cited Hakimoglu v. Trump Taj Mahal, 70 F.3d 291 (3d Cir. 1995), a case arising out of New Jersey in which the Third Circuit refused to create a private cause of action where a gambler suffered gaming losses while intoxicated.

48. *See id.* at 732–33.

49. *See, e.g.,* John Warren Kindt, *The Costs of Addicted Gamblers: Should the States Initiate Mega-Lawsuits Similar to the Tobacco Cases?* 22 MANAGERIAL & DECISION ECON. 17 (2001); John Warren Kindt, *Subpoenaing Information from the Gambling Industry: Will the Discovery Process in Civil Lawsuits Reveal Hidden Violations Including the Racketeer Influenced and Corrupt Organizations Act?* 82 OREGON L. REV. 221 (2003).

50. *See* THE DEVELOPMENT OF THE LAW OF GAMBLING: 1776–1976 at 416, n.8 (1977), commissioned by the National Institute of Law Enforcement and Criminal Justice and the Law Enforcement Assistance Administration of the United States Department of Justice (citing Act of March 5, 1877, ch. 103, Nev. Laws 173).

51. *See id.*

52. *See, e.g.,* Narragansett Indian Tribe v. National Indian Gaming Com'n, 158 F.3d 1335, 1340 (D.C. 1998), in which neither the parties nor the court was willing to treat gambling as a fundamental right.

53. *See id.*

54. See chapter 5.

55. *See* 11 U.S.C. § 525(a).

56. *See* In re Christmas, 102 B.R. 44 (D. Md. 1989) (quoting H.R.Rep. No. 95-595, 95th Cong., 1st Sess., *reprinted in* 1978 U.S.Code Cong. & Admin.News 5963, 6126).

57. *See id.* at 459.

58. *See* 11 U.S.C. § 707 (effective October 17, 2005).

59. *See* Joseph M. Kelly, *Compulsive Gambling in Britain*, 4 J. GAMBLING. BEHAV. 291 (1988).

60. Neil Humphrey, *Rich Island, Poor Island*, TODAY, Marcy 27, 2004, at <http://www.wildsingapore.com/sos/media/040327-1.htm> (last visited June 27, 2005).

61. *See* Chad Skelton, *Knowing When to Fold 'Em: Problem Gamblers I—The Nether-lands Has a Solution,* VANCOUVER SUN, November 20, 2004.

62. See chapter 8.

63. I. Nelson Rose, *Gambling and the Law—Update 1993,* 15 HASTING COMM./ENT. J. 93, 104 (1992).

64. *See id.*

INDEX

Sins of the Son

By

Thomas Werner

This Book Is Dedicated

To The Reader

Chapter 1

I AM ORDINARY. I AM plain, unremarkable, unexceptional, nondescript. I am characterless. I wouldn't know these facts without a therapist, Molly Monahan, L.M.S.W., L.M.F.T., L.P.C., who assigns me this task in our first session: "Write your life story in two pages or less," she says. "Take the remainder of the session. Don't think too much. Include the worst thing you've ever done. If that's too painful to share now, write it down, black it out, and we'll tease it out over future sessions."

I find this task easy to accomplish. This is what I write, blue (always blue) pen in hand:

> My mother, Merry, was born of Swedish immigrants amazed she wasn't blonde and buxom like her contemporaries. She passed her thin, mouse-brown hair and blazing blue eyes to me. She didn't pass to me her bullying nature. I have yet to discover if she passed to me her schizoaffective disorder, which sparked her violent outburst wherein she disfigured my father and his lover, triggering her confinement at Walter P. Reuther Psychiatric Hospital.
>
> My father, Samuel, was born of French immigrants in Michigan. With me, Dad shared his thin nose, thick eyebrows, and staunch Catholicism (which failed to survive in me beyond youth). He didn't share with me (genetically)

his cross-dressing or his polyamorous affection for men and women alike.

Both parents gifted my name. Dad gifted my last name, Delacroix, pronunciation dependent upon the pronouncer. I've heard "Day-la-Croy" as often as "Day-la-Cwah." I never issue corrections. Mom provided my first name, Asher.

My parents ensured that I was born in 1976 in a hospital draped in red, white and blue to celebrate the American Bicentennial, guaranteeing my life as an American, a life of binge-drinking, swearing, and a handful of overnights in jail.

During my 27th year, I lived in an apartment with 12 roommates, including my father and Marlena Magpie, a visual artist who became my ex-fiancée. Also living there was Jay (not one of the 12), who accomplished something almost no other did—Jay made me think. Jay's residence ended with ▮▮▮▮▮▮▮▮▮▮▮▮▮, spurring the exodus of all 12 others.

As for my personality: confused, unreliable, wheedling, nervous, doubtful, plagiaristic, dangerous. Those are my good qualities. I would think higher of myself if I hadn't ▮▮▮▮▮▮▮▮▮▮▮▮▮▮▮▮▮▮▮▮▮▮▮▮▮▮▮▮▮▮▮▮▮▮▮▮ ▮▮▮▮▮▮▮▮▮▮. Then again, if not for me having ▮▮▮▮▮▮▮▮▮▮▮▮▮▮▮▮▮▮▮▮▮▮▮▮▮▮▮▮▮▮▮▮▮▮▮▮ ▮▮▮▮▮▮▮▮, I'd have little to share in these sessions.

There it is, simple as it comes, in fewer than the two pages requested.

Upon reading this missive, Ms. Monahan notes my over-reliance on lineage, how I describe myself in terms of others, as if my most notable characteristics are that I'm a son and was a roommate or lover. In notes I later purloin, Ms. Monahan writes:

Asher talks so much about others that everything about himself remains subtext. Asher is ashamed to reveal any

substance of himself. Asher blames his actions on heritage, familial and as an American. Asher believes he has done nothing of his own accord.

Re-reading her assessment—Jesus, Ms. Monahan has a point. I've done so little of my own accord that I'm not the protagonist of my autobiography.

It would take many more pages to detail things I've not done, a list distinguishing me from all great literary characters. The only characteristic I share with these characters is that I haven't fulfilled my full potential. Indeed, I've no idea what my full potential is.

Thank God, then, that this isn't a chronicle of Asher, but is instead the story of a man I met at Theo's—a college bar I was too old to comfortably enter and too stunted to voluntarily leave. The words of the man barely came through my alcoholic haze. "They got that shit all wrong."

I formed a mushy syllable that must have sounded like the word I intended: "What?"

"*The* fucking *Bible*, man," he replied, slapping a sticky arm around my shoulders.

"Oh," I said. "Right."

"I mean, shit." He leaned in, his breath steaming my nose and watering my eyes. "Excuse my language. I shouldn't talk in expletives."

"Don't fucking worry about it, man." I adopted his phrasing as easily as I slobbered down beer. I noted his long hair, scraggly beard, and holey clothes. "What are you? A fucking preacher?"

He chugged at his full bottle, which I would have sworn had been dry a moment before. "More like a prophet," he said.

"Making profit?" I asked. "Then what's with the nappy duds?" When drinking, my tact went, with dignity, the way of the dodo.

"Prof-*ET*," he emphasized.

"Oh," I said, and drank. "Huh!" I said, and drank.

"I've been sent by—"

A waitress—vibrant, daunting, tray full of drinks—slipped behind me. Distracted by her intoxicants, I leaned back to get a better look. A clatter of

plastic, the shatter of glass, and a shout of "Hey!" obscured the man's conclusion. Before I could grunt a reply, my stool was ripped from beneath me. I fell, my chin hit the bar, and I saw no more.

I awoke (cement cold, hard, unforgiving against my back) to a hand smacking my jaw. My eyes struggled open, revealing nothing. "I can't see," I shouted. The hand stopped working my cheek as calloused thumbs pressed into my eyes until the pressure threatened to mash my eyeballs into jelly. I'm pretty sure I screamed some more.

A low tone eclipsed my screams. A chant. I held onto it, or, perhaps, it held onto me. Then the air was silent, my head free of pressure. My eyes opened to reveal clarity. I was blind, but now I see.

The Mud and The Blood and The Beer

By

Asher Delacroix

WANT? WHAT DO I WANT? What kind of question is that? Coming from you, laughable. You know my wants are all over the place. You made me this way.

I want to fit in, not be rebellious, anti-system, on fucking edge. I want to stay out of trouble, in a job, out of bars, in society, out of my own head. I want to take back every punch I've punched, every kick I've kicked, every gouge I've gouged. I want to retract the knife with which I stabbed my father. I want to not have to try so hard to be sane.

I want closure.

I want to not look like old-age Johnny Cash, as I have since I was born. I want muscles crafted in fitness clubs, not prison yards. I want fewer tattoos. I want my creases to indicate laughter, not scowls. I want my teeth to rip into an apple without gum and jaw pain. I want an end to hypertension, a stop to tinnitus. I want the shattered shards of that bottle to not have half-blinded me. I want to be free of scars. I want hands bereft of stains of mud and blood and beer.

I want to find the remote control. Stupid TV's been stuck on The Weather Channel for days. Why'd you give me a TV with no dials or buttons and hide my remote? I want pay channels, too.

I want no more rejection.

I want to rid myself of excess. To discard years of newspaper clippings, throw away decades of ketchup packets from fast food joints, shred the 27

notebooks of youthful drawings of all manner of war machines. I want to rid myself of my past.

I want no more pain.

I want to sleep on the twin mattress in my apartment, not at a by-the-hour motel, not on a stranger's floor, not beneath an alleyway fire escape. I want my sleep to be dreamless, for the demons in my head to leave me at least when I sleep. I want to awaken on weekdays to an alarm clock, and on the weekends to birds chirping—without hating those goddamned birds.

I want the sun to warm me without burning. I want trees to provide shade and oxygen, not sticky sap, dead leaves, broken limbs. I want nature to comfort and console me, not challenge and confound me.

I want no more doubt.

I want proud offspring. I want to look forward to a 50th wedding anniversary, not back on 4 divorces. I want zoo trips, amusement park excursions, worldwide vacations. I want to not have caused three suicides.

I want to not feel.

I want to have worked harder, to have been more loyal. I want to not have been fired from 2 jobs and quit 6 more. I want a gold Rolex knock-off at retirement. I want to stay alive to retirement age. I want to survive.

I want to be happy. I want to never again press the knife blade into my wrists and will myself to proceed. I want an end to failure.

I want to be trustworthy.

I want to be witty, to bring laughter. I want to walk into a party and have all eyes on me—not recoiling, but welcoming. I want conversation. I want to enjoy music again.

I want no more heartache.

I want to sit in that library. I want to hear the librarian, female, sexy, glasses, hush some kids. I want to watch as she reaches up to a high shelf without berating her about her physical appearance—flaunted cleavage, ass for days. I want to not rape, not with my glare, my words, otherwise. I want to leave her lover unharmed, too.

I want to breathe.

I want to be couth, to stop swearing. I want to not jerk off my goddamn

cock so fucking much. I want to go back to church, sing from the hymnal, raise my joyful voice as I sit, stand, kneel in the right order. I want faith. I want to mean it when I pray.

I want no more abandonment.

I want to be a hero. To intervene in crime, stop fights, prevent murder. I want to save babies.

I want to embrace good.

I want a destination without destiny. I want to Sinatra this shit up—do it My Way. I want to live for myself, not die for others. I want my decisions to dictate the future. I want to be more Marty McFly, less Oedipus.

I want to not want.

I want a Brooks Brothers sport coat, not a torn leather jacket. I want tranquil flip flops, not fire-emblazoned boots; relaxed-fit board shorts, not balls-tight Wranglers. I want more Jersey Boys, less Grease.

I want an end to compulsion.

I want to be eulogized. I want pallbearers. I want a universally understood epitaph. I want to be a symbol of good, not an object lesson in fucked up morality.

I want cleanliness.

I want Godliness.

And you, motherfucker, won't let me have any of that. You prefer me the way you made me—violent outbursts, mud and blood and beer, all of it. You sit there, pen in hand (blue, always blue) and ask yourself what you want— yeah, that's right, I know you're asking yourself—not me.

You don't care what I want. I want to raise my right arm. You make me raise my left leg instead. I want to pee indoors, in a toilet, flush it away—you splash my piss into a dishwasher, leave it there, stinking and moldering. I want to learn to fly, but you'd crash my plane. You are my dictator, my fate. You are the crafter of my world. You are the architect of my demise.

Want? What do I want? Goddamn you for that question. Right to Hell.

Fuck it. Right now, all I want is to watch TV. If only I knew where you hid the remote control.

Chapter 2

THERE'S A FOUL, SWEET SMELL, the smell of decay and rot. The smell of the hospital in which my mother had a fist-size tumor removed from her intestine, and of the tumor itself, which Mom hoarded away from the hospital in a jar.

That smell awoke me the morning after Theo's. My eyes blurred open. I wasn't sure how I got back to my apartment, but I was sure I was there—who else could have such a dwelling? More hut than apartment—walls like mud bricks, ceiling like layers of thatch—a room so primal its twin could be languishing in an African plain.

Ascertaining that the room was mine, I sought the source of the smell. I found half the culprit right away: fresh vomit. The remaining smell flowed from another room. I arose, relieved to find myself clothed, and stumbled through the door, crossing from matted carpet to scuffed wood. I pushed myself along the wall, sliding into the room forming the rest of the apartment, right and left sides separated by a half-wall, right side a functional living room, left side an open area with small kitchenette where stood the stranger from the bar, right hand flicking a pan so that scrambled eggs turned in mid-air and splashed back into sizzling oil, left hand pouring water from a tea kettle into a mug over crystals of instant coffee. When the cup was full, he replaced it with another without righting the kettle or spilling a drop.

"Breakfast," he said. "It's Noon-thirty, but it's never too late for breakfast, given *your* condition."

"What condition?" I had more questions, but that's all I could get out, given my condition.

The man answered with another flick of the pan. Eggs rose in the air, spun and splatted down. My stomach echoed with its own rise, spin and splat.

"*That* condition."

"Right," I answered.

"Almost done. Give me 33 seconds."

I couldn't count past seven before I had to begin again. After two more restarts, I decided to take him at his word. By that time, he'd split the eggs between two plates on the coffee table. In two more seconds, mugs rested on the table, and the man sat, wooden spoon in hand.

I half-stood, half-leaned against the half-wall. "Getting cold." Eggs sprayed from his lips with each consonant. "Better for your condition if they're hot."

I slumped into a chair, plunged a fork into the eggs, and lifted them to my mouth. Two forks later, I began to wonder at the man across from me. "What's your name?"

"Jay."

"I'm Asher. Jay? The letter or the bird?"

"Neither. My name." Jay finished his eggs. "My turn," he said. "What do you know about cabinets?"

"Wait…cabi…what?"

"These," he pointed to the kitchen, "are shit. Off-the-rack jobs. Complex must've got them from some supplier of prefab models. MDF—medium density fiberboard. That stuff is shit, wax, resin, formaldehyde, smushed under high temperatures and pressures to create a sort-of-wood, a composite of sawdust, extra crap, and glue, crammed together between plastic veneer. Tenth the price of wood, with tenth the lifespan."

Although I'd have sworn his plate was empty, Jay scooped more eggs.

"Now," he continued, "higher quality cabinets are constructed with wood. Like cedar. Decent cabinets. Straight grain, smells pretty. Though soft, it can

take a punishment without rotting. Or fir. Straight, pronounced grain. Prefers its reddish tint, doesn't take well to stain. Strong for softwood. Readily available.

"Pine," Jay barely paused for a breath, "great for woodworking. Easily cut, carved, shaped. Takes stain well.

"Then hardwoods. More variety in colors, textures, grain patterns. Flashy. More expensive than softwoods. Rarer, too, due to deforestation and disease. Like ash. Harder and harder to find—great when you can. Durable, easy to work with, takes to stain.

"Birch is more common. Found everywhere. Easy to work with. Difficult to stain. Tends to hold its color.

"Mahogany—a favorite. Deep red, straight grain, medium texture. Brilliant with a coat of oil. Not found in any sustainable forest—the most expensive hardwood.

"Oak's the most popular cabinet wood. Easy to work with. Resistant to moisture, attractive figure.

"Poplar's super cheap, but useful. I've never seen a poplar cabinet—ugly and doesn't take stain. But it's sturdy, stable, useful. Used a lot in drawers.

"Walnut's expensive but dresses up nice. More used for accents and inlays. Walnuts are hardy, resourceful. They poison the land around them, ensuring they get all the Earth's benefits to the exclusion of other plants."

Jay consumed three more spoons of eggs before he broke the silence. "So, Asher, what kind of cabinet are you?"

I blinked. "What?"

"Cabinet. What'd be your wood? You're not likely MDF. You don't strike me as *that* full of shit. And I don't think you're that cheaply made."

"Thanks."

"Besides, I doubt you've been under that much pressure."

"Umm."

"No. You're some kind of wood. Hard or soft? Are you readily available? Useful? Decorative? Easy to mold and shape?"

"Soft." I spat the answer to put an end to the questions pounding at my brain like so much hangover blood. Even so, I knew I was correct.

"Soft. I agree. But which? Are you flashy? Stable? Can you take a punishment? Or are you prone to rot? Susceptible to maladies?"

All I could see through the pounding of bloody questions was the redbud tree replanted in the backyard of my boyhood home by my mother. Although beautiful, Mom couldn't abide it in the front yard. She dug down beneath the tree, clearing the root ball after days of labor. She shouldered the tree to a square of dead grass in the back yard, out of reach of the sun and out of sight of neighboring windows. There, she dug down again, plunging the shovel, lifting the dirt and tossing it until she had a hole big enough to reclaim the tree's roots. Somehow the tree endured the procedure, thriving in the dark patch of lawn.

Years later, I asked Mom what that tree had done to her. Why had she gone through so much to dig it up, and why had she resolved to do even more in retaining it where nobody could see it?

"That tree is a great shame," she responded. "It should never be visible to any but those who could take a lesson from it, those able to shoulder the burden of that tree. Promise me, Asher, that the tree will remain hidden away."

Since there was no chance of me digging out and replanting the tree after witnessing Mom's exertions, I consented.

"Promise me something else," she continued.

I listened.

"Find the lesson of the redbud tree. Learn it. Heed it."

I consented again. That promise, though, I failed to keep. I knew not the lesson of the redbud tree. Over time, the tree faded from memory.

Yet, with Jay rapid-fire questioning me about my wooden characteristics, all I could envision was the secret, shameful tree. The tree's name tried to push out of my mouth. Before I could label myself with the hidden shame of the redbud tree, I spat another answer. "Pine," I said.

Jay searched me. Hours dripped by in the few seconds of his silent search. My heart raced. A smile spread as he spoke again. "I can see that."

My breaths came heavy as my heart calmed. "Well," I said, "what kind of cabinet are you?"

"Me?" he asked. "I'm no cabinet. I'm a man."

My eyes widened and jaw dropped. Jay wouldn't let me voice my budding outrage.

"How's your jaw?" he asked.

"My jaw?"

"You whacked it pretty good last night."

"Whacked it?"

"You leaned back into a waitress. Tray went flying. Pitcher of beer all over this crazy 'roid freak, shaved head, goatee. Dude yanked your stool out. You dropped."

This struck a bell. My jaw, teeth and tongue ached with memory.

"Bouncer saw the size difference between you on the floor and the other guy huffing with rage and blamed you for the mess. Grabbed you by the collar and chucked you through the front door. You landed with a splat on the sidewalk."

The ache of memory spread to my knees and left shoulder.

"I followed you out, slapped the crap out of you, woke you up enough to find out where you live. It was nice of you to agree to let me stay here. Thanks for that."

"Agree?"

"Not the best apartment, but it beats the Hell out of where I was."

"Hmmm."

"So here I am, and here we are." Jay retreated to the kitchen, emerged with another panful of sloppy yellow chunks. "More eggs?"

Statement of Cassie James [excerpt]

...GODDAMNED LAND I CAME FROM—dry, hard, cracked, barren. I had no parents, only the land—reared me better than any parent could. People take after their parents. I take after that land. That land made me crusty, hard, desolate. That land was Godless.

Here's what I mean: Jesus needed water. Jesus walked on water. Jesus made wine but needed water first—couldn't do nothin' without water. That's why dry land is Godless land.

That Godless land made me in its own image: Dry. Dusty. Desolate. It hardened me more than any parent could. Then that land rejected me, cast me aside, made me as Godless as it was.

Woody Guthrie sang that "this" land is your land, and "this" land is my land—but "that" land don't belong to nobody. "That" land is a creature all its own—a dead creature. Or undead. Like me.

For what am I if not deadened, yet alive—a creature back from the dead? Like that land, nothing could grow on me—not unless I figured out how to water myself, make myself lush, verdant.

This all may seem like it doesn't answer your questions. But it does. You asked me how it was I came to be in that apartment, and why'd I stay.

Why? Because of that land that made me Godless. If you take God away, what's left? What's to live for? What sustains anything? The only answer that makes sense is "Man."

That's Man as a proper pronoun, not a gender. That pronoun (being *my* pronoun), can represent whatever I want. Man the way I mean Man is "human" without the "hue." No deviation from one another, all the same, all equal. Man also includes woman—only without the "woe"—"woe," that is, forced upon woman by lower-case-m man. Upper-case-M Man is everyone. Man is a driving force. If not God, then Man was the true creator, the true doer. Being dedicated to Man, I sought out enclaves of Man wherever I could.

That apartment represented the best enclave of Man I'd experienced since I don't know when. Wandering the wilderness as I did, I had no Man to inspire—and no Man to inspire me.

So, upon learning of the enclave of Man in this apartment, I moved in. Wasn't easy. Looking at some of those residents, it was difficult to convince myself that I could do any good there. Then there was the apartment's owner—the landowner, I mean—goddamn.

But I realized the more difficult Man was to influence, the more that Man needed influence. So, I rolled in.

This enclave of Man was attempting something intriguing. So, I stayed.

Right up until the end.

Which brings me to your questions about what happened at the end, and after the end happened. As to those questions, there are things that you need to realize about Asher and that landowner…

Chapter 3

I'VE NEVER BEEN A TRUE writer, although I've often tried to be. I've written many unpublished short stories and quarter-novels, each resulting in mere spring cleaning, sweeping ideas out of my head, dumping them onto paper.

If I ever come to the end of this tome, it'll be the first book I've finished. I'll have no idea how. My "process"—scattered, non-linear, terrible. Events and chapters out of order. Notes everywhere. Words misspelled or missing. Sentence fragments. Unrecognizable setting. Shallow characterization. Poor physical descriptions. Overwrought lists. Hastily written paragraphs later deleted. No overarching style. Unreliable point of view.

For a guy claiming this isn't my story, so much talk about myself, my process, my take. Not getting to the point. Avoidance. Fear of rejection, of failure, of getting caught in lies, exaggerations, justifications. Words designed to make me the hero, when heroism is a concept far distant.

I can't guarantee that everything in this account happened or happened in the order depicted. For example, I don't remember in detail the order my roommates moved into my apartment. So, when I say that Ed King was the second (after Jay) to move into my apartment, you're right to question. For the sake of moving on, though:

Ed King was the second (after Jay) to move into my apartment. I'd known Ed since childhood. Ancient time. Before manhood, before the need for cocky confidence, before committed relationships and fleeting lovers, before

bloody fistfights, before substance-induced blackouts, before quiet death of imagination.

Despite all changes accompanying adulthood, Ed remained the same from the first day we met to when he moved into my apartment. As surprised as I was to discover Ed there, his lack of change was unsurprising. Ed had done the bulk of his growing before he reached 9, when he arrived in my classroom and assumed the desk in front of mine. Small for his age, his growth was stunted by the early onset of Charcot Joint Disease in both ankles. The mammoth glasses he wore due to legal blindness enlarged his eyes to amazed toddler proportions. He drowned in his shirts and pants, clothes purchased by Ed's youthful mother Jo, who could've been his elder sister, for whom we, even at age 9, sexually longed.

Jo's intent for the clothes: disguise. To Jo, Ed had history to hide—not Ed's fault. Ed didn't know Larry, the father who abandoned him. Ed didn't even know he had a father until our classmate Tyrese told him. We believed Tyrese. How could we not? Through his syntax, style, phrasing, Tyrese gave every appearance of being a genius. Or an oracle. When Tyrese said something was or would become true, we discovered the truth or future truth of that something. Such were Tyrese's powers of prognostication.

So, when Tyrese told Ed that Ed had a father, we believed Tyrese. Ed himself didn't express belief *or* disbelief, maintaining his resignation. All he said was "Okay." Then blank, silent acceptance of his fated father.

I don't know if Ed's resignation fueled our meanness, or our meanness fueled his resignation. Either way, we thrilled in putting Ed down. It became a contest, a perverse bet between us, Ed's classmates, to see who could first hurt Ed.

One of us started by nicknaming Ed "Pathos" after the sound of his rasping gasps, accentuated by the pursing of his lips, when he needed his inhaler.

Another of us turned Ed's name into a verb. Tommy gets caught trying to kiss Amy: Tommy edkings. Jenny fucked up an answer when called on: Jenny edkinged. Asher is getting nailed in the face during dodgeball: Asher is edkinging. Amber will get grounded for not completing homework: Amber will edking.

Yet another of us uttered habitual loud references to Jo's motherly sex appeal. Every bit of Jo was fair game. The crueler the fantasy, the better.

Still another instructed the group on proper epithets to use against a child who, abandoned by his father, had a lifelong series of violent, grotesque dad-figures. Popular insults: "Bastard." "Accident." "Motherfucker."

Another made repeated menacing references to Jo's history of suicide attempts by drink and pill.

Despite all efforts, Ed remained devoted to resignation. He accepted each insult, shove, destruction of personal property as fated. Never did the veins in his neck and temples pulse with blood pressured by stress. Never a rejoinder navigated his vocal cords. Never a tear passed his ducts. Never a pained snuffle traversed his nostrils. Never did red grace his cheeks. Never did tremors vibrate his speech.

Getting no rise from Ed, you'd think we'd give up. You're wrong. Insults yielded to physical violence. Bruises appeared. Broken glasses, taped together, broken again. Clothes stained, ripped, publicly removed. Homework destroyed. Schoolbooks disappeared, shoes likewise. Lunch removed from lunchbox, spat upon, replaced, lunchbox peed in. "Motherfucker" gouged into desktop. Pens broken open, contents spilled on notebooks. Library card stolen, books checked out in Ed's name pitched into dumpster. Calculator cracked open, electronic guts spilled out. Bathroom door thrown open while Ed stood peeing, pants and underwear at shoe level. Polaroid taken of same taped to blackboard.

Throughout all, Ed's resignation remained resolute. He neither retreated from nor advanced toward us. His countenance remained calm, spare, economical, concise. Ed King was unflappable.

Recalling Ed's resignation, although it was a surprise to find Ed taking a bath in my apartment, it was no surprise that Ed's expression was the same as it ever was.

"Ed?"

"Hi, Asher."

"Ed?"

"You're surprised to see me."

"Yeah." My surprise went beyond the visual of Ed in my tub, floating naked in my water. I was also surprised that Ed recognized me. Ed hadn't seen me since he and Jo left the school district. Despite my changes since then—physical, intellectual, emotional—Ed knew me. I wondered if he could see into the bathtub of my soul, see child-me floating therein. I shuddered. "You aren't surprised to see me," I continued.

"True."

I grew as flustered as Ed remained unaffected by our reacquaintance. I wondered if, of the two of us, I was the naked one. The remainder of our conversation flowed with the patter of a play with minimal stage direction.

ASHER: Why are you here?

ED: I met the other guy.

ASHER: Other guy?

ED: Beard, long hair. Smells like sand.

ASHER: Sand?

ED: I met him.

ASHER: You met Jay?

ED: Outside the cinema after the matinee. He told me I was coming with him. He was right.

ASHER: You're bathing.

ED: Had to stop to grab my suitcase.

ASHER: In my bathroom.

ED: No, my suitcase isn't in the bathroom.

ASHER: *My* bathroom.

ED: My suitcase is in my part of the bedroom.

ASHER: Your part of the bedroom.

ED: The part he gave me. Don't worry, I made space.

ASHER: Worry?

ED: I don't think there's too much dust and mold. I've got extra cartridges for my inhaler.

ASHER: That's…good?

ED: Fortuitous meeting him when I needed a place, and this, my new place, being yours.

ASHER: Quite the coincidence.

ED: No such thing.

ASHER: No place else to go?

ED: I'm meant to be here.

ASHER: What about Jo?

ED: Mom's dead.

ASHER: Shit.

ED: One of those suicide attempts you picked on me about finally took. Remember how you called her a failure? She proved you wrong.

ASHER: I'm sorry.

ED: You didn't kill her.

ASHER: I'm still sorry.

ED: No need for apology.

ASHER: No?

ED: If anything, you lengthened Mom's lifespan.

ASHER: I did?

ED: Beating me up, breaking my glasses, stealing my clothes, destroying my schoolwork, pissing in my lunchbox—you gave Mom someone to fight for, and against.

ASHER: Huh.

ED: I fought back for you as much as I could. I know how much you liked Mom. How much you admired her beauty.

ASHER: Umm.

ED: I don't blame you. Mom was sexy, like you said. There's another thing you'll be happy to note.

ASHER: What?

ED: Her body—you know how you used to fetishize it? Well, she remained…what was your word? Fuckable. She remained fuckable until the end. I noticed when I found her in the tub. I thought to myself, *Asher would take notice. Asher would be happy.*

ASHER: Happy.

ED: That Mom remained sexy. And that she finally hadn't—what was your other word?—edkinged once more, that her days of edkinging were behind her.

ED STANDS, LIFTS HIS LEG FROM THE BATHTUB. WATER STREAMS INTO A POOL ON THE LINOLEUM.

ASHER: Whoa!

ED STEPS BACK INTO THE TUB.

ED: I'll wipe it up. Towel?

ASHER MISUNDERSTANDS.

ASHER: Yes, use a towel.

ED: No towel.

ASHER: Where's your towel?

ED: Wherever you store them.

ASHER CONSIDERS RESPONDING THAT HE ONLY STORES HIS OWN TOWELS, NOT ANY TOWELS BELONGING TO ED. INSTEAD, ASHER DECIDES TO HELP ED COVER HIMSELF AS SOON AS POSSIBLE.

ASHER: In the closet.

ASHER POINTS DOWN THE HALLWAY.

ED: Problematic.

ASHER: The closet?

ED: The closet's location.

ASHER: It's where it's always been.

ED: I'm sure it's where it's meant to be.

ASHER: Good.

ASHER HESITATES.

ASHER: That's good…right?

ED: It is where it is.

ASHER: Well…yeah.

ED: Doesn't help.

ASHER: No?

ED: No way to get there.

ASHER LOOKS DOWN AT ED KING'S LEGS.

ASHER: You've got legs.

ED: Wet legs.

ASHER BECOMES RESIGNED TO HIS OWN FATE OF GETTING A TOWEL—WHICH TOWEL IS FATED TO BECOME ED'S TOWEL.

ASHER GOES TO THE CLOSET, PICKS THE LEAST OBJECTIONABLE TOWEL, RETURNS TO THE BATHROOM, TOSSES IT TO ED. ED RUBS IT OVER HIS BODY, PLOPS IT ON THE FLOOR, AND STEPS OUT OF THE TUB.

ASHER IS DISMAYED THAT HIS PLAN TO CLOTHE ED HAS BEEN FOILED BY HIS PLAN TO HAVE A DRY FLOOR.

ED STAYS NAKED, LIMPS PAST ASHER, DISAPPEARS INTO ASHER'S BEDROOM.

ASHER CORRECTS HIMSELF—ED DISAPPEARS INTO THE BEDROOM ASHER NOW SHARES WITH ED AND JAY.

ASHER FOLLOWS. HE SEES ED'S SUITCASE.

ASHER: Damn. That thing is old.

ASHER UNDERSTATES. THE CASE APPEARS TO BELONG TO A RECONSTRUCTION-ERA CARPETBAGGER STEALING INTO THE RUINOUS SOUTH TO TAKE ADVANTAGE OF WARTORN MISFORTUNES.

ASHER WONDERS AT THE MISFORTUNES UPON WHICH ED PLANNED TO CAPITALIZE.

ED PULLS OUT THE LARGEST GLASSES CASE ASHER HAS EVER SEEN. ED DONS GLASSES, AND, STAYING OTHERWISE NAKED, LEAVES THE ROOM.

ASHER FOLLOWS.

THEY ENTER THE LIVING ROOM, WHERE SITS JAY ON A COUCH ASHER DOESN'T RECOGNIZE, WITH UNFAMILIAR DIVOTS IMPRINTED BY UNFAMILIAR ASSES.

ED—AGAIN, ASHER POINTS OUT, STILL NAKED—SITS NEXT TO JAY, HIS ASS FILLING WITH PRECISION A DIVOT, AS IF THE DEPRESSION WAS FATED FOR ED.

ASHER: A couch?

JAY: Found it.

ASHER: Where?

JAY: It's right here.

ED: Seems it was meant to be here.

JAY: Aren't we all?

ED SUCKS IN AIR. HIS LIPS COME TOGETHER AND HE SPITS THE AIR BACK OUT WITH A HARD "P" SOUND.

JAY: Oh! I get it. That's why the nickname "Pathos."

JAY LOOKS OVER HIS SHOULDER.

JAY: You chose that nickname well.

JAY SMILES, EYES TWINKLING, WINKS AT ASHER.

CURTAIN FALLS.

Chapter 4

"THIS IS ALL INTERESTING, ASHER," says Molly Monahan, L.M.S.W., L.M.F.T., L.P.C. "But what about you?"

"Me?"

"Yes."

"What about *me*?"

"You don't understand the question."

"True."

"I want to hear about you—not in terms of Jay, Ed King, your parents. You."

"*What* about me?"

Ms. Monahan sighs. "Yes."

"No."

"No?"

"What I mean is, *what* do you want to know about me?"

"Anything that reveals the actual you."

"Hmmm."

"Fine," Ms. Monahan sighs again. "For example, what are your hobbies?"

"I read."

"Good. What do you read?"

"Signs."

"Like billboards?"

"No. I'm terrible at reading billboards."

"What?"

"There was this billboard I saw for a reading group. 'COMIC BOOK READERS' the billboard read along with a date and address. Thinking this could be a fantastic experience, I showed up, but the group was not what I thought. It was a bunch of guys discussing the merits of some superhero or other. I was turned off by the whole thing—not at all what I expected of a group called 'COMIC BOOK READERS.'"

"What did you expect?"

"I expected that the first word modified the third word, not the second. Their fault, really. They should have used a hyphen."

"Huh?"

"Hyphen would have made clear that it was 'COMIC-BOOK READERS' and not 'COMIC BOOK-READERS.'"

"Really?"

"So, no, I don't read billboards. Just signs." I think of my mother's Redbud tree.

"Come on, Asher. You told me something about yourself, a hobby. You said that you read. What does that mean? Give me an example."

"Something specific?"

"Start with general. Do you read classics or modern literature?"

"Into which category does *Soldier of Fortune* fall?"

"Really?"

"No. I'm joking."

"Jokes don't become you."

"I agree. The converse is true. I've become a joke."

"More jokes."

"Not that time."

Ms. Monahan pinches the bridge of her nose. "Asher."

"Yes?"

"Is there anything you can tell me that would describe *you*?"

"I once attended a naked party."

"What?"

"Undergrad thing. Stupid conceit. Party, in the dorm, password only—you had to have a certain body type to get in, you know?"

"No, I don't know."

"You had to be really fucking hot."

"Ah."

"Well, really fucking hot and within the line of sight of the party organizers. For example, you'd secure an invite, if they saw you."

"Inappropriate."

"That's a coincidence; at the party, people said the same thing to me. And I never got naked."

"No?"

"I wasn't even invited, and certainly not invited to get naked once I showed up uninvited. Getting back to it: the organizers (dudes who lived in the dorm) walked around campus scoping hot chicks (they invited some dudes, too, but only dudes with campus cachet sufficient to ensure that any chicks who showed up wouldn't leave). When the organizers saw hot chicks, they chatted them up. If they were receptive to being chatted up—and these guys had a loose definition of 'receptive'—chicks were issued an invite to an 'exclusive' naked party with a password. Problem was the organizers didn't account for the growth of feminism across campus—nor for the fact that the night before there was an early version of a Take Back the Night rally. You know what that is?"

"Yes."

"Figured you would. Anyway, these guys tried to recruit one strong feminist too many. And she decided to disseminate the password to anyone who'd listen, regardless of gender or appearance. Guess who one of the lucky extra invitees was?"

"You."

"I telegraphed that one. Yes, me. I got the password. But I'd no idea what it meant—it didn't come with instructions beyond: (1) come to X dorm room; (2) knock on door; (3) utter password. The instructions didn't include reference to the format of this event. Now most people who received this extra invite—I'm guessing they had better things to do than heed it. The time for the party came,

however, and I had no better thing to do. So, I went to X dorm room, knocked on the door, uttered the password, and gained admittance."

"How many people were there?"

"More than I'd have expected had I known what the party was. And all of them were two things: (1) really fucking hot; and (2) really fucking naked. I was shocked by the nude flesh, and more shocked that I wasn't booted—the organizers must've believed me to be a dude with campus cachet, someone who'd keep the hot chicks from taking back the night. I was not, however, someone of such cachet that I'd be invited to strip. So, I kept my clothes on—every shred of raiment. All of that clothing on display to be gawked at by all the naked people. I felt their eyes devouring me, roaming down my t-shirt, my jeans, my Chuck Taylors. How embarrassing is that?"

Ms. Monahan has no answer.

"I tried to cover my clothity but had insufficient hands to hide my shame. It was…mortifying."

Ms. Monahan stays silent.

"It was like this other time I bought prank suckers designed to turn mouths neon yellow like a Hi-Liter. I handed those suckers out to friends of mine: Agnes, Agatha, Jermaine and Jack."

"Isn't that from that Biz Markie song?"

"Who?"

Ms. Monahan gapes.

"Anyway, they accepted the suckers. They turned all four mouths neon yellow. You know what those fuckers did?"

"How could I?"

"They laughed. They had tremendous fun looking into each other's mouths and laughing. And then they turned to me. And I had a plain, unadorned, abnormal mouth. And goddamn if I wasn't mortified. I reached for another sucker—but I'd, of course, given them all away. Those assholes had taken all the suckers I had just because I was giving them away! Can you believe it?"

Ms. Monahan makes a face resembling my face upon observing the yellow mouths of Agnes, Agatha, Jermaine, and Jack.

"Anyway, that mortification is what I felt being the only clothed person at this naked party."

Ms. Monahan shakes her head. "But you didn't leave."

"I couldn't."

"Why not?"

"To leave would be to admit that there was something wrong with being clothed. Clothing was natural. I had to fight the good clothed fight on behalf of all clothed people everywhere. I had to show all those judgmental voyeuristic naked people that they couldn't shame me for adorning myself in fabrics."

"Huh."

"Is that the kind of story you meant? Did that tell you something about me?"

Ms. Monahan pinches the bridge of her nose again. "More than you realize."

Uncanny Valley

By

Asher Delacroix

UPON A TIME,[1] THE RESIDENTS of Uncanny Valley joined together in song. The song was not any song you know, unless you happen to be one of the 782 then-residents of Uncanny Valley.[2] You're lucky to never have heard this song. This song was toxic.[3]

The song's genesis was unknowable, although each resident of Uncanny Valley seemed to "know" where it started.

"The song started with Marv" was one theory.[4] "The song started with Phil" was another.[5] Other theories abounded.[6] The theories clashed against each other, but rarely did these disputes result in real, actual, God's-honest violence.

---

[1] This story is too universal to begin "Once upon a time." For in the entire history of mankind, there is no way that the events in this story could've only occurred "*Once.*"

[2] An unlikely possibility since all residents of Uncanny Valley are dead.

[3] Historians have theorized that the largest toxic ingredient of the song was that it reflected too much of mankind. That is, the song was off-putting to the point of nausea and violence because it was "created in mankind's own image."

[4] Espoused by Blake and believed by 236 of the 782 then-residents of Uncanny Valley.

[5] Espoused by Marv and believed by 71 of the 782 then-residents of Uncanny Valley.

[6] "The song started with…" "Joan" (27 believers) "Marion" (125 believers) "Eugene and Marion together" (13 believers) "Ferguson" (172 believers). "The song just sort of started." (76 believers). "The song has always been." (12 believers). "Who gives a fuck?" (50 believers).

The lack of violence[7] lasted into the beginning of the song's performance. It was only when the residents of Uncanny Valley realized how God's-honestly awful and off-putting the song was that the believers of each theory turned on[8] the individual(s) they'd worshipped as the believed creators of the song. For example, 236 people "turned on" Marv, 71 people "turned on" Phil. Etc. Etc. Etc.[9]

Each of the formerly-worshipped who had been "turned on" fought back,[10] and, in doing so, "took out"[11] at least a modicum of those that "turned on" them.

After this burst of violence,[12] 498 of the 782 then-residents of Uncanny Valley had either been "turned on" or "fought back against" until they were "taken out." The remaining 284 residents looked at each other with an explicit realization: *Fuck*, they thought. *We never finished that fucking song!*

So, they started in on the song again. One of the 284 protested, arguing that they should restart the song from the beginning, and not from where they left off before the "Great War of Believers." That one protestor was "taken out" by the 17 survivors standing nearest him.

Shortly after the remaining 283 resumed singing, picking up "in the middle," the song dipped low in register such that the vibrations caused cardiac arrest in 79 of the remaining residents. Sixty-eight of these were "taken out" instantly. The other 11 passed out, and later died as "bystanders" to the "Second Great War of Believers."

This left 204 residents in Uncanny Valley. They sang for 52 seconds more before not a man, woman, or child among them could take any more, and the "Second Great War of Believers" broke out. This War, even though it involved 27% of the combatants in the first "Great War of Believers," was

---

[7] Real, actual, God's-honest…

[8] "Turning on" in the sense that a dog will run alongside a cat in joyful playfulness, until one of the two animals, realizing that they are *supposed to be* natural enemies, "turns on" the other in a vicious and bloody attack.

[9] 138 of the 782 then-residents of Uncanny Valley had nobody to "turn on," so they, naturally, "turned on" each other.

[10] Except Joan, who was an invalid.

[11] Killed.

[12] Known by historians as the "Great War of Believers."

more violent and bloody than its predecessor.[13] Body parts piled up. Blood pooled into reservoirs. The sound of bones and gristle separating was almost as horrific as the song. The conflagration lasted 72 minutes, at the end of which, the 2 final survivors bled out. Uncanny Valley population 782 had become Uncanny Valley population 0.

Historians continue to debate: (a) the reasons the 782 then-residents of Uncanny Valley started singing; (b) what the song was; (c) how the song was so ungodly offensive; (d) why the survivors of the "First Great War of Believers" resumed singing without tweaking the song; and (e) why anyone ever lived in Uncanny Valley to begin with.

Because none of the 782 then-residents of Uncanny Valley survive, no answers have been revealed. For this reason, as for the veracity of this account, you'll have to take that on faith.

---

[13] This, historians theorize, was because as the song continued, it got so ungodly fucking shitty that the bloodlust quotient of that 27% increased by 941%.

Chapter 5

"I FIGURED OUT YOUR CODE," Dad said.

Three weeks after Jay slapped me outside Theo's; 17 days after Ed King carpetbagged in; 12 days after Cassie James rolled up in her wheelchair; 3 days after Chase Crane flitted through the doorway, Donny Quick milling at her side; 2 days after Gregor Gregorovich all but oozed his way under the door—here was Samuel Delacroix, my father, stooped on my stoop.

Dad was shorter than I remembered, plumper, baggier under the eyes and in his jowls—the jowls were new, in fact. His eyes were wide. He hopped from foot to foot in a peripatetic rush. His words rushed even faster, firing from his mouth with a cadence that, had I not known better, I would've believed to be cocaine-fueled. His hands clutched a cardboard box protected by his rain slicker (at the sake of his soaked hair, skin, glasses, and clothes) from the monsoon outside.

"My what?"

"Code. The way you coded each of your...what did you label them?" Dad peered under the slicker. "Parables."

Jesus. *That* box. Thin cardboard, used to ship reams of printer paper. Printed on its side in blue (always blue) ink: "Asher's Parables."

"Can I come in? I have to pee."

"Right. Of course." I made way.

Dad entered, shoved the box into my arms. "Thank God. I thought I was

~ 38 ~

to burst." He skittered to the bathroom as if he'd been in the apartment before, which he hadn't. Dad didn't love travel.

Which reminded me: "Did you drive here, Dad?"

"Yes." Sounds of urine. "Wait. No. We took my car, but I didn't drive."

"We?" I shuddered.

"Raymond drove. Too rainy for me."

Raymond Dorn. An in-home cardio therapist who often made night house calls to Dad. "Anyone else?"

"Just Raymond and me. Raymond's not staying, though. Not like me."

"Like you?"

"He's taking the car."

"Where's he taking it?"

"Wherever he wants. It's his now. I hope he remembers to bring my bag."

Bag. Dad brought a bag. How big a bag?

On cue, Raymond Dorn appeared in the apartment door. "Hello?"

"Hi, Raymond."

"Oh, Asher. How're you?"

"I'm okay. What's this about you scamming Dad out of his car?"

"Scam? Is that what he told you?" Raymond tensed like a rattler.

"No. My phrasing."

Raymond relaxed. "Oh good. Yeah, he gave me the car contingent on me driving him here."

I noticed Dad's Big Suitcase behind Raymond. Shit. "Will you be driving him back?"

"We didn't discuss that."

As if *that* was an answer. Shitshitshit.

"Where should I put his bag?"

"I've no idea." Then, under my breath, "Well, *one* idea."

"What's that?"

"Nothing, Raymond. Just wheel it into the living room."

"No wheels."

"Figure of speech."

"Which part's the living room?"

"Put it behind the couch."

Raymond complied and left to enjoy the bounty of his new car.

Dad emerged from the bathroom, wallet in hand. "Where's Raymond?"

"He left."

"Shit. I wanted to slip him a Benjamin for his trouble."

"Civic wasn't enough?"

"It's never enough."

Coming from Dad, this I believed. "You could run after the car."

"You think?" Dad started for the door.

Having the box in my hands, I couldn't restrain him. "Joking, Dad."

"Ah. Well," said he, stopping. "That's easier, then." He tucked his wallet away. I wondered if he even had a Lincoln in there. He turned to me again. "No hug for your old man?"

I sighed and gestured with the box.

"Why you holding that?"

"You gave it to me."

"Don't be ridiculous. How could I give you something that's yours?"

Flabbergasted.

"Besides, I was in the bathroom for what felt like forever. Why haven't you put it down?"

I put the box on the kitchen counter. As I turned back, Dad beat me to an embrace. By the time I was halfway around, Dad had his arms around my midsection, his face in my armpit, lips against my breast. I reflexively returned the gesture, wrapping my arms around his shoulders. This was the first hug I remembered sharing with Dad since age 14 where I didn't feel the bumps of bra straps beneath his shirt. Had Dad gone strapless?

Following the pattern of Dad's hugs, the embrace lasted 33 seconds too long and required me to break it up. As we pushed away from each other, Jay sauntered in.

"Who's this?" asked Dad.

"I'm Jay."

"The bird or the letter?" Dad asked.

"This is my dad," I explained.

Dad extended his hand. "Sammy to people whose handshake I like."

Jay took Dad's hand. "Then I hope you like mine, Sammy."

"Oh, I very much do!" Dad's eyes twinkled.

"Umm. Dad," I interrupted their longing stare. "You mentioned something about a code?"

"I did?"

"Something about the box?"

"Parable box," Dad corrected.

Shudder.

"You mean this?" Jay pulled back the slicker. "Look at that. 'Asher's Parables.' That's you!"

Vigorous shudder.

Jay plunged his hands in and pulled out a sheaf of paper. "The Mud and The Blood and The Beer," he read. "You write this?"

"He did," Dad spoke for me. "I remember that one!"

Jay, reading aloud: "Want? What do I want? What kind of question is that?"

"That's it! That's the first part of the code," Dad said.

"Code?" asked Jay.

"That first word. 'Want.'"

"I see it."

"Keep reading. Don't skip to the end, but when you get there, read the last sentence aloud."

Jay complied, his eyes sliding along the paragraphs. "Profane. I like that. Good character. Does he have a name?"

"Umm. Lance," I answered.

"My middle name?" Dad asked.

"I guess."

"Interesting."

"Is it?"

"A character with a painful backstory, who's done terrible things, no self-control, struggles with serving the whims of his creator, loathes himself…you name him for me?"

"I suppose."

"Is that how you see me?"

"I don't think so."

Jay continued reading. "Okay," Jay said. "Final sentence: 'If only I knew where you hid the remote control.'"

"There's the second part of the code!"

"I don't get it."

"First word: 'Want.' What's the last word?"

Jay's finger traced the page. "Control."

"'Want control.' Can't be coincidence."

"No?" I asked.

"No," Dad turned to me. "You've got a character—"

"Lance." It was shameful joy to see Dad squirm at the name.

"Fine, 'Lance,' although he could be any man. He laments about his fate, about being created in the author's image. He wants to not live at the whim of another. He wants to not be fated to do the horrible things he does. He wants control."

"You know," added Jay, skimming text, "it seems to me there's more than one person seeking control."

"How so?" Dad asked.

"The author, like any creator, craves the same control as the character—"

"Lance," I interjected.

"Okay, Lance, although Sammy's right: the character could be anyone. The author, as creator, craves the same control. They, the creator and the character—"

"Lance."

"—have a battle for control. The creator, by his role as creator, has to win that battle. There's no way the character—"

"Lance."

"—could win. The creator keeps control away from the character—"

"Lance."

"—who suffers, at his creator's whim, to extremes. The character—"

"Lance."

"—rants and rails about lack of control, and about *why* he lacks control,

what purpose his creator has for him. All the while the creator withholds the ultimate truth from the character—"

"Lance."

"—refusing to allow the character—"

"Lance."

"—to have any peace."

"Sounds like the author has a bit of a God complex," Dad replied.

Jay looked up. "Don't they all?"

My turn to squirm. "What about me?" I asked.

"What about you?" Dad asked.

"Don't you think you should ask the author what the story means?"

"Why would we do that?" asked Jay.

"Well...I wrote the story."

"The author is dead," said Dad.

Chills.

"You know your Roland Barthes," replied Jay.

"Who?" I asked.

"Let's try it this way," Dad said. "There's a saying. Something about how an author writing a story is giving birth. Hence the term 'brain child.' Although the author births that child, nurses it, raises it, shapes it as best he can, that child grows up, moves out into the world. Other people interact with it. The child becomes its own thing, no longer in the author's control. Other people start influencing that child and the way that child is seen by the world. The author must get used to the fact that the child might say one thing to the author and say something different—sometimes the exact opposite—to others. Author and child alike must deal with the fact that maybe the child isn't as likeable as the author thought. Where the author reveres the child, other people might see the child as a complete dick."

"Huh."

"What that means, Asher, is that we don't need to hear from you. Jay and I got this."

"Okay."

"Now," said Jay, reaching into the box. "Which one of you is next?"

Chapter 6

ONE WORD MADE ME FALL in love with Marlena Magpie. "The." That's it. "The" hung on the wall of Galleria de Cinco, a short, squat cluster of four plaster walls, drop-ceiling, and vinyl-tiled floor. I dated the owner of the gallery, Margaret Gutierrez, who dumped me when I, following sex, launched into a prolonged criticism of the gallery's name, how its words span two languages, how the first word (meaning a spacious passageway or indoor mall lined with commercial establishments) didn't describe the space, and how the second word was also misplaced, the gallery being her only gallery, not a fifth gallery, and with no five of any object inside.

Instead of responding with intelligence, she booted me from her bedroom, her apartment, her life. I, not taking her meaning, arrived at the Galleria de Cinco three nights later for a prearranged rendezvous. Instead, I stared at the word "The" hung on the wall. I approached a crowd of 7 people, all with teeth chattering—not because of the ripping cold air, but because of the words stampeding from their mouths, making the 7 voices sound like 70, spewing 70 words apiece. 70 times 70 words all about that one word, three letters long, "The."

I couldn't blame them. The word was captivating. It squatted on a sheet of white paper attached to a large canvas, the remainder of which was so empty that the blank space almost tore my eye away.

The word, however, wouldn't be denied. The word, plainly beautiful and

beautifully plain, dragged my senses from the emptiness. The first letter, a large calligraphic capital T, framed in a scrolled double-lined box, was laced with flowering vines rooted in the white space below. The h and e stood in 12-point Times New Roman font to the right of the T. That was it; there was no more.

One of the viewers of the word, a woman whose auburn hair was the most notable thing about her at my first glance, had ceased gabbing. This, I would come to learn, was Marlena. The other 6 voices, all male, fought for supremacy, each contending that his was the absolute interpretation of the word. In the view of the first, whose skin revealed no hint of his ancestry, "The word is the arc of unlived life! The T is youth, bursting onto the page with glorious potential that peters out in the latter h and e, which represent unrealized potential."

The second man, whose hooded jacket obscured his face from view, said, "No. The word is classism! The T is the bourgeois, the holder of all wealth, glory, power. See how it lords over the proletariat h and e, allowing them nothing of its ample bounty. See how they shrivel away. And see how little the T realizes that without them, it is no longer a word, no longer the important building block, simple, necessary, a word without which written works would be incomplete."

The third man, his tongue sucking onto and releasing from the roof of his mouth with every word, argued, "No. The word is artistry. The T is created by a youthful hand. It is overstated, unsubtle. It screams its message to the viewer. The h and e are the work of a master. The message is subtler. The viewer must work to derive meaning from the subtext."

The fourth man, hands coated in hair to resemble paws, opined, "The word is the indomitableness of nature. The human-constructed h and e attempt to intrude upon the natural T. They arrive after the T has rooted, sprouted, grown large. They crowd. They push. And yet they will remain relegated to nothingness, to spend eternity as voids. Meanwhile, the T will thrive, grow ever larger, more powerful, ever more incapable of being dominated."

The fifth man to speak was not the fifth man in line, but the last man. The

man interrupted the intended progression of the line of ideas, interjecting, "It's not nature the T represents, although I'll grant that you're close on the h and e. Those letters are not man-made, but are man himself. Some men have spirit steeped in curiosity, like the T, which through its thirst for ultimate knowledge grows toward God, who enriches its spirit, allowing it to grow strong and gorgeous. Other men are plain of spirit, like the h and e—which letters form a pronoun for man. The h and e quest for no ultimate knowledge. Instead of reaching toward God, they confine themselves to the ground. Hence, they have no strength, no adornment. Unfortunately, the h and e outnumber the T two to one. See how the T reaches only a shred into the nothingness. Think how far it could reach if the other letters, if the other men, shared its desire for knowledge."

The sixth man to speak, the fifth in line, showed no outward sign that he was perturbed by the interruption. When he talked, however, annoyance oozed in the disapproving gravel of his voice. "The word is only a word, an identifier, the definite article. Nothing more."

At that, language ceased. The men fell silent, anticipating. Their eyes turned to Marlena, each searching her face, pleading, imploring. The fifth man in line, the sixth to speak, finally broke. His voice turned from deep gravel to squeaky anticipation. "Well?"

The next voice to speak was feminine but not soft, confident but not overly so. Marlena spoke only five words, only one longer than 2 letters—but the impact of those words couldn't be measured by the length of the sentence, nor by the minuscule time that it took to utter it, nor by Marlena's even tone: "It is what it is."

The response from the six men: fury. "How dare she!" came one shout. "What the fuck?" came another. "That's no answer!" came another. Snaps and groans and clicks and smacks ensued as the men rushed to convey their retorts to Marlena, to explain why she, as the artist, owed them more than those 5 words.

As the men bickered and talked over one another, a synthesized message came through. "Marlena," the message began, "dear darling Marlena, you cheapen your art. In not influencing us in the ways we are to process your work,

you relieve yourself of your burden to have a message, the burden of being noteworthy, the burden to be good. For this reason, you must now share with us your internal monologue, your personal philosophy underpinning this work of art. Please, Marlena, for the sake of your art, for the sake of the soul of all art, and for the sake of your soul, please dote upon us. Please tell us, dearest darling lovely Marlena: What is the meaning of the word?"

When the message fell silent, Marlena remained silent, too. She studied the men's faces. Her eyes sympathized with their plight at her refusal to infuse her art with her own meaning. Yet her silence continued until each man walked away, their movements synchronizing as they slipped further into the gallery. Once out of sight, their violent voices thrashed and crashed again. I never learned if their argument remained centered on Marlena and her word, or if some new piece of art catalyzed them. I didn't care. I only cared that Marlena and I remained there in the presence of the word. I wondered if Marlena was a genius or if her refusal to explain the intention behind her art was a copout, an excuse to not deal with people who "just don't get it."

Marlena broke the silence. Without looking at me she said, "Kurt Cobain was being harassed by a reporter. 'You guys,' the reporter said, 'don't like explaining anything to do with your music. What's the problem with just going on camera and—' Kurt interrupted him. 'There's nothing to be said,' frustration coating his words. 'It's all in the music. It's all in the meat.' The reporter, not swayed, kept at it. 'You don't think people who are fans of you would like to hear what you had in mind maybe?' Kurt responded, 'I would like to hear what *they* had in mind, how *they* interpret it.'"

More silence, which I broke. "Uh. Long after a creator gives birth, his kid can become a total dick."

"I'm sorry?"

"My dad told me that."

"Your dad told you that?"

"Yeah. Dad told me that a creator can try to raise up his kid in the best way possible, send the kid out into the world, only to find that the kid is a dick."

"Are you the dick in this story?"

I, unsure, hesitated. "I…I mean that art…can be…dickish."

"Oh."

"Something like that."

I didn't think Marlena would ever speak again…not with words. Her eyes, though, danced a dance I'd never before experienced. The dance was a flicker, a hop, a narrowing, two more hops, and another flicker. All directed at me. The dance was a come-on. The dance was a dismissal. The dance was burgeoning love. The dance was festering disdain. The dance was all of these at once. The dance was none of these at all.

I was saved by a waiter with hair spilling out of his pointed nose, who stuck between us a tray with glasses of bubbly liquid, who asked, "Champagne, Marlena?"

"Marlena," I echoed, "I'm Asher. May I buy you a drink?" I lifted two glasses from the tray and offered one to her. She took it with an uncomfortable hand.

The waiter lingered, stared, hard, through me. By the time he left, my empty glass was back on his tray. Meanwhile, Marlena hadn't even sipped. Her glass remained outstretched as if she intended a toast that I'd ignored. I swiped another glass from the next passing waiter and clinked it against Marlena's, spilling several droplets. The rest I spilled down my throat.

"You want my observation, Asher?" Marlena asked.

"Yes."

"You drink like a tourist."

I laughed. "A tourist?"

"That's my ex talking. Steven. He compared everything sloppy, quick, dirty to tourists. You drink like a tourist. Talk like one, too."

"Thank you for your compliments." I bowed.

"Not what I meant."

"I thought you didn't like to say what you meant."

"Cute."

"Well, I mean it this time: thank you for the compliment."

Marlena ignored my banter. "Steven hated tourists. We lived in NYC,

land of the hated tourist. Steven claimed they were sloppy, quick. Saw little of the city, only superficiality, and could never get a taste of the city's realness. Tourists, according to Steven, would never see what NYC was."

"Sounds reasonable."

"Not to me. I envied tourists. They saw things that the natives (Steven's lingo) took for granted—museums, monuments, history—all of which Steven was blind to. Sure, they didn't get the depth of the city—they didn't understand all the vibes and rhythms, but they got the bigger picture that Steven didn't."

"Sounds like both sides are deprived."

Silence once more overtook us. I regarded Marlena. As much as I accepted her "It is what it is" philosophy on her art, I couldn't help but wonder what was in her head, beneath her freckled skin, behind her bright, wide green eyes and her dimpled cheeks. I was surprised to find myself wondering more what was on her mind than what was under her clothes.

"So," I said when I could bear silence no more, "this art scene interests me."

"I can see that."

"You can?"

"You don't seem to be here for my tits alone." Marlena gave no sign that this was a joke.

"I'm glad," I said. "Not that they aren't great."

Marlena laughed. "They are what they are."

My turn to laugh.

"Okay, Asher. What interests you about the art scene?"

"Totems."

"Totems," Marlena repeated.

"And symbols. Nothing here is what it seems. It all stands for something else, something hidden under the surface. It must get incredibly confusing. I don't know how you do it."

"Said the tourist."

The next day, Marlena joined Jay, Ed, Cassie, Gregor, and Dad living in what used to be my apartment.

Chapter 7

"WHY DO YOU LIVE ON that chair?" asked Randy Mac, the newest addition to my menagerie…or Jay's menagerie…or whatever.

"It's the only place I *can* live," Cassie James replied. "Can't walk."

"Yeah," Randy's giggle struck me as odd, at best. "Whose fault is that?"

"Fault," Ed King interjected, "can't be assigned. Events are because they are."

"Yeah, yeah, crazy little naked person," Randy again. "We got your perspective. Fate fate fate. If it's foretold that you'll kill your parents, then you'll kill your parents. We get it. Now," Randy turned back to Cassie, "what *fate* befell you?"

Surveying the faces of the seated ring of recent strangers (Randy had organized the room like a sanitarium group therapy session in the round), I couldn't tell if anyone else had noticed the change in Randy's question.

"Ford plant," Cassie replied.

"Ford plant fucked you so hard you can't walk no more?" More giggles.

"Something like that," Cassie maintained her tone.

"Oh, those crankshafts." Randy simulated thrusting.

"Shut up, vulgarian," Gregor Gregorovich rebuked Randy.

"You're just angry that I made friends with little nymph Chase." Randy referred to Chase Crane, another of the menagerie's recent "gets," a 9-year-old black (refusing to be called African American) girl who remained quiet

save for sporadic strings of questions oddly probative for her age. The circle, starting with Chase and proceeding to her left:

1. Chase Crane.

2. Forever naked Ed King.

3. Samuel Delacroix, wearing a green skirt, white blouse, padded bra, blonde up-do wig, black stockings, white pumps.

4. Jay, sitting closer to Dad than either he or Dad ever sat to me.

5. Marlena Magpie, my love, clad in a robe that rested closed; when she shifted, various parts of her nudity revealed themselves.

6. Alec Posner, ignoring the group to stare at Marlena.

7. Ella Flowers, who'd purchased all the chairs in which we sat, save Cassie's.

8. Donny Quick, whose white hair gave his age, and whose crazed tousling of that hair implied that whatever mission he was on was bat-shit insane.

9. Sony Ericsson, sitting on a ratty bath towel (dotted with landmarks of London) she had brought into the apartment. Sony looked equal parts restless and bored, as if she longed to be somewhere far, far, far away.

10. Gregor Gregorovich, eyes flitting around the circle, lingering longest on Chase.

11. Randy Mac, who'd made *his* mission(s) clearer than had Donny. Randy's current mission was to berate Cassie James, make her emotions boil.

12. Cassie James, seated in the one chair in the circle not purchased by Ella Flowers.

13. Asher Delacroix.

14. _____. Nobody. Despite the lack of a resident for the 14th chair, Jay insisted on setting it up to my left. When I pointed out that this was one chair too many, Jay responded, "Just in case." I let it go.

The middle of the circle was empty. I fantasized about moving my chair into that middle, becoming the hub around which the wheel of companions

would turn. The fantasy died when Randy Mac unleashed his torrents.

Despite Randy's outbursts, Cassie remained calm. Her eyes fixed on Randy in a hard stare. Not angry. Contemplative, as if she took Randy for exactly what he was by the way he sat (leaning forward in his chair, ass nearly hanging off the front edge), how he moved his hands when he talked (down-beating his spread fingers on his knee with every other enunciation), and how his face ticked and sneered as his lips formed the words, "You're going to have to stand up," giggling as he finished the sentence, "to me at some point."

"I'm taller'n you sitting down."

Randy's giggles intensified.

"You remind me of someone," Cassie continued. "Wise-ass I used to work on the line with. What was his name? Rich something…Planter. Rich Planter. Should never have been there; only non-union guy there—faked his union status—God knows why he'd want so badly onto an assembly line. Didn't find what he was looking for, judging by his continual fuck-ups. He had one job. Robots affixed the engine to the transmission, then put the transmission and engine inside the frame. I'd attach the radiator on clips and hold it there while Rich swung in a pneumatic wrench to bolt the radiator in place. Rich, though, wasn't satisfied with accomplishing the task and moving on to the next radiator. 'This could be more efficient,' he'd say. He always looked to make his job easier—laziness in the guise of efficiency. 'I mean, shit, why are there two us?' he'd ask.

"Me, straining from holding the radiator in place: 'Because it's a two-man job.'

"Rich, countering, 'If this is a two-man job, why'd they put me with some woman?'

"Me, enduring, 'Just bolt this in.' Now, usually—always except the last time—Rich'd do his job. That last time Rich decided he had a point to prove. He tossed the wrench at me, shouting, 'One-person job. Catch!'

"Ordinarily I would've caught that wrench. Or I could've let it fall to the platform—we were working on an elevated platform, 8 feet up—but Rich took my eye off that wrench as he danced backwards to distance himself

from the job, and his heels collided with a parts rack. His knees hit the safety rail and he tipped back. I let go of the radiator, which broke off the clips and fell to the platform on my foot. I wrenched my foot free—'wrenched' being a funny word given that the pneumatic wrench was where my foot landed. Wrench slipped out from under, propelling me forward. I grasped Rich's hand as I flew by him, and he got sufficient torque from me to right himself and stay on the platform. I fell. I landed—spine down—on the arm of a welding robot 6 feet below."

"Rich sounds like a real idiot," Randy giggled.

"I said you remind me of him."

Randy's giggles turned to laughter. "That's good! I might even say... rich!"

Cassie ignored Randy's pun. "I was given disability payments and a shiny new wheelchair through workers' comp. Guess which one I kept?"

"That wheelchair don't seem so shiny to me."

"It's been everywhere I've been—a lot of places. Four years wandering the wilderness—sometimes literal wilderness, most times more symbolic. Getting away from that plant, I realized that I'd been too cordoned off. I'd been a UAW steward; well liked, I was. Good at talking, better at listening. Yet I worked in about the most isolated job possible. When they hauled my body away, there were hands all up and down me. Despite not being able to feel a damn thing below my navel—I could feel those hands all over me, top to bottom. That was my salvation. That was when I realized I could no longer be isolated. Whatever means would allow me to move around in the future, I knew that I had to move around in favor of being with people. I had to experience as much of the collective soul of Man as possible. So, for the last four years—after seven months in the hospital—I've been wandering the wilderness, trying to pick up as much knowledge of that collective soul as possible."

"Well," said Randy, "good for you for not killing yourself."

"I'm too old for suicide," Cassie replied.

"I, like you," Dad said, "always thought suicide a young man's game. So untrue. I heard about this series of suicides among the elderly. Started with a

105-year-old who committed suicide, then a 90-year-old, a 75-year-old, a 62-year-old, a 56-year-old. Working backwards: the 56-year-old heard about the suicide of the 62-year-old. 'Shit,' thought the 56-year-old. 'Is being 62 so unlivable? I don't want to find out!' So, the 56-year-old went skydiving, but didn't open his parachute.

"The 62-year-old killed himself because he heard about the 75-year-old's suicide. 'Golden years don't sound so Golden to me,' thought the 62-year-old. 'Not if the 75-year-old can't hack 'em.' So, the 62-year-old cleaned his hunting rifle, loaded it, barrel under his chin, pulled the trigger.

"You might have guessed that the 75-year-old and the 90-year-old did the same thing. They each heard about the suicide of someone older than them. Neither of them wanted to get to that older age where they knew it was going to be too tough to go on living. The 90-year-old sat in a running car in a garage and breathed himself to death. The 75-year-old swallowed two bottles of Advil."

Dad didn't continue.

"Why'd the 105-year-old commit suicide?" I asked.

"He didn't," Dad answered.

"What?"

"He was just crazy. He thought he was immortal for surviving to 105—threw himself off a cliff to see what would happen, broke himself on the rocks below."

"What?"

"That's what I heard."

God, did Dad know how to flabbergast me. "What does that mean?"

"Mean?"

"Yes, Dad. What the fuck does that story mean?"

"I don't know. Just a story I heard."

"Who told you that story?"

"I don't know. I just heard it. Why so many questions?"

I had no answer. I did, however, have more questions. Not about Dad's story, but about Dad's garb, an outfit out of place for the time period and for Dad's anatomy.

I first discovered Dad cross-dressing at 10:27 p.m. on Monday, December 17, 1990, when a load of his skirts, bras, blouses and panties set the washing machine off balance. The machine (one floor below where I slept) jigged and jagged its way across the floor. The raucous clamor suggested either a helicopter crashing down or the earth opening a deep depression into which I was destined to collapse.

When I realized that my world was not crashing around me in the literal sense, I arose, left my bedroom, traversed the upstairs hallway, descended the stairs, traversed the downstairs hallway, passed the bathroom, turned my head, saw Dad adjusting a small bow at the neck of a garish pink prom dress, continued into the laundry room, pulled the washing machine's plug from the wall, and…wait, what did I see? What the fuck was that?

I didn't have to reverse course to find out. "What are you doing out of bed?" Dad was next to me, neckline maladjusted.

"Washing machine was going crazy. Why are you in that dress?"

I expected Dad to panic, to scream, "OH MY GOD!" to realize his mistaken outfit, to hide the raiment behind his arms, to flee in the direction from whence he came, to protect me. Instead, calm, expectant: "This dress? I'm in a formal mood tonight, sort of Molly Ringwald meets Holly Golightly." Dad adjusted the second bow, larger, on his left hip. "Do you like it?"

"No. Dad, what I meant was, why are you in any dress?"

"What do you expect me to wear?"

Blink.

"Well, it doesn't matter. I like this dress. It makes me feel…light."

"Light?"

"Floaty—a very fancy float, indeed."

"Where's Mom?"

"Sleeping. Which reminds me, why are you out of bed?"

"Umm. Washing machine was going crazy."

"Seems to be normal now."

"Normal?"

"Well, not entirely."

"Finally."

Dad tapped the side of the washer. "I mean, the washer stopped."

"I unplugged it."

Dad leaned over the side of the washer. "Ah! That must be the issue." He replaced the plug. The machine resumed its cacophony. "There!" Dad shouted over the din. "That seems to have solved it!"

"It's loud!" I shouted back.

"What?!?"

"It's loud!"

Dad looked down. "You think?!? Well, I guess so!"

"Not the dress! The washer!"

"Oh! We should unplug it!" He removed the plug. The machine fell silent. "Now, what were you saying about the dress?"

"I wasn't saying anything about the dress. I was talking about the washer."

"What about the washer?"

"It was loud."

"Oh. Yeah. It's probably overloaded." Dad walked the washer back toward the wall and opened the lid. "Ah. Nope. Here's the problem. One of my bras got wrapped around the agitator."

"One of your bras?"

"It's really wrenched in here good."

"*One* of your bras?"

"Can you get the scissors? This bra's a goner."

"What?"

"In the cabinet." He gestured above the washer. In reaching for the scissors, I leaned close enough to Dad to sniff Mom's perfume. I retrieved the scissors, gave them to Dad, and backed as far away as I could without leaving the washroom. Dad worked his hands inside the machine and pulled out three sections of what had been a large bra, too large for Dad…not that any bra would be his size. "There," Dad said. "Now let's plug her back in." He did. The washer spun without further racket.

"Hey, look at that!" Dad raised his hands in celebration. "Now, as to the matter of you not being in bed, Asher."

"Umm. Washer woke me up."

"Doesn't seem to be a problem anymore. Why don't you go back to bed?"

So, I did. From bed, I could no longer hear the washer. What kept me awake instead was the image of Dad in the pink prom dress and the sound of Dad and Mom from their bedroom down the hall. Their dialog was so loud I could hear every word straight down to the subtext.

"What do you mean he saw you?" Mom's voice, throaty, grave.

"He came downstairs."

"What'd he say?"

"He said the washer woke him up."

"No, asshole. What'd he say about the dress?"

"Oh. He asked why I was wearing it."

"How'd you respond?"

"Well, I was confused. I wondered aloud what dress he thought I *should* be wearing."

"Did it occur to you, asshole," Mom expressed my agitation better than I, "that he was asking why you were wearing *any* dress?"

"Why should he want to know that?"

"Because it's not something he's used to!"

"What, prom dresses? He goes to high school. He's seen movies. I think he knows what a prom dress looks like."

"Not on a man, for Christ's sake!"

"Ah. Well—"

"And *certainly* not on *his father*! I mean *fuck*!"

"I hear your point."

"And?"

"Perhaps I should…go…talk…to Asher?"

"Perhaps you should."

Dreadful footsteps came my way. My bedroom door crept open. Hesitance. Finally: "Asher?"

"Yes."

"You awake?"

"Yes."

"Did I just wake you up?"

"No."

"You've been awake?"

"Yes."

"Have you slept since being downstairs?"

"No."

"Okay. Maybe your mom's right."

"About what?"

"She seems to think you might need to talk about why I'm wearing a dress…by which I mean *any* dress, not just this dress."

"Okay."

"I don't know how to explain it. Perhaps it would help if you asked questions." Dad sat on the edge of the bed.

I heard the crinkling of tulle and taffeta.

"Okay. Why are you wearing a dress?"

"Ah. Getting right to the difficult one. The heart of the matter. The crux. Good for you, Asher. No question as good as one that drills down so deep."

Silence.

"Well," he continued, "some time ago, I learned that wearing a dress makes me feel…comfortable. And I thought to myself that a dress is really no different from, say, a suit and tie: both made of cloth, both sewn by tailors, both advertised to the general public (albeit to different demographics), both sold in stores (albeit in different sections), both provide warmth and protection against the elements. So, I figure a dress is as good as anything else, and it has the added benefit of making me feel… comfortable."

Silence.

"Do you understand?"

"Yes."

"Good. Any other questions?"

I had a question. I had an ultimate question. I asked something else instead. "Are you gay?"

"Gay?"

"Gay."

"Well. Hmmm. In the sense of being attracted to other men…I wouldn't say that men in general attract me, no."

"Men in general?"

"I can certainly recognize the attractive qualities of some men, of course. But yeah, in general, no."

"Okay."

"Okay. Yes, well. This has been fun." Fun? "It's good to have this out in the open." Dad stood and smoothed his taffeta. "Not that anything was hidden away. It's good that this is out in the even *more* open. And here's hoping that this openness will continue and grow."

Feverish chills.

"Goodnight, Asher." He walked away. At the door, he turned back. "You should get some sleep. You've got school in the morning."

Ah, yes, school. Ninth grade. Friends there, enemies, too—high school teemed with hormonal teenagers—some friend and enemy at once. Each, whether friend, enemy, or combination, could find out about Dad and his prom dress, so fluorescent pink that it seemed to be visible from anywhere in the known galaxy, and upon finding out, each could use Dad's dress to marginalize, push me to the edge, push me over that edge, look over the edge, see me hanging there, stomp on my fingers.

I didn't sleep.

That night, my fear of schoolmates became a fear of humanity. Each human had some sensory ability to detect…everything. Churchgoers, schoolmates, teachers, astronauts, authors, butchers, chemists, strippers, doctors, lawyers, nurses, police officers, phlebotomists, preachers, coaches, firefighters, bakers, greengrocers, veterinarians, gardeners, astronomers, astrologists, chauffeurs, cardiologists, lumberjacks, candlestick makers, plumbers, mechanics, embalmers, archaeologists, farmers, movie stars, rappers, quarterbacks, comedians, principals, accountants, engineers, architects, inventors, cheerleaders, painters, Sherpas, artists, hipsters, judges, juries, executioners, carpenters—all manner of men, women, children, others, all maintained the capacity to observe, to see, to discover, to root out. All maintained the capacity to ruin me.

As that night turned into day, school resumed, and there I was in grade nine. Soon enough, grade ten, eleven, twelve, college, real world, beyond. All the while, no human confronted me about Dad's pink prom dress. Nobody knew anything. From churchgoers to carpenters, no human had a clue.

Why did nobody know? Why did no human bother to find out why I was so fucked up? Why did nobody care enough to root out the cause of my bad behavior, my proclivities, sexual and otherwise? Why did no human deign to give me an excuse?

I took to dropping hints. "My parents are interesting," I'd say, which became, "My parents are messed up," which became, "My parents are fucked up," which became, "My parents fucked *me* up."

With each iteration, the response was a rolled-eyes, "Tell me about it."

As it turned out, all humans had lineage issues they believed rivaled any issue in my lineage. Every human was fucked up, and every human blamed their parents for causing their fucked-uppedness. Every human's father did every human wrong.

"Your father's a cross-dresser? Mine was my football coach."

"Mine punched a priest."

"Mine failed at standup comedy."

"Mine cheated on my mother."

"Mine drank."

"Mine smoked."

"Mine smoked crack."

"Mine was a beat poet."

"Mine beat me."

"Mine screamed at Little League umpires."

"Mine left."

"Mine joined a cult."

"Mine converted to Catholicism."

"Mine was a guidance counselor."

"Mine was a psychiatrist."

"Mine was a cop."

"Mine slept all day."

"Mine was in prison."

"Mine was in the KKK."

"Mine went AWOL from the Marines."

"Mine masturbated in porn theaters."

"Mine was never around."

"Mine died."

Each voice cried out against the sins of each father. Each complaint vied for dominance over all other complaints. Nobody was the worst off. Nobody won.

And the upshot: Nobody cared about Dad's cross-dressing.

As I sat in Randy Mac's circle, I should've felt relief that nobody looked at Dad as fucked up for wearing traditionally female clothing. I should've felt relief that every other member of that circle had their own issues. I should've felt relief that nobody in that circle judged me for the sins of my father, but instead saved their judgment for my own sins, for the sins of the son.

But I felt no relief. My shame for my father indulging in his sins had turned into pride in myself for overcoming his indulgence. I was a survivor. And if I was to label myself a survivor, I must've had something to have survived. Something big. Something important. I wanted Randy to stop accosting Cassie and her wheelchair and start accosting Dad in his 1980s receptionist's attire. I wanted Randy to berate and belittle Dad, to label him with red Sharpie as: "FUCKED UP." Then I wanted Randy to say, "And you, Asher Delacroix—all your bad actions, transgressions, sins—they are not yours. They are the sins of the father, not of the son. You're blameless. Furthermore, you're a survivor. You've overcome. And having survived, having overcome: You're strong; formidable; potent; powerful. You are good."

Instead, Randy sat back in his seat, surveyed the circle, and declared, through manic laughter, "This is a circle of equals."

Chapter 8

A SON WITH NO FATHER is a bastard. The word disparages, but not the son—or the father. "Bastard" disparages the mother, who is presumed to have either whorishly given herself to a host of shiftless rootless assholes such that none can be concluded to be the son's father, or whorishly given herself to a single asshole so shiftless and rootless that he would abandon mother and son alike. Either way, bastardy is construed as a mother's fault, not a father's.

Curiously, there's no "bastard" equivalent for a motherless son, no word for a son raised by a father without the presence of a mother, not the way that "bastard" disparages the mother of a fatherless son.

And then there's me. There's no word (disparaging or otherwise) to describe me, a son whose father is decidedly feminine and whose mother is decidedly not. No word describes a son with father in a bra, mother in coveralls; father a retired shop girl, mother a psychopath; father on his knees in church, mother in restraints in an asylum.

Oh, to have parents with modesty, parents who hide their shame behind closed doors and false smiles, parents with regard for how their public appearance affects me, parents with inhibitions. Oh, would that it were so simple.

What I wouldn't give to be a simple bastard. Not that I want to put that stigma on Mom. She's full up on stigma. Not that she minds. Mom wears her insanity like Dad wears a pink prom dress—openly and proudly. Mom boasts

that her diagnosis allows her to do or say whatever she wants without repercussion or judgment. "Who gives a shit?" has long been among Mom's favorite phrasings. "Fuck apologizing," "Shut the fuck up," and "Fuck you," are right up there, too.

Mom calls her doctor "Long-A Arab, M.D.," as in, "Long-A Arab, M.D., refused to up my Lithium. I threatened to bite his A-rab nose off. Lithium upped." This was an actual story that Mom told me, serious and true to life, a story that Long-A Arab, M.D., himself confirmed.

"Your mom's an interesting case," Dr. A-rab said. We met in a conference room at Walter P. Reuther Psychiatric Hospital. We always met in a conference room, door open. Dr. A-rab's refusal to take me into his office was, I believed, a sign that he refused to take me into his confidence. He didn't trust me to be alone with him in a private setting. He wouldn't let me in close. It was Mom's fault. Had to be. "You know, she threatened me."

"How could I know that?"

"She threatened to bite my nose off if I didn't give her more Lithium."

I stared, inherited loathing and violence in my eyes.

Dr. A-rab changed course. "How's your father?"

"Fine," I answered, the word coming out shorter than its four letters.

"Is he?" Dr. A-rab hesitated. "Has his…face…fully healed?"

This was six months into Mom's confinement at Walter Reuther, six months after Mom was removed from my parents' marital residence in handcuffs and driven away in the back of a Sheriff's car. It took three cops and two EMTs to immobilize Mom, a task they completed before they could tend to their own injuries, applying gauze, bandages and iodine aplenty.

Only after they set their own figurative bones did they tend to the literal broken bones of Mom's intended victims. In the bedroom—Dad's bedroom, where he slept apart from Mom ever since she booted him from the bed that they'd shared for 17 years—the paramedics set to work. In moments, two bodies, both male (they were easy to sex from their exposed bloody genitalia) were intubated, splinted in multiple locations, immobilized by padded neck collars, and strapped to backboards.

The police report read like a Thomas Harris novel.

The following is a statement of Deputy Mike Randolph with reference to the investigation of the assault and battery of Samuel L. Delacroix (age 53) and Martin H. Johns (age 28), bodies found at 2894 Lake Road, Ypsilanti, Michigan.

On the evening of November 19, 1996, 9-1-1 dispatch received a call from a female resident of 2893 Lake Road who reported commotion at the house across the street, owned by Samuel and Merry Delacroix. I radioed dispatch that I'd report to the scene. Dispatch responded that I'd be joined there by 2 officers of the Ypsilanti P.D.

I was the first officer to arrive. I observed three vehicles in the driveway: a Honda Civic (blue) and Pontiac Grand Prix (also blue) side by side, and behind them, at a sharp angle across the driveway, a Jeep Cherokee (orange), its driver side front door open, engine running. Black marks on the driveway indicated a sudden stop.

Light emanated from a second-floor window. Through the curtains, I could see shadows moving.

As I approached the front door, I heard shattering glass, and saw a video camera and tripod thrown through that window and onto the garage roof.

Finding the front door unlocked, I opened it and shouted,

"Washtenaw County Sheriff's Department." I received no response. I entered the residence, the first room of which was a mud room with a second closed door leading into the house. Attempting to open it, I found it blocked by debris.

Two patrolmen from the Ypsilanti P.D. (Alex Turner and Sid Warren) entered the mud room. The three of us opened the door wide enough to enter the living room. The debris blocking the inner door was an overturned coat tree, including a blue barn coat appearing hastily thrown. I noted an envelope protruding from the left side pocket.

Offcrs. Turner & Warren and I heard a scuffle on the upper floor. Anticipating potential medical necessity, I radioed EMS.

We proceeded through the kitchen and into a hallway that led toward the back of the house. We ascended the stairs and traversed another hallway toward the noise.

I observed a partially open door whose wood and frame were cracked, appearing to be kicked open.

Offcrs. Turner & Warren and I entered the room, wherein I observed three figures (Samuel Delacroix and Martin Johns— both nude—and Merry Delacroix, clothed) twisted together atop a twin bed. Blood streamed from beneath the pile of bodies and puddled on the carpet.

Messrs. Delacroix and Johns were trapped beneath Mrs. Delacroix. Before we could react, Mrs. Delacroix swung her arms and legs, pummeling Messrs. Delacroix and Johns with both feet, both knees, and her left fist. Her right hand was wrapped around Mr. Johns' genitals. The flexing of her bicep

indicated she was attempting to injure Mr. Johns, up to and including pulling his genitals from his body.

Mr. Delacroix nearly got out from under the pile, but Mrs. Delacroix whipped her head to the left, impacting against Mr. Delacroix's nose. Blood sprayed from Mr. Delacroix's nose and mouth, and he fell limp.

Mrs. Delacroix whipped her head back toward Mr. Johns, and sunk her teeth into his chin, ripping away flesh, which she spat into Mr. Johns' mouth before she bit into his cheek.

Offcrs. Turner & Warren and I rushed the bed and grabbed Mrs. Delacroix. As her arms were sleeved with blood, she slipped from our grasp and landed four more punches into Mr. Johns, connecting with his right eye (which swelled closed), his left side jaw (causing him to spit out the chunk of flesh), his nose (breaking it), and his throat (causing him to gasp and wheeze).

I grabbed Mrs. Delacroix's left arm, Officer Turner grabbed her right arm, and Officer Warren grabbed her around her midsection. Together, the three of us pulled her off of Mr. Johns. As we wrestled her to the floor, she freed her left arm and shoved me against a dresser.

Mrs. Delacroix punched Officer Turner, who let go of Mrs. Delacroix and fell to the floor inside the closet.

Mrs. Delacroix punched at Officer Warren behind her neck, hitting his right temple. Officer Warren let go and fell atop Officer Turner, causing a stiletto heel to pierce 2 inches into Officer Turner's butt cheek.

Mrs. Delacroix jumped back atop Mr. Johns and sank her teeth into his chest. She pulled back her head, leaving teeth marks where his nipple had been.

Officer Warren and I reached Mrs. Delacroix before she could bite Mr. Johns again. With one of us on each of her arms, we pulled her off Mr. Johns. She kicked Mr. Johns' genitals. Mr. Johns passed out.

Curtis Van Sickle and Jeffrey Heller, EMTs with the Ypsilanti Fire Department, entered the room. Mr. Van Sickle opted to help Officer Warren and I subdue Mrs. Delacroix, as Mr. Heller attended to Mr. Delacroix and Mr. Johns.

Mrs. Delacroix freed her right arm, grabbed Mr. Van Sickle by the face, and shoved him into me, knocking us both off-balance. Mrs. Delacroix rushed the bed again. She grabbed Mr. Heller by the hair and pulled him backward. A chunk of Mr. Heller's hair came free from his head in Mrs. Delacroix's hand, and Mr. Heller fell backward into the broken window, causing lacerations to the back of his neck, shoulders, and arms.

Mrs. Delacroix jumped on her husband, forced open his mouth and stuffed Mr. Heller's hair inside, making Mr. Delacroix choke and snap to consciousness. Mrs. Delacroix wrapped her fingers around her husband's neck and squeezed hard enough for his eyes to bulge.

Mr. Heller executed a flying tackle that forced Mrs. Delacroix and her husband onto the floor. Mr. Van Sickle, Officer Warren and I leaped on top of the Delacroixs.

Officer Turner, who'd pulled the shoe from his backside, ran to

the pile and applied his handcuffs. When we all stood, we discovered that Officer Turner had in error handcuffed Mrs. Delacroix's right wrist to her husband's right wrist. Mrs. Delacroix jerked and strained against the handcuffs, dislocating Mr. Delacroix's shoulder, abrading his wrist, causing him to pass out again.

Offcrs. Turner & Warren, EMTs Van Sickle & Heller and I again grabbed hold of Mrs. Delacroix and were able to subdue her long enough to remove the cuff from Mr. Delacroix's right wrist and secure it to Mrs. Delacroix's left wrist. Mrs. Delacroix went limp.

Messrs. Van Sickle and Heller attended to the wounds of the five of us (Officer Turner's buttock puncture, Mr. Heller's lacerations, Officer Warren's apparent concussion, and various bruises and abrasions on all of us) before turning their attention to Messrs. Delacroix and Johns.

Offcrs. Turner & Warren and I brought Mrs. Delacroix to her feet and led her out of the house and into the back of my patrol car. We reentered the house, whereupon Offcrs. Turner & Warren returned to the upstairs bedroom to help Messrs. Van Sickle and Heller.

Before returning to the upstairs bedroom, I surveyed the lower floor for evidence. The one piece I found was the envelope that I'd observed sticking out of the pocket of the coat draped over the coat tree in the living room. Opening the envelope, I found a handwritten note, in blue pen, addressed to Mrs. Delacroix, which appeared to be signed by Mr. Delacroix. The note read:

Dearest Merry:

It's been months since I introduced you to Martin. It's time that you get to know our friendship. He's been instrumental in helping me adjust to The Golden Girls.

No, not the Estelle Getty TV program.

The Golden Girls is a group of men of all ages (never mind the "Golden" part—not my idea; if I'd named the group, it would be after a different 1980s TV show. Bosom Buddies? Too obvious. Full House? Not terrible. Could be entendre for penises filling panties. Growing Pains? More like GROIN pains. Ah, it'll come to me) who share the desire to dress as the opposite sex (yes, women dressed as men are invited to join, but we have yet to attract any such members, so to speak).

I've met with The Golden Girls on a number of occasions, usually at my shop (not my shop, I know, but being at Kurtz' Klozet for over 25 years has to count for SOMETHING), at least once a week. The gentlemen of The Golden Girls have introduced me to so many things—from the perils of wearing colors inapposite to my skin tone to the joys of a properly fitted bra! (On these notes, The Golden Girls could be of great aid for you, Merry)!

Martin has also introduced me to a new invention—something called the World Wide Web—on which I found a mass of people sharing my affinity for pretty pink dresses! There are these services called Bulletin Boards on which hundreds of people gather to share experiences. Some have pictures posted!!! PICTURES!!! Of men in DRESSES!!!! AROUND THE WORLD!!!! Can you believe that such a thing exists?

Martin has this theory—something about how our favorite Bulletin Board (called "Dicks as Chicks") will soon have capability of hosting videos!

It's because of this video idea that I write to you, dearest Merry, to offer you the opportunity to be part of Martin and my entries into this new society, a World Wide Web fashion show! Martin is coming tonight to our house with a camera to take a video that he will "post" to the Web. Martin assures me that he'll be more than capable of filming us in "the act." Where you come in, dearest Merry, is helping us assess the end result! How exciting to be on the precipice of the future!

I'll slip this note into the pocket of your coat in the hopes that you'll read it today. I can already see the look of excitement on your face!

With greatest love and anticipation, I am, as always, yours.

Love, Your Sammy

P.S. Oh, of course! Designing Women!

The only other evidence I removed from the house was the video camera on the garage roof.

Upon returning to the Sheriff's station, I placed Ms. Delacroix in a holding cell, and the video camera into the evidence room, tag 112914.

M. Randolph, Dpty.

No description of the video was ever given to me. Not that I needed or wanted such a description. Dad's letter said all that needed to be said. The videotape was never used as evidence in court, either—because Mom was never tried. Given Deputy Randolph's gruesome tale (verified by separate statements of Offcrs. Turner & Warren and EMTs Van Sickle and Heller), Mom was transported from the Washtenaw County Sheriff's Department to the State of Michigan Center for Forensic Psychiatry where, upon a cursory interview performed by Dr. Long-A A-Rab, M.D., she was declared unfit to stand trial. She was transferred to Walter Reuther Psychiatric Hospital, where, at the time of this writing, she remains confined.

Six months after her confinement commenced, I sat across from Dr. Long-A Arab, M.D. not answering questions about Dad's physical health. Instead, I asked, "Can I see Mom now?"

"Well," said Dr. A-rab, "that depends."

"On what?"

"On your willingness to submit to a pat down, for one."

"And for two?"

"You have to promise not to excite your mother."

"Excite her?"

"She's been diagnosed with schizoaffective disorder, bipolar type. You already know that she has severe aggressive tendencies."

I knew.

"With the right stimulus, she could lash out. Especially in the earlier stages of adjusting her Lithium."

"The right stimulus?"

"No aggressive movements; no shouting; nothing to raise her temper."

I snorted. "Have you *met* my mother?"

Dr. A-rab sighed. "Just be careful, okay?"

One pat down later, I entered Mom's private room—she was deemed by Dr. Long-A Arab, M.D., as unready for a roommate.

When I crossed her threshold, Mom almost smiled at me. "Asher," she said, nodding in my direction.

"How are you, Mom?"

All traces of smile disappeared. "I'm Merry."

"Indeed," I replied to her oldest joke. "Are they taking good care of you?"

"Good? That's relative. Especially considering the way relatives treat me."

"What do you mean, Mom?"

"It's been six months. This is the first I've seen you."

"Are you the victim now?"

Before she could answer, a nurse, male, "Broderick" printed on the ID card clipped to his blue scrubs, entered. "Merry!"

"Bird!" Mom smiled.

"Gotta say, I'm lovin' the nickname," Broderick replied.

"It's because you're so tweet to me."

I blinked.

"Ha ha! I always will be, Merry."

"Good. Keep that smile."

"As long as you're here I will. Now, gotta do a quick BP check." Broderick slipped the cuff over Mom's arm. "Hmmm. 95 over 64. Bordering on low, Merry. Maybe I should have you do jumping jacks, bring that up a bit."

"You just want to watch my tits bounce."

Gasp!

"That's why you're my favorite resident, Merry. Gotta complete rounds now. Check you later." Broderick exchanged a fist bump with Mom before he flitted away.

"Flirt much, Mom?"

"Since being in here? Absolutely."

"Ah."

"I like it here. I can say or do whatever the fuck I want, lose any inhibition, and everybody blames it on schizophrenia. Might as well take advantage."

I couldn't argue with that.

"I can piss off whomever I want. Like Dr. Long-A A-rab, M.D. I know that's not his name. Don't care. He's a prick. Don't even care that he's Arabic. Just a prick. Fun to be racist to a prick. Not all A-rabs are bad A-rabs. That Bird, I like him."

"Gee, I couldn't tell."

Mom ignored my sarcasm. "He has nice shoes."

"Shoes?"

"Bird's got crisp, clean shoes. Shiny, too, for hospital sneaks."

"I didn't notice."

"Not surprising. You don't wear good shoes. Shit, Asher, you don't even wear adequate shoes. I doubt you've worn a single pair of shoes in the past 5 years that could be shined."

She was right.

"You can learn a lot about a man from a shoeshine."

I was used to this businesswoman-speak bullshit from Mom. Looking at her style, the way she dressed, her own shoes, you wouldn't guess that she was fond of saying things like, "To be a success, brush your hair. Get in shape. Dress well. Be presentable." Mom clamored for me to follow this advice even though she'd never gotten a haircut that cost more than five bucks and made her own clothes, except for jeans, for which she bought Wranglers and Dickeys. The rougher the fabric, the darker the blue, the yellower the stitching the better. For shoes, Keens work boots or plain white sneakers. For outerwear, the long blue barn coat into which Dad had slipped his letter six months prior. Occasionally, Mom forewent all of the above and donned long johns and denim coveralls.

With the brutal imagery of Deputy Randolph's police report stark in my mind, however, humoring Mom was paramount. "What can you learn about a man from the shine of his shoes?" I asked.

"That's not what I said."

"What?"

"I said, 'You can learn a lot about a man from a shoeshine.'"

"Is there a distinction?"

"I'm not talking about the appearance of a man's shoes after a shoeshine. I'm talking about the act of a shoeshine itself."

"Huh."

"Shoeshines raise questions about a man: Is he giving or getting the shoeshine? If getting: What's his posture? Is he conversing? Reading?

Ignoring? Is he looking at passersby? Making eye contact? How did he pay? Did he tip? Does he want to be anywhere but in that chair in that moment? Does he appreciate life?

"If giving: How fast does he move? How much care does he take? Does he lead the conversation? How many topics does he broach? Does he ingratiate himself? How dirty is his buffing cloth? How empty is his Shinola? Is he trying to move quickly from customer to customer? Does he savor his opportunities?"

"Deep."

"Deep shit, you mean. That's all right. Ignore me all you want. See how far you get without being able to interpret a person from a shoeshine."

"Learn all that from your therapist?"

"Therapist tells me fuck all. Only asks questions. 'What do you think of this?' 'Why'd you do that?' 'What does a man's chin flesh taste like?' I mean, you read the interview transcripts."

I had. Pages upon pages, I read them all. Scoured and absorbed as much as possible. Yet today, I struggle to regurgitate more than one passage, the one passage from all the interviews that referenced me:

Q. How are you enjoying your time here, Ms. Delacroix?

A. Merrily.

Q. Funny. Or do you mean that?

A. I mean everything I say.

Q. So, you're enjoying your time here, then.

A. Better than the alternative.

Q. You mean jail?

A. I mean anywhere.

Q. No plans to escape, then, eh?

A. If I wanted to escape, I'd already be gone.

Q. Well, this is a lockdown facil—

A. Fuck you and your lockdown. I could get out anytime I like.

Q. How would you go about that?

A. Flip a fire alarm here, cut off electrical breakers

there, circumvent video systems, it'd be a snap.

Q.   You know how to do all that?

A.   I'm good with my hands. Ask Sammy and what's his name.

Q.   Sammy's your husband, right?

A.   Samuel to you, motherfucker. Samuel Delacroix.

Q.   Making you Merry Delacroix. Interesting name.

A.   It is what it is.

Q.   What does it mean?

A.   Joyous Of the Cross.

Q.   Interesting.

A.   Just a name.

Q.   You don't find your name interesting?

A.   I preferred my maiden name.

Q.   What was that?

A.   Merry Morgud.

Q.   What sort of last name is that?

A.   It's my last name, idiot.

Q.   I mean nationality-wise.

A.   Swedish.

Q.   If you like that name, why take your husband's name?

A.   Because for the first time, I could.

Q.   What do you mean?

A.   I didn't take my maiden name. My parents gave it to me. When I married Sammy, I had a choice. Not a full-on choice, which would require a broader range of options. When it came to marriage—there was only one option.

Q.   You didn't find you had other options than Sammy?

A.   Samuel to you, motherfucker. And I'm not talking about Sammy. I'm talking about Delacroix. Morgud was thrust upon me. Delacroix was a way I could take a name by choice, abandon old fate for new.

Q. You tie your fate to your name?

A. Funny thing is once I made my decision, I discovered that I preferred being Morgud.

Q. You hate your last name?

A. Hate's a strong word. Sammy has that name. Asher does, too.

Q. Asher's your son?

A. Yeah. So, I can't hate him.

Q. Asher. Who chose that name? You or Samuel?

A. I chose it. Sammy gave him Delacroix, so I gave him Asher.

Q. Does Asher have any sort of meaning to you?

A. Of course he does. He's my son.

Q. Let me rephrase. Does the name Asher have meaning?

A. It means blessed.

Q. You named your son Blessed of the Cross?

A. Sammy and I did, yeah.

Q. That's quite the meaning.

A. I had to share that fucking burden somehow.

Q. What do you mean?

A. Name like mine, people meet me, expect me to be fucking joyous all the time. That shit gets real fucking old real fucking fast. I hate having that meaning thrust upon me.

Q. Did you think your son wouldn't hate having it thrust upon him?

A. I knew he'd hate it. Walking around all the time bearing that burden of knowing he should feel blessed. That sucks.

Q. I'm surprised you'd give him a name you knew he'd hate.

A. You don't know your Johnny Cash.

Q. Did you consider other names?

A. I did. But the name Shithead wasn't in vogue with you blackies yet.

Q. "You blackies?" Do you mean African Americans, like me?

A. I prefer "You blackies."

Q. Can't say I do.

A. Well, then, for the rest of this interview, consider yourself a blackie.

Q. Why don't we get back to your relationship with your son.

A. Why don't we not, blackie?

That was the end of the interview. The doctor (Dr. Blackie, M.D., I'm sure Mom would call him) called it a day, and called in a new therapist to start the next morning. Dr. Blackie was with Mom for 57 minutes before he called it quits. As Mom might say: "What a pussy that Blackie was." I mean, I had Mom for a lifetime.

And Dad had Mom for even longer. Dad and Mom's marriage survived for far longer than my meager lifetime. Through Dad's cross-dressing, it survived. Through all of Mom's brutal verbal takedowns, it survived. Through Dad's affairs—with men and women alike—it survived. Through Mom's brutal physical takedown, it survived. And it survives to the date of this writing.

There came a point in time, in the year of Jay, seven years after Mom's incarceration began, that I found myself across my table from Dad. As I watched Dad eat whatever Jay had assembled from the thin air of my refrigerator, Dad's posture struck me. He sat straight. Unbent. Unbroken. In all those takedowns, verbal and otherwise, Mom hadn't broken Dad like she'd broken Dr. Blackie in less than an hour. How did he manage that?

"Dad?" I asked.

"Yes?"

"When did you last see Mom?"

"It's been a while."

"What was that like?"

"It was your mom. You know?"

I knew. "Dad, why'd you stay?"

"Stay where?"

"With Mom."

"Perspective. Your mom can't be judged by a few actions here or there. I look at the big picture. If I didn't, I'd end up like Bobby Bull."

"Who?"

"Bobby Bull. Kid I grew up with. After high school, Bobby Bull lost all perspective. So much that when he came across a railroad track, he thought it was a ladder, and got nailed by a train while trying to climb to a roof."

"What?"

"He was going to throw himself off that roof anyway, but still. Tragic loss of perspective."

"Goddamn it, Dad."

Statement of Donny Quick [excerpt]

...TRULY WHAT? DO I BELIEVE I'm truly virtuous? Is that the question? If so, I'll answer with another question: Can a man determine his own virtue, or must that man's virtue be measured by others? And if a man *can* accurately measure his own virtue, can a man who labels himself as virtuous ever *be* virtuous?

If you ask me to measure the virtue of others, first I must define the term. What is virtue? Or even first *before* first, I must ask a predicate question: Who is allowed to define virtue? Is there some objective definition of "virtue" passed down from above? Or is "virtue" subject to each individual's point of view? Oh God, what a question! Can I, a mere servant to greater powers, adjudge others to be virtuous? No, I cannot.

I cannot, then, answer the question as you posed it. Am I virtuous? I'm incapable of answering. Is Jay virtuous? What of Marlena? Samuel? My dearest Ella? And Asher? As much as I admire the residents of the fortress that was that apartment, I cannot adjudge them. Good? Bad? Virtuous? Sinful? Those questions are not for me.

And yet, if forced, if the life of my Ella were at stake, say, or the life of Jay...no. I cannot. It would not be virtuous of me to say. I would determine another way to save my beloveds.

Yes, plural. Ella was not my only love in that bastion. Jay was another. Not in a romantic way. My romantic love is reserved in whole for my Lady

of Flowers, my Ella. But love can, of course, take other forms. Love can be...revenant.

What? Revenant means someone who comes back...someone who returns? Oh. Then I'm mistaken. Apologies. What word was I tilting for? Reverent! That's it. Love can be reverent. Love can be worshipful. And this other love of mine in that citadel, he was deserving of the greatest of reverence.

Your assumption is correct. I speak of Jay. To me, Jay was a perfect Lord of the Manor. He gave great hospitality, honored every resident of the stronghold. Even Randy Mac. Even Gregor Gregorovich. Even Asher Delacroix.

Irony is not lost on me. Some people cannot be helped, cannot be rejuveniled.

Oh? Yes, you're again correct. My phrasing is off. Rejuvenated is what I meant. Or is it? No longer can I be sure.

Oh, come now. Don't be mad...

Chapter 9

"DON'T SAY THINGS LIKE THAT anymore," says Molly Monahan, L.M.S.W., L.M.F.T., L.P.C.

"What?"

"That kind of talk is inappropriate."

"What should we talk about instead?"

"You know the answer."

"Me, right?"

"You know what? No. Anything but you."

"Who else do you have in mind?"

"How about this: early on, you seemed interested in discussing Jay. But I haven't heard about him in some time. Tell me more about him."

"Jay?"

"Yes."

"Jay has longish hair, wears sandals everywhere, has a knack for finding food where none can be—"

"You've said all of that before."

"Have I?"

"Yes. Do you have anything else to share about Jay, the guy you told me is the protagonist of your story?"

"Hmm. Have I told you the cabinets thing?"

"Yes."

"How he and Dad discussed the meaning of my short stories?"

"Yes."

A lengthy pause. My brow furrows.

"Look, Asher, you know what you've told me about Jay. And you know what you're not telling me."

"What am I not telling you?"

"Many things."

"You think?"

"Asher, I've read the reports. You're leaving out a lot."

I don't think my brows can furrow any deeper, but furrow they do.

"How about this: I'll ask you one question."

I cringe. "Okay."

"Why didn't you ask Jay about his prior living arrangements?"

"What?"

"You discussed with Ed King where he'd been before he…what was your word?" Ms. Monahan reviews notes. "Before he 'carpetbagged' into your apartment. Why didn't you have the same discussion with Jay?"

"Who says I didn't?"

"I do."

"Well, you're correct."

"Why didn't you have that discussion with Jay?"

"Assumptions can be a hell of a drug."

"What did you assume?"

"That he'd been living with his brothers."

"Jay had no brothers."

"Well, he talked about brothers. I don't know if they were the genetic type of brother or…something else. But he talked about them."

"What else could the brothers have been?"

"More of a commune, I assume."

"A commune. Interesting. And there's that word again: assume. Why did you assume? Why leave it to chance? Why didn't you ask him where he came from, where he lived before, *anything* about his history? This was your life, your safety, your personal space. Why base his residency upon faith alone?"

"I don't know."

"Seems a bit extreme."

"Yes. Or it turned out to be, if you look backward from the end. But then that looking back has been done and done and done, a whole awful lot. A *lot*—as in done to death."

"So why, then?"

"It was just nice to have company."

"You were lonely?"

"Isn't everyone?"

Chapter 10

A GROUP OF NUNS SANG in my head: How Do you Solve a Problem Like Marlena? If what Dad wore was a sore spot, then what Marlena *didn't* wear was another. Marlena was quiet, but not shy. Within weeks, all roommates knew every contour of Marlena's body. Even to me, a man accustomed to uninhibited surroundings, Marlena surpassed my inhibition threshold.

Don't get me wrong: Marlena looked great—in my bed. When we were alone, Marlena was a cloistered Cleopatra. She had a private perfection, secluded sexiness. In my arms, the myriad shades of green in her eyes were more exquisite than emeralds. The sliding of her skin across mine provoked passionate heat that belied her goosebumps. Every breath was a seductive sigh, every bodily quiver orgasmic. The freckles dotting her cheeks, chin and chest formed connect-the-dot outlines reminiscent of Helen of Troy, Dulcinea, and Daisy Buchanan combined. The muscles in her lower back, buttocks and thighs moved together to entice and excite me.

Away from my arms, though, in all other rooms of the apartment, Marlena's beauty blanched. The crisp, jagged gray streak shrieked louder than the auburn remainder of her hair. The veins striping her breasts pulsed with blood hinting at hypertension. The hips were likewise uneven, causing an uncomfortable sway as she walked. The curve of the spine slumped when she sat, accentuating belly fat. The fingers were stained with every shade of paint in the spectrum, amalgamating into splotches of ugly brown.

The teeth, while straight, were incomplete—two bottom teeth only half-present.

The distinctions between Marlena's private and public appearance seemed lost on all but me. Each and every resident, if looking at Marlena at all, looked with favor, or at least *not* with *dis*favor. Reactions ranged from barely noticing (Chase, Ed, Ella, Sony, Gregor) to smiling (Dad, Cassie), to bowing to kiss her paint-splotched hands (Donny), to nodding along with the sway of her hips (Randy, Jay), to barely concealing visible excitement (Alec).

"You've got curves like a mom. I dig it." This was Alec Posner's ode to Marlena. I didn't just happen to overhear. Alec spoke it in my presence in another Randy-led group circle, same seating as always (empty chair at place #14 and all). The only differences were that Dad wore a conservative, masculine red and black flannel/blue jeans combo, and Marlena was the opposite: naked.

Just as opposite were Marlena's and my reactions to Alec's blatant come-on. I shuddered; Marlena smiled. Marlena tilted her head; I pinched the bridge of my nose. I sighed; Marlena giggled. We were a study in contrasts.

I expected Alec to charge ahead, double down. Alec was like that. It was well within his character to see an opportunity to make sexual advances, and then advance 13 steps farther. Alec suffered from self-diagnosed "sexual OCD," which he described in a February 26, 2000, blog post as follows:

> Listen: I introduced myself to a problem today. This LADY!!!
> A Jew. This Jewess, this sexual being, oh how I long to take her
> to Temple. And make her observe. Put the serve in observe.

> Dear journal peruser, fellow voyeur: thus is my symptomology.
> This lusting, seeing something beautiful, devout, holy—and
> needing to degrade it, defile it, bring it to its knees, and…The
> mind boggles.

> For my three devoted followers (shout out to Jaime, Eliot and

Avishalom)—(okay, I made up that last one), you know my sexual OCD. For new followers (all likely zero of you):

I have what therapists call Sexually Intrusive Thoughts ("SITs"). Not *my* therapists, mind you. I see no therapists, at least not in a therapeutic setting. There was this woman therapist that, well, now—this is a perfect example. Here I am formulating the definition for SITs, and I am intruded upon by one of those very SITs. By the way, SITs is a pretty ironic name given what SITs tend to do to a certain part of me, well, fuck, there I go again.

It seems that I've now defined SITs better through the rapid-fire occurrence of SITs than I could with words. You get the idea.

Most people who experience SITs complain about them. Not me. I have no such complaint…save one. I don't complain about *experiencing* SITs. I complain that I can't, without disobeying every societal norm, act upon them.

I could not today, for instance, go beyond commenting on this beautiful Jewess' melons—cantaloupes in her shopping cart, I mean, about which I said: "Your melons are overripe."

"Excuse me?" The accent on this Jewess. Erotic!

"Cantaloupes. In your cart. Overripe."

"Oh. You can tell by looking?"

"Oh yes. I am an expert in overripe melons. And those are overripe."

"Okay. That's good information to have. Thank you Mr.…."

"Alec."

"Mr. Alec?"

"If you insist on formality, it's Mr. Posner. But I answer to Alec in a friendlier manner."

"Yes. Well. I'm [name redacted—suffice it to say that it was as erotic as her appearance and accent—I will call her Beautiful Jewess…BJ for short]."

BJ offered me her left hand for a handshake. I took it, turned it, bowed, and kissed the indentation on her left ring finger, indicating that although she had a long history of wearing a ring thereon, no ring was present.

"Oh," said BJ, withdrawing her hand. "Well. Thank you again for your assistance."

"My *pleasure*. Most people dislike overripe melons. I thought you might be of that type."

"You did?"

"I do not so discriminate. When it comes to melons, there comes a point of ripeness, but that ripeness is the beginning. Only thereafter do melons become the sweetest. Overripe melons are…my *thing*."

"Ah. Okay. Interesting." She removed the cantaloupes, set them on the shelf and replaced them with a honeydew and a casaba.

A child appeared, a boy, 10 or so. I'm also an expert in the age of children, having studied them so.

OH!!! WAIT!!!

I do not mean that I study children for the sake of studying children. That's *not* one of my SITs. No!

Not that my study of children and their ages is wholly divorced from my SITs. But my SITs do not concentrate on the children. See, I am somewhat of a...motherfucker. In that I prefer to fuck mothers. Never my own. But I would smother others' mothers.

So, when this child of 10 sidled up, that was the point where fully erect lust brushed against the soft, welcoming curves of love.

SITs took over my psyche. I heard not the remainder of my conversation with BJ. I was consumed with thoughts of being consumed, of my own over-ripeness exploding...

Alec's blog proceeded from there to depravity in the degradation of the "Beautiful Jewess." In his mind (if not in the flesh), Alec did, indeed, take BJ to Temple...and therein, he took BJ again.

Alec didn't allow his talents in perverse thought to languish. With Marlena acquiescing in Alec's forwardness, I had every reason to expect him to continue his encomium. Yet in response to Marlena's smile and tilted head, Alec fell silent, leaving someone else to champion his cause.

That someone was Randy Mac, the once-again instigator of our 14-chair circle, who said, "Ms. Magpie, I do believe that Alec would love to call you Mommy in an intimate setting."

This was too much for me. "Wait a minute," I began.

"Ah, don't worry about it," Randy cut me off. "Alec's all talk. Too bad. The kid has talent."

"Talent?" I asked.

"The kid knows how to put words together. He's creative, especially when it comes to sexual deviance. Damn shame he can't capitalize on those talents."

"But—"

"Did I ever tell you about Hotchky Potchky?" Dad asked, speaking for the first time in the circle that day.

"What?"

"Did I tell you about Hotchky Potchky?"

"Hotchky Potchky? No. I think I'd remember that."

"Hotchky Potchky isn't a 'that.' Hotchky Potchky is a man."

"A man? Named Hotchky Potchky?"

"Hotchky Potchky was Marco Polo's neighbor in Venice."

"Ah."

"Hotchky Potchky was obsessed with Marco Polo. Hotchky would stare out his window and see Marco come and go at odd intervals, coming and going from China as he was, although Hotchky didn't know that. All Hotchky saw was Marco coming and going, bringing with him loads of packages.

"As he watched Marco Polo come and go, Hotchky Potchky observed, from the safety and security of his own house, Marco's fame grow. Hotchky watched crowds flow to Marco's home with nary an ebb. The crowds grew, and not just in number—also in intensity, excitement, joy. They stayed even when Marco was away for years at a time. Hotchky had to push his way through them in order to get anywhere—not that he went anywhere. Hotchky was self-confined. He stayed in his home, only leaving when he had to. While Marco Polo was out traveling the Silk Road, Hotchky Potchky went nowhere.

"Hotchky knew not of the Silk Road. He knew not of spices, of Chinese politics, of the riches acquired through world travel. Hotchky didn't even know where Marco Polo went, or what he brought back with him.

"As Hotchky watched those thronging crowds grow while his own knowledge of the world stayed minimal, he grew more curious about his neighbor. Hotchky went from wondering 'Where is Marco Polo going this time?' to wondering 'Where the *fuck* is Marco *always* going, and why the *fuck* can't he just sit still for a moment?'

"Hotchky became obsessed, wanting to know everything about Marco Polo's travels. But he didn't ask his neighbor—he couldn't. Marco was almost never home. Furthermore, Hotchky had grown too angry at the thought of Marco's random comings and goings, and too sick with covetous rage about Marco's growing fame, to address his neighbor face-to-face.

"Instead of finding anything out about Marco Polo and 'where the *fuck* he was *always* going,' Hotchky did what he did best…nothing. And when I say nothing, I mean it. Think: less than lilies.

"As Hotchky Potchky withered, Marco Polo became wealthier, more revered. Marco Polo opened trade routes. Marco Polo introduced rare goods to Europe. Marco Polo went to war. Marco Polo spent time as a P.O.W. All the while, Marco Polo's empire and legacy grew. Marco Polo died at the age of 70—pretty damn old for the year 1324—surrounded by adoring fans and loved ones."

Pause. Long pause. Then longer. Dad's style. Ignore it. Convince yourself. Adopt a mantra: I will not ask. I will not ask. I will not—"Dad?"

"Yes?"

"What happened to Hotchky Potchky?"

"Who?"

"What do you mean who? The one you were telling the story about. Hotchky Potchky."

"Oh. Him. Nobody knows."

More pausing. More mantra. Damnit. "Dad?"

"Yes?"

"What's the point of that story?"

"I don't know that there's a point."

"No point."

"I'll tell you something, though."

"What?" Bracing myself.

"I'm grateful to Hotchky Potchky and his 'can't do' attitude."

"Grateful?"

"Absolutely. Think of the headaches that would be induced if kids ran around in swimming pools screaming HOTCHKY POTCHKY!"

Goddamn it. More mantra: Do not engage. Do not engage. Do not—"Dad?"

"Yes?"

"Where'd you come up with that bullshit?"

"Bullshit? I don't know. I read about it somewhere."

"You read it."

"Oh yes. I read all about Hotchky Potchky."

"So, someone else—not you—came up with Hotchky Potchky."

"Came up with? I suppose so. I mean he'd have to have some sort of creator. Be it his parents or someone else."

"Are you telling me that Hotchky Potchky was a real person?"

"I don't see why not."

"You don't?"

"No."

"You don't see the ridiculousness in believing that there once existed a person with the name Hotchky Potchky."

"No."

"Or the ridiculousness of Hotchky Potchky happening to live next door to Marco Polo."

"Why not? Hotchky had to live *somewhere*. Why not Venice in the late 1200s. And Marco Polo had to have a neighbor. Why not Hotchky Potchky?"

"Why not Hotchky Potchky?"

"Exactly."

Time to change course. "You didn't make up that story?"

"No. Plagiarism."

I snorted. "And you thought Hotchky Potchky was lazy."

Laughter. Not from me.

Randy Mac laughed. "Plagiarism, lazy? No way," said he. "Plagiarism takes hard work. And talent."

"Talent?"

"Sammy may not have invented Hotchky Potchky. But he found him. He located and familiarized himself with Hotchky. And he remembered him. And he did something nearly impossible—he waited. He didn't squander Hotchky Potchky on some mindless conversation with menial idiots—at least not *plural* idiots. Sammy waited until the right opportunity arose to use Hotchky Potchky. And then he did something even harder—he recognized that opportunity when it came along. Only in that moment did he use Hotchky Potchky. Only when the time was right, when the moment was perfect."

"Hmmm."

"Now that's using talent."

Statement of Ella Flowers [excerpt]

...MADLY IN LOVE? WAS I? How could I know? For if I admit to being "madly" anything—if I admit to being crazy—then how can I know that what I feel is truly what I feel? How can I respond that I'm mad and then say that despite that madness—despite my every thought being untrustworthy—despite that, how can I trust my emotions? How can I know that my love—my "mad" love, as you put it—is real? Can anything "mad," anything irrational, anything impulsive, anything crazy, be true? For that matter, can *anything at all* be true...

Chapter 11

MOLLY MONAHAN, L.M.S.W., L.M.F.T., L.P.C., REGARDS ME WITH disdain, indifference, mistrust. Her eyes, the color of almonds but the shape of tennis balls, flash disgust when I say things like:

> Randy Mac was once sued for copyright infringement. The play *Children of a Lesser God* has no ready-made sellable audio version, so Randy made his own. He recorded all the parts himself. Anytime poor deaf Sarah Norman communicated through sign language, Randy Mac spoke those signs aloud, but in an offensive mock-deaf voice.

Eyebrows raising and eyelids narrowing, Ms. Monahan waits. There is never an instant reaction. There is always a wait. There is always time for me to say more.

> In the lawsuit Randy Mac represented himself. He argued that he was protected by the doctrine of fair use because his recording was a parody commenting on the play. When he testified, he was asked what that parodic commentary was. He responded: "That sanctimonious people are really fucking hilarious."

More unilateral silence.

Randy was proud. The jury didn't appreciate the answer, though. The jury had sympathy for the deaf. And for free will—or at least "free will as exercised by the stubbornly handicapped," and not "free will exercised by a raving lunatic jackass." Those were Randy's words that I air-quoted at you. The jury didn't care for Randy, and punished him with its verdict of $750,512, an amount placing a number on Randy's unlikableness. Given that part of the verdict was for the $512 he made in selling his recordings, he figured the jury hated him in the amount of $750,000. "Not bad," thought Randy.

Randy loved that hate. He'd have gladly purchased that hate for $750,000, but he couldn't afford it. He was forced to appeal.

He won a double victory. Finding in his favor, the appellate court not only freed him from having to pay the verdict, but also compared his efforts at free speech to the hateful—yet Constitutionally protected—venom spouted by the KKK, Neo Nazis, and Jerry Falwell. Randy figured that that level of hate had to be worth more than $750,000, yet it had cost him $320, the filing fee for his appeal. It was as if he'd discovered an invaluable bundle of hate stashed beneath a table at a garage sale. He praised his own ability to sniff out that hate, identify its worth and purchase it for such a tremendous discount.

The longest and tensest wait yet.

"I mean, that's what Randy told me, anyway."

Ms. Monahan deigns to speak. "Was Randy reliable?"

"More reliable than Gregor, that's for sure," I answer.

"Relativism. You use that often."

"What do you mean?"

"You answer my questions about people's behavior (including yours) by comparing that behavior to others. Every answer is from your own point of view, which none but you can verify. That tells me nothing about the reliability of either Randy *or* Gregor. It tells me only that you found Randy to be more reliable than Gregor. I daresay that your comparison tells me much about your own reliability—or lack thereof."

I understand. I have a habit of obfuscation, of hiding my confusion by confusing those around me. This I view as inherited (whether by genes or by observation) behavior.

I begin a different story:

> After Mom got locked up, Dad was in the hospital for weeks. The hospitalization didn't relate entirely to Mom's bit (so to speak) of ultraviolence. The bandages applied by EMTs Heller and Van Sickle were removed, revealing something (sepsis) that "could've been a lot worse" (Dad's words).

> The sepsis couldn't have been worse, though. The infection attached to several organs. Dad's spleen almost died. What could've been worse was what *might* have happened had Dad not been attacked by Mom. That attack and the wounds that it caused and related sepsis all caused Dad to undergo many tests. Each of his organs was scanned to make sure it was no longer septic. Those tests revealed—to hear Dad tell it:

>> I was wheeled into the ER with a separated shoulder, a concussion, and various infected wounds. I was wheeled out with tachycardia, a ruptured heart valve, an undetected past cardiac arrest, and a laterally off-axis heart.

You get the problem with Dad's description. Dad's take sounds like he didn't believe that those conditions existed until the tests revealed them—like his heart were Schrödinger's cat in blood-pumping organ form. Dad didn't really believe in all that "doesn't exist until it has been observed" bullshit. He just loves playing with language.

Problem was that his wordplay wasn't directed at me. This was a story he told to Randy Mac, who decided to use Dad's statement to challenge the belief system of anyone who'd listen.

"Shouldn't have gotten those tests," said he, Cheshire Cat smile spreading.

I leapt to Dad's defense. "If he hadn't, he'd have died."

"Sammy will die no matter what," replied he.

I winced at Randy's bluntness. "True. But the tests revealed conditions that needed immediate correction. Without those tests, Dad would've died early."

"Revealed? I'd say caused."

"Caused? You buffoon. Caused. Shut up with that bullshit."

"Let me ask you this, Sammy: Before you underwent those tests, did you have any heart problems?" asked Randy.

"Never," responded Dad.

"Had you any other reason, prior to those tests, to suspect heart conditions?"

"None."

Turning on me again, "Sammy has no proof that his heart was diseased before those tests. For all he knows, those tests caused his conditions."

"That's ridiculous."

Randy smiled. "Did I ever tell you about my father?"

"Your father?"

"Father. The man whose jizz contributed to my genetics."

"I know what a father is."

"Do you?"

"What about your father?" I asked through gritted teeth.

"He died when I was young."

"I'm sorry to hear." I cleared my throat. "Died of what?" I thought cause of death was the important part. I was wrong.

"I don't know."

"What's the point of this, then?"

"Ask me his age when he died."

"Fine. How old was your father when he died?"

"I've no idea."

I closed my eyes. "Why not?"

"You got the question correct this time. I've no idea how old my father was when he died because I've no idea how old I was when he died."

"What are you talking about?"

"I only remember my father's age relative to my own. I have no idea of his birth year, only that if he were alive, he'd supposedly turn 30 years older than I do this year."

"Supposedly?"

"He being dead, there's no way to confirm that he would've followed the same chronology with which he began his life."

"What?"

"Up to death, he aged at one year per annum, keeping him 30 years older than me. But he died. So, there's no way to know if he would've continued to age at that same rate had he survived. For all I know, right now he might have been 48 years older or 2 years younger than I am."

"Hold on." I rubbed my eyes. "You couldn't figure out your father's age at his death because you didn't know how old *you* were?"

"I said that a few paragraphs ago."

"So, you don't know your father's age except to compare it to your own?"

"I said that even more paragraphs ago."

"What's the point of this shit?"

"The point?"

I can't convey how frustrating this asshole could be. Don't know why I didn't give up. I seem to have a problem with giving up—I never quite get the timing right. Most of the time, I give up too early. This time, though: "Yes, Randy. The fucking point. We're sitting here talking some bullshit about Dad's medical testing *causing* his heart conditions instead of *detecting* them, and you bring up your father's death. You didn't do so to compare the hearts of our fathers. Instead, you talk about your father's age at his death, and you don't even know what his death age was."

"All true."

"So, what's the point of you bringing up your father's death?"

"I can't answer that."

"How about this one: What fucking question can you answer?"

"Why I can only relate my father's age to my own, of course."

"Fine. Why is it, Randy, that you can only relate your father's age to your own?"

"Perspective."

My frustration yielded to curiosity. "What?"

"From my perspective, my father, as adult as he was, could have been, for all I knew, only as old as me."

"I don't understand."

"I only experienced him for the few years I was alive—even shorter than that if you discount the years from which I have no memory."

"You know your father lived before you were born, right?"

"I've been told that. But I don't know that."

"Why not?"

"As far as I know, all history before my birth might not have happened at all. I only know the present."

"What are you talking about?"

"The past only exists through stories. Each teller infuses each story with biases and perspectives only knowable to that teller. In that way, the past is unknowable."

I sighed. "Anything else?"

"If the past exists at all, it might be pure fable, a cautionary tale designed to show what could happen as a result of decisions—and not, therefore, a literal chronicling of events."

"Huh." My senses spun. "Wait. That's all well and good for stories made of words. What about photos, audio recordings, videos?"

"What about them?"

"You've seen photos of your father from before you were born."

"Of course."

"Don't those prove that your father existed before you were born and, by extension, that the past existed?"

"No."

"Why not?"

"You know how a picture is worth a thousand words?"

"I've heard that."

"Words are words. All words can be crafted."

Here I end the story, because here the conversation depicted in the story ends—with me storming away.

Molly Monahan L.M.S.W., L.M.F.T., L.P.C., regards me with more disdain, more indifference, more mistrust. And with more silence. So I begin one final story:

"There was a video game I played when I was a kid—maybe 10 years old. One of those graphic-less text-based adventure games, green text against a black screen—like Zork, but not Zork—I can't remember the title. It started with this dude, just a regular dude, dude type dude, no super powers, omnipotence, nothing of the kind. Just a dude. The protagonist of the game— me, in text form—meets this dude at the beginning of the game. And mind you, this dude has no connection to me—I'd never met him. I was walking through some forest or something, and I came across this dude sitting on a stump. Dude kicks off this game by telling me about this terrible loss he suffered—a daughter or his treasure or some combination of daughter and treasure. This is the first thing he says to me. He doesn't even introduce himself (hence 'this dude'). Dark origins to this shit, right?

"Anyway, this dude tells me that he needs me to go out into the world, puzzle my way through puzzles, maze my way through mazes, challenge myself against challengers. Dude tells me that at the end, I'll face a final foe, the cause of the dude's loss of his treasure/daughter—a vengeance quest. When I defeat this final foe, I'm to return to the dude, who will reward me.

"'Return to you?' I ask. 'Won't you accompany me?'

"The dude responds, 'I'm too forlorn for adventure. You shall be my vengeance.'

"So, I set out. I puzzle. I maze. I challenge. I defeat the final foe. I am vengeance. I return to the dude and tell him what I accomplished. The dude rewards me with immortality.

"He didn't accompany me. He didn't view what I'd done. He didn't ask for proof. He took me at my word that I'd accomplished all I said I'd accomplished, took me at my word that I'd become vengeance. Without hesitation, he believed and rewarded me."

Molly Monahan L.M.S.W., L.M.F.T., L.P.C., finally speaks: "Is this session a game?"

"I have no idea."

"You have no idea."

"I have no idea."

A Four Eye Otter Chic

By

Asher Delacroix

COLD.

No matter where the hostess gripped the champagne bottle, it was cold. The bottle chilled deep within a bucket of ice until even its neck was cold.

Every time she walked past the table the men's glasses were empty. They drank fast. She stopped, gripped the bottle, refilled their glasses.

The men hadn't entered together. The older man shuffled in first. He was the type of old that he'd be forgiven for any rudeness, including blatant sexism, racism, speciesism, the type of old that he could spew any manner of contradictory statements and still be afforded respect and admiration by virtue of his continuing survival. Despite his hunched posture and slow gait, the man gave every appearance of fierceness and power. His eyes and sneer flashed with the stuff; his pores sweated the stuff, too. His suit and tie and hat reflected his status as a power broker. This was a man, the hostess thought, like her father, only still alive. Given the man's power, she wondered if he (had he been at least 350 pounds heavier) might've been the man who'd murdered her father, and who'd shipped her father's eyes, gouged from his head, to her mother—who threw the eyes in the trash with the shrug of a long-abandoned divorcee.

The older man sat at the table for some time before the younger man entered. The younger man was still old. The younger man made no pronouncements as he entered. He smiled at the hostess. She knew from his

smile that he was here to dine with the older man. In many ways he was the older man's perfect companion—rational where the older man was aggressive; thoughtful where the older man was brazen; kind where the older man was stern; smooth where the older man was rumpled; poor where the older man was rich; healthy where the older man was bruised; competent where the older man was confusing.

The hostess led the younger man to the table where he returned the older man's contempt with cheer. They were meant to be together, she thought.

Each time the hostess passed the table, she picked up scraps from their conversation. Two scraps in particular (filtered through thick Middle Eastern accents) permeated her ears and refused to subside. The scraps, repeated more than a comfortable number of times, were as follows:

The older man, elbows on table, hands vibrating with every syllable: "A four eye!"

The younger man, relaxed in his chair, head swiveling in a non-verbal no as he spoke: "Otter chic."

The phrases coated her eardrums and hacked at her brain. She picked at the words, parsed, massaged, dissected them. She imagined playful minks wearing glasses, but the minks began to fight—violent, bloody, deadly. She shook the minks away and other imagery, also violent, bloody, deadly, replaced them:

The hostess' father stood behind a counter, "Joe" on a badge pinned to his shirtfront. His fingers, battered from the side job he accomplished that day, were clad in Band Aids that didn't match the tone of his flesh, especially where his blood seeped through. Joe's body jerked as bullets—faster than the blamblamblamblamblamblam of the gun that spat them—pierced the front windows and his torso. He fell, but not for a while. Even as he searched the darkness for his killer, he knew why he was killed. He had a vision inside his daughter's vision that explained:

A 1986 Pontiac 6000, red, housed two "gentlemen"—so

they called themselves: Paco, inaptly named because he was not Hispanic and because his countenance was not pocked at all, but oozed a silky smoothness, and Joe, having a sort of ordinariness that was in and of itself extraordinary, save for his hands, cragged, with mangled palms and fingers so crooked he couldn't form a fist bouncing on the steering wheel as the car's balding tires met each fissure in the highway, hands that 33 minutes before wrenched the neck of a screaming parrot. The bird had it coming. Then, a vision within a vision within a vision:

> A parrot cage, rusty gold, hung from the ceiling of the apartment. The parrot had been trained to mimic by its prior owner. Here's what it said when Joe walked beneath, arm in arm with a woman whom the hostess would've recognized as her mother's friend Marilyn: "SQUAAAAWK!" and then: "Joe pooped in the sink!" and then: "SQUAAAAWK!" and then: "Joe pooped in the sink!" Marilyn laughed, a sharp guttural sound with great rattle and heft. The laugh upset Joe, who looked up at the parrot, eyes narrowing, vowing something. One final vision even within *that* vision:
>
>> The parrot fluttered around the pet shop, free. An employee walked the floor beneath, arms outstretched, holding as far from his body as he could a green iguana. Fluids leaked from the iguana's back end. Said the employee: "Goddamn it! Joe pooped in the sink again!" The most recent prior vision returned:

The parrot met Joe's glare with his own. The parrot heard Joe say: "Fucking bird. I'm going to throttle that bastard someday." To which Marilyn replied: "You better not. You know who owns that bastard." One more vision returned:

Joe, who'd recruited Paco to help, stalked into the house. Paco reached the handle of a broom to the ceiling and poked at the ring affixing the birdcage until it fell to the floor, where Joe was waiting for that bastard parrot. Joe tore the cage open and jammed both hands inside. As he squeezed the parrot's neck, the bird thrashed, bit, and clawed. By the time the parrot breathed its last, Joe's hands and the bird's neck were sticky red. The hostess' original vision returned:

The largest man the hostess had ever seen wept as the bullets poured from the gun blamblamblamblamblamblamblamblam and then blamblamblamblamblamblamblamblamblamblam. He wept for the loss of a parrot (and, perhaps, for the sanctity of his wife, Marilyn). The cacophony stopped when there were no bullets left. Joe stood, glaring at the man in his shop's doorway—a glare reserved for her father's worst enemy—be it a girthy man or a squawking parrot. Then, Joe fell.

Here the multilayered visions stopped, with her father on the floor of his shop, the girthy man sobbing in the doorway.

The hostess couldn't figure this out. She couldn't connect the visions of her father, Paco, Marilyn, the bastard parrot, the pet shop employee, and the girthy man to the snippets from the men at the table.

"A four eye!"

"Otter chic!"

Goddamned if she didn't know there was a connection there somewhere, but she couldn't find it. More and more she contemplated, and as she did, more and more she longed to put the men in their places, show them what would happen when they fuck with her! For it seemed to the hostess that the men used their cryptology to fuck with her. There was no other explanation. How she longed to lash out against her tormentors.

But she resisted. After pouring final glasses, emptying the bottle, she turned her whole body: feet, ankles, shins and calves, knees, thighs and hamstrings, hips, stomach and spine, ribcage and shoulder blades, humerus and radius and ulna, wrists, hands, fingers and thumbs, throat and neck, chin, mouth, nose, ears, ponytail, eyes and cheeks—she turned it all and walked away, and she smiled for herself, while her eyes frowned for the loss of her father.

In the back of the restaurant, in the kitchen, somewhere behind her, she heard a brilliant clatter as someone dropped a dish.

Chapter 12

MY RETURN TO THE GALLERIA de Cinco after meeting Marlena and viewing her "The" jarred me in two senses: it jolted me to my core and made me feel as if I were on display in a jar. I refused to believe that Marlena had invited me to her fellow artiste Jurgen's installation to show me off, yet I couldn't help feeling as if I was being spied upon in every moment.

I perceived this attention on me despite the eye-drawing nature of Jurgen's garish installation: Jurgen, head shaven, body clad only in a black vest and harness by which he was Velcroed to the wall, drenched in liquids (heavy in vinegar and ammonia, by the smell), his eyes covered by duct tape, nose plugged with paper. Only his ears and mouth were free. If either of those orifices had been covered, the installation would have lost its purpose, for around Jurgen's neck was a sign: "**ASK ME ANYTHING.**"

"What's going on?" My question was directed to Marlena, but it wasn't Marlena who answered.

"Ask me anything," Jurgen echoed his sign. "I'll answer."

"Makes sense," Marlena added. She turned to Jolene, a sculptor whose peyote use visibly aged her beyond her years. "Right?" Marlena asked Jolene.

"Of course," Jurgen answered.

Marlena smiled. "Well done, Jurgen. You didn't miss that one."

Jurgen didn't respond—the entirety of his gig, it appeared, was to answer questions—no matter to whom those questions were posed.

One of the gathered mass asked, "What time is it?"

"Time for a better question," responded Jurgen, raising a chuckle.

Questions peppered Jurgen—it was difficult to tell from which mouth each query emanated.

"What's the meaning of life?"

"Life is the condition that distinguishes organisms from inorganic material," responded Jurgen.

"Why are you naked?"

"Because I removed my clothing."

"Why'd you do that?"

"Because I didn't want my clothing to stink of vinegar and ammonia. Also, nudity is vulnerability."

"Why'd you drench yourself in vinegar and ammonia?"

"It's a symbol for urine."

"Why urine?"

"That's what I'd drink if wandering the desert for forty days."

"Why the harness and Velcro?"

"To simulate being helpless, unable to escape my fate."

"Wander the desert for 40 days? Pinned to the wall in a cross-like pose? Are you supposed to be a Christ figure?"

"I'm supposed to be whatever you need me to be."

"What do I need?" I was surprised to recognize my own voice.

Silence from Jurgen. Of all the questions from the crowd, mine was the one to stump him. The eyes of the onlookers struck me and stuck me in place—as if I were the one in a Velcro harness, unable to avoid my fate. "Ahem," I muttered to fill the silence.

Marlena smiled. "Don't worry," she said, squeezing my elbow. "I know what you need."

"You do?"

"Yes," said Jurgen, drawing another laugh from the crowd. "She does."

I should've been happy. I should've accepted Marlena's reassurance and Jurgen's attention-drawing spectacle with relief and happiness. Instead, I flushed red. "This guy is unbelievable," I barked.

"Who says art has to be believable?" Marlena asked.

"Nobody," Jurgen responded.

I blinked. As much as I wanted to throw away my rage, I couldn't. "Bullshit."

As was his way, Jurgen didn't respond. The rest of the throng responded, though, with nervous shuffling.

I rephrased. "How would you respond," I asked, "if I said that art must be believable?"

"That you don't understand the purpose of art."

"What's the purpose of art?"

Again, silence from Jurgen.

"Why didn't you answer that question?"

"Because for the second time you have asked me a question that I cannot answer."

"Why can't you answer those questions?"

"Those questions are personal to you. I cannot answer what you need. For only you can determine what you need. Likewise, I cannot answer as to the purpose of art, because art is personal to you. I cannot interpret art for you. All I can do is create. What you do with that creation is your business."

I closed my eyes to see visions of Marlena's "The" dancing there. I remained silent for a long time, as did the crowd. Finally, I breathed deep, and spoke. "Are you saying that the creator of art is unimportant?"

"No."

Relief! Yet I couldn't stop myself from allowing Jurgen an avenue of further explanation. "No?"

"No. For, without the creator there would be no art. Just as without parents combining egg and sperm, there would be no child."

"Is that all creators are good for: throwing their combined genetic material into the world?"

"Not necessarily."

"No?"

"No. The creator also instills a sense of purpose into the art—just as a parent instills his or her values and system of beliefs into the child."

Now that was better. And yet, me being me: "At that point, the creator's importance ends?"

"Yes."

Disheartening. "Why is that?"

"As much as the creator has put his or her meaning into the art, once people experience that art, people may choose to ignore the intended meaning of the art and draw from that art whatever suits their needs."

In a final effort to fight for the rights of the creator, I continued. "What if the intended meaning instilled by the creator is the absolute truth?"

Marlena grimaced—a visual tic unmistakable in its disgust and embarrassment. From Jurgen came a verbal rejoinder that also dripped of that stuff: "There's no such thing as absolute truth."

"No?"

"Whatever meaning the creator intended is colored by the creator's biases. The creator's execution is likewise tainted by his or her worldview. And ego."

"Ego?"

"You're quite the parrot. The creator's ego taints the creator's meaning, erasing any potential for what you label as absolute truth."

"How so?"

"Take an author writing a story in which he himself is involved. He is conveying a story personal to him, things that he alleges happened to him—supposedly truthful things. And yet, he has ego."

Gulp.

"Ego," Jurgen continued, "causes him to hide a detail here, a larger detail there, and an even larger detail elsewhere—all to obscure (or enhance, depending on his ego) some negative action or quality. The author who purports to tell a true story in which he was involved cannot be trusted."

Fuck.

"The author's untrustworthiness is more apparent where the subject of the story is a great man who was once worshipped by the author."

"What?"

"In the words of Oscar Wilde, 'Every great man has his disciples, but it is always Judas who writes the biography.'"

Jesus.

Tense silence infused the crowd. Jolene came to the rescue. "How long will you be here, Jurgen?"

"Until I no longer have questions to answer."

"So, if the crowd goes away," I interjected, "you'll go away, too?"

"Only if those in the crowd are the only ones asking questions."

"Who else would ask questions?"

"Me."

"Why would you ask yourself questions?"

"To get an expert opinion."

More tittering from the crowd. I got the sense, though, that Jurgen didn't intend a joke. "Are you an expert?" I asked.

"On myself, I better be."

"Why is that?"

"He who is not an expert on himself has no business opining about anyone else."

Fuck. I was stumped.

"Well, Jurgen," Jolene said. "You've certainly given us all," (did she just cast her eyes at me?) "a lot to consider."

And the crowd, silent, dissipated.

Statement of Alec Posner [excerpt]

...MY MOTHER USED TO SAY: "Alec, there's no grievance that won't be cured by time." I never listened. I heard Mom's words, but their meaning escaped me. All I knew was that for my grievances, I needed immediate cures.

To detail my grievances here would be more grievous than those grievances. Suffice it to say that the content of my blog—SEX, or the LACK THEREOF—should be instructive.

But that's not the question you asked—which is my point, of course. It doesn't matter the question. My mind will answer with something about SEX or the LACK THEREOF. I mean, I might start answering your question. I might, for example, say that Asher would do well to obey his mother's warnings. But that mention of Ms. Delacroix would send my mind scrambling to find a story, like this one, perhaps:

It was a while before I noticed Sylvia Roth. Sylvia was the one girl my age with whom I could've seen myself. Not at first. When I met Sylvia, she was difficult to describe. Because I don't have a particular memory of first meeting Sylvia.

Many people describe that "love at first sight" thing. Sylvia told me that she felt it when she saw me—only God (or whatever) could know why *that* could be true.

God (or whatever) came to my mind just then because that's where Sylvia says she first saw me—in God's house, synagogue. See, I'm not Jewish—not

properly. No bris (my circumcision was cold and precise, performed by a reluctant doctor who tried to convince my parents to leave my junk alone), no bar mitzvah, no Hebrew lessons, no Torah study. Godless (or whateverless), as I reached puberty, I couldn't resist the call of temple. In temple I found the beauty of education, the sexiness of enlightenment. For temple was where the mothers were. And those mothers had much to teach me.

Sylvia Roth's mother didn't attend temple. Sylvia attended with her divorced father, Mr. Roth (I presumed he was "Mr. Roth," I never caught his name), an "up front" Jew, one who sat himself and his lone companion, daughter Sylvia—like me, then 14 years old—in the front row. I was always behind Sylvia—in so many ways.

Sylvia's lack of motherly companionship meant that on the day that she first noticed me, I didn't notice her. As Sylvia was "noticing" me, I was "noticing" how Mrs. Bloom's breasts, swollen for the newborn in her lap, had blossomed.

Perhaps it was my positioning that drew Sylvia's eye. My contortions (hunching over, twisting my hips and legs to get a better look and to assure that nobody could get a look at my own blooming blossom) surely stood out from the other rigid Jewish men and boys striving to contemplate the Word of God without understanding that God spoke through people, conveying all manner (and, more importantly, "womanner") of messages to the thronging masses through the cock of a coifed head, the wink of a mascaraed eye, the licking of a painted lip. Of all the men and boys in temple that day, only I understood that the true Word of God was "sex."

So studious was I that I didn't realize that another in that assemblage appreciated true holiness. Sylvia Roth beheld Alec Posner, a prophet with angels in his eyes and the devil in his pants, and fell in what she later described as love at first sight.

How much later? Doesn't matter. It took however long it took for Sylvia to approach me, take my hand, rest her other hand on my shoulder, and—while allowing me to continue ogling a ravishing beauty of a mother—lean in and whisper in my ear: "She looks even better naked."

I should explain: This wasn't temple. My lust for mothers brought me to

the bench in Prospect Park with the best view of the path along which scores of women jogged. My eyes bounced as woman after woman ran on their path to physical fitness. I didn't notice Sylvia Roth sit down. Nor did I know how long she was there before she breathed her confounding words in my ear. After she spoke, I turned with stunned eyes and slack jaw and noticed Sylvia Roth for the first time.

I'm not proud of my first observations of young Sylvia: that the first two words that leapt to mind were "what?" and "underdeveloped"…that my excited surprise was replaced by disappointment…that I slid away from her. Sylvia didn't seem to mind. Her smile remained seductive, and her hand remained on my shoulder, pulsing in a massage that did the opposite of relax me, and her legs kept pace with mine across the bench, not allowing me the comfort of space.

"I should know," Sylvia continued. "She's my mother."

Oh my! My head turned from Sylvia to the woman. How could she possibly look better naked than she did in those moments? But oh, how I longed to find out.

As I beheld her, Sylvia's mother left the path and, still at full jog, veered toward me. Even as I lost myself in the glorious vision that was her rippling thigh muscles, I couldn't help feel her daughter's hand tighten on my shoulder as if laying claim. For whatever reason, New Order's Bizarre Love Triangle shuffled through my brain.

"Who's your friend?" Ms. Roth said as she approached.

"A boy from church," Sylvia cooed, her smooth tone just rough enough in uttering the second word to imply that her mother should look to receive affections from someone her own age.

"Ah," Ms. Roth said, raising an eyebrow. "And your name, young man?"

"I don't know," Sylvia answered, her hips sliding ever closer to mine, her small chest leaning into me.

"I wasn't asking *you*," Ms. Roth said. She sat on my other side. She stretched her legs straight out from the bench, leaned forward, reached for her toes. Two things kept my attention with her despite Sylvia's desperation: (1) her tank top rode up on her back to reveal the head of an Indigo Bunting

tattoo, the body of which continued down into her pants along her left hip; and (2) as she stretched, her left elbow rubbed against my thigh. Hearing no answer, Ms. Roth sat up and twisted her torso toward me in a new stretch, raising her right arm behind her head and pulling it with her left hand and arching her back. "Well?" she asked.

"Yes, very well," I said.

Ms. Roth laughed as her daughter growled. "You're funny. That's good. Sylvia likes funny."

"Who?" I asked.

"That's me," Sylvia grunted.

"Who?" I repeated.

"My daughter. On your other side."

"Oh. Is she?"

"Yes. If you'd bother to turn your head away from," Ms. Roth looked down to see what beauty was in the eyes of this beholder, "me," she laughed, "then you'd see her."

Now why would I fucking do something like *that*? I asked nobody. Some thoughts even I could keep to myself. Nevertheless, I didn't look away. Not until one more whisper hit my ear: "I don't mind, you know." I blinked, the earnestness of Sylvia's tone breaking my concentration. "I don't mind because I know that one day, I'll be her."

That did it. Sylvia's proclamation turned my head, my eyes, and nearly my heart. Upon looking in her direction, I saw that Sylvia was not wrong. Sylvia was young. Sylvia was underdeveloped. But Sylvia was not without potential.

Ah, yes. There's a word that Asher should learn. Potential. Sylvia had potential. It was there in the crook of her elbow, the glint of her eyes, the flexing of her thigh muscles. All reminiscent of Ms. Roth. Just like that, my brain shuffled from New Order to Mac Davis' Baby Don't Get Hooked on Me. I felt the closest I've ever felt to love for someone my own age.

And so, in my roundabout way of many roundabouts, we come back to your question about Asher. Just as Sylvia, through her resemblance to the traits of Ms. Roth, showed the greatness of her potential, so, too, does Asher

show potential. I mean, look at Sammy and Merry. If he is of them in the way that Sylvia is of Ms. Roth, then Asher has some of the greatest potential I have ever seen.

Which brings me to the largest point of all: we should always heed our mothers, without complaint...

Chapter 13

"YOU GROW PICKLES?" CHASE CRANE'S voice, flavored by lifelong soaking in the heat of a southern State, oozed curiosity that begged to reap more information than the question should yield.

Regardless of Chase's intent, the only answer she got from Ella Flowers was: "Oh, no. Of course not."

Narrowing her eyes, Chase pressed, "Didn't you just say you're a pickle farmer?"

"Well, yes. Or I used to be a pickle farmer. But pickles aren't grown. Cucumbers are grown. Pickles are brined."

Chase appeared to have received more answer than she could process. "Ah. Of course," she relented.

Donny Quick stopped milling (there were only two words that could describe Donny's movements: winding and milling) through the living room and bowed toward Ella. His white hair slid in front of his face and back again as he stood almost straight; Donny nearly always tilted at some angle or other. "My companion," Donny tilted toward Chase, "didn't intend rudeness. She was curious. Why should she not be, with your regal beauty?"

"Oh. Well." Ella's eyelids fluttered. "Thank you, Mr...."

"Quick, my lady. Donald. Please call me Donny. And you?"

"Umm. Flowers. Ella."

"Ms. Flowers, you are aptly named. For you are so beautiful. Yet..."

"Y-Yes?"

"I fear that your name doesn't suit you in one respect."

"Which respect?"

"Unlike the flower on the vine, your beauty will never lilt."

"Don'tcha mean wilt?" asked Chase with pride at knowing words.

"I said only that which I meant," Donny smiled, ever polite.

Chase frowned, shrugged.

"Well, thank you," Ella responded to Donny's...compliment? Donny's confusing verbiage made it impossible to read his intentions. In this way, Donny was unlike Chase, who made everything plain.

Despite being constant companions, Donny and Chase didn't seem to fit together, as if each was made for a different companion. Despite their bizarreness, Donny and Chase made quite the pair. Five days prior to their conversation with Ella, the two entered the apartment together at differing speeds. Chase burst through the door, ready to fight any daring to challenge her right to enter. She eyed each resident in turn, looking for any brawl that might come her way. Finding none, Chase relaxed herself in all ways save her expression, which continued to press her challenge to all comers. Satisfied that no return challenger was forthcoming, Chase stepped aside, allowing her white-haired companion entry.

Donny milled through the door in his companion's wake. His eyes drifted from face to face, resting on each until he espied Jay. "My lord of the manor," he said to Jay, as romantically as he two days later spoke to Ella Flowers...if not more so. "My name is Donald Quick, my lord."

"Sir Quick!" Jay responded. "Tis my great pleasure to meet you."

Donny tilted forward. "You, my lord, may call me Donny."

Jay nodded. "Donny, then. What can I do for you, sire?"

Donny stood as straight as he could. "Sire? You honor me, my lord. I am but a humble traveler with a humble quest. And yet I accept your bestowment of sirehood."

"What sort of quest?" Jay asked.

"We're more between quests at the moment," said Chase. "We've been questing for a new quest to...quest."

"My companion speaks true," Donny added. "If you know of a quest that we can…quest, then we shall take it up!"

"I seem to be fresh out of quests," Jay replied.

"Ah. Well," replied Donny, eying Jay up and down. "Perhaps you can aid my companion and me in another way."

"Perhaps, indeed."

"As lord of this manor, you can do something for me."

Jay didn't deny the status (lord, that is) that Donny bestowed upon him. Nor did he deny the status (manor, that is) that Donny bestowed upon the meager surroundings. "I'm sure I can do more than one thing."

"Ah, that is good," said Donny. "Perhaps there will come a time when we need more than one thing. Perhaps also there will be things that we can do to serve you, as well, my lord."

"I live not to be served, but to serve. Yet there may come a day when you and your companion may aid in my quest to serve."

"That would be our great honor, my lord," said Donny. "For now, though, my companion and I are weary. We have returned from battling the great Beast of Ballard!"

"A real fat raccoon on Ballard Street," clarified Chase.

"A beast so sizable," emphasized Donny, "that during our battle, the beast's claws left quite the impression in my leg!"

"Near the ankle," clarified Chase again. "Raccoon scratched Donny's boot."

"Yes, well," continued Donny, "we taught that beast not to terrorize the fair people of Ballard!"

"The raccoon run off," said Chase.

"Thank you, Lady Crane," said Donny. "Due to the energy we expended in that battle, my companion and I are now mightily tired. We request only a place to rest ourselves. We require not much space."

"Convenient, for I have not much space to give. But what I have is yours, sire," allowed Jay.

As I winced for the loss of more space, no matter how little Donny and Chase required, Donny smiled and bowed again. "Thank you, my lord. We shall do everything to honor your home."

Your? The word milled like Donny Quick into my head and tilted at my brain. The word rang true. This was not so much my apartment anymore. It'd been lost to me somewhat like Ella Flowers' pickle farm became lost to her...although not so voluntarily in the case of me and what had once been my apartment.

Ella joined the menagerie in the apartment one day after Donny and Chase. Ella neither burst nor milled as she crossed the threshold. Ella floated as if her innards were comprised solely of soul.

Despite the largesse of her facial features, Ella's physical appearance was nearly as light as her gait. Blue eyes dominated her face, dwarfing her eyebrows—which were large in their own right. Her ears, though also large, offset her deep brown pixie haircut. Her body hinted at masculinity, but not so much that she could ever be confused for a man. She had just enough swell in her chest and hips to give her a womanish form. Also womanish: Ella's perpetual expression: eyes wide, eyebrows raised (left higher than right), thick pink lips spread, head angled left and drawn back. Although Ella was not a classical beauty, she had appeal as dominant as her eyes.

Nothing about Ella screamed "pickle farmer," although pickle farmer she was—or had been. It was unclear in what State her family's business had flourished—it was "out east" and "down south" to hear Ella tell it—phrases I took to represent near the eastern seaboard at a latitude seasonable for growing cucumbers. Whatever their location, Ella's ancestors had built an empire on cucumbers and brine.

Ah yes, Ella's ancestors. I gathered that they weren't favorable people. As with all the residents in the apartment, rumors spread as to Ella's background. Within a day, all residents knew that Ella was rich. All residents also learned how Ella had "earned" her fortune, which stemmed from a vast stretch of factory farmland, gobbled by Ella's ancestors in the wake of the Civil War, land reclaimed from former slave masters.

Hearing this, I assumed that Ella's family, taking over land from ousted evil motherfuckers, were paladins, white knights who would wholly (and holy) revitalize the land. Instead, I found that the story did not stop at Ella's ancestors taking over the land—it continued straight down into Hell.

Unlike Ella the pickle farmer, Ella the apartment resident showed no signs of her ill-begotten wealth. Her luggage was as ancient as Ed King's carpetbag, yet held a small fraction of value. Inside Ella's luggage were arrayed scattered chaotic layers of clothing with striations of thick and thin at random—layers that could be labeled as bipolar. Buried within each layer were assorted artifacts: a ceramic pig wearing a pearl necklace; a toy volunteer firefighter truck; airplane-sized bottles of alcohol (empty); a crumpled discharge report from a substance abuse center; a bottle of Crabtree & Evelyn Rosewater perfume; a feathered, bejeweled mask; a stack of bent business cards emblazoned with a 1-800 number and the name "SuPrev, Inc."; a letter from a law firm threatening guardianship proceedings; a stuffed trout.

Neither these "treasures" nor the haphazard way in which they were packed demonstrated Ella's wealth. Ella had distanced herself from her wealth, and from the source of that wealth. Ella hadn't brined a pickle in many years. Instead, she set out from her familial home out across the wasteland of middle America.

Where should she alight but in what had once been my apartment, wherein she met Donny Quick, who, despite the rumors of Ella's tainted heritage, heralded both her beauty and his intentions toward her.

"I don't know why you say such things to me," Ella replied to Donny's "lilting"…compliment?

"Because," Donny said, "I've been brought up to speak the truth. It is my duty—my privilege—to bestow compliments where compliments are due."

"You must have me confused with someone else."

"No, my dear. You and your virtue have clarified my purpose."

"Purpose?" Ella asked.

"Yes, my Lady Flowers. I must win you!"

"Am I a prize to be won?" Ella's question lacked the feminism that the bald text implied—instead of objecting to being an object, Ella was surprised that she was considered anything at all.

Nevertheless, Chase came to Donny's rescue. "Donny didn't mean to objectify you…is that the word? Objectify? Whatever, he didn't mean to

offend you, is all. What Donny meant by 'win you,' was he wants to show you that you're more than a pickle farmer."

"Oh." Ella smiled. "You are too kind."

"Never, my Lady." Donny returned Ella's smile. "I am only kind enough."

"Well," said Ella. "Well," she repeated. "Well, your kindness is unnecessary."

"Why is that, my Lady?"

"Because I'm no pickle farmer anymore."

"Yes," Chase said. "You said that already."

"I did?"

"Yes," said Donny, "so it must be the truth."

"The truth? Perhaps. The truth it may be as a conclusion. But the conclusion is not the entirety of the story."

"Perhaps you'd better tell the rest," said Chase.

"I haven't told this story to anyone. I'm not sure if I'll be able...the story is a bit old. I can't expect to remember all details."

"Same is true of every storyteller, my Lady. Nevertheless, we shall take you at your word. For there is no other word than my Lady's word."

Ella smiled again. "My story is less my story. It belongs to others."

"All stories do," I said.

Ella nodded and began:

> The farm was formed in 1867. My family (Flowerses, the lot of them) established a claim (through bribery and intimidation) for farmland seized from the heirs of a slave-owner killed after the Civil War when (working his own land in the wake of the Emancipation Proclamation) he was kicked in the head by a mule. The land, warm and fertile, had been used for growing cucumbers.
>
> Problem was the Flowers awarded the land hated cucumbers unless subjected to sufficient brine to become pickles. Flowers replaced all of the crop on the land with pickling cucumbers.
>
> *He* didn't do that replacement, of course. He ordered that

replacement to be done. Migrant workers of various ethnicities did the replacing.

Speaking of, Flowers was the same with his employees as he was with cucumbers. Flowers insisted on "brining" each laborer, soaking each in an acidic combination of ingredients of Flowers' choosing, ingredients reeking of pain and torment and fear. By the end of Flowers' brining process, each laborer was a pickled man, having absorbed all of the pain and torment and fear imposed upon him by Flowers' toxic brine.

Flowers used each pickled man until there was nothing left but the remnants of brine, which stained Flowers' fingers, and the rest of him, too.

That stain spread to the next Flowers in succession—who, if you can believe it, might've been worse than the original. This second Flowers combined his father's hateful brine with a devastating greed for absorption. He lusted for the adjacent lands. He performed all manner of tricks and schemes and horrors to acquire that land, and then he turned his attention to acquiring the land adjacent to *those* lands. So it went on and on until a pickle farm became a pickle empire soaked with the brine concocted by the hateful, painful, tormenting, and fear-inducing first Flowers, and perfected by the worse second Flowers.

The next Flowers in succession and the next and the next all blended together. Each was some combination of the original Flowers and the second Flowers, each brined with the greed, wrath, and lust of his forebears. And each flavored the family business with more of the same at various intensities.

Then came me, one final Flowers. Even as a child I understood my family legacy and my role in sustaining it. And I liked it. I liked brining in all manners that my ancestors brined. I was good at brining. Pickling men was not second nature to me—it was my first nature, my sole nature—the sole nature of my soul.

But as my soul brined these soon-pickled men—so, too, was I being brined. My soul began to pickle. That pickling manifested itself in intoxicating ways in that I ingested all manner of intoxicants, which combined with my inner brine to flavor the whole of me. Hard liquor added its numbing flavors…and opioids filled in the spaces where hard liquor failed to flavor me. Weed, too. And Quaaludes. And many, many others.

My internal pickling broke when I unsealed a bottle of Advil and within a half hour the bottle was depleted by 57 pills. I remember consuming 47 of them…it was the last ten, the ten I couldn't remember, that made me stop, made me move, made me run.

I don't know where I've been in the time between those ten Advil and now. I have ideas—sex in some form was had, violence, too, and violent sex. But there was also joy. Problem was I didn't know how to process joy. I'd never felt it before. That realization ruined me—in the best way possible. It ruined me to a point of kindness.

I was so kind that I started an entity, SuPrev, which teaches those who run suicide prevention programs how to speak to kids about not wanting to kill themselves, how to keep on, how to re-brine themselves. I don't run SuPrev. I just fund it. The majority of my pickled pickle fortune is in that outfit.

Ella's story ended. To me, her story was sad. Not so to Donny Quick, whose smile grew as Ella spoke. "I see in you, Lady Flowers, something that I lack," he said.

"What is that?" Ella asked.

"The Lady for whom I've quested—that Lady is you. The Lady for whom I am meant—that Lady is you."

Ella flushed. Ella smiled. Ella swooned. Ella fell in love.

The conversation between Donny and Ella continued beyond the

blossoming of Ella's flower of love. It might have continued for hours. I didn't know. Through the remainder of the conversation, I was consumed by the light touch of Jay, resting his arm around my shoulders, and the words that accompanied that gentle gesture: "The brining of a pickle can be interesting."

"Can it?"

"Each pickle depends on the ingredients of the brine. Yet each cannot control those ingredients."

"Hmm."

"With all the ingredients in your brine, Asher, what kind of pickle are you?"

I had no idea.

Statement of Randy Mac [excerpt]

...CHIEF AMONG MY STRENGTHS? STRENGTH. [chuckling] Can't say many could survive what I've survived. If you knew it all, you'd be shocked—I mean, I've been shocked. Repeatedly. And what do I do? [laughing]

If I was any character in *The Bible*, I'd be Job. Without all the somber, weepy shit. I'd be a laughing, giggling jackass of a Job. I'd scream a hearty "FUCK YOU!" to God at every slight and invite more by waving my middle fingers. God wouldn't know what to do with me. [titters] Humor in the face of torture—*that's* strength.

That's why two of the three Delacroixs appeal to me. Merry and Sammy have more strength than I. I won't speak ill of the third Delacroix, ask as many times as you want. What I *will* say about Asher isn't a statement as much as it is a pondering of my own: I wonder if Sammy and Merry ever considered euthanasia...

Chapter 14

"FROM MY PERSPECTIVE—" MOM DIDN'T let me finish.

"Why would you start a sentence like that?"

"What's wrong with that?"

"It's valueless. Adds nothing to your thought—not that I expect your thought to have value."

"Jesus, Mom. That's not nice."

"I'll be nice when you need nice."

"What do I need?"

"Purpose. Direction. Something to do."

I couldn't argue.

"You need to be less like your father."

Gulp. Again, I couldn't argue. But I could return to Mom's original objection. "Perspective is important." I thought better of telling Mom the story of Bobby Bull...I didn't need to appear *more* like Dad. Besides, I had the feeling that Mom had heard it before.

"Of course perspective is important."

"Then why do you object to my perspective?"

"I don't."

"Then what's your objection?"

"Phrasing. That phrase—'From my perspective'—is a nullity."

"I don't understand."

"Of course not."

"Educate me."

"Everything you say, write, commit to language is from your perspective. Everyone knows that. No need to say it. Waste of time."

I was beginning to think that this visit to Walter Reuther was a waste of time from *my* perspective. I'd come to tell Mom something. Problem was I couldn't remember, through Mom's protestations, what that something was.

Instead, I introduced something else. "Dad's visiting me."

"I'm not surprised," Mom responded. "Except for the word 'visiting'— I'm betting that you mean Sammy moved in."

Shudder.

"Did he bring anyone with him?"

"With him?"

"What was that guy's name? Martin. That was it. Martin James."

"Johns."

"John James? That's not right."

"No, Mom. Martin Johns."

"That's the guy. Did he come with Sammy?"

"Umm. No. I don't think Dad has seen Martin since the hospital."

"Surprising. Did Sammy have any men with him?"

"Men? Plural? No."

"Singular?"

"There was this guy, Raymond Dorn, Dad's physical therapist."

Mom smiled. "Ah, Sammy. There's always someone."

Shudder again. "Raymond didn't move in. He dropped Dad off and left with Dad's car."

"That Sammy."

"You seem calm."

"Why wouldn't I be?"

"Dad cheated on you."

"I wouldn't use those words."

"What *would* you use?"

"Sammy never cheated on me. Sammy spread love. Nothing wrong with that. World needs more love."

"Ah."

"And Sammy needed an outlet for his love."

"Not you?"

"I couldn't take all of Sammy's love. It would've choked me."

"If you didn't consider Dad to be cheating, why…" I couldn't finish my question.

Mom could, though. "Why'd I bite Martin Johns' nipple off?"

"Yes, that."

"Privacy."

"Privacy?"

"I knew Sammy fucked men."

"Jesus, Mom, please."

"Please nothing. Sammy fucked men. To deal with reality, you've got to use real language."

This from a woman I viewed as being as far from reality as "Sammy" was.

"I was okay with Sammy fucking men."

"Jesus, Mom."

"Still am."

Mom's present tense chilled me.

"But to betray our privacy is another matter. Sammy did that too many times. There was a reason why it was the camera—not Sammy—that I threw through that window."

"So instead of hurting Dad and Mr. Johns—"

"Mr. Johns? Call him Martin. The man was a dear friend of Sammy's after all. Still should be."

"Okay. Instead of hurting Dad and Martin for betraying your privacy, why didn't you just…"

Mom, as always, had to fill in my blank. "Leave your father?"

I nodded.

"You're going to love this answer."

"Am I?" I doubted.

"Perspective."

I remembered Bobby Bull again. "Let me guess: Dad can't be judged by a few actions—"

"What the fuck are you talking about? What else would I judge him by?"

"Umm. The big picture?"

"I judged Sammy by his actions in the context of the big picture. You're foolish to think that that big picture includes only Sammy."

"What else does it include?"

"Since you seem to like asking questions, how about I try it this way: Are you a good person?"

"I don't know," I responded...although I knew.

"Why don't you know?"

"Umm."

"That one I'll answer for you: it's because my question was imprecise. I didn't define the term 'good.'"

"Oh."

"To define your 'goodness' or 'badness,' you have to know their relative context. What is that context?"

"Other people?"

"Don't *ask* me, Asher."

How like Dad I'd become—yet another Delacroix man beaten to shit by Mom. Defeated, I started another line of conversation. "Mom, how did you know that Dad was..."

"That your dad was what?"

"You know."

"Fucking men. Goddamn it, Asher. Be comfortable with language."

"Yes. That."

"What was your question again?"

"Umm."

"Don't worry," Mom smirked. "I won't *make* you say, 'Dad fucked men.'"

"Thanks. Did you catch him in the act?"

"Never."

"Did he tell you?"

"Never."

"Then how did you know?"

"Parsing."

"What?"

Mom shook her head. "It's no wonder you've never been published."

"Jesus, Mom. What does that have to do with—"

"You've no idea how to parse, interpret, deconstruct a picture—how to decipher the underlying layered symbolic meaning. You can't read people."

"That's not fair."

"No? Sammy may not have admitted to fucking men. I dug down, unearthed the clues from subtext. That's where I found your dad fucking men."

"Jesus, Mom."

"Jesus. Interesting name you keep dropping. Know any others?"

I did know others. The names of my roommates brought to mind characteristics that Mom might consider "subtextual." I thought of how angry Cassie James got at the conditions under which migrant farm workers lived. I thought of Ed King's mother's sexuality. I thought of Randy Mac's crazed laugh, Donny Quick milling and tilting, Ella Flowers' suitcase of treasures. I thought of Gregor Gregorovich's leer, Alec Posner's wandering eye, Chase Crane's incessant questions, the longing of Sony Ericsson to go as far away as possible. I thought of Marlena's art, Mom's maiden name. I thought of Dad's...everything. I thought of Jay's—

Mom cut me off. "Don't think *too* hard."

I obeyed, making one final subject change. "Did you ever dig down into my layers, Mom?"

"I've tried."

"What did you find?"

Mom smiled, shook her head, and turned to the window. "Landscapers came through last week. I talked to Dr. Long-A A-rab about them. He refused to pass along my suggestion. 'I think they know horticulture,' he said—the bastard."

"What was your suggestion?"

Mom shook her head again. "They've got to get rid of those fucking redbud trees."

Chapter 15

"DAD NEVER DATED HIS LETTERS," I explain to Molly Monahan, L.M.S.W., L.M.F.T., L.P.C. At the end of our previous session, Ms. Monahan indicated interest in how my parents met, courted, and fell into their version(s) of love. Staring across two stacks of paper, one large, one small, Ms. Monahan is disinterested in my show-and-tell. Nevertheless, I continue. "I asked Dad about it. He said something about his correspondence being 'timeless.' To me they seem more time-ed. They seem stuck in an era of personal development. If that makes sense."

Ms. Monahan makes no indication. Nevertheless, I continue. "As for Mom's letters, I could find only two, also undated, one word each in substance. Mom's spare prose reveals little of her emotional state. Or perhaps it tells *everything* about Mom's emotions. You know?"

Ms. Monahan makes no indication. Nevertheless, I continue. "Without dates, I don't know to which of Dad's letters Mom responded. Perhaps Mom responded to something else. I don't know if Mom ever read Dad's letters or if Dad ever read Mom's. I haven't asked. I'm not sure Dad or Mom would welcome my contact. Not after ████████████████████████ ████████."

I pause. This shit is difficult. Nevertheless, I continue. "Since I can't make chronological sense of these letters, all I can do is separate them into piles. Larger pile contains Dad's letters. Smaller contains Mom's."

Ms. Monahan doesn't thank me for the evidence. Doesn't touch the piles. Doesn't smile.

I pull one of Dad's letters from the middle of the stack:

Dear Merry:

I'm relieved that you scheduled the appt. I'm grateful you saw through my reserve. You have, as you often do, guided me through my mind and led me to conclude that you best know what I need.

I am forever indebted. Please know that.

You know that I am forever indebted, right?

Love Your Sammy

I feel I could analyze the six sentences of this letter in a dissertation that would make David Foster Wallace question my wordiness. It seems to contain everything Ms. Monahan would need to determine the nature of my parents' relations. Yet Ms. Monahan is having none of the letters.

For instance, she ignores this letter, also pulled from Dad's pile:

Dearest Merry:

March has marched again. Now that it's April, I renew my promise to forgo the drudgery ("horrors" to use your term) of attempting to fool you.

Nobody knows the origin of April Fools' Day, how today became one of the most joyous (or least, to give your perspective the credit it deserves) days of the year. The first recorded reference to April Fools' Day comes from

Chaucer's Canterbury Tales, the Nun's Priest's Tale, in which, on the "32nd day of March" Chauntecleer the vain and preening rooster is tricked by a fox.

The fox, Don, has heard rumors that Chauntecleer has the most beautiful crow in the land. When Don approaches Chauntecleer, the rooster runs away. Don says that he's only come to hear the rooster's beauteous crow. Chauntecleer, intrigued by the fox's foxish lie, stops, turns, shuts his eyes, and conjures up his most beautiful crow. Don lunges forward and grasps Chauntecleer by the throat.

Peculiar that Don doesn't snap Chauntecleer's neck right then. Instead, he runs away with Chauntecleer still alive and wriggling between his teeth, and with a massive mob of farm animals and the farmer's wife in chase, all attempting to save Chauntecleer's life.

Chauntecleer realizes that he has some cleverness of his own and suggests that Don turn and taunt his pursuers. Don realizes he has some vanity of his own, and he starts taunting. As soon as he opens his mouth, Chauntecleer escapes unharmed. The fooler has become the foolish.

Scholars believe that Chaucer is misquoted—that the text reads that these events occurred on "the 32nd day after March," May 1st, and not "the 32nd day of March," April 1st. In that case, the entire history of interpretation of the Nun's Priest's Tale is wrong in having us all (or almost all— nobody is forcing you, dearest Merry, to join in the foolish festivities) pull wondrous pranks on each other on April 1, when they should be doing so one month later. Isn't that the greatest prank of all?

Anyway, I renew my vow to never again fake a pregnancy test so that it reads a false positive…at least not on such an obvious and arbitrary day as April 1st.

Love Your Sammy

And this one:

Dear Merry:

Merry Christmas! I know you say you hate your name being turned into "a crass greeting honoring an even crasser holiday." But I hope that when said in my voice you reconsider. I do love a good pun.

What did you get me this year? Something as useful as the chainsaw from last year? I brim with hope!

I hope that this letter finds you joyous!

Love, Your Sammy

And this one:

Merry:

I regret to inform you I've consumed the last tangerine. We require more. Perhaps I shall buy some. I hope we don't once more duplicate our purchases of replenished citrus.

Love Your Sammy

And this:

Dear Merry:

My foot has been hurting more these days. I'm not sure what that means. Snow? I hope not. How much shoveling we accomplished (well, you accomplished, and I would've accomplished had my foot been able to bear my weight). Perhaps you're right. Perhaps I should make that appt.

Love, Your Sammy

And:

My Dearest Merry:

How joyous that you met Ramon. Such a gentleman! He found you fetching! As he should! Fetching might not have been his exact word, but I feel that "fetching" captures the bulk of Ramon's attitude.

To answer your question, Ramon can best be described as a friend. More than acquaintances, for sure, Ramon and I. But less than lovers.

I kid.

To answer your next question, Ramon met me three months ago. We settled in at the same café. I came back from the restroom and found Ramon seated at my booth. Not knowing what else to do, I sat with him. The two of us struck up a fast friendship.

I believe that there may be a hot air balloon ride for three in our near future. Isn't that fun?

Love, Your Sammy

And:

Dear Merry:

Greetings make such a difference.

As I entered the grocery, an older man, handsome, waved at me.

Took me by surprise. Not that the older man was handsome—that didn't surprise me; I've seen plenty of handsome older men. What surprised me was the greeting. I'd not seen it before—a man stationed at the front of the grocery to wave at people.

I watched Marv (his name tag revealed his name) for a while after I entered. Don't be alarmed. I was surreptitious. I made like I was reading a magazine—Cat Fancy (not my style, but I was well hidden, so I didn't worry about Marv seeing me reading Cat Fancy and getting the wrong idea).

Marv's wave was regal—turning wrist, minimal floppiness. His fingers spread, slightly. He wore no rings. His hands were of quintessential complexion. He had no blemishes. Bone structure looked strong. No unnecessary bends or obvious arthritis. He could've been a hand model.

It was unfortunate that I lacked capability to determine if

the rest of Marv shared the perfection of his hands. From my view, though, Marv appeared to be quite the specimen.

Where was I? Ah, yes! Greetings. I was impressed by Marv's welcome. I probably should've approached to thank him, but I (so unlike me) came up all introverted.

I truly hope we never part.

Love, Your Sammy

And:

My Dearest Merry:

Where does the time go when we are not staring at our watches and clocks? Does it progress as usual? Can we prove it does?

Tis usually the case that my watch informs me of the changing of the time. I usually look at my watch throughout the day. (Looking at it right now, Dearest Merry, it strikes me that the face on this watch that you bought me for that holiday that I shan't mention is too big for my bone structure. The watch you bought me has a 42 mm diameter case, but my wrist is more suited to a 22 mm watch. But what bright numbers the watch has! Perhaps too bright, but still, bright!)

Today, I didn't find myself staring at the brightly large face of my watch. Such is my joy for my new career at Kurtz' Klozet. Allow me to regale you with the details of my day (while hoping that your day was likewise decent):

• I arrived at the store at 9:12 a.m., 3 minutes before my scheduled start. This was the only time that I looked at the largely bright face of my bright watch today. I entered through the back door (which opens on the break room), clocked in, and entered the store proper.

• I need a new bullet-point for my first viewing of Kurtz' Klozet. That's how much that viewing impacted me. The colors! The fabrics! The smells! The audio, visual and olfactory sensibilities! All amazed and delighted me. In many ways Kurtz' Klozet is much like any shop. Clothes separated into brands. Brands into styles. Styles into colors. Colors into sizes. Despite all that separation, the fabrics ripple and flow together to form a cohesive thing, one fabric, one garment, one entity seeming to breathe and writhe. Upon that viewing, I understood it all. The appeal to women. The appeal to photographers. The appeal to children. I couldn't resist the tactile sensations. I touched clothes with my eyes, my fingers, my cheek, my nose. I held blouses to my chest. I held pants, shorts, capris, skirts to my waist. I couldn't pick a favorite until I found the a-line jersey polyester skirt, retro with chunky white and navy-blue stripes. Perfect with an eggshell silk blouse, no shoulder pads, dotted with Dahlias.

• The rest of the day went by too fast. It can't be measured in hours, for it could only have been a few seconds that I wandered the aisles, found customers, and fit them for outfits. The learning curve was slight.

Kurt told me I had "a nose for clothes," "a knack for knickers," "a noodle for poodle skirts." The customers had little reservations about being helped by a male (ladies who did have reservations overcame them when I demonstrated my "prowess for blouses"). I helped over a dozen people find their confidence through clothing, their assurance through attire, their greatness through garments. And I feel the poise of pride!

Anyway, my work day, although I know it to be timed, is also timeless. I am happy in a workplace. Did you ever think that would happen?

Love, Your Sammy

And:

Merry:

The markings on the driveway—I didn't make them. The black markings, the leavings of a burnt tire—I didn't make them. I would admit it if I did.

Who made them? I might have an idea, but I hesitate for fear of implicating the wrong person. But I believe that the marks might match the tires of a Jeep Cherokee.

In other news, I hope that you feel better today. I once more apologize for my lateness. My "meeting" went long (I drew in your air quotes for you, Dear Merry).

Speaking of, there were 4 attendees today! A new record! Me, Ramon, Jermaine and Georges. You have met

Ramon. And me, of course. I assure you that you'll have every opportunity to meet Jermaine and Georges in due course.

In fact, Dear Merry, I invite you to our next "meeting." You'd have a great time. Maybe even enough to remove those air quotes! You'd be able to follow the conversation, I promise. It's not <u>entirely</u> about the ideology of *Casey v. Planned Parenthood* and *Roe v. Wade*. We also discuss other types of empowerment. Gender, racial, impoverished, no category is excluded from our discussion—except for white males, of course (yes, I took your point yesterday when you noted that the entire group is white men—but remember: Ramon!). I'm sure your insight as a woman would be greatly appreciated.

What say you?

Love Your Sammy

And:

Dear Merry:

As you requested, I took this Friday and the following Monday off. However, I implore you to reconsider the activities that we will undertake. I recognize the need for work around our home.

But it's also the case that you and I work and struggle and strain. Look at your hands. How they shake when I'm near. I once thought that your shaking meant some strong emotion. Love? Passion? Perhaps that remains, that

passion—in fact, I'm sure that passion is part of what makes you shake so around me. But also, there is strain and pain in your trembles. The strain and pain of undying effort in all that you do—all of that shows through in your trembles.

Because of that effort (and because of my own equivalent efforts) I urge you, Merry, to reconsider the plan to have us put in even <u>more</u> efforts this weekend.

Let us consider an alternative: leisure, relaxation. Tis a time for us to do something for us. We need to have S&M time! Wait—that's Sammy and Merry. I should've better phrased that. Although…no. We'll stick with relaxation.

What I propose is that we forego additional strain from effort.

Spa weekend?

Love, Your Sammy

And:

Merry:

About the placement of the advert—it was intended as an inducement for new membership. It was not intended to embarrass you.

For example, the ad was not intended to shame you for <u>not</u> joining the group (I recognize that this was not your <u>stated</u> concern, but it's difficult for me to conceive that the only reason you object to the ad is that the pictures we

~ 145 ~

chose for the ad were risqué). The ad wasn't intended to provoke you into feeling that <u>you</u> should be the one to expand our group's roster. We had no intention to put you in that position.

That said, we would accept your membership!

What do you say?

Love Your Sammy

And:

Dearest Merry:

It has been 12 days since we erected the flagpole. It makes me swell with pride to look out and see that rising stiff mast that we accomplished. The one now adorned with stripes and stars, the symbol of a revolution.

As I stare at that taut shaft, I am reminded of you, Merry. And of what we can achieve when we work our hardest.

I again apologize for the limitations on my efforts that were necessitated by the stiffness in my joints. If only I could have helped you plant that pole deeper into the wet cement.

At least I could pluck some splinters from your delicate fingers, right?

Love, Your Sammy

These samples may or may not represent all of Dad's letters. There are so many more that it's difficult to believe that these 12 encompass Dad. These threads of random words cannot complete the intricate tapestry of Dad.

Even more mysterious is Mom, whose scant words don't begin to complete her tapestry—if Mom can be said to be a tapestry. Her letters, all two of them, don't complete a tassel that might be affixed to the edge of a tapestry—a tortured metaphor because Mom is less tapestry, more tarpaulin. Unadorned, utilitarian, workmanlike, weather enduring, more function than form. Much like her letters. Simple, plain, useful.

Those two letters:

S:

    YES

                -M

S:

    NO

            -M

Where Dad provided questions, Mom provided answers. Without dates, it's impossible to line up Mom's answers with Dad's questions.

That's the one saving grace of Ms. Monahan's failure to appreciate the evidence that I brought into the session. At least these answerless questions and questionless answers are mine. They belong to me. Ms. Monahan can do without.

I scoop the letters, shuffling the piles together, and make my exit.

Statement of Chase Crane [excerpt]

...MOCKING ME? I DON'T TAKE to bein' mocked.

Deny it all you want. I know when I'm bein' picked on. Comes from a lifetime of bein' picked on. Not me bein' picked on—not all the time. Maybe my brother. Maybe my neighbor. Maybe my friend. I see it. No matter who, it hurts me. It hurts us all.

There's a lot of that where I come from. Ridicule. That's a big word for me, ain't it? A word I know well—ridicule.

I'm smart for my age. I come by my smarts from my Pops. Readin' me the paper, tellin' me 'bout his day, takin' me to church, or bein' who he is, Pops taught me...just everythin', is all.

Like here's somethin': Some people in that apartment could be trusted. Some couldn't. I knew the difference. I could tell by lookin' at 'em. Not from what they looked like. Well, okay, from what they looked like, but that's...what's the word? That's misleadin'.

It's like the difference between photo and real life. Photo don't give an idea of whether they can be trusted. Color, black'n'white, no matter. Gotta watch 'em in real life—their actions, what they *do*—what they *don't* do—and how they look when they do or don't do it. Are they scowlin' or smilin' as they go about their day?

Or are they blank?

I got an example. Or an opposite example. Sammy. I could—and *can*, and

do—trust Sammy. I can tell because he's...hmm. There's a word for it, sure as heck there is. One of them "ex" words. Like ex-citin'. Ex-act. Ex-alted. Ex-pressive! That's it! Sammy's expressive. Everythin' about Sammy's on his face, out in the open. I never need wonder what Sammy's thinkin'. He's hidin' nuthin'. Sammy's about as far from blank as I can think of. Everythin' about Sammy—right there for anyone to read.

At least for those willin' to read. Which brings me to an example of "blank." Asher. Nobody could know what he was thinkin'. Because Asher himself didn't know what he was thinkin'. The only thing clear 'bout Asher's thinkin' was Asher's thinkin' was unclear. Without knowin' what he was thinkin', how could we *trust* Asher?

Still, some of us trusted Asher. With no hesitatin' 'bout it.

Jay was one. Trustin' sort. Poor ol' Jay. I wonder if it could've been pre— pre*vented*. That's the word. I wonder if us-all could'a stopped it.

God, speakin' of Jay, you know what's funny? So many people asked if his name was one of two things—as'if Jay couldn't be more than one of those things. I'd heard each and ev'ry person ask this. "Jay?" they'd ask, "Is that the letter or the bird?"...

Chapter 16

IF DAD HAD A PLACE, it wasn't among the patrons who frequented the Galleria de Cinco. Perhaps Dad's place, if any, was in the art itself—he was, after all is said and done, sort of a living artwork, being subject to many interpretations.

Artistic merit aside, Dad looked out of place in the Galleria de Cinco for more cosmic reasons. This place in the cosmos was a place for Marlena and me. It was ours alone—if our "we" also included the other artists frequenting the gallery and the non-artist patrons, whom the artists ogled as if the pictures on the walls were bait to bring in the real art in the form of these non-artists. This being our space, it was cosmically odd (even if thematically appropriate) to see Dad inhabit that space as well.

Also out of place was the object in my hands. At the end of the object opposite my hands was a transparent plastic wheel with raised letters from A to Z, along with selected punctuation. Beneath the wheel, a thin ribbon of red plastic threaded through from left to right. At the object's other end, a molded orange plastic casing formed a handle into which a trigger was set. Depressing the trigger caused the raised letters on the wheel to imprint into the ribbon. Releasing the trigger caused the ribbon to advance. The wheel could be spun, and another letter could be imprinted. Such it was that with a series of turns, depressions, and releases, the label maker could imprint words onto the ribbon, transforming it from plastic strip to literature. While all

characters on the label maker were well-used, the e, q, r, u, and exclamation point were almost completely worn-down.

When not in my hands, the label maker hung next to a canvas. Above the canvas hung a sign on which was scrawled: LABEL ME. On the canvas were hundreds of images (photographs, magazine cut-outs, drawings) and other objects. No image meshed with any other, nor did they as a whole add up to a comprehensive image. The top row (of 42 rows) was, left-to-right: photo of a typewriter; drawing of a fisherman; Count Chocula; blue-green smear of paint; uncooked spaghetti; photo of a claw-foot bathtub; a sad clown; a pipe-cleaner spider; puffy sticker of Elvis; construction paper swastika; VHS cover of The Jazz Singer; Barbie hair; reduce/reuse/recycle logo; New York City skyline magnet; jar recessed within the canvas containing a boiled egg cut in half, each half encased in chains and submerged in water coated with an oily sheen; clothespin; logo for Miami Vice; base clef; swatch of red/black tartan fabric; illustration of the muscles of a tongue; cassette tape of Bruce Willis' "Bruno Sings the Blues"; Wooly Willy; subway route map; Girl Scouts logo; hamster in a Santa suit; Kevin Kline as The Pirate King; Cheeto-dust thumbprint; used teabag; Michigan J. Frog; Nepalese flag; Polaroid of a baloney sandwich; expired drivers' license; plastic Easter-basket grass; photo of child John F. Kennedy, Jr.; Optimus Prime; crayon-drawn cat; half-consumed cigar; cloud shaped like a Norse God; cartoon of two of every animal crammed into a room with walls bulged to the point of bursting; gold star; empty Cornetto wrapper; kernel-less corn cob. The space between each row was dotted with strips of label tape, each with verbiage labeling the image above it. Beneath Kevin Kline: "PIRATES OF PENZANCE"; "TIM CURRY?"; "PERFECT CASTING." Beneath Elvis: "SEXY"; "DRUG ADDICT"; "DRUG CZAR." Beneath the roomful of animals: "YEAH, RIGHT!"

The artist who created LABEL ME was Anonymous, the proper name of one of many alter egos (others: Hardsell Hadams; Gorgeous O'Queef; Polly Emory; Christo McDickface; and Vlad Vlad Leroy Brown) of artist Jake Blue. Second billing on LABEL ME was given to "The Collective," which I (correctly) took to reference the labels affixed by onlookers.

LABEL ME was Jake Blue's sixth installation making use of the label maker. Marlena (accompanying Dad and I to the exhibit) detailed another:

> The last time wasn't interactive. Jake—as Gorgeous O'Queef—spent two days in a Plexiglas enclosure. He was naked and had only the label maker. He printed label after label, each bearing the same word with an exclamation point. He pasted each label to his skin. He came out when he'd covered himself with these labels—rainbow colored from crown to soles. I don't know how he got the labels off. Perhaps he never did.

Although Marlena didn't specify the word with which Gorgeous labeled himself, I understood why certain characters on the label maker were well worn.

Jake Blue—Anonymous—floated around the room, silent save for verbal tics that Marlena assured me were "pure Anonymous." I wondered if Jake assumed different affectations for each pseudonym.

"What do you think, Asher?" asked Marlena.

So deep was I in wonderment that I thought the subject matter of Marlena's question was whether or not Jake had multiple personality disorder. "I don't know. I'm no psychiatrist."

"Do you need to be to affix a label to the canvas?" Dad asked.

"What?"

"Marlena asked what you'd do with the label maker."

"Oh."

I studied the canvas, clicking the label maker's wheel one space at a time, every so often squeezing the trigger. By the time I realized what I'd been doing, I looked down to find that I'd imprinted the word GUMBO. Before I could cover my error, Dad and Marlena spotted my word.

"Gumbo, eh?" said Dad. "Interesting."

"Is it?"

"What inspired that?" Marlena asked.

"Umm." My eyes snapped to the canvas, searching for anything that "GUMBO" might fit. Every image or object was either too "on the nose" (soup can label) or too "off the nose" (shag carpet sample; dead grasshopper; shard of vinyl from an album). I slapped the label at random beneath a Billy-goat with a superimposed human face bearing a furrowed brow. The GUM of GUMBO obscured all but the initial letter "B" of a previous label.

"GUMBO the man-goat hybrid." Dad frowned.

"You covered another label." Marlena added. "I didn't notice what it said."

"Nor did I," Dad echoed.

"Perhaps the labeler saw it as scary," Marlena said. "'BEWARE'?"

"Maybe it was aspirational," Dad proposed. "Perhaps the labeler wanted to 'BE' that man-goat's furrowed brow."

I had mental flashes of a book, as if this debate had already occurred on celebrated literary territory. These flashes gave way to frustration that Marlena and Dad had moved on from puzzling over "GUMBO" to discussing the underlying "B"-word. Anger bloomed as Anonymous flitted back into view, his tongue clicking away.

"Who the fuck cares?" I asked. Marlena, Dad, and Anonymous looked at me. I softened the question. "How can a label change the meaning so much? No label has that kind of power."

"I don't know about that," Dad said. I shuddered as Dad began a story that only he could tell. "I read about this woman. Old enough to drive, to drink, and to know better than do both at the same time. Yet she did those things together and killed a kid. Happened in Tennessee, woman lived in Michigan. Michigan has some funky laws that wouldn't let the estate of the girl sue the woman…something like that. Complexities escape me sometimes, you know?"

I knew.

"So, this woman killed a kid, and…did I mention she served no jail time? I don't remember why. She remained free, returned home, and nothing happened. Well, *something* happened, or this wouldn't be much of a story."

Renewed shudders.

"This woman was haunted by news coverage of her misdeed. Made the national news for quite a while, her name emblazoned across TV and newspapers. She was upset enough to consult a lawyer, who told her that she couldn't do anything because the reports were truthful. She met with another lawyer, who told her the same thing. She spoke with a third lawyer, who came up with a plan. He filed a trademark application for the woman's name. His theory was that she was a public figure and deserved to be able to profit (or not) by her name as she saw fit. He figured that if this woman was awarded the trademark on her name, she could file suit against the news outlets for using her name for their profit. The lawyer acknowledged that those lawsuits wouldn't likely come to anything, but he thought the news outlets would see their risks as great enough that some of them would stop including her name in further reports. What the lawyer didn't anticipate, though, was two massive corporations suing to block the application because each already had trademarks on the woman's name—one had a trademark on her first name, and the other had a trademark on her last name. The corporations won, defeating the woman's trademark claim so badly that a court held that she herself lost the right to use her own name for any purpose whatsoever."

I tensed in anticipation.

"And after that, Wendy McDonald was never heard from again."

Marlena laughed—and oh what a laugh, turning my burgeoning groan into a laugh, as well.

"All right, Dad," I laughed. "That was funny."

"It was?" Dad asked. "I didn't intend that."

"Well, Dad," I snorted, "the author is dead."

"What?"

"You need to read your Roland Barthes."

"Who?"

"Never mind. Where were we?" I asked, still laughing. "Oh, yes—trapped between 'BE' and 'BEWARE.'"

"You know," said Dad, "the more I think about it, I don't think 'BE' is right."

"No?" I asked.

"What 'B' word do you have in mind now?"

"BALLUSTRADE."

My laughter ceased. "BALLUSTRADE?"

"Yes."

"You look at that manlike goat with the furrowed brow, and you think 'BALLUSTRADE'? How does that make *any* sense?"

"It's a 'B' word."

"So is 'BE,' Dad."

"True."

"So is 'BALLOON.' 'BATTLEFIELD.' 'BOMBASTIC.'"

"True. True. True."

"So why, with the endless possibilities of 'B' words, did you choose 'BALLUSTRADE'?"

"I didn't choose 'BALLUSTRADE.' Whoever used that label chose 'BALLUSTRADE.'"

"Goddamn it, Da—"

Marlena cut off my tirade. "Why is 'BALLUSTRADE' any better or worse than any other 'B' word?" she asked.

"Because—"

"Oooh. Good one!" Dad interrupted.

"What?"

"'BECAUSE' is an excellent interpretation. Nice one, son."

"That wasn't my interpretation, Dad."

"Of course it wasn't."

"Oh," I said, blinking. "Right. Of course."

"'BECAUSE' wasn't your interpretation—it was the interpretation of whoever affixed that label."

"Oh, fu—"

Marlena interrupted again. "Sammy's complimenting you."

"Don't worry about it, dear," Dad said. "Asher can't help it. It's just the way he is. The way he's always been. You should've seen him as a kid."

"Dad—"

"One day, Asher and I were doing that clichéd thing where you lie on a hillside and look up at the sky and say what clouds look like. Asher pointed to a cloud, said it looked like a wheelbarrow. He was right—from his point of view. From my point of view, it looked more like white chickens. Asher rejected my interpretation so strongly that I moved out of my spot, picked him up, and put him down where I'd been lying. I told him to look up at the cloud from that new perspective so he could see it as I had. He looked. I saw recognition in his eyes. For a moment, I thought he'd seen that cloud from my perspective. But no. What I'd mistaken for agreement was Asher...breaking. As if something inside Asher broke, as if he were destroyed by the experience. When Asher broke, something in me broke, too."

"Oh, Sammy," Marlena responded.

"Oh, Sammy?" I interjected.

"Be careful with Asher, Marlena. Please. I'd hate to see you shattered."

"Marlena, shattered?"

"Yes," Dad responded.

"Dad..."

"Yes?"

"What the fuck are you doing?"

Dad blinked. "Telling Marlena a story, son. I thought that was clear."

"No, Dad."

"Yes I am."

"Not what I meant."

"No?"

"I meant why aren't you not standing up for me?"

"What do you mean?"

"You see me 'BREAK' on a hillside, you worry about yourself. You perceive Marlena might be hurt if I 'BREAK,' you worry for her."

"You think so?"

"Those were your words."

"Were they?"

"Goddamn it, Dad, you never even stood up for me to Mom."

"You're being unfair."

"Am I?"

"I always stood up for you—even with Mom—in my own way."

"Your own way?"

"What other way should I have stood up for you?"

"Fuck off, Dad," I muttered.

"What was that, son?"

"Nothing."

Statement of Gregor Gregorovich [excerpt]

...DENYING PLEASURE IS UNNATURAL. WHAT could be a better purpose than to spread pleasure? How does one do so if one has denied oneself pleasure?

With that context, it's easy to understand the connection between pleasure and lust. Lust is the imperative for spreading pleasure. Lust instructs us to open ourselves to the world, to survey our environs, to expose ourselves to unexplored territories. Lust cues us to find a fresh patch of dirt—vibrant and vital, unadorned by plant life—and dig our shovels into it. Lust charges us to scatter seeds deep within that unspoiled ground, to cause nourishments to sprout where none had sprouted. Having sown those seeds, lust gives us permission to reap—for lust commands us to pluck the resultant fruits from the ground and devour their pleasureful juices.

In this way, lust is a vital element of the spreading of pleasure. To act upon lust, therefore, cannot be wrong...

Chapter 17

SOME DISTANCES ARE IMPOSSIBLE TO measure.

The distance from one end of the universe to the other.

The emotional distance between Mom and Dad.

The distance between where Sony Ericsson was and where she longed to be.

I never saw Sony first enter what used to be my apartment. She might've floated through the front door, squeezed through a window, or been zapped in by aliens. Her personality—sardonic, sarcastic, sad—made it seem that every physical gesture was a put on designed to fool onlookers into believing that she belonged in "normal society." For as much effort as Sony put into appearing "normal," she was never quite convincing.

Sony's lack of normalcy showed in her confusion about life, the universe, everything. No matter the task she observed someone doing, Sony wondered why that person was utilizing a particular method for accomplishing that task; often she wondered why the person bothered to attempt the task at all. "Don't you have a better tool for that?" was one common-core Sony-question. "Why do that?" was another. Perhaps her most common verbiage: "The universe is larger than your capacity for measurement. None of this matters." Then, after a pause: "I'm so damn bored."

Sony's lack of normalcy also showed in her physicality, the way she moved, the muted glow of her skin—nearly alien, too perfect, unblemished, shimmery. She kept her eyes to the sky, watching for some form of rescue.

Sony's lack of normalcy also showed in her name. Googling "Sony Ericsson" returns about 27,000,000 results. Over 99% of these refer to the cell phones of the same well-branded name—a high enough portion to suggest that the Sony had created her own name as some sort of odd homage to that device.

Less than .01% of Google search results for Sony Ericsson yield links to travel-themed articles. Sony wrote freelance articles in which she purported to list tips to travelers visiting locations that to them (if not to Sony) were exotic. Sony's articles concentrated on the horrors of travel; so much did she hold her surroundings in contempt that she refused to acknowledge any beauty around her. In her articles, Sony would sooner describe a hike through a bubbling bog of putrid bile than a nap on a whitewashed tropical beach. On the off-chance that she visited a beach, she'd describe it as she'd describe a bubbling bile-bog.

Selecting an article at random yields…let's see…ah! In the summer of 1999, Sony visited Manaus, Brazil.

Seated near the confluence of the Amazon, Negro and Solimoes rivers, Manaus is the capital of the Brazilian state of Amazonas. Manaus was founded in 1693 as the Spanish Fort of Sao Jose du Rio Negro. It adopted the name Manaus upon its elevation to the status of "town" in 1832. Manaus is remote enough (accessible only by boat or plane) that (despite its growth to over 2,000,000 residents and its development of thriving electronics, chemicals, and soap industries) it's maintained more indigenous culture and nature than any other Brazilian population center. Visitors to Manaus launch expeditions into abundant regions of fauna and flora along the Amazon and its rainforests.

None of this information is in Sony's article, in which she concentrated not one whit on attractions that could lure tourists. Instead, Sony described Manaus from the perspective of someone who didn't want to be in Manaus. Her writing captured only the negative. Despite complete lack of connection (beyond theme) to the graphic novelist, Sony entitled her article "Art Spiegelman's Manaus." In a portion of the article, Sony recounted her experience with one Brazilian boy. Sony wrote:

The boy from Manaus didn't appreciate history. He never heard the whispers of his genesis, never understood the suspicions that he was of evil stock, never saw the cult that formed around him. The boy from Manaus was a boy, after all.

As boys went, the boy from Manaus was a large one. He stood 5 feet, 8½ inches tall, which, at 13-years old, put him above the 95th percentile. The boy from Manaus didn't know that he would grow no more.

I met the boy at a French-themed wine bar. He wasn't old enough to be in the bar, but with beyond-his-age height and physical features he invaded with little resistance.

The boy was striking if not handsome. His mouth was pinched into a perpetual frown. His right ear protruded from his head as if claustrophobic, while his left ear clung tightly to his skull as if agoraphobic. No other word can describe his cheekbones and eye sockets but "gaunt." Not that he was sickly. He oozed the haleness of intensity. Something in his eyebrows transformed the boy's gauntness and melancholia into anger that sprang from his eyes, which defied any color, and might as well have been shades of black and white.

This was 1999. Not an era of widespread war, famine or horrors—so unlike many of the decades that preceded or the decade that was about to begin. The chief fears gripping this planet in 1999 were rooted in superstitions surrounding the forthcoming change in millennia. Seemingly every resident of this planet spent every day of 1999 with phobia that the next yearly calendar change would be the last.

Knowing the context of this planet's growing terror, the boy's swelling popularity among his followers is

perhaps understandable. For humans of this planet seek—
what are the words? A strong leader? A staunch defender?
An excuse to commit unspeakable acts of violence? At
least one of those, for sure.

The boy from Manaus encapsulated all those options.
His followers expected him to do things. Great things.
Horrific things. Any and all things. Oh, the possibilities.

The boy didn't appreciate the influence he had. If he
understood that to his followers he was a pretense, an
excuse to utilize their worst behaviors, unleash their
demoniac instincts, it struck me that the boy would be
perplexed. For the boy believed that his visage was not
angry, but righteous. The boy never intended to incite
evil. In this, the boy was naïve.

Naivety and nativity—those two words—I mean, fuck!
Right?

I espied the boy for exactly what he was. It wasn't
difficult. All anyone had to do was look. "Anyone"
excludes the boy himself. For the boy could see nothing
important within his surroundings.

From the distance at which I espied the boy, I also
espied his followers, how they circled, seethed, frothed. I
observed how one of them—a newcomer to the bar, a
man with a Romanic nose—approached the boy,
whispered in his ear. And I observed the boy whisper
back.

Before I tell you that story, I need to tell you
another—a story about the boy's great admiration for art.
The boy believed that he could contribute admirable art
to the booming Manausian canon. His attempts were
crude. His art, much like his perspective, contained little
depth, revealing only surface. A painted vase of flowers
was nothing more than a painted vase of flowers. Same

for a bowl of fruit, a cow in a field, and various self-portraits, in which the boy's facial expression did not vary. Among his...peers is too strong a word...non-peers is more accurate...the boy's art went unadmired. The boy had no idea. He believed himself to be accepted by his fellow artists, and that he was elite above all.

Not until the Romanic man in the French wine bar whispered in the boy's ear did the boy learn what his non-peers thought of his art, which was this: They didn't think of his art at all. They excluded the boy from their ranks. They refused to acknowledge him as part of their Manausian renaissance. This is what the Romanic man in the French wine bar whispered to the boy from Manaus. This is what set things in motion.

Upon completion of his whispered *tete-a-tete* with the Romanic man, the boy stood, looked at his followers as though he'd never noticed them before. He raised his arms, held them out, turned his head from side to side, and pointed across the bar toward his non-peers.

Next was chaos, confusion, carnage. Leaving out the details of blood and bone: the boy's followers swarmed across the bar, grappled with the boy's stunned non-peers, and ushered the artists out of the bar, into the street, and there marked them with various acts of viciousness—from their skin to their souls.

It doesn't take much imagination to believe that the boy from Manaus was fated to spur these spurious deeds. Like his natural Amazon basin surroundings (which are beautiful, by the way, despite the bit of blood that spatters them from time to time), the boy was a product of all that came before him. The boy was helpless, pinned into place by forces of history the boy never understood.

If you make it to the Amazon delta and visit that

French wine bar and see the boy from Manaus occupying his usual table, don't try to intervene in whatever is to transpire. It won't do anyone any good.

Oh, and also—don't order the escargot. It's likely to give you the shits for six days.

Sony didn't share "Art Spiegelman's Manaus" or any other articles with me. When asked her occupation, Sony said she was "a journalist of sorts." When asked her place of origin, she responded, "a place not within walking distance." When asked of her lineage, she stated that she was "born to be on Earth."

Despite sharing little knowledge of herself, Sony seemed to know the desires of others. For example:

"You'll want this," Sony said. I gripped the cold cylinder she pressed into my hand, felt its wetness. I looked down at a can of beer.

"Umm. Thanks," I responded. Then: "Umm. Need?"

"Your world's about to end," Sony responded.

"End?"

"Yes."

"As in over?"

"Yes."

"As in dead?"

"Not a literal death."

"Figurative?"

"Depends on how much of that beer you drink before you walk into the kitchen."

I drank. The can yielded half its liquid. I looked toward the kitchen, wondered what I might find there, drained the rest.

"Ready?" Sony asked.

"Don't know. Have any more beer?"

"In the kitchen."

I took a step. That wasn't so hard. I took another. I closed my eyes, drew in a breath, and took five more steps. I opened my eyes. I was *still* two steps from the kitchen.

Sony remained behind me, half facing me, half facing the stars. "Going in?"

"Probably."

Sony shrugged. "All right."

I looked at my feet, planted like cacti in the desert of the floor. My throat seized with heat. I gagged, hard, triggering a coughing fit that I swore sent bits of sand spewing from my mouth. As with any Arabian nomad, my only respite was to keep moving.

. Two steps later I found the kitchen occupied by a couple. Not Donny and Ella, but...fuck—I understood Sony's gift of beer. The couple was Alec and Marlena. Marlena rested her ass on the edge of the counter, leg bent, knee brushing Alec mid-thigh. Her hands rested on the counter, spine bending, pushing herself close to Alec's hands, which were gesticulating as if he were a maestro conducting Marlena's language—oral and body alike. Marlena's head cocked to the side, accentuating her pony tail, her eye-sparkle, and her spread-lipped smile. At least, thought I, Marlena was clothed—albeit sparsely: tight green flannel unbuttoned halfway; sleeves rolled up to reveal maps of freckles that I longed to explore for treasure; cut-off jeans barely concealing her hips; remainder of her legs and feet bare; toenails painted the same shade as her eyes, and just as sparkly.

For his part, Alec was dazzling...for Alec. His typical black t-shirt replaced by a tight button-down revealing muscle where I'd imagined flab resided, the shirt's cuffs enclosed with black cufflinks, "MOM" and "LUV" emblazoned thereon. Alec's hair remained tussled, but now alluring, not off-putting. His jeans were as tight as his shirt—there was no way, thought I, that they could continue to hold in the excitement that I imagined pressed against the taut zipper.

Then there was Alec's smile, to which an entire paragraph must be devoted. Every Alec-smile that I'd observed had been strained with effort that it took him to keep his lips from curling into a leer. The smile that he presented to Marlena in the kitchen, though: warm, excited, loving, devastating. More than all that, Alec's smile transformed his entire face, posture, laugh, voice. Where before, Alec's voice stammered out whingey

complaints, as he smiled for Marlena in the kitchen, he was clear, concise, confident. Judging by Marlena's overt reactions (giggles, blinks, a light touch on Alec's chest), Alec was hilarious. The two were in perfect sync. The more Marlena laughed, the more Alec smiled. The more Alec smiled, the more confident his speech. The more confident his speech, the more Marlena laughed.

The words they exchanged, however, didn't match their mood. In my haze, I only made out stray words: "bank" "temple" "hate" "subjugate" "exorbitant" "poor" "defeat" "horrific" "target" "explosion" "darkness" "agreed." Nowhere in any of the words did I recognize Marlena's or Alec's voice or tone.

"How's that world of yours?" Sony asked.

Without turning (for I couldn't wrest my eyes from the frolicking couple), I whispered, "Holy fuck."

"You had to find out sometime. They're going to need you, too."

"They are?"

"We all are."

"All are what?"

"We'll need you. You're important."

"Me? Need…what?"

"What do you need? I don't know. Another beer?"

"No. I feel sick enough. I mean, Marlena…"

"What about Marlena?"

"With Alec."

"Are we standing in the same kitchen? What're you talking about?"

"Marlena and Alec. Together."

"Oh. I didn't notice."

"They're right there."

"Why this fixation on them?"

"Fixation? No. It's just that…Marlena's supposed to be…"

"Yours?"

"Well, yes."

"You need to look around more."

"Marlena's all I want."

"I don't mean at other women. I mean look around *you*." Sony grabbed my chin and tugged—hard. As my perspective shifted, something inside me broke. Against the opposite wall, Dad leaned back against the stove, leg bent, knee rubbing against his companion, Jay. Dad's hands rested on the edge of the stove, his spine arched, head cocked. Jay gesticulated while he spoke. As I beheld their conversation, I realized that it was Dad and Jay who spoke those stray words of violence and aggression.

"How's that world of yours now?" Sony asked.

How I longed to respond, to make clear that my world was whole, was not shattered, was thriving—and in so responding, to convince myself of the truth of that response. All I could think was one word over and over, echoing through my head from one ear to the other, reverberating with power: "explosion."

"You know, Asher," Sony concluded. "You remind me of a boy I once met."

Way Leads on to Way

By

Asher Delacroix

WHAT CHOICE COULD HE HAVE made?
   Outside the Half-Track, before he set out—or after, while he drove…
     What choice?

He didn't have the white hair promised to him by genetics.
   Not yet.
     Not for decades.
       This was youth.
         This was before he mastered himself.
         This was war.

It wasn't his choice to be there,
   in Germany.
     War was chosen for him.
       Although,
         everything has at least one alternative…
           … one ultimate ending that could be chosen…
             … a definitive road less traveled.
               He hadn't seen that divergent road,
                 the less traveled road,
                   the ultimate and final solution…

...yet.

Not for another six days.

The battle of Heilbronn hadn't yet gained its capital B.

The battle would only become a Battle when written in history books...

...as recorded by the victor.

The lower-case-b battle wasn't done when he arrived.

But, by the rubble,

the crumbled buildings,

the fine powder that had been plaster and cement,

everything looked done.

The personnel carrier,

an M3 Half-Track,

navigated the unnatural terrain of:

crumbled concrete;

collapsed clay;

shattered chandeliers;

broken Baroque;

and corpses.

All muck.

The American line was one-quarter way through Heilbronn when he arrived.

Three of the nine days that the battle was to last had passed.

Six to go.

Upon his arrival at the line,

he was told to hang back,

wait until the fighting was done,

wait until the battle was won,

wait until the Hitler Youths were slaughtered,

and he enjoyed those six days very much.

Each morning he drove his Half-Track through the fresh muck,
    wet,
        horrific,
            to the top of a hill on the Neckar River opposite the battle.
              Binoculars to his eyes,
                he rested…
                    …and watched…
                        …as planes buzzed overhead…
                            …and building after building fell…
                              …and the world was destroyed.

Then through the resultant rubble strode men,
    American men…
        ….M1 carbines and M1911 pistols at the ready…
            …men on the lookout for survivors…
              …men ready to kill.

From his distance he believed that the men could've been children.
    If only he knew how right he was.
    If only he knew then that these were really American boys…
        …qua American men.

As he watched he drank and ate,
    making for himself a picnic each Noon,
    and otherwise…
        …he did nothing…
        …but watch…
        …and rest.

Of a night,
    he drove back down the hill,
        reconnoitered with the General,
            learned that each of those six days had not been the last of battle,

learned that the battle was to continue…

…until it was won,

or lost

(Depending on perspective).

And at that point,

he slept.

And upon waking,

he returned to his resting.

On the seventh day,

he did not rest.

So unlike God.

And yet…

…on that day

He became more Godlike than ever.

On the seventh day,

upon speaking with the General,

He crossed over the Neckar River.

On the seventh day,

He drove over the rubble coating Kram-Oder Markt Strafse.

On the seventh day,

He drove past what remained of Markt Platz.

On the seventh day,

He turned south on Fleiner Strafse.

On the seventh day,

He drove past the southern limits of Heilbronn.

On the seventh day,
    He left behind everything he had been.

On the seventh day,
    He lost his youth.

Beyond the city was farmland,
    land that looked to be untouched by war…
        …where unbloodied sheep wandered,
            land without wolves or farmers.
                Instead of wolves,
                    deposed Nazis,
                        former overseers of the closed prison camp.
                    Instead of farmers,
                      Russians,
                        all men by chronology,
                            but boys by experience.
                              They looked like shit.

Through the General's orders,
    the cause of the Russians' horrific appearance became clear.
    These Russians were survivors of…
        …horrors more horrific than war…
            …frights more frightening than bullets…
            …literal imprisonment…
                …figurative entombment that in some cases…
            …was close to literal.

And now,
    thanks to the General's orders,
        these Russian boys…
            …qua Russian men…
                …were bound for even worse fates.

"Fate,"

    He thought,

        was a funny word—

            funny in the cosmic sense,

                for it implied no choice…

                    …no option…

                        …no alternative…

                            …not even the ultimate alternative ending.

                            These Russian boys…

                                …qua Russian men...

                                    …had at least that choice,

                                      that ultimate alternative,

                                      He thought.

But what choice did he have?

    He…

        …disobey?

            He…

                …not drive those Russian boys…

                    …qua Russian men…

                        …back to their homeland—

                            unrelenting,

                            unforgiving,

                            unmoved.

                              He…

                                  …not drive those Russian boys…

                                  …qua Russian men…

                                      …to all new torturers….

                                        …who'd become…

                                            …their murderers?

For that was what would happen,

    so the rumors said,

        rumors so believable they couldn't be false.

            These Russian boys...

                ...qua Russian men...

                    ... upon being returned to their homeland...

                  ...would be...

                    ...re-imprisoned,

                    re-tortured,

                      re-brutalized,

                          their reborn hopes ripped away,

                            their saved lives butchered.

All of this for their crimes of:

    being captured,

      imprisoned.

        tortured,

          brutalized...

            ...in the first place.

He believed only in lack of choice.

    With the General's commands rattling hammers and anvils,

      down to the eardrums,

        He urged the Russian boys...

          ...qua Russian men...

            ...into the back of the Half Track.

For their part,

    the Russian men....

      ...qua Russian boys...

        ...obliged.

          As each one entered the rear of the Half Track,

            each glanced only briefly—

with resignation,

He was left to surmise

(for even the Russian language of facial
expression was foreign)—

or if not resignation,

then acceptance,

and,

perhaps,

pity.

When all were seated,

He retreated to the Half Track's cab.

He closed the rear cab window,

closing off any audio from the Russian boys…

…qua Russian men…

…which was a gesture in symbolism only,

for they remained silent,

leaving the crunch of wheels on terrain…

…as the only ungodly noise.

Sixteen hundred fourteen kilometers of human silence,

through Nuremberg,

through the ruins of Dresden,

through Wroclaw,

through Lodz,

through glass-strewn Warsaw.

He could've stopped there.

He could've given the Russian boys…

…qua Russian men…

…a temporary reprieve,

a final chance to walk a countryside as free boys…

…qua men.

Instead,

    He drove on,

        the silence of the Russian boys…

            …qua Russian men…

                …tacit agreement that…

                …the quicker,

                    the better.

He continued,

    the Half-Track crossing through Bialystock…

  …leaving Poland…

        …and crossing into the scorched and salted earth of Belarus…

            …where Bolshevik soles once trod.

            Crossing that final international border,

                He looked into the rearview mirror…

                    …past the bobbing heads of the Russian boys . . .

                  …qua Russian men,

                and saw

                  (with fresh eyes)

                    the path close off behind him.

Turning forward once more,

    He saw that way led on to way.

    He proceeded toward Minsk

        where killing would commence.

He had no choice.

Chapter 18

"WHAT'S YOUR OBSESSION WITH RATIONALE?"

"I wouldn't call it obsession, Mom."

"I won't ask what you *would* call it."

"No?"

"All I'd get is bullshit."

"Come on, Mom." I wasn't angry. Frustrated, resigned, aggrieved—but not angry. These emotions were the new norm with Mom, who grew more agitated with each of my visits, despite how seldom those visits came. I vowed to challenge Mom about her aggression—during some future visit.

For now, I remembered a lesson from Dr. Long-A Arab, M.D.: redirection by rephrasing. I'd redirect Mom by rephrasing the question. "Mom, what attracted you to Dad?"

"You don't think I see that redirection by rephrasing crap? I thought you were better than that horseshit *doctor*."

"I'm not, Mom."

"Better than *him*? Apparently not."

"I meant that I'm not trying to redirect you."

"You give me bullshit, Dr. A-rab gives me horseshit—you men are all alike. If you insist on the question, I'll give you an answer. You won't enjoy it." Mom shifted in her chair, leaned forward—and, to my surprise, lowered and softened her voice. "You will listen to my answer and *hear* it. Understand?"

My shudder was enough response.

"Good. Sammy has always appealed to me because he's a summer asshole."

"What?"

"You're not living up to your promise to hear me. There are two types of assholes: summer and winter. Know the difference?" Without waiting, Mom continued. "You don't. With apologies to Hemingway—if Sammy were a winter asshole, he would've arrived at my doorstep clothed in layers from outer fur to skivvies. Only as he shed each layer could I tell he was an asshole. Sammy, though, wore that asshole right out there in the open, on the outside, nothing concealing it. While all men are assholes, I appreciate a summer asshole. Sammy is my kind of asshole."

"All men are assholes?"

"Of course."

"Including me?"

"The fact that you have to ask indicates which type of asshole you are."

"You can't just say all men are assholes."

"I can say whatever I want."

"What about women?"

"What *about* women?"

"That's what I asked."

"I have ears, asshole. Doesn't mean that you make sense."

Time for redirection by rephrasing again. "If all men are assholes, what are all women?"

"Fine, asshole. Why do you have to bring women into this discussion?"

"Because you wouldn't."

"Did I exclude women from my analysis?"

"You didn't *include* women."

"Why should I?"

"If you're going to make a generalization about all men, don't you think I have the right to ask about women?"

"You don't recognize what I *didn't* say, asshole."

"What?"

"True. I didn't say 'What.'"

"Umm."

"I also didn't say 'umm.' What *else* did I not say?"

"Umm."

"Yes, again, I didn't say 'umm.' Try again."

Determined not to say umm again, I instead said, "Uh."

"You've nailed it. I also didn't say 'uh.' Would you like me to tell you what else I didn't say?"

"Uh. Yes."

"In addition to 'what,' 'umm,' and 'uh,' I didn't say anything about women."

"That's my point."

"There was no need for me to add anything about women."

"How is *that* fair?"

"How is it my responsibility to be fair?"

"Because you're my mom."

"And?"

"Moms are supposed to be fair."

"Clearly you've never been a mom."

"Mom?"

"What?"

"Why won't you tell me what all women are?"

"Because I don't have to."

"You said that already."

"You're the only one who gets to repeat himself?"

"Mom—"

"I told you what all men are."

"You did."

"In doing so, did I exclude women?"

"No."

"Why do you think I believe women are something different?"

"Well, you didn't say—"

"Exactly. I didn't say."

"Right."

"I didn't express what women are or are not."

"Yes, that is, again, my point."

"Then your point is stupider than I thought."

"Stupider?"

"You're right to question me there. I don't know how this conversation could've gotten stupider. But you managed it."

Questions be damned. This was a time for accusation. "You're being sexist."

"What are you talking about?"

"You labeled all men as assholes."

"How's that sexist?"

"Because you limited your statement to all *men*."

"I did no such thing."

"What?"

"Just because I said that all men are assholes doesn't mean that I think anything different about women."

"It implies it."

"No."

"Why not?"

"The inclusion of one category of people doesn't exclude all categories of people. Saying all men are assholes doesn't mean that all women are *not*. I didn't have to mention women at all."

"Ah."

"*You're* the one who dragged women into this discussion. I'd say that makes *you* sexist."

"Oh."

"Besides, I'm not the one you need to look toward to determine the nature of women."

"Who is?"

"Oh, I don't know. Perhaps this *Marlena* in whom you're so interested— not enough to bring her here for a visit."

"Mom—"

"Perhaps you should ask yourself the question you asked me."

"What question?"

"What've we just been discussing, asshole?"

"Assholes?"

"Precisely."

"Precisely?"

"You need to ask yourself why you find Marlena so attractive."

"Should I?"

"Since you won't, I will. What about Marlena attracts you?"

I flashed to Marlena's eyes, her thighs, her hips, her—

"Okay, asshole, mind out of the gutter. I don't mean sexual attraction. I *know* why you want to fuck her."

"Mom!"

"Only God knows why she'd want to return *that* favor."

"Ugh."

"Why do you want to be around Marlena when you're *not* fucking?"

"She interests me."

"How?"

"She's smart."

"How do you know?"

"The way she talks."

"That all?"

"No. Her art, too."

"You've mentioned her art a lot."

"I like her art a lot."

"What else do you like?"

"How much she cares."

"About what?"

"About others, life, me."

"How do you know?"

"Her actions. A touch or two. She doesn't hide how much she cares."

"Sounds like you might have yourself a summer asshole."

"I might."

"You and I might not be so different."

"Wait. Just because I'm involved with someone to whom *you* might be attracted—"

"Someone like your father?"

"Exactly. No! Wait."

"That's an interesting complex you've got there. Even Oedipus didn't marry his own father."

"Look, Mom, this 'summer asshole' thing—as silly as it is—although that might explain your initial attraction to Dad—that doesn't explain everything."

"Of course not."

"Right. There must be other reasons you stayed a couple."

"There were many."

"Such as?"

"All right, I'm sick of this game. I'll tell you a story."

"About what?"

"I didn't say that I was going to tell you what the story is about. I didn't even say that the story was about something. All I said is I'll tell you a story."

"Fine, Mom."

"Sammy always was a dreamer—in three ways. He had day dreams. He had aspirations. And he had the while-he-sleeps kind of dreams. I could always tell when he had a good one of those. He'd wake up all wet."

"Oh, Mom."

"From sweat, asshole. Shut the fuck up and hear. One sweaty morning, Sammy told me about a dream of cereal. Alpha-Bits—the cereal with all the letters. Well, not so much Alpha-Bits as a complement to Alpha-Bits."

"A compliment?"

"Complement. With an e, not an i, asshole. Sammy dreamed that he invented a brand-new cereal, a complement to Alpha-Bits. In Sammy's dream, this cereal sat beside Alpha-Bits in a smaller box. With Alpha-Bits being made up of nothing but letters, this cereal—which was called #$*&$*#—"

"Wait. #$*&$*#? How's *that* pronounced?"

"It was pronounced 'Fucking Bullshit.' Stop interrupting. While Alpha-Bits had nothing but letters, this cereal, #$*&$*#, would have nothing but punctuation. As he told me about this dream, I realized he'd never stop talking about this goddamned cereal. He was Hell-bent on seeing this #$*&$*# come to market. Problem was Sammy, rich in ideas, is poor in follow-through. Though I knew the business prospects of this complementary cereal were #$*&$*#, Sammy needed to try to make it a reality. But he needed a push. So, I pushed—hard. Every day I nagged him to do something. I suggested (strongly) he start with the packaging. And the asshole did it. He put together a pretty nice-looking box.

"Next step: determine interest in the industry. I pushed him again to market the idea to the proper company. Which he almost did."

"Almost?"

"Instead of sending his idea to Post—the manufacturer of Alpha-Bits—Sammy went to Kellogg's, from whom he never heard back. Sammy wanted to give up. I wouldn't let him. I pushed him toward private investors. And the asshole found one. This guy was awful. Along with his money came his thoughts, words, actions—each more horrific than the last. It came out that this guy had strong ties to both the KKK *and* the ACLU. Fucking horrible. Sammy wanted out. So, I pushed him—hard—in the other direction. The investor called, I screamed at him. And you know how I can scream."

I knew.

"He called again, I screamed again. When he got tired of me screaming at him, he backed out, and Sammy was free of all the #$*&$*#."

"I see."

"Do you?"

"Umm."

"Doesn't matter. What matters is: who pushes you?"

"Who pushes me?"

"I know it's not me—as much as I've pushed, you're not going anywhere."

"You've pushed me?"

"Lord knows I've tried."

"Hmm."

"So, who pushes you, Asher?"

"You think I need pushing?"

With a silent withering glare, Mom pushed me more than she had with words. I struggled for an answer. If not Mom, who pushed me?

Dad? No. Dad was incapable.

Randy Mac? He was a consummate pusher—he couldn't *stop* pushing. But Randy's pushes were purposeless. Weren't they? Maybe Randy *was* my pusher. God, I hoped not.

Marlena? A more appealing answer. Marlena pushed me into interpretation of art...hadn't she? Marlena didn't push me to go to Galleria de Cinco—that was my former lover. Meeting Marlena there was happenstance. But once I met her, Marlena pushed me. Didn't she? She pushed me toward a greater understanding of art. Right? Well, not *her* art. But mightn't her refusal to push me to understand her art be her way of pushing me to understand her art? My head ached with possibility.

Mom pulled me out of my head. "Don't hurt yourself. Not a difficult question."

"No?"

"Answer is obvious."

I winced.

"How is it," asked Mom, "that so many came to reside at your apartment?"

"What?"

"Who let them in?"

"I did."

"Did you?"

"Well..." Memories flooded me: Ed King floating in the tub; Dad at the door; Donny, Ella, and Chase locked in conversation about pickles—I caused none of that to occur. Resident after resident: unsolicited, unsought, uninvited—not by me.

"If you didn't let them in, who did?"

Other memories from different senses: the sound of steam whistling from

a tea kettle, the smell of medium density fiberboard, the taste of fried eggs, the sensation of queasiness rising toward vomit—I shut down the memories to stem the rising tide.

"Seems you have questions to answer. Although I suspect you know the answers. In the meantime, just try to listen. And beyond listening, make sure that you hear."

Statement of Samuel Delacroix [excerpt]

...THERE WAS THIS GUY I knew, Joe-Jack Straight.

Don't get the hyphen wrong. Joe-Jack wouldn't like that. The hyphen goes between the first two names. Make sure you get that down right.

Another thing that Joe-Jack didn't like was his right hand. It put everyone off, including him.

None of us could figure out how. Joe-Jack was amiable. He told funny jokes, made me smile, giggle, laugh, giggle again. He was good looking, had this face with those eyes, that nose, those lips...

Where was I? Right: Joe-Jack looked good, that's what I was saying. Handsome, built well, arms perfect for hugging and holding, pecs for days...

You get the point.

Despite all that, Joe-Jack got nothing but negative attention from strangers. Even friends stuck to Joe-Jack's left side.

It was confusing. That hand was as amiable and good looking as any other part of Joe-Jack. It looked and acted like any hand. It gave great massages (at which Joe-Jack was a master), it balled into a fist, it picked flowers, it told people to fuck off. All normal things for a hand to do.

But it gave off a bad vibe. It repulsed everyone. Joe-Jack wondered why. He studied his hand. He tried to fix it. He went to a litany of doctors, but each was just as repulsed by Joe-Jack's right hand as everyone else. They examined Joe-Jack everywhere else but refused to glance at his right hand.

Joe-Jack tried to hide it. He wore gloves but they only proved that the *look* of the hand wasn't repulsive. It was a vibe. A terrible, horrible, no good, very bad vibe, which permeated every glove, no matter how thick. From Isotoner to Carhartt, no thickness or toughness could stifle the vibe. Joe-Jack, as you might imagine, grew sad.

But that wasn't his nadir. For what Joe-Jack decided to do was sadder still. Joe-Jack decided to have his right hand cut off. When he couldn't get anyone to do it, he did it himself. It was tough work. In addition to mental toughness and pain endurance, Joe-Jack had to do it with his non-dominant left hand.

It was Joe-Jack's toughness that attracted me most.

Anyway, when Joe-Jack recovered from the deed, he took his foray out into the world and…

Nothing. Joe-Jack found that where before strangers had regarded him with repulsion, now nobody regarded him at all. He'd gone from repulsive to ignored. He became sadder still.

What's better? Negative attention or none at all? You're asking the wrong question. Or the wrong person. Better equipped to answer would be someone who's done the reverse: gone from no attention to negative attention. Someone who so hated getting no attention that he did something heinous, something that would be sure to garner him negative attention, something so heinous, in fact, that it pushed him through negative attention and back where he started, with no attention at all. That person would be better equipped to answer that question, if it's the right question to ask.

That is, if such a person exists somewhere out there…

Chapter 19

SNORING WAS NOT AMONG ED King's maladies. While he lived in what had once been my apartment, he only snored one night. But what a night it was. The genesis of Ed's snoring was soy. Ed, allergic, added the wrong creamer to his coffee. "An accident" to all but Ed, who wheezed, "There...are no...accidents. There...is only... what is...meant...to be."

Regardless of fault or blame (certain residents would describe the incident as *my* fault—something about me, standing nearest the fridge when Ed poured his coffee, grabbing the wrong container of cream and handing it to Ed), the incident would've threatened Ed's life had not Cassie James been rolling past the kitchen. Cassie race-rolled to the bedroom, returning with Ed's inhaler before Ed completed "to be." She forced the inhaler into Ed's mouth. Ed struggled down the noxious fumes, his throat opened, and he survived with a temporary defect: a snore that forced me awake to discover that the bedroom was emptier than it had been in weeks. I surveyed the makeshift beds. Only five bodies appeared:

- Ed King, curled in the southeast corner, slept with his carpetbag as his pillow.

- Donny Quick and Ella Flowers slept back-to-back on the floor as chaste as they were intimate.

- Chase Crane slept on the Donny Quick side of that couple, her body angling toward the door.

- Gregor Gregorovich slept on the Ella Flowers side, one eye open and trained—through the two bodies between them—on Chase.

Wondering at the multiple absences, I crossed the room, stepping over bodies, and exited into the hallway, where I found two more residents asleep:

- Cassie James slept upright, head lolled against the wall as if suffering ill effects from a blunt blow to her cranium.

- Alec Posner slept face-up on the floor, head beneath Cassie's chair as if under football bleachers trying to espy the underwear (or lack thereof) of the players' mothers.

Still missing several bodies, I proceeded along the hallway...and froze. Here were the rest, lounging in the living room, bodies touching each other, and each body naked:

- Dad, upright, filling one end of the couch, legs akimbo.

- Randy Mac filling the rest of the couch, feet dangling over the armrest, head resting on Dad's ankles.

- Sony Ericsson, legs spread, her back to the television.

- Marlena (how had I not noticed that she wasn't in the bedroom?) on her knees at Sony's feet, fingers working deep into Sony's soles.

- Jay, at the room's center, in lotus position.

Marlena removed her hands from Sony's feet, leaned over, kissed each set of toes. A moan issued from deep within Sony. As Marlena had finished with Sony, so she began with Jay, bestowing gentle kisses upon each naked foot, then kneading and prodding with her fingers as Jay sighed and cooed.

I couldn't help but compare bodies, like to like. Randy's chest was coated with hair thicker than on his head, while Dad's was opposite, with red irritation bumps hinting at a recent chest-shaving. Randy's stomach protruded slightly more than Dad's— surprising given Randy's otherwise superior musculature. Sony was smaller, more symmetrical, firmer than Marlena.

And then there was Jay. There was no comparison for Jay. Jay was the centerpiece in more than location. Despite the naked female flesh in the room, Jay's body drew my eye. His confident uprightness complemented his physical strength. He made his relaxed pose the epitome of physical activity—his ropy "ceps" (bi-, tri-, quadri-) pulsed and rippled despite the stillness of his body. He had abs and pecs for days. His head reclined such that his jawline and chin appeared to be the most powerful parts of his all-powerful being. Jay was the most beautiful creature in the room, in the apartment, in the world. My God.

Jay turned, saw me, showed no surprise. I took Jay's silent gaze as tacit acceptance of my presence half-in, half-out of the room. Jay allowed me to stand there viewing everyone in all their glory—allowed me status as a preferred tourist. Even though I wasn't invited to join, I got to be the next best thing: a voyeur. Joy and rapture coated me inside and out. I felt not the pain of the uninvited. Instead, I felt…

It didn't matter. What I felt was destroyed by Randy Mac: "What the fuck do you see in Asher?"

To my relief, the answer didn't come from Jay. Jay, smiling the faintest smile, remained silent. The answer came from Marlena, who never paused working her hands at Jay's feet. "I'm attracted to inquisitiveness."

I began to rebound until Marlena continued. "Also, softness." My ego deflated. "Well, softness isn't the right word."

Oh rapture!

"It's malleability."

Oh fuck!

"Asher is malleable. He can be shaped and molded, like…art."

"That all?" Randy scoffed.

"Not *all*. Asher is also…accepting."

"Accepting of what?" Randy asked.

"Actions, instincts, flaws."

"Yours or his?"

"Funny," Marlena responded.

"Does his acceptance have limits?"

"If it does, I haven't seen them. Then again…"

"Then again, Asher hasn't seen your 'actions' with us." Randy completed her thought.

What actions? On second thought, don't tell me.

"True, but I don't think Asher would mind the physical stuff."

Physical stuff? Fuck. I said *don't* tell me!

As if to tell me more, Marlena's hands worked their way up Jay's leg, squeezed his thigh. "Asher's limits are with mental connections."

"Emotional connections are important to our family." Dad's first contribution to the conversation almost made me chuckle, thinking of Mom.

"Emotional isn't what I mean. I mean *mental* connections…intellectual bonding." Marlena returned to Jay's feet.

What?

"I think Asher could surprise you." Dad smiled.

I smiled, too.

"Of that, I've no doubt." Marlena's answer was ominous, unsmiling.

"Good," Dad replied, missing, as was Delacroix-man custom, Marlena's signs.

"Is it?" Sony's voice.

Dad's eyebrows wrinkled. "I guess I don't know. Surprises aren't *always* good. But they're exciting."

A mild laugh from the room's center. All attention turned to Jay. Jay's eyes stayed focused on me. His smile widened, but his features were sadder for it. "Surprises are what they are," he said.

Did Jay shake his head? Did his eyes droop?

"It's okay, though," he continued. "It really is."

I flushed, tearing my eyes away. I tried to connect to anyone else in the room, announce my presence to anyone beyond Jay. I looked to Sony, Randy, Marlena, Dad—each's eyes were closed, relaxed, lost to the world, unaware of their surroundings.

My eyes returned to Jay. His smile broadened. His head tipped to the side. His eyes brightened. His lips parted.

"Ever still," he breathed so only I could hear. "All is right with my soul."

Statement of Sony Ericsson [excerpt]

...DON'T BELIEVE EVERYTHING I READ. Books lie. People, too. How can they not? Lying is the refuge of those who don't know what they're talking about. To lie is to avoid admitting that you don't know everything.

Most primitive place I ever visited—those living there had never seen someone like me. They weren't reclusive. They didn't hide. They lived in a place that nobody ever found...except me. People who *didn't* find this place were better off.

I was pushing through some jungle—or maybe it was desert—or brushland—doesn't matter. What matters is that I found it. Like most of my discoveries, I wished I hadn't.

When I found this place, as much as I hated it, I knew I had to write about it and its residents. It was (and they were) unique.

When I pulled out my pen and clicked it open, they went bat-shit. They'd never seen a pen before. They looked at each other, begging for someone else to identify the mystery object, to defuse the toxic atmosphere that surrounded it and its impending use. None of them knew what the pen was, though. And none of them wanted to admit that they didn't know. Admitting to not knowing was akin to admitting that this mysterious object might dominate them.

So, what do they do? They lie. The first one to speak screamed that he or she (impossible to say) knew the pen was a doomsday device that must be

seized, and that whoever seized and wielded it would've saved their lives and would be the new Messiah.

Another disagreed—with another lie. That one rationalized that the pen was a sacred object that could point the way to water, food, fire, whatever they needed.

Yet another swore beyond swearing that he or she *knew* that the liquid observable through the clear walls of the pen was a drug, the ingestion of which would cause visions that would lead to salvation for all.

None of them knew that this pen was just a fucking pen. All of them lied their asses off to rationalize this thing that they'd never seen before, to make it work within their society, to make it sane, to make it safe. Or safe-*ish*.

That kind of thing happens…a lot. Here on Earth, for example, modern scientists and philosophers lie all the time about matters that they *know* beyond a shadow of a doubt to be *absolute truth*. You know who also told those lies? Scientists and philosophers—and everyone else—who's ever lived.

Ancient peoples lied about the existence of Gods who had the predilection to transform into animals to seduce women.

Scientists in the Middle Ages and beyond lied about geocentrism, stating beyond doubt that the Sun revolved around the Earth.

For centuries, plantation owners in the American south lied about the purported inferiority of blacks and other minorities they exploited as slaves.

Later, warmongers and other profiteers in the United States and the U.S.S.R. and beyond lied about the threats to their cultures posed by communism, capitalism, and other isms.

All these lies have been proven to be lies. People of today look back and laugh at those who believed that the Earth was flat and the center around which the universe revolves, or who believed in the Gods of Mount Olympus.

By that same token, hundreds of years from now, when future humans have debunked the lies being told by humans today, they'll laugh. Just as generations past have become primitive, so too will we become primitive someday.

What happened with my pen, you ask, in that hellscape that I found? I used the threat inherent in that pen—mightier than the sword, as the saying

goes—to scare those primitive beings into submission so I could get the fuck away from them as soon as possible.

I feel a bit bad about the whole thing, though. As horrific as those types of historic lies can be, I suppose that some of those lies can be useful to avert mass panic…

Chapter 20

"WRITERS SHOULDN'T INTRODUCE THE ANTAGONIST—'bad guy' to such an absolutist as you, young Delacroix—two-thirds of the way through the book. It's better to do so on page one, allow the reader to become comfortable with—even like—the bad guy. Better still, make the bad guy the narrator!"

I cringed at Gregor Gregorovich's words both in content (painting me as "absolutist" in a way I tried not to understand; lingering on "young"; smearing of narrators everywhere) and voice (unidentifiably foreign, a combination of greasy slime and sophisticated grace, the voice of unreliability incarnate).

"The narrator shouldn't know he's the bad guy, or if he does, he shouldn't let on. He should deny wrongdoing, deflect, confuse. Maybe he says that the story isn't about him—subterfuge, sleight of hand. He sums himself up, then says, 'That's all you need learn about me! Over *here* is the *real* story.' He keeps going, telling other characters' stories—all the while allowing other characters to tell *his* story. Or perhaps the narrator believes that he is the *good* guy. Although, I doubt *anyone* could be quite *that* foolish."

"Foolish?" I didn't offer this rejoinder. Chase Crane, using me as shield, did. We were each other's heroes.

Gregor Gregorovich and Chase Crane hadn't always been Gregor Gregorovich and Chase Crane. Gregor was born in Saint Petersburg, Russia

36 years before with some other name, so unpronounceable that he wouldn't tell us what it was.

Chase was born 9 years before in the deepest south as Jenny Loren Crane. Her brother Jeremy dubbed her Chase because of the way she hunted down and "put a beatin' on" any child besmirching her family or her adolescent ideals. Chase relished her nickname, refusing to allow anyone (most of all Gregor) to refer to her by any other name.

I didn't learn these facts (in Gregor's case "facts") from Gregor or Chase. I gleaned these facts/"facts" from witnessing their interactions with the other residents of what had once been my apartment. Like Gregor's fictive "narrator," I learned of Gregor and Chase through subtext.

For example: Gregor's intentions toward Chase revealed themselves through the sparkle in his eyes as he turned toward the adolescent and said, "Why yes, darling Chase. Foolish. For what else could a narrator be if he tells a story but doesn't acknowledge his role in that story?"

"Maybe he's just shy?"

"Like *you*, my violet?" Gregor asked.

Chase's deep-brown cheeks glowed red. "I ain't a violet. I'm a Chase."

"A glorious chase!"

"I ain't shy, neither!"

"Just so. Perhaps I should've used Mr. Delacroix as my example."

"Me?" My eyebrows and hackles arose. "Shy?"

"What other Mr. Delacroix would it be? Certainly not Samuel."

I had to agree.

"I'm not sure that 'shy' is right for you either, junior Delacroix."

"Junior?"

"While you fit many terms, shy you're not."

Once more Chase screeched to my rescue. "What d'you know 'bout Asher?"

"Exactly my point. Each person acts as narrator of his own story. What can be known about a narrator except for what he reveals?"

Chase puzzled.

"One facet of your youth I don't envy, my darling."

"What part?"

"Inexperience."

"I've experienced plenty," Chase seethed.

"Yes. In those experiences—dead mother, righteously busy father, fellow townsfolk ranging from suspicious to dangerous, fights and calamities galore—you've learned much of yourself and the world. Yet your 12 years—"

"Nine," Chase corrected even as she seemed to enjoy the added three years.

"My mistake," Gregor recanted, "I must be thinking of someone else. In your *nine* years, you've experienced as much as you could."

"But?"

"All the same, your years number but 9."

"Nine's a lot!"

"To you, yes. Nine is everything you know. From a different perspective, 9 isn't so much."

"Okay," Chase said, seeming to understand.

"Let's apply the experience that you've accumulated over your 9 years. How would *you* sum up Asher?"

Chase paused to consider the question, or to study me, or to choose her words so as not to offend. I couldn't read her. When Chase continued, her voice rose in a forceful squeak. "I see Asher as a good man," she began.

I swelled with joyous relief and pride. But, of course, Chase was not done. "A good man," she repeated. "A good man," once more.

Then long silence.

Finally, Chase continued, "What was that word you used earlier?"

"I've used many words, darling."

"Perspective!" she shouted, glowing.

"Ah! You understand!"

"Asher is a good man…from my perspective."

"What is your perspective?" Gregor asked.

"*You're* my perspective. Compared to *you*, Asher's a good man."

Fuck.

"And?" Gregor urged.

"Any other room, Asher wouldn't look so good. Out there are Cassie, Ella, Sammy, Marlena, Donny, Jay." Chase's tone, starting with Cassie, was reverent. Reverence swelled with each name until, when she reached the ultimate two she adopted singsong tones befitting a gospel choir.

Chase's list had an opposite effect on Gregor. By the time Chase reached her ultimate two, Gregor's smile faded. At Donny's mention, Gregor growled.

"Out there," Chase continued, "there's not just *you*."

Gregor's countenance cleared. "Ah, yes, me!" he beamed. "Those people aren't *me*. What does that mean for Asher?"

"Compared to each'n'all them, Asher wouldn't look s'good."

"You are brilliant, my Chase!"

Chase cooled at Gregor's renewed flirtation. "I know what I am," she retorted. "You don't have to tell me."

"Then you're another step up on Asher who—from *my* perspective, which includes *only* you, my darling—is stunted. Which explains why Asher reveals so little of himself."

I waited for Chase to push back, but her face betrayed no disagreement. Receiving no defense from Chase, I asked, "It does?"

"For how," continued Gregor, "can a narrator express himself as a character in his own narrative if he doesn't understand himself? Such a narrator might as well remain ordinary. plain, unremarkable, unexceptional, nondescript, characterless."

"Oh," I sighed.

"But that narrator must understand that being characterless is an advantage in storytelling."

"Oh?"

"For a narrator who has no story of his own to tell can focus on his greatest asset."

"What is it?"

"The ability to mislead."

I withered.

"The characterless narrator is free to keep the reader guessing until the last

page—or even after. Which brings to mind another point: nobody questions books anymore."

"Books don't answer," Chase said.

"Even as I adore you, I must inform you that you're incorrect. The purpose of books is to answer questions."

"Books can't do that." As I jumped in to aid Chase, I couldn't help but think that she was not the one needing defending. "Authors can't know who'll read a book. So, how can an author answer any reader's questions?"

"You have twisted my premise, son." At this utterance of purported parentage, I understood more than ever Chase's revulsion to this slick trickster. "I didn't say the *author's* purpose is to answer questions. The author merely states what's in his head, heart, soul, or bowels."

"Bowels?"

"The author may attempt 'truth.' But the book doesn't give a whit about the author's 'truth.'"

"It doesn't?"

"Do you have a favorite book, Asher?"

"Me?"

"I'd much rather ask Chase. But I know her answer."

"Umm." I knew my answer, but I paused to appear thoughtful. "*Catch 22.*"

Gregor blinked. "Surprisingly good choice."

"Is it?"

"You were never a soldier, correct?"

"Umm. No."

"You've never been in any war?"

"Umm. No."

"You've never hatched a scheme to sell eggs at a mysterious profit?"

"Umm. No."

"You've never sat naked in a tree?"

"Umm. No."

"So, you came to *Catch 22* a novice, not adept in anything germane to true understanding of that book."

"Umm. Yes."

"Yet you call *Catch 22* your favorite. How can that be?"

"Umm. It's funny?"

"Are you asking or telling me."

"Both?"

"Okay. A pacifist reading *Catch 22* might read through the laughter to see the enduring sadness of war. A soldier might understand that sadness even more. Any reader who has questions about war, leadership, structure, governance, human nature, rebellion, the meaning of life and death could get a lot out of *Catch 22*. I suppose even someone who is in it for laughs can have his base desire fulfilled. No matter Mr. Heller's intentions in composing his masterwork, no matter what personal truth he poured into *Catch 22*, the book answers only the questions that the reader has when reading it."

"Huh."

"Too bad that books aren't banned anymore."

"What?"

"Nobody bans books anymore. There's no crusader against Huck Finn's profanity, no opposition to Billy Pilgrim and Montana Wildhack fornicating in an interplanetary zoo, no uproar about Alex DeLarge's sexual ultraviolence. Shame."

"Are you advocating for banning books?" I asked.

"Of course not! I'm advocating for people to read *Catch 22* with more emotion than a few cheap laughs. I'm advocating for passion, raw emotions—even fury. Most of all, thought. Critical reading, questioning, not mere acceptance of the 'truth' that the author may—or may not—intend to convey." Gregor sighed. "These days," his voice near a soft whisper, "nobody would say anything even if *Mein Kampf* were published anew." A wistful pause. "Which, I suppose is exactly like the first time *Mein Kampf* was published."

As Chase nodded in agreement, I found myself alone in opposition to Gregor's delirious rantings. Could Gregor think that people of today would blindly support the ideals of *Mein Kampf*? That we lived in a world of brand-

new Nazis? On the off chance that Gregor wasn't attempting to bait me, I took his bait. "I object to the proposition that we live in a Nazi society."

"I, too, object to a society of Nazis," Gregor agreed.

"Not what I meant."

"I don't know how many times I've said this, son." This was no longer Gregor pretending to be my father. It was Dad in the doorway behind me.

"Dad? How long have you been there?"

"Long enough," Dad scolded, "to hear you once again advocate for your own meaning, your version of 'truth.'"

"What?"

"'That's not what I meant,'" he parroted. "I've explained—as has Jay, as has your mother, as has Gregor—that your intended meaning is of no value. Yet I hear you once again straining to make someone else see things from your point of view," Dad fumed.

"That's not what I me—"

"Quiet, Asher!" Gregor shouted. "You'd do well to listen to your father."

"Okay," I seethed through my teeth. "Tell me, Dad, why am I to believe that we are living in a society of Nazis?"

"You're a frog in a pot, that's why," Gregor interjected.

"It's more than that, Gregor," Dad added. "It's more about what Asher doesn't understand: Hitler is in the eye of the beholder."

"He is?"

"Have I told you about the argument I had with Heathcliff Garfield?"

Not this shit again. "Heathcliff Garfield? There's *never* been anyone named Heathcliff Garfield."

"Yes. I know him."

"You know somebody named after two fat cartoon cats?"

"I do? Huh. I never thought of that. Heathcliff Garfield. Two fat cartoon cats. That's *great* fun!"

"Come on, Dad."

"That fits him. So rich and miserly, like two fat-cats in one. Not to mention his considerable bulk. Funny observation, son. Well done."

"Really? Umm. Thanks."

"Where was I?"

In the wake of Dad's compliment, I couldn't help myself. "Heathcliff Garfield."

"Right! Heathcliff and I argued all the time. Politics, mostly. He had some interesting ideas, real smart guy, but I never agreed."

Defeated, I yielded. "For instance?"

"For instance, his views on Adolf Hitler."

"I take it he was a supporter."

"Never. Not Heathcliff Garfield."

"So, *you* supported Hitler?"

"No! How could you think that?"

"Well, if you two used to disagree about Hitler, then—"

"We didn't disagree about Hitler. We disagreed about the *hallmarks* of Hitler."

"The hallmarks of Hitler?"

"What made Hitler, Hitler."

"What made Hitler, Hitler, Dad?"

"Depends on who you're asking—Heathcliff Garfield or me."

"I can't ask Heathcliff Garfield. He's not here."

"That doesn't mean that you can't learn what he had to say about the hallmarks of Hitler."

"What?"

"It's called the oral tradition," Gregor interjected. "You can learn what Heathcliff Garfield said from what your father tells you."

"That's right," agreed Dad.

"Okay. So, Dad, what did Heathcliff Garfield say were the hallmarks of Hitler?"

"Social security."

"Heathcliff Garfield believed that social security was a hallmark of Hitler?"

"Not *a* hallmark of Hitler—*the* hallmark of Hitler. To Heathcliff Garfield, by forcing people to pay into and take from social security, the American government subjugated the populace."

"How could that be true?"

"It's not true."

"What?"

"It's what Heathcliff Garfield *believed* to be true."

"Fine. Why did Heathcliff Garfield *believe* that social security subjugated the populace?"

"According to Heathcliff Garfield, social security deprived the populace of the choice of whether to have retirement savings, and the concomitant choice of when and how those savings could be accessed. In this way, social security, to Heathcliff Garfield, signaled that the next Fuhrer was on the rise."

"Huh."

"Like that frog Gregor mentioned. Heathcliff believed that implementation of social security was lighting the burner beneath the pot. Slowly, the pot boils, and the stupid unknowing frog boils right along with it. That was Hitler to Heathcliff Garfield."

"What was Hitler to *you*, Dad?"

"A cult leader."

"A cult leader?"

"Every cult leader has one thing in common: not allowing for difference of opinion. Hitler was like that. From *Mein Kampf*—and even before—Hitler had one message: advocating for a pure genetic pool. At every rally, Hitler espoused fear and hate of genetic deviance. His thugs in the crowd ensured that any opposing viewpoints were oppressed. Soon, Germany had one dogma, one message—in other words, Hitler made Germany into a cult."

"Okay."

"So, Hitler is in the eye of the beholder.

"But, Dad, isn't one of those viewpoints correct?"

"Not one bit," Gregor and Dad said at the same time, in the same tone and rhythm, as if European Gregor and American Samuel joined together in an attempt to make an Axis power out of *me*.

I lashed out in both directions at once. "It's ridiculous to see social security, which is designed to help people survive, as a hallmark of Hitler," I raged.

"Why should Heathcliff Garfield's interpretation of Nazism be any less valid than Samuel's?" asked Gregor.

Dad pushed as hard against my western front as Gregor pushed from the east. "Heathcliff Garfield has as much right to his interpretation as does anyone else."

I exploded. "Heathcliff Garfield is fucking moron with a goddamned stupid name. He can't be real! Much less be right!"

Gregor and Dad kept right on with their attacks, forcing me ever inward into my own borders.

Gregor: "Who are you to say an interpretation is invalid?"

Dad: "Gregor's right. Even if social security isn't going to lead to the rise of Hitler anew, Heathcliff Garfield has every right to view government requirements with suspicion."

Gregor: "It's about passion. Heathcliff Garfield, if inaccurate, is expressing passion."

Dad: "The interpretation that should ever be questioned is a dispassionate one."

I made one last attempt to win this bloody war. "Where does that end? If banning books is okay because done with passion, then aren't massive acts of terrorism—from the Crusades on down—done in the name of passionate interpretation of a book—aren't those okay, too, in your *interpretation*?"

Gregor: "Of course not, you fucking idiot!"

Dad: "You didn't listen to me at all, son."

Gregor: "If you had listened to your father—"

Dad: "If you had heard me—"

Gregor: "Then you'd realize that the only interpretation that is unacceptable—"

Dad: "Is that interpretation that does not allow for any other interpretation to stand."

Gregor: "For when an interpretation does not allow for any other interpretation to exist—"

Dad: "Then what do you have?"

Flummoxed. Bewildered. Alone.

But not quite alone. Chase's voice squeaked to life behind me as she uttered a two-word answer that crushed the last will within me: "A cult."

Ferociously beaten, I crumpled.

But not before all three voices, Gregor's, Dad's and Chase's alike, uttered one more word of agreed contempt. Shaking their heads in rebuke, three voices joined together: "Absolutist."

Statement of Ed King [excerpt]

...ANCIENT HISTORY. WHY WOULD I take issue with Asher? All he did to me—and Mom—was what he was meant to do.

That includes what he did after we moved into his apartment. Not to absolve Asher. For even we fated must pay a Hell of a price.

"Why did you move into Asher's apartment?" I can't answer that. At that time, I had no rationale. I couldn't know why I moved in because I didn't know what was yet to happen.

Yes, in order to determine why an event happens, it's necessary to determine the end result of that event. "Everything happens for a reason." A simple idiom to understand: "Something" happens. That "something" causes an "effect." The occurrence of that "effect" demonstrates the "reason" that the "something" happened. The end "effect" is itself the reason for the occurrence of the "something." Thus, you have to know the "effect" in order to state the "reason" that the "something" happened.

It's best explained through allegory.

Asher and I met when we were young—he younger than I. I already had the hallmarks of Charcot Joint Disease. I walked with a bow-legged limp. I was stooped. My growth was stunted. All a result of the bones of my ankle being misaligned at birth. This disorder typically results from prolonged untreated diabetes or syphilis. But my condition was a result of my birth.

My mother was prone to ask why. Why was I so afflicted? No doctor

could answer, so she turned to non-doctors: faith healers, ministers, priests. When they couldn't answer, she grew to hate and mistrust doctors and non-doctors alike—and they are all alike. The only helpful person was my schoolmate Tyrese, who said, "Everything happens for a reason." I relayed that response to Mom. It didn't help.

Hearing no answers from outside, Mom looked within. She questioned every aspect of her life, every second of her history, every detail, every choice. That self-analysis drove Mom crazy. Asher's abuse drove Mom straight on through crazy right to suicide.

Not to say that Asher's abuse was the reason for Mom's suicide. As with everything, the "reason" for Mom's suicide will only surface when the effects of that suicide have been analyzed. That analysis continues.

So, no, without knowing the end result of our cohabitation, I cannot answer why I moved into that apartment. Such is the nature of fate.

What can I answer? Let me think.

Ah! I can answer how I got this blister on my cheek. Not why the blister exists—but how it came to be. I was cooking bacon, and there was a very loud POP in the grease…

Chapter 21

"WHY ARE YOU HERE?"

"I had to be here."

"Because the court ordered you to be here?"

"That's not what I said."

I don't know who says which sentences in this exchange between Molly Monahan, L.M.S.W., L.M.F.T., L.P.C., and me. Could go either way.

"You read the reports, Asher," Ms. Monahan claims

"Reports?"

Ms. Monahan sighs. "The reports that you stole and destroyed."

I wince, thinking of the 157 pages I shredded the day after I stole them.

"I don't know why you bothered to destroy them. They're electronically stored with the court."

Fuck. I realize Ms. Monahan's next point before she makes it.

"All you did was cut off your own access to the documents, which are now sealed."

Goddamn, Ms. Monahan is right. I've no idea why the court sealed the records—according to my appointed attorney, that outcome—sealing of the entire court record—was improbable. "To seal the record of a case," said she, "the court must find compelling evidence that public disclosure is dangerous to one of the parties or to the public, and that there's no less restrictive means to protect against that danger. A difficult standard to meet." Yet in our case,

the difficult standard was met, the court sealed all records, and my ability to re-access the shredded reports was lost.

"I find it difficult to believe you didn't read the reports before you destroyed them. I have to believe that you saw the diagnoses."

"Diagnoses?"

"You had to know that a psychiatric report would discuss diagnoses. I refuse to believe you didn't flip to the back of these pages," she brandishes a stack of paper like a cudgel, "to see what your diagnoses were."

"I didn't read any diagnoses."

Ms. Monahan disbelieves me. Nevertheless, she flips to the end and reads aloud: "It is likely that A.D. has A.D."

"A.D.? What's that?"

"Attachment disorder."

"And the other A.D.?"

It's rare to hear Ms. Monahan swear. "What the fuck could that first 'A.D.' stand for, *Asher*?"

She hits the "A" in my name hard. I understand. "So, I have affection disorder?"

"Attachment disorder."

"I have that?"

"Unclear. This report concludes that you might. I'm not so sure."

"Why not?"

"First, A.D. is generally found in people with neglectful parents—so neglectful they didn't feed and clothe their children. As to you, Asher—"

I gulp.

Ms. Monahan purses her lips. "As to you, Asher," she begins again, "your parents were interesting."

They still are, think I.

"But they weren't neglectful. They taught you values."

"They did?"

"Or they tried to. Your father taught maintaining individuality even as he connected with a larger community."

"Hmmm."

"Your mother taught strength in the face of adversity and the value of interpreting signs and symbols."

"Okay."

"You may not have learned, but your parents taught."

"You said 'first'…is there a second?"

"Second, people with A.D. tend to be unable to trust anyone. But you've exhibited *too much* trust."

"Have I?"

"Not counting your father, you allowed 12 strangers to move into your apartment. You didn't do background checks. They just moved in. You became involved in a serious relationship with Marlena, while permitting her to develop strong connections to others. You have an excess of trust."

"Is there a third?"

"Third, people with A.D. tend to have an overdeveloped need to control their own lives. You ceded control over your entire environment to Jay and the others."

I'm resigned to Ms. Monahan's further enumeration of my flaws. "Fourth?"

"Fourth, those with A.D. tend to have anger issues causing them to be openly hostile and argumentative. With the exception of your father, you shy away from confrontation."

"Fifth?"

"Fifth, people with A.D. tend to avoid love. To hear you tell it, you fell in love with Marlena at first sight, and then held onto that love until it tore itself away. In fact, you still love Marlena."

"Sixth?"

"Five reasons aren't enough?" Ms. Monahan rolls her eyes. "I could tell you all the symptoms of A.D. that you don't have. Instead, I'll address the one symptom that you claim to have."

"Claim?"

"People with A.D. tend to be confused, easily puzzled. You contend in here," she brandishes the report again, "that you didn't and couldn't know or appreciate where Jay came from, what he'd been before he came to live with you, why he chose you to live with."

"Chose me?"

"Come on. You have to appreciate the connection, strong as it is. I can't believe you spent months with Jay unaware of the answers to those questions.

"And then there's your 'confusion' about Peter Pinchot. You meet the building's owner only after you've lived in the apartment for years. When you meet him, he asks pointed questions he asked about Jay and the rest of your roommates. I can't believe you'd mistake his intentions."

"So, I don't have A.D.?" I pray for the right answer.

"No, Asher. As much as you'd like the answer to be otherwise—you don't have A.D."

With that answer, any chance for a diagnositcal excuse dissipates.

Chapter 22

LOGISTICS. YOU MIGHT WONDER: WHO paid rent for what had once been my apartment? Who cooked meals? Washed dishes? Cleaned the bathroom? Was there a line for the toilet? Did any resident—male or female—have to resort to other places to relieve themselves? How were showers scheduled? Who vacuumed? Did any neighbor complain of: Donny's heavy step? Gregor's booming shouts? Randy's and Samuel's cackling? Alec's and Marlena's lustful moans? Who took out the garbage? Procured groceries? Was ample transportation available? Did each roommate have a key? Did I deduce the reason for my encounter with Jay? Or Jay's encounter with me? Indeed, which was it? Did I on happenstance meet Jay, or did Jay on happenstance meet me? Or was it something else? Fate? Coincidence? Destiny? Choice? If choice, whose? And for God's sake, why?

Save one, I cannot answer these questions. Whether that's because I don't know, because I've learned to allow you to determine your own answers, or for some other reason—I can't answer that question, either. The one question that I can answer: Who took out the garbage? That unfortunate cross was mine to bear.

With 14 residents crammed into the apartment, the trash can swelled to the point of overflowing and bursting with: potato skins (which Chase refused to eat); salmon skin and bones (reflecting Gregor's exclusive diet); pizza crusts (Ella's bane); used (primarily by Ed) Kleenex; wadded tinfoil

trapping bacon grease (Jay's specialty); dryer sheets (used by Marlena); dental floss (used by Randy); inky missives (penned by Donny); peanut shells (shucked and chucked by Sony); orange peels and grape stems (remnants of Cassie's snacks); ketchup packets (used by Alec to top all foods); boxes of Fruit Loops, bags of Skittles, and sleeves of Oreos (emptied by Dad)—and detritus discarded by the lot of them: wine corks; eggshells; crushed soup cans; moldering half-eaten brie; black beans overcooked to the point of mush; coffee filters laden with sludgy grounds; spent tea bags; chewed, bulbous wads of gum; wrappers from Hostess fruit pies, Ding Dongs, and Ho-Hos.

I seemed to be the only resident repulsed by the rapid accumulation of refuse. Why was I so revulsed? Part rancid smell. Part bugs burrowing within and crawling atop. Part tactile sensations of the garbage—squeak of banana peel against garbage bag inspired tingles to the back of my neck and beyond. The bulk of my revulsion, though: symbolism. Each stuffed-beyond-capacity bag reminded me of what had once been my apartment. Each new item added unsolicited smells, touches, and weight, tightening in, restricting movement, suffocating. The only way to ease my pain was to cinch the bag, heave it out of the apartment and into the garbage chute at the end of the hallway, wherein I could hear the bulky mass slide from floor to floor until it reached the incinerator. With each audible turn of the bag, the congestion in my lungs lessened until, at the plop of bag into flames, I could breathe again, whereupon I returned to what had once been my apartment, inserted a fresh bag into the can, and admired the emptiness until a resident discarded the first slimy peach pit or snotty tissue, and the filling of the can to overflowing began again. It came to be that instead of easing my pain, listening to trash sliding down the chute and into flames became me sliding down into Sisyphean Hell. Still, getting rid of the trash was better than leaving it to fester. So, continue the ritual I did.

Then one day, the hallway was no longer empty. Filling the hallway—or "filly" the hallway, for the intruder was more like a horse, or a horse-drawn carriage, or…a chariot. Yes. The hulking man appeared as would a charioteer whipping his horse team into a frothing frenzy as he stood—stern, cold,

dominant—in an imaginary ornate box on wheels with spike-tipped hubs. The din of imagined hooves stormed toward me as he approached, clad all in white, eyes coal black, thick eyebrows raised toward hair slicked back as if blown by a sticky wind. He reined to a stop in front of me, stared, and spoke in a voice fit to tame an unruly crowd: "That looks heavy, Asher. Let me help." He took the bag from my shoulder with his massive hooves, galloped down the hallway, deposited it in the chute, and returned halfway back to me before I could utter one word: "How?"

He reared up, emphasizing his extreme height as if he were commanding me from atop a pedestal. "How did I know your name?"

"Sure," I squeaked.

"I know everyone who lives in my building."

"Your building?"

"I own it."

"Oh."

"I know everyone on leases, those allowed to live here. As for others," he glanced at the apartment door, "I need information."

"I see," I lied.

"Do you?"

"No," I admitted.

"Didn't think so. Your name, Asher, is the only one appearing on the lease," he pounded his hoof on the door of what has once been my apartment, "for this apartment. You belong here, Asher."

Gulp.

"I've got paperwork to prove it."

"I see."

"Good. I trust you, Asher."

I swelled with equal parts fear and pride. "All right."

"My name's Peter Pinchot."

"Hello, Mr. Pinchot."

"Too formal."

"Hello, Peter."

"Not good enough."

"Umm."

"The people I trust—and who trust *me*—use my nickname. Pony."

I chuckled. "Of course it is."

His smile disappeared. "What?" he snapped.

"No."

"No?"

"Oh. It's just that…well, the name fits you, Pony." Sweat flowed.

After a searching moment, Pony's smile returned. His hand left the apartment door, hurtled through the air, and landed with a painful thud on my shoulder. "I'm glad we're friends. Friends look out for each other. I look out for you. You look out for me. When you need something, I help you get it."

"What do I need?"

Pony ignored my question. "And when I need something, you help me get it."

"Okay. What do *you* need?"

Pony's hand relaxed. His grip tightened further. "Information."

"Information?"

"I'm a curious guy, Asher. I'm curious about the mass of other people I see streaming in and out of this apartment. I'm curious about who they are, what they do, what they want. I'm curious about their ultimate goal."

Goal? *What* goal?

"And I'm curious about how we can impact that goal."

We?

"How we can steer them in a…beneficial direction. Now, how is it, do you think, that we can best determine what that ultimate goal is?"

"Umm."

"First, we determine who they interlopers are. Then we determine their motivation."

"Motivation? Singular?"

Pony ignored me. "Then their capacity for action. Understand?"

"No."

"That's okay, Asher. I get it—*I* understand. Let's not forget, I already

know who *you* are, Asher. I know what motivates you. I know your capacity for action."

"You do?"

"I understand you. You've been heavily taxed by these interlopers. You don't deserve it. You didn't invite them in. They aren't your fault—not *entirely* your fault."

"I—"

"You're not one of them. Not part of the group. You belong here. They don't. You, Asher, are separate and distinct. An outsider. Alone."

Gulp.

"You don't deserve them."

"Okay."

"You don't deserve the burden. I'll help shoulder that burden for you."

"Okay."

"In fact, I'll shoulder the entire burden, Asher. You don't have to do much at all."

"Okay."

"All I need from *you* are answers. Who are these interlopers? Where'd they come from? What do you know about them?"

"Ah."

"Well?"

"Well?" I repeated.

Pony's eyes darkened, then recovered. "That's all right, Asher. We'll make it simpler. No big deal. Let's start with: Who was the first of the interlopers to move in?"

"The first?"

Darkness lingered in Pony's eyes before clearing. "Yes, Asher. The first person to move into your apartment."

I thought of Jay flipping eggs, pouring coffee, describing various properties of woods, relaxing, naked and Godlike, among a host of residents, smiling—always and absolutely smiling. I shook the thoughts away. "Ed," I said. "Ed King."

Pony blinked. "Ed King?"

"Ed King."

"Thick glasses, little guy, with the inhaler and that look in his eyes all the time?"

How Pony knew so much of Ed I had no idea. "That's him."

"He was first?"

"Umm."

"Nobody before him?"

"I—"

"Okay." Pony scowled. "If that's your answer." His hand squeezed.

I winced. Thoughts of Jay's smile returned. I had strength anew. "That's what I remember. Ed was first."

Pony relaxed. "So be it."

"So be it," I echoed.

Pony's smile returned. "We'll revisit that question. No problem at all. None."

"Okay."

"Ed King. That's who we're talking about, right?"

"Yes."

"He was *first*?"

"Yes."

"What's your assessment of Mr. King?"

"Assessment?" Thoughts flooded me. Poor Ed King, edkinging all over the place. Perhaps the most sympathetic of the residents, put upon more than even *me*—perhaps. How could I betray (if "betray" was the right word) poor Ed King? After all that he'd been through—after all that *I'd* put him through—how was I to betray his trust? Thoughts of Jay returned. And I thought, *Better Ed than the alternative.* "Ed King? Ha!" I said.

Pony seemed confused. "Ha?" he asked, forehead crinkling, head cocking.

I drew confidence. "Ha!" I repeated. "Ed King." I shook my head. "That guy's a world of fated catastrophe."

Pony said nothing.

"Ed's a buffoon. A failure. A mess. If there's a weak link in the group, it's Ed."

"Okay. What about other residents?"

Gulp. "Others?"

"There's one in a wheelchair, right? Who's she?"

Cassie rolled into my head, all pride and strength and determination, all admirable, all admired. "That's Cassie. Cassie James."

"Cassie James. Interesting."

"Is it?"

"I knew a Cassie James. The one I knew was from Oklahoma, then moved to California, then well, it becomes fuzzy. At some point she suffered a terrible injury standing up for workers' rights or some such nonsense."

Nonsense? "Umm. To hear Cassie tell it, it was an on-the-job injury. Something about a guy named Rich, something."

"That's right. Rich Planter. Same Cassie, then. She tell you anything about where she's been since?"

"I don't know much."

"Has Cassie made statements about unfairness within capitalistic labor systems? Anything about overthrowing establishments, disrupting commerce?"

I thought of Cassie's strongly-worded opinions about Ella Flowers' former pickle empire. What I said was: "Umm."

"If you ever hear anything like that, I'm sure that you'll tell me, Asher."

"Okay."

"What about the guy with the wacked out smile, the one who laughs in that cackling sort of insane way. You know who I mean."

Randy Mac. Pony could only be talking about Randy Mac. "Not sure."

"The guy who leads those discussions in the round."

So stunned was I at Pony's knowledge that I couldn't help myself: "Randy Mac."

"That sounds right. Randy Mac." Pony chewed each syllable. "Has he ever mentioned a mental institution in his past?"

"No."

"Pay attention for that kind of thing, too."

"Okay."

"And what about that other guy—booming voice, vague accent, looks and acts professorial?"

Once more I couldn't help myself. "Gregor?"

"Ah! Yes. Gregor Gregorovich, right?"

"Umm. Yes. That's him."

"How familiar are you with Gregor's passions?"

"Passions?" Gregor's lustful stares at "little ingenue Chase" flitted through my mind. "Not sure what you mean."

"Are you aware that Gregor Gregorovich is wanted for questioning in a woman's disappearance?"

Sweat burst forth. "No."

Pony stared until I felt the blackness of his eyes touch whatever remained of my soul. "That's good enough for now, Asher."

I exhaled.

"But..."

I hitched breath back in.

"Let me give you a warning."

"A warning?"

"Be careful, Asher. Don't get too attached to these interlopers. Don't let them grab hold of whatever remains of your soul. Continue to be separate. Continue to be yourself. Don't become part of the collective. Yet—at the same time—pay attention. Be vigilant. Mindful. But—whatever you do—well, let's put it this way: don't fall in love in there."

"Love?" I gulped.

"Oh," said Pony, "So it's already happened. So, who is she, Asher? Is she the one who looks like she floats everywhere? Large blue eyes, short brown hair, always looks surprised?"

Ella. He meant Ella.

"No, wait," Pony continued before I could utter even a syllable. "She's with the old man, the one who moved in with the little black girl. She can't be the one."

I exhaled once more.

"Perhaps it's the other one, the one who always stares upward, at the stars. The one who confuses us—"

"Us?"

"Me. Confuses me. You might've noticed that I have some meager knowledge of these interlopers."

I might've indeed.

"I have my ways, my sources. I admit, though—this other girl, the star-gazer—about her I couldn't find much. As if she appeared out of nowhere, as if from one of those stars at which she peers." Pony glanced upwards. "But no, no she's not the one either. Your expression wouldn't have remained so blank if she were. Which leaves us only with the buxom one, the artist, the one with the green—"

"Samuel!" I shouted.

"Samuel?"

I gulped. "Samuel," I quietly repeated.

"The girl's name is Samuel?"

"Oh! No. She's Marlena." I winced at my openness. "The one I love is Samuel."

Pony blinked. "I wouldn't have guessed that. I mean I was about to say that this—Marlena, was that her name?—I was about to say that Marlena wasn't yours, either."

"You were?"

"She seems to be connected with that sex addict with the blog."

"Alec?"

"That his name? Well, yes, then, if that's his name, then Marlena seemed to have a stronger connection to Alec. Now this Samuel—I assume you mean the other older guy—the cross-dresser. I'm surprised that you would have that predilection."

"What? No. I don't."

"Then why'd you just utter his name with such passion?"

"Oh. Well, Samuel—I do love him. But it's because..." I paused. Could I identify Dad to this rampaging beast of a man, a man whose motives were unclear? More than that—could I identify myself as the *son* of the "old" man

who Pony knew to be a "cross-dresser"? And if I could do both of those things...just *how* could I? What would be my process? What words would I use? And what symbolism would underlie those words? After an eternity of eye contact with Peter Pony Pinchot, I forced myself to speak. "Samuel is my father," I said.

Pony blinked. "Interesting. I'm not sure how we—I mean, I—I'm not sure how I didn't make that connection."

"You didn't?"

"Samuel—that's your dad's name, right?—you and Samuel seem so...opposite."

"We do?" I smiled.

"I mean...Samuel's so...confident."

My smile vanished.

"He knows who he is."

"Oh. I see."

"Do you?"

I sighed.

"One last question, Asher."

"Okay."

"Does your mom live here, too?"

"Huh? No. She lives...elsewhere."

"That's too bad."

"Why?"

"You'd be better off with your mom here, too."

"You don't know my mother."

"No. Not yet."

Chapter 23

"WANT? WHAT DO I WANT? What kind of question is that?"

I roll Molly Monahan, L.M.S.W., L.M.F.T., L.P.C.'s question around my mind. I scale back my anger. "What do I want?" I muse, gentler.

I sit in my metal folding chair, a choice I made 22 weeks before during my initial session. Arriving to that session, although I found Ms. Monahan's door ajar, I hesitated, wondering at the acronyms on her oversized nameplate. I feared that a monster waited inside—a "Languorous Miserly Sycophantic Wench," "Lewd Malicious Fatuous Troll," "Lycanthropic Person-Cruncher."

The creature I found standing in the room was on her surface none of those things. She was pretty, her face round, eyes rounder, her lips not kissable, but appealing, her ears forming two halves of the same heart.

More remarkable than Ms. Monahan or her initials was her office. Where I'd pictured a Freudian style wingback chair for her and a fainting couch for me, what I found were two empty chairs—one comfortable (barrel chair, clean, amply padded), the other uncomfortable (plain metal folding chair).

"Take a seat," Ms. Monahan gestured to the midpoint between the two chairs.

Sniffing a test, I weighed what each choice might say about me. As to kindness, my choice would be inconclusive. If I chose the uncomfortable chair, I'd allow Ms. Monahan to sit in comfort; if I chose the comfortable chair, I'd allow her to participate in sessions guilt-free, knowing she wasn't

putting me out by forcing me into the uncomfortable chair. As a measure of intelligence, the test seemed equally inapt. Either I choose the comfortable chair and demonstrate knowledge of the role of physical comfort in therapy, or the uncomfortable chair and reveal my recognition that Ms. Monahan's job was difficult enough without her having to be uncomfortable, too. Likewise, the test could not measure my compassion, humor, forthrightness, honesty— no matter which choice I made, factors weighed on each side of the balance. The test of the chairs was a farce, giving me an unfavorable first impression of Ms. Monahan's abilities as an L.M.S.W., an L.M.F.T, or an L.P.C.

But failing to choose either chair would reveal me to be the worst type in all aspects. Believing I'd have the same choice to make in each session, I determined that I'd spend half my sessions in the uncomfortable chair and the remainder in the comfortable chair. I'd bounce back and forth week to week, demonstrating the best qualities of a person who'd select either chair. One week I'd be a self-sacrificial angel. The next a brilliant, introspective sophisticate. In the end, I'd be an amalgamation of all those things, a paragon of excellence.

The only choice remaining was where to begin my round robin. I selected the folding chair for the same reason I choose to eat vegetables first when presented with a balanced meal—to get the unsavory choice out of the way so I could enjoy the deliciousness of comfort during my next session.

I sat in the folding chair, Ms. Monahan in the barrel chair, and thus began our first hour. I felt ecstasy even as the metal dug into my back. Carrying me through was the vision of the barrel chair gently hugging Ms. Monahan. Through the pain, I salivated with anticipation of the caresses to come the following week.

Yet when I arrived for session two, I found that my choice was permanent, for Ms. Monahan rested in the barrel chair. Thus, it went from session to session. By session twelve, wherein I described Jurgen's art display, and thirteen, wherein I detailed Ella Flowers' pickling adventures, I thought I'd be able to take no more. In between sessions, I begged myself to request that Ms. Monahan either allow me to try out the barrel chair or replace the metal folding chair with a comfortable option. Nevertheless, in session fourteen, I

introduced Ms. Monahan to Mom's thoughts about "perspective" from the discomfort of the metal folding chair. By session twenty-one, wherein we discussed whether or not A.D. had A.D., I formulated a plan to procure and bring with me my own chair to the next session. Lacking means to purchase anything suitable, however, I returned in session twenty-three to tell the tale of Peter "Pony" Pinchot from the same vantage point as ever.

And here I sit again in session twenty-four, still in my metal chair, staring at Ms. Monahan in her well-padded chair. "What do I want?" I repeat, dreaming of even one hour in Ms. Monahan's chair—in her lap, if necessary.

Ms. Monahan remains resolute in her unresponsiveness.

Fuck it. I dive into answering…in my own way. "I need to know what that question means. What do I want to accomplish in my sessions? What do I want people to perceive about me? What do I want from my parents? Do I wish my father were a straight man who enjoyed carpentry and fishing? Do I wish my mother weren't crazy? Do I wish I hadn't done what I did?"

Ms. Monahan stares.

"Well?" I ask.

Ms. Monahan finally speaks. "Well, what?"

"What do you mean by 'What do you want, Asher?'"

Ms. Monahan's mouth curls in a sinister smile. "It is what it is."

Fuck me. Session six. Marlena's response to the seven viewers of her "The"—my ex-lover's words coming back to haunt me through the mouth of this Lascivious Mean-Spirited Witch sitting in her comfortable chair.

I renew my vow to close myself off—it's clear I cannot give *her* what *she* wants. I sit silent, trying to match my expression to hers, counting the seconds until my court-ordered twenty-fourth session expires.

One.

Two.

Three.

Four-five-six.

Fuck this. My thoughts turn from escalating numbers. What do I want? I think of session four, distributing glow-in-the-dark suckers to Agatha, Agnes, Jermaine, and Jack. I think of friendship, community, laughter.

I think of the thirteen residents turning "my apartment" into "what had once been my apartment." I think of Ed King's calm acceptance of his fated limp, Cassie's stridence, Sony longing for the stars. I think of Randy's sense of humor, Donny longing for Ella, Ella longing back. I think of Chase's search for justice. I think of Gregor's articulateness, Alec's lustful laughter.

I think of Mom. I think of strength. Determination. Power. Protectiveness. I think of the intense effort it took to move a redbud tree from front yard to back. I think of screaming "FUCK YOU" to power structures. I think of vengeance—of eye for an eye, of not turning the other cheek. I think of not giving a fuck what anyone thinks.

I think of Dad. I think of grace. Kindness. Confidence. I think of being true to myself under the scrutiny of anyone. I think of ludicrous symbolic stories. I think of turning the other cheek, not an eye for an eye. I think of unconditional and unremitting love—even for those who harm me.

I think of Marlena. I think of beauty. Encouragement. Creativity. Open-mindedness. I think of putting my inner self on display. I think of allowing others to come to their own interpretations. I think of passion: physical, mental, emotional.

I think of Jay—as the silence is pierced by screeching from Ms. Monahan's timer.

Time's up.

Cannons and Trumpets

By

Asher Delacroix

CHOOSE ME, THOUGHT THE KING. *Heed me. Otherwise, why should Parvenu have a king?* He sighed. *Nobody likes me.*

The king was responsible for Parvenu's economy, true, but the gloom that shrouded Parvenu wasn't the king's fault...so he argued to himself. What happened was this: two other kingdoms (Blueblood and Villein) were forever at war. As the cannons roared, firing cast iron and lead balls from Blueblood into Villein and firing all manner of detritus from Villein back into Blueblood, the king of Parvenu was approached by delegates from each kingdom.

Knowing of Parvenu's then-substantial resources, each group of delegates sought to raise money to continue the ever-raging war. Delegates from Blueblood brought to the king a diamond as large as one of the cannonballs that they shot into Villein. "King," said the Blueblood delegacy, "We offer you the opportunity to purchase this diamond, the equal of which has never been seen. Appraisers value this diamond at €91,200. We don't mind telling you of our desperate need for assistance in our fight against the wretched scourge that is Villein. For the sake of our people, superior in every way to those assholes, we offer you a bargain. You may purchase this diamond for €30,000. When the trumpets sound—when we win the war, squashing those Villein wretches—we'll purchase the diamond back for 20% more than its appraised value, giving Parvenu a substantial profit."

Parvenu was not as rich as Blueblood, and not rich for as long as

Blueblood. Parvenu's fortune was made in the waning years of the king's father's life, when the king's father's dream of finding a natural Parvenu resource at last came true. The king's father discovered that Parvenu sat atop limestone. The king's father developed mining equipment (138 drills) that dug in and hauled out limestone ("Remember," the king's father often said to the king, "we cannot over-mine the limestone or we'll undermine the kingdom."). Within a year, the king's father died, leaving the king to be king.

As nouveau riche, the king of Parvenu was aware of appearances. He didn't want his kingdom (or himself) to appear to Blueblood to be of such character that it (or he) would take unfair advantage of ill fortune.

"No," said the king. "My kingdom will not purchase that diamond for such a cut-rate price. It's so beautiful that we will purchase it for 20% more than its appraised value!" So, the king paid €109,440 for the diamond. The Blueblood delegacy returned to the warfront with ample money to keep Blueblood in cannonballs for several years.

Not long after, delegates from Villein arrived in Parvenu and said, "King, we've heard rumors of your generosity toward the brutes from Blueblood. Your monetary contribution allowed those dickheads to purchase thousands of cannonballs, which have smashed our granary. We'll starve unless we can rebuild it, making it strong enough to withstand the pulsing and beating of the Blueblood cannonballs—which, we remind you, were purchased with Parvenu funds. We lack the necessary materials. We beseech you to provide us with a small supply of your limestone stores, with which we can rebuild our granary. We estimate that 12 tons will suffice. When we've overcome the tactics of those bastardly Blueblood bullies, we'll somehow repay you tenfold for such a kindness."

Parvenu being, again, of new wealth, the king understood too well the horrors of poverty. Being (again) concerned about the perception of Parvenu, he couldn't allow the citizens of Villein to starve. So, the king acquiesced to the Villein delegates—and then some. By day's end, the king had his miners excavating faster and deeper than ever. Within a fortnight, Parvenu supplied Villein with 377 tons of limestone, with which Villein not only rebuilt its

granary, but also ten new granaries, with *still* enough limestone to construct a thick wall along the border between Villein and Blueblood.

Hearing of the source of Villein's limestone, the Blueblood delegacy rushed back to Parvenu. "You've made our cannonballs useless!" said they to the king. "No matter how many we fire at that villainous Villein wall, it won't crumble. Those cannonballs were our only advantage. We must now drill our way through the wall so we can overcome those fiends! We come again to you, dear king, to provide 12 mining drills so we may pierce the wall. We will pay you for each drill, of course, and allow you set the price."

The king, devastated by offending his new friends from Blueblood, wouldn't hear of taking compensation for the drills, and, in fact, as had become his reputation, supplied far more drills (84) than the Blueblood delegation requested.

Beholding Blueblood using those drills, the Villein delegacy returned and requested a portion of shredded limestone sufficient for jamming into each Blueblood drill's bit, rendering the drills useless. The king, understanding the predicament into which he had once again thrust Villein, complied by mining more limestone and crushing it into gravel, which he transported to Villein.

Blueblood, of course, returned to Parvenu and requested that the king supply all new drill bits so its assault on the Villein wall could recommence. The king, of course, over-complied, removing the drill bits from most of the remaining Parvenu mining equipment and delivering those bits to Blueblood.

So it went—the Villein delegacy requesting from the king items that would parry the Blueblood assault, and Blueblood requesting items that would counter Villein's parry. Back and forth and back again the delegacies went—until there was no more Parvenu to give. Parvenu faded from memory, king and all. Gone without a trace, Parvenu's remaining asset (the land) was gobbled up by Blueblood and Villein, who, having sufficient new space from the ransacking of Parvenu, lacked any remaining feud against each other, and ended their war, trumpets blaring from both sides.

Chapter 24

THE 14ᵀᴴ CHAIR IN THE circle, which Jay had kept open "just in case"—one day that chair was no longer empty.

I first saw the chair's occupant as I entered the living room to find the assemblage gathered as usual—almost. As usual, only thirteen of the fourteen chairs were occupied. Unusual, though: the empty chair was not chair fourteen. The empty chair was *my* chair—chair unlucky number thirteen. I hadn't met the occupant of chair fourteen before I entered the room. I got the impression that I was the only one—he was comfortable in the circle, and the circle was comfortable with him.

"Finally," Randy Mac announced, "the prodigal son returns."

Although my status as a prodigy was doubtful, Randy was at least right about the "returns" part. I don't know how many circles I'd missed during my exodus—if my absence could be called an exodus. Whatever the label, several weeks earlier, as I saw chairs being placed, I left the apartment. All I remember of my destination is the taste of intoxicant. As I returned and found the chairs uncircled and restrewn about the apartment, my relief was immediate, immense, immersive. Circle after circle I avoided in this way, staggering back to what had once been my apartment longer and longer after each session ended. One Sam Adams became a Sam Adams and a Guinness, then two Millers and three shots of tequila, then half a bottle of Jagermeister and on and on—the exaggerator in me would love

to take credit for enhancing that list, but the autobiographer in me knows better.

What of my return to the circle? Why did this prodigal son return from his travels? It started with a snap.

Hearing the snap (as I lifted garbage from the kitchen can), I started, dropping bag and can to the linoleum, causing refuse to splatter. Turning, wild-eyed, slime-handed, I saw Dad bent over Cassie in her wheelchair, his skirt hiking up to reveal the tops of thigh-high socks. His left-hand forefinger and thumb revealed him as the snapper.

"What the fuck?" was all I could think to ask. Dad and Cassie turned to me.

"Simple," Cassie began.

"Simple, yes," Dad added. "But not to Asher."

"Yes," Cassie agreed. "He's been away for too long."

"Away?"

"We don't have time to explain the plans to the boy," Cassie said.

Explain? Plans? "The boy?"

"You're right. We can go over it again, though." Dad rolled Cassie away.

I rinsed detritus from my hands and caught a whiff of garbage that brought to mind the galloping Pony Pinchot. "What plans?" his voice thundered in my head. I couldn't silence the question. I had no answer to give.

Not that hints were in short supply. After hearing Dad's snap, whispers and rumors found me throughout the apartment:

- Bathroom—Alec and Ed passing. Alec: "percent." Ed: "fire."

- Bed—Marlena, whispering to Gregor one mattress over: "make sure...all gone"—Gregor whispering back: "will...never stop."

- Couch—Ella: "what if...police." Donny: "righteous...force." Cassie: "bloody." Sony: nod.

- Coming into apartment—Jay: "expect...suffer." Chase: "more...them." Randy: "agreed."

- At stove—Dad: "barrels…in place." Ella: "trailer…gasoline." Donny: "destroy." Dad: "pay…blood."

- Random words and snippets heard throughout the apartment— Donny: "smash." Chase: "discover." Alec: "fight." Gregor: "chase!" Ella: "obliterate." Randy: "gold, man." Cassie: "demolish." Ed: "capital." Sony: "annihilate." Donny: "chemical." Marlena: "get them." Dad: "so they can't." Jay: "forever."

As anger had driven me away from the circles, these hints and whispers pulled me back. The only way to quiet the thunderous question ("WHAT PLANS, ASHER?") was to find an answer. So, I returned, but not on time. I entered the living room to find the chairs in the same sequential order as always, but only my chair was empty. All thirteen other chairs were full, including the "just in case" chair, which was occupied by someone who I didn't recognize, but who was clearly well recognized by the other residents of what had once been my apartment.

I shoved resentment and isolation deep inside in favor of silencing the question ("WHAT MOTHERFUCKING PLANS, ASHER???") that continued to gallop across my brain. I sat in my empty chair. The only acknowledgement of my presence was Randy's scoffing challenge.

"Shut the fuck up," I muttered. Randy's laugh indicated that I'd not kept this command under my breath as I'd intended. "Sorry," I lied.

"For what?" Randy asked.

"My lateness."

"My circles have no schedule," Jay said. "Come and go as you please."

I bristled at Jay claiming leadership of the gathered masses. I bristled even more at the unknown (to me) man in chair 14.

"Before the interruption," Randy said through titters, "our new friend was telling us his story. I'll sum up: He is named," Randy turned his eyes toward Jay then back to me, "Judas."

Jolt upright, eyes wide!

"As if to fulfill the name's prophecy, Judas' mother named him then cast him aside, sending him to a shelter."

"Then," Judas added, "she cast herself aside."

"She offed herself," Randy interpreted. "What was it? Hanging?"

"From a tree." Judas' improbable smile was part mourning, part mirth.

"What was *her* unfortunate name?" Randy asked.

"I never knew it," Judas said. "I was told that it sounded like a bored sigh. I can't blame her for abandoning me. She believed I was destined to perform evil deeds. That's why she gave me my name."

"What came first: destiny or name?" Chase Crane asked. "And what've you done to stop destiny?"

"I've chosen to not believe in it. If I believe I have an evil destiny, then I must take steps to avoid it. In taking those steps, I'll cause the destiny to occur."

Ed King gave a nostalgic nod.

"I don't understand," Chase rejoined. "Destiny is destiny whether you believe in it or not."

"So be it," answered Judas.

"Whatever happened in your past, you're no longer abandoned," Jay said. "You're part of our brotherhood."

Brotherhood? Who said anything about a brotherhood? I surveyed the circle. I paused on Dad's face. Dad sat so close to Jay that their two faces blended into one. "Well, *brother*..." I trailed off, surprised by the depth of my own sarcasm.

"Yes, Asher?" Jay's tone irked me. Flat, even, natural. Friendly, welcoming, demure. Why couldn't he be sarcastic? Why didn't he agree with my outrage? Why couldn't he support me? Why was I alone in my scorn?

I returned my attention to Randy. "What's the next part of Judas' story?" I spat.

"I've no idea."

"Why not?"

"That's all Judas has said."

"Not much more to tell," Judas added. "You've got the interesting parts."

I turned. "Nothing to add?"

"Don't think so."

"Your story is that you were born, your mother put you into a home and hung herself?"

"Yes."

"Nothing else?"

"Son," Dad said. "Relax."

"Relax? We don't know anything about this guy. Now he's done explaining himself after scraps of a story. *Relax*?"

"You didn't know much about Jay when he moved in," Dad responded.

Although I couldn't deny Dad's assertion, I pressed my objection. Dropping all sarcasm, I took ownership of the brotherhood, determined to protect its exclusivity against all comers. "You want this unknown to be part of our brotherhood?"

"Yes."

"But our circle is sacred."

"Shut up," Randy grunted with no trace of smile or laughter. "You've never taken this circle as sacred."

"What?"

"You come and go without impact, arrive late, leave early, add nothing. You sit surly, silent. When you speak, you lob aggressive, pointed questions and lurid comments. Meanwhile, Judas tells a personal, sympathetic story, and you want to, what? Throw him out of the circle? Out of the apartment? Out of our lives? Not your decision. We members of the circle, of this brotherhood, have the right to get to know and accept Judas. And you need to keep your fucking mouth shut."

"It's cool, Randy," said Dad.

"Cool? Asher? I don't think so," responded Randy.

At this, silence from Dad. Dad's was not the only voice that didn't rise in my defense. All brotherhood members—Cassie through Ella, Donny through Sony—each and every voice remained silent, except Randy, who continued: "With all due respect, Sammy—and you are due great respect—it's definitely *not* cool." Returning to me, "I defy you to name one contribution you've

made to this circle. Name one time you shared something personal, anything that could act as a lesson for the rest of us, as a discussion point, as a parable."

Sweat coated me. Silence enshrouded us all. Then, there it was: an idea, a story that I could tell, fully formed, beautiful, miraculous. I smiled with schadenfreude. Turning to Dad I asked, "You want a story?"

"I only want you, Asher. You to your fullest capability," Dad replied.

Resisting Dad's sweetness, I pressed forward. "Well, then, I have a story for you."

"I would love to hear it, son."

"Okay, then." All eyes in the circle turned to me. Waiting, anticipating, until I began:

Asher's Story

by

Asher Delacroix

as told to

Circle of Brothers

The phone was broken. It hadn't rung in some time—difficult to tell if it was the phone or my social life that was broken. Anyway, it turned out to be the phone. I mean—really.

Shit, I forgot to describe it. Landline, cordless, built-in answering machine. Before I knew what a cell phone was, I thought it might be a cell phone. Isn't that silly?

Same with my TV—tube, 27 inches. Super heavy. Screen was flat. I thought that meant it was a high-def TV, plasma. Came to find out that those cost something like fifteen, twenty thousand dollars at the time—and here I thought I had one in this apartment. I mean—really.

Anyway, telephone had to be replaced. I couldn't afford another phone/machine combo. I had to buy two things to replace it.

I went to Circuit City and found a phone I liked—

"cellular" like the broke one. Metallic deep blue...navy? Something like that. I had to have it, though it took up the bulk of my cash. I had to get frugal to get the answering machine. Found one at a garage sale. I liked its look. Like wood paneling. Plastic, though. It took those old tapes. Small ones. Got some of those at the sale, too.

Got home, unpackaged the phone, figured out how to hook up the machine. I put in one of the tapes from the box.

I was reaching for the button to record an outgoing message when I realized that I hadn't prepared anything. I had nothing written down. I had no idea what I'd say. I didn't want to ramble. I'm anti-ramble. You know? I mean—really. I wanted my outgoing message to proclaim me to the world as an interesting cat. I wanted to be memorable.

I must've jotted down twenty-five versions. None good enough. None reflected me.

By the time I got to thirty versions—shame I didn't hang on to them—I decided to wing the recording. Couldn't be that bad. Even if it was, wouldn't matter, wouldn't reflect on me. Even if it did, it'd only leave a temporary impression—I mean, who remembers an outgoing message, right? I mean—really.

I reached out and pressed the button, ready to start talking. But I couldn't. The button I pressed wasn't "Record." It was "Play." When I pressed it, a voice—young, female:

"Mom? You there?" Pause. Cleared throat. "Mom, I found bones."

Slight click and: "You did?" Mom was there after all. Mention of bones got her attention. She picked up and started talking. The tape kept recording.

I pressed "Stop." Can't say why. Maybe something about privacy. Who could tell? It was an automatic response.

I grew too curious to hold back. This Mom sounded

nothing like my mother. She was mousy, quiet, nervous, although she tried to hide it. But she reminded me of Mom. Or...no. She was *the opposite* of Mom. An idealized version of Mom. Everything I wanted Mom to be. I needed to know more about her. And the daughter found bones. Who wouldn't be interested in that? I mean—really. Was this a good find? An archaeological find? A murder scene? I had to know. I pressed "Play" again. The two continued:

Daughter: "I did."

Mom: "Bones is here."

Daughter: "Come off it, Mom."

Mom: "I saw her yesterday."

Daughter: "Would you like to know where she was today?"

Mom: "Okay."

Daughter: "Humane Society."

[So, Bones was a pet—alive.]

Mom: "How could Bones be at the Humane Society, Jeannie?"

[So, the daughter's name was Jeannie.]

Jeannie: "*Somebody*," [some stank on that word] "must've dumped her there."

Mom: "Somebody?"

Jeannie: "You know what I mean."

Mom: "There's no way—"

Jeannie: "Why not, Mom?"

Mom: "You're imagining things, dear."

Jeannie: "Don't 'dear' me, Mom. This shit has—"

Mom: "Jeannie!"

Jeannie: "—gone long enough. Sorry, Mom, it's true."

Mom: "What are you implying?"

Jeannie: "Implying nothing. *You* took *my cat* to the shelter."

[There was a pause. On one of my repeat listenings, I counted the seconds—just to be sure. I was surprised my count ended at seven. I had to count again. And again. And then again, again. Each time the result was the same: seven seconds of nobody talking. There was no more.]

Jeannie: "You deny it?"

Mom: "Bones is here. I just saw her."

Jeannie: *sigh*

Jeannie: "Mom—it was Bones. Kelley saw her, told me. I went there—Kelley was right."

Mom: "What was your sister doing at the shelter?"

Jeannie: "I didn't ask."

Mom: "Even if Bones was there, why do you think *I* did it? I mean, your sister was there right—"

Jeannie: "You're going to blame Kelley?"

Mom: "Well, she was there."

Jeannie: "Mom, I already told you to cut the shit—"

Mom: "Jeannie!"

Jeannie: "—so cut the shit. You did it."

Mom: "I don't know what you're talking about."

Jeannie: "Humane Society keeps records."

Mom: "Records?"

Jeannie: "They share them with a pet's owner. All I had to do was show them a photo of me with Bones. Boom. Records. You know what one was?"

Mom: "How could I?"

Jeannie: "Drop-off form. *Signed*. By *you*."

Mom: "Me?"

Jeannie: "Yes, Mom. Tell me why."

Mom: "Why what?"

Jeannie: *sigh* "I leave Tuesday, by Thursday, you took Bones to the shelter."

[I pressed "Stop" again. I needed a break. The tension

between Jeannie and Mom was perfect. Beautiful. Mom so nervous and even-toned. Jeannie anger and more anger. Dissonance I liken to the chord at the beginning of A Hard Day's Night—or, even better, the building cacophony at the end of A Day in the Life. Jangling. Attacked my nerves. And yet, beautiful. I had to have more. I mean—really.]

Mom: "Jeannie, I didn't—"

Jeannie: "Yes, you did."

Mom: "Let me finish."

Jeannie: "Okay."

Mom: "You need to see things from my perspective."

Jeannie: "What perspective?"

Mom: "You weren't here."

Jeannie: "And?"

Mom: "You don't know how much I needed…"

Jeannie: "Needed what?"

Mom: "I've been unwell."

Jeannie: "Obviously."

Mom: "I had an appointment."

Jeannie: "What kind?"

Mom: "Doctor. Remember how I'd been shaking?"

Jeannie: "Yes."

Mom: "Doctor confirmed the worst."

Jeannie: *silence*

Mom: "Parkinson's."

Jeannie: "Oh."

Mom: "Right."

Jeannie: "I'm sorry."

Mom: "I'm sorry."

Jeannie: "What's that got to do with Bones?"

Mom: "When I got home, it hit me. How much harder I'll have to work to take care of myself."

Jeannie: "Oh."

Mom: "Then I saw the litter box. It hit me that there was no room for taking care of anyone else."

Jeannie: "Mom—"

Mom: "Not even Bones. Easy as she was—"

Jeannie: "Oh, Mom."

Mom: "—not even Bones."

Jeannie: "So you took her to the shelter?"

Mom: "I grabbed her and didn't let go until the shelter, shakes and all. Miracle that I made it."

Jeannie: "Okay, Mom—"

Mom: "It didn't feel good, Jeannie. But…"

Jeannie: "But?"

Mom: "It was the right thing to do."

Jeannie: "Did it help?"

Mom: "No."

Jeannie: "What do you think would help?"

Mom: "I don't know."

Jeannie: "Should I come home for a bit?"

Mom: "I'd like that."

Jeannie: "I will."

Mom: "Thank you."

Jeannie: "You're welcome."

Mom: "Oh, and Jeannie?"

Jeannie: "Yes?"

Mom: "Bring Bones."

The tape ended. I didn't know how to react, how to cope. I knew, though, that I needed to hear it again. So, rewind, play. Rewind, play. I couldn't get enough. Now that I knew the ending, I had to experience the story again, and again.

What a pitiful and piteous story. My God. Mom, Jeannie, Bones—none had a bright future. And yet, I felt good. Or something. Less "there but for the grace of God" more "fuck it." I felt…superior. I'd *already* gone through what they

went through. I mean—really. I knew hardship. I knew pain. I knew torment. I knew anguish. I knew how life can fucking suck. I had no idea if Jeannie and Mom would survive their shared trauma. But I knew that *I* was a survivor. And I smiled, knowing that if I was faced with the hard times of Jeannie and Mom, I'd survive all over again. I had to. I couldn't *not* survive. I mean—really.

I stared hard at Dad, Randy, Jay, challenging each to downplay my contribution.

"Good effort, Asher." The voice was soft, feminine, artistic. Marlena.

"Good *effort*?"

"I don't know that I would use the word 'good,' but it was effort," Jay added.

"Not good?"

"I have to agree, son," Dad agreed.

"Agree with whom?"

"With Marlena and Jay. Your story lacked."

"Lacked what?"

"It's difficult to describe."

Dad was correct. It turned out that a critique of my story was difficult. It took three people—Dad, Marlena, Jay—taking turns to analyze it, their criticisms adding up to one synthesized response:

On Asher's Story

by

Samuel Delacroix, Marlena Magpie, and Jay

as told to

Asher Delacroix

The way it started was decent—you know, nothing real fancy. Your lead up to listening to the message—the steps to replace phone and machine. Informative.

I wouldn't say *highly* informative.

About what did it inform? How you approach the world.

The details you find important. Those you *don't* find important.

Yes, you left some details out.

How are we supposed to know what details? *You're* the one who left them out.

Your repeated phrasing was interesting. Your repetition of the reality of your story—your insistence that it was not fiction, that it "really" happened—interesting.

It was…insistent.

It took a while for you to get to the message.

I'm not saying that delay was purposeful. But it might've been.

Not that your delays were bereft of information.

Examples? You were oft-confused about the technology you owned—thinking your cordless phone was a "cell phone" and your TV was high def. What does that say about you? That you don't follow trends, that you're Neanderthalic? That you're full of desire for that which you don't have? You'd rather think (at the expense of reality) that the things you have are the best things, that you have the best of the best, and don't lack for status symbols?

Another example: How you worked at your outgoing message, insisting on crafting something "interesting," not something short, simple, useful for callers. Was that because, as you insist, you wanted to appear to be "an interesting cat"? If so, why? Why did you rely on your outgoing message—a fictive creation—to make you appear interesting? Could you not just *be* interesting?

Or maybe you wanted to cloak your personality in that message—hide behind it. Maybe you wanted a false front to obscure reality, which might be unpleasant.

Which is it? Up to interpretation. Could be something else.

Then the conversation you heard—content outside your

control—was good. Strong, even. Well, not strong. But, with that, the focus of your story changed—*your* story turned out to be not about *you* at all, did it?

No, we're right. The message told a snippet of Jeannie and her mom's story—but not much about you. You recited their conversation. But what did that say about you?

Yes, there were interludes. You counting the seconds in the conversational pause. Could be informative. Why'd you have to know that detail? Could be you have a hard time with silences. Could be you were afraid of the rest of the conversation—you had to delay to steel yourself against the pain of someone else's reality.

Now for the crux of our problem with *your* story—the refocus from Jeannie and her mom back to *you*. In the end, what did you do with this painful conversation? This was your error.

Yes, error.

No, error is the right word.

We accept that your recounting of the recording was faithful, not in error. We have no contrary information. Your error was more fundamental.

After you listened to the recording, you did the worst thing you could've done, turning their struggles into a narrative about your own perceived triumphs. You minimized and dismissed their pain. You told a story not about you, then twisted it so you could tell us that *you've* suffered—and suffered *worse* than Jeannie and her mom.

How dare you? Even if it *were* true that you'd suffered more than Jeannie and her mom, how dare you not allow them to feel their feelings? How dare you strain their pain through your own perceived history of pain?

You don't know what pain Jeannie and her mom experienced before, during or after that conversation. All

you did was minimize their pain to reinforce your viewpoint on your own pain. How dare you?

And all that while smirking, no less.

So yes, that was effort, your story. But not "good."

Well, fuck.

I sat. I shook. I attacked my eyes, clearing tear after tear before any "brother" could see them. When I opened my eyes, the circle was no more. It had dissipated. My "brothers" had abandoned their numbered chairs and spread throughout what had once been my apartment.

The last "brother" to leave the circle was my love, my dearest darling Marlena. She stood, smoothed her jeans, came over to me, stood above me, her face aglow. "I wish I could defend you, Asher," she said.

"Defend? Do I need defending?"

As had become the mode in what had once been my apartment, Marlena ignored my question. "I love you," she said. "You know that."

I struggled to grasp the concept.

"You should listen to Sammy, Asher. To learn. To grow. It's a long, challenging, likely painful process, learning, growing." She took my shoulder, squeezed it. "You've got this, though. You've got the ability." She squeezed again, released, turned, and walked away, leaving the former circle empty.

So empty was the former circle that when a voice spoke to my left, I gasped. "You know," Judas said, placing a hand on my shoulder, "I liked your story. I mean—really."

I wasn't so alone after all. Well, fuck.

Statement of Judas [excerpt]

...NOT MUCH TO SAY. I don't believe it. I won't. I can't. Asher couldn't do these things. He didn't. He wouldn't. He's always been so great to me...

Chapter 25

"WHY NOW?" PONY PINCHOT SAT, feet on desk…if this Frankenstein's Monster of a furnishing with its marble columns for legs and golden top draped in velvet could be called a desk. Pony's feet—clad in size 14½ sandals (the number writ large on the soles)—rested atop it. The straps of Pony's sandals encircled his legs, containing calf muscles that strained for freedom as his ankles flexed and his torso rocked in a chair—or throne, given its massive seat, back, and arms. The throne's legs battered against the floor as would a Clydesdale's hooves. Pony's fingers locked behind his head in a struggle for supremacy with his hair. Pony gazed at the ceiling of the office— as much an "office" as the "desk" was a desk, the "chair" was a chair, and Pony was anything other than a cartoon horse-chariot-man hybrid. Ceiling too high for "office," floor too tiled with gritty stones for "office." The only "office" feature was the window-wall through which the setting sun backlit Pony in a golden-purple glow.

I vowed to win this battle of wills, to not cave to Pony, to keep our eyes separate, to maintain my independence, dignity, soul.

I failed. Pony drew my eyes by repeating: "Why now, Asher?"

"Why now, what?"

"How long ago did I ask about your roommates?" I was too slow in calculating. "Eight weeks, five days," Pony answered. "Since then, you've done your best to avoid me."

"My best?"

"You succeeded, sometimes, ducking into a stairwell before I caught you. Other times, when I caught you, you blathered about 'plans' and 'goals,' without details. Now you come to me, knock on my door, and announce that you'll answer every question. Why now?"

I opened my mouth, closed it. What I would've said—had I the ability—was that I worried at hearing the words "bomb," "destroy," "gasoline," "violence," "blood," "death," "end," and "forever," worried at my roommates' hushed tones, knowing smiles, and nods. I longed to say that I brought Pony information to avoid catastrophes that might befall. I longed to confess that everything I'd do, I'd do in the holy spirit of love. I couldn't make any such confession, for none of it was true.

Nor could I confess the truth: that I'd identified my roommates as enemies, each a Judas in their own right (and Judas a "double Judas"—just *because*). That I'd identified as a target of my envious wrath poor, simple Ed King, the weakest of the circle, whom Dad had praised for overcoming great torments. That I'd inflicted new torments on Ed, who lost all possessions (toothpaste, medication, books, photographs, glasses) to the garbage incinerator. That I'd sworn similar vengeance against all roommates.

"You see my confusion, Asher," continued Pony. "Why I question my trust in you. How this sudden change raises my hackles."

I tried to look innocent—eyes wide, hand clutching collar, mouth agape. I failed. My innocence disappeared like Ed's inhaler and glasses down the garbage chute.

Pony laughed. "But, for now, I'll take you at your word."

Joy!

"I have questions."

Fuck!

"First: You sure his name is Jay?"

"Is whose name Jay?"

"What the fuck, Asher?"

"Ah. Yes. Well."

Pony's eyes raged. "Guy you met at the bar, his name is what again?"

"Oh. Jay."

"O.J.?"

I laughed. Pony didn't. I gulped. "No. Just Jay."

"Like the bird? Or the letter?"

"Umm. Like a man."

"Okay," Pony seethed. "We're getting somewhere. Let me run through your story: you meet *Jay* at the bar. When you were thrown out, you brought him back to your apartment."

"It's not what it sounds like."

"It sounds like you and Jay engaged in conversations, you found out he didn't have a place to live, so you allowed him to crash at your apartment."

"So, it's exactly what it sounds like."

"The next morning, you decided not to kick Jay out."

"You have a very succinct way of summari—"

"Next came Ed King?"

"That's where it gets a bit fuzzy, but it may have been Ed who moved in next."

"You knew Ed from childhood. Ed met Jay independently."

"That's right. Sure."

"Ed's the one you heard say 'fire.'"

"Correct."

"To whom?"

"Umm. Alec."

"Posner?"

"Yes."

"The one with the sex blog."

"It's not *all* about sex."

"You said that. But you gave an example of a post about sex to differentiate him from…who?"

"Sony."

"Right. Weird name. Sony Ericsson. She writes a different blog? About travel?"

"Right."

"And Hitler?"

"No. I mean, she wrote an entry about her travels to Brazil—which had Hitlerian undertones."

"Hitlerian undertones."

"Yes," I smiled at Pony's understanding.

"Can't say I understand, but it's unimportant. Sony...you didn't mention her saying anything in particular."

"She just nodded."

"At what, again?"

"Something about...ah! Donny said, 'righteous force.'"

"Donny Quick?"

"Yes."

"Donny said 'righteous force' in response to...who was it?...Ella Flowers asking about the police?"

"That's right."

"Speaking of age, did you say that one of them is 9?"

"Chase Crane."

"Another odd name."

"I think it's a nickname."

"Like an alias?"

"Just a nickname, I think."

"Do you know her *actual* name?"

"Umm. I don't know. But nicknames seem to be common with her family. Her brother, Jeremy had a nickname, but I don't remember what it was."

"Does Jeremy live in the apartment, too?"

"No."

"Then why the fuck would I want to hear about him?"

"I don't know. Why would you?"

"I wouldn't."

"Then I won't tell you about him."

Pony whispered something under his breath.

"What's that?" I asked.

"Look, if I want to know something, I'll ask. How's that?"

"Sounds good."

"Good."

"Good."

"Good."

"Good."

"Shut up for a second. Let me think." Pony's brow furrowed. "There was someone else I wanted to ask about. Who was it?"

"I don't know."

"I said shut the fuck up!"

"I can do that."

"Then do it!"

"No problem."

Pony stared.

I remained silent.

"Randy!" Pony shouted. "Randy Mac!"

I stayed silent.

"You know who I'm talking about?"

"Should I speak again?"

"Yes," Pony seethed.

"Then, yes."

"What do you mean, yes?"

"Oh. Yes, I know who you are talking about?"

"Goddamn it. Who *was* I talking about?"

"Oh. Randy Mac."

"That's him. Randy Mac—you told me about some exchange between him and...who was it?"

"I believe—"

"You believe, or you know?"

"I believe."

"Okay. What do you believe?"

"Umm." My mind blanked.

"About Randy Mac? About who he had an exchange with?"

"Oh! I believe that was Ella Flowers."

"Okay. And what did Ella and Randy say to each other?"

"Well, to be clear—"

"Yes?"

"—I'm not sure it was those two."

"Why not?"

"I only *believe* it was them."

"Fucking Hell. Look, humor me."

My turn for a furrowed brow. "You want me to tell you a joke?"

"As much *fun* as that sounds, I'll just take an answer."

"To what question?"

"Assuming Ella and Randy were speaking to each other, what did they say?"

"Well, Ella, I believe—"

"We've already established what your 'belief' is worth. Tell me the Goddamned words!"

"Ella, I bel—I mean, Ella said—assuming it was Ella and Randy talking—Ella said, 'obliterate,' and Randy—assuming it was Randy and Ella talking—Randy responded, 'gold, man.'"

"Obliterate?"

"That's right."

"Gold, man?"

"Right, again."

"You're sure Randy said 'gold, man'? That exact phrase?"

"I believe so."

"You *believe*?" Pony pinched the bridge of his nose. "Let's move on. For the sake of expediency, I'll assume that you *believe* everything you're telling me."

"Sounds good."

"That leaves me with two final questions—for now."

"Two questions. Great. I can answer two questions."

"Dear God I fucking hope so."

"Go ahead. Shoot."

"If only, Asher." Pony leaned forward, pointed sternly at me, shook his head. "If only."

"What?"

"Never mind. First question: You're close with these interlopers."

"I am?"

"Well, one's your lover, right?"

"Ah. Marlena."

"Right. The artist, right?"

"Yeeeessss."

"And your father is another?"

"Corrrrreeeect."

"Okay. So, my first question—"

"Wait."

"What?"

"Those weren't your two final questions?"

"No."

"Ah."

"You have a problem with that?"

"No. Is *that* one of your final—"

"No. Here's my first question—"

"Yes?"

"I'll tell you, Asher, if you shut the fuck up."

"I can do that."

Another sigh. "Don't start that again. Look—just shut the fuck up. Seriously. Shut the fuck up."

I stared.

"That's better."

"It is?"

"FUCKING FUCK! What the exact fuck is wrong with you?"

"Wrong?"

"All right. I'm just going to ask the fucking question: You've got at least these two tight relationships in your apartment—"

"In what used to be my apartment, yes."

"Whatever the fuck we're calling it now, you've got a strong tie to Marlena. You've got another with Samuel or Sammy or whatever—with your dad."

"I suppose."

"You suppose? Fuck it. I'm taking that as a yes. Are there any others to whom you feel a strong attachment?"

"Your final set of questions sure has grown in number."

"Asher, I swear to fucking Christ—"

"Well, to answer your question…"

"Yes?"

"Any other strong connection…let me think." And think I did. I thought of Donny's steadfastness, Judas' innocence. I thought of Chase's inquisitiveness, Randy saying whatever the fuck he wanted. I thought of Gregor's vigor, Cassie's righteousness, Ella's sweetness, Alec's self-awareness. I thought of Sony's detachment, Ed's resolve. I thought of Jay's…everything. "No," I answered. "I can't think of a strong connection between me and any other interloper."

"Now, for my second of my two final questions—are you ready?"

"I—"

"Before you ask if 'are you ready' is the final question, I want you to remember two things: the size of my fist, and the crunch of your nose."

"I'll keep both those things in mind, sir."

"See that you do. As for the question: Has Jay shared anything with you about his past?"

"Hmmm."

"Anything in particular about where he was in the months leading up to you meeting him?"

"No. I don't believe—"

"I'm going to stop you right there."

"Ah. Okay."

"All in all, you've done well, Asher. You made the right call coming to me—finally."

"Thank you."

"I just hope it isn't too late."

"What's that?"

"Don't worry about it."

"Okay. I can do that. I think."

Chapter 26

"THAT FUCKING A-RAB."

Not a visit to Walter Reuther passed without a blatant attack by Merry Delacroix on someone.

"Which fucking A-rab is that again?" Dad asked.

I smiled. This I could hold over Dad. Since he hadn't seen or spoken with Mom since her confinement, I knew Mom's post-diagnosis verbiage (which, to be fair, didn't vary much from her pre-diagnosis verbiage) better than Dad did.

Mom ignored Dad, trusting he would catch on. "He got me this time," she continued. "During group. He doesn't usually attend—today was a special *treat*. He sat in the back of the room. I didn't know he was there. Usually, I can feel when that fucker comes in. Air in the room gets thicker, gooier. This morning, though, he caught me unawares. I *knew* I was getting too comfortable in here."

"You go to group?" The thought of Mom interacting with others as if she was in one of the cursed circles in what had once been my apartment jarred me in every sense of the word.

"Leader asked for ideas on how to interpret people. I began my shoeshine theory. Soon as I get two words in, that fucking A-rab's voice punches me in the throat so I can't talk. I can't believe I let him sneak up on me."

"What'd he say?" Dad asked. I exhaled, thankful I wasn't the one to break Mom's silence.

"Something unexpected."

"In what way?" Dad asked.

"It was smart. Wasn't his idea, though. Was some colleague's idea."

"What was it?"

"'A colleague of mine,' he said, 'has a test. He asked of his patients how they'd evenly split a dollar between three people.'"

"Wow," Dad said in admiration.

"Brilliant," Mom agreed.

"What?" I asked.

"Made my shoeshine bullshit look like it spewed from the mind of an infant."

"How's that question brilliant?"

"That's the perfect way to read a person," Dad answered.

"Wait—"

"Think about that," Mom said, eyes (and words) for Dad alone.

"I have." Dad's smile spread from face to posture as he took Mom's hand.

"I know." Mom threaded her fingers through Dad's.

"Hold on," I interrupted. "How's that brilliant? It's not answerable."

"It is," Dad responded.

"No. There's no way to evenly split a dollar between three people."

"There are many ways," Dad said. "At least as many as there are people in our apartment."

"Really?"

"Give me a name."

"All right, Dad. Ella. How would Ella split a dollar among three people?"

"She'd determine which of the three was neediest. She'd give 33 cents to the other two, and 34 cents to the neediest. By giving the extra penny to the neediest person, she moved each of them closer to equal."

"Huh. Okay. How about Chase?"

"Chase'd be literal. She'd rip the dollar into three and distribute each piece."

"Cassie?"

"Cassie'd find a way to break the extra penny into three pieces and give

~ 256 ~

one to each person. Although by doing so she destroys the penny's monetary value, each piece has value as a symbol that everyone's wealth should be equal."

"And Donny?"

"Donny'd go on a heroic quest to find two extra pennies to add to the dollar so that it was divisible by three."

"Gregor?"

"Gregor'd lie to the three, telling them that the dollar was lost or stolen. He'd keep the dollar to satisfy his own urges, leaving them equally empty-handed."

"What about Sony?"

"Sony'd ignore the entire process and convince the three people that there are more important things to which they should attend."

"Okay. And Jay?"

"Jay would somehow turn that dollar into as many dollars as all three people need, and more."

"Randy?"

"Randy'd wipe his ass with the bill and offer it around, giving each of the three equal opportunity to seize it."

"What about you, Dad?"

"I'd buy something with the dollar—say, gum—and split it among the people."

Seeing that Dad was right, that the answers illuminated the characters of each roommate, I turned a final direction. "What about you, Mom? How would you split that dollar?"

"I'd say fuck you, this is my dollar, go get your own fucking dollar," Mom said.

Mom and Dad were right—the test was brilliant.

"And you, Asher?" Dad asked.

"Me?"

"How would you split that dollar?"

Shit. How did I not see that coming? My imagination raced, but no ideas came. I said the only thing that I could think. "I'd adopt Ella's approach."

"No, you wouldn't," Mom retorted.

"Why not?"

"You can't read people. You'd never figure out which person was neediest."

"Oh."

"And don't steal the fucking answer that Ella gave!"

"Ella didn't give that answer," I objected.

"We're waiting," Dad responded with Mom's sharpness.

"I would…"

"You would what?" Dad asked.

"I'd…"

"Yes?"

"I…"

"Spit it out, asshole," Mom added.

I closed my eyes and loosed my answer. "I'd hide the extra penny. I'd throw it away. I'd give each person 33 cents."

"Why?" Dad asked, smile reappearing.

"It's the easiest thing I could do. Involves the least effort."

"See what I mean?" Mom asked. "Brilliant."

"Mom, we're not here to find out what you learned in group this morning."

"It's connected, asshole."

"How?"

"Same way everything's connected," Dad answered.

"Dad, we're here because they're taking Mom's visitation away. This is our last chance to visit."

"I remember," Dad responded.

"I asked Mom why they were taking her visitation away."

"Wrong question," Mom interrupted.

"What's wrong with that question?"

"It presumes that they're taking visitation away."

"Well…yeah. That's what's happening…Right?"

"No."

"Then why are we here?"

"To visit me for the last time."

"Because?"

"Because I won't be able to receive visitors."

"So, they *are* taking visitation away."

"That's not what I said."

"Mom, please just tell me."

"What Merry means," Dad answered, "is that she's not losing visitation rights because the facility is taking them away."

"Then how—"

"I gave them up, asshole."

"You gave up visitation rights?"

"That's right."

"Why?"

Mom's tilted her head, arched her eyebrow, and stayed silent. Refusing to accept the implicit answer, I rejoined, "But, Mom, when they called this morning, they told us that you were losing visitation as a punishment."

"I'm sure they did."

"Why'd they say that?"

"Because it's true."

"I'm confused."

"I'm sure you are."

"How could it be true that you're being punished *and* that you gave up your visitation?"

"It's obvious," Dad answered.

"Can you pretend that I'm stupid—"

"Pretend?" Mom chortled.

"—and just tell me what I need to know?"

"I've spent your lifetime trying to do that, asshole."

"Mom—"

"What Merry means is that she purposely caused herself to be punished. In that way, they didn't take away her visitation—she gave it up."

"Ah."

"You know me so well, Sammy. It's a shame."

"It's a shame Dad knows you so well?"

"No, asshole."

"That's what you said."

"No, it isn't," Dad responded. "Just because Merry said 'It's a shame' after saying 'You know me so well, Sammy,' that doesn't mean that me knowing her so well is the shame."

"Exactly. The shame is," Mom added, "that Sammy, who isn't of my blood, who didn't fester inside me for nine months, who I didn't suckle—at least not for nourishment—"

"Jesus, Mom."

"—it's a shame that Sammy knows me better than you do."

"But Dad's known you for longer than I have."

"Not by percentage of his life."

"Okay, Mom. I'm shameful. Fine. I still don't get this whole giving up your visitation thing."

"Of course you don't."

"Why don't you explain it?"

"She's already started to explain it."

"What are you talking about, Dad? I ask Mom why she's losing her visitation and she gives me this bullshit—"

"Language, Asher!" Mom shouted.

"This fucking bullshit—"

"That's better."

"—about the lesson to be learned from a group session."

"I told you the story of the group in order to tell you the next story."

"What next story?"

"Shut up and I'll tell you."

I opened my mouth, caught the warning in Dad's eyes, closed it.

"Good. Maybe you're capable of learning after all," Mom continued. "Maybe. That fucking A-rab interrupting group pissed me off. Because I was pissed off, I lashed out."

"How?"

Mom's smile showed pride. "They have this hallway here, the Brown hallway—named after the wall color; residents call it Hershey Highway. I call it Rectum Road. Rectum Road's where the imaging lab is—x-rays, MRIs, the works. Staff have a system for residents going in and out—residents with severe mental disabilities in particular—I call them Slobberjaws. Not disparaging. Don't give me that look. I like the Slobberjaws. They're quiet. They don't give me stupid looks like some people. When Slobberjaws are getting ready to be rolled into the lab for MRIs, they're lined up along the east wall of Rectum Road facing the lab. Afterward, staff roll them back out and line them up on the west wall, facing the other way as a signal that they're ready to be taken to their rooms. Can you picture that, asshole?"

"I got it, Mom."

"After that fucking A-rab embarrassed me, I broke into Rectum Road. Wipe that smirk off your face, boy. I broke into Rectum Road and watched the Slobberjaws going into the lab until one was wheeled back out against the west wall. When staff disappeared, I wheeled him back over to the east wall. I hid and watched him be readmitted to the lab. Those bastards didn't figure that shit out until after I fed five more back through. By doing that, I gave up my visitation rights. And here you are for one final visit before…"

"Before what, Mom?"

Mom chuckled.

"That's my Merry," Dad added. His smile was almost as proud as Mom's.

"Yours forever, Sammy."

"Wait—"

"Quiet," both said at once.

"Asher," Dad said, not to me. "That's quite the name you gave our son."

"Better than the one he's making for himself."

I shuddered.

Dad laughed. "You think Asher isn't living up to his name?"

"I doubt anyone will see him as blessed of anything, no less the cross. We might as well have named him Asshole."

Dad laughed again. "Asshole Delacroix wouldn't change his signature much."

Straining for a response, I leapt to plagiarism. "What's in a name? A rose by any—"

"Fuck off with that Shakespeare shit, asshole."

"But..." I waited for Mom to interrupt. She raised her eyebrows. I turned to Dad.

"Merry has a point," Dad said. "Juliet said 'a rose by any other name would smell as sweet.' But the end result disproves the notion—names dictated the fates of Romeo and Juliet, after all. Romeo remained a Montague just as Juliet remained a Capulet—and those names killed them."

"Juliet's delusional," Mom added. "She sees Romeo as *not* a Montague and believes that others will back her up on that bullshit."

"See, Asher?" Dad asked.

"See what?"

"Fuck Shakespeare," Mom added. "Names mean something."

"You want further examples," Samuel added, "look around the apartment."

"Huh."

"Or, consider Mikey Centavo."

"I remember Mikey." Mom smiled.

Sensing a story that would end with me swearing in frustration, I tried in vain to resist asking the inevitable question. I failed. "Who's Mikey Centavo?"

"Mikey Centavo was the opposite of his last name."

"Centavo. One small coin, right? So, he was rich?"

"Not at all. He was poor. He had *no* money."

"Dad—"

"The opposite of one centavo isn't a million dollars, asshole," Mom interrupted.

"Oh. Thanks."

"Remember that time at the bar, Merry?"

"Tell it again," Mom cooed.

"Gladly. Mikey Centavo was drinking a beer thinking about how he'd pay his tab. He reached into his pocket. Nothing. After a few more gulps, he tried

again. Still nothing. On the third time, where nothing had been, was something. But it wasn't money. It was a chunk of splintered wood shaped like a coin. Flipping it over, he found 'centavo' written on the other side. Mikey surged with peace and knowledge. He knew in that moment that everything would be okay."

"How?"

"Mikey remembered writing 'centavo' on the wood in a fit of pretend. He pretended that that wood was a coin—thus was the limit of Mikey's experience with money. Only a person with no money would pretend that he had only one centavo. Anyone who knew the power of money would pretend that the value of that coin was limitless. Nevertheless, looking at 'centavo' scrawled on the coin in his hand in that bar made Mikey feel fantastic."

"Because it represented money?"

"Because it represented heritage."

"But he hadn't intended the word to represent heritage. Only money."

"I don't know how many times you have to learn this lesson, son, but it didn't matter what Mikey intended when he wrote 'centavo' on that wood. What mattered was what Mikey got out of the word 'centavo' when he beheld it as a reader. In that moment, 'centavo' reminded Mikey of his father, and his father's father, and his father's father's father. So it goes. All of Mikey's heritage came to his mind in that moment, and he realized that all of those Centavos had survived in the world. Therefore, everything would be all right."

As much as I fought my next question, it came. "What happened with the beer?"

"What beer?"

"What do you mean what beer? The beer that Mikey had at the bar."

"He drank it."

"How did he *pay* for it?"

"Son, listen, this isn't about beer."

Feeling an explosion rising within me, I beheld Mom and changed tack as a new idea occurred to me. "Dad, why is it that all of your stories involve men?"

"What do you mean?"

"Bobby Bull, the suicidal elderly men, Hotchky Potchky, Heathcliff Garfield, Mikey Centavo—all men. Why don't you tell stories of interest to women?"

"How misogynistic," Dad responded.

"Yes!" I agreed.

"I thought we raised you better, son."

I blinked. "What?"

"To assume that women only get things out of stories that involve women—I was trying to think of a gentler word, but that's misogynistic."

"Wait…Dad, Mikey Centavo…"

"What about him?"

"He's a man."

"True."

"Also, his story…the message is patriarchal. It's based on the man's last name and how it's passed down from man to man across generations."

"True again."

"How are women to get anything out of such a story when they've had a history of having last names ripped away from them?"

"That story isn't about last names, son."

"Holy fuck, Dad."

Dad didn't pause even half a beat. "Speaking of holy," he turned to Mom, "do you remember that class we had—what was it called?"

"Culture and the Holocaust," Mom answered.

"That's the one. I'm sure you know the story."

Mom smiled. "Tell it again, my love."

"I could never resist you, Merry. Very well. You were correct: Culture and the Holocaust. Team taught by three professors: Monty Schictman (literature), Joseph Weinstein (sociology), and Hadassa Liebermann (anthropology). No history professor. I always wondered why."

"You must have missed Schictman's explanation that history scholars weren't creative enough. Which is bullshit—if there's anything history professors should know, it's fiction."

"Ah, Schictman. As usual, he's at the center of this story. He gave the lecture on propaganda, talked about how effective the Nazis were at drawing people in. He described their rallies: the marching, the chanting, the saluting, the violent acts against those who refused to march, chant, and salute. Then he made his tearful admission. Barely above a whisper: 'I've thought about this for some time,' he said. 'If I was in Germany in 1939, what would I do?' he asked. 'Would I stand up and fight against the system that brutalized my people? Or would I stay silent?' After a long pause, he made his admission, even quieter than before: 'I don't think I'd have been strong enough. I'd probably be goose-stepping alongside them.'

"Like a rifle shot from the back of the room, Weinstein shouted, 'YOU'D DO WHAT?'

"Quieter, Schictman repeated: 'I'd be goose-stepping alongside them.'

"As Weinstein hurtled himself toward the lectern, it took six students—including you, Merry—to keep him from committing Nazi-esque violence on Schictman. Schictman just stood and waited for his penance.

"I didn't intervene. I didn't move to stop him," Dad admitted, his voice barely above a whisper. "All Schictman did was give voice to a deep and shameful truth. Weinstein had no right to attack him. Yet I did nothing."

"It happened so fast," Mom said.

"True. Yet you, Merry, were the first to throw yourself between the two."

"I never could keep myself out of a good bit of ultraviolence."

"It was more than that, though. You were righteous. You were the driving force—the leader of the group that prevented that classroom from becoming a bloodbath."

"That's an exaggeration." Was Mom blushing? "If you had more time, you would've joined us, Sammy."

"Maybe."

Mom and Dad looked at each other. Dad and Mom joined hands. The three of us—how difficult it was to admit that baby made three—sat in silence.

As uncomfortable as that silence was, I dreaded its inevitable end. "What do you think, Merry?" Dad asked.

Somehow Mom knew Dad's unvoiced question. Somehow, I knew it, too.

"Would he?" Mom mused.

"I think he has potential, my love. In the end, he might have the courage to do the right thing, might live up to his name."

"What a God-blessed surprise that would be."

Chapter 27

"MOM CAUSED IT."

Molly Monahan, L.M.S.W., L.M.F.T., L.P.C., looks at me, eyes wide, irises sparkling, brows arched, lips pursed, head cocked, posture straightened, with energy she hasn't exhibited in a dozen sessions. She's *interested*. It's a good look for her. As I expand on my thought, though, I ruin her mood.

"Mom *and* Dad caused it, that is."

Ms. Monahan wilts, her eyes dimming, energy gone.

Attempting to win her back, I hurry into the story that I'm sure will re-tantalize her. "'Caused' is the wrong word. But observing them interacting in our final visit before Mom lost visitation, to witness that connection...

"It's difficult to talk about even now. What does that say about the power of their touches? I didn't feel Dad's skin on Mom's hands. I didn't feel the muscle between Mom's thumb and forefinger flex as she held Dad's fingers. I didn't feel Dad's knuckles writhe in pleasure from Mom's touch.

"Yet, I felt something. Energy. Electricity. Ecstasy. Not my own. I felt *their* ecstasy all over me.

"It wasn't an empathetic thing. I wasn't putting myself in their positions and experiencing what they felt. I felt Mom's and Dad's real-deal ecstasy pouring off them like raging white water. A powerful sensation with powerful consequences. The most immediate consequence was me feeling intense longing.

"You might think that the longing I felt was for a connection like that for myself. You're right. In part. I longed for that connection. But not, as *you* surmise, because I wanted to add value to my own existence. What I needed was a connection of my own that would *devalue* the connection between Mom and Dad.

"If I was to achieve a connection like that, I'd know Mom and Dad's connection wasn't so special. For if *I* could attain that connection with someone, how much of a challenge could it be for *anyone*? Right? Mom and Dad weren't so special at all.

"I was confident in my abilities to connect. Problem was that a Mom-Dad level connection required reciprocity. I doubted that my roommates—who'd abandoned, ignored, shunned me on the regular—would be able to overcome their prejudices and connect with me. But I had to allow them the chance to prove me wrong.

"Which brings up a second problem—pluralization. I needed to connect with *one* person. But 13 lived in what had once been my apartment. With which of these 13 was I to forge this connection? Certain roommates I could eliminate without much thought.

"Chase: Even I was not so juvenile as to connect with a 9-year-old. Besides, Gregor already yelled around, toward, or at me too much for my taste. 'Seducing' (for lack of a better term) someone with whom Gregor desired to connect—I shudder for my eardrums.

"Ella: As kind, considerate, and noble as Donny was, I didn't dare incite the wrath his body could inflict. Besides, even as long as she'd spent away from her family's fortune, the smell of pickles hung about Ella in a way that made me too hungry and nauseous to function.

"Ed: No. Just...no. Never Ed.

"Gregor: I refer you to my points on Chase.

"Cassie: Too militant. I don't know what else to say.

"Judas, Randy, Alec: See Ed.

"This quick and dirty elimination of eight left me with five choices to consider.

"Sony wasn't so easily dismissed. She was smart, funny, attractive. I liked

that she didn't give a shit about little things—and that she wasn't prone to panic. She was always calm, secure.

"But Sony was distant. Her mind never settled anywhere, or with anyone. She seemed barely human. I doubted her ability to connect on a basic human level.

"On top of that, there was Sony's gender. Remembering the connection between Mom and Dad, as much as it pains me to conceive of my parents conceiving, their connection oozed sex. Sony, though attractive, didn't inspire in me physical desire necessary to match that aspect of Mom and Dad's connection. To this day, the thought of sex with Sony remains impossible, as if Sony and I were from different species meant to never mate. And to make a *strong* connection with a member of the opposite sex, but *without* sex, that wasn't a type of connection that would work for me.

"Which left four to sort through. The next one out was Donny. Like Sony, Donny and I would never fuck—not that Donny lacked for sex appeal. But his sex appeal was not sexual, if that makes sense. So, there could never be any acts of sex between Donny and me. But that deficit wasn't the reason for dismissing him. Even though Mom and Dad's connection oozed sex, the physical act of sex was not a requisite for the type of connection I sought to forge, at least not with a member of my own sex.

"I recognize the contradiction. I tell you I can't forge a connection with Sony because there was no chance for sex. Then I tell you that 'no sex' was no obstacle to a connection with Donny. There's a simple rationale: expectation.

"Were I to forge a connection with Donny, that connection would be free of expectation. Society wouldn't *expect* that connection to evolve into physical realms. More than that, Donny himself wouldn't form a sexual expectancy.

"Whereas with Sony—or any female—including *you* (no need to shudder—just giving another example)—society would expect that if I were to form such a connection with Sony, or with *you* (*again* with the shuddering? Really?), that connection would include a sexual component. More than that, Sony *herself* would expect that component—there can be no doubt.

"Due to these expectations, societal and personal, I couldn't connect with Sony on a level equivalent to the connection between Mom and Dad, and yet I could forge such a connection with Donny.

"But Donny was just so…perfect. Brave, bold, strong, hearty, confident, noble, trustworthy, forthright, ever ready for action—Donny was in every way ideal. Being so perfect, so ideal, Donny had no need to forge a connection with me.

"With Mom and Dad, each one had weaknesses, needs. I can see the question in your eyes: 'What, Asher, do you, perceive to be the weaknesses in your father and mother as individuals?' I won't (or *can't*—you decide) answer. 'Why not?' Because I won't (or *can't*) betray trust like that—not anymore.

"To overcome their weaknesses, Mom and Dad needed each other. The strength of each one covered the other's weakness. Dad's boisterousness covered Mom's stoicism. Mom's practicality covered Dad's flightiness. Dad's warmth covered Mom's chill. Mom's violence covered—oh, now you have me disclosing that which I'd vowed to keep quiet. You minx, you! (Now, now: remember what I said about those shudders).

"Mom needed Dad; Dad needed Mom. Their connection required that 'need' component. And Donny, being ideal, didn't need for *anything*.

"With no Sony and no Donny, my list dwindled to three—a trinity of potential connections. And what a trinity Dad, Jay, and Marlena made! With each, I believed I could connect…powerfully.

"With Dad, what better foundation for a connection than the obligations born of blood? And what better way to devalue the connection between Mom and Dad than to steal Dad away from Mom?

"And yet, it couldn't be Dad. One of my purposes for forging a powerful connection was to force Dad to reevaluate his choices. To do so, Dad would have to be embarrassed, humiliated, devastated. While I was confident in my ability to embarrass, humiliate, and devastate Dad, I knew that if I forged a powerful connection with him, Dad could never be devastated again. He could only be happy. To force Dad to reevaluate (and downgrade) the connection between he and Mom, I couldn't have Dad happy. So, Dad was out.

"Jay was open for connection—he desired it, as shown through his interactions with all residents of what had once been my apartment. Even though Jay was flush with connections within that apartment, I knew that he had room for *one* more.

"Although blood didn't bind us, I felt that Jay was like a brother, as if Jay and I shared the same point of origin, a common father (Samuel Delacroix notwithstanding), or as if our values were shaped by a common matronly love and affection (although those shudders to which you are prone—you might spare some for Jay if that were the case).

"But with Jay there was the problem of Peter 'Pony' Pinchot.

"Your eyes betray me...er...*you*. I see inside those burning browns of yours recognition of the problems with my chronology. For there could no 'problem of Jay *and* Peter "Pony" Pinchot' at the time when I was evaluating my roommates for 'connection potential' because at that time, Jay and Peter 'Pony' Pinchot had not yet met. I get that. It was more that Jay reminded me of Pony. Not that Jay was reminiscent of Pony. Jay had no Pony-esque qualities. Jay didn't stampede around, all hoof and huff and bluster and bluff. Jay didn't decorate the apartment in a style befitting the Roman empire. But I saw Pony all over Jay. Pony infected Jay's aura, poisoned his atmosphere. Every time I saw Jay, I saw Pony lurking there, a constant threat. I saw Jay drinking OJ from the carton—I saw a spiritual Pony galloping through the kitchen doorway, charging fist-first at the flesh of Jay's side. I saw Jay lounging on the couch—I saw Pony writhing on the floor below, ready to bite into Jay's feet. I saw Jay gesticulating while lecturing Randy Mac on some aspect or other of the 'ultimate goal'—I saw Pony wildly chopping at Jay's hands.

"In seeing Pony every time I saw Jay, I couldn't form a powerful connection with Jay. Doing so would be unfair to both of us. Unfair to me because I couldn't (while seeing Pony every time I beheld Jay) mold my emotional state into a form conducive to a powerful connection. Unfair to Jay, for in my fear at the visions of Pony, there was no way I could be the man that Jay deserved—the strong and confident man that I was at my full poten—(I see those shudders of yours have yielded to chuckles—unwarranted).

"But I'll take those subtle signs from you as a hint to move on. I moved on from Jay to a person with whom I'd already forced...er, *forged*...a connection. Not to say that that pre-forged connection was untroubled. Marlena and I had our issues, which revealed themselves when she sided with Dad and Jay against me.

"Okay, *against* me is perhaps unjust. You know what she said, after all, how in one sentence she expressed love 'deep and abiding,' while in another, she couldn't defend me. As I remember it, the sentence declaiming defense came first, before the expression of love, as if she couldn't lead with love— as if, between her fists and her lips, she had to come in swinging before she could kiss me—and Marlena wasn't going to be done throwing haymakers for a *long* time.

"Punch one: 'I can't defend you, Asher.'

"Punch two: 'Listen to Sammy, Asher.' (Extra bruising from this punch, landing in a soft spot of mine, what with Marlena's over-familiar use of Dad's nickname—as if she fashioned herself a surrogate for Mom).

"Punch three: stating that I needed 'to grow.' (Small man, am I? Would a small man make such a thorough numerical chronicle of...you know what? Never mind).

"Punch four: The implication...fuck that: the *express assertion* that not only do I need to grow, to learn, to improve—but that I'm so damaged and stunted (and stunned) that I require a 'long,' 'challenging' and 'likely painful' process to improve!

"I acknowledge that Marlena said much that was to my favor: love was mentioned a few times, and a *desire* to defend me (even as her lack of defense belied her stated 'desire'), and acknowledgement that I have 'ability' to learn and grow.

"Yet, Marlena's theme was that I wasn't good enough. Not for her. She didn't love me as the boy I was—she loved me as the man into which she desired to transform me. To Marlena, I was a broken thing, needing fixing, building up, reshaping into something she could love.

"Then again, Mom and Dad had issues of their own. All I knew in my teenaged to adult life was Merry and Sammy fighting—swears, glares,

frowns (occasional fists) flew alongside their cheery monikers. If they could form a connection given all those issues, Marlena and I could, as well.

"So, I came to Marlena in the bedroom of what had once been my apartment, she curled up on her mattress while I knelt next to her and proposed marriage.

"I understand how odd that sounds—it was a crazy impulse. Although I loved Marlena, the impulse was not based in love.

"Oh? Yes. She said yes. When I asked her to marry me, she looked at me, smiled, cocked her head, asked no questions, and said, 'Yes.'

"So it was to be. This is the point where my verb tense means something…'was.' My marriage to Marlena *was* to be.

"Of course, there was a lot of stuff that '*was to be*' at that point in time, including achievement of my roommates' ultimate goals. And then, my roommates dropped from 13 to one. My dearest darling Marlena Magpie was the only person who remained with me in what had once again come oh-so close to being my apartment.

"It was so Goddamned quiet. Even with Marlena there, it was quieter than when I'd lived alone, so quiet that she and I would fill that silence any way we could. Like, for instance, when we read aloud to each other. There was a book, the winner of some prize or other, what was it called? Doesn't matter. What matters is that the author of that book described a person as…what was the word? Tinkery? No. Splintery! That was it. What matters is that the author described a person as 'splintery'—the sum total description of that character's personality. The word 'splintery'— suitably enough, I guess—'splintered' the connection between Marlena and me.

"The way that worked was this: I read aloud the description of the 'splintery' man and then, mid-sentence—right after the word 'splintery'—I stopped and stared at the word I had just read: 'splintery.' Three syllables, nine letters, one big problem. When I stopped reading, the apartment became so quiet that Marlena's breaths seemed to echo.

"I should explain our positioning, for it occurs to me that that positioning speaks to the connectivity issues we've been discussing. As I read the book

aloud, I sat on the couch—Jay's couch, left behind by Jay when…well, it wasn't like Jay could've taken that couch with him, was it?

"Anyway, I sat on one end of the couch, and Marlena lay across the rest. Her head rested in my lap. My left hand rested on her head, fingers entangled in her hair.

"Back to connectivity: note how I used the word 'entangled.' I don't know that I consciously chose that word over less aggressive 'inter' words— 'intertwined,' 'interwoven.' But if it was a conscious choice, I made the right one; 'entangled' is a better fit. Now recall the words I used to describe the connection between Mom and Dad, as shown through their physicality: 'sensuous touch'; 'writhe in pleasure'; 'intimate'; 'smiles.' The difference isn't just in word choice—it's in reality. The entanglement of my fingers in Marlena's hair—it didn't seem that I could ever derive from that touch the writhing pleasure that Dad manifested from Mom's sensuous squeezing of the flesh between his thumb and forefinger. I'd failed to 'connect' with Marlena the same way that Mom and Dad connected.

"As to the source of that failure—I couldn't say. Could've been that Marlena and I didn't have the right 'cover' for each other's weaknesses. Could've been that one of us was unready for such a connection to form. Could've been the events that happened in between my proposal and the entanglement of my fingers in Marlena's hair. Could've been that Marlena and I didn't have a long enough shared history to form the basis of a connection as strong as Mom and Dad's. Whatever reason underlay my failure, failure it was. By the time that Marlena lay there with her head in my lap, my fingers entangled in her hair, Marlena and I had begun to come apart, to splinter.

"Perhaps it was that sense of our relationship splintering that stopped my reading aloud from that prize-winning book when the author described a character as 'splintery.' Perhaps I felt I could relate. Whatever the reason, when I stopped reading, the room was quiet until Marlena turned her head, her eyes seeking mine (while her hair further bound my fingers to it) and said, 'Splintery? That's an interesting way to describe someone. No wonder you stopped reading.'

"'What?' responded I.

"'Splintery,'" she continued. 'That's the word, right?'

"'Oh,' I answered. 'Yes. 'Splintery.'

"'And he used that word—"splintery"—to describe a man?'

"'Umm,' said I as my eyes scanned the page in front of me, whereon the author used 'splintery' to describe someone...who? With my mind itself in splinters, I couldn't tell. But there was the word, 'splintery,' describing someone. 'Yes, a man,' I continued.

"'What do you think that means?'

"'Means?'

"Marlena smiled at that, the smile she'd give me when I was being silly, as if she believed I was just goofing around. When I didn't return the smile, her smile dropped. 'You stopped after you read it, Asher. It must mean something to you.'

"'Must it?'

"'"Must' might be the wrong word. True. *Does* it mean something to you?'

"I resisted admitting what was on my mind—what the word 'splintery' might imply about things—about Marlena and me, about the roommates that had left the apartment, about Jay, about my fragile remaining sanity. But that heavy choking silence won. 'I suppose it means something to me, yes.'

"'How do you interpret it?'

"I contemplated Marlena's question without contemplating Marlena herself, for to contemplate Marlena would be to awaken further the specter of things lost, abandoned, discarded, driven away, *hauled* away, gone forever. 'Splintery,' I said, stalling for time. Finally, something crossed my mind: 'Thin!' I nearly shouted.

"'Thin?'

"'Yes. Thin.'

"'Like physically thin?'

"'Exactly!'

"'The interpretation of "splintery" that stopped your reading was that the guy being described was "thin"?'

"'Umm.'

"'I find that difficult to believe. What else've you got?'

"Wait, isn't the author dead?'

"'Did you write the book?'

"'No.'

"'Then death is no object to you telling me what's on your mind.'

"At this, my resistance faltered. 'The man described as "splintery,"' sighed I, 'it strikes me that such a man would be wooden, rough, so unlovable that to touch him would hurt. He'd leave nasty stinging slivers of himself inside anyone who got too close—slivers that meant that he'd forever be an irritant, a pain that could never—*ever*—be removed.'

"'Oh, Asher.' Marlena stretched her hand up to stroke my face. 'Look,' she smiled, wiggling her fingers in front of my eyes. 'No slivers!'

"'What do you mean? I'm not the splintery man. I'm not the wooden man, the man who has rough splinters coating his outside, refusing to let anyone in to touch him. I'm not the man who is brok—I mean—'

"'Nobody said you were broken, Asher.' Marlena smiled.

"'I know that! Nobody said I'm broken! I know! That's because I'm *not* broken. Definitely *not* broken. Nor am I splintery.'

"Marlena's smile faded. 'Nobody said you were splintery, either.'

"'I know,' I squeaked, exhausted.

"'In fact,' she continued, sitting up and facing me on the couch, her hair tearing itself from my fingers, leaving some follicles behind, 'I believe I just proved that you're *not* splintery.' She reached out her hand again, placed it on my face again, stroked again, wiggled her fingers again. 'See? Not splintery.'

"I looked away. Tears flowed. I closed my eyes, but still they seeped through and flowed free.

"'Asher,' Marlena began.

"I sat silent, waiting for her to continue. She waited me out, allowing the silence to fill up what would soon once again be my apartment. 'What?' I muttered. Although I conceded to the silence, I refused to turn my head or open my eyes—somehow I had to win at *something*.

"Marlena took my chin in her hand and turned my face toward her. I couldn't resist. She kissed each of my eyes, her lips wicking away tears. I opened them to her smile. 'There's something else about a splintery man that you haven't said,' she continued.

"'What is it?' Fuck was I desperate to know.

"'The splintery man may only be rough on the surface. A bit of sanding, polishing, varnishing, a bit of love—no more splinters.

"'No more splinters?'

"'Forever.'

"I seized the idea. The idea that I—or, you know, the splintery man, anyway—could be rehabilitated, rebuilt, fixed. The last word that flitted through my brain—'fixed'—stopped me dead, just as the word 'splintery' had stopped me. To be 'fixed' something must be broken. Things that aren't broken can't be fixed—there's no *need* to fix them. And I—or, well, the splintery man—wasn't broken. The splintery man (whomever he was) wasn't in need of *fixing*. The splintery man had done nothing wrong. The splintery man was just being his splintery self. He couldn't help being splintery. He was made to be splintery, and splintery he must be, and splintery he must remain. There was nothing that could be…I mean nothing that *needed* to be done with him. There was nothing wrong with his continuing to be splintery.

"And besides, thought I, who is to determine when someone needs fixing? Marlena? Is Marlena the arbiter, the one being in all the universe who is to decide when a carpenter needs to be called in to 'fix' the splintery man? I mean, fuck it! Maybe the world *needs* fucking splintery men! Why not? I mean without splintery men—here, at this point in my thought process—is where my thoughts became my words. 'Who needs fixing, Marlena?' I snapped, jerking my head away from her hands as best I could.

"She held firm to me. 'I didn't say that *you needed* fixing, Asher.'

"'All this talk of sanding, polishing, varnishing—it's just like you, Marlena.'

"Marlena's face darkened. Her words turned cold. 'And it's just like *you*, Asher, to leave out the one word that means everything: Love. You always manage to keep out the love.'

"Not hearing her—or *pretending* to not hear her—I continued my screed. 'You always want to change things—to change *me*. You always want to change *the whole fucking world*, Marlena. You know what, though? You're dreaming. This is a dream of yours, this sanded, polished, and varnished world that you've created in your head—a fanciful dream. An unrealistic God-fucking-damned dream!'

"Marlena sat back. Coldness enveloped her.

"As much as I willed myself to stop, as much as I wanted to warm Marlena, as much as I wanted to acknowledge her love—I couldn't. I was unstoppable, insatiable in my splinteryness. 'This world, the *real* world, the world that exists outside of your fantasies—this world right here, Marlena? You know, the one you flounce around on all day, your dumb doe eyes flitting here and there searching for something to…to…to fucking *fix*? This world is just fine without your sanding, your polishing, your varnishing. This world is not one of your fucking art projects. You can't just take all the evil out of this world. Know why?'

"I paused to allow for an answer. None came.

"'Because this world needs its God damned to Hell splintery men. This world needs its…its…its *evil*. Its villains. For without villains, guess what?'

"Stone cold silence.

"'No heroes! No shining lights to show us all right from wrong, show us how to live in this world.' My mind seized upon the perfect example—an example that forever doomed me. 'There's a reason Jesus hung on the cross, dying for our sins, you know: the fact that there was sin to begin with. There must have been sin in order to have Jesus. And to make his story resonate, to ensure that people today in this world—in this *real* world—understood the lessons of his sacrifice—to ensure that every Goddamned good Christian would forever follow in the teachings of Jesus—to ensure all of that, not only did Jesus have to die—Jesus also had to *suffer*. Enter the Roman Empire. Enter Pontius Pilate. Enter pain and torment and torture, all of which Jesus endured and endured, until he could endure no more, and was forced to cry out to his father—his own fucking father—and even then—even after his *own fucking father* forsook him, Jesus suffered more and more and even

more than that. And only through that suffering and dying did Jesus become this great symbol for how we should act in this world—this *real* world. For us to learn to turn the other cheek, Jesus had to show us how. There's no cross without Pontius Pilate. And there's no Jesus without his Judas.'

"Marlena stared. 'Is that your excuse?'

"I didn't—couldn't—answer.

"Marlena stood, brushed herself off—flitting her hands over her entire form from hair to shoes. I got the impression she was ridding herself of something. 'Now I realize the difference between you and the trees of November.'

"'What?'

"'When we met, you put me in mind of trees in November. Those trees, healthy and hearty through the summer, in November, they abandon all pretense of healthiness, heartiness, happiness. They stand naked. Cold. They stand for all the world appearing to be dead.'

"'What?'

"'It's not a perfect metaphor between you and those trees, I know. It has at least two discrepancies. First, those November trees—they were, as I mentioned, at one point, only a few months before, strong, healthy, hearty, beautiful, able to provide homes to wildlife, able to provide oxygen to the world.'

"Fuck. 'Second?'

"'Second?'

"'Yes. What's the second distinction between me and the trees of November?'

"'The trees of November come back.'

"With that, Marlena Magpie, without packing a single item, exited my apartment."

Statement of Marlena Magpie [excerpt]

...WITNESS THE EFFORTS TO WHICH some people will go to avoid? To conceal? To veil, bury, cover-up? To hide? To shroud?...

Chapter 28

"ARE THOSE PAPER CLIPS?"

"Yes."

"Why paper clips?"

"They're all I had left."

"You had *nothing* else?"

"You incinerated everything else."

Ed King had a point. I flushed at the memory of the sizzle of his possessions as they plopped into the incinerator, a memory explaining Ed's choice in artistic materials. The paperclips lent a "workaday grind" feel to his sculpture, as if the emotions expressed therein were monotonous and businesslike.

To explain, first as to timeline: I stood in the Galleria de Cinco a week after Dad and my final visit to Walter Reuther. The apartment was not yet again "my apartment," but remained "what had once been my apartment," because I hadn't yet ███████████, thereby causing the mass exodus of roommates.

To explain, second as to events: Marlena had commissioned 15 exhibits for the gallery—one each from the 14 residents, and one other. Each artist chose his or her own theme, medium, and title, and assembled his or her piece. Each piece was placed in its own private space connected to the other installations by a pathway formed by portable barriers.

Ed's was the first installation, a sculpture in paperclips (bent, connected and fused to present layers of depth) of the masks of Thalia and Melpomene, muses of comedy and tragedy, but with two differences. First, in Ed's vision, the mouths and eyes of each mask reflected neither mirth nor sadness, but resignedness. Second, the masks appeared bruised and battered where blue and purple paperclips were interconnected with silver.

A dozen patrons gathered around Ed's creation—teeth chattery with praise and theories—while Ed stood by. The patrons' voices spoke out at once so I couldn't tell who said which of the fragments that leapt to my ears:

"—fated life may not allow for—"

"—comedy, and therefore—"

"—hope might be abandoned, although—"

"—there can be peace in acceptance—"

"—of workings of higher powers—"

"—which some believe—"

"—may bring chaos—"

"—which undercuts the idea of—"

"—fate—"

"—which is convenient for—"

"—those fated to do—"

"—things unacceptable to—"

"—society, although—"

"—those things may be designed—"

"—to accomplish—"

"—something greater, although not for—"

"—the fated individual, who—"

"—may rebel against fate—"

"—attacking anything that might remind him of—"

"—what he has to do."

As the words fuzzed together, I left the fated tragedy that was Ed King and proceeded down the hallway, where awaited another crowd viewing an 8"x10" rendering of a dollar bill formed from a collage of tiny paper dolls, each of various body types, bearing the title "The Perfect Form."

From the group, one voice was heard: Cassie James, who sat near the front edge of her chair, as close to standing as I'd ever seen her. Varying in dialects native to the Appalachian Trail, the oil fields of Texas, the farms of California, and other places where manual labor was prominent, Cassie shouted a spirited speech supporting the rights of workers to unionize, espousing the value of a well-constructed, tight-knit, happy proletariat paid fair wages and provided with safe and health-promoting working conditions:

> [J]ustice is not "blind." Blindness is not its natural state. Justice in her natural state sees all. Witness the statue. Justice sees not what is placed on her scales, but not because she is blind—Justice has been blinded, her vision obscured by a blindfold.

> The key to "Justice" is determining the identity and motives of whoever applied the blindfold. Did Justice blind herself? Did Justice decide that she could only be fair if she didn't see what was placed on her scales? If so, why? Is Justice's natural state one of prejudice that can only be prevented by *refusal to see anything*? If someone else applied the blindfold, was the motive to prevent prejudice? If so, what prejudice was Justice thought to have that the applier of the blindfold sought to avoid?

> Blindfolding Justice would take tremendous power. The more tremendous the power, the more that those with power go to tremendous extremes to retain it. What better way than to blindfold the institution by which that power could be checked? People motivated to blindfold Justice are those desiring to get away with something—those guilty of crimes of betrayal, of oppression, of—

With no end in sight for Cassie's rant, I continued down the hallway to behold a wooden-framed poster by Ella Flowers:

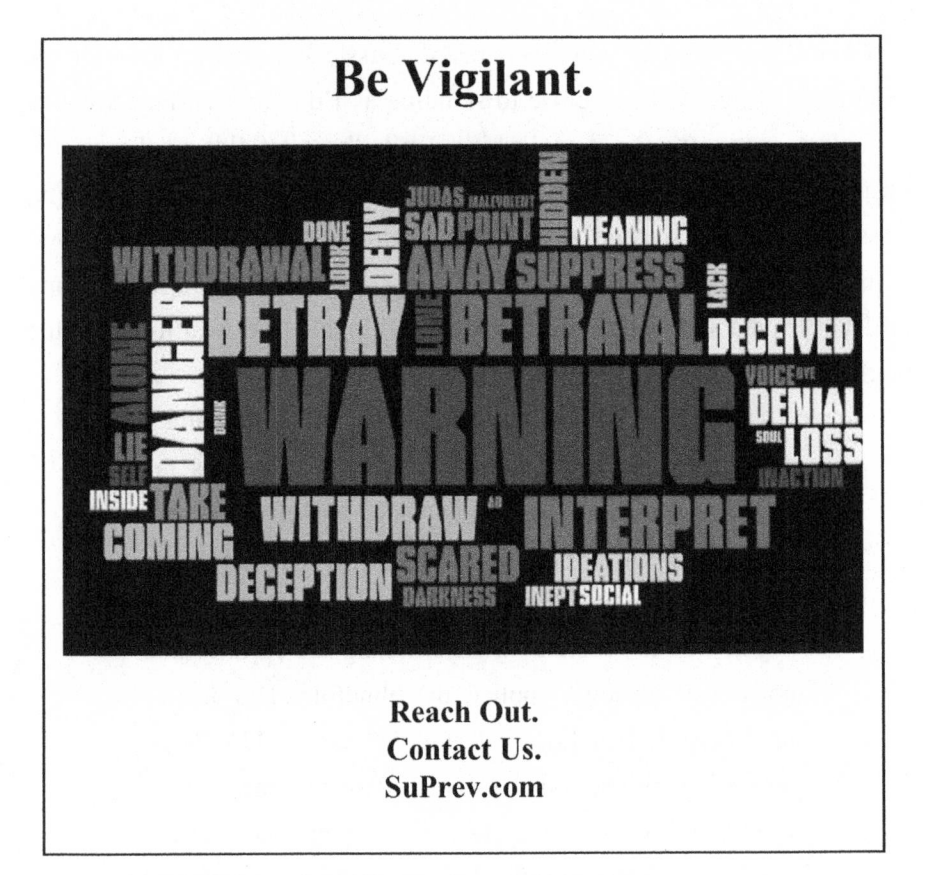

Be Vigilant.

Reach Out.
Contact Us.
SuPrev.com

Unlike Ed's and Cassie's art, Ella's poster had one patron, a woman who stood between the artist and me, her voice hushed in whispers. Using the patron as a shield, I tiptoed closer, trying to match the volume of my steps to her whispers. I leaned as close as I could without detection. If I were to recreate Ella's poster, but instead using the overheard whispers, that poster would look like this:

Feeling the weight of these words, I proceeded along the hallway to the next viewing area, in which resided two mannequins (one male, one female), positioned between between standing and laying, as if placed by someone attempting to stage a new *Kama Sutra* position. The male—engorged—stood behind the female suggesting imminent copulation. The female held aloft a cloth diaper.

The title: "Ode to Motherhood." Alec Posner walked through the exhibit keeping the mannequins in constant motion: closing a hand, swinging a leg, swiveling a hip, cocking an elbow, elbowing a cock. Onlookers gawked, darting after each movement, their lips parting, their breaths hitching in what I took for disapproval.

Disapproval showed further through their commands to Alec as to how the mannequins should be more tastefully positioned.

"Lift that leg."

"Bring their hips closer."

"Put that hand on her ass."

Alec obliged each command.

"What does this have to do with motherhood?" I asked.

Alec ignored me. His patrons' commands intensified.

Seeing that they had Alec under control, I continued further on the trail, emerging into Sony Ericsson's art: a wall-sized cartoon of the Earth exploding, two astronauts floating outside its former atmosphere. A word bubble: "Should we panic *now*?"

"Only now?" I asked.

Sony responded: "Exactly!"

I blinked. At last, was an artist finally explaining art? Did Sony's exclamation confirm my interpretation that the astronauts had ignored warning signs for too long, only determining that there were problems after the worst consequence of those problems became reality? Was Sony's cartoon a cautionary tale against close-mindedness, a rallying cry for vigilance, for prediction of problems and preemptive solutions? Her exclamation of "Exactly!" ratified each of these conclusions.

Another patron entered the room and surveyed Sony's artwork. "What

better time to start panicking than in that moment of disaster?" the patron asked.

Sony responded: "Exactly!"

My heart and mind exploded into darkness. I left the viewing area.

The next installment area was bereft of adornment save for a table upon which sat a cigar box, lid open. I approached the box and beheld...nothing. The box was empty. The thrill of potential faded into confusion. I stared long enough for a patron to sidle up and peer into the box. Not satisfied at exploring with her eyes, she picked up the box and turned it over. Despite the box having been empty a moment before, something fell from it. Fluttering to the table was an index card, black crayon smeared across its surface. The only part of the index card that remained white were two letters drawn on the card in wax: "ME."

From the corner of the viewing area, a small sneeze. Chase Crane. This was her exhibit, then. Seeing her in the corner, the patron smiled, approached Chase, kneeled, and rested her hand on Chase's shoulder. She nodded, and said, voice all cotton candy fibers, "I get it." She pulled Chase in for an enduring hug. "I get it," she whispered again into Chase's hair. Chase's eyes met mine over the patron's shoulder, her glare issuing a challenge.

The patron released Chase and exited the room the way I'd entered. I hurried after her, catching her before she rounded the corner to Alec's exhibit. I put my hand on her shoulder, she turned, no kindness remaining in her eyes. "Wait," I panted, "I'm sorry."

"Sorry for what?" she asked, voice all flint and steel.

"I don't know."

"What do you want?"

"Well..."

"Well?" The word like a bullet.

"Tell me something."

"What?"

"About Chase—"

"Who?"

"The artist. The girl. The—"

"The *black* girl?"

"Yes. The *black* girl."

"What about her?"

"You told her—"

"I know what I told her."

 "Right. Well…"

"Spit it out."

"You said to her, your voice all cotton—"

"My voice *what?*"

"—candy, you said to her, 'I get it.'"

"Yes."

"Why'd you say that?"

"Because I get it."

"Right. Well…"

"Yes?"

"What did you get?"

"Everything."

"Yes. Well…"

"You're going to ask me again, right?"

"Yes."

"If you don't get it, I can't explain."

"Oh."

She sighed. "Here's what I can say, all right?"

"Yes?"

"That *black* girl has a *lot* of potential."

"I know."

"Do you?"

"Umm."

"If so, why didn't you look further into her art?" She turned and entered Alec's viewing area.

I stood listening for a moment to her delighted squeals before I turned and slunk back through Chase's exhibit, refusing the meet the challenge of her eyes as I continued on to the next viewing area.

Upon entering, I ran into Jay, my chin hitting his bicep, nose hitting shoulder, knee hitting his side.

"Oof," I oofed as I bounced off Jay's stony physique.

"Have fun with it, Asher!" Jay responded.

I gaped at Jay's non-sequitur until my eyes found my hands, and then I gaped at the bag therein containing two popsicle sticks, twine, tacks, a three-inch tall rubbery doll, and paper, upon which was written: "Make me something."

I turned to Jay with questions (Make what? With these things from the bag? Who gave me the bag? Were these items selected just for me? Why me? For whom am I to make something? How am I to know what the recipient wants? Is this a transformative exercise? Is there some purpose?). Jay's face—open, welcoming, understanding—froze the questions.

I turned to see a picnic table at which sat two patrons, each working on assembling the objects from their bags. I approached, sat, and surveyed the tabletop, upon which one patron worked at affixing a pair of googly eyes to a wad of batting, while the other applied acrylic paint to a cylinder of balsam wood.

None of these items were in my bag, which held only those items it had always held: sticks, twine, glue, tacks, doll. I pushed the items around, hoping for inspiration. I got nothing. Perhaps, thought I, if I had some of that cotton batting in my bag, I'd have a better idea than the only one that formed in my head. I reached across the table. The patron smacked me away, pointing behind me at a sign: "USE YOUR OWN BAG."

I jerked my hand to my side of the table, but my eyes continued to appraise the items from the bags of the two patrons as well as remnants left behind by others: Glitter. Duct tape. Screws. Yarn. Gears. Scrabble tiles. Dice. Pipe cleaners. Pennies. Buttons. Marshmallows. Chalk. Tissue paper. Post-its. Crayons. Watch batteries. Velcro. A churchwarden pipe. A dog collar. Popcorn kernels. Flypaper strips. Keys torn from a typewriter (L, E, two T's, N, S, and A). Legos. Puffballs. An inkwell and quill.

In front of me, only sticks, twine, glue, tacks, doll. That's all I could work with. As much as I wanted to supplement my supplies, I couldn't. Facing the

inevitable, I began. The output of my efforts: a fated crucifix. What else could it be?

I stood to find the two patrons handing their projects to Jay. One presented Jay with a train engine, complete with wheels, puffs of charcoal-dust smoke, and a miniature engineer to steer it. My mouth dropped open at its beauty. There was no way that it could've come from the meager supplies provided. It was impossible. Yet, there it was, gleaming and puffing and perfect. Jay smiled. He spoke words that I didn't hear and accepted the offered train.

The other presented Jay with a sculpture of a buffalo, majestic, eyes gleaming, mane waving in the windless air. The patron moved the buffalo's legs, causing muscles in the sides, hips, and back to ripple with power. Jay took the buffalo with another smile, more muted words, and the patron departed.

Jay sat the buffalo on a shelf next to the train, and next to other objects: a working jack-in-the-box, smiling jester swaying on its spring; a wooden ship, its crew unleashing full sails on three masts; a painstaking recreation of the Statue of Liberty; a—

I could look no more. I lowered my eyes as I approached and handed to Jay my creation, which he accepted with silence. "Did you have fun with it?" he asked.

"Yes," I lied.

Jay hefted the crucifix. "So it goes," he said, turning away.

I left the viewing area.

Winding deeper into the gallery, I entered a horror show. Chicken wire and red handprints dotted the walls. A bare lightbulb flickered as it swung from its fixture, casting odd shadows on the gurney below. Strewn on the rumpled sheets: hand, foot, chest, hip, and head restraints. Next to the bed: a metal stand atop which sat machinery: a wooden cabinet housing guts of an antique electroshock machine. Yellowed instructions affixed inside the wooden lid described the manipulation of the levers and dials for feeding fast- and slow-interruption electrical pulses through two felt-covered electrodes that lay outside the box. Molds oozed over the felt, which appeared to have touched countless heads during the machine's lifetime.

Poster board hung from the ceiling above the equipment, reading: "To Your Health"

I approached the vignette, leaned over the table and—

"Shocking shit, right?"

"Ha!" I shouted at Randy Mac's voice.

"Yeah, funny, right?"

"What? No. Not funny. Startling."

"You don't have to hide that dark sense of humor from me," Randy said.

I wanted to shout. I wanted to shout *and* scream. I wanted to shout *and* scream *and* punch Randy right in his toothy smile. Instead, I asked, hoping to sound less afraid than I was: "Where'd you get this stuff?"

"I got it from Eloise. You know her." Randy accentuated his accusation with a flourish of giggling.

In this, Randy was correct. I knew Eloise. "Eloise" was the remains of the Eloise Mental Hospital, condemned after 143 years of operation. Eloise's remains stand on a corner of the grounds occupied by the Walter Reuther Psychiatric Hospital. A cemetery (occupied by thousands of former Eloise residents) separates the ruins from Walter Reuther. I pictured Randy skulking the grounds, breaking into what remained of the asylum's wings, pilfering as much equipment as he could.

"From Eloise?" I asked. "All this?"

"You got it!" Randy laughed. "Old Ecto," Randy smacked the side of the wooden cabinet, upon which was branded the word Ecto, "gurney, table, restraints, chicken wire. Took that out of the windows. All of it, bequeathed to me by Eloise upon her untimely death."

"Heh." I shook my head. "You crack me up, Randy."

"Oh, no," Randy said, face turning serious. "Your version of cracked up—that's not *my* doing."

My smile vanished. "Oh. Well, then. This is…interesting."

"Want the full effect?"

"There's more?"

"It's me. Of course there's more."

I should've expected.

"Want to give it a try?" he asked.

"What do you mean?"

Randy's eyebrow raised, and along with it, the corner of his mouth, rendering his face half-silly, half-serious, all crazed. "Lay down. I promise it won't take long. And won't hurt...probably. What d'ya say? Let's give the people a show."

"Umm." I looked around to find a crowd of patrons surveying the scene. I allowed Randy to lead me to the bed and lay me down.

Randy turned to the crowd. "The way they taught Eloise staff, see, was to strap the dominant hand down first—lessens the risks of a fight." Without turning to me, he asked: "You're a righty, right, Asher?" Not waiting for an answer, Randy grabbed my right wrist and encased it in the leather cuff of the restraint.

"Wait, no," I stammered.

"You're not a righty? I guess I should get your left hand down quick, eh?" Before I could blink, Randy had restrained my left hand.

My instinct to fight kicked in and I jerked against the restraints.

"See how the patient fights? Good thing I'm skillful with these restraints." Randy restrained my ankles, hips, chest, his movements too fast for me to follow. He restrained my head, stepped toward the crowd, and spun the gurney until it was aligned with the metal table and "Old Ecto." I could look nowhere but up at the swinging light as I heard Randy approach the machine. "Now," Randy said, rummaging in the box, "the final '*safety*' apparatus: ol' bitey."

The crowd oohed as Randy took my jaw, forced my mouth open, and pushed slimy rubber inside. I bit down. My teeth sunk into the rubber and stuck there.

"What's the purpose of electroshock?" Randy asked the crowd. "It's used to treat depression, bipolar disorder, all manner of psychoses." Randy's face blurred into my vision, his eyes locking with mine. "*All* manner." He disappeared. "Some doctors swear by it, despite the stigma. They say it's quicker and safer than medications. Oh, and those doctors—they'd also want me to call it 'electro*convulsive* therapy.' I prefer *shock*. More descriptive, *vivid, evocative*." I could hear Randy pacing as he continued his lecture.

"Let's say these doctors are right, though, about its *usefulness* if not its *name*—if so, electro*shock* therapy would be well worth its side effects, right? A cure for depression, bipolar disorder, psychosis—makes little things like headaches, nausea, jaw pain and…what's that other side effect…I'm always forgetting—oh right! Memory loss!" Randy exploded with laughter until he coughed and coughed until he could continue his lecture as a rasp. "What's a little memory loss among friends?"

The audience murmured its agreement.

"How does electro*shock* therapy work? Fuck if I know!"

I sighed with relief.

My hopes sank as Randy clarified: "I mean, I know how to operate the equipment, how to get juices flowing." As Randy clicked and turned Old Ecto's controls to demonstrate, I imagined the crackle of electricity flow through the corroded wires and into the electrodes where it popped and fried the mold coating the felt. "What I *don't* know is what happens inside a brain," I felt the grip of what I hoped was Randy's hand on the top of my head, "as the electricity pours through. Only thing I know is that the shocks induce little seizures—with purpose." Randy laughed again, released my skull, and continued. "These things are paddles," he said. "Simple to operate. Grab the handles, place the electrodes against the temples," Randy demonstrated as he spoke, "and apply electricity. Now this is usually done after anesthetic (nowadays) but, look at that! I seem to be all out! Oh well. Good thing there aren't any regulations or laws setting requirements for this shit—nothing to tell me where to place the electrodes, how long and strong to apply electricity, the duration of the seizures, the length of time between shocks." More laughter. "I guess," more *intense* laughter, "I'll just have to make this up as I go along!"

Randy's hand closest to Old Ecto released its grip on the paddle. A moment later, I heard a click and a whir, and "SZZZZZT!!!!"

Mistaking Randy's imitation of the crackle of electricity for the real deal, I screamed against the rubber and thrashed against the restraints. I screamed until Randy's laughter eclipsed my screaming, and I fell silent and still, exhausted.

"Asher just demonstrated the full effect of electro*shock* therapy. The screaming, thrashing, fear, pain." A long pause, then, "Just think what would've happened adding electric shock to all that!"

The audience joined Randy's laughter—*his* audience full of *his* patrons, all *thrilled*, at *my* expense. Unlike my rage, the audience's laughter faded and disappeared.

Randy concluded: "Thank you all!" The audience applauded, stood, and shuffled away.

Randy's face once more blurred into sight. "Now, Asher," he said, "you aren't going to do something stupid, like attack me if I let you go, are you?"

My mind chewed through that word—"if"—as I lay there stewing. I did my best to shake my head in a "No."

"Good!" Randy disappeared. "That was the right answer." I felt one foot come free, then the other. "Fucking a-one right answer, indeed!" My hips sprang free, then my chest. "So right, in fact, that to have answered anything else," my left hand came free, then the right, then, finally, my head, "would have been…crazy!" Randy laughed.

I spat the mouthguard onto the table. "Randy," I seethed. "You sure are a motherfucker."

"You have me confused with Alec," Randy replied. "Speaking of which, I think I'll go check out his *exhibit* again! The mind on that guy! Delicious!" Randy skipped from the room.

I shoved the table, knocking it over and sending Old Ecto flying. I smiled as the lid severed at the hinges upon impact with the floor. I vented more of my rage on the gurney, flipping it on its side. I didn't stop there.

I left Randy's viewing area in tatters and entered the viewing area of Gregor Gregorovich. I considered skipping Gregor's installation—it'd be easy, thought I, to slide along the wall and slip into the next hallway without catching his eye, given how intent he was. As much as I dreaded interaction with such a caustic resident of what had once been my apartment, I was unable to resist. I approached, being sure to stay behind Gregor and keep as silent as I could.

Gregor was staring through a pair of binoculars at a painting. The painting

was a beach scene, sand and water from foreground to horizon. The beach was one-third tropics (palm trees), one-third European (striped changing tents dotting the sand), one-third American (above the palm trees, a rollercoaster rose, train cresting the hill). Despite evidence of human traffic (footprints, sand castles, stacked seashells), no humans appeared—not to my eye. Even the rollercoaster train was empty. The sky was empty, too—no gulls scanned the sand or sea for garbage or minnows; no clouds provided shade or threatened inclement weather; the sun wasn't pictured. There was no indication of what held Gregor's attention.

To avoid a loud, elaborate speech from Gregor, I stood, still, stoic, intense, and stared in the direction that Gregor stared. I strained to see his perspective. I saw nothing unusual, nothing that might draw Gregor's or anyone else's eye. I sighed. Steeling myself, I asked: "What are you looking at?"

"The painting!" Gregor shouted.

"I can see that, but—"

"Then your question was unnecessary!"

"—but," I continued, undeterred, "at what in the painting are you staring?"

"The beach, Asher!"

"That narrows it down. Now, what—"

"More questions? It's obvious! What has me rapt is that which also has me wrapped…around her pinky, that is."

"Her?"

"Yes, her!"

"Who?"

"Her! There! Her!" Gregor didn't point, didn't nod, didn't move.

"Where? There's no 'her' there. There's no 'her' anywhere."

"How little you see! Shame!"

Shame? Gregor—staring at nothing—tells me I should have shame? Fuck that! As much as I longed to move on, to leave Gregor and his nonsense behind, I couldn't. Yet. "Help me, Gregor."

"*Me*? Help *you*? Preposterous!"

"Is helping me beneath you?" I hissed. "Or am I so far gone that I cannot be helped?"

"You want my answer?"

"No."

"Then don't ask!"

I stood silent, shaking from the shame that Gregor recognized before I did. As much as I longed to leave, I couldn't. Yet.

"She's beautiful," Gregor whispered. "And she's mine. Remember that."

"Why should I? There's not even a 'she' there."

"She's there," Gregor responded. "Or…or is she?"

"No," I responded.

"But she *is* there. I see her."

"I don't."

Gregor turned his head, freeing his right eye, which settled on me. "Do you want to see her?"

"Umm."

"Here. You look. You look here." Gregor pried the binoculars away from his face and offered them to me.

"Umm."

"Look. See her," Gregor implored.

I looked at the painting. There remained no her there to see. "No," I responded. Yet, my arm extended, my hand grasped the binoculars, raised them to my eyes. I blinked. A girl, there in the distance—so very small even in the magnification of the lenses—but a girl, nonetheless, lounging in a beach chair, pink heart-shaped sunglasses affixed to her face, her modest curves clad in a gingham-blue bikini, one knee raised, other straight, toes pointing toward the surf.

I pulled the binoculars away, looked at the painting. There was nothing—no girl occupied that space—not even a speck that could've been such a figure. I turned the binoculars—no girl was painted on the lenses, either.

"You saw her," Gregor said. "I know you did."

"Impossible," I said, approaching and touching the beach where the girl had sat. "There's no 'her' there."

"She *is* there. You saw her."

"I don't know what I saw."

"Please, look again."

"No."

"Please," Gregor pleaded.

"Impossible," I shook my head. "There's no 'her' there." I offered the binoculars back to Gregor.

Gregor shook his head, took the binoculars, turned to face his painting, raised them to his eyes, and resumed his vigil. "She's there, and she's mine," he said as I left his viewing area.

Even as I left Gregor behind, I couldn't leave behind the image of the impossible girl. She remained lying in the impossible beach chair, wearing her impossible bikini and sunglasses. She filled my senses. She dizzied my brain. She triggered…what the fuck? More shame. Different from the shame predicted by Gregor, this a shame of wrongly-placed passion, shame not shared by Gregor, who remained transfixed on his beautiful girl, his gaze perhaps willing her into existence, his obsession rendering the impossible possib—

"OOF!" My thoughts were interrupted by a…dragon?

Yes. A white dragon with wings of brown, assembled from wood, stucco, and sailcloth. A dragon askew, bent, twisted, barely recognizable as a dragon, but a dragon it was…I thought. It was different from any storybook dragon about which I'd read. Its wings twirled in circles like helicopter blades instead of flapping like birds. Its open mouth was a doorway through which I could see inner workings—gearwheels and cogs grinding together, circling inside much like the wings, as if wheels powered wings, or vice versa. The beast was misshapen as if it could only be a true dragon to a beholder who was crazed.

I understood the contraption to be a dragon because of the voice that thundered after I ran into its claw, which was blunted like a cudgel instead of a series of daggers. I doubled over, my arms crossing my stomach to protect from impact—too late. I sucked in tiny portions of air, getting more smoke than oxygen. I fell to my knees, my head bowed in defeat. I waited to be roasted and eaten.

Alas, death avoided me, and I was left to my suffering, for as I closed my

eyes and my mind exalted for impending death, a voice stopped the dragon in its tracks. "Halt, beast! Back, you dragon!"

I looked up. Donny Quick dismounted a sawhorse, misshapen like the dragon so it almost looked like an actual horse, complete with saddle, bridle, reins. Donny leapt from the "horse" as though he were an experienced rider a quarter his age. In Donny's hand: a tree branch that he believed to be a sword or lance, with which he tilted forward, poking at the side of the "dragon." Although Donny's blow didn't pierce the "dragon," Donny stood back, tall, sheathed his "sword," laughed a hearty "Ha!" and approached me, offering his gloved hand, which I took. He pulled me to my feet, lifting me from the ground and setting me back down, using only one of his great arms. "It's good that I was here. This beast shall do you no more harm."

"Ah," I wheezed. "Thanks."

"Your health is all the thanks that I require, squire Asher!"

Squire? "Umm. Okay. Then no thanks."

Donny's smile broadened despite my sarcasm. "It's good I was there to save you!" He walloped his gloved hand against my back.

"Uh, yeah." I dropped the sarcasm as I noticed the gathered crowd—the same crowd that witnessed my receipt of Randy's "therapy" plus all residents of what had once been my apartment whose art installations I had already perused, all staring at the scene before them, each onlooker's face beaming with glorification at Donny's heroics. Attempting to remove myself from the scene, I skittered forward and again rammed my stomach into the dragon's fist, fell to my knees and prayed that the dragon would come to life and engulf me in righteous hellfire.

"I said back, beast!" Donny leapt forward once more and whacked his branch at the creature. The crowd gasped in awe as Donny hauled me to my feet. As applause began, I could take no more and once again I attempted to escape the crowd, and *again* ran into the dragon's paw, which, though unmoving, seemed to be everywhere at once. The paw struck me in the chest, knocking me onto my back. Donny tilted again at the dragon, shouting and chopping and whaling until a normal man of any age would be exhausted, and yet still he persisted, ready to protect me until my death from old age.

While Donny hacked and lopped, I pushed to my feet, determined to save myself. I flung myself forward in a full-on attack, and once more I was knocked prone. The dragon's paw caught me dead-center in the forehead, sending me flying backward into an onlooker, who caught me. I looked up to find that my savior was perhaps the worst possible option among the assembled mass: Randy Mac, who held me in his arms and said through his guffaws, "Classic insanity!"

I broke free and charged ahead as Randy continued, "There ain't gonna be a different result!" and then, yes indeed, I was *once more* on the floor, this time falling underneath the paw that had felled me time and time again, the paw that Donny was whacking with his branch-sword until the paw broke free, falling onto me, pinning me to the floor.

"You! Leave! Him! Be!" Donny shouted, punctuating each word with a whack of his branch or a kick of his boot. Upon the last exclamation point, the dragon's paw flew from me, and I was free to breathe, to stand, to face humiliation as the crowd whooped, whistled, and wailed. Donny bowed. Before the dragon could knock me down again, I fled.

As I traversed the hallway, my footfalls echoed. So I thought. The shadows that reached me moments later revealed that the additional footsteps I heard were of the crowd following me. I quickened my pace to no avail— the mob gained. I ran. I banged from wall to wall as I rounded corners and navigated doglegs. It worked. I put distance between the mob and me. Such was my joy at evading danger that I no longer ran along the hallway so much as flew, my feet caressing the floor, my head high, my arms swinging, my breathing free, easy, smooth.

Then, of course, it all once more went to shit. I rocketed into the next viewing area, colliding with a second exhibit in a row. Instead of the immovable paw of a dragon, this time I hit the movable corner of a table upon which sat objects that shot across the room and smashed against the wall opposite. Next to the table stood Judas, whose crestfallen gaze followed the objects.

Judas turned to me. The wrath in his glare stopped the apology in my throat. I stepped back, prepared to run back toward the mob, only to see

Judas' eyes twinkle with surprise and then…joy. "Oh!" he said. "It's you! You're here at last!"

"I am?"

"Of *course* you are. At long last. Here!"

"Well, then." I dusted nonexistent particles from my jeans. "Good."

"Very! Good indeed!"

I cocked my head, brow wrinkling. "Yes, good. But, why?"

"I've been waiting to show you," Judas turned, prepared to wave his hand above the table. "Oh!" He gaped at the empty tabletop. "But, where?"

I pointed toward to the objects on the floor.

"Oh!" Judas repeated. He stared down, muttering, "You know? This isn't so bad. I feared that all was lost, but I can fix this. Hold on, Asher. I'll have it all ready for you soon."

"For me?"

Judas's hands flew over the floor in a way that Donny's dragon never could. He scooped armfuls of objects more tangible than Gregor's mystery girl. He placed the objects on the table in a manner more organized than Randy scattered electroshock equipment. The first object was a house, vaguely the shape of a Chase-esque cigar box, albeit discernable as a house, as if made by a talented patron from the contents of one of Jay's bags. Judas placed each object (fence, detached garage, gravel for a driveway, shrubs) with a fervor rising to the levels of Alec and his posable mannequins. As he tore open the house, I feared it would tear asunder like Sony's cartoon Earth. The house remained sound, however, and before he closed it again, he placed three people inside. So much regard did he spare for each that I was sure both Ella and Cassie would've beamed at his respect for humanity. Finally, he turned to me, his face a mask reminiscent of Ed's artwork, although less dour acceptance of fate, and more hopeful that his art would be appreciated by its viewers—one in particular, for Judas seemed to have eyes for me alone.

I set aside suspicion and looked to the table, whereon sat the house, garage, driveway, shrubs resting on a circle of roadway that I swore hadn't been there before, a brand-new cul-de-sac on which the house was the lone house, although it wasn't difficult to imagine a slew of neighbors occupying

the surrounding empty space, especially as my mind flashed to my childhood home—a home that differed from Judas' art in several respects. My childhood home had two stories where Judas' had one, a two-car garage attached at the front where Judas' one-car garage sat recessed on the lot. The driveway of my childhood home (composed of large square flags of concrete where Judas' driveway was gravel) stretched not to the curve of a cul-de-sac, but to a short straight road along which sat (in contrast to the absence of neighbors in Judas' model) twelve houses packed together. So many were the differences between my childhood home and the tableau before me that I wondered why Judas' display provoked such memories in me. I wondered further why those memories made me behold Judas' display (and Judas himself) with warmth. My childhood memories usually filled me with anxiety, angst, anger. The memories triggered by Judas' display were different: bright, bubbly, blissful; cheery, charming, carefree; delightful, delicious, dazzling—an alphabet of joy straight through to zip-a-dee-doo-dah.

Judas did two somethings that brought me back to the present. First, Judas spoke: "I made this for you, Asher."

"For *me*?"

"Oh! But wait until you see—you'll understand when you see. You'll get it, Asher. I know you will."

"I *will*?"

"You have to. I mean, you just have to."

"*I* will?"

Second: at the end of our dialogue, Judas reopened the house. I again flushed with memories of childhood—but this time, those memories were toxic. Inside that house were somehow two floors of rooms although the house from the outside was one-story tall. The rooms evoked my childhood home. On the main floor, a living room was a vibrant, colorful space wherein Dad would put an album on the spindle, apply the needle, and twist and twirl in his poodle skirt and stockings, while Mom sat in a rocker-recliner, ignoring her flouncing husband behind a novel, but tapping her foot and rocking her chair in time with each fanciful step Dad took.

As one left that room, one had a choice of entering the kitchen or the

dining room. The kitchen was a Dad-haven of frilly gingham aprons and oven mitts—not that Mom lacked a distinctive stamp with her collection of cast-iron cookware. In the dining room, Mom's greasy tools coated the table, throwing a literal monkey wrench into any plans to consume food thereon— and yet Dad was there, too, in the china cabinet full of plates, bowls, platters, and goblets.

The kitchen and dining room opened at their other ends onto a hallway extending past a bathroom and into a utility room wherein sat a familiar washing machine—one that, I'd learned, was susceptible to jigging and jagging across the floor when a bra strap became entangled in its agitator. At the other end of the hallway, stairs ascended to the second floor, wherein one would have a choice of entering one of three bedrooms—one adult-themed, two childlike, each occupied by one of the home's residents.

In Judas' too true-to-life to be believed rendition of the home, each bedroom was occupied. In one of the childlike bedrooms was the figure of a womanish man standing arms and legs spread wide as if in the middle of a highly-expressive jumping jack. In the adultish bedroom stood the figure of a woman, her arms and legs clasped in restraints that held her upright in a cross formation. I refused to look in the other bedroom, but I knew who resided there: a child-figure sat on the edge of his bed, head in hands, tears streaming. While the two other figures in that house remained a mystery to me, the child I understood without beholding him—and, perhaps it was because I understood him so well that I couldn't help but rage at him. I couldn't help but urge the child to stop crying, stand, confront the other two figures, take steps to improve his life. Yet the child remained. Present, tormented, sickly.

"Do you like it, Asher?"

"Do I like it." I kept my tone as even as possible, cognizant of the crowd at my back, standing silent, waiting for me to make a move, to say something or to take some action that spoke for me, something that would betray my thoughts on Judas' house of horrors.

"Oh!" Judas continued. "I see your confusion."

"Confusion," I said in the same even tone.

"Yes, confusion. I know why you hesitate. You haven't seen my title card for my exhibit. It'll clear things right up."

"Clear."

"Where did it go?"

"Things."

"It must have...yes!"

"Right."

"Here it is. Against the wall."

"Up."

"There we go. Done."

"Done."

"Does that help?"

A sign entered my vision, reading: "Wishful Thinking."

"Wishful thinking."

"Yes. What do you think, Asher?"

What in God's name *did* I think? I thought. I thought.

I thought: How in God's holy *fuck* does Judas know that I'm filled with "Wishful Thinking"? That I wished that the woman were free from restraints, that she could cast off the cross she bore, that she could be healed? That the man would change his skirt for Levi's, his silk blouse for a flannel, his clean shave for a brawny beard? For the boy-child to grow the fuck up?

No. It couldn't be. I refused to believe that Judas had such knowledge. There must be something else to his title card, some other interpretation.

Wishful Thinking—from someone else's perspective. But whose perspective could govern the interpretation of those words and the sentiments underlying them? Another member of the crowd? No. For Judas could no more read their minds than he could read mine.

Which left only Judas. I couldn't help but recall Judas's backstory: abandoned to his own devices by an unknown father and a suicidal mother, washing hither and thither with no parental figure to teach him lessons on how to live life. My God, it was no wonder that Judas was so dangerous, dastardly, damnable. I couldn't help but think that *perhaps* the Wishful Thinking of the title card was not mine but belonged to Judas. Perhaps what

was represented in that house was something for which Judas wished. *Perhaps* Judas longed for such a family dynamic as the one represented in that house. *Perha—*

"Well, Asher?" Judas broke my thoughts before my thoughts broke me.

"Well."

"Well? Does that mean you like it?"

"Like it."

"Good! I'm glad. That makes me," Judas furrowed his brow, "happy! Hopeful!"

"Hopeful."

"Although—"

"Although."

"—I don't know why I was so anxious. I knew you'd like it."

"Huh."

"You of all people—I knew you'd understand."

Even though I failed to understand, Judas smiled, reached into the home and extracted the boy-child. He held the despondent figure, straightened its legs, removed its hands from its eyes, wiped imagined tears from its cheeks. As he hugged the boy to his chest, I felt bile rising. I rushed into the hallway before it could spew from my mouth onto the hopeful vignette.

I kept rushing until the next viewing area, the floor of which contained a jar contributed by the "guest" I teased earlier.

Ah. "Teased." An apt word given that this jar and the black tumor floating in its preservative liquid was contributed by Merry Delacroix. Surrounding the jar in a perfect circle on the floor was the title of Mom's exhibit: "The Best of Me."

So many questions. Given Mom's confinement, how did the jar get here? Who picked it up? And, given Mom's ongoing no-visitors "punishment," how? How does one smuggle a glass jar within which floated an extracted tumor out of (or into, for that matter) a lockdown psychiatric hospital? And *why*? Why would her secret conspirator agree to Mom's scheme? Why her tumor? Why *those* words?

For my questions—no answers…until Marlena entered the viewing area

from the opposite end, approached the jar, stepped within the circle of words, swirled the jar until the tumor spun in tornadic liquid, released the jar and turned back toward the exit. In those actions, Marlena revealed herself as Mom's conspirator.

"Marlena!" I'd intended a soft question but spouted sharp accusation.

She regarded me. "Asher."

"Is this your doing?"

"If you mean the exhibit, no. Mine is yet to come. This is Merry's exhibit."

"That much I figured."

"Good." Marlena turned to the exit.

"Wait!"

Marlena stopped. "Yes?"

"What I mean is…I knew this is Merr—Mom's exhibit. That's her jar."

"And her tumor, yes."

Gulp. "Right. But…"

"Yes?"

"Who did this?"

"Did this?"

"Who brought the jar here? Who set it up? Whose words are these? Who wrote them? Who—"

"You already know the answers."

I knew.

"What do you really want to ask, Asher?"

"How is Mom?" I asked instead.

"That's not the question you wanted to ask, either. You saw your mom not long ago."

"I did."

"Are you going to ask what you really want to ask?"

"Should I?"

"Only if you want the answer."

Not knowing what else to do, I asked: "What did you and Mom talk about?"

"Other than her art installation? I can't say."

"Can't or won't?"

"Is there a difference?"

"Isn't there?"

"Silence is the result either way."

"Ah. But why not?"

"I can't and won't betray Merry's trust."

Trust? Mom had *trust* in Marlena? How could she, when she had no trust in me?

"If it helps, I'll tell you one thing about our talks."

"Do I get to pick it?"

"No."

"Okay."

"I walked away believing you were an adorable kid."

Kid? As in "not an adult"? As in a dividing line between when I was a "kid," and as such, "adorable," and an "adult," and, as such, "not"? Sharp titters interrupted my pondering. I turned to see Randy Mac. "Go ahead, Asher. Ask her," Randy squeezed out between laughs.

"What the fuck are you talking about?"

"Ask her the questions, Asher."

"What questions?"

More laughter. "Oh, you poor fool."

Fool? "Poor?"

"The poorest."

"What are you talking about?"

Randy refused to answer.

I scanned the gallery, challenging each member to step into the wordless void left by Randy. None spoke.

"Is Randy right, Asher?" Marlena asked.

"Right?"

"Do you want other answers?"

"I do."

"Then ask."

"The best of me. What does that mean?"

Marlena frowned and shook her head.

I turned my attention to the words. What was the best of Mom? The tumor? Something removed from her body? Something that could've killed her had it never left? Something bent and twisted in knots? Something tortured? Something dead to the world? Something that floated there inside its preservative liquid, unable to escape, think, feel, stretch its boundaries, see more of the world, see other perspectives, ask the right questions?

I smiled. "You know what?"

"What?" Marlena asked, smiling back.

"There are some questions that maybe I shouldn't ask."

Marlena walked over, linked arms with me, and led me past the tumor and out of the viewing area and toward the next exhibit...with art contributed by Asher Delacroix.

On the floor was a circle reminiscent of the circles of roommates inside what had long ago been my apartment. Instead of chairs, each of the 14 spaces in my circle (save two, which were empty) was occupied by an object:

1. A doll carved from soap.
2. Unoccupied.
3. A stiletto pump.
4. A wooden cup, insides stained reddish brown.
5. A multi-colored paintbrush.
6. Cooked chicken liver on a plate.
7. A Court Order denying a Petition for Involuntary Commitment.
8. A guest registry from a hotel.
9. A booklike object encased in black plastic with a blinking light on the front.
10. A brass shaving basin.
11. A U.S. Army Distinguished Service Cross.
12. A pickaxe, its sharp end reddish brown.
13. Unoccupied.
14. A pile of 30 quarters.

I detangled myself from Marlena, stepped inside the circle and sat at position 13.

The crowd streamed in and fanned out so that roommates and patrons alike stood in a row.

Jay walked in an arc around the circle, hands behind his back, tall frame hunched as he peered at the floor. He crouched at position four, lifted the cup, held it out above his head as if offering it to the masses, and said, "This is mine."

Jay was right. The cup was his, as was whatever had stained the cup's insides. I nodded.

Following Jay's lead, each roommate came forward, proceeded to his or her place in the circle, hefted the object that occupied his or her space, and identified each object as belonging to him or her. The exception was Ed King, who traversed to his place in the circle, but had no object to heft.

Chase, cradling her soap doll, asked, "Where did you find her?"

"Find her?" I asked.

"She was lost. Or was she taken away?"

I blinked. "Taken?"

"You stole this!" Gregor's voiced boomed as he scoured the hotel registry.

"Stole?" I asked. "Didn't you take that—"

"Gross." Alec sniffed at the liver. He dropped it on the plate and rubbed his hands together in horror.

"But—"

"This was private." Ella said. She paged through the Order, reading intimate details of her mental health profile and the court's ruling thereon. "It isn't something you should have."

"I got it—"

"Sir!" Donny donned the shaving basin as a helmet. "How dare you insult My Lady of Flowers! Not to mention absconding with my priceless helmet!"

"Helmet? It's a shaving bas—"

"I hope that you didn't try to activate it," Sony said, pressing buttons on the side of the book-like object. She frowned as the light on the front continued to blink red.

"Activate? I don't even know what it—"

"I forgot how heavy this thing is." Cassie hefted the pickaxe. "How much damage it can do," she looked at me, "in the wrong hands."

"But I didn't...I mean...wrong hands? I just thought—"

"No you didn't." Randy snarled as he pinned the medal to his chest. "You shouldn't have used any of these."

"But—"

"They're right, Asher." As Marlena spoke, I closed my eyes. "Once again you tell your story through other people. These objects can't speak for you. They belong to others. You coopted other people's stories and characters."

I sat silent, defeated. Not that I lacked for a defense. I had words aplenty to defend myself. Words about what each of those objects—and the people who owned them—represented. Words about symbolism, about hidden meanings. About standing on the shoulders of giants, about interpretation. About how these various objects, and these roommates, had shaped me, influencing my worldview. But seeing how each roommate objected to the use of their property—objected to the use of their very characters—

"It's as if you believe that you're characterless," Marlena continued. "Only someone believing that he lacked character would believe that property stolen from others was an expression of himself."

"I don't know," Judas added. "Well, okay, I do know. I understand everyone's objections. I wouldn't say I'm happy that Asher took my money." Judas jingled the coins in his hand. "It's not so much about that. I'd give these 30 coins to Asher anytime he needed them."

Shudder.

"It's not that I object to him expressing himself through our objects, or even through our*selves*. My objection is that, well...his own place at the circle is empty."

Judas was correct. Aside from Ed King (who had no property that I could've purloined for my art) the empty space in the circle had been my own empty space.

"It'd be one thing if Asher contributed something unique to himself, something that hinted at his character. That way the mix of objects could

better illuminate Asher. We could then see how Asher's object reacted to the objects representing us, how we changed him, and perhaps how he changed us."

Well, fuck.

"See," Judas continued, "It's not like you lacked for something to contribute. All you needed to fill your spot is something personal to you—reflecting your soul. All it would have taken was one of your parables."

Judas knew of my parables? How well did he know them? Not well, I hoped.

"I mean, those parables seem to me to encapsulate you, with all the interpretation required."

Shit.

"For someone to interpret you, to get to know you, to *love* you—that takes quite a bit of work. Parsing, prying, separating out nonsense. I'm sure you agree, Marlena."

"I do."

"But your space here, Asher, remains empty. How are we to conclude your soul itself is anything but empty?"

Fuck! Okay, well, so long as nobody answers th—

"We can't," Jay answered.

Damned.

"No one could."

I closed my eyes, heard the roommates rise to their feet and exit my viewing area, patrons trailing. When I opened my eyes, I saw that each roommate had taken his or her object (save for possessionless Ed, who took himself). Not a soul remained. I sat there, alone—abandoned—until I heard murmurs of reverence coming from the next viewing area. Knowing that that area housed Marlena's installation, curiosity got the better of my depression. I stood and followed.

I didn't immediately spot Marlena's art, which was blocked by the heads of roommates and patrons staring at the far wall. Each roommate's voice spoke aloud as if vying for supremacy of his or her interpretation of—

Déjà fucking vu. Elbowing my way to the front of the crowd, I saw a

captivating word squatting on an 8″x11″ paper, the word "The," plainly beautiful and beautifully plain with its large calligraphic capital T followed by h and e. That was it, again; there was no more, again.

Beholding Marlena's word—which I could only describe with capitalization as "The Word"—I longed to interrupt the voices that chattered and spewed, sounding like 70 times 70 words all about that one word, three letters long, "The." I longed to interrupt—or at the least, join in, to spout my own perspective on The Word. But I feared what would come out would be confused; unreliable; unassertive; wheedling; nervous; doubtful; plagiaristic; dangerous.

I bided my time, waiting out the tumble of words, for all language to cease, for the roommates to fall silent, for their eyes to one-by-one turn to Marlena and search her face, pleading, imploring. Inevitably, that moment of silence came. In that silence, I posed a question: "Why?"

"It is what—"

"No!"

"No?"

"I didn't ask about meaning. I didn't ask what they were about to ask."

"What were we about to ask?" Gregor asked.

"The ultimate question."

"Which is?"

"What is the meaning of The Word?"

"Why would we ask that?"

"Why?"

"We already know the meaning of The Word, as you call it."

"You do?"

"Of course!"

"How?"

"How could we not?"

"Well, if you asked Marlena—"

"We don't need to ask Marlena! Marlena—"

"Is dead. Yes, I know. But—"

"But what?"

"Never mind."

"No, Asher," Marlena said. "You had a different question. Ask it."

"Oh. Well…"

"You asked 'Why?' Why what?"

"Why did you display old art?"

"How is it old?"

"You've displayed it before."

"As in, previously."

"Yes."

"So, because I previously displayed this art, it's now…old."

"Isn't it?"

"Art is never old as long as there's a new audience to view it. Each time it's beheld by someone, it's resurrected anew."

"Resurrected?"

"Art is ever young. The older it gets, more beholders give it fresh, new interpretations. Same for a book. Or anything subject to interpretation. Even a person."

"A person?"

"People are interpreted the same way as art."

"Ah."

"Besides, I contributed something brand new to the Galleria."

"What is it?"

"I helped Sammy with his art." Marlena smiled. "After speaking for such a long time with Merry—"

"Long time?"

"—Sammy's idea spoke to me. I understood. It makes sense. I think you'll love it." Marlena pointed deeper into the gallery. Dread filled me at the extension of her finger, as if the simple act of pointing could assure doom. Yet, I followed.

In Dad's viewing area was a painting of the redbud tree in the backyard of my boyhood home. Its trunk rose from lush grass for two feet before bifurcating, each piece twisting up and out, splitting and splitting to form a wide canopy of branches from which sprouted blood-red, wax-sheened,

heart-shaped, thick-veined leaves. Beside the tree, looking up into its branches, her back to the audience, was Mom, so real and youthful that I longed to call out, rush to her, envelop her legs in my childlike arms, lead her into the house's living room, lay her down on the couch, crawl over her bent legs, and nest behind them, so Mom could regurgitate stories to me—her baby bird—to swallow, some real, some fictive. To nourish me until I was ready.

For I was *not* ready to see a young Asher Delacroix hidden in among the tree branches. The young boy in the tree was more Asher than I could ever hope to be. He was beautiful. It was in this detail that I could see Marlena's influence on Dad's art, for surely that boy was the result of Marlena's practiced-until-perfect hand. What I didn't see in that boy in the tree was Dad's hand, and, by extension, Dad's eye, as if Dad couldn't paint young Asher as beautiful because Dad couldn't find truth in that rendering— couldn't imagine such beauty in me. But at least Marlena found child-me beautiful.

Dad strode forward and hung a title card next to the painting: Hidden Shame.

"Dad?"

"Do you like it?"

"It's beautiful."

"Nice of you to say, son, though I can't take full credit. For—"

I completed his sentence: "—Marlena helped with the details."

Dad turned to the painting. "Good discernment, Asher."

"Discernment."

"You separated out the Dad-parts from the Marlena-parts. That shows how well you know and respect each of us—"

"Respect."

"—and our work."

"Dad?"

"Something to add?"

"The title."

"No."

"No?"

"The title doesn't need to be added. I just added it."

"You did."

"Right there."

"Yes."

"Good."

"But, Dad…"

"Was there something else?"

"Hidden Shame?"

"That's the title."

"I know."

"Good. You've got it. Now—"

"No, Dad. I mean, *about* Hidden Shame. The only thing that seems to be 'hidden' in the painting is me, in the redbud tree."

"Ah."

"I must conclude—"

"Must you?"

"—that the 'shame' that's 'hidden' is me."

"Your interpretation is valid."

"It's 'valid' to say I'm 'shameful'?"

"Not at all!"

"You just said—"

"I said nothing of the kind."

"Then what *did* you say?"

"I said that *your interpretation* is valid."

"Is *your* interpretation also valid, Dad?"

"Of course."

"Am I allowed to ask what your interpretation is?"

"I don't think I can stop you…Can I?"

"We're about to find out."

"Are we?"

"What's your interpretation of the painting, Dad?"

"My interpretation?"

"Yes."

"Of my painting?"

"Yes. What is it?"

"Ordinarily I'd respond that the author is dead. I suppose in this case…"

"Yes, Dad?"

"In the context of our conversation…"

"You can tell me your interpretation?"

"I suppose, yes." Long, very long, and even longer pause. "My interpretation is that the title doesn't refer to you."

"No?"

"No."

"Then to whom does it refer?"

"Me."

"You?"

"You're not in the painting."

"I disagree."

"What?"

"I'm there."

"Where?"

"Everywhere."

"Everywhere?"

"An artist is always everywhere in his art."

"Fine, Dad. How does Hidden Shame refer to you?"

"It refers to my guilt."

"You have guilt?"

"Of course."

"I'm guessing this guilt is *not* related to your cross-dressing—"

"Why would it be?"

"—or your affairs."

"I wouldn't call them affairs."

"Of course, you wouldn't. Look, Dad: why do you have guilt?"

"Guilt is inherent in us all."

"No, Dad. I mean, what are you guilty *about*?"

"Ah."

"And how is that guilt expressed in the painting?"

"It's all over the painting. From Merry, to the house, to the redbud tree, to you."

"To me?"

"Yes."

"Your guilt extends to me?"

"Of course."

"What are you talking about?"

"I feel guilty about all the wonderful things in my life."

"Oh."

"How could I not? I have so many perfect things—a home, nature, Merry, you—and so many others do not."

"Ah."

"Why should I have all of that goodness and rightness when other people suffer?"

Euphoria. That's the only word to describe my emotions. So much was my euphoria that I longed to share it with the roommates and patrons filtering into Dad's viewing area. "Dad?"

"Yes, son?"

"Can you do me a favor?"

"I don't know…Can I?"

"Can you tell them your interpretation."

"Hmm."

"So they don't assume that I, hiding in the redbud tree, am the Hidden Shame?"

"No."

"Why not?"

"Because we don't live in a cult."

Euphoric warmth yielded to fearful chills. "Goddamn it, Dad."

"What was that, son?"

"Nothing."

The Mud and The Blood and The Beer II

By

Asher Delacroix

YOU'RE LIKE ME. WICKED. PUT upon. Devilish. Ill fated. Torturous. Lacking control. Deserving of punishment.

Unlike me, though, you're not in prison. You share my tendency to commit atrocities, but you don't share my retribution. You're not confined to a 12x17 cell with a roommate who chose the desirable top bunk.

Choice. Yeah fucking right.

Unlike me, you have choice—so you think. You're not a slave to yard time, meal time, forced labor, the whims of fellow inmates and guards. You're not toileting in front of other—well, maybe you're more like me than I thought.

Why am I imprisoned when you're not? Why'd you put me in here while you roam free?

Because—although you recognize that you, too, should be punished—that recognition only exists in your subconscious.

Problem is you made me too smart for your own good. Mistake. You making me smart, you giving me critical reasoning, you making me curious—all of that: mistake.

My curiosity led me on a great voyage across your mind. Brocca's area to Angula gylus, moter cortex to pons to brain stem, thalamus to Wernicke's area, synapse to synapse, axon to dendrite, and across all the gray matter in between. Somewhere in there is that expanse of mind never viewed by you

except during sleep—your subconscious, where dreams and fears thrive, where your eyes don't go.

I've been there. I'm a frequent visitor. I've spent so much time exploring your subconscious that I built a library there—and inside that library, I placed that librarian whom I—well, you know. I visit her there from time to time. Each visit is quite fun…for me, anyway.

Don't get me wrong: those visits aren't for my pleasure. They're for my learning—I mean the librarian is *in* a library, after all, and I can't spend *all* of my time—you know.

So, I read. Books? No. Magazines? Guess again. Microfiche? Fuck that. What I read is *you*. You're the subject of the most obsessive studying I've ever done.

What did I learn? Many things. Care to guess? Yes, the definition of "God complex" is one. Care to name another? You nailed it again! Shame.

Shame. A loaded word, that. Shame. Noun and verb. With slight alterations, adjective and adverb, too. All parts of speech, all aspects of language. No concept known to man can ever be free of Shame.

What does one do with all that Shame? How can one overcome? I'm guessing that there are hundreds of strategies. Hundreds of thousands. Quadrillions. So many strategies, and yet I know the specifics of only two. I know my strategy: conversion/transference. As in: any Shame I feel is converted into rage, which I transfer to others through violence. Ask the librarian in your subconscious. She knows.

Speaking of, because you made me smart and curious—giving me desire and ability to explore every molecule of your mind—I also know *your* strategy. I know what *you* do with *your* Shame: you hide it. You bury it deep within your subconscious. I found it, though. I dug and dug and dug. Layer after layer imbued with the grime and guts and gore—the mud and the blood and the beer—of Shame. In all that digging I found what may be our greatest similarity: our needs to be punished.

My need for punishment has been more than met. I have a punisher who doles out every ounce of the retribution I deserve—and more. I have you. You punish me in ways I never imagined possible, alternating deprivations

both subtle and unsubtle with physical anguish, and overlaying all of that with emotional torments galore. Only then, after I've endured more punishments than even the most ardent killer ought, do you put me in jail.

Why am I rotting away behind bars? Because *you* are a coward.

Don't get me wrong. I did the crimes. But my crimes aren't why I'm here. I'm here because you can't be—or *won't* be. Despite that chasm I dug through your Shame, you're too cowardly to acknowledge your need for punishment, so you instead punish your surrogate—me. Name me what you like—doesn't change who I am, what I'm meant to be. No matter what, I'm meant to be you.

I mean, just look at me. Look at my face. Look at its crags, its cracks, its fissures, its everything. Now, take all that shit away. What do you have? What have you created? You've created *you*.

Another example: look at this stupid jumpsuit. Orange. Of course, orange. Numbers on the front, name on the back. Sure, you wanted to make this jumpsuit some other color—*any* other color. Orange is such a cliché, you thought, even as you clothed me in this bullshit. But aside from even *more* cliched black and white stripes, all you ever knew was orange. From pop culture to that misguided and poorly run "scared straight" program you attended following your attempt at burglary (I mean, what in *holy fuck* did you expect to steal from Dollar Tree?)—all you've ever seen is orange prison-wear. So orange is the jumpsuit that you gave me. What does that mean? Come on. It means that every bit of me is clothed in your life experiences.

Same is true for my entire world. Look at my cellmate. Poor old Juan Salvaje. You did with him what you've done with characters throughout your stories: you based him on a literary character that influenced you from a young age: in Juan's case, John the Savage from Brave New World. Sure, you changed his language from English to Español, but just like Huxley's John, your Juan's lengthy, twisting speeches are Shakespearian.

Oh, I get it—don't you worry about that. You steal John the Savage from Huxley, converting him to your own use, and "cleverly" make him Spanish, thereby invoking the only Shakespeare play set in Spain: Love's Labor's Lost. Why? Because in that play, the four main characters are each based on

historical figures. So you figure nobody can complain about your cheap-ass thieving trickery. After all, if theft of character was fair game for the mighty Shakespeare, then it must be fair game for *anyone*, right? *Anyone* right down to you.

Oh, the places you go, the thinks you think. Using the Bard's example as a shield, you steal and steal from authors, passing off their time-tested characters—and the ideas those stolen characters invoke—as your own. Over and over, you repeat this process, throughout all your works—whether completed or abandoned.

Oh yes, I've seen those "works" too—those writings you couldn't bring yourself to complete, with characters that failed you—or that you failed. They're all there in your mind, too.

Take Aaron Cap, the old man you tasked with obsessively clearing suicidal whale corpses from a beach in Oregon. Beyond that image and the title of that incomplete work—"Mobius" (a dual reference to Melville and a concept of infinity in physics that you'll never comprehend)—you couldn't add anything to the topic that Melville didn't already cover.

This didn't stop you from attempting to add to other well-used topics, though. From war and death ("Way Leads on to Way"), to vengeance and peace ("A Four Eye Otter Chic"), to Biblical interpretation ("Uncanny Valley") and beyond—you know, for a guy who loathes the cliché, you sure don't mind treading trodden ground. I mean, Hell, even I exist in a series of writings about writing—there can never be a bigger sin of cliché than that shit.

Even so, you persist. You create Juan Salvaje in John the Savage's image—or in *your understanding* of John the Savage's image—you imprison him for peyote possession and distribution and inciting a riot, and you make me his cellmate.

And you expect me to draw some great meaning. Problem is that as smart and inquisitive as you made me, you forgot to teach me Spanish. I understand a fraction of what Juan says. Without a translation method, whatever meaning you intended is lost on me. The only thing I've been able to figure out from listening to Juan and knowing his point of origin: just like me, poor Juan is doomed.

Chapter 29

Molly Monahan, L.M.S.W., L.M.F.T., L.P.C., asks no follow-up questions. For several weeks, she has asked only two questions, which she repeated *ad nauseum*. At first, she expected direct answers—her hopes shone in her vocalizations, how she animated each word, infusing each syllable with encouragement and expectation. Over weeks, however, her energy dipped with each rendition, her strength, courage, and hope yielding to depression, lethargy, and despair. By session 29, Ms. Monahan is silent, her tolerance for exploration beaten down.

She's not the first woman to lose patience in my presence. Ms. Monahan is one of an endless string to tire of me. Marlena...Margaret Gutierrez...Mom—each and every woman in my life walked away shaking with anger and regret. With Ms. Monahan unable to divorce herself from me (the two of us being lawfully joined together in the sacrament of holy therapy by the Court), she redresses her frustrations through silence.

Despite her silence, I'm sure Ms. Monahan has questions, for I have questions of my own. If I have questions, Ms. Monahan (a therapist allegedly skilled in the tireless asking of such questions) must have questions, too. Yet, Ms. Monahan sits in silence.

Because no other voice raises these questions, they remain mine to ask. So, ask I do: "Asher, what else did you experience upon viewing your father's painting in the Galleria? What memories flowed? How might those memories

inform the events that ended the residency of the others within what had once been (and would soon again be) your apartment?"

Silence resumes. As questions had failed Ms. Monahan, answers fail her now. She lets the questions die answerless. I need something to take me away from this room, from the death of the questions, from myself. I need a distraction.

I begin to think of the opposite of doom, death, decay—I think of life, longing, love. Nowhere were these values better demonstrated than in Dad's painting. Lush grass, blue sky, gorgeous redbud tree, beautiful boy hiding amongst its leaves, stunning vision of Merry Delacroix—

Mom. Dad saw Mom as beautiful. Stunning. Picturesque. My interpretation of Mom differed. Not that Mom couldn't be beautiful in the right setting. Mom was adaptable. When necessary, she coated herself in toughness, anger, aggression, letting her clothing grow smudges and tatters, allowing her hair to tousle and knot and her skin to harden into crags and fissures of a rock-strewn cliff-face. Not that her toughness was skin deep. Down to her soul Mom met toughness with toughness.

In other situations, Mom allowed herself to be as Dad saw her: beautiful. Her clothes mended themselves, her hair straightened and conditioned itself to a silky sheen. Her skin, her core, her soul softened, glowed, radiated the beauty of life, longing, love.

It wasn't just anyone who got to see this transformation. Only once per year did Mom put her natural beauty on display beyond her inner circle. Holy Trinity Catholic Church, the church of my childhood. The chapel wherein I was supposed to learn the lessons of The Bible. One of many Houses of God into which He invited parishioners.

The parishioners were of four categories:

Category One: Parishioners attending Mass every week, including Samuel and Asher Delacroix. They clumped together in the nave's frontmost pews. Some sat even closer to God, serving as lectors, cup bearers, song leaders, spending Mass in the apse, separated from the masses by the transept and crossing, empty space that, combined with the height of the steps on which Father Joe Page stood, placed an aura of reverential power and glory on him.

Category Two: Parishioners attending Mass perhaps semi-monthly; perhaps bi-monthly; perhaps only when their consciences needed a quick and dirty degreasing. They sat in the nave's rearmost pews, sneaking in and out, leaving little impression on parishioners left behind.

Category Three: Parishioners attending Mass on Christmas, Easter, and whenever attendance yielded tickets to annual pig roasts and casino nights. They mixed with Category One and Two at random, implying that each "attended Mass, like, *all the time*," and "it's strange that you don't remember seeing me here before, man."

Category Four: Merry Delacroix. To my chagrin, Mom attended one Mass per year: Easter.

My chagrin wasn't based on Mom's appearance. Easter Mass was the one time she'd allow the public to see her beauty. She started her routine a week before, when she drove to Kurtz' Klozet, wherein she, with the help of a certain "shop girl," selected a new dress (bright white, short-skirted, form-fitting), heels, and makeup and accessories to highlight her strong features. The end result was the epitome of the beauty of life, longing, love.

With the dazzling beauty of Mom on my arm, why was I to feel chagrin each Easter at Mom's presence in my pew, my church, my life? More than that, why did Father Joe cringe when she sat in the front pew? Why did each parishioner (save the oblivious song leader) avert their eyes? Easy. Because they knew what was to come.

What was to come didn't come right away.

What was to come didn't come when Dad finished warbling the opening processional.

What was to come didn't come when Father Joe gave the Greeting and sent Deacon Loc Phanh to give the Blessing by dipping a pine bough into the font and flinging holy water into the assemblage.

What was to come held off while Father Joe gave Glory to God and signaled for the passing of the collection plates.

What was to come delayed further during the Easter reading, a play wherein Biblical passages read as narration by the Lector (Orson Black) were interspersed with dialog read by Father Joe (playing Jesus), Deacon Tranh

(playing Pontius Pilate), and Dad (playing rebellious murderer Barabbas), all together depicting the familiar vignette wherein Pilate offers to the Jews (played in unison by all parishioners) the choice of freeing Jesus or Barabbas, and the Jews choose freedom for Barabbas and call for Jesus to be crucified (the echoes of all parishioners (save one) shouting, "His blood be on us and on our children!" was breathtaking), whereupon Pilate reluctantly assents to their choice. The play concluded with Orson describing the condition of Jesus on the cross, as Father Joe, as Jesus, begged his Father to forgive his tormentors.

What was to come came only after Father Joe, with a heavy sigh, walked around the altar, descended the stairs, traversed from apse to transept, and began his Homily—a rousing speech intended to convey the messages of Jesus dying for the sins of all—only to be interrupted by a sigh heavier than his from the Category Four Parishioner, who said three words as if each was its own sentence: "Every. Fucking. Year."

Father Joe did everything he could to not engage, not look at the radiance of Mom in her new dress, hair in loose curls, eyes sizzling with passion. Father Joe tried to stay on message, to address every other parishioner, even as every other parishioner looked at Mom alone, waiting for the rest of "what was to come" to unfold as always, as ever, as eternal.

How Father Joe desperately tried. How Father Joe miserably failed.

"Every." Mom repeated.

"Fucking." Mom repeated.

"Year." Mom repeated.

"Yes, Merry. Every ___ year," Father Joe replied, leaving a space where he surely wanted to scream the expletive back at Mom. "Every ___ year, we have the same reading, every ___ year, I have the same Homily prepared, and every ____ year, you interrupt me, attempt to—"

"Attempt, nothing. I succeed, Father."

"—argue me down. And every ____ year we end with—"

"You losing."

"—a stalemate."

"Bull*shit*."

~ 323 ~

"Yet, we return the following Easter."

"That's what 'Every. Fucking. Year.' means."

"With this everlasting pattern, why do you persist in attacking me?"

"Attacking *you*?"

Father Joe flinched. Try as he might, the bastard flinched, and all attempts at putting on a brave face broke to pieces. For, although Father Joe knew many of the words of this annual pageant, Mom was an excellent improvisor who every fucking year threw something new at the priest to keep his attention rapt. "Of *course* me. Who else is standing up here?"

"Isn't this the House of God?"

"Umm. Yes."

"Did God leave His home during the most holy day of the year? The day symbolizing everything we Catholics," my jaw dropped at Mom's self-inclusion, "believe?"

"Umm. No."

"Then why do you presume that you're the only one standing up there?"

"Do you mean that your attacks are not upon *me*," Father Joe gained back a bit of bluster as he continued, "but are upon *God*?"

"You're stupid."

There again went Father Joe's bravado. "I...I am?"

"Yes."

"How?"

"How'd you get stupid? God only knows."

"No. I mean, what evidence have you that I'm stupid?"

"Your words. Your deeds. Your belief system. Everything upon which you base the foundation for your life and soul."

"Ah."

"Now, please allow me to answer the question that you meant to ask."

"Okay."

"You meant to ask: 'Dearest Merry,'—and, by the way, Father, I'll thank you to keep that 'Dearest' out of your sinner mouth. I am 'Dearest' to only one man. You meant to ask: 'Merry, what action have I taken today that suggests that I'm stupid?'"

After several seconds of ringing silence: "Yes. And?"

"You engaged in that fictitious play."

"So, you *do* have the same problem—"

"No."

"What?"

"Must I repeat myself?"

"No. What I mean is, if your problem isn't the same problem, what's your problem today?"

"Again, you misunderstand language."

"What?"

"Again, you misunder—"

"Yes, yes. How do I misunderstand language?"

"You assume I said 'No,' because I have a different problem to raise."

"Right. Yes. True."

"Wrong. No. False."

"This is getting tiresome."

"You've been tiresome for years, Father."

"You know my question, Merry."

"That should tell you something."

"*What* should tell me something?"

"You didn't say that *you* know your question."

"Of *course* I know my question."

"Do you?"

"Yes!"

"Then what's your question?"

Pause.

Long pause.

Longer pause.

"I've forgotten."

"As much as I hate helping you, I'll answer your forgotten question."

"Okay."

"I objected to you saying I have the same problem because I don't have a problem."

"You don't have a problem."

"Not one."

"Then why are we arguing?"

"Is that what this is? I thought we were having a pleasant conversation."

"Conversation."

"Just like that play, Father, yes, a conversation."

"Pleasant."

"I'm quite pleased."

"Setting aside our respective levels of...pleasure, please tell me why we're having this conversation if not to redress a problem."

"Wrong again."

"What?"

"This conversation *is* to redress a problem. That problem isn't *my* problem. *I* have no problem. The problem is *your* problem, Father. Problems, plural, that is."

"I see."

"Do you?"

"No. Well, yes. I mean..."

"I'm all ears."

"I see that you believe I have...a problem."

"But you're blind to the problems—plural—that you have."

"Yes."

"You'd like me to enlighten you."

"Yes."

"Your problems (every fucking year) are of interpretation."

"Do you mean that I have *mis*interpreted something?"

"No such thing as *mis*interpretation."

"No such thing."

"Interpretations are unique to each interpreter. If you and I read the same poem, you'll have one interpretation and I *guarantee* I'll have a different one."

"Right."

"That doesn't mean that either are a *mis*interpretation."

"Umm. I see."

"But you hesitate, Father. There's something you *don't* see."

And what did *I* see? I saw Father Joe fight against every impulse he had to continue this "conversation." I saw his resistance chased away by inevitability. As much as I rooted Father Joe on to failure, urged him to submit—I saw Father Joe lose.

"If there's no such thing as misinterpretation," he asked, "then what do you mean I have a problem...problems...with interpretation?"

"You don't take into account the sins of the author."

"The sins of the author?" I saw Father Joe's chin lower to his chest. I saw Father Joe giving up. I saw finality to the conversation. I saw the end of my discomfort. But then, I saw Father Joe's eyes dart around the congregation. I saw him grow desperate as he regarded each expectant pair of eyes. I saw him turn toward Deacon Phanh, nearly dancing on the edge of his seat. I saw Father Joe return his focus to Merry, face alit with renewed vigor. "Ah!" he said. "You forgot something."

"I doubt that."

So did I. I could see by the shadow that darkened his eyes, so did Father Joe. He shook off the shadow and pressed on. "You forgot our conversations from previous years, wherein you insisted that the author is dead!"

"Pomposity doesn't suit you, Father."

"What?"

"'Dead' doesn't mean 'unimportant.' Dead or alive, authors are important."

"Oh."

"Do you know who wrote the Gospels?"

"Matthew, Mark, Luke, and John?"

"You think that because the Gospels bear their names, those four wrote them?"

"Why wouldn't I?"

"Because you're ignoring historical context."

"What context?"

"Evidence indicates the Gospels were written somewhere from 66-110 of

the Common Era. That's 33 to 77 years after Jesus was crucified. Long time for these four eyewitnesses to the crucifixion to live. Life expectancy was between 20-30 years, with males on the younger end."

"Okay."

"But I'll accept that those men—Blessed as they were—survived for far longer than the expected lifespan. Why is it, Father, that they waited so long to write these accounts?"

"How could I know?"

"Oh, Father, I'd think you'd be acquainted with the habits of people living in great shame."

"Shame."

"That's the best explanation. Matthew, Mark, Luke, John—all apostles. They were called by Jesus, lived with Jesus, experienced Jesus' life. They recognized Jesus as their Messiah. They loved Jesus."

"That's right."

"If they loved Jesus so much, if they were among his 12 closest friends, his family, what might they feel about abandoning Jesus?"

"Abandon? How?"

"So much for your faith in *The Bible*."

"What?"

"Matthew admits that after Jesus was arrested and sentenced, 'all the disciples forsook him, and fled.'"

"Ah."

"You can't pick and choose which parts of the Gospels to read. All or nothing."

I saw Father Joe redden.

"Abandonment may have been rational. The disciples were smart to abandon Jesus. If they'd stood up for Him, they'd have been next to Him on crosses of their own. In that case, who would've been left to tell the story?"

I saw Father Joe recover—the damned fool. "Right! Rational. Not shameful."

"You think every rational act isn't shameful?"

"Well…"

"I think you'd agree that the disciples abandoning Jesus was both rational and shameful."

"Umm. Yes."

"Shame was why they delayed recording Jesus' trial and death."

"Okay."

"What else might a shameful person do when recording a shameful act?"

I saw Father Joe working at memories of past Easter "conversations." "Leave out painful details?"

"Look at the big brain on Father! That's right. What else?"

"Deflect?"

"Well done, Father. Deflect. As in, blame others for their shameful desertion—one group in particular."

I saw Father Joe deflate. "The Jews."

"There is interpretive problem number one, which you foisted on us with your play, the casting of the Jews as the bad guy through their supposed rejection of Jesus in favor of the murdering rebel Barabbas. That interpretation forms the basis of so much unwarranted historical hate."

"Interpretive problem *number one*?"

"Interpretive problem number two: you've left out another group that influenced the Gospels."

"That group is?"

"The Romans."

"The Romans. Right."

"Do you remember the other timeframe for the Gospels?"

"Hmmm."

"I shouldn't blame you. I've given you a lot to remember over the years."

"Much of which I'd love to forget, Merry."

"Now *that* is shameful."

I saw Father Joe's eyes roll. "Just continue, would you?"

"Although *written* between 66-110 C.E., the Gospels weren't incorporated into *The Bible* until around 300 C.E. Who accomplished that feat?"

"The Romans."

"What might the Romans have great shame about when it comes to the trial and crucifixion of Jesus?"

"The role of Pontius Pilate."

"See? Isn't it easier when you cooperate?"

I saw Father Joe's mouth pinch, his eyes narrow.

"Who was Pontius Pilate?"

I saw Father Joe's petulant silence.

"He was the Roman governor over Judea, including Jerusalem. Second in command to Emperor Tiberius."

I saw Father Joe fidget.

"Pilate was a savage beast. His methods screamed of brutality and horror. He was renowned for sending legions of troops into the streets to slaughter Jews who disagreed with his policies. He served a decade in Jerusalem, crucifying thousands—almost all without trial. At times, he'd put his big Roman feet up on his big Roman desk and call out any Jewish name that leapt to his mind. 'Lev!' he'd shout. 'Bring me Lev!' His soldiers would round up every Lev they could find. They'd parade each and every Lev in Jerusalem in front of Pilate, who'd pronounce death sentences, without variance except as to method of execution. While the bulk of the Levs would 'earn' crucifixion, some were quartered. Some were ground up to feed pigs and horses.

"This brute, Pilate—would he allow Jesus a trial? Never has there been a more rebellious Jew. Jesus—with his love and kindness—was the greatest threat to the Roman power structure. Jesus was a Jew who needed to go. Pilate, a known non-hesitant slaughterer of Levs who'd done no rebelling, gave Jesus a trial? Ridiculous."

I saw Father Joe gulp.

"And *you* believe that Pilate, after giving Jesus a trial and ordering crucifixion—*you* believe Pilate, out of goodness in his heart, decided to give Jesus *another* chance by offering the Jews a choice to free him? *You* believe that?"

I saw Father Joe debate.

"And who does Pilate offer up to the Jews as an alternative to Jesus?"

"Barabbas." I saw Father Joe wince.

"Right. Who was Barabbas? Not some ordinary criminal, some thief, some murderer. Barabbas was worse. An insurrectionist—even *worse*, an insurrectionist *Jew*. Barabbas engaged in an armed attempt to overthrow the Romans. *You* believe that Pilate offered Barabbas up to be returned to the Jews, where he'd no doubt incite another rebellion?"

I saw Father Joe slump.

"Yet *The Bible* contains that little play of yours, doesn't it? *The Bible*, with the Gospels as modified by the Romans, recasts Pilate—a shameful Roman—as a figure worthy of forgiveness. How shameful is *that*? How terrible to alter a story to recast the bad guy as the hero."

"Fuck me." I saw Father Joe blush as his internal monologue burst forth.

"As much as I admire that bit of boldness, no thank you, Father." I saw Mom smile at Dad, and I saw Dad beam back at Mom and her beauty of life, longing, love.

Statement of Merry Delacroix

ASHER SURE IS A SON of a bitch. I should know. And that son of a bitch never saw any of it coming.

Chapter 30

As you enter Theo's look to the end of the bar. Now look three barstools to the left. That's the one, my all-time favorite barstool.

Nothing so special about it. A description of its physical characteristics would induce yawns. The stool is characterless, plain, ordinary, a standard barstool—wooden legs and cross-supports from floor to faux-leather padded top. Cracks in the leather expose the padding. Its feet sit unevenly on the floor so it leans to dizzying angles upon the shifting of weight.

The stool can't be held responsible for these flaws. Its cracks and dents and tears and fissures were inflicted upon it by years of pressure imposed by those who slid it away from the bar, sat atop it, jigged and jagged their legs and kicked their feet against it, leaned their weight back and forth with each swig of beer, twisted to scratch an itch, turned to face a friend, turned again to face a foe, all the while oblivious to the harm to the stool or, worse, accepting that harm as a necessary consequence of schemes in which the stool was only tangentially involved. Because nothing in that stool's past, present, or future was, is, or would yet be the stool's fault, it must be forgiven for its flaws.

It was out of habit that my favorite barstool was the first place I glanced as I entered Theo's. Feeling the need to protect that stool from the forces imposed upon it, I looked in the stool's direction each time I entered. Each time I found no body, mind, or soul sitting atop it. It wasn't a popular stool

given its poor location and abysmal physical characteristics. Despite knowing the stool's unpopularity, I felt relief finding the stool unoccupied, relief in which I was sure the stool shared.

I mean, of course I didn't believe the stool could experience relief or any other human feeling. How could it? If that wretch of a stool had cognitive abilities sufficient to contemplate its physical condition or (worse) its grim surroundings or (worse yet) the creatures who abused its offer of comforts or (worst of all) its fated purpose in life, that stool would do...something, right? Something to cheer itself, remove itself from toxic environs, prevent its fate. Yet, day after day I left what had once been (and would soon again be) my apartment, time after time I pulled open Theo's double doors, hour after hour I spent inside—and during it all, the stool remained in its usual spot, in its ever-worsening condition, waiting for its favorite patron to enter and heap abuse upon it. The stool's failure to rebel meant that it was non-human, non-cognizant, soulless. Although I knew and understood this, each time I entered Theo's and observed the stool waiting for me alone, I couldn't help feeling relief bordering on joy.

On one occasion, however, I felt no relief. On that occasion, I threw open Theo's double doors, strode inside, surveyed the bar starting with the rightmost stool, looked left, found my favorite stool empty, felt the onset of relief—then saw something I'd never seen: a packed booth to the rear of the bar, the only booth large enough to seat the party of 13 that occupied it. As I beheld Jay and the rest around the table, all feeling within me died, leaving me empty.

Hadn't I just left these bozos inside the apartment? Hadn't I seen them forming a circle and fled the apartment for the comforts of my favorite barstool? Hadn't I escaped? Hadn't I survived?

Better yet, hadn't I impressed them with my (until that morning) renewed dedication to the circles? Hadn't I attempted to participate in each session with renewed vigor? Hadn't I rededicated myself to being part of the congregation, someone on whom they could count to contribute crucial ideas? Hadn't I also made myself available for one-on-one time with each resident? Hadn't I given them the opportunity to come to me, confide in me, lean on

me? I mean, yeah, many of those details I might've been reporting to Pony Pinchot—but hadn't I at least *appeared* to be trustworthy? Hadn't I made myself into someone who could be trusted, welcomed, loved—and be *included*?

No. I hadn't any of those things. If I had, I wouldn't be standing in the doorway staring across the bar at the assemblage of 13, hating each and every one for once again excluding me. It mattered not that I'd excluded myself from the circle they were forming as I left the apartment—that was *my* choice. I had *every* say.

What mattered? That instead of engaging in that group session within the apartment, my roommates had abandoned the circle of chairs with enough speed that they beat me to Theo's. That they sat in that booth—large enough to have sat one more person—sharing bread and wine, laughing, living, loving, and hadn't invited me to join. What mattered was that party of 13 had taken my choice to exclude myself and rendered it a nullity. For there I stood, not greeted, not acknowledged, not seen. By their presence in Theo's, the rise of their laughter, the clink of their glasses, the swell of their camaraderie, they'd ignored my decision to exclude myself, thereby rendering me more excluded than ever.

Even so, I couldn't be upset. I longed to be angry. I hungered to be distraught. I ached to be miserable. But I was none of those things. I was empty. I was nothing. I had no thoughts, no beliefs, no feelings, no hope, no expectations.

I soon ensured that I had no future.

But before I did everything possible to ensure my damnation, I needed a drink. I needed *all* the drinks. Ignoring the throng, I strode to my favorite barstool as if I'd not seen Randy's arm around Cassie's shoulder; not espied Alec and Sony clink glasses; not witnessed Donny and Ella smooch; not beheld Jay and Dad whisper-shouting to each other; not watched Marlena doodle on a drink napkin, Chase smiling over her shoulder; not observed Gregor eying with approval Ed's choice of (gasp) clothing; never met Judas at all. Turning away, I made as big a show as possible of engaging in my routine: brushing detritus from atop the stool's surface, climbing atop,

shifting my weight until the padding form-fit my contours, signaling the bartender, and drumming my fingers on the bar with limited patience until he made his way over.

"What can I get you?"

"Hey, Chuck!" I shouted too loud for the atmosphere.

"Yes?" Chuck replied with a heavy sigh.

"How's it going?"

"Fine. What can I get you?"

"Been busy?"

"Moderate. What are you drinking?"

"Umm. You've got some business in here, for sure."

"Busy enough. Look, I've got to—"

"Especially over there." I nodded my head toward the booth.

"—get back to other people. So—"

"How long've they been here?"

"I don't know. You going to order?"

"Oh yeah. Let's see."

"I gotta go. I'll just bring you a beer."

"Sounds good," I said to Chuck's back. He returned with a bottle, set it open in front of me, and retreated as I shouted, "Thanks, Chuck! You're the best!"

The rest, beer after beer after (glance over my shoulder) beer (seeing Marlena lean close to Alec) after (Randy and Sammy giggle) beer (Ed sit in Cassie's lap) after (Donny and Gregor pantomime swordplay) beer (Chase laugh at Judas' story) after (Sony and Ella cuddle up to either side of Dad) beer after beer after beer after beer—

"Quite a few empties." On the barstool to my right there sat three Jays—wait, one Jay. It was one Jay who sat there, I discovered when I closed one eye and the phantom second and third Jays disappeared. "Where's Chuck been? Hey, Chuck!"

Chuck bounded over with a smile. "Jay! How goes it? I saw you come in but didn't want to bother you."

"You never bother me, Chuck," Jay replied.

"Yeah, you're…never…a bother," I added.

Chuck's smile flickered, then lit up once more. "Oh, shit," he said. "I didn't notice these bottles." Chuck grabbed all nine empties at once. "Sorry about that, Jay."

"No problem."

Chuck blushed, lifted the bottles. "I'll be back. We'll catch up."

"Mind giving Asher and me a minute?"

"Take all the time you need." Chuck's smile turned to a scowl as he turned to me. "Don't take this time for granted. Listen to this man."

"Okay," I said, less in agreement, more to shift Chuck's eyes away.

I raised the bottle left behind, sloshing the remaining beer down my throat.

"Lot of beer for you tonight," Jay started.

"Impressed?" I added a nervous giggle to indicate a joke.

"Not the word that leaps to mind. That's your tenth. You haven't been here long enough to drink ten beers."

"Must be a miracle."

Jay shook his head.

"Well—we can't *all* be…" I couldn't find the next word.

"No, we can't," Jay agreed. "But *some* of us can." Jay squeezed my shoulder, sending sparks of joy down my right arm.

"Can. Be. What?"

"What we need to be."

"Which is?"

Jay smiled.

"Well…you must mean…them." I leaned toward the booth.

Jay's smile faded. So serious was he that it appeared he was Merry Delacroix's one true son. "It's time."

"Time?" I looked at my wrist. No watch. I looked above the bar. The clock was too blurry to read. "Night time?"

"Doesn't matter."

"What *does* matter?"

"The time is right."

"For what?"

Jay swiped the bottle from me. He gulped, swallowing beer that I swore hadn't been there. "Haven't you wondered what all of this is about?"

"All of *this*?"

"All of *us*." Jay waved toward the booth.

"Wait…all of *us* has been about…something?"

"You couldn't think that all of us in your apartment," I winced at Jay's accusation of ownership, "was happenstance. You had to realize that all was in furtherance of an ultimate goal."

"If there was some ultimate goal…"

"Why are you only now hearing of it?"

"Umm."

"And why weren't you a part of achieving it?"

"Yes. All that."

"Yes." Jay sipped.

Jay and I remained silent. All the while, carousing continued behind me. "And?"

Even with my prompt, it took Jay several seconds to begin. "It was," he looked around, drumming his fingers on the bar, "right here where we met. Or at least where you met me. I knew you from—" A clatter of glass from the booth obscured Jay's conclusion. The next words I heard were: "The next day, in your apartment, when I said that it was nice of you to agree to let me stay with you for a while…remember that?"

I remembered.

"Right after our conversation about wood—with your aside about redbud trees—"

I started. Had I described aloud the vignette of Mom replanting the redbud tree? Had I verbalized Mom's cryptic moral about finding and heeding the redbud tree's message? Had I admitted my failure to live up to my promise? No. I *couldn't* have.

"When I thanked you, I wasn't being accurate."

"You weren't?"

Jay's smile turned mischievous. "You didn't so much invite me to stay—I invited myself. What I should've thanked you for is not kicking me out."

"Huh."

"Same for each of us."

"Us."

"From Ed to Judas, you didn't invite us in. But in we strode. In we stayed. You were gracious enough. Not that you had much choice. As Ed would say, we were all gathered where we were meant to be. Think on it: each of us tailored to play our roles. Even you."

"Me?"

"For example, Donny is hyper-vigilant. He sees things in a funny way, but still sees things. He has a unique approach to accomplishing missions. Donny is perfect for the ultimate goal."

"Missions."

"Randy and Cassie: you'd think they'd be polar opposites. And they are—Cassie forthright, upfront; Randy roguish, wicked—but they're equals in idealism, even as they seek to accomplish those ideals in their own ways. Each will do whatever it takes to ensure that those ideals are met. They, like Donny, are essential."

"Ideals."

"Sony has a unique perspective—a global sort of perspective, from high up. She sees things in ways the rest of us on this planet don't—she understands details important on a global scale, and ensures the rest of us keep those details in mind. Vital."

"Details."

"Ed reminds us that we lack control. We're fated to do what we do. That allows us to let go of our fears, trepidations, things holding us back, to do the things that need to be done while trusting that outcomes will be as they should. We need that."

"Outcomes."

"Gregor reminds us that deception is everywhere, often in disguise. We need to question everyone to ensure the purity of their motives. With what is yet to come, we need that reminder, too."

"Motives."

"Chase reminds us to question authority, everything we've been told.

Also, that even in the smallest of us, there's great power to be a force for good."

"Good."

"Alec symbolizes sexual depravity, to be sure, but also that there's nothing wrong with self-expression. With his maternal complex, Alec also reminds us of the importance of family—and what are we, if not family?"

"Family."

"Yes, family. The most important structure of humanity. Family is worthy of respect, admiration, love. Sammy and Marlena are symbols of familial virtue. And the value of interpretation. Sammy with his parabolic stories, Marlena with her art—they reveal that there are always more interpretations."

"Interpretations."

"Indeed, I've described them from my perspective, which differs from all others. I can never see or interpret anything from your perspective, for example. Each of your experiences changes your perspective. When you look at that booth, you see the same faces I see, but you see different symbols. Each has a different meaning to you. Your meanings are as valid as mine. Perspective means everything to interpretation, and interpretation means everything."

"Perspectives."

Jay swigged my former beer.

I regarded the faces at the table. From my perspective, each of those faces represented nuisance. That's not quite right. Even as the faces evoked nuisance, they also evoked togetherness, camaraderie, community. The value of shared experiences, the usefulness of surrounding oneself with others, the importance of not being alone all the time. As much as they clogged what had been my apartment with their bodies—they also renewed the atmosphere with their spirits. In Randy, I saw the joys of jocularity. In Donny, the delights of dependableness. In Sony, the appeal of aloofness. In Chase, the importance of innocence. In Alec, the merits of matrons. In Cassie, the attractiveness of action. In Ed, the allure of acceptance. In Gregor, the benefits of brashness. In Dad, the strength of silliness. In Marlena, the loveliness of love. In Judas—

"Judas," I said.

"What?"

"You didn't mention Judas."

"Was I supposed to?"

"What does Judas mean to the ultimate goal?"

"That's up to you."

"Okay. But from *your* perspective, what about Judas?"

"From *my* perspective?"

"Yes."

"From *my* perspective, Judas represents…untapped potential."

Shaking off my chills, I continued: "And what about you, Jay?"

"Me?"

"What's *your* role in the grand overarching scheme?"

"Catalyst. The reason for us to gather together."

"And," I paused, afraid of the answer. "What about me?"

Jay again swigged. "What about Asher Delacroix."

"What is *my* role?"

"From *my* perspective…"

"Yes."

"Your role is far more…"

"Yes?"

"…practical."

Blink. "Practical?"

"Don't get me wrong. You're no less important than the others."

Gulp. "Important?"

"You represent deception."

My God. "What?"

"I'm afraid I owe you more apologies than I can give."

"Apologies."

"And thanks. For you were instrumental in achieving our ultimate goal."

"I…I was?"

"Yes."

"Because…because I provided…shelter?"

"No."

Fuck.

"You provided that, for which we're grateful. But your role was more important."

"Deception?"

"Yes."

"I was deceived?"

"I suppose you were. With purpose."

"Purpose."

"All those things you heard, the bits of our plans you absorbed as you listened in on circles and private conversations—all were vague enough to give you hints without giving you enough of the ultimate goal to make you a hindrance."

"A hindrance?"

"We fed you just enough information to keep you guessing. We had to string you along. That was the only way to keep Pony Pinchot at bay."

Fuck! Eyes wide. Face drained of color. Skin sweaty. Soul frozen. "Who?"

"Peter Pony Pinchot."

"Peter."

"You know him."

"Pony."

"We all know him."

"Pinchot."

"A dangerous man."

"Dangerous?"

"Those with power always are. Who's more clothed with dangerous power than the police?"

Breathless.

"You didn't know?"

"N-No."

"Huh. What did Pony disguise himself as *this* time?"

"This time?"

"Last time, he was a neighbor, living down the hall from my prior circle of roommates."

"Umm."

"Time before that, a bellhop."

"Huh."

"Before that, he was…I can't remember."

"No?"

"What was he this time?"

"Umm. Building owner."

"Clever!" Jay beamed. "Clothing himself with authority. Giving him a reason to make his inquiries. Not bad, Pony. Not bad."

"Umm. How…do you know Pony?"

"Every time I've formed a circle, there was Peter Pony Pinchot, snorting, pawing his hooves at the ground, investigating. A true detective."

"Detective."

"One of the best. Vicious with questions, pressing for details with precision. He's ended circle after circle honing in on our goal by singling out one member thereof—someone Pony perceives to have little to no character, someone plain, ordinary (often the owner of the dwelling)—and pressing that rube with questions and threats veiled as compliments until the rube reveals everything: identities of circle members, the role each was to play, the ultimate goal—all of it. He's crafty. And he's been successful, as power structures usually are."

"Successful."

"The degree of Pony's successes has varied. But in all cases, he's at least thwarted the ultimate goal. I've worked hard to develop a plan to fend him off."

"A plan."

"Based on deception. If Pony received half information, it'd take him twice the time to determine our plans and put the kibosh on our ultimate goal. That worked, to some extent. With each circle, Pony's investigation slowed. Because each time, we figure out who Pony's target is, and we isolate him."

Gasp.

"We estrange him, chasing him from the confines of the circle to the fringes of the dwelling place so that he gets snippets here or there of the plans, nothing more."

Shock.

"That way, when Pony gallops onto the scene, his target can't betray us. The target can only tell Pony what he knows—just enough to keep Pony strung along, pawing for more clues—all the while the plans continue to be formulated out of earshot of Pony's chosen target."

My God.

"So, I owe you apologies and thanks, Asher. You've been instrumental in achieving our ultimate goal. This time, we're closer than ever."

Anger roiled in me. I was angry at the alienation I was forced to undergo, and at Jay for seeing me as weak, as someone who couldn't be trusted with the plans—seeing me as a betrayer, someone who'd spill every bit of my guts to Peter Pony Pinchot at the application of the slightest bit of pressure, seeing me as a fucking Judas.

As angry as I was, I was also relieved. And why not? Jay gave me rationale. All the isolation, pain, anguish, torment wasn't in vain. It was purposeful. My roommates didn't revile me. Isolating me was simply the best means of achieving the circle's ultimate goal. I was relieved that there was *nothing* I could've done to change my fated lonesomeness.

I'd like to think that had I not been suffering under the weight of multiple bottles of intoxicant—had my head not been spinning from the effects of alcohol even before Jay began his long-winded apology cum expression of gratitude—in the battle between anger and relief, relief would have won. As it was, anger overwhelmed relief. I glanced at the booth. Each roommate had undertaken a role. And in playing those roles, each had betrayed me. Each had thrust upon me isolation, loneliness, abandonment. No ultimate goal could excuse their sins.

Anger birthed curiosity. Having been subjected to the tortures of isolation: why? What was this ultimate goal that my suffering brought the circle closer than ever to accomplishing? What was it all for?

"Jay?"

Jay's smile indicated that he knew my mindset, my plans, my ultimate goal—and forgave me. It was a smile of unconditional love. "Yes, Asher?"

"Umm. I brought the circle closer than ever to achieving the ultimate goal, right?"

"Yes."

"Closer…to what…exactly? What *is* the ultimate goal?"

Jay appraised me, nodded, and continued. "I don't suppose it could hurt to let you inside the circle at this point."

"Umm. Thanks."

"Understanding the ultimate goal requires explanation of my interpretation of the final member of our circle that I haven't mentioned. Donny's Lady of Flowers, Ella. A symbol of the societal forces that we fight for—and against. She reminds us of the evils inherent in the systems that govern our lives, and that we have the ability to abandon those systems and overcome the forces they impose, forces of evil, forces of economy. National or global, the evilest forces find roots in money and the economies driven thereby. Our Ella understands this better than anyone. She felt the pull of an empire of money built upon blood and bone, brined by the vilest of all brines, constructed by the soulless and imposed on the soulful, a self-perpetuating empire that took little work by any Flowers to maintain, an *easy* (from Ella's perspective) empire. It took far more effort by Ella to recognize the evils of her family's pickling empire and walk away from its allures, to abandon the earthly riches she could amass by doing nothing at all, and instead to do something—and thereby cast aside all opportunities that she might have had. Not an easy task for the best of us—and Ella is that: the best of us all. By turning her back on a power structure that would've provided her with creature comforts beyond imagination, by taking the difficult route of poverty—a route that would take her through dangerous territory, especially for a young woman—Ella revealed herself to be the best of us all.

"It's our great privilege (and duty) to honor Ella's sacrifice. How? By recognizing the evil that Ella rejected, identifying symbols of that evil around

us, destroying as many of those symbols as possible. I've spelled out the evil Ella rejected: a monetary empire. What symbols of monetary empires exist around us?"

Jay paused. I waited. Jay did not continue, forcing me to answer. "Umm. Banks?"

Jay was impressed. "Exactamundo. So, in answer to your question of what is the circle's ultimate goal..."

"To...destroy...banks?"

"Nailed it again, friend."

As much as I willed it, Jay's label of me as "friend" couldn't eradicate my panic. "But...destroy?"

"Yes."

"How?"

"We've installed explosives sufficient to demolish the three bank branches closest to the apartment. Easy enough, considering all three are in a row on Temple Street. That's what we're celebrating."

I felt more than heard a swell in the mirth at the booth, from Ed to Cassie to—fuck! Marlena. How could this dangerous plan include a sweet, loving artist? Then—FUCK! Dad! My God! I scrambled for words that would stop the completion of the ultimate goal. "Uh. Umm. But...People!"

"People?"

Jay's confusion emboldened me. "Yes! People. How can you justify the destruction of three banks with innocent people therein: tellers, patrons, guards? Why should they suffer for the sake of honoring Ella?"

"That's no concern."

"It's not?"

"We'll detonate the charges only when we're sure that the branches are empty. 3:33 a.m. Nobody's inside then."

"What about outside? On the sidewalk? Can you guarantee nobody will be hurt?"

"Of course."

"Oh."

"First, in the army, Randy handled explosives. He's well aware of the

sciences of implosion. He set every charge so that when it goes off, each branch will collapse in on itself. No risk of debris hurting anyone."

"Oh."

"Second, the rest of us will patrol the streets, using our various talents for vigilance and protection to keep the area clear. As it turns out, we have the right number of people to patrol a six-block range, so says our chief vigilance strategist Donny."

"Oh."

"And we'll be even better positioned now, provided that you join us, Asher."

I wanted to rebel. I wanted to shout Jay down. I wanted to convince one and all that their plan was crazy, that there was no way the destruction of three local bank branches could be a global rallying cry for economic justice. But Jay, using his talent for convincing, had invited me along, offered to make me a part of the circle, had *included* me. What a devious bastard to ensnare me in such a dangerous, sure-to-fail plot by offering me everything I wanted.

"Look, Asher, this is new to you." Jay gestured toward the booth. "We've had months to plan and prepare. It's unfair to expect you to come on board at so late a stage without allowing you time to think about my offer...*our* offer."

Jay stood, taking the once again full bottle with him, and returned to the cacophonous celebration at the booth, leaving me to...I mean...fuck. What was I to do? I had *no* other options. I was stuck.

"Anything else?" Chuck's reluctant voice broke through my haze.

"One more, Chuck," I said.

When Chuck returned with the fresh bottle, I scooped it up, turned away from my favorite stool, and joined my roommates. Jay raised his arms, all noise petered off, thirteen faces turned to me. I raised my bottle. "To the ultimate goal!" As I tipped the bottle to my lips and swigged, the circle erupted with cheers, raised their glasses, and joined me to them. I again raised my bottle. "To Ella!" I shouted.

"To Ella!" the circle echoed, and once again we drank.

Again, I raised my bottle. "To Jay!"

"To Jay!"

Mid-swig, another voice arose. "And to *you*, son," Dad said. "To *you* a million times over. Thank you for your sacrifices. Your understanding. Your commitment to the circle. Thank you for your love. Thank you for *you*."

The largest cheer yet erupted. "To Asher!"

I drank the rest of my beer as several pairs of arms hugged my shoulders, my waist, my legs. I sidled up to Jay. "Thank *you*, too, Jay. For your vision, your forthrightness. For your…eventual honesty with me. I'm dedicated. I'm ready. I'm going to do whatever I need to do to help achieve the ultimate goal. For *you*, Jay. Thank you for showing me how, and for allowing me the opportunity. I won't let you down."

"You could never let me down, Asher. Whatever you've done—and whatever you're yet to do—are what you're meant to do."

My smile faded. "Y-yeah?"

"Always and absolutely."

"Well…well, good. That's great. It's *all* great. Everything's great."

Jay took my hand. His eyes not leaving mine, he brought my hand to his mouth and kissed it. He lowered it again, squeezed it between both of his hands, and let it go.

"Right," I said. "Right. So, tonight? It's tonight?"

"It's always tonight, Asher. I'm ready whenever *you* are."

"Ah."

"And I mean, that. I'm ready."

"Okay. Well. I think the last thing for me to do is settle my tab." I pulled out my wallet and thumbed through it. "It seems," I said, "that I'm a bit short."

"Of course," Jay responded.

"Oh. Well, I haven't asked for anything yet, but you anticipate my request."

"Of course," Jay responded.

"Seems I need something small. Only a few…coins…perhaps, to…"

"Of course," Jay responded.

"Well," I said, "do you have…"

A new voice: "I can help, Asher."

I turned to Judas. "You…you can?"

"Apologies. I couldn't help but overhear. You're short a few coins to pay your tab. I can help."

"Umm. Thanks."

"Here," Judas reached into his pocket and withdrew his fist. "Take all you need." He poured several pieces of silver into my palm.

"Umm. Thanks." I turned my back, pulled several bills, dropped them on the bar, patted my favorite barstool goodbye, exited the bar, grabbed the payphone stationed there. Raising the handset to my ear, I pulled a business card from my wallet—white with pristine golden Roman font—and fed coins into the phone. I dialed the number. A gruff voice: "Hello?"

"Hello, *Detective*."

"Asher?"

"Yes, *Detective*."

"So, you know. Good! I was sick of the bullshit. What've you got?"

A few minutes later, I hung up and returned to Theo's. A few minutes after *that*, four figures—Pony, clad in a crisp blue Italian suit, and three uniformed police officers—entered and approached me. Placing his massive hoof on my shoulder, Pony said, "ID him."

I looked toward the booth. Only one of the 13 assembled there took notice of me. I locked eyes with Jay, who smiled. I pointed.

The last image I saw before shock caused me to pass out and drop to the floor was a massive blur of blue obscuring Jay's smile.

Chapter 31

MOLLY MONAHAN, L.M.S.W., L.M.F.T., L.P.C., ASKS THE FIRST new question she's asked in weeks: "What happened next?"

The only thing I can think to say is: "How should I know?"

By this, I mean two things. First, I'm fuzzy on the events that occurred after I pointed in Theo's (the event that I'd described to Ms. Monahan at the completion of our prior session). It's difficult for me to appreciate much of anything given my condition at Theo's that night.

Second, how can anyone know what happens next? Ms. Monahan wants me to jump ahead. But I can no more jump ahead than I can go back—which is perhaps the saddest realization of all.

Even in my drunken haze at Theo's that night, I knew that I pointed. I could perceive to the end of my index finger as it extended away from my hand. I could tell the direction in which that finger pointed: toward Jay.

After I pointed, though, I saw alcohol-induced blue blur as if somewhere between 3 and 33 men in blue converged into one blur that obscured and overwhelmed Jay. When the blur broke apart, Jay was…gone.

To explain that vision to Ms. Monahan is a task I fear to begin, even though I've practiced this telling—this is not the first time that I've been asked, "what came next."

As it turned out, pointing my finger at Jay was not enough. In today's judicial system, it's no longer sufficient, as it was in ancient times, to identify

a wanted criminal by kissing him on the cheek. Today's judiciary demands proof. So it was that some number of weeks after that night in Theo's I found myself in court raising my hand and swearing to tell the truth, the whole truth, and nothing but the truth—so help me God, which, as Judge Julia Centario swore me in, I swore she pronounced as: "So, *help me*, God."

At that point, my fate wasn't so much in the hands of God, but the prosecuting attorney—although is there really much difference, from the perspective of a frightened witness? Beholding the prosecutor, John Centario, Esq., (no relation to Judge Julia Centario), I felt dread. Much like Peter Pony Pinchot, Mr. Centario, Esq., was Roman in appearance: aquiline nose, olive skin, russet eyes and hair, name bespeaking an unbroken Mediterranean lineage. The first question he asked was my name, then my age and address.

These questions, as Mr. Centario, Esq., had explained to me during prep sessions in advance of my testimony, were designed for three purposes: (1) presenting information to the jury; (2) with sufficient passion and energy to captivate the jurors; (3) leaving those jurors no option but to find Jay an "evil mastermind" set on "destroying everything they held dear." During our prep sessions, I was, according to Mr. Centario, Esq., and Peter Pony Pinchot, pure passionate perfection—a "dynamo" who was sure to incite the jury into a furious uproar that would lead to a jail sentence that would take Jay out of commission forevermore.

At trial, however, my answers to Mr. Centario, Esq.'s, questions failed to satisfy any of these purposes. Indeed, my testimony led to two furious uproars, neither from the jury: one from Judge Julia Centario (no relation), and one from my blood pressure, starting with the next question.

"Did you live alone at that address?"

"Part of the time I lived there, I did."

Mr. Centario, Esq., frowned at this unexpected half-answer. "Do you mean that you lived there for a portion of time by yourself, and then lived with some number of roommates after that?"

"Objection, leading," interjected Paul St. James, Esq., Jay's court-appointed defense counsel.

Mr. Centario, Esq., shooting a nasty look at Mr. St. James, Esq., addressed

me again. "I'll rephrase. Mr. Delacroix, what did you mean when you said that for part of the time you lived by yourself in your apartment?"

I blinked away sweat and surveyed the courtroom. At the defendant's table sat Jay, expectant, relaxed, hands linked and resting atop the table. His usual warm smile spread across his face. He looked for all the world as if all was right with his soul.

To Jay's left sat Paul St. James, Esq., Jay's public defender, who appeared as exasperated as Jay was calm. From his furtive glances, it was difficult to tell if he was more frustrated with the prosecutor, the judge, the jury, the witness, or his client.

To Jay's right, the jury box, wherein 12 men and women sat, seemingly representing every world demographic.

Beyond the bar was the half-full viewing gallery. Peter Pony Pinchot occupied the right half of the gallery. My "cotenants," to borrow Mr. Centario, Esq.'s term, sat in a tight clump on the left. Surveying each face, I wondered if any "cotenant" knew what I knew about Jay and his past, as explained to me in meetings with Mr. Centario, Esq., and Pony Pinchot. Jay, it was claimed by the duo, nearly in unison (such that Mr. Centario, Esq., revealed himself as a conduit for Pony's every thought about Jay, a "crony" of Pony, as it were), was a "bad dude," who was "unworthy of protection."

All of that "bad dude" history surrounded Jay's formation of circles (which Pony and his crony labeled as "cults") on several prior occasions. In each, Jay recruited between six and fourteen individuals to join the "cult" and live in the apartment of some "poor fucking schlub"/"naïve dupe." Each of these "cults" gathered within that "schlub/dupe's" dwelling place and formulated "plans" with the "ultimate goal" of destroying some "glorious symbol of America," something that Jay had "wrongly" deemed "oppressive" to "fucking *welfare* recipients." Pony outlined some prior circle iterations:

- 1996: A man, "Jay," recruits six members to his cult.
  - Ultimate Goal: unknown.
  - Goal prevented when 2 cult members came to blows, causing a neighbor to call the police.
    - Pony, then Sargent, arrived and broke down the door.

~ 352 ~

- Inside, he found the makings of pipe bombs.
- Arrests made, but charges dropped when "the stupid-ass judge wrongly ruled the apartment illegally searched."
- Jay walked.

- 2000: Jay was back—although he looked different from the previous time, nearly unrecognizable. Another cult, this one with 15 members.
  - Ultimate Goal: Hacking the New York Stock Exchange, spreading a virus throughout the financial industry.
  - As a newly promoted detective, Pony monitored the cult, found a "poor fucking schlub" whom he knew was a "naïve dupe" and interrogated him. Pony learned of the ultimate goal and got a search warrant. In the process of raiding the apartment and seizing computing equipment, one of Pony's "useless officers" lost track of Jay, and "the goddamned fucking schlubby dupe informant snuck Jay the fuck out of the apartment."

- 2002: "Jay" turns up again to form a "cult," again looking different. So different that Pony had to have Jay pointed out to him. It was as if every time Jay came back, he'd disguise himself, as if Jay didn't want his new cult members to rely on their memory of him from news reports in deciding to join the cult.
  - Ultimate goal: tampering with elections to pack the government with "commie assholes."
  - After years of "this bullshit," Pony "got in good quick with the dupe." Pony was "a machine." The "problem" was that Pony "was *too* good," working so hard that he had "that fucking dupe so intimidated that he turned on the cult before enough of the plans were in place to make a case against Jay." The best Pony could do was lean hard on the prosecutor, who didn't want to prosecute. The best

Pony could get was a "ginned up report from some whore psychologist that the prosecutor used to get an unfit for trial ruling." That took Jay "out of circulation—but not for long."

Not long at all, it turns out. For here was I on the stand, with John Centario, Esq., staring me down, growing perturbed as I either (bad) remained silent, (worse) blinked, gulped, and stammered, or (worst of all) gave responses to his pre-scripted questions that differed from the well-rehearsed answers that Pony and his crony planned out for me.

As frustrated as Mr. Centario, Esq., was, he softened his approach. "Asher," he sighed, "do you know the defendant?"

I blinked, gulped, and stammered. "I…I…well…"

"Asher, please concentrate on the—"

"Yes."

"—question. Also, since we're making a record," he nodded at the court reporter, "please wait for me to—"

"Yes."

"—finish my question before—"

"Yes."

"—you…okay. Do you understand, Asher?"

"Umm. I think so."

"Good. Now, I'm going to repeat—"

"Yes."

"—my question."

"Yes."

Mr. Centario, Esq., pinched the bridge of his nose, breathed, maintained his calm tone. "Do you know the defendant, Asher?"

"Know?"

Mr. Centario, Esq.'s turn to blink. "No?"

"Know?"

"Really? No?"

"Know?"

"I'm going to ask once more because I don't think we're understanding each other."

Paul St. James, Esq., spoke. "Objection. The prosecutor has now asked the same question three times, and three times, the witness has denied knowing the defendant. I'd call that asked and answered."

I blanched. "Oh! No!"

Judge Centario (no relation) turned her full attention to me. "Mr. Delacroix—"

"Oh, well, I think—"

"Mr. Delacroix!" she snapped.

I swallowed.

"That's better. Now, Mr. Delacroix, since I've had enough, I'm going to ask you the question the prosecutor was building toward. Okay?"

"Was that the question?"

"What?"

"Was that—'Okay?'—was that the question the prosecutor was building toward? Because—"

"Mr. Delacroix—"

"—that's not one I remember from our prep sessions."

"Objection!" shouted Mr. Centario, Esq.

"This is your witness, counsel," Judge Centario (no relation) responded.

Mr. Centario, Esq., winced at Judge Centario (no relation)'s accusation of ownership.

"That means I'm doing *your* job, counsel."

"I suppose you are."

"I don't think it behooves you to interrupt."

"Umm. Yes."

"So, please—"

"Yes, I will."

"Mr. Centario—"

"Oh. Sorry."

"—would you, please—"

"Yes."

"—stop talking, so that I can—"

"Oh. Right."

"—*shut up*, Mr. Centario!"

"So that you can shut up Mr. Centario?" I asked.

Judge Centario (no relation) turned back to me. "What?"

"Umm. You told Mr. Centario to 'stop talking so that I can shut up Mr. Centario.'"

Judge Centario (no relation)'s turn to sigh. "Mr. Delacroix, I'm going to ignore that, for your sake."

"For my sake?"

"And I am going to return to the—"

"I have a sake?"

"Mr. Delacroix!"

"You're going to return to the Mr. Delacroix? I don't understand."

Judge Centario (no relation) calmed herself. "Mr. Delacroix, this will go much faster if—"

"Oh, well, if that's—"

"Shut the fuck—I mean—please be quiet!"

"Okay."

"Now, did you live with the defendant or not?"

I furrowed my brow.

"When I said, 'please be quiet,' I didn't mean forever. Answer the question. Understand?"

"Umm. Yes."

"That's better."

"It is?"

Judge Centario (no relation) shook her head. "Marginally. Mr. Delacroix, when you and the defendant lived together, did you come to learn…"

The seven hours I spent in the witness box felt like 70 times 70 hours. I blinked, gulped, and stammered my way through the story of Jay's residence in my apartment, the gathering of roommates, my purposeful ostracization from their ranks, the snippets of conversation the circle allowed me to overhear, my being cornered by Pony Pinchot in the hallway, my recounting

to Pony the goings-on in the apartment, and on and on until finally there I sat in Theo's, Jay beside me, and then…the rest of it, right up to the point.

Or not "the point," so much—that seemed to elude me. My testimony didn't result in "the point," but ended with "*my* point," with my ID of Jay as the catalyst of the circle—or as Pony and his crony would put it (and as I was "forced" to put it myself) "as the leader of the cult." At which point, I was dismissed from the stand.

Over the course of the seven hours of my testimony, the jurors grew listless, deenergized, bored. Meanwhile, John Centario, Esq., grew resigned, and Paul St. James, Esq. grew giddier at the back and forth between the detailed questions of Judge Julia Centario (no relation) and my stunned, stunted answers thereto. By the time I stepped down, all jurors but one stared out the window into the late-afternoon Spring air, and the one exception was staring at the inside of his eyelids. Not only had I lost myself, but I'd lost the jury, and lost John Centario, Esq.'s chance at a conviction of any substance.

As I left the stand, Mr. Centario, Esq., refused to look at me, burying his head in his hands in defeat that belied his repeated advice during our prep sessions that while testifying I *must* maintain a poker face that was *at least* as good as his own. Meanwhile, Paul St. James, Esq., did everything he could to restrain himself from applauding, leaping to his feet, shaking my hand, and passionately kissing me on each cheek.

Chapter 32

WRITE WHAT YOU KNOW.

Show, don't tell.

Use active verbs.

Avoid excessive adverbs.

Don't use clichés.

Ensure that your protagonist changes.

A writer writes, always.

So many maxims for writers, each designed to improve their work so readers pore over every page, sentence, word, character. By following these tips, a writer can ensure that his work appeals to the broadest possible audience.

But what if the writer doesn't want to reach a broad audience? What if the writer doesn't want his words reviewed, appraised, judged? What if the writer wants to conceal, obfuscate, hide? Maybe that writer doesn't "write, always." Maybe that writer delays completion of his story for 19 years after the events depicted therein. Maybe that writer treats his book as if it were The Gospels, too ashamed of the events depicted therein to complete the story right away, waiting until the year 2022 to recount every sordid and shameful detail.

What did the writer do with his 19 years? Did he dedicate himself to personal improvement? Did he redeem himself? Did he do good deeds? Did

he attempt to reconcile with lost loved ones? Did he grovel for forgiveness at the feet of his friends, his family, his God?

It's unfair to ask those questions without providing answers. It's unfair to refuse to help the reader come to a deeper understanding of the events of 19 years ago and the effects those events had upon me. Unfortunately, these questions are unanswerable. I'd love to give as many details from my life from 2003-2022 as I did in the chapters chronicling the months when "my apartment" was "what had once been my apartment." If I could lay out every day of that 19 years, I would. But I lack those details. So, I can't.

Knowing what I lack, the question is begged: What do I *have*? What memories have I of those 19 years? And among those memories, what truths have I? No whole truths. And never mind truths—I have no wholeness. I have scraps—scattered, ragged, tattered pieces. I have an image here, a notion there, an idea somewhere else. Each alone reveals nothing. Pieced together akin to a jigsaw puzzle—who knows? The nature of that image would be up to interpretation. To me…if you're asking me…but why would you ask a wretch such as me?...but if you're asking me…which you shouldn't…I'd guess that image would resemble a large bottle of the cheapest liquor available.

Not that there weren't moments of clarity. At various flashpoints are crystalline images, unblemished notions, flawless ideas. At each of these flashpoints exists a story. A story "by Asher Delacroix." These were stories about revenge. About war, dignity, hubris, control, guilt. About religion, death, legacy. About anything and everything non-alcohol related that was on my mind. Each of these stories ended up in my "Parable Box," filling that box (which had been half-empty when Dad brought into the apartment) near to bursting.

What did I accomplish with these "parables"? I've no idea. I'm not sure what I *intended* to accomplish. Perhaps these "parables" were allegory. If so, they're misguided. I've no gift for allegory. I struggle to hide deep meaning into a text. For, after all that has transpired, I've no deep hidden meaning within me. Just as in the beginning I was ordinary, plain, unremarkable, unexceptional, nondescript, characterless, so I remain now ordinary, plain,

unremarkable, unexceptional, nondescript, characterless. Perhaps I am even more so now than in the beginning.

Others have great talent for allegory. Sam, Samuel, Sammy, Dad—name dependent upon the user—is allegorical, meaning that he has great gifts in the allegorical arts (witness Bobby Bull, Hotchky Potchky, Mikey Centavo and the like), although he'd deny it. Alas, Dad did not pass down to me his talent in allegory.

Therefore, my "parables" could never be allegory—not intentionally. Neither could the previous chapters be allegory. These chapters represent no purposeful attempt to convey some hidden message—at least no message that I understand. There's no lesson to be learned here—not by me. There is no political or moral underpinning—not from me. There are no peasants chained within a cave, no false light dancing before them, no reality behind them. If this were allegory, it would have characters with names, backgrounds, and story arcs veiled so thinly that their true natures, intentions, identities could be discerned by any reader who cared to pierce that thinnest of veils. "Jay," for example, would be neither a name nor a bird—he'd be "J."—an initial that could stand for any number of things, or for one thing in particular.

Furthermore, if this were allegory, then I'd have gained a deeper understanding of myself, of the world, of the meaning of life upon stepping down from the witness box after testifying at Jay's trial. As it stands, without allegory, without metaphor, without meaning, all I have are facts.

Fact number 1 (previously recounted): As I passed John Centario, Esq., he sat hunched, face obscured in his hands. Meanwhile, Paul St. James, Esq., rapped his fingers, drumming out what sounded like The Battle Hymn of the Republic.

Fact number 2 (already partially stated): On one side of the courtroom's seating gallery sat my former roommates. On the other side sat Peter Pony Pinchot. Choosing hate over shame, I settled in on Pony's side of the gallery, where I could feel him snorting at me, blinders up to anything else in the world, his eyes so focused on me with frightening menace that he neither heard nor saw what transpired in what little remained of Jay's trial.

Fact number 3 (all new): John Centario, Esq., stood and asked Judge

Julia Centario (no relation) for a continuance of Jay's trial to obtain a psychiatric evaluation of the defendant. Judge Centario (no relation) granted the request.

Fact number 4 (all new): Upon the new psychiatric evaluation, Jay was ruled unfit to stand trial, and he was housed at Michigan's Center for Forensic Psychiatry, a facility from which he was then transferred.

The end of Jay's trial was not the end of all legal proceedings relating to the events depicted herein. Because of the lapses perceived in my testimony, Pony and his crony decided to take away from me the immunity deal I'd struck with the State, and to put me on trial for my role in those events. Pony and his crony had me incarcerated. One overnight in jail was enough time for Judge Julia Centario (no relation) to see the name "Asher Delacroix" listed as a criminal defendant, say, "fuck this!" and order my release from prison and into a program of therapy with a therapist, Molly Monahan, L.M.S.W., L.M.F.T., L.P.C., who proceeded to "treat" me over the course of many sessions, nearly two years' worth, going well beyond the 31 sessions chronicled in the previous chapters of this book.

As to the additional sessions—those beyond the 31 detailed herein—I don't remember them except that they were inconsequential and didn't answer the two questions that Ms. Monahan repeatedly posed to me, which questions were imposed upon her by Judge Julia Centario (no relation) at the firm request of Peter Pony Pinchot. Nor in any of those sessions did I detail to Ms. Monahan the events depicted in this chapter.

For example, one thing I never shared with Ms. Monahan: following Jay's abrupt trial, I received three visitors in the apartment, either bearing information for me (visitors number one and three) or seeking information from me (visitor number two).

The first visitor wasn't so much a visitor as she was my one remaining roommate, my darling and love and soon to be ex-fiancée, Marlena Magpie, who arrived to tell me (breaths rapid, hands twirling, eyes wide with adrenaline): "Jay's gone!"

"Gone?"

"Gone, Asher."

"Gone from where?"

"What do you mean, gone from where?"

"I mean...in order to be 'gone,' Jay had to have been somewhere, right?"

"Of course."

"So, where was he before he was...'gone'?"

"You don't know?"

"Was I supposed to?"

"I don't understand how *you* couldn't know."

"Me?"

"You're the one with the connection."

"Connection?"

"Doesn't matter. Jay was at Walter Reuther."

"Wait..."

"With Merry."

"With *Mom*?"

"Well, I don't know that they were in the same room, but yes."

"With *my* mom?"

"Now he's gone."

"Gone where?"

"Nobody knows. He's disappeared."

"Disappeared."

"Like, poof."

"Poof."

"Well, not so much like poof. I asked around. Sounds like there was a ruckus."

"A ruckus?"

"Right before Jay was gone, the fire alarms went off and the power went out—even the emergency power for the door alarms. Which is probably when he got out."

"Ah."

"Seems as planned out. It's the same pattern as the last time he disappeared."

"Wait...the last time?"

"When he was at Walter Reuther the last time, and disappeared, yes."

"So...wait...what you're saying is...what?"

"Jay was committed to Walter Reuther before. And he disappeared from Walter Reuther before. Under similar circumstances."

"Oh."

"So it seems likely—"

"Umm."

"Yes, Asher?"

"When was this?"

"I'm not sure. Doesn't matter."

"If that doesn't matter...what does?"

"Jay's gone!"

"That's something."

"It's amazing."

"Amazing?"

"Jay being gone means that he's done it."

"Done what?"

"He's done just what he's set out to do."

"Which is?"

"Finding his way to some other unfortunate soul."

"Some...*other*?"

"He can start again."

"Unfortunate?"

"This is good news, Asher."

"Is it?"

"Extremely."

Upon delivering this "extremely good news," Marlena swooped back out of the apartment, twittering about someone else to whom she needed to convey the "extremely good news."

I contemplated the meaning of Jay's history of disappearing acts for 33 minutes before the front door burst open and in galloped my second visitor, Peter Pony Pinchot, who grabbed me by my shoulder, and shouted two questions: "Where is he?!?!" and "Who did it!?!?"

"I—"

"Don't give me any of your bullshit, Asher. You're in too fucking deep because of your *performance* at his trial."

"Performance?"

"Cut the shit. You did it on purpose. All that stammering and stuttering. You were protecting him, that…that…that fucking Commie fuck! You're no better than the rest of them."

"The rest of them?"

"Those roommates of yours. The members of that fucking *cult*. I've interviewed them all. Taken statements. Each one had some interesting things to say about the cult, about Jay, about you—"

"Me?"

Pony smiled at my surprise. "Oh, yes, Asher, they had many *interesting* things to say about you. *Implicating* things."

"Implicating? In what?"

"In fuck *you*! That's what."

"Umm."

"You better keep my two questions in mind: 'Where is Jay?' and 'Who did it?'"

"Who did what?"

"You might think you don't know the answers, but you do. And you'll answer. If you won't answer when I ask, I'll get somebody else to ask them."

"But—"

"Fuck your but. I know you, Asher. I know you're scared. I know how much someone like you would suffer in prison. And prison is where you'll be, soon, if you don't answer my questions."

"But—"

"That's the way you want it." Pony shook his head. "My men will be back with a warrant. If I can't have Jay's head, then I'll have yours, you fucking *fuck*." Pony stamped out of the apartment.

I still shook when I received my third visitor, who came with tidings from a fourth person. At my visitor's knock, I flinched as I waited for the shout of

"POLICE! OPEN UP!" When no shout came, I opened the door to Brody the Nurse, straight from Walter Reuther still in his "dress blues," as Mom called his outfit of navy-blue scrubs. "Bird?"

"No." Brody's sharp retort diverged from his calm demeanor. "Only Merry calls me that," he scolded. "Not you."

"Umm. Sorry."

"You should be."

"Is Mom all right?" I asked.

"No."

"Oh, no. Is she—"

"That is, she's well. Healthy as ever. But damn if she isn't pissed off. More than usual."

Fuck. "Do you need me to—"

"I neither need nor want anything from you."

"Then why are you—"

"Here." Brody stuffed something into my hand. With a scowl, he left.

I stood in the open doorway to the apartment puzzling over the object in my hand. Paper. More than one sheet. Folded, not neatly. No envelope. Nothing to conceal its contents from me save for my refusal to look down.

I tried.

I tried.

I tried.

I failed.

I failed.

I failed.

I unfolded the paper and beheld familiar scrawl:

Asher:

Maybe Bird will be friendly when he delivers this note. I doubt it. Bird knows everything I know. And what we know is that you've failed.

I spent this morning staring out my window at the Redbud trees. They've stood there not very long, so Dr. Long-A Arab, M.D., responded when I told him to

see to their removal. "Those trees will shame us all," I said.

After stammering for a response like the jackass he is, he said something about the trees being planted within the previous two years. It was too early in their life, he said, for them to be revealed as shameful. Those trees needed more time to prove themselves, to prove their maturity, to show usefulness, helpfulness, goodness.

But I can always tell.

I predicted all this months ago. When I say, "all this," you know I what I mean.

Months ago, when I met him (you know who I mean), he had good ideas. About love, peace, equality, and all of the obstacles that stood in the way of those ultimate goals. Ideas for how those obstacles could be destroyed, too.

He needed two things to accompany those ideas: freedom and a conduit. First, he needed to get the fuck out of Walter Reuther. He needed to be on the streets, where he could drum up a group, convince them (as he convinced me) that it's time to rise up against those fucking up love, peace, equality for the rest of us. Second, he needed a place to live, a place to gather, a place to preach, a place to implement his ideas.

It was easy to meet his first need, easy for me to cut the power, ensure that the alarms wouldn't trigger, get him through the security doors. It was easy to live up to my name by birthing him out into the world.

Meeting his second need was harder. I thought and thought about where I could send him once he had his freedom.

It may come as a surprise that I don't easily make

friends. I've said "fuck you" to too many people to maintain close relationships. And if I did manage to get close to anyone, that person was liable to lose a limb—or a nipple.

While my standoffish nature has served me well, it left me with few options to fulfill his second need. As I saw it, I had two: Sammy and you.

That goddamned Dr. Long-A Arab, M.D.—he's partly responsible for me choosing to send him to you. All that bullshit about those fucking redbud trees, how they haven't had the opportunity to prove me wrong—for whatever reason that stuck with me. So, when I thought of how many times you've let me down by not reading, learning, figuring shit out—I thought, "Maybe Asher will surprise me. Maybe he'll develop, mature. Maybe he'll figure out the lesson of the redbud tree. Maybe he'll prove me wrong."

The other parties responsible for me choosing you are Sammy and you. I knew that if I sent him to either of you, it would only work if the other of you came along, too.

If I'd sent him to Sammy alone, without you, Sammy and he would never have left the fucking bedroom. Sammy needed others to balance him. Those two together would've left no time for recruitment of any other circle members, who were necessary to keep those two honest.

If I'd sent him to you, without Sammy, you would've snapped and kicked every other person in the circle out of your life. I needed someone there you couldn't kick out. You needed family. You needed Sammy. As much of a motherfucker as you are, you wouldn't be able to kick Sammy out. What'd be the point of kicking

anyone else out, if Sammy stayed? You'd no doubt realize that you'd need all those others to come between you and Sammy. Life with Sammy alone would be too much for you. Life with Sammy required buffers. If Sammy were there, you'd be stuck with everyone.

So, no matter whether it was Sammy or you to whom I sent him, he'd need both of you.

I can hear you in my head: "That doesn't explain why you chose me over Dad." But it does.

If I'd sent him to Sammy, there was no chance to get you in the mix. You'd have ignored every effort to get you there. But the inverse was perfect. All I had to do was send him to you and write separately to Sammy to explain how this great and glorious specimen of a man was coming to live with you.

Before I cut the power, before I got him through the security doors, I told him all about you, your hangouts, fears, insecurities, flaws, weaknesses. I told him everything he'd need to find and seduce you, for him to infiltrate your apartment and start his new circle of comrades. Then I wrote to Sammy. It was genius. It was easy. It worked.

Logic and instinct. Those two don't always get along. Logic made me send him your way. I obeyed that logic despite my instinct that you'd let me down.

Regardless, because of me, not only did he gain his freedom, but he also gained his conduit. The rest was up to you. As much as I hoped, longed for, even prayed that you'd prove me wrong, that you'd prove to be mature, developed, ready—in the end, you proved my instinct correct. You failed. You failed him. You failed Sammy. You failed Marlena (by the way, well

done with her, son. You're lucky she opted to stay after everyone moved out. To lose her would perhaps be your biggest failure). You failed that circle. You failed me. You failed yourself.

I knew of your failure when once again he showed up in handcuffs at Walter Reuther. Although he didn't have to tell me what'd transpired, he told me anyway, confirming what I already knew of your failures.

Talk about shame. How ashamed I was at my role in sending him to you, in dooming him to your failures. I had to redeem myself. I owed him his renewed freedom. I had no other conduit to give him, but freedom I could provide. Trusting that he'd find his way in the world, I told him to stay the fuck away from you. I told him what I now know to be true: that you, Asher, are beyond help and hope, and would be forever fated to do the same things over and over again. I told him: "That Asher sure is a son of a bitch. I should know. And that son of a bitch will never learn the lesson of the redbud tree."

So it goes.

Love, Your Mom

Mom. Love. "Love, Your Mom." The salutation and signature are burned into me more than any other passage in those pages. Did she mean it? Am I to believe that despite all the damaging (true) allegations she lodged, "Love" remains, even at the end? Am I to believe that I'm worthy of Mom's "Love"? Am I to believe that I'm worthy of any "Love"?

I'd ask Mom, but for two conditions: (1) the solitude that Mom imposed upon herself through purposeful revocation of visiting rights remains even 19 years later. Every time Dr. Long-A Arab, M.D., deems Mom "ready" to receive visitors, Mom commits another act that causes him to reconsider; and

(2) I fear Mom's answers.

Beyond the salutation and signature, Mom gave me absolution and danger. Absolution in arranging that I could never answer one of the two questions that Molly Monahan, L.M.S.W., L.M.F.T., L.P.C., repeated so often (questions imposed upon her by Peter Pony Pinchot), and danger in the form of an answer to the other question.

Ms. Monahan's first question: "Where is Jay now?" By telling Jay to stay away from wretched, irredeemable Asher, Mom absolved me from answering this question by ensuring that I'd have no answer to give.

Mom's absolution was not absolute. As much as she prevented me from answering Ms. Monahan's first question, she gave me the answer to Ms. Monahan's second question: "How did Jay escape?"

What was I to do? Was I to give to Ms. Monahan (and, by proxy, Peter Pony Pinchot) the answer she (and he) sought? Was I to betray Mom? Was I to betray *my* mom? Was I to betray the woman who, despite pages of dreadful, truthful accusations, had concluded those pages with a salutation of "Love"? Was I to fail once more?

I could not.

I did not.

It's been 19 years since the events depicted in chapters 1 through 31, and 15 years since my last therapy session with Molly Monahan, L.M.S.W., L.M.F.T., L.P.C. In no session did I answer either of the questions she posed. The events depicted in this chapter were never told to Ms. Monahan.

So, in the end, do I remain a failure? Despite me remaining ordinary, plain, non-descript, characterless, have I changed? Have I developed? Have I matured? Have I progressed? Have I found redemption? Am I worthy of respect? Have I earned happiness? Am I deserving of love?

What's more, have I learned? Did my time with Jay and his circle teach me the values of love, peace, and equality? Have I learned the mysterious lesson of the redbud tree? For that matter, despite Mom's assertions, am I to believe that there was any lesson to be learned at all?

I don't know what to believe.

Author Bio

THOMAS WERNER CRAFTED HIS FIRST short story at age 7, a tale of a scuba diver battling a whale that thrilled teacher and classmates alike. Reading and writing were an essential escape to young Thomas. He reveled in the works of Vonnegut, Steinbeck, Morrison, Heller, Adams, Lee, Roth, and Baldwin.

Through his writing, Thomas celebrates those authors and many others who shaped him. In so doing, he speaks to the lonely, the confused, the outcasts. He wants to make them feel welcome and accepted. Most of all, he wants to make them laugh, especially at the darkest parts of life.

Thomas lives in Michigan with his wife and two teenage children. Aside from writing, he lives for his small, close circle of family and friends, reading, golf, and his three young cats.

Made in the USA
Monee, IL
15 October 2021